A TREATISE

ON THE

LAW OF PATENTS

FOR USEFUL INVENTIONS,

AS ENACTED AND ADMINISTERED

IN THE UNITED STATES OF AMERICA.

BY

GEORGE TICKNOR CURTIS.

FOURTH EDITION,

REVISED AND ENLARGED.

THE LAWBOOK EXCHANGE, LTD.
Clark, New Jersey

ISBN 978-1-58477-580-5

Lawbook Exchange edition 2006, 2016

The quality of this reprint is equivalent to the quality of the original work.

The Lawbook Exchange, Ltd.
33 Terminal Avenue
Clark, New Jersey 07066-1321

Please see our website for a selection of our other publications and fine facsimile reprints of classic works of legal history:
www.lawbookexchange.com

Library of Congress Cataloging-in-Publication Data

Curtis, George Ticknor, 1812-1894.
A treatise on the law of patents for useful inventions / George Ticknor Curtis.
p. cm.
Originally published: Boston : Little, Brown, 1873.
Includes bibliographical references and index.
ISBN 1-58477-580-7 (alk. paper)
1. Patent laws and legislation--United States. I. Title.
KF3114.C8 2005
346.7304'86--dc22

2004030209

Printed in the United States of America on acid-free paper

A TREATISE

ON THE

LAW OF PATENTS

FOR USEFUL INVENTIONS,

AS ENACTED AND ADMINISTERED

IN THE UNITED STATES OF AMERICA.

BY

GEORGE TICKNOR CURTIS.

FOURTH EDITION,
REVISED AND ENLARGED.

BOSTON:
LITTLE, BROWN, AND COMPANY.
1873.

CAMBRIDGE:
PRESS OF JOHN WILSON AND SON.

PREFACE TO THE FOURTH EDITION.

THE first edition of this work, published in 1849, has been the foundation of all the succeeding ones. The second was published in 1854; the third, in 1867. The present edition is believed to contain references to most of the important decisions in England and in this country that have appeared since the edition of 1867. In preparing it for the press, I have been ably assisted by Mr. E. S. DRONE, of the New York Bar, whose abstracts of the recent decisions and of the statute of 1870 have been made and adapted to my text, with clearness and precision.

NEW YORK, November 1, 1873.

CONTENTS.

CHAPTER I.

CHAPTER II.

CHAPTER III.

CHAPTER IV.

CHAPTER V.

CHAPTER VI.

CHAPTER VII.

INDEX OF CASES CITED.

NOTE.—The references, unless otherwise indicated, are to the sections, and not to the pages. Where the volume of Webster's Patent Cases is not given, the reference must be understood to be to the first.

PRELIMINARY OBSERVATIONS.

Writers on the law of patents for useful inventions have often introduced their discussions of this branch of the law, by tracing the history of monopolies in the law of England. This example has not been followed in the present work, because it is believed that it tends to encourage incorrect conceptions of the legal nature of a patent privilege. A patent for a useful invention is not, under our law, or the law of England, a grant of a monopoly, in the sense of the old common law. It is the grant by the government to the author of a new and useful invention, of the exclusive right, for a term of years, of practising that invention. The consideration, for which this grant is made by the public, is the benefit to society resulting from the invention; which benefit flows from the inventor to the public in two forms: *first*, by the immediate practice of the invention under the patent; and, *secondly*, by the practice of the invention, or the opportunity to practise it, which becomes the property of the public on the expiration of the patent. As the exercise of the invention is wholly within the control of him who has made it, who may confine his secret entirely within his own breast, it is apparent that his consent to make it known and available to others, and finally to surrender it to the public, becomes a valuable consideration, for which, upon the principles of natural justice, he is entitled to receive compensation, in some form, from the public to whom that consideration passes. Inventors, in this respect, stand upon the same broad ground with authors. Both of these classes of persons have created something intellectual in its nature, the knowledge of which it is desirable to others to possess. Both of them have, at first, the complete right of disposition over that which they have created; and when they part with the exclusive possession of this knowledge, and confer upon others the opportunity of reaping the benefits which it confers, they manifestly consent to something for which they are entitled to receive an equivalent.

Whether we regard the knowledge, remaining for the present in the exclusive control of him whose intellectual production it is, as property, or as a possession of ideas, to which some other term might be more appropriate, it is still a possession, of which the owner cannot by any rule of natural justice be deprived, without his consent. In this view it may, as it seems to me, justly be termed property; for although in political economy, and in common speech, material possessions, or the rights growing out of them, are the objects generally included under that term, yet no one will question that ideas constitute, in ethical contemplation, a portion of a man's possessions entirely under his own control; and in the case of useful inventions, or of written thought, there is to be added to the power of control the further economical fact, that other men will part with valuable possessions of all kinds, in order to obtain that invention or writing in exchange. For these and for other reasons, which I have endeavored more fully to develop elsewhere, in relation to the rights of authors, I do not hesitate to affirm, that in natural justice, — the ethics of jurisprudence, by which civil rights are to be examined, apart from all positive law, but on which positive law is usually founded, — the intellectual conception of an inventor, or a writer, constitutes a valuable possession, capable of being appreciated as a consideration, when it passes by his voluntary grant into the possession of another. If, by the same voluntary grant, this possession is bestowed upon the public, the logical justice of compensation, in some form, will appear at once, by supposing the benefit to have been conferred exclusively upon any one of the mass of individuals who form in the aggregate the moral entity termed the public.

Let us suppose that A, by the exertion of his inventive faculties, has ascertained that by placing matter in certain positions to be operated upon by the forces of nature, a result will be produced, in the shape of an instrument, wholly unknown before, and capable of being usefully applied to the wants of mankind. Let us suppose that B, seeing the result, but wholly ignorant of the process by which it may be attained, desires to possess that instrument. Common gratitude would prompt him to return something valuable for it, if it were given to him; common policy would lead him to offer something for it, if it were not freely given; and common justice requires that he should not take it without an equivalent. How does it alter the case, if, instead of a single specimen of the instrument, we suppose A to have retained in his recollection the process by which copies of that instrument may be indefinitely multiplied, and that it is the secret process of making the thing, the intellectual conception and knowledge, which B desires to possess? If he obtains it, he can make the thing for his own use, or for the use of others, and by so doing can acquire valuable possessions in exchange; all of which A could do exclusively by retaining his own secret. But if he imparts that secret to B, he is surely entitled to receive for it some reward or remuneration.

This secret the inventor undertakes to impart to the public when he enters into the compact which the grant of a patent privilege embraces. In that compact he promises, after the lapse of a certain period, to surrender to the public completely the right of practising his invention; and, as a guaranty against his concealment of the process by which it is to be practised, and to prevent the loss of this knowledge, he is required to deposit in the archives of the government a full and exact description in writing of the whole process, so framed that others can practise the invention from the description itself. The public, on the other hand, through the agency of the government, in consideration of this undertaking of the inventor, grants and secures to him the exclusive right of practising his invention for a term of years.

In all this, a patent right, under the modern law of England and America, differs essentially from one of the old English Monopolies. In those grants of the crown, the subject-matter of the exclusive privilege was quite as often a commodity of which the public were and long had been in possession, as it was any thing invented, discovered, or even imported by the patentee.

Nothing passed in such cases from the patentee to the public in the nature of a consideration for the enormous privilege conferred upon him; but the public were robbed of something already belonging to them, viz., the right to make or deal in a particular commodity, for the benefit of the favored grantee of the crown. So broad is the distinction between these cases and that of the meritorious inventor or importer of something new and useful, that when Parliament, in the 21 James I., taking encouragement from the courts of law, prohibited the granting of exclusive privileges in trade, by the Statute of Monopolies, they introduced an exception in favor of "letters-patent and grants of privilege for the term of one and twenty years or under, heretofore made, of the sole working or making of any manner of new manufacture, within this realm, to the first and true inventor or inventors of such manufactures, which others at the time of the making of such letters-patent and grants did not use, so they be not contrary to law, nor mischievous to the state, by raising the prices of commodities at home, or hurt to trade, or generally inconvenient," &c.

Upon this exception, the law of England, concerning Patents for Useful Inventions, stands to this day.

The modern doctrine, in England, and undoubtedly the

doctrine of our law, is, that in the grant of a patent right, a contract, or, as it has been said, a bargain, takes place between the public and the patentee. As far as the old cases on the subject of monopolies furnish, like other cases of grants by the crown, rules and analogies for the construction of this species of grant, so far the history of monopolies has a bearing upon this branch of jurisprudence. But it should always be remembered that in the grant of a patent privilege, as now understood, a contract takes place between the public and the patentee, to be supported upon the ground of mutual considerations, and to be construed, in all its essential features of a bargain, like other contracts to which there are two parties, each having rights and interests involved in its stipulations.

It is necessary also to have clear and correct notions of the true scope of a patent right, because its nature and character will show whether there is any close analogy between such privileges and those to which the term monopoly is correctly applied. In this connection, therefore, I shall attempt a brief general description of the subject of protection, in patent rights; without, however, designing to lay down definitions, or to draw exact lines, within or without which controverted cases may fall; but solely with the purpose of stating certain general principles and truths, the application and development of which may be found to assist, in particular cases, the solution of the question, whether a particular invention or discovery is by law a patentable subject.

In this inquiry it is necessary to commence with the process of exclusion; for although, in their widest acceptation, the terms "invention" and "discovery" include the whole vast variety of objects on which the human intellect may be exercised, so that in poetry, in painting, in music, in astronomy, in metaphysics, and in every department of human thought, men constantly invent or discover, in the highest and the strictest sense, their inventions and discoveries in these departments are not the subjects of the patent law. Another branch of jurisprudence, of a kindred nature, aims at the protection and establishment of property in literary productions, and in some of those which fall within the province of the fine arts. The patent law relates to a great and comprehensive class of discoveries and inventions of some new and useful effect or result in matter, not referable to the department of the fine arts. The matter of which our globe is composed is the material upon which the creative and inventive faculties of man are exercised, in the production of whatever ministers to his convenience or his wants. Over the existence of matter itself he has no control. He can neither create nor destroy a single atom of it; he can only change its form, by placing its particles in new relations, which may cause it to appear as a solid, a fluid, or a gas. But under whatever form it exists, the same matter, in quantity, that was originally created, exists now, and, so far as we now know, will forever continue to exist.

The direct control of man over matter consists, therefore, in placing its particles in new relations. This is all that is actually done, or that can be done, namely, to cause the particles of matter existing in the universe to change their former places, by moving them, by muscular power or some other force. But as soon as they are brought into new relations, it is at once perceived that there are vast latent forces in nature, which come to the aid of man, and enable him to produce effects and results of a wholly new character, far beyond the mere fact of placing the particles in new positions. He moves certain particles of matter into a new juxtaposition, and the chemical agencies and affinities called into action by this new contact produce a substance possessed of new properties and powers, to which has been given the name of gunpowder. He takes a stalk of flax from the ground, splits it into a great number of filaments, twists them together, and laying numbers of the threads thus formed across each other, forms a cloth, which is held together by the tenacity or force of cohesion in the particles, which nature brings to his aid. He moves into new positions and relations certain particles of wood and iron, in various forms, and produces a complicated machine, by which he is able to accomplish a certain purpose, only because the properties of cohesion and the force of gravitation cause it to adhere together and enable the different parts to operate upon each other and to transmit the forces applied to them, according to the laws of motion. It is evident, therefore, that the whole of the act of invention, in the department of useful arts, embraces more than the new arrangement of particles of matter in new relations. The purpose of such new arrangements is to produce some new effect or result, by calling into activity some latent law, or force, or property, by means of which, in a new application, the new effect or result may be accomplished. In every form in which matter is used, in every production of the ingenuity of man, he relies upon the laws of nature and the properties of matter, and seeks for new effects and results through their agency and aid. Merely inert matter alone is not the sole material with which he works. Nature supplies powers, and forces, and active properties, as well as the particles of matter, and these powers, forces, and properties are constantly the subjects of study, inquiry, and experiment, with a view to the production of some new effect or result in matter.

Any definition or description, therefore, of the act of invention, which excludes the application of the natural law, or power, or property of matter, on which the inventor has relied for the production of a new effect, and the object of such application, and confines it to the precise arrangement of the particles of matter which he may have brought together, must be erroneous. Let us suppose the invention, for the first time, of a steam-engine, in one of its simplest forms, the use of steam as a motive-power having never been discovered before. Besides all the other powers of nature, of which the inventor avails himself almost without thought, by which the different parts of his machine are held together and enabled to transmit the forces applied to them, he has discovered and purposely applied the expansive power of steam, as the means of generating a force that sets his machine in motion. All that he actually does with the matter in which this expansive power resides is to turn certain particles of water into vapor, and to bring that vapor in contact with an obstructing mass of matter, to which it communicates motion, by pushing it from its place. But the invention consists in observing and applying this natural power, the expansive force of steam, to produce the effect or result of moving the obstructing mass of matter from the place where it was at rest. It would be singularly incorrect and illogical to say that a man who should take a certain other quantity of water, and convert it into a certain other quantity of steam, and bring that steam in contact with a certain other obstructing mass of wood or iron, for the purpose of moving it, would not produce the same effect by the same means, as the person who first discovered and applied the expansive power of steam to move a piece of wood or iron.

Again, let us take the case of an improvement in the art of manufacturing iron, which consisted in the discovery that a blast of air introduced into a smelting furnace in a heated state produces an entirely different effect on the iron manufactured from the ore, to that produced by blowing the furnace with cold air. What the inventor did, in this case, was to introduce a certain amount of caloric into the blast of air, on its passage from the blowing apparatus into the furnace, thereby creating a blast of a new character, productive of a new effect; and any other person who should introduce caloric into a certain other quantity of atmospheric air, and use that air, so heated, to blow a smelting furnace, would do precisely the same thing. The invention consisted in the discovery and application of the law or fact, that heated air produces a different effect from cold air, in a particular art, and in thereby accomplishing a new result in that art.

In these and in all other cases, there is a particular arrangement of matter, which consists in the new relations and positions in which its particles are placed. But beyond this, there is also the effect or result produced by the action of the forces of nature, which are for the first time developed and applied, by the new arrangement of the matter in which they reside. The use and adaptation of these forces is the direct purpose of the inventor; it is as new as the novel arrangement of the particles of matter; and it is far more important. In fact, it is the essence and substance of the invention: for if no new effect or result, through the operation of the forces of nature, followed the act of placing portions of matter in new positions, invention would consist solely in new arrangements of particles of inert matter, productive of no new consequences beyond the fact of such new position of the particles.

However inadequate, therefore, the term may be, to express what it is used to convey, it is obvious that there is a characteristic, an essence, or purpose of every invention, which, in our law, has been termed by jurists its *principle*; and that this can ordinarily be perceived and apprehended by the mind, in cases where the purpose and object of the invention does not begin and end in form alone, only by observing the powers or qualities of matter, or the laws of physics, developed and put in action by that arrangement of matter, and the effect or result produced by their application. Even in cases where the subject of the invention consists in form alone, the principle or characteristic of the invention is the result produced by the aid and through the action of the qualities of matter. As, for instance, to take the simplest case: if I make a round ball, for the first time, of clay, or stone, or wood, I do so by putting the particles of matter in those relations and positions in which, through the attraction of cohesion which holds them together, the result of spherical form will be produced; and this result, so produced, is the essence or principle of the invention. In the case of inventions which are independent of form, we arrive at the principle of the invention in the same way. As if I, for the first time, direct a column of steam against a piece of wood or iron, for the purpose of producing motion, the characteristic or principle of my invention consists in the use and application of the expansive force of steam and the effect of motion thereby produced; and these remain logically the same, whether the form and size of the wood or iron, and the form or size of the column of steam are the same as mine, or different.

It is apparent, then, that the mere novel arrangement of matter, irrespective of the purpose and effect accomplished by such arrangement through the agency of natural forces or laws, or the properties of matter, is not the whole of invention; but that the purpose, effect, or result, and the application of the law, force, or property by means of which it is produced, are embraced in the complex idea of invention, and give the subject of the invention its peculiar character or essence. And if this is true, it is easy, — and as correct as it is easy, — to advance to the position that the discovery and application of a new force or law of nature, as a means of producing an effect or result in matter never before produced, may in some cases be the subject of a patentable invention. When it has been laid down that a "principle," — meaning by this use of the term a law of nature, or a general property of matter, or rule of abstract science, — cannot be the subject of a patent, the doctrine, rightly understood, asserts only that a law, property, or rule cannot, in the abstract, be appropriated by any man; but if an inventor or discoverer for the first time produces an effect or result, practically, by the application of a law, he may so far appropriate that law, as to be entitled to say, that whoever applies the same law to produce the same effect or result, however the means, apparatus, forms, or arrangements of matter may be varied, practises or makes use of his invention, unless the variation of means, apparatus, method, form, or arrangement of matter introduces some new law, or creates some new characteristic, which produces or constitutes a substantially different result. For, in all such cases, the peculiarity of the invention consists in the effect produced by the application of the natural law, as an agent; and this effect is not changed by the use of different vehicles for the action of the agent, provided there is still the same agent operating substantially in the same way, to produce substantially the same effect or result.

This may be illustrated by several inventions or discoveries, for which patents have been granted, and which have been the subjects of litigation. One of the most striking of these cases is that already mentioned, of the application of a hot-air blast to the production of a particular effect in the manufacture of iron. It is very easy to say, in general terms, that no man can appropriate to himself the use of caloric, which is a substance, or element, or force in nature, bountifully supplied, as the common property of mankind. But if any man has discovered that the use of caloric in a particular manner, never before observed, will, as a universal fact, produce a particular effect of a new character upon matter, what reason can exist why he should not appropriate to himself the production of that effect by the use of that particular agent? His appropriation, in such a case, would embrace strictly what he has invented. It may be more or less meritorious; it may have been more or less difficult or easy of discovery; it is still his invention, and any one else who does the same thing after the inventor, however he may vary the particular means or apparatus, practises that invention which the inventor was the first to discover and announce to the world. If the patent law were to say, in this case, that the invention or discovery could not be appropriated by him who had made it, because caloric is the common property of all men, it would be obliged, in consistency, to say that a certain arrangement of wood and iron, constituting a new machine, could not be appropriated by the inventor, because cohesion, gravitation, and the laws of motion, which are all applied by the inventor to the accomplishing a certain effect, are the common property of every man. But the patent law does not come to such determinations. It proceeds upon the truth, that while the properties of matter, the forces or elements of nature are common property, any man who applies them to the production of a new and useful effect in matter may rightfully claim to have been the inventor of that application to the purpose of that effect. The effect itself is what is commonly regarded as the patentable subject; but as that particular effect must always be produced by the application of the same properties of matter, or the same forces or elements in nature, it is correct to say that the appropriation rightfully includes their application to the production of the effect, and that to this extent they may be appropriated.

Inventions which consist in the application of the known qualities of substances extend the appropriation of the inventor to those qualities in the same manner and in the same sense. For instance, in the case of Walton's improvement in the manufacture of cards for carding wool, &c., which consisted in giving elasticity and flexibility to the backs of the cards, by making the sheet on the back, in which the teeth are inserted, of india-rubber, instead of leather. The qualities of elasticity and flexibility in india-rubber were common property; but this did not prevent the inventor from sustaining a patent, which was held to cover the general ground of giving to the backs of cards elasticity and flexibility derived from india-rubber, by whatever form of application of the india-rubber the effect might be produced.[1]

[1] See *post*, § 312, § 322–327.

In the same manner, inventions which consist in the application of a well-known law of physical science involve and admit of the appropriation of that law in its application to the production of the particular effect, however the machinery or apparatus may be varied. There is a known law of physics, that the evaporation of a liquid is promoted by a current of air, and this law is common property. An invention of certain improvements in evaporating sugar consisted in applying this law by forcing atmospheric air through the liquid syrup by means of pipes, the ends of which were carried down nearly to the bottom of the vessel containing the solution; and it is obvious that any person who should apply the same law to the same purpose, though by a different apparatus, would practise the same invention. Although, therefore, it is not safe, in reasoning upon the patent law, to lay down general rules of an abstract character, with the purpose of describing what every inventor appropriates to himself, without regard to the particular circumstances of the invention, yet it is, on the other hand, equally unsafe to assume, because the properties of matter, or the laws of physics, or the forces of nature are common property, that no inventor can establish a claim of a general character, irrespective of particular methods or forms of matter, to the application of such properties, laws, or forces in the production of a certain effect.

It is, in truth, wholly incorrect to say that the inventor in such cases, because his patent is held to embrace such a general claim, monopolizes the law, property, or quality of matter which he has applied by a particular means to the accomplishment of a certain end. His patent leaves the law, property, or quality of matter precisely where it found it, as common property, to be used by any one, in the production of a new end by a new adaptation of a different character. It appropriates the law, property, or quality of matter only so far as it is involved in the subject with which, the means by which, and the end for which the inventor has applied it; and this application constitutes the essence and substance of the invention in all cases, and is in reality what the patentee has invented. He cannot be deprived of it without violating the principles on which all property in invention rests, and denying the whole policy of the patent law. The test which marks the extent and nature of his just appropriation is the same that is applicable to every invention.

This test may be stated thus: That the truth, law, property, or quality of matter, which, by reason of its application, enters into the essence of an invention, may be appropriated, to the extent of every application which, according to the principles of law and the rules of logic, is to be deemed piracy of the original invention.

One of the most well-settled as well as soundest doctrines of the patent law is, that where form, arrangement of matter, proportion, method of construction, or apparatus employed are not of the essence of the invention, any changes introduced in them which do not effect a change in the characteristic or purpose of the invention, are changes in immaterial circumstances. When the patent is a patent for form, or particular arrangement, or for the apparatus devised to accomplish a particular effect, changes in these respects will be changes in the subject-matter of the invention; but in cases where the invention has a characteristic or an aggregate of characteristics, independent of particular form, method, arrangement, or apparatus, changes in these things amount only to the substitution of one equivalent for another, unless they cause a change in the characteristic, essence, or, as it is commonly called, the *principle* of the invention. This is very clearly seen in the case of machinery. The characteristic or principle of the invention consists in producing a certain effect by the application of motion, through a form of apparatus adapted to that result. But if the same effect of the combined operation of the different parts of the mechanism can be produced by substituting a different contrivance, which does not change the characteristic of the machine, but is a mere equivalent for the part for which it is substituted, such a substitution is only a different mode of practising the same invention.

In this sense, all inventions are independent of form, except those whose entire essence, purpose, and characteristics begin and end in form alone; as would be the case with the manufacture of a sphere or a cube for the first time; and as is the case with all manufactures, the utility and advantage and proposed object of which depend on form. But where there is a purpose that does not begin and end in form alone, where the form or arrangement of matter is but the means to accomplish a result of a character which remains the same through a certain range of variations of those means, the invention is independent of form and arrangement to this extent, that it embraces every application of means which accomplishes the result without changing its nature and character. In other words, it may be stated as a general proposition, that in the characteristic or principle of an invention are embraced the truth, law, property, or quality of matter which is applied to the production of a result, and the result of such application; and that, by reason of such application, the truth, law, property, or quality of matter is appropriated, to the extent of all other applications which a jury, under the guidance of the law, shall consider as a piracy of the former.

In coming to this result, the patent law establishes no monopoly beyond the fair fruits of actual invention. It protects the real inventor in the enjoyment of what he was the first to produce; and it recognizes, as substantive inventions, all changes which may be produced in the same line of experiment, or in the same department of labor, which introduce new characteristics, new results, or new advantages not embraced by the former invention. As long as the patent law exists at all to afford protection to the labors of ingenious men, it must proceed upon this fundamental principle. It is now too late in the history of civilization to question the policy of this protection, which forms a prominent feature in the domestic polity of every nation which has reached any considerable stage of progress in the arts of civilized life.

It will be seen in the following pages how far these views have prevailed in the administration of the patent law, in England and America, and to what extent they have been developed in particular cases. They have led, in the construction of patents in England, to a somewhat different spirit from that which formerly animated the courts of law; for, formerly, the judges exercised their ingenuity to defeat every patent that came before them, if it could by possibility be defeated. This was done upon the notion, that a patent is the grant of a privilege against common right; and hence some judges were in the habit of saying that they were "not favorers of patents." But within the last forty years a different view has been adopted; the more just and liberal doctrine has been acted upon, that public policy requires the encouragement of the inventive powers of ingenious men, and that this policy is supported by every consideration of justice. The consequence has been, that the patent law has made greater advances, in England, within the last forty years, towards a consistent and admirable system of justice, than it has ever made before during the whole period that has elapsed since the enactment of the Statute of Monopolies.

In America, the more liberal policy has always prevailed, from the time when patent rights came under the protection of the general government; and the rule has been often laid down by the Courts of the United States with a good deal of strength, — as if in obedience to the spirit of the Constitution, — that patents ought to be construed liberally. Perhaps the general language which has thus been employed by judges would lead to the conclusion, that the leaning of the courts is, systematically, in favor of the patentee and against the public; but this tendency has not been exhibited so strongly, in practice, as to derange the administration of the law.

The truth is, a patent should be construed as, what it really is, in substance, namely, a contract or bargain between the patentee and the public, upon those points which involve the rights and interests of either party. These points relate to the extent of the claim, and to the intelligibility of the description for the purposes of practice. The first is universally a question for the court; the last is generally a question for the jury, under the direction of the court. As to the first question, the extent of the claim presents at once the relations between the patentee and the public; for it involves, among other things, the inquiry, whether the patentee has claimed any thing beyond what was really his own invention. If, in representing himself as the inventor of the thing for which he has asked and received a patent, the inventor has included in his claim any thing that existed before, he has made a representation untrue in point of fact; and whether he has made this representation intentionally or unintentionally, the grant of the patent proceeds upon it, and, if it is not true, the grant is not supported by an existing consideration, such as the inventor has represented it to be. In determining this question whether the patentee has really included in his claim something which he did not invent, two things are to be ascertained; *first*, whether he makes use of any thing not new; and *second*, whether that thing, according to the fair import of his language, is represented to be a part of the invention which he claims to have made. The fact of whether he makes use of any thing not new, is a question depending upon evidence, if it is not manifest on the face of the description. It is upon the second branch of the inquiry, whether the old thing is really included in the claim of invention, that the true principles of construction have to be applied. Recollecting, on the one hand, that if the public have been misled, the patent ought not to stand, because of the false representation; and, on the other hand, that a construction, which will destroy the patent, ought not to be adopted lightly, it would seem to be the true rule, to construe the patent fairly, and so as to arrive at the just import of the language in which the claim is set forth. But if, after applying this rule, the question remains doubtful whether the claim is not broader than the invention, then the rule should be adopted, in favor of the patent, that the patentee is to be presumed to have intended to claim no more than he has actually invented. Every patentee is presumed to know the law, and to know that if he includes in his claim something which he has not invented, his claim is void. Such a claim is a kind of fraud upon the public, with whom the applicant offers to enter into a contract, when he asks for his patent; and fraud is never to be presumed, but is always to be proved. The rule, therefore, which presumes, in doubtful cases, that the patentee intended to claim no more than his actual invention, is founded in a maxim of general application to contracts; and it will be seen, in practice, that it has no tendency to support patents which ought not to be supported, or to encourage loose and sweeping claims. In all cases which are not doubtful, — where it is manifest that the claim admits of no construction but that which makes it too comprehensive to be valid, — this rule will have no application. The imposition attempted will be apparent, and the fraud — so far as it is a fraud — will not require to be presumed, but will stand proved.

This rule, although not distinctly announced by any of our courts, has much to support it, in several authorities. Judges would seem to have had a rule of this kind in view, when they have construed patents under the guidance of the maxim, *ut res magis valeat, quam pereat.* The use of this maxim, which has often furnished the spirit of construction in particular cases, implies that the claim is to be supported, if it can be done without a violation of principle. But the rule has been distinctly applied, in England, by the Court of Common Pleas, that the patentee is not to be presumed to have intended to claim things which he must have known to be in common use, although, in describing his invention, he has not expressly excluded them from the claim. There are also cases, in this country, where it has been held not to be necessary to use words of exclusion, in reference to details, where it appears from the whole description of the invention that the new is capable of being distinguished from the old.

The same rule, in cases of doubt, should be applied to the construction, where the question is, whether the patentee has claimed as much as he has invented; that is to say, the specification should be so construed as to make the claim coextensive with the actual invention, if this can be done consistently with principle.

But beyond this rule it is not necessary or wise to go, in the construction of patents. By giving the patentee the benefit of this presumption, in cases of doubt, the doubt will be removed, and the patent will remain good for the real invention. But where there is no room for doubt, and no occasion for the application of the rule, but the claim is manifestly broader or narrower than the real invention, there can be no hesitation about the judgment to be pronounced, especially since the provisions of our law, by which a patent may remain valid *pro tanto*, after the real invention of the party has been judicially ascertained.

THE LAW OF PATENTS.

THE LAW OF PATENTS.

CHAPTER I.

OF THE SUBJECT-MATTER FOR WHICH LETTERS-PATENT MAY BE GRANTED.

§ 1. THE patent system of the United States, having grown up under a positive grant of authority in the Federal Constitution, is to be considered, in respect to the subjects of the exclusive privilege, with reference to that grant, and to the legislation which has been had under it. In England, the corresponding system has rested upon a proviso in the Statute of Monopolies, which excepted from the prohibitions of that act letters-patent granted by the crown for "the sole working or making of any manner of new *manufactures*, within this realm, to the first and true inventor or inventors of such manufactures, which others at the time of the making of such letters-patent and grants did not use, so they be not contrary to the law, nor mischievous to the state."

§ 2. The distinction thus established between those exclusive privileges which the crown may and those which it may not grant proceeds upon the principle, that a monopoly, in the prohibited sense, is a grant which restrains others from the exercise of a right or liberty which they had before the grant was made;[1] whereas the exclusive privilege intended to be secured by letters-patent for an invention contemplates something in which other persons than the inventor had not, before his invention, a right to deal, or which they had not a right to use, because it did not exist. Other persons than the first inventor of a thing had the same right to invent it that he had; but as he has been the first to invent it, the patent system — proceeding upon the policy of encouraging the exercise of inventive talent by securing to the

[1] Sir E. Coke's definition of a monopoly, 3 Inst. 181, c. 85.

inventor an original property, which, without protection, would have rested only upon a principle of natural justice—takes notice of the exclusive right of that first inventor, and makes it effectual by assuming that he who has first exercised the right of invention has bestowed something upon society which ought to procure for him thereafter, at least for a time, the exclusive right to make or use that thing.

§ 3. This being the leading idea of the patent system, the executive and judicial departments of the English government had for a long time no other guide by which to distinguish the proper subjects of patents, which the crown could lawfully grant, excepting the description in the proviso of the Statute of Monopolies. Accordingly, the English system of patents for inventions has grown up under the constructions given to the term "manufactures." Taking into view the clear policy intended by the proviso of the statute, and the principle, that while the subject could not lawfully be restrained in the exercise of any right of trade which he possessed before a particular grant to another, yet that he might be lawfully restrained from the exercise of any trade in respect to a thing which did not previously exist, and which another had invented, the English judges had to consider what could be regarded as falling within the meaning of the term "new manufactures." The term itself, as well as the purpose of the statute, evidently contemplated something to be done or produced in matter, as distinguished from a philosophical or abstract principle. The subjects of patents which could be lawfully granted were to be "new manufactures," or "the working or making of new manufactures," invented by the grantee, and which "others," at the time of the grant, "did not use." Hence, it was apparent that something of a corporeal nature, something to be made, or at least the process of making something, or of producing some effect or result in matter, or the practical employment of art or skill, and not theoretical conceptions or abstract ideas, must constitute the subjects of the exclusive privileges which the crown was authorized to grant.[1]

§ 4. But, subject to this restriction, the words "any manner of new manufactures," in the Statute of Monopolies, have received in construction a comprehensive import. According to the con-

[1] See the comments on the statute, in The King *v.* Wheeler, 2 B. & Ald. 349, 350.

struction of the courts, the word "manufacture" is used in the statute in a literal and a figurative sense. It is used in a literal sense, because it clearly includes any species of new manufactured article, or tangible product of industry; or a new machine, the construction or production of which, as an arrangement of matter, is the result at which the inventor aims. But when it is extended to include the mode of producing an old or well-known substance, or an old and well-known effect upon matter, by a new method or process, it seems to be used in a sort of figurative sense; because, in such cases, it is the method or process of producing the thing or the effect that is new, and is the real subject of the invention; and the manufacture, or the result attained in matter, is then made to stand in the place of the new method or process of attaining it.

§ 5. Thus, "manufacture" has been defined to be "something made by the hand of man";[1] and it has also been held to include the practice of making a thing, or of producing a result.[2] As in

[1] Per Lord Kenyon, in Hornblower *v.* Boulton, 8 T. R. 99.

[2] "It was admitted, at the argument at the bar, that the word 'manufacture,' in the statute, was of extensive signification; that it applied not only to things made, but to the *practice of making*, to principles carried into practice in a new manner, and to new results of principles carried into practice. Let us pursue this admission. Under *things made* we may class, in the first place, new compositions of things, such as manufactures in the most ordinary sense of the word; secondly, all mechanical inventions, whether made to produce old or new effects, for a new piece of mechanism is certainly a thing made. Under the *practice of making*, we may class all new artificial manners of operating with the hand, or with instruments in common use, new processes in any art producing effects useful to the public. When the effect produced is some new substance or composition of things, it should seem that the privilege of the sole working or making ought to be for such new substance or composition, without regard to the mechanism or process by which it has been produced, which, though perhaps also new, will be only useful as producing the new substance. Upon this ground Dolland's patent was perhaps exceptionable, for that was for a *method* of producing a new object-glass, instead of being for the object-glass produced. If Dr. James's patent had been for his *method for preparing* his powders, instead of the *powders themselves*, that patent would have been exceptionable upon the same ground. When the effect produced is no substance or composition of things, the patent can only be for the mechanism, if new mechanism is used, or for the process, if it be a new method of operating, with or without old mechanism, by which the effect is produced. To illustrate this. The effect produced by Mr. David Hartley's invention for securing buildings from fire is no substance, or composition of things; it is a mere negative quality, the absence of fire. This effect is pro-

Watt's patent for "a method of lessening the consumption of steam and fuel in fire-engines," which was held, after great consideration, to be a good subject-matter.[1] The distinction to which this case gave rise, and which greatly extended the meaning of the term "manufacture," is this: that although a principle, or a rule in mechanics, or an elementary truth in physics, cannot be the

duced by a new method of disposing iron plates in buildings. In the nature of things, the patent could not be for the effect produced. I think it could not be for making the plates of iron, which, when disposed in a particular manner, produced the effect; for those are things in common use. But the invention consists in the *method of disposing those plates of iron* so as to produce their effect; and that effect being a useful and meritorious one, the patent seems to have been very properly granted to him for *his method* of securing buildings from fire. And this compendious analysis of *new manufactures*, mentioned in the statute, satisfies my doubt, whether any thing could be the subject of a patent but something organized and capable of precise specification. But for the more satisfactory solution of the other points which are made in this case, I shall pursue this subject a little further. In Mr. Hartley's method, plates of iron are the means which he employs; but he did not invent those means; the invention wholly consisted in the new manner of *using*, or I would rather say of *disposing, a thing in common use*, and which every man might make at his pleasure, and which, therefore, I repeat, could not, in my judgment, be the subject of the patent. In the nature of things it must be that, in the carrying into execution any new invention, use must be made of certain means proper for the operation. Manual labor, to a certain degree, must always be employed; the tools of artists frequently; often things manufactured, but not newly invented, such as Hartley's iron plates; all the common utensils used in conducting any process, and so up to the most complicated machinery that the art of man ever devised. Now let the merit of the invention be what it may, it is evident that the patent, in almost all these cases, cannot be granted for the *means* by which it *acts*, for in them there is nothing new, and in some of them nothing capable of approbation. Even where the most complicated machinery is used, if the machinery itself is not newly invented, but only conducted by the skill of the inventor so as to produce a new effect, the patent cannot be for the machinery. In Hartley's case it could not be for the *effect* produced; for the effect, as I have already observed, is merely negative, though it was meritorious. In the list of patents with which I have been furnished, there are several for new methods of manufacturing articles in common use, where the sole merit and the whole effect produced are the saving of time and expense, and thereby lowering the price of the article, and introducing it into more general use. Now I think these *methods* may be said to be *new manufactures*, in one of the common acceptations of the word, as we speak of the manufactory of glass, or of any other thing of that kind. Per Eyre, C. J., in Boulton *v.* Bull, 2 H. Bl. 492.

[1] Boulton *v.* Bull, *ut supra;* Hornblower *v.* Boulton, *ut supra.*

subject of a patent, yet a new principle, rule, or truth, developed, carried out, and embodied in the mode of using it, may be the subject of a patent. A mere principle is an abstract discovery, incapable of answering the term "manufacture"; but a principle so far embodied and connected with corporeal substances, as to be in a condition to act and to produce effects in any art, trade, mystery, or manual occupation, becomes the practical manner of doing a particular thing. It is no longer a principle, but a process.[1] Mr. Watt's invention was the discovery of a practical means of lessening the consumption of steam, by protecting the cylinder from the external air, and keeping it at a temperature not below that of steam itself. He thus brought a principle into practical application, by the invention of a process carried on by a newly contrived machine.

§ 6. In like manner, a patent for the application of the flame of gas, instead of the flame of oil, to remove the superfluous fibres of lace, was sustained.[2] So, too, where the invention consisted in the use and application of lime and mine-rubbish in the smelting of iron, Lord Eldon said there might be a patent for a new combination of materials previously in use for the same purpose, or for a new method of applying such materials.[3] But this distinction has been made still more prominent by two more recent cases. In one the patent was for the application of anthracite, combined with hot-air blast, in the smelting or manufacture of iron from iron-stone, mine, or ore; and the patent was sustained.[4] in the other, the invention was of a mode of welding iron tubes, without the use of a maundril, or any internal support; and this patent was also sustained.[5]

§ 7. These cases show that the term "manufacture" has been extended to include every object upon which art or skill can be exercised, so as to afford products fabricated by the hand of man, or by the labor which he directs.[6] In this sense it includes a pro-

[1] See the remarks of Eyre, C. J., *ante*.

[2] Hall *v.* Jervis, Webs. Pat. Cas. 100.

[3] Hill *v.* Thompson, 3 Mer. 626; Webs. Pat. Cas. 237. In Morgan *v.* Seaward, 2 Mees. & W. 544, Mr. Baron Parke said: "The word 'manufacture,' in the statute, must be construed one of two ways; it may mean the machine when completed, or the mode of constructing the machine."

[4] Crane *v.* Price, Webs. Pat. Cas. 393, 408.

[5] Russell *v.* Cowley, Webs. Pat. Cas. 459.

[6] Webster's Law and Practice.

cess; so that a patent may, it is said, be taken for a process, method, or practical application of a principle, that will cover every means or apparatus by which that process or method can be carried on, or by which that principle can be applied, provided the patentee has not only discovered the principle, but has also invented some mode of carrying it into effect.[1] Such has been the construction given to this important clause in the Statute of Monopolies, upon which the English patent system has been built. The recent English statutes, which have employed only the word "inventions," when referring to the subjects of this class of patent privileges, manifestly assume that the settled law has sufficiently defined them.[2]

§ 8. In this country, when the Constitution of the United States was framed, and the clause was inserted giving power to Congress "to promote the progress of science and useful arts, by securing, for limited times, to authors and inventors, the exclusive right to their respective writings and discoveries," the terms "inventors" and "discoveries" had a well-understood meaning, founded not only upon the practice and law of England, but upon a similar practice of some of the States before the adoption of the Constitution, which, by special grants in particular cases, often protected new and useful inventions. Accordingly, in the first general patent law passed by Congress, and entitled "An act to promote the progress of useful arts," the subjects of the patent privileges to be granted were described as the invention or discovery of "any useful art, manufacture, engine, machine, or device, or any improvement therein not before known or used."[3] In the next statute, the phraseology was first introduced, which has since been employed, and was continued in the patent law of 1836, namely, "any new and useful art, machine, manufacture or composition of matter, or any new and useful improvement on any art, machine, manufacture or composition of matter, not known or used before the application" for a patent.[4]

§ 8 *a*. The language of the present patent law (Act of 1870) is: "That any person who has invented or discovered any new and useful art, machine, manufacture or composition of matter, or any

[1] Forsyth *v*. Riviere, Webs. Pat. Cas. 97, note. Per Alderson, B., in Jupe *v*. Pratt, ibid. 146, and in Nielson *v*. Hartford, ibid. 342.

[2] 15 & 16 Vict. cap. 83 (July 1, 1852).

[3] Act of April 10, 1790.

[4] Act of February 21, 1793.

new and useful improvement thereof, not known or used by others in this country, and not patented or described in any printed publication in this or any foreign country, before his invention or discovery thereof, and not in public use or on sale for more than two years prior to his application, unless the same is proved to have been abandoned, may, upon payment of the duty required by law, and other due proceedings had, obtain a patent therefor." [1]

§ 9. I. AN ART. What is meant by the statute when it describes the subject of a patent as "any new and useful art," or "any new and useful improvement on any art," it is not difficult to understand, if we bear in mind the general purpose of the patent laws, and the other classes of subjects which they embrace. We have just seen that, in order to make a new process or method of working or of producing an effect or result in matter a subject of a patent in England, a somewhat liberal construction of the term "manufacture" became necessary, by which an improvement in the art or process of making or doing a thing was made constructively to be represented by the term which ordinarily would mean only the thing itself, when made or done. It was doubtless to avoid the necessity for this kind of construction that the framers of our legislation selected a term which, *proprio vigore*, would embrace those inventions where the particular machinery or apparatus, or the particular substances employed, would not constitute the discovery, so much as a newly invented mode or process of applying them, in respect to the order, or position, or relations, in which they are used. Thus, for example, in the art of dyeing or tanning, it is obvious that an old article of manufacture may be produced by the use of old materials, but produced by the application of those materials in new relations. In such cases it might not be practicable to claim the article itself, when made, as a new manufacture, for it might, as an article of commerce or consumption, differ in no appreciable way from the same kind of article produced by the old and well-known method. At the same time the new method of producing the article might be a great improvement, introducing greater cheapness, rapidity, or simplicity in the process itself. Again, other cases may be supposed, where the manufacture itself, as produced by a new process, would be better than the same manufacture produced by the old process, as in the different modes of making iron from the native ore; and yet the really new discovery, in

[1] § 24.

such cases, could not well be described as a new "manufacture" or a new "composition of matter" without a figurative use of those terms which it is desirable to avoid. This difficulty is avoided by the use of the term "art," which was intended to embrace those inventions where the particular apparatus or materials employed may not be the essence of the discovery, but where that essence consists in using apparatus or materials in new processes, methods, or relations, so as to constitute a new mode of attaining an old result; or a mode of attaining a new result, in a particular department of industry, which result may not of itself be any new machine, manufacture, or composition of matter; or finally, an entirely new process of making or doing something which has not been made or done before, by any process.

§ 10. A case which occurred before Mr. Justice Washington furnishes an illustration of an "art," as the subject of a patent. The plaintiff alleged himself to be the inventor of a new and useful improvement in the printing of bank-notes, which was said to furnish an additional security against counterfeiting. The invention, as summed up in his specification, was "to print copperplate on both sides of the note or bill; or copperplate on one side and letter-press on the other; or letter-press on both sides of a bank-note or bill, as an additional security against counterfeiting." The art of printing with both letter-press and copperplate was not the invention of the plaintiff. He made use of old materials and processes in a new manner, for the purpose of producing a new effect, namely, a new security against counterfeiting. His patent, therefore, was for the new application of the process of printing by copperplate and letter-press, by printing on both sides of the note; and this new application was held by the court to be an art, within the terms of the statute.[1]

§ 11. Another illustration is presented by a patent for a mode of casting iron rollers or cylinders, so that, when the metal was introduced into the mould, it should receive a rotary motion, by which the dross would be thrown into the centre instead of upon the surface of the cylinder. This was effected solely by changing the direction of the tube which conveyed the metal to the mould from a horizontal or perpendicular position to a direction approaching a tangent of the cylinder.[2]

[1] Kneass *v.* The Schuylkill Bank, 4 Washington's R. 9, 12.

[2] McClurg *v.* Kingsland, 1 Howard, 204. See also Gray *v.* James, Peters's Circ. C. R. 394.

§ 12. Another very instructive illustration is presented in a severely litigated case in England, where an old machine was made use of in a new process. This case exhibits in a striking manner the advantage of a statute provision by which a patent may be granted for an improvement in an "art." The plaintiff had taken a patent for an invention, which was one thing according to his real discovery, but which, as described by the title, specification, and claim, was in truth another thing. The improvement which he in fact invented constituted a new *process* in the art of spinning flax; while his patent was taken for a new or improved *machine* for spinning flax. Before his invention, the common machine for spinning fibrous substances was fitted with slides by which the "reach" (the distance between the retaining and the drawing rollers) could be varied according to the length of the staple or fibre of the article to be spun; and the well-known principle of spinning fibrous substances in a dry state was to vary the "reach," according to the length of the fibre, — the distance for spinning dry flax into thread being from fourteen to thirty-six inches. But it was not known before the plaintiff's discovery, that by macerating the flax it could be spun at a shorter "reach"; and the plaintiff had ascertained by his experiments that in a macerated state flax could be spun at a "reach" of two and one half inches, and that thereby a much finer thread could be produced than had previously been made in any machine driven by steam power. In order to accomplish this new process the plaintiff invented an apparatus for macerating the flax, which was then new, and he reduced the "reach" of the ordinary spinning machine to two and one half inches. But, unfortunately, his patent was taken, not for a process, or an improved process, of spinning flax, but for "new and improved *machinery* for macerating flax and other similar fibrous substances previous to drawing and spinning it, which is called the preparing it; and also for improved *machinery* for spinning the same after having been so prepared. The patent was thus made to cover not only the machinery employed, but two distinct parts of the machinery, namely, that for preparing and that for spinning the flax after it had been prepared. The former was a new invention of the plaintiff, but the defendant did not use it; he made use of another mode of macerating, which had been discovered subsequently. The latter part of the patent was used by the defendant; but he denied that the

placing of the rollers at the distance of two and one half inches, when they had been before placed at greater and less distances. was a patentable invention. As this was a material part of the invention claimed, and the only part used by the defendant, the question as to the validity of the patent necessarily turned upon the inquiry whether the plaintiff had made a new invention of a machine, or had made a patentable invention by changing the "reach" in the old spinning-machine. It was held, upon the greatest consideration, both at law and in equity, and finally in the House of Lords, that this part of the invention described in the patent and specification was not a patentable subject, as it was but the application of a machine already known and in use to the new macerated state of the flax.[1]

§ 13. This decision resulted necessarily from the improper form in which the invention was claimed. At the same time, it is clear that the plaintiff had made a very important invention. He had discovered, by a long course of experiments, that flax in a macerated state presents a much shorter fibre than it has in a dry state, and that this new state of the flax admits of its being spun at a very short "reach," so as to produce much finer thread than had been made before by any spinning-machine driven by power. The case is therefore not to be regarded as deciding that this real invention of the plaintiff could not be the subject of a patent, but that the patent before the court was invalid, because it *claimed* a subject not patentable. There can be no question that the plaintiff should have described his invention as an improved process in the art of spinning flax, making his improved process to consist, first, in reducing the flax to a state of maceration, and then spinning it at a "reach" of two and one half inches. There could then have been no ground to say that the use of the old spinning-machine (previously capable of spinning at variable distances), for the special purpose of spinning macerated flax, could not be the subject of a valid patent. When the invention in this case was claimed as a new *machine* or new *machinery* for spinning flax, on account of the adaptation of the spinning-machine to the new macerated state of the flax, the objection that it was only the use of an old machine on a new occasion was fatal to the patent. But if the patent had been obtained for a new process in the art of spinning flax, consisting of, first, the macera-

[1] Kay *v.* Marshall, 2 Webs. Pat. Cases, 34–84.

tion, then of the spinning at a shorter "reach" than that at which dry flax could be spun, this objection would not have prevailed; for the invention, as claimed, would not have consisted in altering the "reach" of the old machine, but in a process of spinning never before used.[1]

§ 14. Although there may be cases where a patent might be taken either for a process (that is, for a new art, or an improvement in an art) or for a new manufacture, or a new machine or combination of machinery, indifferently, yet it may often become necessary to ascertain whether the subject-matter of a particular patent which has been issued is a process or something else; because the alleged infringement may depend on the construction that is to be given to the claim of the patentee in respect to this question. Thus an important invention in the manufacture of iron, consisting of a new mode of rolling what are called puddler's balls, was announced in the preamble of the specification as "an improvement in the process of manufacturing iron." The real invention consisted in causing the mass of iron as delivered from the puddling furnace to pass between vibrating and reciprocating curved surfaces, which subjected it to a pressure that was found to expel the impurities of the metal in a better manner than the old methods of making puddler's balls. Now it is obvious that this inventor might either have taken a patent for a new machine operating upon this principle, and covering all devices which could be substituted so as to operate substantially in the same way, or he might have taken a patent for the new method or process of making puddler's balls by passing the metal through vibratory and reciprocating curved surfaces, and thus have entitled himself to cover all machinery which accomplished this process, provided he had given proper directions for the construction of some machinery by which this process could be applied. But the misfortune of his case was, that, while he claimed to have invented a process of manufacturing iron not before known, he so described the machine by which he effected the operation, and so ambiguously summed up his claim in respect to the machine, that the Supreme Court of the United States construed it to be a patent for a machine, and not for a process. It was held, therefore, that evidence on the part of the defendant that his machine differed in mechanical structure and mechanical action from the plain-

[1] See the note of Mr. Webster on this case, 2 Pat. Cases, 83.

tiff's, which had been rejected at the trial, should have been received and submitted to the jury.[1]

§ 14 *a*. The Supreme Court of the United States held, in a very recent case,[2] that a process and the product of a process may be both new and patentable, and are wholly disconnected and independent of each other. On this occasion, Mr Justice Swayne, in delivering the judgment of the court, remarked that "patentable subjects, as defined by the patent law [Act of 1836, § 6], are 'any new and useful art, machine, manufacture or composition of matter, or any new and useful improvement on any art, machine, manufacture or composition of matter.' A machine may be new, and the product or manufacture proceeding from it may be old; in that case, the former would be patentable, and the latter not.

[1] Corning *v.* Burden, 15 Howard, 252. I am not disposed to dispute the correctness of this decision, although the specification manifestly disclosed a discovery of a new process, and as clearly evinced the intention of the patentee to secure the benefit of it. But the instrument was unskilfully constructed, and the decision of the court may be defended. But I must express my dissent from some of the comments made by the learned judge, who delivered the judgment of the court, upon the distinction between the patentable character of a process, and the patentable character of a machine. I agree with him, of course, in the observation that a process, *eo nomine*, is not the subject of a patent under our laws, and that it is included under the general term "useful art." But the explanations given by the learned judge of the distinction between a process and a machine, as the subjects of patents, seem to carry with them the idea that a patentable process is confined to such means or methods of producing a result as are not machinery; but that if the means or methods are effected by mechanism, or mechanical combinations, the patent must necessarily be for a machine. If this is a correct view of his meaning, I must dissent from it. A process may be altogether new, whether the machinery by which it is carried on be new or old. A new process may be invented or discovered, which may require the use of a newly invented machine. In such a case, if both the process and the machine were invented by the same person, he could take separate patents for them. A new process may be carried on by the use of an old machine, in a mode in which it was never used before, as in the example above referred to, of spinning macerated flax. In such a case, the patentability of the process in no degree depends upon the characteristic principle of the machine, although machinery is essential to the process, and although a particular machine may be required. The case of Le Roy *v.* Tatham, 14 Howard, 156, exhibits a similar instance of a claim so unfortunately constructed as not to embrace the new *process*, which was the real invention, but making the novelty to depend on the apparatus made use of.

[2] Rubber Company *v.* Goodyear (1869), 9 Wal. 788.

The machine may be substantially old, and the product new; in that event, the latter and not the former would be patentable. Both may be new, or both may be old; in the former case, both would be patentable; in the latter, neither. The same remark applies to processes and their results. Patentability may exist as to either, neither, or both, according to the fact of novelty, or the opposite. The patentability, or the issuing a patent as to one, in no wise affects the rights of the inventor or discoverer in respect to the other. They are wholly disconnected and independent facts. Such is the sound and necessary construction of the statute."

§ 15. These illustrations will suffice to show the importance of a careful discrimination between an improved process and an improved machine, manufacture, or composition of matter, when a specification is to be prepared, — a discrimination that must be guided by the nature of the invention and its essential character. In order to assist the reader in forming the habits of investigation on which such an inquiry is to be conducted, it may be useful now to proceed to the discussion of the following question: Assuming that an invention has been made, and that it is *primâ facie* to be regarded as a new process, and not a new manufacture or machine, in what is the novelty to consist, that will entitle the inventor to claim it as an improvement in an art, in distinction from an improved machine or manufacture or composition of matter? Thus, for example, supposing that the object of the process be to make a vendible article, useful in the arts, such as is described in the statute by the general term "composition of matter": must the article, when made by the new process, possess properties which render it more valuable than the same kind of article when made by the old process, or is it sufficient, in order to sustain a patent for the new process of making it, that the process itself is different from the old process, while the article itself is not improved in respect to its properties, and in what must that difference consist? Again: suppose that there is novelty, both in the process of manufacture, and in the article or substance produced; how should the patent be taken?

§ 16. One of the most simple cases of this kind is to be found in Hall's invention of a new process of manufacturing lace, by singeing off the superfluous fibres of the thread, by directing upon it a flame of gas. The flame of other substances had been used for the same purpose before. The plaintiff did not rest his claim upon any particular apparatus for applying the flame of the gas, although he described an apparatus fit for the purpose. What he claimed was, the application of the flame of gas to the singeing of lace; and it appeared that the fibres of the thread could be more effectually removed by this process than by the use of other flames. The case, therefore, was one where the article manufactured by the new process may be said to have possessed other properties, namely, a superior finish, as compared with the article manufactured by the old process. The patent was sustained; and the case is, therefore, an authority for the position, that whether the process itself, or the means employed in the manufacture, be cheaper or dearer, simpler or more complex, than the old process, or means employed, yet if it be different in respect to the agency used, and the article produced by it is improved in quality, the process is patentable, as an improvement in the trade or art of manufacturing lace.[1]

§ 17. A similar case is that of an improvement in copperplate printing, consisting in a new mode of preparing the paper, by putting upon it a glazed enamelled surface, by means of white lead and size; the effect or advantage gained being the better exhibition of the fine lines of the engraving than could be attained by the old modes of preparing the paper.[2] So, also, in another case, where the object of the plaintiff's invention was to render fabrics water-proof, at the same time leaving them pervious to air. Before the plaintiff's patent, a solution of alum and soap was used, and the fabric to be rendered water-proof was immersed therein. But this produced a water-proof surface only, which was, moreover, not lasting. The plaintiff's new process consisted in immersing successively in two solutions, — first, in a solution of alum and carbonate of lime, and then in a solution of soap. The effect was to make each fibre of the cloth water-proof throughout, while the whole fabric remained pervious to air.[3] In these and similar cases, where it appears that a superior article is produced by a change in the method or process of making it, the true subject of the patent is the improved process, and it is supported as an invention by the improved effect, whether the process be dearer or cheaper, simpler or more complicated, than the old one.

[1] Hall *v.* Jarvis, 1 Webs. Pat. Cas. 100.
[2] Sturz *v.* De La Rue, 5 Russ. Chancery R. 322.
[3] Halliwell *v.* Dearman, 1 Webs. Pat. Cas. 401, note (*t*).

§ 18. Another very important case is presented by Crane's patent for "an improvement in the manufacture of iron"; the improvement consisting in a new process of making iron, followed by extremely important effects. Before the plaintiff's patent, the use of a hot-air blast, in the manufacture of iron with bituminous coal, was known, and the use of a cold blast, with anthracite coal, was known; but the plaintiff's invention consisted in a new process of making iron with a hot blast and anthracite coal. The effect of the change in the process was, that the yield of the furnaces was more, the nature, properties, and quality of the iron better, and the expense of making it less, than under the former process. Upon the question whether this was a patentable invention, Tindal, C. J., delivering the judgment of the Court of Common Pleas, said: "We are of opinion, that if the result produced by such a combination is either a new article, or a better article, or a cheaper article, to the public, than that produced before by the old method, that such combination is an invention or manufacture intended by the statute, and may well become the subject of a patent."[1] By defining this as a new "manufacture," the learned judge did not simply mean that the iron produced was a new iron; although, in respect to its being of better quality, it may be said to have been a new article of iron; since that which has new or superior properties is, in a metaphysical sense, a new thing, although it is still iron. But the word "manufacture" was here used, as it must be used, in reference to any new process, by an English judge, when dealing with such a case, as meaning the art or process of manufacturing. Keeping this in view, it will be seen that the comprehensive proposition laid down by the court in this case, and the comments which follow it, embrace the cases where the process itself presents the advantages of the change from the old to the new, or where the article manufactured presents such advantages, or where they appear both in the process itself and in the result of using the process. Thus, if the article made be either new or better, having different or superior properties, the advantages are presented by the thing itself, as made by the new process. If the article, as made by the new process, is of as good or better quality, and cheaper, the advantage of cheapness is gained by a more economical process than the old one, and the improvement appears in the process, while the article made by it

[1] Crane *v.* Price, 1 Webs. Pat. Cas. 375, 409.

may or may not be new; that is to say, may or may not possess other new properties than cheapness.

§ 19. There is a class of cases, some of which have been already mentioned, where the distinction between a mere process and a machine has come into view, in the construction of the particular patent in controversy, in pursuance of the general rule of construction, by which the real invention is to be beneficially secured to the patentee, if the terms of his specification will admit of it. These cases will come under review hereafter, in considering the application of this rule.

§ 20. II. A MACHINE. The next subject of letters-patent recited in the statute is a machine, or an improvement of a machine. When the supposed invention is not a mere function, or abstract mode of operation, separate from any particular mechanism, but a function or mode of operation is embodied in mechanism designed to accomplish a particular effect, it will be a machine in the sense of the patent law.[1] A very concise statement of the distinction between a machine and a method or process is to be found in a *dictum* of Mr. Justice Heath: "When a mode of doing a thing is referred to something permanent, it is properly termed an engine; when to something fugitive, a method."[2] But without recurring to the distinction between a machine and a process, it may be said that a machine is rightfully the subject of a patent whenever a new or an old effect is produced by mechanism new in its combinations, arrangements, or mode of operation.

§ 21. If the subject of the invention or discovery is not a mere function, but a function embodied in some particular mechanism whose mode of operation and general structure are pointed out, and which is designed to accomplish a particular purpose, function, or effect, it will be a machine, in the sense of the patent law.[3] A machine is rightfully the subject of a patent when well-known effects are produced by machinery entirely new in all its

[1] Blanchard *v.* Sprague, 3 Sumner, 535, 540.

[2] Boulton *v.* Bull, 2 Hen. Blackstone, 463, 468. The meaning of the learned judge, expressed in a more amplified form, appears to be this: that an engine or machine has been invented, when mechanism has been constructed, which does something in a particular mode; and that a method or process has been invented, when the mode of doing a thing has been devised that is capable of being carried out by various mechanisms, and does not require one permanent mechanism.

[3] Blanchard *v.* Sprague, 3 Sumner's R. 535, 540.

combinations, or when a new or an old effect is produced by mechanism, of which the principle or *modus operandi* is new.[1] The word "machine," in the statute, includes new combinations of machines, as well as new organizations of mechanism for a single purpose. There may be a patent for a new combination of machines to produce certain effects, whether the machines constituting the combination be new or old. In such cases, the thing patented is not the separate machines, but the combination.[2] A single instance of such a combination is presented by the telescope, in which a convex and concave glass of different refracting powers are combined to make the object-glass.[3] What constitutes a claim for a combination only, and what will be a claim for the specific parts of a machine, as well as for the combination, is a question of construction on the patent and specification, the rules for which will be stated hereafter.

§ 22. The statute also makes a new and useful "improvement" of a machine the subject of a patent. A patent for the improvement of a machine is the same thing as a patent for an improved machine.[4] Improvement, applied to machinery, is where a specific machine already exists, and an addition or alteration is made, to produce the same effects in a better manner, or some new combinations are added, to produce new effects.[5] In such cases the patent can only be for the improvement, or new combination.[6] The great question, of course, when an alleged invention purports to be an improvement of an existing machine, is to ascertain whether it be a real and material improvement, or only a change of form. In such cases, it is necessary to ascertain, with as much accuracy as the nature of such inquiries admits, the boundaries between what was known and used before, and what is new, in

[1] Whittemore *v.* Cutter, 1 Gallis. 480; Boulton *v.* Bull, 2 H. Bl. 463, 468. When a mode of doing a thing is referred to something permanent, it is properly termed an engine; when to something fugitive, a method. Per Heath, J., in Boulton *v.* Bull.

[2] Barrett *v.* Hall, 1 Mas. 474; Evans *v.* Eaton, 3 Wheat. 454, 476, 506; Prouty *v.* Draper, 1 Story's R. 568; Park *v.* Little, 3 Wash. 196; Pitts *v.* Whitman, 2 Story's R. 609, Ames *v.* Howard, 1 Sumner, 482.

[3] Dolland's Case, Webs. Pat. Cas. 42, 43.

[4] Per Heath, J., in Boulton *v.* Bull, 2 H. Bl. 463, 482; and per Story, J., in Barrett *v.* Hall, 1 Mas. 475.

[5] Whittemore *v.* Cutter, 1 Gallis. 480.

[6] Ibid.; Odiorne *v.* Winkler, 2 Gallis. 51.

the *mode of operation*.[1] The inquiry, therefore, must be, not whether the same elements of motion, or the same component parts are used, but whether the given effect is produced substantially by the same mode of operation, and the same combination of powers, in both machines; or whether some new element, combination, or feature has been added to the old machine, which produces either the same effect in a cheaper or more expeditious manner, or an entirely new effect, or an effect that is in some material respects superior, though in other respects similar to that produced by the old machine.[2]

§ 23. This inquiry will therefore involve the question, whether the alleged improved machine operates upon the same principle as the former machine; or, in other terms, whether it produces the same effect by the same mechanical means, or by means which are substantially the same. One machine may employ the same mechanical power in the same way as another machine, though the external mechanism may be apparently different. At the same time a machine may have an external resemblance to another, and yet may operate upon a different principle.[3] It is therefore necessary, where the effect is the same, to determine whether the *modus operandi*, the peculiar method of producing the effect, is substantially the same. Where the effect is different, the test of a sufficient "improvement" to sustain a patent will be the character and importance of the effect itself.

[1] Whittemore *v.* Cutter, 1 Gallis. 478, 481. Whether an improvement is trifling and insignificant, or real and important, is a question for the jury. Losh *v.* Hague, Webs. Pat. Cas. 205.

[2] Whittemore *v.* Cutter, 1 Gallis. 478; Brunton *v.* Hawkes, 4 B. & Ald. 540.

[3] Barrett *v.* Hall, 1 Mas. 470. In this case, Mr. Justice Story said: "The true legal meaning of the principle of a machine, with reference to the Patent Act, is the peculiar structure or constituent parts of such machine. And, in this view, the question may be very properly asked, in cases of doubt or complexity, of skilful persons, whether the principles of two machines be the same or different. Now, the principles of two machines may be the same, although the form or proportions may be different. They may substantially employ the same power in the same way, though the external mechanism be apparently different. On the other hand, the principles of two machines may be very different, although their external structure may have great similarity in many respects. It would be exceedingly difficult to contend that a machine which raised water by a lever was the same in principle with a machine which raised it by a screw, a pulley, or a wedge, whatever in other respects might be the similarity of the apparatus."

§ 24. There may be a patent for an improvement of a machine that is itself the subject of an existing patent. It has been held in England, that a patent including the subject-matter of a patent still in force is valid, if the improvement only is claimed in the specification. In such cases, the new patent will come into force after the expiration of the old one, or it may be applied by using a license under the former patent, or by purchasing the specific machine which the former patent covers, before its expiration.[1]

It has also been held, that, in an action for an infringement of a patent, professing to be an improvement on a former patent, the specification of that former patent must be read. But it is not

[1] Crane *v.* Price, Webs. Pat. Cas. 333, 413. In this case, Sir W. C. Tindall, C. J., said: "Now, it is further argued, that, in point of law, no patent can be taken out which includes the subject-matter of a patent still running or in force. No authority was cited to support this proposition; and the case which was before Lord Tenterden, and in which he held, that where an action was brought for an infringement of improvements in a former patent granted to another person, and still in force, that the plaintiff must produce the former patent and specification; that at least affords a strong evidence that the second patent was good. (Lewis *v.* Davis, 3 Car. & P. 502.) The case of Harmar *v.* Playne (14 Ves. Jr., 130, 11 East, 101; Dav. Pat. Cas. 311; Fox, *ex parte*, 1 Ves. & B. 67) is a clear authority on the same point; and upon reason and principle there appears to be no objection. The new patent, after the expiration of the old one, will be free from every objection, and whilst the former exists, the new patent can be legally used by the public by procuring a license from Neilson, or by purchasing the apparatus from him, or some of his agents; and the probability of a refusal of the license to any one applying for it is so extremely remote, that it cannot enter into consideration as a ground of legal objection."

See also Fox, *ex parte*, 1 V. & B. 67. Mr. Webster puts this very clear illustration: "For suppose a particular article — starch, for instance — to be the subject of letters-patent, and that all the starch in the country was patent starch; there are attached to the making and selling of that article certain exclusive privileges; but the individual who has purchased it of the patentee has a right to sell it again, and to use it at his will and pleasure; the exclusive privileges are, in respect of that particular portion of the article so sold, at an end, and do not pursue it through any subsequent stage of its use and existence, otherwise every purchaser of starch would be obliged, according to the terms of the letters-patent, to have a license in writing, under the hand and seal of the patentee; the absurdity of which is manifest. Hence it is obvious, that if a person legally acquires, by license or purchase, title to that which is the subject of letters-patent, he may use it or improve upon it in whatever manner he pleases, in the same manner as if dealing with property of any other kind."

material whether a machine, made according to that specification of the first patent, would be useful or not, if it be shown that a machine, constructed according to the subsequent patent, is useful.[1]

§ 25. III. A Manufacture. It has been stated, in a former part of this chapter, that the term "manufacture" was used in the English statute 21 Jac. 1, to denote any thing made by the hand of man; so that it embraces, in the English law, machinery, as well as substances or fabrics produced by art and industry.[2]

§ 26. We have seen also that it came, by construction, to include the process of making a thing, or the art of carrying on a manufacture; so that all the various objects which are now held in England to be the subjects of letters-patent are included under this term, which alone saves them out of the prohibition of the statute of monopolies.[3]

[1] Lewis *v.* Davis, Webs. Pat. Cas. 488, 489.

[2] In Boulton *v.* Bull, Heath, J., said: "The statute 21 Jac. 1 prohibits all monopolies, reserving to the king, by an express proviso, so much of his ancient prerogative as shall enable him to grant letters-patent, and grants of privilege, for the term of fourteen years and under, of the sole working or making of any manner of *new manufactures* within this realm, to the true and first inventor and inventors of such *manufactures*. What, then, falls within the scope of the proviso? Such manufactures as are reducible to two classes. The first includes machinery, the second, substances (such as medicines) formed by chemical and other processes, where the vendible substance is the thing produced, and that which operates preserves no permanent form. In the first class the machine, and in the second the substance produced, is the subject of the patent. I approve of the term 'manufacture' in the statute, because it precludes all nice refinements; it gives us to understand the reason of the proviso, that it was introduced for the benefit of trade. That which is the subject of a patent ought to be specified, and it ought to be that which is vendible, otherwise it cannot be a manufacture."

In Hornblower *v.* Boulton, 8 T. R. 99, Lord Kenyon defined the term as "something made by the hands of man." In The King *v.* Wheeler, 2 B. & Ald. 349, Abbott, L. C. J., defined it thus: "The word 'manufacture' has been generally understood to denote either a thing made which is useful for its own sake, and vendible as such, as a medicine, a stove, a telescope, and many others, or to mean an engine or instrument, or some part of an engine or instrument, to be employed, either in the making of some previously known article, or in some other useful purpose, as a stocking-frame, or a steam-engine for raising water from mines. Or it may perhaps extend also to a new process to be carried on by known implements, or elements, acting upon known substances, and ultimately producing some other known substance, by producing it in a cheaper or more expeditious manner, or of a better and more useful kind."

[3] See Hindmarch on Patents, p. 80.

§ 27. Our statute, however, having made an enumeration of the different classes of subjects which in England are held to be patentable, it is to be presumed that this term was used to describe one of these classes only, namely, fabrics or substances made by the art or industry of man, not being machinery.[1] It may sometimes require a nice discrimination, to determine whether one of these classes does not run into the other, in a given case; as, for instance, when a tool or instrument of a novel or improved construction is produced, to be used in connection with other machinery, or to be used separately. As an article of merchandise, found and sold separately in the market, such a production would be a manufacture; but, regarded with reference to its use and intended adaptation, it might be considered as a machine, or part of a machine. In determining, in such cases, how the patent for the article should be claimed, it would probably be correct to range it under the one or the other of these classes, according to the following test. If the article is produced and intended to be sold and used separately, as a merchantable commodity, and the merit of it, as an invention, consists in its being a better article than had been before known, or in its being produced by a cheaper process, then it may properly be considered simply as a manufacture. But if its merit appears only after its incorporation with some mechanism with which it is to be used, and consists in producing, when combined with such mechanism, a new effect, then it should be regarded as a machine, or an improvement of an existing machine. These distinctions, however, are not vitally important, to be taken in the patent itself, since it is not necessary to the validity of a patent, that the thing should be

[1] Perhaps the best general definition of the term "manufacture," as the subject of a patent, would be, any new combination of old materials, constituting a new result or production, in the form of a vendible article, not being machinery. In one sense, all materials are old; as the amount of matter in existence does not depend on the will or the skill of man, whatever he uses is, in one sense, an old material. In this sense, therefore, all that he does, in producing a new manufacture, is to bring old materials into a new combination, and by so doing to produce a new result in matter. It is this new combination, carried into, or evinced by, a new result or production, that is the subject of a patent. The use of all the materials in other combinations may have been known before; but if they are used in a new combination, producing a new result, there will be a good subject for a patent for a "manufacture," as there is in respect to "machinery" when the same thing is effected. See Cornish *v.* Keene, Webs. Pat. Cas. 512, 517.

described with entire accuracy as "a machine" or "a manufacture." If the thing itself is correctly described, and it appears to be novel and useful, and unites all the other requisites of the statute, it may be left to general interpretation to determine whether the subject-matter ranges itself under the one or the other of these classes, or whether it partakes of the characteristics of both. But if the subject-matter be neither a machine nor a manufacture, or composition of matter, then it must be an art. There can be no valid patent, except it be for a thing made, or for the art or process of making or doing something.

§ 28. IV. A COMPOSITION OF MATTER. The last class of patentable subjects mentioned in the statute is described by the term "composition of matter." It includes medicines, compositions used in the arts, and other combinations of substances intended to be sold separately. In such cases, the subject-matter of the patent may be either the composition itself, the article produced, or it may be the mode or process of compounding it. Generally speaking, the patent covers both, because if the composition is itself new, the process by which it is made must also be new, and the law will protect both as the subjects of invention. But if the article itself be not new, but the patentee has discovered merely a new mode or process of producing it, then his patent will not be for a new "composition of matter," but for a new "art" of making that particular thing.

§ 29. With regard to this class of subjects, it is sufficient to observe, that the test of novelty must, of course, be, not whether the materials of which the composition is made are new, but whether the combination is new. Although the ingredients may have been in the most extensive and common use, for the purpose of producing a similar composition, if the composition made by the patentee is the result of different proportions of the same ingredients, or of the same and other ingredients, the patent will be good.[1] The patentee is not confined to the use of the same precise ingredients in making his compound, provided all the different combinations of which he makes use are equally new.[2]

§ 29 *a*. DESIGNS. By the Acts of 1842[3] and 1861, provision was made for granting letters-patent for designs. This class of articles is now embraced within the patent law of 1870, section 71 of

[1] Ryan *v.* Goodwin, 3 Sumner's R. 514, 518.

[2] Ibid.

[3] Act of 1842, ch. 263, § 3.

which provides: "That any person who, by his own industry, genius, efforts, and expense, has invented or produced any new and original design for a manufacture, bust, statue, alto-relievo, or bas-relief; any new and original design for the printing of woollen, silk, cotton, or other fabrics; any new and original impression, ornament, pattern, print, or picture, to be printed, painted, cast, or otherwise placed on or worked into any article of manufacture; or any new, useful, and original shape or configuration of any article of manufacture, the same not having been known or used by others before his invention or production thereof, or patented or described in any printed publication, may, upon payment of the duty required by law, and other due proceedings had the same as in cases of inventions or discoveries, obtain a patent therefor."[1] Patents for designs may be granted for the term of three years and six months, or for seven years, or for fourteen years, as the applicant may, in his application, elect.[2] Section 76 provides: "That all the regulations and provisions which apply to the obtaining or protection of patents for inventions or discoveries, not inconsistent with the provisions of this act, shall apply to patents for designs."

[1] Act of 1861, ch. 88, § 11.

[2] Act of 1870, § 73.

CHAPTER II.

OF THE QUALITIES AND POSITION OF AN INVENTION WHICH WILL MAKE IT THE SUBJECT OF LETTERS-PATENT.

§ 30. In the foregoing chapter, the different kinds or classes of inventions described in the statute as the subjects of letters-patent have been considered. It is now necessary to ascertain, with as much precision as the inquiry admits of, what is the nature and character of a supposed invention, that will entitle it to be the subject of a patent privilege. And it is to be observed, at the outset of this inquiry, that it is the *discovery* or *invention* of any *new* and *useful* art, machine, manufacture, or composition of matter, or any *new* and *useful improvement* on any of these things, which the statute makes the subject of a patent. One of the first questions to be considered, therefore, in this connection, is, whether there is any special quality or character necessary to a patentable invention, apart from its novelty and utility; and if so, what that quality or character is.

§ 31. In discussions on the patentable character of a particular subject, the question has often been raised, whether there is a "sufficiency of invention" to support a patent. This, it is said, does not depend on the quantity of thought, ingenuity, skill, labor, or experiment, or on the amount of money, which the inventor may have bestowed upon his production. And it is undoubtedly true, that, whether the invention was the result of long experiment and profound search, or of a merely accidental discovery, is not the essential ground of consideration in determining the patentable character of any subject.[1] Still, we read in many of the adjudged cases frequent discussions of the question, whether the inventive faculty has been at work in the production of a particular thing. And nothing is more common than to witness at the bar, in the trial of patent causes, a great expenditure of

[1] Crane *v.* Price, 1 Webs. Pat. Cas. 411; Earle *v.* Sawyer, 4 Mason, 6.

evidence and argument upon the inquiry whether a particular change from an old to a new article, process, method of operation, or combination amounts to an invention, within the meaning of the patent law.

§ 32. It may be doubted, whether all the different forms of stating or investigating the question of sufficiency of invention are any thing more than different modes of conducting the inquiry, whether the particular subject of a patent possesses the statute requisites of *novelty* and *utility*, both of which qualities must be found uniting in it. Thus it may, in a particular investigation, be necessary to consider, not whether an invention, in point of fact, *was* the result of much thought, design, or ingenuity, but whether it *may* have been so. It may not be necessary that there should be positive or direct evidence of the expenditure of more or less thought, design, or ingenuity, or of a greater or less degree of exercise of what is sometimes called the inventive faculty. Still, it may be important to see, that the possibility of there having been an exercise of that mental process which is called invention is not excluded by the character of the supposed product of the act or process of invention; because the possibility that the thing made, or the result produced, was arrived at by study and experiment, and not by mere accident, although not an ultimate test of the right to a patent, is one test by which we can determine whether there is a substantial novelty in the alleged invention, as compared with what existed before. While the law does not look to the mental process by which the invention has been reached, but to the character of the result itself, it may still require that the result should be such as not to exclude the possibility of some skill or ingenuity having been exercised. It requires this, because it requires that the subject-matter of a patent shall be something that has not substantially existed before, and is useful in contradistinction to being frivolous. Now, while a thing that is both new and useful may have been produced by accident, and not by design, yet it may also have been the fruit of study and design. If, however, the character of the alleged invention be such that no design or study could possibly have been exercised in its production, then its character tends strongly to show that it does not differ substantially from what had been produced before; or that it is frivolous and immaterial. While, therefore, the law does not regard the process by which an invention has been produced as a decisive test of its patentable qualities, it is often necessary to see whether the character of the invention excludes the possibility of thought, design, ingenuity or labor having been exercised in its production, or exercised to any considerable extent.

§ 33. Thus, if an alleged invention is absolutely frivolous and foolish, though it may have the element of novelty, in one sense, it is not the subject of a patent. So, too, mere colorable variations, or slight and unimportant changes, will not support a patent; as the immersion of cloth in a steam-bath, with the view of damping it, instead of immersing it in hot water; [1] and the substitution of steam as the means of heating hollow rollers over which wool was to be passed, instead of heating them by the insertion of hot iron bars.[2] In such cases, if the consequences resulting from the change are unimportant, and the change consists merely in the employment of an obvious substitute, the discovery and application of which could not have involved the exercise of the inventive faculty in any considerable degree, then the change is treated as merely a colorable variation, or a double use, and not as a substantive invention.[3]

§ 34. On the other hand, the comparative utility of the change, and the consequences resulting therefrom, may be such as to show that the inventive faculty may have been at work; and in such cases, though in point of fact the change was the result of accident, its comparative utility and importance will afford a test of the amount of invention involved in the change. Thus, in Crane's patent the invention consisted in the use of anthracite and hot-air blast, in the manufacture of iron, in the place of bituminous coal and hot-air blast; and the Court of Common Pleas said: "We are of opinion, that if the result produced by such a combination

[1] Rex *v.* Fussell, cited in Webster on the Subject-Matter of Patents, p. 26.

[2] Rex *v.* Lister, cited in Webster on the Subject-Matter of Patents, p. 26.

[3] The illustrations put by Lord Abinger, in Losh *v.* Hague, Webs. Pat. Cas. 208, present the distinctions here taken in an amusing form. "If a surgeon had gone to a mercer and said, 'I see how well your scissors cut,' and he said, 'I can apply them instead of a lancet, by putting a knob at the end,' that would be quite a different thing, and he might get a patent for that; but it would be a very extraordinary thing to say, that because all mankind have been accustomed to eat soup with a spoon, that a man could take out a patent because he says you might eat peas with a spoon."

be either a new article, or a better article, or a cheaper article to the public than that produced before by the old method, that such a combination is an invention or manufacture intended by the statute, and may well become the subject of a patent." [1] But if the change be immaterial, and productive of no beneficial result, so that the end can be attained as well without as with the supposed improvement, it will not support a patent.[2]

§ 35. A concise and lucid *dictum* of Buller, J., presents a capital test of the sufficiency of many inventions: "If there be any thing material and new, which is an improvement of the trade, *that* will be sufficient to support a patent." [3] The term "improvement of the trade" was obviously used by the learned judge in the commercial sense, meaning the production of the article as good in quality at a cheaper rate, or better in quality at the same rate, or with both these consequences partially combined.[4] There are many cases where the materiality and novelty of the change can be judged of only by the effect on the result; and this effect is tested by the actual improvement in the process of producing the article, or in the article itself, introduced by the alleged invention. To these cases this test is directly applicable. Thus, in Lord Dudley's patent, the change consisted in the substitution of pit-coal for charcoal in the manufacture of iron, and it was new both in the process of manufacture and in the constitution of the iron.[5] In Neilson's patent, the change consisted in blowing the furnace with hot air instead of cold; and in Crane's, the substitution of anthracite as fuel, in combination with the hot-blast. Both these

[1] Crane *v.* Price, Webs. Pat. Cas. 409. It has been suggested, that if the immersion of cloth in steam instead of hot water had been attended with any considerable improvement in the manufacture, the change would have been held a sufficient substantive invention to have supported a patent. Webster on the Subject-Matter, p. 26, note (*t*).

[2] In Arkwright's case, there was evidence that the filleted cylinder had been used before, both in the way in which he used it and in another way. Buller, J., said: "If it were in use both ways, that alone is an answer to it. If not, there is another question, whether the stripe in it makes any material alteration? For if it appears, as some of the witnesses say, to do as well without stripes, and to answer the same purpose, if you suppose the stripes never to have been used before, that is not such an invention as will support the patent." Rex *v.* Arkwright, Webs. Pat. Cas. 72, 73.

[3] Rex *v.* Arkwright, Webs. Pat. Cas. 71.

[4] See Mr. Webster's note on this *dictum*, *ut supra*.

[5] Webs. Pat. Cas. 14.

processes were great improvements, leading to a cheaper production of iron of as good or a better quality.[1] In Derosne's patent, the invention was by the application of charcoal in the filtering of sugar, being a change in the process of manufacture, so as to produce sugar in a way unknown before.[2] In Hall's case, the use of the flame of gas, to singe off the superfluous fibres of lace, effected completely what had been done before in an imperfect manner.[3]

§ 36. In these cases, the subject of each invention was not the particular machinery or apparatus by which the new application was to be made available, but it was the new application itself of certain known substances or agents, to produce a particular result, differing either in the process or in the article produced from the former methods of producing the same thing, and thereby producing a better article, or producing it by superior and cheaper processes. It is obvious that the result, in such cases, furnishes a complete test of the sufficiency of invention ; because the importance of the result shows that, whether actually exercised or not, the possibility of the exercise of thought, design, ingenuity, and skill is not excluded. The merit is the same, whether the invention was the fruit of accident or design ; because the merit consists in having realized the idea, and carried it out in practice. But if the idea and the practice involve no beneficial results, superior to what had been before attained, there could have been no scope for the exercise of the inventive faculty, because the result excludes the supposition of its having been exercised.

§ 37. The same test is also indirectly applicable to another class of cases, where a particular instrument or machine, or combination of machinery, is the subject of the patent. As in Arkwright's case, the gist of the objection was, that the alleged new machinery did not serve the purpose of spinning cotton better than the machinery formerly used.[4] In the case of Brunton's patent, which covered two inventions, the one was for an improvement in the construction of chain cables, and the other for an improvement in the construction of anchors. As to the first invention, chain cables had been formerly made with twisted links, a wrought-iron stay being fixed across the middle of the opening of

[1] Webs. Pat. Cas. 191, 273, 375.

[2] Ibid. [3] Ibid. 97.

[4] The King *v.* Arkwright, Webs. Pat. Cas. 71.

each link to keep it from collapsing. The alleged improvement consisted in making the links with straight sides and circular ends, and in substituting a cast-iron stay with broad ends, adapted to the sides of the link, and embracing them. This combination of the link and the stay was calculated to sustain pressure better than the old form. The court considered the substitution of a broad-headed stay in the link, in place of a pointed stay, under the circumstances, a sufficient invention to support a patent, on account of the utility of the substitution, in connection with the principles to be carried out, viz., the resistance of pressure according to the action of forces.[1]

§ 38. In respect of the anchor, the invention consisted in making the two flukes in one, with such a thickness of metal in the middle, that a hole might be pierced through it for the insertion of the shank, instead of joining the two flukes in two distinct pieces by welding to the shank. The hole was made conical or bell-mouthed, so that no strain could separate the flukes from the shank, by which means the injury to the iron from repeated heating was avoided, only one heating being necessary to unite the end of the shank perfectly with the side of the conical hole. But it appeared at the trial that the improvement in the anchor was the avoiding the welding by means well known and practised in cases extremely similar. It was a case of the simple application of a mode known and practised for a similar purpose in other like cases; and it did not appear that anchors so made were superior to those which had been made before. The court were therefore

[1] Brunton *v.* Hawkes, 4 B. & Ald. 540, 550. Abbott, C. J., said: "As at present advised, I am inclined to think that the combination of a link of this particular form, with the stay of the form which he uses, although the form of the link might have been known before, is so far new and beneficial, as to sustain a patent for that part of the invention, if the patent had been taken out for that alone." Bayley, J., said: "The improvement in that respect, as it seems to me, is shortly this; so to apply the link to the force to operate on it, that that force shall operate in one place, namely at the end; and this is produced by having a bar across, which has not the defect of the bar formerly used for similar purposes. The former bars weakened the link, and they were weak themselves, and liable to break, and then if they broke, there might be a pressure in some other part. Now, from having a broad-ended bar instead of a conical one, and having it to lap round the link instead of perforating it, that inconvenience would be avoided; and therefore the present impression on my mind as to this part of the case is, that the patent might be supported."

unanimously of opinion that the patent, in respect of the anchor, could not be sustained.[1]

§ 39. It appears, then, according to the English authorities, that the amount of invention, as being sufficient or insufficient to support a patent, may be estimated from a compound view of the change effected, and the consequences of that change. If the change introduced is so considerable as to warrant the conclusion that it may have been the result of thought, skill, and design, and the consequences produced by it are important and considerable, there will be, it is said, a sufficiency of invention. But in applying this test, it is obviously necessary to view the change and its consequences as a sum, and to see whether both, taken together, are considerable or inconsiderable, important or unimportant. The change alone may be very slight, or in point of fact accidental; yet, if it leads to consequences and results of great practical utility, as in the case of Dudley's, Crane's, Hall's, and Daniel's inventions, and others above mentioned, the condition of a sufficiency of invention is satisfied. But if both change and consequences are inconsiderable and unimportant, the condition is not satisfied.[2]

§ 40. I am persuaded, however, that at least under our statute the question of the patentability of an invention depends upon its satisfying the statute requisites of novelty and utility, after the subject is ascertained to belong to one or the other of the classes mentioned in the statute.[3] I shall proceed, therefore, to the consideration of those statute requirements, drawing the illustrations of their proper scope and application alike from the English and the American decisions. And first, as to the requisite of *novelty*.

§ 41. The subject-matter of a supposed invention is new, in the sense of the patent law, when it is substantially different from what has gone before it; and this substantial difference, in cases where other analogous or similar things have been previously known or used, is one measure of the sufficiency of invention to support a patent. Our courts have, in truth, without always

[1] Ibid.

[2] Webster on the Subject-Matter, pp. 29, 30.

[3] There are some observations by Mr. Justice Nelson, in the case of McCormick *v.* Seymour, 2 Blatch. 240, 243, which appear to me accurately to describe the qualities belonging to a patentable invention.

using the same terms, applied the same tests of the sufficiency of invention, which the English authorities exhibit, in determining whether alleged inventions of various kinds possess the necessary element of novelty. That is to say, in determining this question, the character of the result, and not the apparent amount of skill ingenuity, or thought exercised, has been examined; and if the result has been substantially different from what had been effected before, the invention has been pronounced entitled to a patent; otherwise, the patent has failed.[1]

§ 42. Thus, where the patent was for an improvement in *copperplate* printing of bank-notes, by printing copperplate on both sides of the note, or copperplate on one side, and letter-press on the other, or letter-press on both sides, *as an additional security against counterfeiting;* and the defendants had used steel-plate printing; the question was, whether "copperplate printing" included "steel-plate printing." The plaintiff's counsel contended, that even if copperplate did not include steel-plate printing, still the use of the latter by the defendants, applied to bank-notes, to produce the effect stated in the patent, was a mere evasion, and virtually an infringement. Washington, J., instructed the jury, that if the use of steel plates was an *improvement* upon printing from copperplates, for which a patent might have been obtained by the inventor, the use of steel plates by the defendants could with no propriety be considered as an infringement of the plaintiff's right, unless it appeared that they had also used the plaintiff's improvement.[2]

§ 43. This is in substance the test applied by Mr. Justice Buller, of "any thing material and new that is an improvement of the trade."[3] If the process of printing by steel plates was an improvement, in the manufacture of notes, upon the process of printing by copperplates, so as to be a benefit to the trade, of manufacturing notes, it would have been a substantive invention, and therefore not an infringement upon the plaintiff's patent, if standing alone.

§ 44. So, too, upon the clause in the former statute, "that

[1] The application of these tests is most frequently found in cases, not where insufficiency of invention has been expressly the ground of defence, but where the question has been, whether the patent did not claim something that was not new.

[2] Kneass *v.* The Schuylkill Bank, 4 Wash. 9, 11.

[3] Cited *ante*.

simply changing the form or proportion of any machine shall not be deemed a discovery," Mr. Chief Justice Marshall held that the word "simply" was of great importance; that it was not every change of form or proportion which was declared to be no discovery, but that which was *simply* a change of form or proportion, and nothing more. If by changing the form and proportion a new effect is produced, there is not simply a change of form and proportion, but a change of principle also. The question will be, therefore, whether the change has produced a different effect.[1] If the result of a change is beneficial in a considerable degree, its character will reflect back upon the change itself, and aid in determining its extent.[2]

§ 45. In like manner, Mr. Justice Livingston decided that a patent was invalid, upon substantially the same test as that of Mr. Justice Buller. The patent was for an alleged invention in folding and putting up thread and floss cotton in a manner different from the ordinary mode, so that it would sell quicker, and for a higher price than the same cotton put up in the common way. The article itself was imported, and underwent no change. The whole of the improvement consisted in putting up the skeins or hanks in a convenient quantity for retailing, with a sealed wrapper, and a label containing the number and description of the article. The court declared that the invention, upon the patentee's own showing, was frivolous; that it was in no way beneficial to the public, not making the article itself any better, or altering its quality in any way. In other words, it was no "improvement of the trade" of making the article sold, but it was a mere improvement in the art of selling it, by which the retailer could get a higher price for the same article than could be obtained by putting it up without the label.[3]

[1] Davis *v.* Palmer, 2 Brock, 298, 310. See also Pettibone *v.* Derringer, 4 Wash. 218, 219.

[2] Hall *v.* Wiles, 2 Blatchford, 194–200.

[3] Langdon *v.* DeGroot, 1 Paine's C. C. R. 203. The learned judge said: "The invention is for folding the thread and floss cotton in a manner a little different from the ordinary mode, in which form the cotton will sell quicker and higher by twenty-five per cent than the same cotton put up in the common way. The cotton thus folded is imported from the factory of Holt, in England. The article itself undergoes no change; and the whole of the improvement — for it is a patent for an improvement — consists in putting up skeins of it, perhaps of the same size in which they are imported, decorated with a label and wrapper; thus rendering their appearance somewhat more attractive,

§ 46. So, too, where the question was whether, in a patent for a machine for making wool-cards, the patentee had not claimed what had been substantially done before, — his claim being for the whole machine, which comprehended several distinct operations or stages in the manufacture, — Mr. Justice Story said the question was, whether either of these effects had been produced in the machines formerly in use by a combination of machinery, or mode of operation substantially the same as in the machine of the patentee. That it would not be sufficient to protect the plaintiff's patent, — it being for the whole machine, — that his specific machine, with all its various combinations and effects, did

and inducing the unwary, not only to give it a preference to other cotton of the same fabric, quality, and texture, but to pay an extravagant premium for it. When stripped of these appendages, which must be done before it is used, the cotton is no better in any one respect than that of Holt's retailed in the way put up by him. All this came out on the plaintiff's own testimony.

"Now, that such a contrivance — for with what propriety can it be termed a useful art, within the meaning of the Constitution? — may be beneficial to a patentee, if he can exclude from the market all other retailers of the very same article, will not be denied; and if to protect the interest of a patentee, however frivolous, useless, or deceptive his invention may be, were the sole object of the law, it must be admitted that the plaintiff has made out a satisfactory title to his patent.

"But if the utility of an invention is also to be tested by the advantages which the public are to derive from it, it is not perceived how this part of his title is in any way whatever established. Is the cotton manufactured by himself, which is put up in this way? The very label declares it to be that of another man. Is any thing done to alter its texture or to render it more portable, or more convenient for use? Nothing of this kind is pretended. Does the consumer get it for less than in its imported condition? The only ground on which the expectation of a recovery is built is, that he pays an enormous additional price, for which he literally receives no consideration.

"It is said that many ornamental things are bought of no intrinsic value, to gratify the whim, taste, or extravagance of a purchaser, and that for many of these articles patents are obtained. This may be so; but in such cases there is no deception, no false appearances; and the article is bought to be used with all its decorations and ornaments, which may have been the principal inducements to the purchase, and which will last as long as the article itself. In this the sight or pride of the party is gratified. But here it is the cotton alone which it is intended to buy, and the little label and wrapper appended to it, and which constitute the whole of the improvement, however showy, are stripped off and thrown away before it can be used. And when that is done, which may be at the very moment of its purchase, the cotton is no better, whatever the buyer at the time may think, than when it first left the factory.

not exist before; because, if the different effects embraced in it were all produced by the same application of machinery, in separate parts, and he merely combined them, or added a new effect, such combination would not sustain his patent for the whole machine;[1] that is to say, without looking at the apparent

"When Congress shall pass a law, if they have a right so to do, to encourage discoveries, by which an article, without any amelioration of it, may be put off for a great deal more than it is worth and is actually selling for, it will be time enough for courts to extend their protection to such inventions, among which this may be very fairly classed."

[1] Whittemore *v.* Cutter, 1 Gallis. 478. In this case, the learned judge said: "It is difficult to define the exact cases when the whole machine may be deemed a new invention, and when only an improvement of an old machine; the cases often approach very near to each other. In the present improved state of machinery, it is almost impracticable not to employ the same elements of motion, and, in some particulars, the same manner of operation, to produce any new effect. Wheels, with their known modes of operation, and known combinations, must be of very extensive employment in a great variety of new machines; and if they could not, in the new invention, be included in the patent, no patent could exist for a whole machine embracing such mechanical powers.

"Where a specific machine already exists, producing certain effects, if a mere addition is made to such machine, *to produce the same effects* in a better manner, a patent cannot be taken for the whole machine, but for the improvement only. The case of a watch is a familiar instance. The inventor of the patent lever, without doubt, added a very useful improvement to it; but his right to a patent could not be more extensive than his invention. The patent could not cover the whole machine as improved, but barely the actual improvement. The same illustration might be drawn from the steam-engine, so much improved by Messrs. Watt and Boulton. In like manner, if to an old machine some new combinations be added, to produce *new effects*, the right to a patent is limited to the new combinations. A patent can in no case be for an effect only, but for an effect produced by a given manner, or by a peculiar operation. For instance, no patent can be obtained for the admeasurement of time, or the expansive operations of steam; but only for a new mode or new application of machinery to produce these effects; and therefore, if new effects are produced by an old machine in its unaltered state, I apprehend that no patent can be legally supported, for it is a patent for an effect only.

"On the other hand, if *well-known effects* are produced by machinery in all its combinations *entirely new*, a patent may be claimed for the whole machine. So, if the principles of the machine are new, either to produce a new or an old effect, the inventor may well entitle himself to the exclusive right of the whole machine. By the principles of a machine (as these words are used in the statute) is not meant the original elementary principles of motion, which philosophy and science have discovered, but the *modus operandi*, the peculiar device or manner of producing any given effect. The expansive powers of steam, and

amount of skill or invention involved in bringing these several modes of operation into one machine, which was not the invention claimed, if the result accomplished thereby did not differ substantially, in respect to the processes embraced in it, from what had been done before in separate machines, the subject-matter claimed as the invention was not new.

§ 46 *a.* So, too, where the claim was for "an elastic erasive pencil head," the court viewed it as a claim to "a piece of india-rubber

the mechanical powers of wheels, have been understood for many ages; yet a machine may well employ either the one or the other, and yet be so entirely new, in its mode of applying these elements, as to entitle the party to a patent for his whole combination. The intrinsic difficulty is to ascertain, in complicated cases like the present, the exact boundaries between what was known and used before, and what is new, in the *mode of operation.*

"The present machine is to make cotton and woollen cards. These were not only made before the present patent, by machinery, but also by machinery which, at different times, exhibited very different stages of improvement. The gradual progress of the invention, from the first rude attempts to the present extraordinary perfection, from the slight combination of simple principles to the present wonderful combinations, in ingenuity and intricacy scarcely surpassed in the world, has been minutely traced by the witnesses on the stand.

"The jury, then, are to decide whether the principles of Mr. Whittemore's machine are altogether new, or whether his machine be an improvement only on those which have been in use before his invention. I have before observed that the principles are the *mode of operation.* If the same effects are produced by two machines by the same mode of operation, the principles of each are the same. If the same effects are produced, but by a combination of machinery operating substantially in a different manner, the principles are different.

"The great stages (if I may so say) in making the cards by Whittemore's machine, which admit of a separate and distinct operation in the machinery, are, — 1. The forming and bending the wire; 2. The pricking the leather; 3. The sticking the wire into the leather; and, 4. The crooking the wire after its insertion. Were either of these effects produced in the machines formerly in use by a combination of machinery or mode of operation substantially the same as in this machine? If so, then clearly his patent could only be for an improvement, and of course it is void; if not, then his patent is free from any objection on the ground of being broader than his invention. It will not be sufficient, to protect the plaintiff's patent, that this specific machine, with all its various combinations and effects, did not exist before; for if the different effects were all produced by the *same application* of machinery in separate parts, and he merely combined them together, or added a new effect, such combination would not sustain the present patent, any more than the artist, who added the second-hand or repeater to a watch, could have been entitled to a patent for the whole watch."

with a hole in it," and held it to be invalid for want of invention.[1]

§ 47. On the other hand, where the patent claimed, as the invention of the party, a new and useful improvement in the making of friction-matches, by means of a new compound, and it was said that the ingredients had been used before in the making of matches, the court said that the true question was, whether the materials had been used before in the same combination, and if not, that the combination was patentable, however apparently simple it might be. That is to say, if the result at which the inventor had arrived — the production of a friction-match, by a particular combination of materials — was new, there was a sufficiency of invention, without looking at the apparent facility or difficulty of accomplishing it.[2]

§ 48. So, too, where it was said in the defence that a machine for cutting ice was but an application of an old invention to a new purpose, it being likened to the common carpenter's plough, the court distinguished the machine from every thing that had been made before, by pointing out that such a combination of apparatus had not been known before.[3]

[1] The Rubber Tip Pencil Co. *v.* Howard (1872), 9 Blatchf. 490.

[2] Ryan *v.* Goodwin, 3 Sumner's R. 514, 518. In this case, Mr. Justice Story said: "It is certainly not necessary that every ingredient, or, indeed, that any one ingredient, used by the patentee in his invention, should be new or unused before for the purpose of making matches. The true question is, whether the combination of materials by the patentee is substantially new. Each of these ingredients may have been in the most extensive and common use, and some of them may have been used for matches, or combined with other materials for other purposes. But if they have never been combined together in the manner stated in the patent, but the combination is new, then, I take it, the invention of the combination is patentable. So far as the evidence goes, it does not appear to me that any such combination was known or in use before Phillip's invention. But this is a matter of fact, upon which the jury will judge. The combination is apparently very simple; but the simplicity of an invention, so far from being an objection to it, may constitute its great excellence and value. Indeed, to produce a great result by very simple means, before unknown or unthought of, is not unfrequently the peculiar characteristic of the very highest class of minds."

[3] Wyeth *v.* Stone, 1 Story's R. 273, 279. In this case, Mr. Justice Story said: "Assuming the patent to be for the machinery described in the specification, and the description of the invention in the specification to be, in point of law, certainly and correctly summed up, (points which will be hereafter considered,) I am of opinion that the invention is substantially new. No such

§ 49. But where an invention was claimed to be a mode by which the back of a rocking-chair could be reclined and fixed at any angle required, by means of a certain apparatus, the patent was declared void, because the same apparatus or machinery had been long in use, and applied, if not to chairs, at least in other machines, to purposes of a similar nature.[1] An examination of the result attained by the plaintiff showed that he had accomplished nothing which had not been done before, but had merely applied an old contrivance to a new purpose.

§ 50. The question will arise, then, in reference to any supposed invention, in what is the novelty to consist? or, in other words, what is the nature of the change that has been effected, which will entitle it to the protection of a patent? It is a leading general principle on this subject, as we have already seen, that there must be something more than a change of form, or of the juxtaposition of parts, or of the external relations of things, or of the order or arrangement in which things are used. The change, or the new combination or relations, must introduce or embody some new mode of operation, or accomplish some effect not before produced. This is what is called, in the judicial sense, introducing a new principle. But then it is plain, from the nature of this subject, that no rules can be laid down which will admit of application to all supposable cases. All that can be done in the way of exhibiting the doctrines which are to be applied in judicial inquiries into the novelty of inventions, is to classify the adjudged

machinery is, in my judgment, established by the evidence to have been known or used before. The argument is, that the principal machine, described as the cutter, is well known, and has been often used before for other purposes, and that this is but an application of an old invention to a new purpose; and it is not therefore patentable. It is said that it is, in substance, identical with the common carpenter's plough. I do not think so. In the common carpenter's plough there is no series of chisels fixed in one plane, and the guide is below the level, and the plough is a movable chisel. In the present machine there are a series of chisels, and they are all fixed. The successive chisels are each below the other, and this is essential to their operation. Such a combination is not shown ever to have been known or used before. It is not, therefore, a new use or application of an old machine. This opinion does not rest upon my own skill and comparison of the machine with the carpenter's plough; but it is fortified and sustained by the testimony of witnesses of great skill, experience, and knowledge in this department of science."

[1] Bean *v.* Smallwood, 2 Story's R. 408, 410.

cases, and to observe the illustrations which they furnish of the different modes in which this patentable requisite of novelty may present itself. One class of the adjudged cases consists of those in which the supposed invention has been held to be nothing more than a double use, or double application, of what had in fact existed before; and another class embraces the cases where there has been held to be something involved which may be the subject of a patent.

§ 50 *a*. In a case in the Circuit Court for the Southern District of Ohio, the improvement claimed related mainly to the construction of portable steam-engines. The most desirable qualities in this class of machines were stated to be compactness and lightness, combined with strength and simplicity, so as to adapt them to purposes of transportation. The invention consisted, according to the specification, "in the arrangement of a hollow continuous bed-plate between the boiler and the engine, upon which, and to which, the entire working parts of the latter are supported and attached; the hollow bed-plate being for this purpose provided with suitable flanges on its upper and outer sides, by which the operative parts of the engine are supported and secured to it; there being others cast on its under side, by means of which the bed-plate itself is attached or riveted to the boiler. This hollow continuous casting, or bed-plate, may be also used as a heater for the supply water. By this plan the engine will be rendered insulated, as it were, from the boiler, so that the relative position of its working parts to each other cannot be affected by the expansion and contraction of the boiler so as to impair their regular and easy working; and, on the other hand, the boiler will not be subject to the injurious effects of the vibration and direct straining of the operative parts when at work. . . . The bed-plate, if desired, may be used as a heater for the supply of water, by passing the exhaust steam, as it escapes from the cylinder, through a pipe suitably arranged within the bed-plate."

The claim of the patentees was construed by the court to embrace: 1. A hollow continuous bed-plate placed between the boiler and the engine; 2. The bed-plate to have flanges on its upper and outer side cast with it; 3. The attachment and securing of the operative parts of the engine upon its upper and outer side, by means of the flanges. The essence of the invention consisted in the construction of the bed-plate and its lateral attachment to the engine.

To defeat the claim of novelty in this case, evidence was adduced to show the prior existence of a similar bed-plate; this plate consisted of a frame cast in one or four pieces, the sides consisting of hollow boxes from four to eight inches square, and extending the whole length of the boiler. The frame was placed upon it, while the parts were secured to the boiler by feet or flanges cast with them, and secured by bolts. Upon the bed-plate so attached, the engine was placed, and firmly fixed by bolts or rivets. Both the bed-plate and engine were directly over the boiler. Feed-pipes for the supply of water were introduced into the bed-plate, along which the exhaust steam from the cylinder was passed, thus heating the water before its entrance into the boiler. The object of the feet or flanges on the plate was to effect, as far as possible, the insulation of the engine. Admitting that there were striking points of analogy between the two engines, the court, in deciding in favor of the validity of the patent, concurred with the scientific experts that the differences were not merely mechanical, but were radical in their character, and pointed out the essential diversities to be in two particulars: 1. The bed-plate covered by the complainant's patent was a single continuous shell or tube, giving a combination of lightness and strength not found in other similar structures; 2. The engine was attached to the outer side of the bed-plate, instead of being placed upon it, or over the boiler.[1]

[1] Blandy *v.* Griffith (1868), 3 Fisher's Pat. Cas. 609. In delivering the judgment of the court, Mr. Justice Swayne said: "Here are certainly some striking points of analogy to the engine of the complainant. But able scientific experts have testified that the dominant conceptions in the two cases are totally distinct from each other, and that the differences are not merely mechanical, or equivalent, but that they strike deeper, and are radical in their character. Whether they are so is the test to be applied to the solution of the question before us. We have already held that the use of the plate as a heater is not a part of the invention patented. This subject may, therefore, be laid out of view. The essential diversities are to be found, it is said, in two particulars: The bed-plate covered by the patent is *a single continuous shell or tube*. It is proved that this gives a combination of lightness and strength beyond any other configuration or structure which has yet been devised. The engine is attached to the outer side of the bed-plate, and is not placed above it, or over the boiler. The attachment is lateral. In both these points the proof is that it is essentially different from the Talbott engine, and from any other which preceded it.

"In these views, after much reflection, we have found ourselves able to con-

§ 50 *b.* In the case of Stimpson *v.* Woodman,[1] the invention claimed consisted in producing a pebbled or boarded grain or finish on leather, by subjecting it to the pressure of a short revolving cylinder or roller of metal, having the required design or figure engraved on its surface. But this machine was antedated by another, substantially the same in its combination and arrangement, and in its working and effect upon the leather, except that the metallic roller in the latter had a smooth, and in the former a figured surface. It further appeared that this figured roller was old, and had been used in pebbling leather by pressure. Upon this state of facts, it was held that the engraving or stamping of the figure upon the surface of the smooth roller, or the substitution of the old figured roller for the purpose, involved simply mechanical skill, and was therefore not patentable.

§ 50 *c.* An important case, illustrating the sufficiency of invention, is that of Treadwell *v.* Parrott,[2] decided by the Circuit Court for the Southern District of New York, in 1866. The invention claimed consisted in the improvement of cast-iron cannon, by surrounding them with wrought-iron hoops or bands, in the manner described, so as greatly to increase their strength. The patentee disclaimed the discovery of "hoops generally in making cannon, as the earliest cannon known were formed in part by hoops brazed upon them"; but limited his invention to "constructing cannon with hoops screwed and shrunk upon a body in which the calibre is formed in the manner herein described."

cur. It is not our business to form any opinion of the *comparative* value of the complainant's engine. The question is not whether the invention is better or worse than its predecessors, but whether it is new, useful, and different from any thing before used or known. Those who hold the negative are at liberty to use any thing older to which the proofs in this case relate. All required of them is that they shall not use, either in form or substance, what is patented to the complainants."

[1] (1869), 10 Wal. 117. At the trial in the Circuit Court (3 Fisher's Pat. Cas. 98), the court was asked to charge the jury in substance that if the plaintiff's machine had been anticipated in every part of its construction except the figures or designs on the roller, which roller was old, he was not entitled to recover. The refusal to give this instruction was regarded as erroneous by the Supreme Court of the United States, and the judgment rendered by the Circuit Court for the plaintiff was reversed. In the Appellate Court, Mr. Justice Clifford, placing a different construction upon the claims of the patentee, delivered a dissenting opinion.

[2] 3 Fisher's Pat. Cas. 124; s. c. 5 Blatchf. 369.

According to the mode of construction described, the cannon was cast, having at its largest part a diameter about twice as great as the calibre. It was then bored, the outside turned, and a screw cut on the body. Hoops or rings of wrought iron, having a diameter about one-thousandth part less than that of the body to be encircled, after being expanded sufficiently by heat, were screwed upon the body of the cannon, where contraction was caused by a change from heat to cold. The gun might thus be encircled by an indefinite number of hoops or rings, while others might be formed in the same way over the first series. The claim of the patentee was: "First. In making a cannon consisting of a body (in which the calibre is formed), the walls of which are of one piece, surrounded by rings, hoops, or tubes, in one or more layers, placed upon said body under great strain, by which said body is compressed, and the natural equilibrium of the molecules or particles of which it is composed disturbed by their being brought nearer together; and this is accomplished in the manner herein set forth, namely, by making the hoops smaller than the part which they are to surround, and then expanding them by heat, and suffering them to shrink or contract after having been put in their places. Second. I also claim the method of securing the hoops to the body of the gun, and the several layers of hoops to each other, by screw threads, when they shrink to their places as above described."

In explanation of the principles that led to the invention, reference was made by the patentee to the Barlow law, so called, viz., that hollow cylinders of the same materials do not increase in strength in the ratio of increase in thickness, but that the ratio of increase in strength is such, that, when they become of considerable thickness, the strength falls enormously below that given by the ratio of thickness. This diminution in the power of resistance was thus stated by Barlow: "Suppose such a cylinder to be made up of a great number of thin rings or hoops, placed one within the other, and exactly fitting, so that the particles of each hoop shall be in equilibrium with each other; then the resistance of these rings, compared one with the other, to any distending force, will be inversely as the squares of their diameters."

The object of the patentee's invention was "to obviate the great causes of weakness arising from the conditions before stated, and to obtain, as far as may be, the strength of wrought iron instead of cast iron"; and after describing the mode of construction he adds: "This compression [the compression of the body of the gun by the hoops] must be made such that, when the gun is subjected to the greatest force, the body of the gun and the several layers of rings will be distended to the fracturing point at the same time, and thus all take a portion of the strain up to its bearing capacity."[1]

Upon the construction of the specification and claim, the court held that the improvement of the patentee was intended to be confined to cast-iron guns, as a gun of this material was mentioned, and no other.

The defence relied upon was that the patentee was not the original inventor of the improvement, and evidence was adduced to show that it was well known as early as 1834 that the hooping of the body of cast-iron guns with wrought-iron bands, very much after the manner of the patentee, increased the resistance of cylinders of cast iron against the explosion of gunpowder; that the compression of the cast-iron metal, by the contraction of the heated hoops or bands, increased very much the strength of this resistance; and that the smallness of the diameters of the hoop, compared with the exterior diameters of the barrel, was governed by the principle of the law of expansion of wrought iron. As early as 1834, Thiery, a French officer, had discussed, in a publication of that date, the improvement of a cast-iron gun by combining with it a wrought-iron envelope; and in that year, as well as in 1840, had constructed guns according to his principle and theory. Thiery's mode of construction was substantially the same as that of the patentee. The body of his gun, however, was not purely of cast iron, but contained longitudinal

[1] The patentee adds: "There may, at first view, seem to be a great practical difficulty in making the hoops of the exact size required to produce the necessary compression; but wrought iron and all malleable bodies are capable of being extended without fracture much beyond their power of elasticity. They may, therefore, be greatly elongated without being weakened. Hence we have only to form the hoops small in excess, and they will accommodate themselves under the strain without the least injury. It will be found best in practice, therefore, to make the difference between the diameters of the hoops and the parts they surround considerably more than one one-thousandth part of a diameter." The result reached is that "a gun thus made will be nearly four times as strong as a cast-iron gun of the same weight, wrought iron being taken at only twice the strength of cast iron."

strips of wrought iron, which had been immersed in the metal in casting the gun. The court considered this circumstance as one of great importance, and held "that although the use of wrought-iron hoops in the way stated, and used for strengthening the barrel of a gun, had been known as early as 1834 or 1840, yet if the patentee was the first to apply the device to a cast-iron gun, he must be regarded as the original inventor, and entitled to a patent; and that the application of it to a wrought-iron gun, or a barrel composed of a combination of cast and wrought iron, prior in point of time, would not of itself be any objection."

It was held, however, that the complainant was not entitled to a patent, upon the ground that his gun was constructed upon substantially the same principles and method as the Frith gun, also having a cast-iron barrel, the patent for which had been granted in England in 1843.

§ 51. The application of an old contrivance to a new use, in the case of the rocking-chair, furnishes an instance where there may be a clear line of demarcation between the invention of a new thing and a double use of an old thing.[1] So, too, where the change consisted in the substitution of potter's clay, or any kind of porcelain, as the material for making door-knobs attached to a spindle or shank, the Supreme Court of the United States, proceeding upon a state of facts which ascertained that knobs made of wood or iron had been previously attached to the shank in the same way, and that the sole change consisted in the substitution of one material for another, held the subject not patentable.[2]

§ 52. Another case of a double use, or double application, of a well-known mode of manufacture, is presented by the case of the anchor, already referred to. The supposed invention consisted in manufacturing ship's anchors having two flukes, by making the two flukes of one piece of metal, and piercing it in the middle by a hole for the insertion of the shank, instead of making the two flukes in separate pieces and welding them to the shank. The advantage of the change consisted in avoiding the injury to the iron occasioned by repeated heating, and using a method of manufacture which required but one heating, namely, for the

[1] Bean *v.* Smallwood, 2 Story's R. 408, 410. See a somewhat similar case, Hovey *v.* Stevens, 1 Woodb. & Minot, 290.

[2] Hotchkiss *v.* Greenwood, 11 Howard, 248.

purpose of welding the end of the shank to the side of the hole in which it was inserted. Now, if anchors or other similar instruments had not been made before in this mode, there could be no doubt that a patent might be supported for anchors of this particular manufacture. But the principle of this mode of manufacture was not new, and nothing was new but its application to the making of what are called ship's anchors, or anchors with two flukes, which of themselves were an old instrument. It appeared that the mushroom anchor, the adze anchor, the common hammer, and the pickaxe had all been made in this way. There was no invention, therefore, of a new process of manufacture, or of an article as made by a new process; but the novelty consisted solely in the application of an old process of manufacture to a new occasion; that is, it was a double use. Had this mode of manufacture not been used before in cases extremely similar, an inventor of it might have patented its application, not only to anchors, but to other instruments.[1]

§ 53. Hence it appears that the presence or the absence of the *patentable* quality of novelty depends in some degree on the position in which the supposed inventor stands with reference to the history of the art; for there may be in what he has done an element of novelty, and yet that novelty may consist only in the new occasion, or new use to which he applies an old or well-known method. Thus the principle, that is to say the method of operation, or the order of combination, under which his invention ranges itself, may have been discovered and applied before, but not on precisely the same occasions or uses, or with the same materials. When this is the case, the question to be determined is, whether the new application is any thing more than a double use, or whether something has been discovered, or some effect produced, which goes beyond the mere skill of a constructor in adapting a well-known method to different occasions, and enters the domain of what is called invention.

§ 54. Illustrations of this distinction may be seen in the application of well-known medicines, drugs, and chemical substances upon new occasions, or for new specific purposes. If it is discovered that a medicine, known and used as a valuable remedy in one class of diseases, has also great efficiency in curing another

[1] Brunton *v.* Hawkes, 4 B. & Ald. 540, 550.

and different disease, there is a new application of a known thing, but it is only a double use of that thing.[1]

§ 55. In order to escape the objection of a double use, it is necessary that the new occasion or purpose, to which the use of a known thing is applied, should not be merely analogous to the former occasions or purposes to which the same thing has been applied. There is a very material distinction between applying a new contrivance to an old object, and an old contrivance to a new object. The former may be patentable, but the latter cannot be, when the new object is merely one of a class possessing a common analogy. Thus, where a certain description of wheels had been used on other carriages than railway carriages, Lord Abinger, C. B., held that the plaintiff could not claim a patent merely for the use of such wheels upon railway carriages;[2] and where a patent claimed, as the invention of the patentee, a process of curling

[1] In Boulton *v.* Bull, 2 H. Bl. 487, Buller, J., said: "Suppose the world were better informed than it now is how to prepare Dr. Janes's fever-powder, and an ingenious physician should find out that it was a specific cure for a consumption, if given in particular quantities; could he have a patent for the sole use of Janes's powders in consumptions, or to be given in particular quantities? I think it must be conceded that such a patent would be void; and yet the use of the medicine would be new, and the effect of it as materially different from what is now known as life is from death. So in the case of a late discovery, which, as far as experience has hitherto gone, is said to have proved efficacious, that of the medicinal properties of arsenic in curing agues, could a patent be supported for the sole use of arsenic in aguish complaints? The medicine is the manufacture, and the only object of a patent; and, as the medicine is not new, any patent for it, or for the use of it, would be void."

[2] Losh *v.* Hague, 1 Webs. Pat. Cas. 207. In this case his Lordship said to the jury: "The learned counsel has stated to you, and very properly, and it is a circumstance to be attended to, that Mr. Losh has taken out his patent to use his wheels on railways. Now, he says, the wheels made by Mr. Paton, or by the other workmen who were called as witnesses, were never applied to railways at all. That opens this question, whether or not a man who finds a wheel ready made to his hand, and applies that wheel to a railway, shall get a patent for applying it to a railway. There is some nicety in considering that subject. The learned counsel has mentioned to you a particular case in which an argand lamp, burning oil, having been applied for singeing gauze, somebody else afterwards applied a lamp supplied with gas for singeing lace, which was a novel invention, and for which an argand lamp is not applicable, because gas does not burn in the same way as oil in an argand lamp. But a man having discovered by the application of gas he could more effectually burn the cottony parts of the gauze by passing it over the gas, his patent is

palm-leaf for mattresses, but it appearing that hair had long been prepared by the same process for the same purpose, Mr. Justice Story held it to be a mere double use of an old process.[1]

good. (1 Webs. Pat. Cas. p. 98, Hall's Patent.) That was the application of a new contrivance to the same purpose; but it is a different thing when you take out a patent for applying a new contrivance to an old object, and applying an old contrivance to a new object, that is a very different thing; if I am wrong I shall be corrected. In the case the learned counsel put, he says, if a surgeon goes into a mercer's shop, and sees the mercer cutting velvet or silk with a pair of scissors with a knob to them, he, seeing that, would have a right to take out a patent in order to apply the same scissors to cutting a sore, or a patient's skin. I do not quite agree with that law. I think if the surgeon had gone to him, and said, 'I see how well your scissors cut,' and he said, 'I can apply them instead of a lancet, by putting a knob at the end,' that would be quite a different thing, and he might get a patent for that; but it would be a very extraordinary thing to say that, because all mankind have been accustomed to eat soup with a spoon, that a man could take out a patent because he says you might eat peas with a spoon. The law on the subject is this: that you cannot have a patent for applying a well-known thing, which might be applied to fifty thousand different purposes, for applying it to an operation which is exactly analogous to what was done before. Suppose a man invents a pair of scissors to cut cloth with, if the scissors were never invented before, he could take out a patent for it. If another man found he could cut silk with them, why should he take out a patent for that? I must own, therefore, that it strikes me if you are of opinion this wheel has been constructed, according to the defendant's evidence, by the persons who have been mentioned, long before the plaintiff's patent, that, although there were no railroads then to apply them to, and no demand for such wheels, yet that the application of them to railroads afterwards, by Mr. Losh, will not give effect to his patent, if part of that which is claimed as a new improvement by him is, in fact, an old improvement, invented by other people, and used for other purposes. That is my opinion on the law, and on that I am bound to direct you substantially."

[1] Howe *v.* Abbott, 2 Story's R. 190, 193. In this case the learned judge said: "In the first place, it is admitted on all sides that there is no novelty in the process by which the stripping, or twisting, or curling the palm-leaf is accomplished. The same process of twisting, and curling, and baking, and steaming has long been known and used in respect to hair used for beds, mattresses, sofas, and cushions. It is, therefore, the mere application of an old process and old machinery to a new use. It is precisely the same as if a coffee-mill were now, for the first time, used to grind corn. The application of an old process to manufacture an article, to which it had never before been applied, is not a patentable invention. There must be some new process, or some new machinery used, to produce the result. If the old spinning-machine to spin flax were now first applied to spin cotton, no man could hold a new

§ 56. When, therefore, the principle is well known, or the application consists in the use of a known thing to produce a particular effect, the question will arise, whether the effect is of itself entirely new, or whether the occasion only upon which the particular effect is produced is new. If the occasion only is new, then the use to which the thing is applied is simply analogous to what had been done before. But if the effect itself is new, then there are no known analogous uses of the same thing, and the process may constitute such an art as will be the subject of a patent. Thus, the use of scissors to cut one substance produces a particular effect, entirely analogous to that produced when they are used to cut another substance; the effect, therefore, is not new. In like manner the use of a machine in the water, which was originally intended to be used on land, has been held to be no invention.[1] But the use of gas to singe off the superfluous fibres of lace was the use of an agent for a purpose not analogous to any other purpose for which the same agent had ever been used before; and therefore the effect, as produced by that agent, was new. Great discrimination, however, is to be used in determining whether the analogy is such as to justify the inference that the occasion only is new, and that the effect is not new. Of course, if any new contrivances, combinations, or arrangements are made use of, although the principal agents employed are well known, those contrivances, combinations, or arrangements may constitute a new principle, and then the application or practice will necessarily be new also.[2] But where there is no novelty in the preparation or arrangement of the agent employed, and the novelty professedly consists in the application of that agent, being a well-known thing, or, in other terms, where it consists in the practice only,

patent to spin cotton in that mode; much less the right to spin cotton in all modes, although he had invented none. As, therefore, Smith has invented no new process or machinery, but has only applied to palm-leaf the old process and the old machinery used to curl hair, it does not strike me that the patent is maintainable. He who produces an old result by a new mode or process is entitled to a patent for that mode or process. But he cannot have a patent for a result merely, without using some new mode or process to produce it."

[1] Bush *v.* Fox, 26 Law & Eq. R. 464.

[2] As where anthracite and hot-air blast were used in the manufacture of iron, in the place of bituminous coal and hot-air blast; and where sail-cloth was made, with the omission of an ingredient before used, that is, by a different combination from that before used.

the novelty of that practice is to be determined according to the circumstances, by applying the test of whether the result or effect produced is a new result or effect never before produced.[1] If a new manufacture is produced by an old process, or if an old manufacture is produced by new means, then the result or effect is new, as produced by that particular means, and the new case is such as can be protected by letters-patent. But if only an old manufacture is produced, or an old result is attained, by means analogous to what the same means have produced when applied the same way in other cases, the new occasion of using those means does not constitute a case that can be protected by a patent.

§ 57. The distinctions that are applicable to this question of a double use may be more readily perceived, however, by considering several of the adjudged cases, where the supposed invention consists in the application of an old process, or a known machine or combination of materials to a new use or occasion. Of this class there are two English cases, to which reference has already been made, and which require to be re-examined in this connection. In one of these cases (Kay *v.* Marshall) the real invention of the plaintiff was of a new mode of spinning flax. It consisted in first subjecting the crude flax to a process of maceration, and in then spinning it, by the well-known spinning-machine, at what is called a "ratch" of two and a half inches, that is, by adjusting the drawing and retaining rollers at that distance from each other, the existing machine having a well-known capacity for such adjustments. The invention was therefore the spinning of macerated flax at a short ratch. This had never been done before, and consequently the doing it was a new manufacture, and, *as such*, entitled to be protected by a patent. But the patent taken out made the invention to consist in "new and improved *machinery* for preparing and spinning flax," &c. And as it appeared at the trial that an old machine was used by the plaintiff, capable of being adjusted at different ratches according to the length of the fibre to be spun, although it had not been used at a ratch of two

[1] As in the case of the application of bells to fire-engines, to be rung by the motion of the carriage, for the purpose of alarms or notice, which Washington, J., instructed the jury might be a subject for a patent. Park *v.* Little, 3 Wash. 196. The application of steam for propelling boats is another illustration of novelty in practice. Ibid.

and a half inches to spin macerated flax, it became necessary to support the patent upon the ground that this new use of the old machine could be patentable as a "*new and improved machine.*" It was held otherwise, upon great consideration, both by the Court of Common Pleas and in the House of Lords.[1]

§ 58. It should be recollected, in examining this case, that the facts presented by the record reduced the question simply to this: whether the construction or modification proposed by the patent was a patentable improvement of the spinning-machine. It was upon the ground that no new or improved *machine* had been invented, but that a new occasion only had been discovered for using the old machine in a manner for which it was before adapted, and because the patent claimed an improved machine, that it was held that there was a want of novelty. But there can be little doubt that a patent would have been good for a new or improved process in the art of manufacturing flax, consisting of two parts, the maceration of the flax, and the spinning it, when macerated, at a ratch of two and a half inches, provided that both parts of this process had been new.

§ 59. A question might arise upon this case, however, of a different nature. Assuming that the plaintiff had made no alteration in the structure of the spinning-machine other than to adjust the rollers which he found in it at a distance from each other at which they had not been before used, and assuming that this adaptation of the machine led to a manufacture of flax in a mode never before practised, would such an adaptation of the machine to a new use be a patentable invention? It was suggested by Lord Chancellor Cottenham, in delivering the judgment of the House of Lords in this case, that if "he" (the plaintiff) "has discovered any means of using the machine which the world had not known before the benefit of, *that* he has a right to secure to himself by means of a patent; but if this mode of using the spinning-machine was known before, (and the indorsement upon the *postea* states that it was known before,) then the plaintiff cannot deprive them (the defendants) of having the benefit of that which they enjoyed before."[2] The meaning of this *dictum* appears to be this. If the capacity of the spinning-machine to have its re-

[1] Kay *v.* Marshall, 2 Webs. Pat. Cases, 34–84.
[2] Ibid. p. 82.

taining and drawing rollers used at variable distances, according to the length of the fibre to be spun, was previously unknown, and the plaintiff discovered it, although he may not have altered the construction of the machine so as to produce this capacity, by adding any new parts, or taking out any old ones, he might have a patent for the new application or use of the machine ; or, in other words, he might be considered as the inventor *quoad hoc* of an improved machine, which differed from the old one in the position and relations of its rollers. But if the capacity of the machine to have its rollers adjusted at variable distances was known, the fixing them at a particular distance could not, of itself, be an invention.

§ 60. The second of the two cases above referred to presents a good illustration of the doctrine of double use, and of the manner in which that fatal objection may be created by an improper mode of claiming what would have been entitled to a patent if the real invention had been correctly described. The plaintiff was the inventor of a method of making excavations, and building foundations of structures beneath the surface of water, such as lighthouses, piers of bridges, &c., &c. For this purpose he constructed a caisson of iron, divided into chambers, and made air-tight, which was sunk in the water, the lowest chamber being open at the bottom. By means of an air-pump the atmospheric pressure upon the water within the chambers was sufficiently increased to force the water out at the bottom. The workmen placed in the lower chamber excavated the soil at the bottom, which was raised to the top of the machine in buckets through a system of valves arranged so as to retain the compressed air. The chamber was then filled with solid masonry, and the iron cylinder left on the outside as part of the structure. The next chamber was proceeded with in the same manner, until the structure had risen above the level of the water. The plaintiff had stated his claim thus: "What I claim is, the mode of constructing the interior of a caisson in such a manner that the workpeople may be supplied with compressed air, and be able to raise the materials excavated, and to make and construct foundations and buildings as above described." It is obvious enough that this claim hazarded the entire patentable quality of the invention upon the single question of the novelty of the caisson, and the manner of its operation in enabling the work to be done. For although the making and constructing foundations in the manner described is stated as the object for which the caisson is used, yet it is clear that the caisson itself, in its peculiar structure and operation, was claimed as a very material part (to say the least) of the invention. Now it was shown at the trial that such an apparatus for excluding the water by forcing air into a series of chambers, in making excavations, was not new; and that the contrivance for enabling the workmen and the material excavated to be passed from one chamber to another, without permitting the compressed air to escape, was also previously employed by Lord Dundonald, who had invented and patented such an apparatus to be used in making excavations on land. So far as the apparatus was concerned, therefore, the only difference between the plaintiff and Lord Dundonald was, that the former used it under the surface of water, the latter under the surface of land. The new or double use of the thing operated no change in the character of the thing.[1] But then it is quite certain that the real invention of the plaintiff, provided his method of operation in building foundations under water was new, was entitled to a patent. It consisted in making the excavations by means of a machine adapted to the purpose of working under water as well as on land, and then in building the structure of masonry within the successive chambers of the machine, leaving them one after the other as parts of the permanent structure. He had thus developed a use of the machine to which it had not been before applied; and had he taken care not to claim the structure of the machine, and had claimed his proper improvement in the art of building foundations under water, he might perhaps have had a valid patent.

§ 61. Of a somewhat similar character was the American case of Le Roy *v.* Tatham. The real invention in this case consisted

[1] Bush *v.* Fox, 26 Law & Eq. R. 464. In this case, the Chief Baron, at the trial, after comparing the two specifications, heard two witnesses, who testified that the apparatus described in each worked in the same way, in respect of the process of excavating in a chamber of compressed air, and of raising the materials excavated from that chamber. He thereupon directed the jury to find a verdict for the defendant, if they believed this evidence. When the same case was before the House of Lords, on error from the Court of Exchequer, Lord Chancellor Cranworth, in delivering judgment, intimated that the Chief Baron might have gone much further, and might have directed the jury to find for the defendant, without any evidence at all, because it was for the court to compare the specifications and declare what each covered. Bush *v.* Fox (House of Lords), 38 Law & Eq. 1, 5.

in the discovery and practical application of a new method of making lead pipe, by forcing the metal, when recently set, but still under heat, by great pressure, from a receiver through an aperture and around a core, so as to make the metal reunite where it had been separated. Wrought pipe, as an improvement upon cast pipe, had been previously made from set or solid lead by great pressure; but before the discovery of the plaintiff's method, such wrought pipe could not be made with uniformity of thickness, and a true centrality of bore. The former mode of making wrought pipe from set or solid lead was founded on the supposition that the metal, when once set after being molten, would not unite perfectly if separated; and it was in consequence of the want of knowledge of the property of such metal to unite under heat and extreme pressure, that a mode of making the pipe was resorted to by which the contact of the particles of the metal would remain unbroken. This mode consisted in the use of the following apparatus. Lead in a fluid state was introduced into a cylinder in which a piston played from one end to the other. In the solid end of the cylinder opposite to the piston an aperture was fitted with a die, which formed the exterior of the wall of the pipe. To form the interior wall of the pipe, a core, or mandril, consisting of a long cylindrical rod of steel, was attached to the face of the piston, and extended through the cylinder, and through the centre of the die. When the metal in the cylinder had become set, the piston was forced through the cylinder by hydraulic pressure, carrying the metal to the die, and driving it through the annular space between the die and the core, and thus forming a continuous pipe from the whole charge of the cylinder, because the continuity of the particles composing the wall of the pipe was nowhere broken. But the liability of the long core to be warped out of a true line by the great pressure necessary to form the pipe, rendered it impossible to produce uniformity of thickness and an even bore.

§ 62. On the other hand, the great feature of the invention which the plaintiffs claimed consisted in the discovery of the fact, that lead, when recently set, and still under heat, will reunite perfectly around a core, under extreme pressure, *notwithstanding* the particles have been separated, and will thus form pipe of great solidity and unusual strength. This beautiful discovery was made available by the substitution of a short immovable core in front of the die, supported by a bridge or cross-bars, and extending into and through the die, so that the true centrality of the core in reference to the die was constantly preserved; and although the particles of the metal, when forced through the apertures in the bridge, were necessarily separated, they reunited perfectly around the core, and formed a pipe superior in quality and cheaper in production than had ever been made before.

§ 63. The patent which was to protect this remarkable invention, after duly describing the apparatus and its mode of operation, and after disclaiming any design of patenting the machinery independent of the arrangement and combination set forth, summed up the claim as follows: "What we do claim as our invention, and desire to secure, is the combination of the following parts above described, to wit, the core and bridge, or guide-piece, with the cylinder, the piston, the chamber, and the die, when used to form pipes of metal, under heat and pressure in the manner set forth, or in any other manner substantially the same."

§ 64. It does not appear with sufficient distinctness, from the report of this case, whether the precise combination of the bridge or guide-piece with the cylinder, the piston, the chamber, and the die, had been used before; although evidence was offered in the defence tending to show that substantially the same combination had been used before in the manufacture of lead pipe, of clay pipe, and of the confection called macaroni. It may be assumed, however, that the evidence did not show any previous manufacture of lead pipe by the substitution of a bridge for the long cylindrical mandril, for the purpose of making available the capacity of lead, when recently set, to reunite after separation. From the charge of the judge who tried the cause, and from the finding of the jury, it is to be inferred, that before the plaintiff's invention this combination of machinery had not been used for the development and application of this property of lead, and that this was a newly discovered property, for the first time made known, and made of practical consequence by the invention of the plaintiff. The jury were instructed, in substance, that the invention of the plaintiff did not consist in the combination of the machinery separate from the manner in which and the purpose for which it was used by him, but that the novelty of the invention consisted in the application of a combination of machinery, which might of itself be old, to a new end, by making a newly discovered property of lead practically useful, and producing thereby an article of manufacture which was both new in respect to the process by which it was made and in respect to its superior qualities, and that such an invention was patentable. That this instruction was correct, provided the patentee's summary of his claim had not made the novelty of his machinery essential, there can be, I conceive, no doubt. But in the Supreme Court of the United States it was held, by a majority of the judges, that the claim did not admit of a construction that would support this direction; but that the patentee had made the novelty of his machinery essential by claiming it as part of his invention, and that therefore the novelty of the machinery was a material fact for the jury.[1]

§ 65. Two questions obviously arise upon this case: *First*, whether it was a correct construction of the claim, to hold that the patentee had limited his claim, in part, to the novelty of the machinery; and, *secondly*, whether, assuming that his claim correctly described his invention, namely, the application of that machinery to a new method of making lead pipe, through the instrumentality of a newly discovered property of lead, such an invention is patentable. Upon the first question, it is only necessary in this connection to remark, that although the claim was not skilfully stated, the purpose of the patentee to claim the combination of the machinery only "when used" for the purpose and in the manner of his new process of making lead pipe, which his patent set forth, was sufficiently manifested; but the second question, namely, whether the application of the machinery, assuming it to be old as a combination of devices, to the new purpose of making lead pipe through the instrumentality of a newly discovered property of lead, was a patentable subject, or was only a double use, belongs to the topic now under consideration.

§ 66. In all the cases which have heretofore been cited, in which the objection of a double use has prevailed, it is to be observed that the new occasion or purpose to which an old contrivance, device, or method of operation has been applied, without any alteration of the agent itself, there has been no new effect produced, or no new development of properties of matter heretofore unknown, or no application of the agent to any uses that were not strictly

[1] Le Roy *v.* Tatham, 14 Howard, 156. Justices Nelson, Wayne, and Grier dissented from this view of the patent. See the case again in 22 Howard, 132, where Judge McLean explained.

analogous to the former ones. It may therefore be practicable to state a rule which will furnish a safe general principle in the following terms: viz., that in order to escape the objection of a double use, it is necessary that the new occasion or purpose to which the use of a known thing is applied should not be merely analogous to the former occasions or purposes to which the same thing has been applied. The meaning which should be given to the term *analogous use*, in this connection, will be sufficiently illustrated by the adjudged cases. Thus, in the case of the rocking-chair, the ship's anchor, and the wheel for railway carriages, an old contrivance or a well-known mode of manufacture was applied to a purpose which, considered by itself, was new; but that application developed no new mode of operation, and exhibited no effect differing from what had been done before. In like manner, the use of the machine for making excavations under the surface of water, in the same way in which it had been used for the strictly analogous purpose of making excavations under the surface of land, could not make it a new machine, although the new use, as part of a new method of building solid structures under water, was so far patentable as it entered into a new method of building such structures. So, too, the application of the spinning-machine, with its rollers fixed at a particular position, to the purpose of spinning flax with a very short fibre, was not an invention of a new machine, because the use was purely analogous to the former uses of the same machine; but as one of the elements of a new process of spinning flax, of which the other element consisted in the previous maceration of the flax, the spinning at a particular distance was new.[1]

[1] To these may be added another illustration of the doctrine of merely analogous or double uses. A. took out a patent for improving the texture of threads of *cotton* or *linen* yarns, by exposing the threads in a distended state to the action of beaters, which gave them smoothness and polish. B. took a subsequent patent for producing the same effect upon yarns of *wool* or *hair*. On comparing the two specifications, it appeared that the machinery and method of using it were the same in both, although their mere application to wool and hair was shown to be new. Upon the ground that this was but the application of an old machine in the old manner to an *analogous substance*, a rule to enter a nonsuit was made absolute in the Queen's Bench (Brook *v.* Aston, 8 Ell. & Bl. 478). But it was admitted by the court that novelty in the application of an old invention to a new purpose will support a patent. When this case came before the Exchequer Chamber on appeal, some effort was made by the plaintiff's counsel to support the patent, upon a ground

§ 66 *a*. An important case illustrating the degree of novelty essential to a valid patent was recently decided in the House of Lords. The case was that of Harwood *v.* the Great Northern Railway Company.[1] The invention in controversy was made by one Wild, and was for "improvements in fishes and fish-joints for connecting the rails of railways." The function to be performed by this invention is clearly explained in the following language of Mr. Justice Blackburn : "The rails meet but-end to but-end, and, as the engine passes along the rails, its weight has a tendency to depress the rail on which it rests below the rail to which it is approaching, on which the engine does not yet rest; and unless this tendency is counteracted, the end of the rail to which the engine approaches being more elevated than that on which the wheel of the engine rests, there will be a jolt when the wheel passes over the joint. The mode of counteracting this tendency is by attaching to the sides of the rails plates called 'fishes' by means of bolts and nuts. The plates are at the sides of the joint and in the hollow of the double-headed rail, and, so long as the fishes are held in that position, the one rail cannot be depressed below the other, except in so far as the fish bends. The main strain, therefore, which the fish has to bear, is a strain tending to the flexure of the fish in the vertical plane, which is also the plane of the fish or plate attached to the side of the rails, the forces which tend to push the fish off from the rails being comparatively slight, and being counteracted by the bolts and nuts."

The fish in use at the time of the patentee's invention was a solid plate of equal thickness throughout; and as a strain in the

which was not adverted to in the Queen's Bench. It was argued that, under the earlier patent, the process was accompanied by the use of sizing, which had a beneficial effect on the thread of cotton or linen ; whereas under the plaintiff's patent no sizing was used, as it would *not* have a beneficial effect on wool or hair. But the court, on comparing the two specifications, did not find the sizing process to be an essential part of the old patent; although it was admitted that it was intended to apply the machinery and mode of operation to articles sized. But it was said the question was, whether the plaintiff could take the process as applied to cotton and linen yarns sized, and apply it to woollen yarns unsized; and it was held he could not (Brook *v.* Aston, 32 Law Times Reports, 341). It is very easy to see the distinctions to which a practitioner should attend, who has occasion to advise on the patentability of similar inventions.

[1] 11 House of Lords Cases, 654.

plane of a plate, and tending to produce flexure in that plane, is chiefly borne by the upper and under parts of such plate, there was a considerable part of the iron in the centre of the plate which did not contribute to the resistance of the strain. The inventor conceived that this superfluous material might be removed, by constructing a groove which would serve as a bed for the heads of the bolts, thus producing economy of material without diminution of strength.

The nature of the invention will sufficiently appear from passages of the specification : " The fishes are made with a groove or recess in their outer surfaces, which groove serves to receive the square heads of the bolts, and prevent them turning round when the nuts are screwed on or off. Washers are placed in the groove of the fish which is next to the nuts, so as to allow of the nuts being turned round; or the fish on this side may be made without the groove. The position of the bolts and nuts may be reversed, if preferred, so that the nut may be prevented from turning round while the bolt is screwed into it. The groove renders the fish lighter for an equal strength, or stronger for an equal weight of metal, than a fish which is made of an equal thickness throughout. The top and bottom of each fish is a plane surface, and the parts of the rail with which they come in contact are also plane surfaces, forming the same angle as the top and bottom surfaces of the fish. The fishes are thus made to fit into their places with greater facility than if these surfaces were of curved or irregular forms. If, however, the surfaces of the rails are curved, the fishes may be made to fit them." Another important advantage claimed was that the heads of the bolts, nuts, or rivets, being imbedded in the groove, would not be exposed to contact with the flanges of the wheels.

Such was the invention the validity of which was contested for want of novelty. It was proved that fishes of different kinds had been used prior to this invention for the same purpose; but such fishes had not been made with a groove in their lateral surfaces, so as to receive the square heads of the bolts, and render the fish lighter for equal strength, or stronger for an equal weight of metal. It was also proved that, before the date of the patent, in the construction of bridges, beams of timber had been laid horizontally, one above the other, and fastened or bolted together with bolts or nuts; that horizontal bars or plates of iron were placed beneath, and parallel to, and in contact with, the horizontal beams, and were also fastened or bolted by the same bolts and nuts, and that each of these bars or plates of iron was constructed with a groove in its under surface, which received the square or horizontal heads of the bolts. This was done for the purpose of strength, and also to prevent the heads of the bolts from turning. But in these bridges there were not joints to be fished by the bars or plates of iron, nor were there corresponding bars or plates of iron above the horizontal beams.

It was further proved that in 1847 Mr. Brunel had constructed a bridge, known as the "Hackney Bridge," over the Teign canal. Owing to the length of the span, the bridge was constructed so as to have upon each side two horizontal longitudinal beams of timber, the ends of which met and were joined together in the middle of the bridge by scarf-joints. Beneath these beams were placed transverse planks, which extended from side to side of the bridge, and constituted its flooring or roadway, and immediately beneath the ends of the planks were longitudinal bars of grooved iron, one upon each side of the bridge, running parallel to, and under the longitudinal beams along the whole length of the bridge, with the grooves or channels downwards. Bolts passed through the grooved iron bars, with square heads resting in the grooves, which prevented them from being turned round.

At the trial below, in answer to questions specially put by the Lord Chief Justice, the jury found "that the channel irons upon the railway bridges (independently of the particular instance of the 'Hackney bridge') were used before the patent, for the double purpose of obtaining increased strength and preventing the bolt-heads from turning round, but they were not used for the purpose of fishing. Secondly, that the fastening of the scarf-joint of the longitudinal beam at the Hackney bridge was a fishing of that joint, but that the use of the channel iron as one of the plates of the fish arose from its being already there for the purpose of fastening the beam and this iron together, and was not adopted by Mr. Brunel with reference to, or in contemplation of, the special advantages in fishing contemplated by Wild's patent."

A verdict was thereupon directed to be entered for the plaintiff; on appeal to the Exchequer Chamber, that decision was reversed, and it was ordered that the verdict be entered for the defendants, upon the pleas denying that the invention was new and that it was the subject-matter of a patent.

An appeal was then taken to the House of Lords, where, after great deliberation, it was held that the patentee had merely transferred a known thing from one use to another, and an analogous use, and that there was not sufficient novelty or invention to support a patent.[1]

[1] The following able discussion of the facts and legal principles involved in this important case was made by the Lord Chancellor, Lord Westbury:—

"At the trial, the novelty of this invention was impeached, on the ground that channelled iron, which altogether corresponded with the grooved fish-plate, had been in use for a considerable period anterior to the patent, and several examples were furnished to illustrate that; but, in particular, one example in the construction of a railway bridge by the late Mr. Brunel, in which channelled iron was used to a very great extent for the purpose of acting as a support to the beams which were placed transversely, and in which there were scarf-joints. In that case, the square heads of the bolts which bolted on the iron that served as a support, or fish, were received in the hollow produced by the channel, and fitted the channel, in order to effect the same object as is here described by the plaintiff, namely, the preventing of the head of the bolt from being turned when the nut was unscrewed.

"I particularly wish to point out to your Lordships the difference between the grooved plate and the channelled iron. The centre of the plate of the channelled iron is not cut away at all; it has the same thickness throughout; but it is constructed with two flanges, one at either end, joining the plate at right angles, and producing therefore this configuration of the plate, that there is a lateral plate forming the base, having on either side a flange at right angles to the plane of the plate. The difference, therefore, between the grooved fish-plate and the channelled iron consists in this: that the centre of the plate of the grooved fish is cut away by the groove, and part of the metal is taken away, so that the plate is not of a uniform thickness throughout; but in the channelled iron the plate is of a uniform thickness throughout; and instead of a groove formed by hollowing out a recess in the plate, the same object is effected by two flanges, one on either side of the plate which forms the bottom (I am speaking in familiar language) of the channelled iron.

"Unquestionably this is a difference, and it would have raised in my judgment a material question whether, if the plaintiff had pointed out and had rested upon this difference of configuration as constituting his invention, it would have been possible to set up the anterior use of the channelled iron as depriving him of all claims to that invention; because the true mode of trying the question of course would be to reverse the order of time of the two productions, and to inquire whether, if any one had now introduced the channelled iron, it would or would not have been an infringement of the plaintiff's patent. If, tried by that criterion, the conclusion should be that the channelled iron

§ 66 *b*. The principles of law decided in Harwood *v*. The Great Northern Railway Company were applied in the subsequent case

would be an infringement of the plaintiff's patent; then, of necessity, it would follow, that as the channelled iron had been in use, and in public and notorious use, preceding the date of the plaintiff's patent, that patent could not be lawfully considered as granted for a 'new invention.'

"My Lords, the learned judges differed on this point. Two learned judges, Mr. Justice Blackburn and Mr. Justice Shee, have in a very learned argument pointed out the difference between the mechanical effects produced by the use of the grooved fish-plate placed so as to resist vertical pressure, in the one case, and the mechanical effect produced upon the channelled iron placed so as to resist transverse pressure, in the other case; but I do not think that that of itself would constitute a material difference. The patent is taken out for a fish of a particular configuration; the patent is not taken out for a saving of metal in the construction of the fish-joint, but the patent is limited entirely to the introduction and use of fishes of a particular shape and configuration. Then the question is simply this: whether the channelled iron, which undoubtedly was a fish (and one of the objects of the patent was to receive the square heads of the bolts and to prevent their turning), is not, in truth, substantially the same thing as a grooved plate with a recess hollowed out in its own plane, instead of a hollow being effected by flanges placed on either side of the plate. Regarding the patent as limited to a claim for fishes of a particular configuration, I cannot for a moment doubt that the channelled iron having the same object, and being capable of the same application, substantially involves the fish-plate made with a grooved hollow in the manner which I have attempted to describe.

"Then, my Lords, the question is, whether there can be any invention of the plaintiff in having taken that thing which was a fish for a bridge, and having applied it as a fish to a railway. Upon that I think the law is well and rightly settled, for there would be no end to the interference with trade and with the liberty of adopting any mechanical contrivance, if every slight difference in the application of a well-known thing should be held to constitute ground for a patent. There is the familiar contrivance of the button to the button-hole, taken from the waistcoat or the coat, which may be applied in some particular mechanical combination in which it has not hitherto been applied; but it would be an idle thing, if it were possible, to take a well-known mechanical contrivance, and, by applying it to a subject to which it has not hitherto been applied, to constitute that application the subject of a patent to be granted as for a new invention. No sounder or more wholesome doctrine, I think, was ever established than that which was established by the decisions which are referred to in the opinions of the four learned judges who concur in the second opinion delivered to your Lordships, namely, that you cannot have a patent for a well-known mechanical contrivance merely when it is applied in a manner or to a purpose, which is not quite the same, but is analogous to the manner or the purpose in or to which it has been hitherto notoriously used. The channelled iron was applied in a manner which was notorious, and the application of it to a vertical fish would be no more than the application of a

of Jordan *v.* Moore.[1] The complainant was the inventor of "certain improvements in the construction of ships and other vessels navigating on water."

In his specification, he claimed, among other things in the construction of ships, "the combination of an iron frame, with an external covering of timber planking for the sides, bilges, and bottoms; and, 6, the construction of iron frames adapted to an external covering of timber for the sides, bilges, and bottoms, *as described*."

On a careful consideration of the specification the court were of opinion that the expression "iron frame" in the first claim was not confined to an iron frame such as that specified in the sixth claim, but comprehended whatever might, according to the ordinary use of language, be called "an iron frame" for a ship, and was therefore "a claim for planking with timber any iron frame of a ship."

Such being the construction put upon it by the court, the main question arose whether the application of wooden planking to the iron frame of a vessel, without any peculiarity in the nature of that planking, could be the subject of a patent in view of the facts that iron had been extensively used in the construction of ships; that ships partly of iron and partly of wood had frequently been constructed; that frames partly of iron and partly of wood had been coated with iron, and that the iron coating of iron vessels had been placed upon iron frames of more or less strength and completeness. It was held that such a patent could not be sustained. In the language of the opinion: "It is not only the substitution of one well-known and analogous material for another, that is, wood for iron, to effect the same purpose, on an iron vessel, but it is the application of the same old invention, viz., planking with tim-

well-known contrivance to a purpose exactly analogous or corresponding to the purpose to which it had been previously applied. Therefore, my Lords, with some anxiety upon this subject, and feeling that the intricacy of the matter must render it impossible to convey one's ideas in words unless one perpetually referred to drawings or models, I think that, upon the whole, I must advise your Lordships, and move your Lordships to confirm the decision of the Court of Exchequer Chamber: that there was no novelty in the patent, and that, therefore, there was a misdirection on the part of the Lord Chief Justice. The consequence will be that I shall move your Lordships to affirm the judgment of the Court of Exchequer Chamber, and to dismiss the appeal with costs."

[1] Law Reports, 1 C. P. 624.

ber, which was formerly done on a wooden frame, to an analogous purpose, or rather the same purpose, on an iron frame."[1]

§ 67. In the case of the new mode of making lead pipe, the new use of the previously existing combination of the devices employed was not analogous to the former uses of that combination. The new use depended on and involved the application of a newly discovered property of the metal of which the pipe was to be made, thus producing, by a new process, an article of manufacture possessing a great superiority over the same kind of article made by former processes. It seems to be quite apparent, that, however old the apparatus, this great improvement in the art of manufacturing lead pipe was not a use of that apparatus, in any legal or logical sense, analogous to the former uses to which it had been applied.[2]

[1] "In this view of the case," continued Mr. Justice Byles, "the recent decision of the Exchequer Chamber and of the House of Lords in Harwood *v.* The Great Northern Railway Company, appears to us to be in point, and decisive for the defendant. These grooved fish-plates having been before used for fastening the scarf-joints of timbers, a patent was taken out for their application to fastening the butt-joints of iron rails; and it was held that the patent was bad, because it claimed the application of an old contrivance to an analogous purpose."

[2] I entirely concur in the following reasoning of Mr. Justice Nelson, embraced in his dissenting opinion given in the case of Le Roy *v.* Tatham, and reported 14 Howard, 156 *et seq.*

"Now, on looking into the specification, we see that the leading feature of the invention consists in the discovery of a new property in the article of lead, and in the employment and adaptation to it, by means of the machinery described, to the production of a new article, wrought pipe, never before successfully made. Without the discovery of this new property in the metal, the machinery or apparatus would be useless, and not the subject of a patent. It is in connection with this property, and the embodiment and adaptation of it to practical use, that the machinery is described and the arrangement claimed. The discovery of this new element or property led naturally to the apparatus by which a new and most useful result is produced. The apparatus was but incidental, and subsidiary to the new and leading idea of the invention. And hence the patentees set forth, as the leading feature of it, the discovery that lead, in a solid state, but under heat and extreme pressure in a close vessel, will reunite, after separation of its parts, as completely as though it had never been separated. It required very little ingenuity, after the experiments in a close vessel, by which this new property of the metal was first developed, to construct the necessary machinery for the formation of the pipe. The apparatus, essential to develop this property, would at once suggest the material parts, especially in the state of the art at the time. Any skilful mechanic, with Burr's machine before him, would readily construct the requisite machinery.

§ 68. A case involving the same distinctions, founded on the discovery and practical use of a new property in a particular compound of metal, was tried in the Court of Common Pleas in England some years before the case of Le Roy *v.* Tatham. The patent was for "an improved manufacture of metal plates for sheathing the bottoms of ships or other such vessels." The invention consisted in making plates of metal of an alloy of zinc and copper, in such proportions of the two metals as would cause in the water a degree of oxidation of the surface sufficient to prevent impurities attaching to it, but not sufficient to wear away the substance of the plate, and in applying such plates as sheathing for the bottoms of vessels. At the trial, evidence was offered tending to prove that plates had previously been made of a compound of zinc and copper in proportions which came within the limits given by the plaintiff in his patent, and that such plates had been sold for the ordinary purposes for which such metal is used; but it did not appear that it had been applied for the purpose of sheathing ships, or that the property of oxidation to a certain degree, and not beyond that degree, when in the water, had been made use of or discovered. Upon this evidence the jury were instructed (by Tindal, C. J.) that the previous existence of plates made in the proportions of metal embraced by the patent was immaterial, provided they had never been applied to the purpose for which the

"The patentees, therefore, after describing their discovery of this property of lead, and the apparatus by means of which they apply the metal to the manufacture of pipe, claim the combination of the machinery, only when used to form pipes under heat and pressure, in the manner set forth, or in any other manner substantially the same. They do not claim it as new separately, or when used for any other purpose, or in any other way; but claim it only when applied for the purpose and in the way pointed out in the specification. The combination, as machinery, may be old; may have been long used; of itself, what no one could claim as his invention, and may not be the subject of a patent. What is claimed is, that it had never been before applied or used, in the way and for the purpose they have used and applied it, namely, in the embodiment and adaptation of a newly discovered property in lead, by means of which they are enabled to produce a new manufacture — wrought pipe — out of a mass of solid lead. Burr had attempted it, but failed. These patentees, after the lapse of seventeen years, having discovered this new property in the metal, succeeded, by the use and employment of it, and, since then, none other than wrought lead pipe, made out of solid lead, has been found in the market, having superseded, on account of its superior quality and cheapness, all other modes of manufacture."

patentee used the plates manufactured by him; for the discovery and application of a new property of such plates, developed by the new use to which the plaintiff had applied them, might well be the subject of a patent. This ruling is in substance the same as that of Mr. Justice Nelson at the trial of the case of Le Roy *v.* Tatham; and although it was not subjected to the revision of any court of errors (the litigation having been compromised), I cannot entertain any doubt of its correctness. The case is a valuable illustration of the doctrine, that when the new use of a thing produces an important effect never before produced, or develops or makes practical some new property of matter not previously known, the new use is not analogous to the former uses, and therefore the novelty of the mere agent is immaterial.[1] But of course

[1] Muntz *v.* Foster, 2 Webs. Pat. Cas. 96–103. In the summing up to the jury, Sir N. C. Tindal, C. J., said upon this part of the case: "I come now to the question, was this a new manufacture within the realm at the time? That is, did people before this patent had been obtained on the 22d October, 1832, know any thing of a manufacture such as this is described in the specification? Therefore it becomes necessary to state what I conceive to be the meaning of the claim, and how far the plaintiff is bound to make out the novelty of it, and how far any objection arising from a user of part of it before can or cannot invalidate the patent which he has got. It appears to me to be properly described in its title, that that is in fact the very discovery for which the patent was granted, namely, 'an improved manufacture of metal plates, for sheathing the bottoms of ships or other such vessels.' He goes on to state that he declares 'his invention to consist in making the said plates for sheathing of an alloy of zinc and copper in such proportions and of such qualities as, while it enables the manufacturer to roll the said compound metal into plates or sheets fit for the said sheathing, at a red heat, and thus makes the said plates or sheets less difficult to work and cheaper to manufacture, renders the said sheathing less liable to oxidation, and consequently more durable, than the ordinary copper sheathing now in use, though at the same time it oxidates sufficiently to keep the bottom of the vessel clean.'

"I look upon the invention to consist in this, that he has, by an experiment, ascertained that a certain mixture of the alloy of zinc with copper will have the effect of producing a better sheathing, by reason and by means of its oxidating just in sufficient quantities, that is, not too much, so as to wear away and impair the sheathing, and render the vessel unsafe, but enough, at the same time, to keep by its wearing the bottom of the vessel clean from those impurities which before attached to it. That I consider to be the meaning of the patent, and the object with which it was taken out. And I cannot think, as at present advised, that if it was shown (as possibly it might be) that sheets had been made of metal before, in the same proportions which he has pointed out, that if this hidden virtue or quality had not been discovered

it is not intended to intimate that it is immaterial in what way the invention is described and claimed. The several cases on

or ascertained, and consequently the application never made, — I cannot think the patent will fail on that ground. That is the opinion which I form upon it. I look upon it that there is as much merit in discovering the hidden and concealed virtue of a compound alloy of metal as there would be in discovering an unknown quality which a natural earth or stone possessed.

"We know, by the cases that have been determined, that where such unknown qualities have, from the result of experiments, been applied to useful purposes of life, that such application has been considered as the ground, and a proper ground, of a patent; and therefore, when I come to that part of the case in which they seek to show this is not so, because these metal plates have been invented before, — that is, persons have used them before, — in my judgment it will not go far enough, unless they can show there has been some application of them before to this very useful purpose.

"There is a third ground upon which they contend that this is not a new invention. They call a class of witnesses, consisting of Emery and Mercer, the casters, and Clarson, who was a caster, and Greson, who was a roller, and Ralph, who was a roller, to state to you, that in 1828, and down from that time to the year 1830 or 1831, they were all employed together in a mill (some of them perhaps not quite so long as the others), but employed in a mill that had once belonged to a person of the name of Rose; that mill is called "Nechell's Mill," I think; and they undertake to tell you (and you heard the mode they gave their evidence, and it is for you to appreciate properly, and to lay what stress on it you think right), they say, so far back as that year 1828, they most distinctly remember that they used the compound of zinc and copper in the proportions of one and a half to one, which would be within the limits mentioned in the plaintiff's specifications, and that they made a quantity of yellow metal from it for the purposes of sale.

"If it was an objection to this patent, that in point of fact any person had made a plate of this compound metal in the interval, — if the patent cannot exist, although no person had discovered what the virtues of this mixture were, but the mere fact of making it and combining the zinc and the copper together was sufficient to destroy the validity of the patent, — then indeed it would be a very material point for you to consider whether the testimony was such as you who have heard it — the cross-examination of some of the witnesses — would entirely rely upon.

"That would be a question I should not take out of your hands, but should leave, as I ought to do, entirely to yourselves. You recollect what the nature of the evidence was; and it is a long time ago (without the attention of the parties being called to it apparently until very lately); the year 1828 is a long time ago. Those are observations I should make to you when you are exerting your own discrimination on the value of the evidence; but, as I have stated already (from which I do not mean to recede), I do not think that the circumstance of showing the combination of these two materials in a metal plate will of itself destroy this patent, when no attention at the time was paid to the purpose for which this patent was taken out, and it was made merely

which the foregoing comments have been made, are apt and forcible illustrations of the necessity of great care in the statement of what constitutes the invention; for if the particular apparatus, agent, compound, or combination employed, is not of itself new, and the novelty consists in the use, which forms a new process, or develops and makes practical a new property of matter, then it will certainly be an error to describe and claim the invention in such a way as to make it necessary to construe the patent as a claim for a new machine, or agent, or combination.

§ 69. The case of Newton *v.* Vaucher rests upon similar principles. The defendant was the earlier inventor of a mode of applying soft metal to the surfaces in contact in a particular class machines, for a specific purpose. He discovered that a lining of soft metal, introduced into the parts of machines where moving surfaces require to be packed so as to be steam tight, could be substituted for the elastic substances which had been used as packing before. The plaintiff afterwards discovered that soft metal had the property of diminishing friction, and of preventing the evolution of heat when applied to the surfaces in contact of machines in rapid motion where there is great pressure; and he embodied the application of that discovery to machines in a patent. It was held that the two inventions were entirely distinct, and that the plaintiff's patent did not cover a mere double use of the discovery made by the defendant.[1]

§ 69 *a*. In the case of Tilghman *v.* Morse, the patent granted to the complainant was for an improvement in cutting and engraving the surfaces of stone, metal, glass, and other hard substances, by means of a stream of sand or grains of quartz driven as projectiles rapidly against such surfaces by any suitable method

in the ordinary course of melters of metal for the various and ordinary purposes of life.

"I do not think that the circumstances of showing that in the long time that has passed before us in the different, and, I may say, infinitely varying combinations that must have been made for the various purposes for which brass and other metal was manufactured for ordinary and common purposes of life, — to call a workman to show that on some occasion or occasions he had combined them in those proportions for another and different purpose, — it does not appear to me that such destroys the patent; and therefore it makes that which was the third head of objection, under the question of new invention or not new invention, immaterial for you to consider."

[1] Newton *v.* Vaucher, 11 Law & Eq. R. 589.

of propulsion; the most common being a rapid jet or current of steam, air, or water. "The invention of Tilghman," said Blatchford, J., "consists in the discovery that a stream of sand, driven with sufficient velocity to cause the grains of sand, through their own velocity and momentum, to act as projectiles against the article to be cut or dressed, will do the work effectually, without any vehicle to carry the sand into contact with the article, and without any contact between any thing and the article, except the sand." The court had no doubt as to the novelty and utility of this process, and sustained the validity of the complainant's patent, which was for a process or art, notwithstanding the prior use of a process in which sand or emery was rubbed against the surface of glass by the wires of a rotating wire brush, and the use on a locomotive engine of a stream of sand combined with a jet of steam to drive cows from the track of a railroad. "Grave reference is made," said Judge Blatchford, "on the question of novelty to patents granted for projecting a stream of sand combined with a jet of steam from a locomotive engine, for the purpose of driving cows from the track of a railroad; and the learned expert, who makes an affidavit on the subject, says with great truth, that the only difference between such use, in combination, of a jet of steam and a stream of sand, and the use by the plaintiff of the combination of a jet of steam with a stream of sand, is that, in the former case, the sand, after having had velocity imparted to it, came in contact with cows, while, in the latter case, it comes in contact with glass, stone, &c. This is the only difference; but in this difference lies the distinction between the two. No one, from observing the temporary operation of the process on the animal, would infer that he could, by the same means, produce the results which the plaintiff describes. Nor is there any resemblance in kind between those results and the result produced on the animal."[1]

§ 70. But there is a class of cases which come much nearer to the line, and in which it is much more difficult to determine whether the supposed invention is to be regarded merely as a double use, or as a substantive improvement entitled to a patent. These are the cases where the change consists in the substitution of one material for another in a particular manufacture or machine, and in the consequences produced by that change. Thus, to take one of the most simple of these cases, — that mentioned by Mr.

[1] Tilghman *v.* Morse (1872), 9 Blatchf. 421.

Justice Nelson in his judgment in the case of Hotchkiss *v.* Greenwood, — in which the patent was for an improvement in manufacturing buttons, the foundation being made of wood, the face being covered with tin bent over the rim. At the trial, the defendant produced a button made long before the plaintiff's in the same way, excepting that the foundation was of bone. It was admitted that the new article was better and cheaper than the old one; but the case was given up on the part of the plaintiff, rightly, as the learned judge thought, since, in his view, the mere superiority of the material, unconnected with any change in the contrivance or mode of putting the button together, could not make the manufacture a new one, in the sense of being entitled to a patent.[1]

§ 71. The case in which this illustration was resorted to was one where a similar substitution of one material for another had been made by the supposed inventor. It consisted of an improvement in the manufacture of door-knobs, and other knobs to be used as handles of locks or other fastenings. Previous to the invention of these patentees, knobs had been made of metal and fastened to the shank by a peculiar arrangement, namely, by making a dovetail cavity in the knob for the insertion of the shank, which had a screw upon its end, and by pouring fused metal into the cavity around the shank, so as to form the proper corresponding screw. It appeared, moreover, at the trial, that door-knobs had previously been made of potter's clay, but not that they had been attached to the shank in the mode in which the metallic knobs had been attached. The patentees described in their specification the method of fastening the knob and the shank together, which proved to be substantially the same as the mode previously used with the metallic knobs; and they claimed the manufacturing of knobs, in this mode of fastening, of potter's clay, or of any kind of clay used in pottery, or of porcelain.[2] It is quite apparent that the invention (if there was one) of these patentees consisted in making door and other knobs of clay or porcelain, in the same way in which knobs had previously been made of iron, or brass, or glass, or wood.

[1] See the statement of this case by Mr. Justice Nelson, in his opinion in the case of Hotchkiss *v.* Greenwood, 11 Howard, 248, 266.

[2] The claim was as follows : "The manufacturing of knobs, *as stated in the foregoing specification*, of potter's clay, or any kind of clay used in pottery,

§ 72. Now the question of the patentability of the application of this new material to the manufacture of door-knobs, in a well-known mode of attaching the knob to the shank, appears, from the evidence adduced at the trial, to have depended upon the single consideration of the superiority of that material in point of cheapness or durability; and both the court below and the Supreme Court of the United States held, that mere superiority of material could not constitute an invention of a new manufacture.[1] It is true that the patentees asked for an instruction to the jury, under which it would have been their duty to inquire whether the attaching of the clay knob to the shank required more skill or invention than to attach the metal knob. But it does not appear from the report of the case that any evidence was offered which would have justified the jury in finding that the patentees' method of attaching the knob differed from the method previously used. The amount of ingenuity or skill or invention involved in the attaching of the knob and the shank was therefore not a material issue in the case; and the sole material issue was, whether the substance of a knob, so attached, was new, and whether *that* novelty made the new knob a patentable invention. The case therefore presented the naked question of the superiority of a new material for the purposes for which that material was used in an old manufacture as the ground for a patent.

§ 72 *a.* It is a question, however, whether a hoop used for ladies' skirts, consisting of a brass wire in the form of a spiral, having a thread of catgut running through it and forming a core, would be patentable, in view of the fact that the large strings of a bass viol and other stringed musical instruments had been made in the same way, with the exception that the wire of the skirt-hoop was heavier and stiffer than that on the viol string, and therefore more elastic.[2]

and shaped and finished by moulding, turning, burning, and glazing, and also of porcelain." The claim is stated in the text as a claim for the manufacture of knobs of clay, in that mode of fastening, because the patent, under all the facts bearing upon it, was capable of no other construction.

[1] Hotchkiss *v.* Greenwood, 4 McLean's R. 456; s. c. 11 Howard, 248. This, it should be observed, is a different question from the one that would arise where the material is itself a new composition of matter; for, in such a case, the superior fitness of the material for particular uses has relation to the question of its novelty as a composition, if it is any relevancy at all.

[2] West *v.* Silver Wire and Skirt Manufacturing Co. (1867), 3 Fisher's

§ 72 *b*. The true test would seem to be that of invention. In the first place, the application to another purpose must be new and useful. Then it must be such as to require invention. If the new application be merely within the knowledge of an ordinary person, or a skilled mechanic, it is not patentable, though its use may have been previously unknown. A discovery is not necessarily an invention. Thus, the application of a fabric, which is not new, to a new use, is not invention, when nothing novel is required for its adaptation.[1] But if any one discovers that a machine or a process may be applied to a new and valuable use, and such discovery is novel and has the qualities of invention, it

Pat. Cas. 306. In referring to this point, Shipman, J., said: "It will be seen by referring to the description of the state of the art, and the defects to be remedied as set forth in the first paragraph, that mere steel, brass, whalebone, or rattan strips, formed into hoops, or combined with a covering of any kind, are not claimed. Hoops made of the material mentioned were old and well known. These materials were only claimed when curved into a spiral form, either with or without a core or central cone, of a flexible character. The specimen presented on the trial as an illustration of the invention covered by the patent was a brass wire in the form of a spiral, having a thread of catgut running through forming a core. Whether such a hoop would be patentable in view of the state of the mechanic arts need not now be determined. But it may be remarked, as it is familiarly known, that the large strings of a bass viol, and other stringed musical instruments, are nearly identical with this core which formed the hoop of the skirt presented on the trial, as one manufactured under this patent, with this exception: the wire of the skirt-hoop was heavier and stiffer than that on the viol string, and therefore more elastic. Both, however, had the same combination and the same mechanical construction. Whether such an article, by simply using a stiffer wire and inserting it in a lady's skirt in circular form, could legally be the subject of a patent, without claiming it in combination with some new element, or as part of some new combination; or whether it is the application of an old thing to a new use, and therefore not patentable, does not arise properly on the pleadings, and therefore will not be decided."

[1] Smith *v.* Elliott (1872), 9 Blatchf. 400. In this case the court remarked: "There are many changes which may be suggested by the judgment or taste of the manufacturer, or by the particular uses to which the article produced is to be applied, which are not invention; and many exhibitions of superior skill, in producing an article of greater excellence, which are not invention. Thus, if a fabric be already known and in use, change of color, change of mere material, change in its degree of fineness, or in the fineness of parts thereof, if these changes involve nothing new in construction, in the relation of its parts, in the office or function of either part or of the whole, do not constitute invention, although for many purposes these may constitute the greater excellence of the fabric."

would seem that such improvement would be patentable so far as its application to the new use is concerned. Thus, in a recent important case, the application of annealing to the manufacture of car wheels was held to be new and patentable, notwithstanding the fact that the ordinary process of annealing metals had been applied to wheels other than car wheels.[1]

[1] Whitney *v.* Mowry (1867), 3 Fisher's Pat. Cas. 157. The facts and the principles of law involved in this case were thus presented by Leavitt, J:—

"1. First, as to the novelty of the invention patented to the complainant. The allegations of the answer assailing the novelty of the patent are: 'That, in so far as the complainant, in his said letters-patent, claims to be the inventor of reheating car wheels after their removal from the moulds, or of a continuing process of removing them, while at a red heat, from the moulds, and, without allowing them to cool, placing them in that state, in a previously heated furnace or chamber, and then reheating them to a high temperature, and then allowing them to cool gradually; such claim is beyond the invention of complainant, and his said letters-patent are void, for the reason that the same process was known and used long prior to such alleged invention by the complainant.' The defendant then specifies more than twenty persons to whom the complainant's process was known, and by them used, in different places in the United States, prior to the date of his patent. He also refers to twenty or more works or printed publications in this country and in Great Britain, in which it is averred the complainant's process is described.

"Before advancing further in considering the question of novelty, it will be necessary to state at least the outlines of the complainant's process, as set forth in his specification and claim. In the patent the invention is designated as 'a new and useful improvement in the process of manufacturing cast-iron railroad wheels. In his specification, the complainant calls it 'a new and useful improvement in the process of manufacturing cast-iron railroad wheels.' And he says: 'My improvement consists in taking railroad wheels from the moulds in which they are ordinarily cast, as soon after being cast as they are sufficiently cool to be strong enough to move with safety, or before they have become so much cooled as to produce any considerable inherent strain between the thin and thick parts, and putting them, in this state, into a furnace or chamber that has been previously heated to a temperature as high as that of the wheels when taken from the moulds. As soon as they are deposited in this furnace or chamber, the opening through which they have been passed is closed, and the temperature of the furnace or chamber and its contents gradually raised to a point a little below that at which fusion commences, when all the avenues to and from the interior are closed, and the whole mass left to cool no faster than the heat it contains permeates through, and radiates from, the exterior surface of the materials of which it is composed. By this process all parts of each wheel are raised to the same temperature, and the heat they contain can only pass through the medium of the confined atmosphere that intervenes between them and the walls of the furnace or chamber; consequently, the thinnest and

§ 72 *c*. In Rushton *v*. Crawley,[1] it was held that the use of a new material to produce a known article could not be the subject

thickest parts cool simultaneously together, which relieves them from all inherent strain whatever, when cold.' After referring to the drawings descriptive of the furnace, the patentee adds: 'To heat this furnace, I have used anthracite coal, it requiring less than one-fourth of a ton to anneal two tons of wheels.' He also provides for other kinds of fuel for heating the furnace, but declares that, by whatever means the heat is produced, the furnace or chamber must be so constructed as that the operator can control the quantity and intensity of the heat used 'by admitting more or less of it into the chamber, and excluding it entirely.' After stating the advantage of annealing car wheels by this process, as adding to their strength and durability, and as being more economical than any other known process, he disclaims the annealing of castings in the ordinary way, and also says he does not 'claim to be the inventor of any particular form or kind of furnace in which to perform the process.' And he adds: 'But what I do claim as my invention, and desire to secure by letters-patent, is the process of prolonging the time of cooling, in connection with annealing railroad wheels in the manner above described, — that is to say, the taking them from the moulds in which they are cast, before they have become so much cooled as to produce such inherent strain on any part as to impair its ultimate strength, and immediately after being thus taken from the moulds, depositing them in a previously heated furnace or chamber, so constructed, of such materials, and subject to such control, that the temperature of all the parts of the wheels deposited therein may be raised to the same point (say a little below that at which fusion commences), when they are allowed to cool so fast, and no faster than is necessary for every part of each wheel to cool and shrink simultaneously together, and no one part before another.' Such is substantially the specification and claim of the complainant, stated in such full, clear, and exact terms as that an intelligent mechanic in that department, according to the testimony of a well-qualified expert in the case, could readily follow the process described.

"Before referring to the evidence offered as impeaching the novelty of the complainant's patented invention, it is proper to remark, that the evidence to sustain such a claim must be strong and conclusive, to justify a judgment setting aside the patent as void for want of novelty. The presumption of law is with the complainant upon this issue, arising not only from the grant of the original patent, but from its extension for seven years after its expiration. The statute authorizing the extension of a patent is too well known to require special reference or citation. It is sufficient to say that it imposes on the head of the Patent Office the duty of a critical revision of the grounds on which the original patent was granted. He must be satisfied, not only that the invention was new, but that it had proved of great practical utility to the public, and that the patentee had used proper diligence in bringing the invention into public use, and had not been sufficiently remunerated, as the conditions on

[1] Law Rep. (1870), 10 Eq. Cas. 522.

of a patent, unless some invention and ingenuity were displayed in the adaptation.

which alone the patent can be extended. And the statute requires notice of the application of the extension, so that all persons opposing it may have the opportunity of making their objections. A patent which successfully undergoes this scrutiny, without any modification of the original claim and specification, has very strong presumptive claims to validity, as being both new and useful. Another fact strengthening this presumption is, that the complainant, for eighteen years before the commencement of this suit, had practically and successfully practised his patented method of annealing car wheels, during which time, as the proof shows, nearly five hundred thousand car wheels were manufactured and sold at his foundry in Philadelphia.

"But how does the issue of novelty stand upon the evidence? The complainant's patent bears date of April, 1848, but it appears that his application for a patent dates back to August 2, 1847, which is to be viewed as the date of his invention. All the witnesses agree, that prior to that time no car wheel, made of cast iron, was known having the required qualities of durability and strength. The art of casting in chills as it is called — that is, casting in a mould, the outer circumference of which was iron instead of sand — was previously known and practised. This produced a hardened surface of the periphery of the wheel; but in casting, the thin and thick parts of the wheel contracted unequally, and the result was an inherent strain between the periphery or tread of the wheel, and its inner parts, that greatly impaired the strength and durability of the wheel. Prior to the date of the complainant's invention, several devices had been resorted to, and patented, designed to remove the injurious effects of this inherent strain. The first remedy for this difficulty was to cast the hub in sections, dividing it into four parts. After the wheel had cooled, and the process of contraction ended, the spaces between the divided parts of the hub were filled with some fused metal, and the hub thus made solid. But this method involved a waste of time, and was too expensive for practical use. It was found, too, that the wheel was sometimes distorted, so as to be useless. It appears that the next device for avoiding the inherent strain was to make the plate, or thin part of the wheel, of a curved form, so that in cooling the curve in the plate would be straightened. There were also patents for other plans, embodying changes in the shape of the wheels to overcome the effects of unequal contraction in cooling, and thus avoiding the inherent strain. But none of these inventors seem to have conceived the idea of making a practical car wheel with straight plates, so annealed and cooled as to leave it strong and durable, and uninjured by the unequal contraction of its parts.

"It is safe to say, that up to the date of the complainant's invention, the process of prolonging the time of cooling the wheel, in the mode described and claimed by him, and thus overcoming the difficulties of the prior methods, was unknown. Several intelligent witnesses sustain this conclusion in a manner that frees it from all doubt.

"I have not deemed it necessary to advert to the publications referred to in the defendant's answer as anticipating the complainant's invention. They

§ 73. The mere quality of cheapness, or other superiority in the material of which an article is made, disconnected with any

prove, undoubtedly, that the process of annealing metals has been long known, and that various plans and modes of accomplishing it have been described by scientific writers. But the evidence is clear, that casting railroad car wheels is a distinct branch of the art of casting, and that none of the printed works referred to describe or apply to that art. One witness examined as an expert, and apparently well acquainted with mechanical science, testifies that in none of those works is the complainant's process of making car wheels alluded to or described. There is some reference to annealing wheels, other than car wheels, but none to any wheel cast with a chill; and therefore it has no application to the process described by and patented to the complainant.

"Without enlarging on the question of the novelty of this invention, I have no hesitancy in the conclusion that the evidence is entirely satisfactory to prove that the process of prolonging the cooling of car wheels, and thus avoiding inherent strains, is due to the thought and inventive talent of the complainant. And I cannot, perhaps, more appropriately close my remarks on this point than by quoting what was said in relation to it by my learned brother, Mr. Justice Swayne, who sat with me on the hearing of the application for an injunction, at the last April term of this court. His remarks on that occasion show a very intelligent apprehension of the subject, and are very pertinent to the question now under consideration. The learned judge, speaking for the court, said: 'Our impression is, that the patent may be sustained on the ground of a discovery. Annealing is undoubtedly an old invention, but, as applied to car wheels, may be valid as a discovery applied to car wheels. It strikes us, as the case is presented, we may fairly hold, and perhaps are bound to hold, that the patentee and complainant did discover a mode of overcoming this difficulty (the inherent strain of the wheels) by his process. That result is a meritorious one, and we should be inclined, at the final hearing, as we are now, to give such a construction to this patent as will sustain his claim to that invention, and give him the fruits of his discovery. There is no proof that he was not the inventor or discoverer of that art, and the application of that art.'

"Such were the views of the learned judge, upon the case as presented on the application for the injunction. I may add, that the evidence on the final hearing, instead of detracting from the correctness of these views on the question of the novelty of complainant's invention as covered by his patent, has strengthened and confirmed them. Several reliable witnesses, familiar with the progress of making car wheels, from their first introduction in this country, agree in their testimony, that, up to the time of this invention, no successful method of making them had been discovered; and that the complainant's process of prolonged cooling was the first known which overcame the defects in all wheels previously made. In the language of one witness: 'It enabled a better wheel to be produced at a less cost than had been the case before his invention.' And again: 'There was a general confidence felt in regard to their strength as well as durability, which never had been the case regarding other wheels.'"

new or different mode of applying that material in the process of making the thing, has not been held to be the subject of a patent. There are *dicta* of judges in which cheapness has been made an important consideration in determining the patentable character of inventions. But it is necessary to observe carefully the nature of these inventions, and the relation which this quality of cheapness bears to the subject-matter. Thus in Crane's invention, consisting in the use of anthracite coal and a hot-air blast in the manufacture of iron, in the place of bituminous coal and a hot-air blast, one test applied by the court, in order to determine whether this change in the process of manufacturing iron was a patentable invention or new mode of manufacture, was to inquire whether the article produced by it was cheaper or better than that produced by the old process. Here the superiority of the article made by a particular process was resorted to as proof that the process is new or improved, in the sense of being a patentable change. So, also, in Lord Dudley's patent, where pit-coal was substituted for charcoal in the manufacture of iron, the different constitution of the iron so made was evidence of a new process of making it. The production of an article, therefore, as good in quality as before, and at a cheaper rate, or better in quality than before, at the same rate, by a process which claims to be new, may be taken as evidence tending to show a substantive difference between that process and any former one. But in the case of a manufacture or a machine, the substitution of one material for another, leading to greater cheapness or durability in the manufacture or machine itself, seems to belong to the province of construction and not to that of invention.

Still, it is not to be laid down broadly that the use of one material in place of another, in a manufactured vendible article or a machine, can never be the subject of a patent. If such substitution involves a new method of attachment or construction, or leads to any new mode of operation, or develops a new application of the properties of matter, so as to change the use of the manufacture or machine, there may be in the use of the new material a patentable invention.[1]

[1] Mr. Phillips takes the same distinction. "There may be cases," he says, "in which the substitution of a different material may be a matter of contrivance and invention, and in such case the particular mode of applying the new material would be a good subject of a patent." Phillips on Patents, 134.

§ 73 *a*. But if any one merely makes a machine out of iron that has been made out of wood, and it is the same machine, producing the same result in the same way, it is no invention; because any constructor can make a machine of iron instead of wood. So the application of horse power, or water power, or steam power to a machine that has been moved by hand power, provided the change is within the ordinary knowledge and skill of any constructor, is not patentable. "The mere means," says Lowell, J., "of giving motion to a machine would not ordinarily be a part of the essence of the machine."[1]

It has been seen, however, that the application of a device to cast-iron guns was held to be patentable, notwithstanding the fact that substantially the same device had been applied to wrought-iron guns, or guns composed of wrought and cast iron in combination.[2]

§ 74. Having presented these illustrations of the doctrine of novelty, as applied to cases of double use, it may be expedient to consider, in reference to the same patentable quality, that class of inventions where there is supposed to be a new process, formed by the substitution of one thing for another, or by the use of a new combination of materials, or by the omission or addition of some step or manipulation, in a manufacture or an art. What is it, in this class of cases, which constitutes the patentable novelty? In other words, what is it that affords proof of a change sufficient to constitute a patentable improvement in the art or manufacture, or to form a new process or method distinguishable as an invention from what had gone before it?

§ 75. The leading case of Crane *v*. Price, involving a new mode of making iron, stands very prominent among the cases of this description. The whole invention in this case consisted in the use of a well-known material, anthracite coal, in the manufacture of

It was in reference to the same distinction that Mr. Justice Nelson, in delivering the opinion of the Supreme Court of the United States in Hotchkiss *v*. Greenwood, laid down the doctrine that superiority of material cannot, *of itself*, be the subject of a patent. The meaning of this doctrine is, that the superiority must extend beyond mere comparative cheapness or durability, or adaptation to the purpose for which the old material was used, and must lead to some change in the construction or mode of operation. 11 Howard, 266. See, in connection, the dissenting opinion of Mr. Justice Woodbury.

[1] Woodman *v*. Stimpson (1866), 3 Fisher's Pat. Cas. 98.

[2] Treadwell *v*. Parrott, *supra*.

iron, in combination with the use of a hot-air blast, after bituminous coal had been used with a hot-air blast, and after anthracite coal had been used with a cold-air blast. The doctrine applied by the court to this state of facts is embraced in the proposition that, if the result produced by the new combination is either a new article, a better article, or a cheaper article to the public than that produced by the old method, the new combination is patentable as an invention or manufacture intended by the statute. The meaning of this proposition, when applied to the English statute (the Statute of Monopolies) is, that the improvement in the article manufactured is proof that the change which has been made in the process of manufacture amounts to a new process or new mode of manufacturing iron. Applied to our statute, which embraces any new and useful art, or any new and useful improvement in an art, and therefore embraces a new process of manufacturing iron, the doctrine means the same thing. The question arises, then, whether this doctrine is sound.

§ 76. It may be observed, that patents of the class to which this case of Crane *v.* Price belongs embrace inventions which consist entirely in the use of known things, acting together in a manner already known, and producing effects already known, but producing those effects so as to be more economically or beneficially enjoyed by the public. That is to say, these inventions consist in a change of process, by the substitution of one thing for another, or the omission or addition of one or more steps, in the manufacture of an article known before as manufactured by a different process. It is quite clear, that, if there is any test capable of being applied to these changes of process, and fit to determine whether there is a patentable novelty in them, that test must be found in the improved effect which the new combination of materials or agents produces. This is the ground on which the decision in Crane *v.* Price was made.[1] The decision has been questioned; but it appears, from the whole of the discussion embraced in the opinion of the court, that it was intended to be put upon the ground that the iron manufactured by the new process was a new metal, that is to say, new in respect to its superior properties, or its cheapness, or both.[2]

[1] See also the cases cited in the opinion of the court, as contained in 1 Webs. Pat. Cas. 407–411.

[2] In Dobbs *v.* Penn, 3 Exchequer R. 427, 432, the Lord Chief Baron is

§ 77. The previous case of Sturz *v.* De La Rue, before Lord Chancellor Lyndhurst, was very similar in principle to Crane *v.* Price. The patent covered "improvements in copper and other plate printing"; and the invention consisted in "putting a glazed enamelled surface on the paper by means of white lead and size, whereby the finer lines of the engraving are better exhibited than heretofore." This was held to be a patentable invention, as an improvement in copper-plate printing.[1] In like manner, the omission of any ingredient previously used in, and considered essential to, a particular process, may constitute such a change in the series of processes pursued as to amount to a patentable invention. As where a patent was taken for "a new and improved method of making and manufacturing double canvas and sail-cloth with hemp and flax, or either of them, without any starch whatever";[2] and where another invention, for rendering cloth fabrics water-proof, consisted in immersing them in various solutions in a different order from that which had been previously followed, although the same solutions had been previously used.[3]

§ 78. It appears, then, that there is a large class of cases where improvements or inventions in the mode of producing a particular known effect will be the subject-matter of letters-patent; and

reported to have said, that the decision in Crane *v.* Price might be put upon the ground that the patent produced a new result, — that the metal produced was a *new* metal; and Baron Parke observed, that upon that ground he could understand the decision, although before he had entertained serious doubts as to the correctness of it.

[1] Sturz *v.* De La Rue, 1 Webs. Pat. Cas. 83, 5 Russel's Ch. R. 322, 324.

[2] Campion *v.* Benyon, 4 B. Moore, 71, cited in Webster on the subject-matter, p. 23, note.

[3] Halliwell *v.* Dearman, 1 Webs. Pat. Cas. 401, note (*t*). "The object of the plaintiff's invention was the rendering fabrics water-proof, but at the same time leaving such fabrics pervious to the air. It appeared that, before the plaintiff's patent, a solution of alum and soap was made, and the fabric to be rendered water-proof was immersed therein. By this means a water-proof surface was produced on the fabric, but it was not of a lasting nature; it wore off. According to the plaintiff's invention, the fabric is immersed first in a mixture of a solution of alum with some carbonate of lime, and then in a solution of soap. The effect is, that by the first immersion every fibre becomes impregnated with the alum, the sulphuric acid of the alum being neutralized by the carbonate of lime, and by the second immersion the oily quality, rendering it repellant of water, is given to every fibre, so that each fibre is rendered water-proof, instead of the surface only; but the whole fabric continued pervious to air."

another large class of cases, in which the discovery and application of new means of producing an effect before unknown will also be the subject-matter of a patent. One of these classes embraces all cases of the new application of known agents and things, so as to lead to a change in the series of processes by which the particular effect, result, or manufacture is produced, or by which an entirely new effect, result, or manufacture is produced. The other embraces all cases of the discovery and application of new agents or things, by which a new effect or result is to be produced.

§ 79. But with respect to that class of inventions which we have been considering, and which consist in a change of process produced by the omission of some step in the old process, or the new application of a particular agent, there are some recent English cases which show the test that is to be applied in determining the patentable novelty. In one of them the alleged invention consisted in a new mode of extracting garancine, the pure red coloring matter contained in madder. Before the plaintiff's patent, garancine had been obtained from fresh madder by the application of sulphuric acid and hot water or steam. The refuse, called spent madder, was regarded as useless. The plaintiff discovered that, by applying the same process to spent madder which had formerly been applied to fresh madder, garancine could still be extracted; and this discovery rendered spent madder very valuable. Upon the trial, — there being an issue which embraced the question whether this was a patentable invention, — the presiding judge told the jury that, if they believed the evidence which had been offered to show the facts above stated, they must find this issue for the defendant. This instruction made the patentable character of the invention an inference of law, to be drawn from too narrow a basis of facts. In the Exchequer Chamber, on a writ of error, it was held that this direction was wrong, and that the jury should have been directed to find certain questions of fact, as inferences from the evidence, which questions are thus stated in the opinion of the court. "There is here no new contrivance, for the process used under the plaintiff's patent with the spent madder is the same as that previously used with fresh madder; neither is the product new, for garancine produced from the one and the other appears to us precisely of the same quality. If, therefore, the patent be good, it must be on account of the old contrivance being applied to a new object under such circumstances as to support the patent. Now, spent madder might be a very different thing from fresh madder in its properties, chemical and otherwise, or it might be in effect the same thing as fresh madder in its properties, chemical and otherwise, with the difference only that part of its coloring matter had been already extracted; again, the properties, chemical and otherwise, of both might or might not have been known to chemists and other scientific persons, so that they could tell whether fresh madder and spent madder were different things, or substantially the same things. These points appear to us to be questions of fact, and material to affect the validity or invalidity of the patent," &c.[1]

§ 80. From this ruling it is apparent that there might be one state of circumstances which would support this patent, and another state of circumstances which would show the supposed invention to be nothing more than a double use of the old process. The proper instruction to have given to a jury in this case would have been to direct them to find whether spent madder, as a substance from which to extract garancine, was, chemically or otherwise, a substantially different substance from fresh madder; or whether it was, chemically or otherwise, substantially the same substance, differing only in the amount of coloring matter remaining in it. If the latter should turn out to be the case, the supposed invention would be nothing more than the repetition of an old process, for the purpose of extracting from the same substance what had not been extracted by the first application of that process. But, if spent madder was a substantially different substance from fresh madder, then there would have been an invention, consisting in the application of an old process to a substance to which it had not been before applied, and obtaining thereby the same result which had formerly been obtained from a different substance.[2]

§ 81. The still more recent case of Booth *v.* Kennard is an in-

[1] Steiner *v.* Heald, 6 Eng. Law & Eq. R. 536. A new trial was directed, but it does not appear that it was ever had. The patent was repealed, on the production of a foreign work which affected its validity. See Webster's argument in Booth *v.* Kennard, 38 Eng. Law & Eq. R. 457.

[2] Just as if the discovery had been made (to use an illustration suggested by *Maule*, J., at the argument of this case) that, by applying to potatoes the process used for obtaining garancine from madder, a valuable coloring matter could be obtained.

stance where there was an invention in making an article by the omission of one step in the process. Before the plaintiff's patent, gas had been made from oils extracted from seeds and other substances. The plaintiff discovered that gas might be made directly from the seeds, &c. The apparatus which he employed was not new, the seeds or other matters from which the gas was made were the same from which the oils had been previously extracted, and the gas produced was the same. The distinction, therefore, between the plaintiff's and former methods consisted in the saving of one step in the process of making gas. This was held to be a substantive invention, capable of supporting a patent.[1]

§ 82. Having thus considered the statute requisite of novelty in respect to the quality and extent of the difference between the alleged invention and other things which preceded it, the next inquiry is, whether this must be an absolute novelty, in respect to all previous time and all other countries, or whether it may, under any and what circumstances, be relative to the existing state of knowledge, and to the knowledge of this or of other countries. And here an inspection of the statute brings into view certain clauses which have an important bearing upon the issue of novelty, and, in one way or the other, qualify or limit the circumstances under which a valid patent may be taken. One of these clauses, found in the sixth section of the act of 1836, provides, as if by way of accumulation, that the subject-matter of the alleged invention must be something "not known or used by others before his or their discovery or invention thereof." The other is the provision, in the fifteenth section of the statute, which declares that, "whenever it shall satisfactorily appear that the patentee, at the time of making his application for the patent, believed himself to be the first inventor or discoverer of the thing patented, the same shall not be void on account of the invention or discovery, or any part thereof, having been before known or used in any foreign country; it not appearing that the same, or any substantial part thereof, had before been patented, or described in any printed publication."

§ 83. The clause of the statute which makes the condition of a valid patent, that the supposed invention was "not known or used by others before his or their invention or discovery thereof," was founded upon a similar clause in the patent act of 1793, and

[1] Booth *v.* Kennard, 38 Eng. Law & Eq. R. 457.

upon the construction which that clause had received. The words of the act of 1793 were, "not known or used before the application." The seeming ambiguity of this language led to the inquiry in what way and by whom a previous knowledge was to vitiate a claim to an otherwise original invention. It was perceived that the applicant or patentee himself must have had a knowledge and use of his invention before his application for a patent; and that others, who might have been employed to assist him in developing or applying it, might have thus derived a knowledge of it from him, and that others still might have pirated it from him, or used it without his consent, before his application. In order, therefore, to give the statute a rational interpretation, it was held by the Supreme Court that it must be construed to mean, not known or used by *the public* before the application.[1] This construction made the clause to mean, that if the public were, at the time of the application, in possession of the invention, whether derived from another inventor or from the applicant himself and with his consent, the patent obtained would be invalid.

§ 84. This construction was adopted into the act of 1836 by inserting the words "by others"; but the previous use or knowledge by others was made to relate to the time of the invention or discovery by the applicant, instead of the time of his application for a patent. Thus altered, the text of the clause "not known or used by others before his or their discovery or invention thereof," obviously gives rise to several very important questions. In the first place, looking at the authority of the decision on which the clause was founded, and at the reasons of that construction, it is apparent that the term "others," although used in the plural, was used to denote that the use or knowledge was to be the use or knowledge of any other person or persons than the patentee himself; and therefore the prior use or knowledge by one person, other than the patentee, is sufficient to defeat his statute claim to be regarded as the inventor, provided that use or knowledge was not such as to be excluded by the further construction which the clause is to receive, or by the limitations which are imposed upon it by some other clause.[2] We have seen, then, that when the Supreme Court inserted the term "others," by con-

[1] Pennock *v.* Dialogue, 2 Peters, 1. See also Mellus *v.* Silsbee, 4 Mason, 108; Treadwell *v.* Bladen, 4 Wash. 703.

[2] See Reed *v.* Cutter, 1 Story, 590; Bedford *v.* Hunt, 1 Mason, 302.

struction, into the statute of 1793, they gave it two limitations: first, that the prior use or knowledge must have been from the invention or discovery of some other person than the applicant for a patent; or, secondly, if derived from his invention or discovery, that it must have been with his consent. The first of these limitations is embodied in the clause in the act of 1836, which is now under consideration; and the second is embraced in another clause of the same statute, which permits the applicant to have allowed the use of his invention for a certain period, —a regulation that will be considered hereafter. With these limitations, then, kept in view, the question arises, what is to constitute a prior "use" or "knowledge" of an alleged invention within the meaning of this statute? Does the "use" or "knowledge" comprehend all time and place, or is it limited, under any and what circumstances?

§ 84 *a*. The language of the present statute (1870) is that the invention or discovery for which letters-patent are sought shall not have been "known or used by others in this country, and not patented, or described in any printed publication in this or any foreign country, before his [the inventor's or discoverer's] invention or discovery thereof, and not in public use or on sale for more than two years prior to his application, unless the same is proved to have been abandoned."

§ 85. It is apparent that, if the whole state of a particular art, past and present, were to become known, on a full investigation, the previous use or knowledge of a thing which is sought to be made the subject of a patent might relate to a foreign country, or a former period of time, or to this country, or the present time. Confining our inquiries, therefore, to the state of the existing knowledge of this country, at the time of a supposed invention, one question to be considered is, whether the former existence of the supposed subject of invention, after the previous specimen of it has been laid aside, lost, or abandoned, is sufficient to prevent a patent being granted to one who has reinvented it. This question has been judicially considered, under our statute, but under circumstances which should be carefully noted. One Fitzgerald was an original inventor of an iron safe for the preservation of papers from fire, of a peculiar construction, patented in the year 1843. In the defence it appeared that one Conner, a stereotype founder in the city of New York, between the years 1829 and

1832, made a safe for his own use of substantially the same construction, and used it in his own counting-room as a place of deposit for his papers, and for their preservation from fire, until the year 1838, when it passed into other hands. There was no evidence to show what became of this safe afterwards, or that the person into whose hands it fell was aware of any peculiar construction making it valuable as a protection against fire, or that it was ever used for that purpose after Conner had parted with it.[1] While in Conner's possession, its construction and supposed value, as a means of protection against fire, were known to the workmen employed in his foundry, but no test was applied to it to ascertain its value in this respect. After it passed out of his possession, he did not make another like it, but used a safe of different construction. The case, therefore, on which the Supreme Court intended to pass, was that of a single specimen, of substantially the same construction as the patentee's safe, used for some years, by the person who made it, as a place of deposit for his papers, then laid aside and lost to the world, but still capable of being described from the recollection of the person who made it, when recalled to his recollection by the subsequent reinvention of it by an original inventor. Does such a state of facts negative the claim of a subsequent original inventor to a patent?

§ 86. In considering this question, the Supreme Court came to the conclusion that it was not the intention of Congress to require that a patentee should be *literally* the original and first inventor or discoverer of the thing patented. This conclusion they deduced from the obvious policy and object of the statute, namely, to reward him who first gives to the public the means of knowledge of a useful discovery, — a policy which is evinced by that provision of the statute which requires that a previous foreign invention must have been patented, or described in a printed pub-

[1] I state the facts of this case as they appeared in the record on which the Supreme Court pronounced its opinion. Unfortunately, the bills of exceptions were somewhat loosely drawn, and it appears to have been true that the Conner safe was in existence at the time of the trial. See the application made to the Supreme Court to open the judgment, after it had been pronounced. 10 Howard's Reports, 509, original edition. But the decision of the Supreme Court must be examined as if this fact were not in the case, and upon the supposition that the Conner safe and all knowledge of it, except such knowledge as was recalled to the mind of Conner by Fitzgerald's invention, had likewise been lost.

lication, in order to invalidate the claim to a patent in this country by an original inventor, who believed himself to be the first inventor. This provision is obviously founded upon the hypothesis that an invention might exist for ages in a foreign country, and yet the means of knowledge would not be within the reach of the public in this country, unless the foreign invention were patented, or described in a printed publication. The policy of the statute, thus deduced, the court seem to have considered would cover the case of a lost art, when reinvented, and also such a case as that of Fitzgerald, which they likened to the case of a lost art, and to the case of the reinvention of an unpatented or unpublished foreign invention. The particular instruction given to the jury by the court below, and in which the Supreme Court held there was no error, required the jury to find two facts: first, whether the Conner safe had been finally forgotten or abandoned, before Fitzgerald's invention; and, secondly, whether Fitzgerald was the original inventor of the safe for which he obtained a patent. The jury were directed, if they found these two facts affirmatively, to return a verdict for the plaintiff. This instruction and verdict were sanctioned by the Supreme Court, mainly upon the ground that the evidence authorized the inference that the Conner safe had been finally forgotten before Fitzgerald's invention, so that there was no existing and living knowledge of the improvement, or of its former use, at the time of Fitzgerald's discovery.[1]

[1] Gaylor *v.* Wilder, 10 Howard, 477. The opinion of a majority of the court (McLean and Daniel, Justices, dissenting) was delivered by Mr. Chief Justice Taney. The following is his view of the subject considered in the text: "It appears that James Conner, who carried on the business of a stereotype founder in the city of New York, made a safe for his own use, between the years 1829 and 1832, for the protection of his papers against fire, and continued to use it until 1838, when it passed into other hands. It was kept in his counting-room, and known to the persons engaged in the foundry; and after it passed out of his hands, he used others of a different construction.

"It does not appear what became of this safe afterwards. And there is nothing in the testimony from which it can be inferred that its mode of construction was known to the person into whose possession it fell, or that any value was attached to it as a place of security for papers against fire, or that it was ever used for that purpose.

"Upon these facts the court instructed the jury, 'that, if Conner had not made his discovery public, but had used it simply for his own private purpose, and it had been finally forgotten or abandoned, such a discovery and use would

§ 86 *a*. The principles of law determined in the case of Gaylor *v*. Wilder were applied in a similar case in the Circuit Court for

be no obstacle to the taking out of a patent by Fitzgerald or those claiming under him, if he be an original, though not the first, inventor or discoverer.'

"The instruction assumes that the jury might find from the evidence that Conner's safe was substantially the same with that of Fitzgerald, and also prior in time. And if the fact was so, the question then was, whether the patentee was 'the original and first inventor or discoverer,' within the meaning of the act of Congress.

"The act of 1836, ch. 357, § 6, authorizes a patent where the party has discovered or invented a new and useful improvement, 'not known or used by others before his discovery or invention.' And the 15th section provides, that if it appears, on the trial of an action brought for the infringement of a patent, that the patentee 'was not the original and first inventor or discoverer of the thing patented,' the verdict shall be for the defendant.

"Upon a literal construction of these particular words, the patentee in this case certainly was not the original and first inventor or discoverer, if the Conner safe was the same with his, and preceded his discovery.

"But we do not think that this construction would carry into effect the intention of the legislature. It is not by detached words and phrases that a statute ought to be expounded. The whole act must be taken together, and a fair interpretation given to it, neither extending nor restricting it beyond the legitimate import of its language, and its obvious policy and object. And in the 15th section, after making the provision above mentioned, there is a further provision, that, if it shall appear that the patentee at the time of his application for the patent believed himself to be the first inventor, the patent shall not be void on account of the invention or discovery having been known or used in any foreign country, it not appearing that it had been before patented or described in any printed publication.

"In the case thus provided for, the party who invents is not, strictly speaking, the first and original inventor. The law assumes that the improvement may have been known and used before his discovery. Yet his patent is valid if he discovered it by the efforts of his own genius, and believed himself to be the original inventor. The clause in question qualifies the words before used, and shows that by knowledge and use the legislature meant knowledge and use existing in a manner accessible to the public. If the foreign invention had been printed or patented, it was already given to the world and open to the people of this country as well as of others, upon reasonable inquiry. They would therefore derive no advantage from the invention here. It would confer no benefit upon the community, and the inventor therefore is not considered to be entitled to the reward. But if the foreign discovery is not patented nor described in any printed publication, it might be known and used in remote places for ages, and the people of this country be unable to profit by it. The means of obtaining knowledge would not be within their reach; and, as far as their interest is concerned, it would be the same thing as if the improvement had never been discovered. It is the inventor here that brings

the District of New York in 1869. The controversy had reference to a machine for stretching chains, which had been patented

it to them, and places it in their possession. And as he does this by the effort of his own genius, the law regards him as the first and original inventor, and protects his patent, although the improvement had in fact been invented before and used by others.

"So, too, as to the lost arts. It is well known that centuries ago discoveries were made in certain arts, the fruits of which have come down to us, but the means by which the work was accomplished are at this day unknown. The knowledge has been lost for ages. Yet it would hardly be doubted, if any one now discovered an art thus lost, and it was a useful improvement, that, upon a fair construction of the act of Congress, he would be entitled to a patent. Yet he would not literally be the first and original inventor. But he would be the first to confer on the public the benefit of the invention. He would discover what is unknown, and communicate knowledge which the public had not the means of obtaining without his invention.

"Upon the same principle and upon the same rule of construction, we think that Fitzgerald must be regarded as the first and original inventor of the safe in question. The case as to this point admits that, although Conner's safe had been kept and used for years, yet no test had been applied to it, and its capacity for resisting heat was not known; there was no evidence to show that any particular value was attached to it after it passed from his possession, or that it was ever afterwards used as a place of security for papers; and it appeared that he himself did not attempt to make another like the one he is supposed to have invented, but used a different one. And upon this state of the evidence the court put it to the jury to say whether this safe had been finally forgotten or abandoned before Fitzgerald's invention, and whether he was the original inventor of the safe for which he obtained the patent; directing them, if they found these two facts, that their verdict must be for the plaintiff. We think there is no error in this instruction. For if the Conner safe had passed away from the memory of Conner himself, and of those who had seen it, and the safe itself had disappeared, the knowledge of the improvement was as completely lost as if it had never been discovered. The public could derive no benefit from it until it was discovered by another inventor. And if Fitzgerald made his discovery by his own efforts, without any knowledge of Conner's, he invented an improvement that was then new, and at that time unknown; and it was not the less new and unknown because Conner's safe was recalled to his memory by the success of Fitzgerald's.

"We do not understand the Circuit Court to have said that the omission of Conner to try the value of his safe by proper tests would deprive it of its priority, nor his omission to bring it into public use. He might have omitted both, and also abandoned its use, and been ignorant of the extent of its value; yet if it was the same with Fitzgerald's, the latter would not upon such grounds be entitled to a patent, provided Conner's safe and its mode of construction were still in the memory of Conner before they were recalled by Fitzgerald's patent.

to the complainant in 1864. The defence relied upon was the prior use by the defendant's father of a machine similar to that used by the defendant. This machine had been kept under lock and key in a cellar concealed from persons in general, its existence being known only to the machinist who constructed it, to the father and the brother of the defendant, and to the defendant himself. The machine was seldom used before the death of the defendant's father in 1862, and was suffered to become rusty and neglected after that time. In 1864 the plaintiff's machine was described to the defendant by a workman who was at that time in his employ, and who had previously been in the employ of the plaintiff and had used his machine. Thereupon the rusty machine was taken from the cellar in July, 1865, and cleaned and fitted up in the defendant's shop, and used to stretch chains. Prior to this, the defendant, in making chains which required the links to be of equal length, stretched the links by means of the hammer and anvil, and not by any machine.

Upon this state of facts, the court, assuming that the old machine, in the condition in which it was while in the cellar, was substantially the same in construction with the machine as used by the defendant after July, 1865, and with the plaintiff's machine, held that it was an abandoned and lost invention, and its existence was no bar to the recovery of the plaintiff, especially as the plaintiff had no knowledge of its existence at the time of his invention. It appeared, moreover, that the machine as used by the defendant was not identical with that taken from the cellar.[1]

"The circumstances above mentioned, referred to in the opinion of the Circuit Court, appear to have been introduced as evidence tending to prove that the Conner safe might have been finally forgotten, and upon which this hypothetical instruction was given. Whether this evidence was sufficient for that purpose or not, was a question for the jury, and the court left it to them. And if the jury found the fact to be so, and that Fitzgerald again discovered it, we regard him as standing upon the same ground with the discoverer of a lost art, or an unpatented and unpublished foreign invention, and, like him, entitled to a patent. For there was no existing and living knowledge of this improvement, or of its former use, at the time he made the discovery. And whatever benefit any individual may derive from it in the safety of his papers, he owes entirely to the genius and exertions of Fitzgerald."

[1] Hall *v.* Bird, 6 Blatchf. 438; s. c. 3 Fisher's Pat. Cas. 595. After referring to the principles of law laid down by the court in the case of Gaylor *v.* Wilder, Judge Blatchford continued: "Now, although the old machine in the present case was constructed in 1852, and had been kept in the

§ 87. It may be suggested that the principles and analogies of the patent law would have furnished another mode of testing this question, which would have led to the same result, and which probably was what the learned judge who tried the cause in the court below intended to embrace in his instruction to the jury, but which does not appear to be distinctly developed in the decision of the Supreme Court. In every question of an alleged priority, there arises the necessary inquiry whether there was a completed invention or discovery by another before the invention or discovery by the patentee. If the thing patented has once been actually and completely invented or discovered before, however limited the use, the patent is invalidated, unless the former article was an unpatented or unpublished foreign invention, never introduced into this country. But what amounts to proof of a completed invention will depend on the nature of the subject-matter, and may also depend on the nature of the previous use. If the subject-matter is a mere structure, whose adaptation or capacity to effect what is proposed requires no test or practical use, then nothing is needed but to ascertain if the structure has been once previously made. The extent of use, or the mode in which the first inventor treated the article, or the fact that he had once forgotten that he had ever made it, are immaterial, provided he had completed the structure. But this is a case which rarely occurs.[1]

cellar of the defendant's father under the circumstances stated, and had been occasionally used there, and although it had not bodily disappeared from view, yet its existence and use were not made public, the knowledge and use of it did not exist in a manner accessible to the public, it had been substantially abandoned, and it had substantially passed away from the memory of those who had used it, as is shown by the fact that when they were called on to stretch the links of chains to a uniform length — a purpose to which it is not shown that the defendant's father ever applied the machine — it did not occur to them to use the machine for the purpose, until after they had learned of the existence and use of the plaintiff's machine. The knowledge of the machine was, therefore, as effectually lost as if it had never been constructed, and the public could derive no benefit from the invention, embodied in it, until such invention could be discovered by another inventor. As it clearly appears that the plaintiff made his invention by his own efforts without any knowledge of the machine in the cellar of the defendant's father, he invented an improvement which was then new, and was at the time unknown, because the old machine was recalled to the memory of the defendant, and of his brother, and of the machinist who put it up, by the success of the plaintiff's machine."

[1] A case was once tried before Mr. Justice Nelson, upon a patent for an

In the larger number of inventions, some amount of actual use is necessary, in order to determine whether the structure did effect in practice the supposed theory of its construction; and until this use has been had, until the capacity of the structure to effect what is proposed is ascertained, it cannot be said that there has been a completed invention.[1] What kind of use this must have been in order to test and ascertain the capacity of the structure, so that the inference of complete invention can be drawn, depends upon the character of the invention. Thus in the case of Conner's safe, the mere structure alone, and its use as a place of deposit for papers, for any number of years, without its having been subjected to the test of fire at all, would not make it a completed invention of such a safe as that patented by Fitzgerald, but would rather leave it all the while in the position of an experiment, or a theoretical structure, whose relation to the question at issue would depend upon the fact of its having been abandoned, or of its having been prosecuted to the required result. Hence it is, that in all inquiries of this kind, the principles which determine how far a former use rested only in experiment, or in preparation for experiment, and how far it is to be regarded as a use in which the proposed result or mode of operation was actually reached by a practical test, are of great significance. There is no real danger of having this inquiry lost in questions of

improved water-wheel, in which a witness testified that ten years before the plaintiff's patent he assisted in constructing a water-wheel embracing the principle of the plaintiff's invention, which was carried away by the person for whom it was made, and the witness never saw it afterwards. The judge instructed the jury, that, if they believed the witness, and the wheel was a perfect wheel and was taken away to be used, the evidence was sufficient to invalidate the patent, without proof that the prior wheel was ever actually used. Parker *v.* Ferguson, 1 Blatchf. 407. This instruction was appropriate to a case where perfect or complete invention could be inferred from the structure alone, without any use whatever. But this class of cases is entirely distinguishable from those where some test of actual use is necessary to ascertain whether the alleged prior invention was any thing more than an experimental effort to do what the patentee has afterwards done.

[1] In the trial of patent causes, on questions of priority of invention, it is very common to hear expert witnesses asked the question, whether the alleged prior machine or other thing *would have worked* as well as, or in the same mode as, that of the patentee. This evidence is not otherwise relevant to the true inquiry, than so far as it tends to the inference that the thing actually did work. This tendency is often very slight.

degree, if it is properly conducted; because the question of complete prior invention does not depend upon questions of degree, or perfection, but upon the inquiry whether the two things actually accomplished a result that may be regarded as substantially the same in kind.

§ 87 *a*. It is not sufficient that another may have previously conceived the idea that the thing patented could be done; he must have reduced his idea to practice, and have embodied it in some useful practical form. The representation of such ideas by means of drawings is not such embodiment into practical and useful form as will defeat a patent which has been granted.[1]

It is well settled that a prior experiment will not invalidate an invention subsequently completed by another. Such experiment must have been brought to a practical, completed form, capable of producing some useful result. He is the inventor, and is entitled to the patent, who has first completed the machine and made it capable of useful operation, although others may have previously had the idea, and made some experiments towards putting it into practical form.[2] Prior machines, in order to defeat a patent for subsequent machines, must have been working machines, and not mere experiments; they must either have actually done work, or have been capable of doing it.

Whether they were in use a greater or less time is immaterial, except so far as that fact may tend to show whether they were or were not mere experiments. The prior machine may have been inferior to the subsequent one, and may not have performed its work so well; but so long as it is substantially the same, and was a perfected invention, it anticipates the latter.[3]

Moreover, it is not necessary that a prior machine should have been actually used for the purpose contemplated; but if it is capable of such use, and its adaptation to such use be within the knowledge of a mechanic of competent skill, it will be a bar to

[1] Poppenhusen *v*. N. Y. Gutta-Percha Comb Co. (1868), 2 Fisher's Pat. Cas. 62; Ellithorpe *v*. Robinson (1859), ibid. 83; Union Sugar Refinery *v*. Matthiessen (1865), ibid. 600.

[2] Agawam Co. *v*. Jordan (1868), 7 Wall. 583; Seymour *v*. Osborne, 11 Wall. 516; Whitely *v*. Swayne, 7 Wall. 685.

[3] Woodman *v*. Stimpson (1866), 3 Fisher's Pat. Cas. 98; Swift *v*. Whisen (1867), ibid. 343; Rich *v*. Lippincott (1853), 2 Fisher's Pat. Cas. 1; Pitts *v*. Wemple (1853), ibid. 10; Waterman *v*. Thomson (1863), ibid. 461; Sayles *v*. Chicago & N. W. R.R. (1865), ibid. 523.

the validity of the subsequent invention.[1] The adoption of an invention in practical use is generally strong evidence that it is a completed invention, and not a mere experiment. But it may be a completed invention, put into practical form, ready for practical use, and reduced to practice, without having been put into use in the general acceptation of that word. The case of Coffin *v.* Ogden is authority for the doctrine that a piece of mechanism, which has been completed and is capable of working successfully, may defeat the claim of novelty in a subsequent alleged invention, though such piece of mechanism was not actually used before the date of the subsequent invention. In this case one Erbe, prior to the date of the plaintiff's invention, had made a lock, embodying the reversible latch, which had been patented by the plaintiff. It was a complete working reversible latch, requiring no alteration, adaptation, addition, or improvement, to fit it for use as a latch, and as a reversible latch. It was therefore a complete and perfected invention. It does not appear that Erbe had made more than one lock prior to the plaintiff's invention, or that such lock had been in any way used. But it had been exhibited by its inventor, and its construction and operation explained to three persons skilled in the mechanism of locks. This was construed by the court to be imparting to the public such knowledge of it as a completed invention, before the complainant's assignor had made his invention, as to deprive the latter of the right to be considered in law as the first inventor, notwithstanding he was an original and independent inventor of the improvement. The principles of law applicable to this statement of facts were thus stated by the court: —

"A putting of an invention into use is generally a strong evidence of a reduction of it to practice. But it may be a completed invention, put into practical form, ready for practical use, and reduced to practice, without being put into use in the general acceptation of that word. If the adaptation to use, or even the use itself, is merely experimental, the invention is not perfected. But use is not necessarily required in order to show perfection or completion. In respect to most inventions, use, not merely experimental, is one of the best proofs of the reduction of an invention to practice. But the particular invention in question is an illustration of the fact that a piece of mechanism may be shown to

[1] Pitts *v.* Wemple (1865), ibid. 10.

have been completed, and not to have rested in experiment, and to have been capable from its structure of working successfully, so as to deprive of the merit of novelty, in the patent law, a subsequent independent invention of the same thing, without its being shown that such piece of mechanism was actually used before the making of such subsequent invention.[1]

§ 88. A great deal of light may be thrown upon the particular question now under consideration, by an examination of some of the English cases; for while our statute is not precisely the same as the British Statute of Monopolies, in its description of the qualities and circumstances of a patentable invention, it is substantially the same in its provisions respecting prior use and knowledge, and the requisite of novelty.[2] But in examining the

[1] Coffin *v.* Ogden, Blatchford, J. (1869), 7 Blatchf. 61; s. c. 3 Fisher's Pat. Cas. 640; Reed *v.* Cutter, 1 Story, 590; Bedford *v.* Hunt, 1 Mason, 302; Whitely *v.* Swayne, 7 Wall. 685.

[2] The difference between the English statute and ours, in the particulars referred to in the text, is as follows: The clause in the English Statute of Monopolies, on which the patent system rests, embraces the two conditions: *first*, that the manufacture is *new* within the realm; *second*, that others did not use it at the making of the letters-patent. The object of the last condition was to prevent a patent being held for a thing which the patentee had — although it was new within the realm at the time he invented or introduced it — permitted to go into public use. Our statute has put these two conditions into distinct clauses; and therefore the clause "not known or used by others before the discovery or invention thereof," by the applicant for a patent, is to be taken as a repetition of the quality of novelty, and is to be construed in connection with the clauses which allow the special defence of want of priority of invention, and the previously stated condition that the subject-matter must be "new." For this reason the principles laid down in the English cases, by which the fact of priority has been ascertained, are equally applicable under our statute, where the alleged prior use or knowledge was in this country. The question which has sometimes been raised in the English cases, as to the prior use being a public use or not, is not founded upon the conditions of their statute, but upon the proviso in the letters-patent, which makes them void if the invention is not new "as to the public use and exercise thereof" in England, and which has been supposed to add to the conditions of the statute. As to this, it is well settled that the phrase "public use," introduced into the proviso, means use in public, or in a public manner, in opposition to a secret use, and that it does not mean use by the public generally. Carpenter *v.* Smith, 1 Webs. Pat. Cas. 530, 534; Hindmarch on Patents, 108–112; Stead *v.* Williams, 2 Webs. Pat. Cas. 126; Stead *v.* Anderson, 2 Webs. Pat. Cas. 147. But in this country there can be no such distinction, since our letters-patent do not contain this proviso, and the validity of

English cases on priority of invention or introduction, it is necessary to bear in mind that the judges, in giving instructions to juries, and in deciding cases *in banc*, have often brought into the discussion the inquiry whether the subject of the patent was in "public use" before or at the time of granting the patent, in opposition to any secret or entirely private use. This has arisen from two circumstances, which have had a tendency to blend two distinct issues into one. The first of these circumstances is that the English law allows a patent to the first introducer of a thing from abroad, as well as to the first inventor. Hence a question may arise, whether the public were already in possession of the thing, or were already using it, at the time of a patent being granted. The other cause for the consideration of this question of prior "public use" is to be found in the proviso of the letters-patent, which makes them void if the subject was not new as to the "public use and exercise thereof." But in all the cases, whether the issue to be found was directed expressly under the statute, on the question of novelty, or under the proviso of the patent, on the question of prior "public use," this point of a perfected invention, as distinguished from mere experimental trials or efforts, has been alike involved; and if we examine the facts of the several cases and the tests applied to them, taking care to remember that under our law, on the question of novelty, the publicity of the prior use is not otherwise important than as a circumstance tending to show that there was or was not a completed invention, we shall find the English cases of great value.

§ 89. Thus in the case of Jones *v.* Pearce, which bears some resemblance to the case of Gaylor *v.* Wilder, and which was an action on a patent for making wheels on a principle of suspension, evidence was offered, in the defence, to show that, many years before the plaintiff's invention, a Mr. Strutt had caused a pair of wheels to be made for his own use, and had used them on a cart until they had become broken and laid aside, and that they were constructed and worked on the principle of the plaintiff's invention. On this last point there was conflicting evidence. Mr. Justice Patterson instructed the jury as follows: "If, on the whole

the grant depends upon the same principles, as to the novelty of the invention, which have been applied to that question under the English statute, where the question has arisen directly upon the statute respecting the priority of invention.

of this evidence, either on the one side or the other, it appeared this wheel, constructed by Mr. Strutt's order in 1814, was a wheel on the same principles and in substance the same wheel as the other, for which the plaintiff has taken out his patent, and that it was used openly in public, so that everybody might see it, and had continued to use the same thing up to the time of taking out the patent, undoubtedly, then, that would be a ground to say that the plaintiff's invention is not new, and, if it is not new, of course his patent is bad, and he cannot recover in this action; but if, on the other hand, you are of opinion that Mr. Strutt's was an experiment, and that he found it did not answer, and ceased to use it altogether, and abandoned it as useless, and nobody else followed it up, and that the plaintiff's invention, which came afterwards, was his own invention, and remedied the defects, if I may so say, although he knew nothing of Mr. Strutt's wheel, he remedied the defects of Mr. Strutt's wheel, then there is no reason for saying the plaintiff's patent is not good: it depends entirely upon what is your opinion upon the evidence with respect to that, because, supposing you are of opinion that it is a new invention of the plaintiff's, the patent is good."[1]

§ 90. The trial in the case in which this instruction was given was on a plea of the general issue; and the question raised and put to the jury was, therefore, directly upon the novelty of the plaintiff's invention, that is to say, whether he was the first inventor, and not whether the thing was in public use at the time of the grant. From the form of the issue, therefore, as well as from the obvious meaning of the learned judge, the facts of the open public use of Mr. Strutt's wheel, or the continued use of it down to the time of the patent, or the abandonment of it, were put to the jury as circumstances from which they were to decide whether it was an incomplete and imperfect experiment, or a completed and successful invention; and not because these inquiries as to continued or discontinued use were of themselves important, provided the wheel had once been made and used as a successful and substantial application of the principle of the plaintiff's. This instruction appears to me to have been entirely correct, upon the facts of the case, both under the English law and under our own; for this is one of a class of cases which are entirely distinguishable

[1] Jones v. Pearce, 1 Webs. Pat. Cas. 122.

from the case of what is called a lost art, where evidence may be produced of the prior existence of a thing, but there is no living knowledge of the method or process by which it was made, and where there has been a fresh invention or discovery of some method or process of making it, and where the method or process of manufacture is the essential thing demanded by the public wants. This class of cases will be considered by itself.

§ 91. In the same way, where the issue to be tried was raised technically upon the proviso in the letters-patent, by a plea that the article patented was previously in "public use," Sir N. C. Tindal, C. J., instructed the jury that, in order to sustain this issue on the part of the defendant, the alleged former practice of the invention "must not be such a practice of it as is only referable to mere experiments for the purpose of making a discovery, or something secret, or confined to the party who was making it at the time, but that it must be, in order to set aside the patent, a case where it was in public use and operation among persons in that trade and likely to know it." The action was on a patent for a manufacture of elastic fabrics; and it was put to the jury to find whether the various specimens or proofs of such a manufacture brought forward by the defendants amounted to proof that *the patented manufacture* was in public use in England, or whether they fell short of that point and proved only that experiments had been made in various quarters, and had been afterwards abandoned.[1] Again, it is well settled in a case which went to the

[1] Cornish *v.* Keene, 1 Webs. Pat. Cas. 501, 508, 519. The following was the very lucid instruction given to the jury: "If this, No. 3, calling it technically and compendiously by that title, was, at the time these letters-patent were granted, in any degree of general use; if it was known at all to the world publicly, and practised openly, so that any other person might have the means of acquiring the knowledge of it as well as this person who obtained the patent, — then the letters-patent are void; on the other hand, if it were not known and used at the time in England, then, as far as this question is concerned, the letters-patent will stand. Now it will be a question for you, gentlemen, to say, whether, upon the evidence which you have heard, you are satisfied that the invention was or was not in use and operation, public use and operation, at the time the letters-patent were granted. It is obvious that there are certain limits to that question; the bringing it within that precise description which I have just given must depend upon the particular facts that are brought before a jury. A man may make experiments in his own closet for the purpose of improving any art or manufacture in public use; if he makes these experiments and never communicates them to the world, and lays them by as forgotten things,

House of Lords, and there received great consideration, that where the issue is, whether the patentee was the true and first inventor, and evidence of a prior use or exercise of the invention is offered in the defence, the abandonment or discontinuance by the supposed prior inventor is a material fact for the jury, in considering whether there was a prior perfect invention or not; but that if there was a prior perfect invention, the abandonment of its use or exercise before the date of the patent is wholly immaterial.[1] The

another person, who has made the same experiments, or has gone a little further, or is satisfied with the experiments, may take out a patent, and protect himself in the privilege of the sole making of the article for fourteen years; and it will be no answer to him to say that another person before him made the same experiments, and therefore that he was not the first discoverer of it; because there may be many discoverers starting at the same time, — many rivals that may be running on the same road at the same time, and the first which comes to the crown and takes out a patent (it not being generally known to the public), is the man who has a right to clothe himself with the authority of the patent, and enjoy its benefits. That would be an extreme case on one side; but if the evidence that is brought in any case, when properly considered, classes itself under the description of experiment only, and unsuccessful experiment, that would be no answer to the validity of the patent. On the other hand, the use of an article may be so general as to be almost universal. In a case like that, you can hardly suppose that any one would incur the expense and trouble of taking out a patent. That would be a case where all mankind would say, 'You have no right to step in and take that which is in almost universal use, for that is, in fact, to create a monopoly to yourself in this article, without either giving the benefit to the world of the new discovery, or the personal right to the value of the patent, to which you would be entitled from your ingenuity and from your application.' Therefore, it must be between those two (if I may so call it) limits that cases will range themselves in evidence; and it must be for a jury to say, whether, supposing those points to be out of the question, in any particular case, evidence which has been brought before them convinces them to their understandings that the subject of the patent was in public use and operation at that time, — at the time when the patent itself was granted by the crown. If it was in public use and operation, then the patent is a void patent, and amounts to a monopoly; if it was not, the patent stands good. Now, gentlemen, you will have to apply your understanding to-day to the evidence in this case, which is in many parts contradictory, in order to see whether you bring the case within the one or the other of these two descriptions, and whether this patent is or is not a new invention." See also the cases of Walton *v.* Potter and Walton *v.* Bateman, 1 Webs. Pat. Cas. 585, 613.

[1] Househill Company *v.* Neilson, 1 Webs. Pat. Cas. 673–718. See also the case of Heath *v.* Smith, 25 Law & Eq. R. 165, 168, and the case of Stead *v.* Williams, 2 Webs. Pat. Cas. 126, 135, in which Mr. Justice Creswell, on the

law has been held in the same way in this country for a long period.[1]

§ 92. We may now recur to the case of Gaylor *v.* Wilder, and to the inquiry whether there is a distinction between cases situated

issue of prior public knowledge, pointed out to the jury the distinction between knowledge of an experiment and knowledge of a thing that would answer, in the following terms : "Now as to its being publicly known in this country, I take it that there is a great difference between the knowledge of it as a thing that would answer and was in use, and the knowledge of it as a mere experiment that had been found to be a failure and thrown aside. If you are dealing with an article of merchandise, or with an article of ordinary use,—if a person has had a scheme in his head and has carried it out, but after a trial has thrown it aside, and the thing is forgotten and gone by,—then another person reintroducing it may, within the meaning of this act, be the inventor and the first user of it, so as to justify a patent. There is one instance where a patent was taken out for wheels on the suspension principle, bearing a proportion of the weight from the upper rim of the wheel, as well as supported on the spokes below by perpendicular pressure. It was proved in that case that Mr. Strutt of Derby had used a cart with wheels upon that principle some time before. After using it a year or two, he threw it aside. It was totally forgotten ; and some sixteen years afterwards a man brought the thing to perfection, and took out a patent ; and it was held that that former use by Mr. Strutt, having been abandoned as a useless thing, was no impediment in the way of a patent. So, also, in the case alluded to of Cornish *v.* Keene. An attempt had been made to introduce new elastic matters, combined for the purpose of making braces and bandages, and various articles of that sort. I remember well, in that case, the Chief Justice left it to the jury to say whether these were experiments. Some pieces were actually produced which had been manufactured, and some of those things which had been manufactured had been sold. It was left to the jury to say whether that was an introduction of it so manifest, or whether it was a mere failing experiment, which had been abandoned, so as to leave the way open to any new speculator in it, who yet might bring the patent to perfection. In that case, also, the patent was supported. In this case the defendants, in order to negative the first use, have given some evidence of similar pavements in Surrey, Somersetshire, and somewhere else. The ends of fir or oak, or other things of that sort, just in their natural condition, round, driven down to make a firm flooring either in small houses, fronts of doors, or something of that sort. Undoubtedly a very different thing from this, and no further affecting this question than as showing that wood had in some instances been used as a pavement ; but as a pavement for a carriage-way, none of these

[1] Woodcock *v.* Parker, 1 Gallis. 438; Bedford *v.* Hunt, 1 Mason, 302; Reed *v.* Cutter, 1 Story, 590; O'Reilly *v.* Morse, 15 How. 62.

as that was, and cases of what may be called the reinvention of a lost art. The case of Gaylor *v.* Wilder (and also that of Jones *v.* Pearce) was one where the novelty or priority of invention was sought to be impeached by evidence of the former existence of a single specimen of an article made, as was alleged, in the same way and operating upon the same principle as the invention of the patentee. So far as the mere construction was concerned, the article itself, or the recollection of those who had seen it, disclosed the process or mode of making it. But after this was ascertained, the inquiry still remained, whether it operated upon the same principle as the patentee's invention; and to the trial of this question the success with which it operated, as proved by the continuance or abandonment of its use, or, in other words, the fact of its being a completed invention, or an experiment towards the making of an invention, was a most material issue.

§ 93. But when we pass from cases of this description to cases of what have been called the reinvention or rediscovery of a lost art, we shall find a very important distinction, that requires to be

things appear to have been used. But then comes the question of Sir William Worsley's. Now the principle of that may or may not involve entirely the principle of this, according to your judgment. It appears to have been laid down to support the traffic of carriages, in a small place undoubtedly; a portico which was covered in, — the porch to the dwelling-house of Sir William Worsley in Yorkshire. Undoubtedly it has been put there to sustain the traffic of carriages; that there is no doubt of. They are cut into hexagon blocks of equal sizes. There you have the principle of the angular parts corresponding, so that the flat surfaces would come together, and so sustain each other from any lateral motion. They are not driven horizontally against each other, but driven in from the surface, and there are no dowels; but dowels are not claimed as any part of the present invention. Then if you think (though that is a little more bevelled off), — if you think that is essentially the same thing as the hexagon block introduced by the plaintiff for the purpose of making roads, then I should say, in point of law, that makes an end of the patent, because that appears to have been introduced by Sir William Worsley, or to have been used by him in public, not concealed, no secrecy about it, made known to all persons who came to his house, so far as their ocular inspection could make them. It was intended to be public, not to be made a matter of merchandise certainly, but merely for his own private use; but the knowledge of it exposed to the public an article in public use, and continued to be used down to the time in question. Therefore, if you think that is the same thing in substance as that which the plaintiff claims, I think that it was publicly used before, and that he cannot have his patent. Whether it had been used by one or used by five, I do not think it makes any difference."

carefully considered, in applying the test which is to determine the presence or absence of the patentable quality of novelty, or the meaning of the expression "first inventor." There are *dicta*, both of the English and the American judges, to the effect that a patent may be supported for a new discovery or invention of what was once in existence and use, but has been long lost sight of or unknown. But in what sense or under what circumstances the statute may be so construed as to make one the "first inventor" of a thing that has existed before; or, in other words, to make one the inventor of something "not known or used by others before his discovery or invention thereof," when there is evidence of the prior existence of something of the same character, is a topic that has not been made the subject of direct adjudication. The most important of the *dicta*, in reference to lost arts, are what fell from Lords Lyndhurst and Brougham, in the case of The Househill Company *v.* Neilson, and from Mr. Chief Justice Taney, in Gaylor *v.* Wilder.[1] The latter stated the case of a lost art, by way of illustration of the latitude of interpretation which the term "first inventor" might receive, as follows: "So, too, as to the lost arts. It is well known that centuries ago discoveries were made in certain arts, the fruits of which have come down to us, but the means by which the work was accomplished are at this day unknown. The knowledge has been lost for ages. Yet it would hardly be doubted, if any one now discovered an art thus lost, and it was a useful improvement, that, upon a fair construction of the act of Congress, he would be entitled to a patent. Yet he would not literally be the first and original inventor. But he would be the first to confer on the public the benefit of the invention. He would discover what is unknown, and communicate

[1] In delivering the judgment of the House of Lords, in Neilson's case, Lord Lyndhurst observed: "It must not be understood that your lordships, in the judgment you are about to pronounce, have given any decision upon this state of facts, namely, if an invention had been formerly used and abandoned many years ago, and the whole thing had been lost sight of. That is a state of facts not now before us. Therefore, it must not be understood that we have pronounced any opinion whatever upon that state of things. It is possible that an invention may have existed fifty years ago, and may have been entirely lost sight of, and not known to the public. What the effect of this state of things might be, is not necessary for us to pronounce upon." To which Lord Brougham responded: "It becomes like a new discovery." 1 Webs. Pat. Cas. 717.

knowledge which the public had not the means of obtaining without his invention." [1]

§ 94. In the sense in which the learned Chief Justice probably intended to make use of this illustration, the true distinction seems to be recognized. For there may obviously be two classes of cases coming under the general head of a lost or abandoned or forgotten art: one, where an article of manufacture still in existence, or capable of being proved to have once existed, discloses of itself, without other proof of its origin or of its mode of manufacture, the process or method of its construction; the other, where the process or method of manufacture cannot be proved by the article itself or any description of it, and can only be known by the aid of evidence which would show the process or mode of manufacture formerly made use of. In one of these cases, to possess the thing or evidence of its existence, is to possess knowledge of the mode of its construction. In the other, the thing itself may remain, and yet all knowledge of the means of making it may have been lost for centuries.[2] It is of the last class of cases that Mr. Chief Jus-

[1] 10 How. 477.

[2] Mr. Webster, in a note to Neilson's case, thus states the same distinction: "The third class of evidence is the production of a machine or article of manufacture with or without proof of actual user anterior to the date of the patent. On the authority of the above case, it would appear that the production of such a machine or article of manufacture, without actual proof as to its use, or any evidence as to whence it originally came, or as to its mode of manufacture, would vitiate subsequent letters-patent for such a machine or article of manufacture, as negativing the grantee of such letters-patent being the true and first inventor. With reference to this head, two distinct cases may occur, — the one in which the machine or article of manufacture so produced shows at once its mode of manufacture, the other in which the machine or article of manufacture does not present any means of knowledge to the public, so as to enable any person to reproduce the same. There may be many various modes of attaining a result, and an article of manufacture may be the subject of various patents. The term 'new manufacture' may be satisfied either by a thing that is made then for the first time, or that is made in a new way then for the first time. An arrangement of material parts, as a simple combination of the elements of machinery, discloses its mode of manufacture to the eye on inspection, but with respect to a paint, or a dye, or a medicine, and many other inventions, a mere inspection of the result attained will convey no information as to the mode of manufacture. The distinction just adverted to relates to the doctrine 'that knowledge and the means of knowledge are the same'; but independently of this, this last class of cases, depending upon user, differs altogether from the two first-mentioned classes of cases, depending upon publication in such a form as to preserve and communicate the knowledge to the public." 1 Webs. 718 *seq.*

tice Taney is to be understood as speaking. He supposes the case of an art, "the *fruits* of which have come down to us, but the *means* by which the work was accomplished are at this day unknown," and that some one has discovered a process, or means, by which those fruits can be again produced.

§ 95. Now it is of great consequence to know what relation to the issue of priority is borne, in the one or the other of these two cases, by the fact of the existence or absence of what may be called living knowledge, at the time of the supposed reinvention or rediscovery. In the class of cases first supposed, the production of a previously existing machine, or other article of manufacture, or the production of evidence that it once existed, proves of itself the construction, or mode of manufacture; and therefore it cannot be said that the knowledge of it has ever been lost, since the very case supposes that the means of proving it exist, either in the thing itself or in the recollection of witnesses. It is a case where knowledge and the means of knowledge are the same. When, therefore, the means of knowledge are sought in the recollection of witnesses who speak to the former existence of a thing, which of itself proves its own construction, or use, it must be wholly immaterial, as an ultimate test, whether those witnesses have had the thing recalled to their recollection by the subsequent reinvention of that thing. It may not be immaterial to the accuracy or value of their recollections to inquire whether they had once forgotten the former article, and had been reminded of it by the subsequent newly invented specimen; because they may have unconsciously borrowed from the latter the means of describing the former. But assuming the accuracy of their recollections and their title to belief, it can be of no moment to the issue, to inquire whether they had forgotten the knowledge which they once had, unless the statute is to be so construed as to make "existing and living knowledge" the test of priority. Such appears to have been the construction given to it by Mr. Chief Justice Taney, in Gaylor *v.* Wilder; for the bearing which he assigns to the facts that Conner had forgotten his own safe, and that its construction and use were recalled to his memory by the subsequent invention of Fitzgerald, shows that he and the judges who concurred with him intended to put the case upon the want of such knowledge, at the time of Fitzgerald's invention, as would have enabled the public to construct the safe in question, without resorting to Fitzgerald. But there does not seem to be any satisfactory reason for construing the phrase "not known or used by others before his [the patentee's] invention or discovery," in cases of this class, so as to confine the knowledge or use to what is in the *present* memory of witnesses, in contradistinction to what may be said to be in their *potential* memory. If a witness, however his memory may be aided or stimulated, can recollect or describe a thing, its former existence is proved, and it was "known or used by others" before the invention of it by the patentee. What, then, is the true relation to the issue, of the fact that the former maker of a thing may have forgotten that he made it, and may have had it recalled to his recollection by a subsequent invention? I conceive that this fact has a twofold relation to the issue, in cases of the first class, namely, where the question is simply whether a particular structure alone existed before, or even in cases where the question is whether a particular structure, operating in a certain way, existed before.

§ 96. In the first place, as the priority, in such cases, depends upon the recollection of a witness, it is very important to be able to test the accuracy of his recollection; and therefore the fact that he had forgotten a thing which he had once made, may be important in ascertaining whether he has borrowed any thing from the subsequent invention which recalls the recollection of his own. In the second place, the fact that a thing has been forgotten, has a most material bearing upon the question of complete or incomplete invention. But, beyond this, it seems to be unimportant, provided the thing was once completely invented and can be described.

§ 97. In the other class of cases, namely, an art (to use the description of Mr. Chief Justice Taney) "the *fruits* of which have come down to us, but the *means* by which the work was accomplished are at this day unknown," it is obvious that the discovery or invention relates to those means, or, in other words, to the process or method by which a thing was produced. If, then, the art is once lost, it cannot be said with certainty, in most cases, that the newly discovered or newly invented method was the same as the old, since there is no knowledge what the old method in fact was. The fact, therefore, that all knowledge of the former method has been lost, occupies a very different place in this class of cases to what it occupies in the other class. I conclude, therefore, that in construing the clause "not known or used by others," it is necessary to look closely at the subject-matter of the patent, and to try the issue of prior use or knowledge accordingly.[1]

[1] Upon the whole, therefore, I reaffirm what was said in my former edition upon this subject of lost arts, in reference to the issue of *prior use or knowledge*, as follows: —

"This distinction, if sound, presents two important inquiries: first, whether there is any class of cases where the mere previous existence of a thing, the art of making which has been lost, negatives the fact that a subsequent discoverer of an art of making the same or a similar thing is the 'first inventor,' as those words are used in the statute; secondly, whether the use or knowledge intended by the statute, in cases of this kind, means the use or knowledge of the art of making the thing, or whether it means merely the use of the thing itself, or the knowledge that it exists, without the means of practising the invention itself. Both of these questions may arise, for instance, in reference to an article which has been patented in England, to wit, an encaustic tile, a description of which was well known in the Middle Ages, but the art of manufacturing which has been lost; or in reference to such arts as that of staining glass.

"With regard to the first question, — if the words 'first inventor' are to be taken in their literal import, and without reference to the character of the subject-matter, whether it furnishes or does not furnish, on mere inspection or analysis, a knowledge of the means by which it is produced, — then it is only necessary, in any case, to show that the thing itself has existed before, in order to negative the claim that the subsequent patentee is the 'first inventor.' This might be all that would be necessary in cases of machinery, because the machine is a collection of material parts in a certain combination, the existence of which, at any previous time, shows that it cannot have been again invented for the first time. But with regard to the arts and the products of the arts, it may be very different. The same thing may have been produced at one time by one process, now wholly lost sight of, and at another time by another process, or by the independent discovery of the same process. It can never be known with certainty whether the subsequent process of manufacture is the same with the first, which may always have been a secret, and is, at any rate, now unknown. The product alone is the same or similar; and if the mere existence of the same thing, without the knowledge of the mode by which it was produced, excludes a subsequent independent discoverer of a process of making that thing from being regarded as the 'first inventor,' a large class of what are really original inventions — and inventions 'first,' as regards the state of knowledge — are excluded from the benefits of the patent law. The difference between inventions or discoveries of this kind and cases of machinery is, that, in a machine, the invention consists in the putting together, in a certain combination, material parts, intended to operate upon each other according to certain laws of motion, to produce a given effect; and this, when once done, is done forever, and can only be done upon one principle and plan, that remain always the same as long as the same machine is

§ 98. Such appear to be the principles of law applicable to the question of novelty, in respect to the *time* of a supposed prior use

reproduced; but, in the case of a manufacture or product of an art, the invention consists in the process by which the thing itself is produced, which may be invented in one way at one time, and in another way at a subsequent time, so that the subsequent inventor may be, literally as well as metaphysically, the 'first inventor' of *his* process of making the thing.

"With regard to the second question which arises under our statute, upon the clauses which provide against the prior use and knowledge of the thing, it may be considered that those provisions are cumulative upon the previous requisition that the patentee shall be the first inventor. The statute requires that the patentee shall make oath that he verily believes himself to be the original and first inventor, and that he does not know or believe that the thing, art, machine, composition, or improvement was ever before known or used; and it provides that the negative of these propositions may be proved in defence against the patent. In the case supposed, — that of an art long lost, but of which specimens of the manufacture can be proved to be or to have been in existence, — the patent of a subsequent discoverer of a method of making the same or a similar thing, would be *primâ facie* evidence that he is the first discoverer of his particular process of making the thing. The negative is then to be shown in defence; and whether this can be shown by merely producing the thing, without showing the process by which it was formerly made, depends upon the force to be given to the words 'use and knowledge.' If those words mean merely that the prior use of the thing itself, or the prior knowledge of its existence, is, in all cases, an answer to the allegation of the patentee that he is the first inventor or discoverer, without showing that his process is the same as that by which the thing was formerly produced, then, there is no occasion to inquire further. But if, on the contrary, those words are to be taken with reference to the character of the subject-matter, in each case, then it is apparent that there may be cases where, as in such arts as those above referred to, the invention or discovery is not, strictly speaking, the thing itself, but a process of making that thing. The words of the statute must be taken with separate application to each of the subjects recited as the proper subject-matters of a patent. The language is, that 'he is the original and first inventor of the art, machine, composition, &c., and that he does not know or believe that the same was ever before known or used'; and in the subsequent clause the 'thing patented' is declared to be subject to the defence, that the patentee was not 'the original and first inventor or discoverer,' or that 'it' had been described in some public work, or had been in public use. The 'thing patented' is the antecedent of 'it,' and in the case of an art this may be, not the product itself, but the process of producing it; and where it cannot be shown that the process invented by the patentee has been 'known' or 'used' before the mere production in evidence of a similar manufacture, produced at a former period by an unknown art, does not negative the allegation, that the patentee invented or discovered the art by which he has produced that manufacture." Curtis on Patents, 2d edition, 1854, §§ 36–39.

or knowledge; and the next topic for consideration is, whether the novelty required by our statute is relative or absolute, as to the *place* of a prior use or knowledge. Had the phrase "not known or used by others before his or their discovery or invention," as used in the 6th section of the act, been left without qualification by any subsequent clause or clauses, the novelty required for an invention must have been absolute as to all countries. But by the 7th section of the same act, the commissioner is authorized to grant a patent, if it does not appear that the subject applied for "had been invented or discovered by any other person in *this* country prior to the alleged invention or discovery thereof by the applicant, or that it had been patented or described in any printed publication, *in this or any foreign country*." And in the 15th section of the same act, one of the defences that may be made, under the general issue and a special notice, is, that the invention had been "described in some public work, anterior to the supposed discovery thereof, by the patentee"; and this is followed by the proviso, "that whenever it shall satisfactorily appear that the patentee, at the time of making his application for the patent, believed himself to be the first inventor or discoverer of the thing patented, the same shall not be void on account of the invention or discovery, or any part thereof, having been before known or used in any foreign country; it not appearing that the same or any substantial part thereof had before been patented, or described in any printed publication."

§ 99. These provisions are not very skilfully framed, but when collated, they leave the rights of an original inventor in the following position: that an inventor who does not consciously borrow from a foreign discovery, that is, who believes himself to be the first inventor or discoverer of the thing patented, can only be deprived of the benefit of his patent, by showing that the thing had been before patented, or described in some printed publication. It will not be enough to show that the thing had been known or used in a foreign country, if it had not been patented, or described in a printed publication. Thus, while the statute still continues, the presumption that the patentee has seen the prior description contained in a printed publication, and makes that presumption conclusive,[1] it relieves an original inventor from

[1] Upon the former law the Supreme Court of the United States said: "It may be that the patentee had no knowledge of this previous use or previous

the same presumption, arising out of the mere previous knowledge or use of the thing in a foreign country where it had not been patented or described; and if he can take the oath that he discovered or invented the thing, he will not be debarred of his patent, by a prior invention or discovery and use of the thing in a foreign country. The meaning and operation of the terms "patented" and "described in some printed publication" will be considered hereafter in connection with the subject of Defences.

§ 99 *a*. But when a prior foreign patent, or a printed publication of a prior foreign invention, is relied upon to defeat a patent, the description and drawings therein must "contain and exhibit a substantial representation of the patented improvement in such full, clear, and exact terms as to enable any person skilled in the art or science to which it appertains, to make, construct, and practise the invention to the same practical extent as he would be enabled to do if the invention was derived from a prior patent in this country. Mere vague and general representations will not support such a defence, as the knowledge supposed to be derived from the publication must be sufficient to enable those skilled in the art or science to understand the nature and operation of the invention, and to carry it into practical use."[1] It must be an account of a complete and operative invention capable of being put into practical operation.

§ 100. We now come to consider the next clause in the 13th section of the act of 1836, which imposes a further condition upon the grant of a valid patent. We have seen that the subject-matter must be new, and that there is superadded the condition that it was not known or used by others before the applicant's discovery or invention of it; to which the statute adds, "*and not at the time of his application for a patent*, in public use or on sale, with his consent or allowance, as the inventor or discoverer."[2] The obvious meaning and effect of this clause establish a distinction between an abandonment or dedication of an invention to the public before a patent has been obtained, and an abandonment of the patent right after it has been obtained.

description; still his patent is void; the law supposes he may have known it." Evans *v.* Eaton, 3 Wheat. 454.

[1] Seymour *v.* Osborne (1870), 11 Wal. 516; Hill *v.* Evans, 6 Law Times, N. S. 90; Betts *v.* Menzies, 4 Best & Smith, Q. B. 999.

[2] Act of 1836, § 6.

§ 101. The terms of this clause recognize the principle that, although the applicant or patentee may be an original and the first inventor, yet that he may have so conducted, before applying for a patent, as to have lost the right to obtain one. That an inventor could lose his right to a patent by an abandonment or dedication of his invention to the public, was held by the Supreme Court of the United States, under the Patent Act of February 21, 1793, which made it necessary to a valid patent that the invention should be one "not known or used before the application." It was considered by the court that these words could not mean that the thing invented was not known or used before the application by the inventor himself, since he must possess the knowledge and practise the use of his invention, in order to test its value. The words, to have any rational interpretation, must mean, not known or used by *others*, before the application. But it was further considered by the court in this case, that the clause "not known or used before the application," after receiving by construction the insertion of the words "by others," were to be considered as intended for a requirement that the applicant for a patent should be the first inventor, and not as a substantive enactment of the doctrine of abandonment or dedication by the first inventor, and before he had applied for a patent. Still, it was held, that, without any enactment or statute declaration to this effect, if the first inventor should put his invention into public use or sell it for public use before applying for a patent, he would create another bar to his claim for a patent, distinct from the question of priority of invention ; because his voluntary acquiescence in the public use of his invention would create a disability to comply with the conditions on which alone the proper department of the government was authorized to grant the patent.[1]

§ 102. This construction of the statute of 1793 was not, it must be perceived, entirely consistent; for it did not distinctly rest the doctrine of voluntary abandonment upon general principles, aside from the statute provision, but sought to bring the case of such a dedication within the terms of a clause which were admitted to have been designed to establish the requirement of first invention. This ambiguity led to the incorporation into the act of 1836 of the further condition, that the discovery or invention was "not,

[1] Pennock *v.* Dialogue, 2 Peters, 1–24.

at the time of his application for a patent, in public use or on sale, with his consent or allowance as the inventor or discoverer." The intent of this provision was to cause a public use or sale of the invention in any one instance, if consented to or allowed by the inventor, before his application for a patent, to be a bar to his obtaining a valid patent, and also to recognize such a bar where there had been a general abandonment or dedication to the public.[1] Under this statute, therefore, an invention might be allowed to be in public use by the inventor in two modes. He might allow of its use in public by an individual or individuals, or he might allow the whole public to use it, by having abandoned or dedicated his invention to the public before his application. In either case his patent would be void. But by the act of 1839, § 7, this inconvenience was so far remedied as to confine the forfeiture of the right, in cases of individual use with the permission of the inventor, to such use prior to the two years preceding the application for the patent. This new provision was as follows: "That every person or corporation who has, or shall have, purchased or constructed any newly invented machine, manufacture, or composition of matter, prior to the application by the inventor or discoverer for a patent, shall be held to possess the right to use, and vend to others to be used, the specific machine, manufacture, or composition of matter so made or purchased, without liability therefor to the inventor or any other person interested in such invention; and no patent shall be held to be invalid by reason of such purchase, sale, or use, prior to the application for a patent aforesaid, except on proof of abandonment of such invention to the public; or that such purchase, sale, or prior use has been for more than two years prior to such application for a patent."[2]

§ 103. This enactment relieved the patentee from the effect of the former laws, and the construction that had been put upon them by the courts, and put the person who, by the consent and allowance of the inventor, had had a prior use of the invention, on the same footing as if he had a special license from the inventor to use his invention; and at the same time the patent is valid

[1] McClurg *v.* Kingsland, 1 Howard, 202; Ryan *v.* Goodwin, 3 Sumner, 514.

[2] The words, "any newly invented machine, manufacture, or composition of matter," in this statute, have the same meaning as "invention," or "thing patented." McClurg *v.* Kingsland, *ut supra.*

after it is issued, against all persons except such licensee, who will continue to have the right to use the invention.[1] Inventors may now, therefore, permit the use of their inventions, by individuals, for a period of two years, prior to the application for a patent, and still obtain a valid patent notwithstanding such use. But if the use thus allowed extends over a period of more than two years prior to the application, or if it amounts to an abandonment of the invention to the public, whether for a longer or a shorter period, the patent will be invalid.

§ 104. But to entitle a person to claim the benefit of this statute as a licensee by operation of law, he must be a person who is a purchaser or who has used the patented invention before the patent was issued, by a license or grant or by the consent of the inventor, and not be a purchaser under a mere wrong-doer. What will amount to such a license, grant, or consent, is well shown in a case where a person employed in the manufactory of another, while receiving wages, made experiments at the expense and in the manufactory of his employer, had his wages increased in consequence of the useful result of the experiment, made the article invented, and permitted his employer to use it, no compensation for its use being paid or demanded, and then obtained a patent; it was held, that such an unmolested and notorious use of the invention prior to the application for a patent brought the case within the provisions of the statute.

§ 105. The remaining quality essential to a patentable invention is, that it shall be "useful." Care must be taken, however, to discriminate between what may be called the positive utility of an invention, which is made by the statute a mere description of the class of inventions which can be the subjects of valid patents, and that comparative or relative utility which is sometimes applied as one of the tests of novelty, or of substantial difference of structure or mode of operation. We have already seen in what manner this test of comparative utility may be applied to distinguish one invention from another. But this is not the usefulness which the statute contemplates when it describes the subject for which a patent may be granted as a "new and *useful* invention." Nor must this utility be confounded with the inquiry whether some part of a thing claimed or described in a specifica-

[1] McClurg *v.* Kingsland, *ut supra.*

tion as essential to produce the effect intended is or is not useless to that end. This is an inquiry into the question of whether the patent is void for a false suggestion, or as calculated to mislead the public.

§ 106. But when it is said that an invention, to be the subject of a patent, must be "useful," the term must be construed with reference to the known policy of the law in granting patents for inventions. It cannot be supposed that inventions injurious to the welfare of society are within that policy. But what is not injurious or mischievous to society may be capable of some beneficial use; and when this is the case, that is to say, when the invention is not absolutely frivolous or insignificant, the law takes no notice of the degree of its utility, whether it be larger or smaller as compared with other things of the same class. "By useful invention, in the statute, is meant such a one as may be applied to some use beneficial to society in contradistinction to an invention which is injurious to the morals, the health, or the good order of society. It is not necessary to establish that the invention is of such general utility as to supersede all other inventions now in practice to accomplish the same purpose. It is sufficient that it has no noxious or mischievous tendency, that it may be applied to practical uses, and that so far as it is applied it is salutary. If its practical utility be very limited, it will follow that it will be of little or no profit to the inventor; and if it be trifling, it will sink into utter neglect. The law, however, does not look to the degree of utility: it simply requires that it shall be capable of use, and that the use is such as sound morals and policy do not discountenance or prohibit."[1]

[1] Per Story, J., in Bedford *v.* Hunt, 1 Mason, 301, 303. See also Lowell *v.* Lewis, ibid. 186; Kneass *v.* The Bank, 4 Wash. 9; Many *v.* Jagger, 1 Blatchf. 372; McCormick *v.* Seymour, 2 Blatchf. 240; Wilbur *v.* Beecher, 2 Blatchf. 132; Foote *v.* Silsby, 2 Blatchf. 260; Seymour *v.* Osborne, 11 Wall. 516; Hoffheims *v.* Brandt, 3 Fisher's Pat. Cas. 218.

CHAPTER III.

OF THE SUBJECT-MATTER OF LETTERS-PATENT, IN RESPECT TO UNITY OR DIVERSITY OF INVENTION, AND OF THE RELATION OF THE PATENTEE THERETO.

§ 107. WE have seen that the subject-matter of valid letters-patent must possess certain qualities, and must stand in a certain position relatively to the state of the art to which the invention belongs; and we have also seen what are the limits within which the antecedent state of the art is to be confined in the comparison to be instituted between the supposed new invention and what has gone before it. These requisites having been ascertained, there next arises the important inquiry, how far the unity of an invention is consistent with a diversity of objects in the same patent. The terms of the patent acts do not admit of distinct inventions as the subject of a single patent, but, on the contrary, they imply that the subject-matter must be one invention or discovery. How far is it consistent with this unity, that the same patent should be made to cover a new machine or other invention, consisting of several parts working to a common end, and the several new parts, each as working for its separate purpose?

§ 108. In some of the earlier cases on this subject, language was used by the courts tending to create doubts as to the legality of claiming, in the same patent, improvements on different mechanisms, so as to give a right to the exclusive use of the several mechanisms separately, as well as a right to the exclusive use of those mechanisms conjointly. Thus, in reference to the patent granted, under a special act of Congress, to Oliver Evans, for his improvement in the machinery for manufacturing flour, the Supreme Court intimated a doubt whether such a patent as the special act authorized could have been taken out under the general patent law. Evans's invention comprehended five machines, each of which was designed for, and capable of, a distinct operation for a special purpose of its own, in the process of manufacturing flour, but the whole of which, when combined and operating together, constituted a complete flouring-mill, in which every operation necessary to the converting of the grain into bolted flour could be carried on without the intervention of manual labor, and by the motive-power of the mill. In his specification, Evans claimed the machines both separately and conjointly, giving notice that "they may all be united and combined in one flour-mill to produce my improvement on the art of manufacturing flour complete, or they may each be used separately for any of the purposes specified and allotted to them, or to produce my improvement in part, according to the circumstances of the case." Upon this claim, the Supreme Court said that, under the general patent law alone, it was doubtful whether such a patent would not be irregular; but the special act for the relief of Evans was held to have expressly authorized it.[1]

§ 109. In the subsequent case of Barrett *v.* Hall, Mr. Justice Story made use of the following language: "A patent under the general Patent Act cannot embrace various distinct improvements or inventions; but in such case the party must take out separate patents. If the patentee has invented certain improved machines, which are capable of a distinct operation, and has also invented a combination of those machines to produce a connected result, the same patent cannot at once be for the combination and for each of the improved machines; for the inventions are as distinct as if the subjects were entirely different. A very significant doubt has been expressed on this subject by the Supreme Court, and I am persuaded that the doubt can never be successfully removed."[2]

§ 110. In a subsequent case, however, the same learned judge developed to some extent the distinctions which appear now to be generally recognized between the three cases of, first, a machine new as a machine and an entirety; second, several distinct improvements in an existing machine; and, third, a new combination consisting of elements wholly or partially old.[3] That these three classes of cases are distinguishable from each other, as subjects of letters-patent, there can be no reasonable doubt. An instance of the first class is presented by the sewing-machine invented by Howe, which as an automatic machine for uniting two pieces of

[1] Evans *v.* Eaton, 3 Wheaton, 454, 506.
[2] Barrett *v.* Hall, 1 Mason, 447, 475.
[3] Moody *v.* Fisk, 2 Mason, 112, 117.

cloth by a stitch of thread, in contradistinction to working ornaments of thread on the surface of cloth, is said to have had no predecessor. In such cases where the machine as a whole is claimed to be a new invention, giving rise to an entirely new art, — the art of sewing by automatic machinery, — the subject-matter which it is necessary to secure is the machine itself. This of course can require but one patent; and whether that patent will cover not only the machine as an entirety, but the new sub-combinations embraced in it, will depend upon the manner in which the subject is described and claimed, and upon the character of those sub-combinations. An instance of the second class appears in certain improvements upon the steam-engine, patented by one Emerson, and which became the subject of much litigation, involving the nature and relations of several inventions as capable of being embraced in one patent. The title of this patent was "for certain improvements in the steam-engine, and the mode of propelling therewith either vessels on the water or carriages on the land." The patentee claimed to have invented three distinct mechanisms, contrived with the view of being used conjointly, and as conducing to a common end, namely, the better propelling and navigating a ship; but each of these mechanisms was capable of a distinct use without the other two; and it was suggested in the specification that one of them, by the use of similar gearing, could be applied to the turning of the wheels of carriages on rail or ordinary roads, as it was applied to the turning of the paddle-wheels of a ship. In the Circuit Court it was held, that the patent covering the three inventions was rightly taken, upon the ground that, although each was a distinct invention, yet as they were capable of being used in connection and to subserve a common end, they might be united together in one patent, which would protect the patentee from the wrongful use of either of them separately.[1] This conclusion appears to have been reached in conformity with the views expressed by Mr. Justice Story in the case of Wyeth *v.* Stone, in which he modified his *dicta* in the previous cases of Barrett *v.* Hall and Moody *v.* Fiske. In Wyeth *v.* Stone, it appeared that the patentee had invented an apparatus for cutting surface ice into blocks of uniform size, consisting of two machines capable of being used separately or together. The

[1] Emerson *v.* Hogg, 2 Blatchf. 1, 8.

one, called a cutter, was a contrivance for marking the surface with parallel grooves; the other, called a saw, was a mechanism for working a circular saw in the groove so cut, by means of which the ice could be cut through or so nearly through as to be easily pried off with a chiselled iron bar. The two machines were embraced in one patent, which was construed by the court as a claim, not for the combination of the two, but for each distinct machine as a separate invention, yet conducing to the same common end. It appeared that in practice the patentee had himself discontinued the use of the saw, it being found that after the ice had been marked off in grooves by the cutter, it could be split off without being sawed. The suit was against a party using the cutter only; and consequently the point presented by the case was whether a patent describing and claiming two distinct machines was good as a patent for one of them, it appearing that they were not claimed as a combination. In order to sustain it as a patent for one of the machines, it became necessary to find some rule by which it could be saved from the objection that it embraced more than one subject-matter. Such a rule was supposed to be afforded by the fact that the machines, although capable of distinct use, were auxiliary to one common purpose.[1] Following this rule, the Circuit Court, in Emerson *v.* Hogg, adopted the principle that where distinct inventions are capable of being used in connection, and to subserve a common end, they may be included in one patent, and their actual employment together is not required to sustain the validity of the patent in which they are united; and that the wrongful use of either machine is a violation of the patent right *pro tanto*. Applying this principle to the case before them, the court came to the following conclusion: "We think the specification in this case shows that these three separate machines were contrived with the view of being used conjointly, and as conducing to a common end, in the better propelling and navigating a ship; and in our opinion, their capability of being used separately and independent of each other does not prevent their being embraced in one patent."[2] This case came twice before the Supreme Court, and on each occasion the ruling of the Circuit Court on this point was sustained, although at last there appears to have been a division of opinion among the judges.[3]

[1] Wyeth *v.* Stone, 1 Story, 273, 287.

[2] Emerson *v.* Hogg, 2 Blatchf. 8.

[3] Hogg *v.* Emerson, 6 Howard, 437; s. c. 11 Howard, 587. In delivering

§ 111. The third class of cases embraces what may be called technical combinations. In machinery the distinction between a new combination and a new machine may be illustrated in the history of the sewing-machine, of which there are several different varieties. Assuming that A. was the first person to make a sewing-machine, consisting of certain elemental parts operating together

the opinion of the court in 6 Howard, Mr. Justice Woodbury said: "There seems to have been no good reason at first, unless it be a fiscal one on the part of the government when issuing patents, why more than one in favor of the same inventor should not be embraced in one instrument, like more than one tract of land in one deed, or patent for land. Phillips on Pat. 217.

"Each could be set out in separate articles or paragraphs, as different counts for different matters in libels in admiralty, or declarations at common law, and the specifications could be made distinct for each, and equally clear.

"But to obtain more revenue, the public officers have generally declined to issue letters for more than one patent described in them. Renouard, 293; Phillips on Pat. 218. The courts have been disposed to acquiesce in the practice, as conducive to clearness and certainty. And if letters issue otherwise inadvertently, to hold them, as a general rule, null. But it is a well-established exception, that patents may be united, if two or more, included in one set of letters, relate to a like subject, or are in their nature or operation connected together. Phil. on Pat. 218, 219; Barrett *v.* Hall, 1 Mason, C. C. 447; Moody *v.* Fiske, 2 Mason, C. C. 112; Wyeth *et al.* *v.* Stone *et al.*, 1 Story, 273.

"Those here are of that character, being all connected with the use of the improvements in the steam-engine, as applied to propel carriages or vessels, and may, therefore, be united in one instrument."

In 11 Howard, the same learned judge said, in answer to the same objection: "But grant that such is the result when two or more inventions are entirely separate and independent, — though this is doubtful on principle, — yet it is well settled, in the cases formerly cited, that a patent for more than one invention is not void, if they are connected in their design and operation. This last is clearly the case here. They all here relate to the propelling of carriages and vessels by steam, and only differ, as they must on water, from what they are on land; a paddle-wheel being necessary on the former, and not on the latter, and one being used on the former which is likewise claimed to be an improved one. All are a part of one combination when used on the water, and differing only as the parts must when used to propel in a different element.

"In Wyeth *et al.* *v.* Stone *et al.*, 1 Story, 288, in order to render different letters-patent necessary, it is said, the inventions must be 'wholly independent of each other, and distinct inventions for unconnected objects'; as one to spin cotton, and 'another to make paper.'

"Again, if one set of letters-patent is permissible for one combination consisting of many parts, as is the daily practice, surely one will amply suffice for two or three portions of that combination."

automatically, to make a stitch uniting two pieces of cloth, the field of invention is in one direction closed ; that is to say, no one can afterwards be the first inventor of a sewing-machine. This result has already been accomplished. But there remained to be invented a great variety of new and different combinations of the parts which go to make up a sewing-machine. A combination, therefore, in machinery, may be defined, not as a new machine, but as a new union of elemental parts not before brought together in that kind of machine. The machine itself may have existed before; and the separate elements of the new combination may have existed before; but if those elements have not been before united so as to produce a method of operation differing from what had been done before in that kind of machine, what is called a new combination is created. An instance of this kind appears in certain improvements in the common cooking-stove. This machine had long existed, and one of the varieties of the previously existing machine contained, among other things, an oven extending under the open hearth of the stove, combined with the reverberating flues. To this an inventor added a flue or fire-chamber in front; making, it was held, a new and patentable combination, which may consist of elements either new or old, provided their union is effected for the first time.[1] So, also, where the invention, being an improvement in the power-loom for weaving figured fabrics, consisted in bringing into use in the machine three elemental parts, each of which performed a certain office in producing one practical result, and the claim was for thus combining those elemental parts, it was held that this was a new combination; for the essence of a combination is this, namely, although each of the several elements performs a distinct function, yet as a whole their joint or successive action contributes to one practical result.[2]

[1] Buck *v.* Hermance, 1 Blatchf. 398.

[2] Forbush *v.* Cook, 20 Law R. 664. In this case Mr. Justice Curtis said: "To make a valid claim for a combination, it is not necessary that the several elementary parts of the combination should act simultaneously. If those elementary parts are so arranged that the successive action of each contributes to produce some practical result, which result, when attained, is the product of the simultaneous or successive action of all the elementary parts, viewed as one entire whole, a valid claim for thus combining those elementary parts may be made. Nor is it requisite to include in the claim for a combination, as elements thereof, all parts of the machine which are necessary to its action,

§ 111 *a*. Mr. Justice Clifford has divided inventions pertaining to machines into four classes, as follows: —

First, those which embrace the entire machine, as a car for a railway, or a sewing-machine. Such inventions are seldom made, but, when made and duly patented, any person is an infringer, who without license makes or uses any portion of the machine. Under such a patent, the patentee holds the exclusive right to make and use, and vend to others to be used, the entire machine; and if another, without license, makes, uses, or vends any portion of it, he invades the right of the patentee.

Second, those which embrace one or more elements of a machine, but not the entire machine, as the coulter of a plow, or the divider of the reaping-machine. In patents of this class, any person may make, use, or vend all other parts of the machine, and he may employ a coulter or divider in the machines mentioned, provided it be substantially different from that embraced in the patent.

Third, those which embrace both a new element and a new combination of elements previously used and well known. In such a case the property of the patentee consists in the new element and in the new combination. No one can lawfully make, use, or vend a machine containing such new element or such new combination. They may make, use, or vend the machine without the patented improvements, if it is capable of such use, but they cannot use either of those improvements without making themselves liable as infringers.

Fourth, those where all the elements of the machine are old, and where the invention consists in a new combination of those elements whereby a new and useful result is obtained. Most of the modern inventions are of this kind, and many of them are of great utility and value. In this class the invention consists solely in the new combination; and the rule is, that the property of an inventor, if duly secured by letters-patent, is in all cases exactly commensurate with his invention. Such an invention, however, is but an improvement on an old machine, and consequently the patentee cannot treat another as an infringer who has also improved the original machine by the use of a substantially dif-

save as they may be understood as entering into the mode of combining and arranging the elements of the combination." See further, in the same case, a very apt illustration of what constitutes a new combination.

ferent combination, although the machine may produce the same result.[1]

§ 111 *b*. In the case of Seymour *v*. Osborne,[2] decided in the Supreme Court of the United States in 1870, the validity of a combination of five patents held by the complainants for improvements in reaping machinery was in issue. The leading parts or features of a reaping-machine were stated to be: first, the reel, which gathers or presses the standing grain to the cutting apparatus; second, the cutting apparatus for severing the stalks; third, a platform on which the cut grain is received. The chief characteristics of the platform are its shape and the arrangements for removing the grain therefrom and depositing it on the ground in gavels or bundles ready for the binder. The reaping-machine is drawn by horses attached in front and to one side of it. The desideratum is to cut the standing grain and deposit it on the ground in bundles adapted to being readily bound into sheaves. In the latter mentioned operation it is of vital importance not to discharge the cut grain directly backwards immediately behind the machine where it will be in the way of the horses on their second round, but to deposit it at the side of the machine in the path just passed over by the horses, thus leaving a clear way for the horses on the next round between the stalks so deposited and the standing grain.

The invention of Seymour consisted in constructing the platform for receiving the grain in the shape of a quadrant or sector of a circle, and placing it immediately behind the cutting apparatus, and in such relation to the main frame that the cut grain could be swept around in the arc of a circle and deposited on the ground behind the horses, so as to leave a clear way between the standing grain and the gavels, thereby obviating the necessity of taking up the grain as fast as cut, and at the same time doing the work more perfectly. For this invention an original patent was granted July 8, 1851, and, by successive reissues, two claims, among other things, were allowed to the patentee. One in reissue No. 72 was: —

"A quadrant-shaped platform, arranged relatively to the cutting apparatus substantially as herein described, for the purpose set forth."

[1] Union Sugar Refinery *v*. Mathiessen (1865), 2 Fisher's Pat. Cas. 600.

[2] 11 Wall. 516.

Reissue number seventy-two, as construed by the court, consisted "in constructing the platform of a reaping machine, upon which the cut grain falls as it is cut, in the shape of a quadrant, or of a sector of a circle, placed just behind the cutting apparatus, and in such relation to the main frame that the grain, whether raked off by hand or machinery located behind the cutting apparatus, can be swept around on the arc of a circle and be dropped heads foremost on the ground, far enough from the standing grain to leave room for the team and machine to pass between the gavels and the standing grain without the necessity of taking up the gavels before the machine comes round to cut the next swath."

The other claim, on the basis of the same original patent, was in reissue No. 1683: —

"The combination in a harvesting machine of the cutting apparatus (to sever the stalks) with a reel and with a quadrant-shaped platform located in the rear of the cutting apparatus, those three members being and operating as set forth." The ingredients of this claim are the cutting apparatus to sever the stalks, the reel to incline the heads of the stalks towards the cutting apparatus, and the quadrant-shaped platform, located in the rear of the cutting apparatus, to receive the cut stalks as they fall, before the operation of the sweep-rake begins. In Seymour's machine the grain was discharged from the platform on to the ground by a hand-rake.

The other inventions in controversy were made by Palmer and Williams, and pertained to the employment of an automatic sweep-rake in combination with the quadrant platform, which, as a separate device, was conceded by these inventors to have been the invention of Seymour. The claims for these improvements were allowed in reissue No. 4 and No. 1682. In the former the claim was: —

"Discharging the cut grain from a quadrant-shaped platform, on which it falls as it is cut, by means of an automatic sweep-rake, sweeping over the same substantially as described." "Explained in general terms, the invention secured in the reissued patent numbered four," said Mr. Justice Clifford, "consists in arranging an automatic sweep-rake in a harvesting machine, in such relation to a quadrant-shaped platform, upon which the cut grain falls as it is cut, that it shall vibrate over the same at suitable intervals to discharge the cut grain in gavels upon the ground."

The claim of reissue No. 1682 was as follows: —

"The combination of the cutting apparatus of a harvesting machine with a quadrant-shaped platform arranged in the rear thereof, and a sweep-rake operated by mechanism in such manner that its teeth are caused to sweep over the platform in curves when acting on the grain, these parts being and operating substantially as hereinbefore set forth."

The court construed this combination to embrace: 1. The cutting apparatus to sever the standing stalks of grain; 2. The quadrant-shaped platform arranged behind the cutting apparatus to receive the severed stalks of grain as they fall; 3. The sweep-rake and the described mechanism to operate the same in such manner that the teeth shall move in circular curves over the platform when they are acting on the grain. The letters-patent covering all these improvements, which were designed to accomplish the same object, became vested in the complainants who sought to restrain their alleged infringement by the defendants.[1]

The defence set up was that the combination claimed in each of the several letters-patent was a combination of old parts, the combining of which involved no invention, but merely the skill of an intelligent mechanic, or other person skilled in the manufacture and use of harvesting machines.

In support of this theory, evidence was adduced to show that the improvements claimed had been embodied in other machines alleged to have been in use prior to those of the complainants. Obed Hussey had made a reaping-machine with a square platform, to the rear of which was bolted an angular addition, giving to the whole where the addition was attached an angular form. The court was of opinion that this machine was "substantially different in several respects" from that of complainants, but deemed it unnecessary to enter that field of inquiry, as Hussey's machine was merely an experiment, and had never been reduced to practice as an operative machine. The machine most relied upon by the defence was the self-raking reaper invented by Nelson Platt, and for which a patent had been granted June 12, 1849. In this machine, the grain, after being cut, was received on a rectangular platform whence it was raked by a set of rake, acting from below, on to a second quadrant-shaped platform. From this platform the

[1] An original patent granted to Palmer and Williams, and assigned to complainants, relating to the mode of supporting the reel, was also in controversy; but it is not necessary to describe it in this connection.

grain was discharged by a vibrating rake, which swept across it in the arc of a circle on to the ground, the heads of the grain lying towards the machine. It was not claimed that this was identical in construction with the complainants' invention, but that the improvements of the latter were within the scope of a skilled mechanic, and did not require invention. This view was adopted by the Circuit Court, which also held that the evidence did not show that the defendants' machine infringed, and dismissed the complaint.[1] The Supreme Court of the United States, when the matter came up on appeal, held that the court below had erred in both of these conclusions, and accordingly reversed the judgment.

Mr. Justice Clifford in pronouncing the judgment of the Supreme Court said: "Particular changes may be made in the construction and operation of an old machine so as to adapt it to a new and valuable use not known before, and to which the old machine had not been and could not be applied without those changes; and under those circumstances, if the machine, as changed and modified, produces a new and useful result, it may be patented, and the patent will be upheld under existing laws. Such a change in an old machine may consist merely of a new and useful combination of the several parts of which the old machine is composed, or it may consist of a material alteration or modification of one or more of the several devices which entered into its construction; and whether it be the one or the other, if the change of construction and operation actually adapts the machine to a new and valuable use not known before, and it actually produces a new and useful result, then a patent may be granted for the same, and it will

[1] "The size and particular form of the platform," said Judge Hall, in rendering the decision of the Circuit Court, "whether square, rectangular, or otherwise shaped, was simply a question of mechanical construction, depending upon the form, construction, and operation of the other parts of the machine; and the actual invention of Palmer and Williams was confined to the devices and organization by which the automatic rake was effectually operated and made to produce the desired result. No one who had any pretension to mechanical skill, or even to practical good sense, could have been stupid enough, after placing the circular fence and rail on the old-fashioned rectangular platform, to leave the useless wood outside that fence and rail, to add unnecessarily to the weight of the machine, and consequently to the force required for its operation. To remove this useless wood, or simply to change the position of Platt's quadrant-shaped platform to the rear of the cutting apparatus, required neither ingenuity nor invention."

be upheld as a patentable improvement. "Improvements for which a patent may be granted must be new and useful, within the meaning of the patent law, or the patent will be void, but the requirement of the patent act in that respect is satisfied if the combination is new and the machine is capable of being beneficially used for the purpose for which it was designed, as the law does not require that it should be of such general utility as to supersede all other inventions in practice to accomplish the same object." In overruling the defence that the difference between Nelson Platt's machine and that of the complainant was "so very slight that it required no invention to pass from the former to the latter," the same learned judge said: "Properly understood, that machine does not contain a combination of the quadrant-shaped platform with the cutting apparatus in any practical sense. On the contrary, it has a square platform combined with the cutting apparatus, and the quadrant-shaped platform is combined with the square platform; nor does it contain any quadrant-shaped platform to receive the grain as it falls, but the ingredients of the invention, as well as the combination, are different from those in the complainants' machine, and the mode of operation is also different, which is all that need be said in response to that defence."

§ 111 *c*. A mere aggregation of parts, whereof the patentee has not the exclusive right to either, and in which the parts have no new operation and produce no result which is due to the combination itself, is not invention, and consequently is not patentable. The combination must be new itself, and must produce a new and useful result, not due to the separate action of any one of the devices used in combination, nor attained thereby, but due to the co-operative or reciprocal action of the combined devices. And in such a case any one may lawfully use any one of the old devices separately, or in new combinations, or may use some of them in combination and omit others. Or if the combination of the old devices be supplemented by other and new devices co-operating therewith, thus producing a new and useful result, that is invention.[1] But if a device in one combination performs mechanically and practically, and in substantially the same manner, the same office of another device in another combination, it is none

[1] Hailes *v.* Van Wormer (1870), 7 Blatchf. 443; Sarven *v.* Hall (1872), 9 Blatchf. 524.

the less an equivalent of the latter because it performs an additional office, not performed by the former, by reason of a difference in its mechanical construction.[1]

[1] Sarven *v.* Hall, *ut supra.* In this case the court said: "The second claim is, 'A carriage wheel constructed with a mortised wooden hub, with tenoned spokes, and with flanges which embrace the faces of the spokes in the immediate vicinity of the hub, and are connected together so as to form a metallic band through which the spokes extend into the mortises in the wooden hub, substantially as before set forth.' This claim, construed by the aid of the specification, is for the combination of the two flanges with tenoned spokes, the two flanges being connected together so as to give lateral support to the spokes.

"This second claim raises three questions involved in the present case, which may be most intelligently discussed in the following order: First, have the defendants used this combination? and if so, then, second, is such combination patentable, or is it a mere aggregation of devices not involving patentable invention? and, third, is it a new combination?

"The defendants have not used — it is not claimed that they have used — flanged collars, constructed separately, to be separately applied, and bolted or screwed together. The mechanical construction of the mortised collar, cast in one piece, with divisions between the mortises for the several spokes, and with tapering sides, formed to receive the spokes driven tightly therein, and give them endwise bearings, is not the same as the plaintiff's flanged collars. They perform a different office in the particular last named, which the plaintiff's flanged collars do not and cannot perform. The defendant's mortised collar and the plaintiff's flanged collars are, therefore, not identical, either in mechanical construction or in the office which they perform. It is, nevertheless, claimed that, in the particular construction and office which is embraced within the plaintiff's second claim, they are the precise equivalent of the plaintiff's flanged collars. This claim suggests a question of some interest: Is a device which, both mechanically and practically, performs the same precise office of another device, in substantially the same manner, any less an equivalent of the latter, because it also performs another office or offices, by reason of a difference in its mechanical construction?

"The mortised collar used by the defendants has its two sides in the same form as the two flanged collars of the plaintiff. In reference to the purpose for which the plaintiff's two flanged collars are used — to wit, to strengthen the hub, and to sustain the spokes against lateral pressure or strain, and to co-operate with the tenons in giving firm support to the spokes — they perform identically the same office as the plaintiff's flanged collars, and in the same way. The circumstance that they are held together by connecting cross-pieces, made solid therewith, instead of by bolts or screws, has no effect on the manner of their operation in this respect. Are they, then, to be deemed any less the equivalent of the flanged collars, because, by reason of the greater number of cross-pieces, they are stronger, or because the cross-pieces between each two spokes and the sides of the mortise are tapered, so as to give an end-

§ 111 *d*. In a very recent case the House of Lords held that a new combination of old and well-known things was a proper

wise bearing to the spokes, and enable the spokes to be driven in and be grasped firmly, and held therein? I think not. In the use, and for the purpose, for which the plaintiff's flanged collars are useful, they are identical in the office they perform, to wit, to sustain the spokes against lateral strain. The mechanical construction, in the parts which perform this office, is substantially the same. The crosswise partitions and form of tapering mortises may be improvements upon the plaintiff's flanged collars, but the mortised collars do, nevertheless, operate, for all the purposes for which the flanged collars are used, in precisely the same way. If the question was between a single patented device, conceded to be new, and a device claimed to infringe, because an equivalent, the alleged infringer could not protect himself by showing that, although his device was an equivalent of the patented device, in all its functions, and in its construction and mode of operation, yet, by other or additional features, it possessed other and further useful functions. Such a device would, perhaps, be an improvement upon the patented device, but must be nevertheless deemed an appropriation of the former.

"This view of the subject of equivalents is not stated in order to a conclusion that, as separate devices, either of these parties has the exclusive right to the flanged collars or to the mortised collar. Both, as hereinbefore stated, are old. It does not follow that the plaintiff's combination of flanged collars with tenoned spokes is old; and the question discussed is, whether, in the combination of flanged collars with the tenoned spokes, the substitution of the mortised collar is not, within the meaning of the law, the substitution of an equivalent in the combination, although such device (being equivalent for the purposes, and in all the functions, of the flanged collars) also contains other and additional functions due to its peculiar construction. In this view, the combination of a mortised collar and tenoned spokes with a wooden hub must be regarded as embracing the combination of the flanged collars and tenoned spokes with a wooden hub, claimed in the plaintiff's patent; and, if that patent is valid in respect of that claim, the defendants must be held to infringe it, notwithstanding the combination used by the defendants may also include other functions and produce effects not attainable by the plaintiff's combination.

"The plaintiff's combination referred to in his second claim is distinguished from a mere aggregation of devices in this, that there is a reciprocal action or operation of the parts upon each other and conjointly upon the entire wheel, each part giving to the other increased support and efficiency, and the two co-operating to make a stronger and more durable wheel than is produced by the use of either without the other, — that is to say, the tenoned spokes are strengthened and sustained in position by the flanged collars, and the flanged collars, bound to the spokes by the connecting bolts or screws, are more firmly held in position by the tenons of the spokes. Combined, they unite hub and spokes, enabling the wheel better to resist a blow or strain either laterally or in the direction of its plane. It must be conceded, within the rule on this subject, that a combination of devices would not necessarily be patentable from

subject for a patent; that a patent may be sustained, though each principle or process in it was previously well known to all persons engaged in the trade to which the patent relates, provided, however, that the mode of combination was new and produced a beneficial result. In this case the specification must claim not the old processes, or any one of them, but only the new combination.[1]

§ 112. The present chapter, which treats of the relation of the patentee to the invention, seems to be the proper place to consider the case of a joint invention made by two or more persons. Practitioners may be, and probably often are, called upon to advise, either before or after a patent has been obtained, in reference to a state of facts from which it would appear that more than one person has been concerned in making the supposed invention. That the statute contemplates the case of a joint invention, the product of the ingenuity and skill of more than one person, is evident from its language.[2] But as it is impossible that an invention should be at the same time the separate production of one person, and the joint production of two or more persons, and as all inventions

the mere fact of their union producing a better wheel. If the superiority arose from the fact that the two devices were intrinsically better than others and the wheel combined both, — each, however, operating independently of the other, — the combination would be but the exercise of judgment in the choice of parts, and not invention in discovering new means to produce useful or better results. For illustration, one mode of securing the tire to the felly, or the felly to the spokes, may be better than any other in use. One form of axle-box, or a mode of securing the axle-box to the hub, may be better than any other in use; and it might so happen that both or all had never been used together in the construction of a carriage wheel; and yet, both being old, one who should adopt both in the construction of a wheel, without other change in its construction, would not be an inventor, and his wheel would have no patentable quality. Each device is complete in itself, it performs the same functions and in the same way, in whatever wheel it is used, and without being influenced or affected by the other. This distinction may often be very nice, and sometimes may, for its application, require very close and careful discrimination; but the distinction is itself a substantial one. It reduces the basis of the second claim in the plaintiff's patent to somewhat narrow grounds, but it is sufficient to sustain it. A new relation is established between the efficient means of strengthening and supporting the parts of the wheel in question, and a new and greater efficiency is given to each, which is due not to their inherent quality, but due to the combination itself."

[1] Cannington *v.* Nuttall (1871), 5 H. L. 205.

[2] Act of 1836, § 6.

must be classed under one or the other of these heads, it becomes important to consider whether one of the authors of a joint invention can apply for and take a patent on it in his own name, or in their joint names, under any and what circumstances.

§ 113. A very singular case occurred in 1816–1818, before Mr. Justice Story, under the Patent Act of 1793. In the year 1809 two persons obtained separate patents for the same invention. One of them instituted a suit against the other, to repeal the patent of the latter, upon the allegation that it was obtained surreptitiously and upon false suggestion. Upon an issue joined on this allegation, the jury found that the plaintiff and defendant were both concerned in making the invention; but as they went on to find a general verdict for the defendant, it was set aside by the court for inconsistency and repugnance, and a new trial was ordered.[1] The parties then, 1818, applied for and obtained a joint patent for a joint invention, leaving their several previous patents outstanding; and on this joint patent they brought an action against a third person for infringement, and obtained a verdict. The defendant, among other grounds, then moved to set this verdict aside because the court at the trial instructed the jury that the existence of the prior patents granted to the patentees respectively for the same thing, and their several oaths of invention on which they obtained those patents, were not an absolute bar to the joint patent declared on, and did not conclude them from showing a joint invention. It was held that the prior patents, although very strong evidence against the claim of joint invention, were not conclusive.[2]

[1] Stearns *v.* Barrett, 1 Mason, 153.

[2] Barrett *v.* Hall, 1 Mason, 447, 474. Some observations may not improperly be made upon the point thus decided, in order to guard against a misapprehension of the distinction on which the learned judge appears to have relied. The prior patents, held by the inventors severally, were still outstanding when their action on the joint patent was tried. The question was, whether those prior patents were not an estoppel to the joint patent. The learned judge stated the position, with great strength, that a subsequent patent is an estoppel to the setting up of a prior grant inconsistent with the terms of the last grant; and also that a repeal for some original defect in a prior patent is necessary to the acquisition of a right under a subsequent patent for the same invention. But he appears to have treated the prior patents, in this case, as having been possibly taken under an innocent mistake, which the plaintiffs were at liberty to show; and he treated their subse-

§ 114. It will be seen, on comparing this case with the Patent Act then in force, that it arose under a statute which unequivocally authorized a joint patent to be issued on a joint invention to joint applicants.[1] A very different case might arise under the statute of 1836, the terms of which, either by accident or design, are somewhat different. The sixth section of that act, after providing, by the use of the plural, that a patent may be granted on the application of more than one person, does not continue, in prescribing the form and substance of the specification, which is to be delivered, to make use of the plural, but speaks of what the inventor or applicant is to do, in the singular only. Looking, however, to the obvious intent of the act, it should doubtless be construed to provide that, in case of a joint invention on which the inventors petition for a joint patent, the specification and oath of invention may be signed and made by the joint inventors. But how would it be in the case of a joint invention, where one party only applies, acting for both? Could a patent for a joint invention be issued to the joint inventors, on the application of one? If one of two joint inventors had, before an application, assigned his interest to the other, how should the patent be applied for,—as for a joint invention, taking a joint patent, or as for an invention part of which had been assigned to the applicant before the application? These are some of the questions which may arise in practice, in regard to which it may be prudent to make only general suggestions respecting the policy and purposes of the statute.

§ 115. These suggestions are : *First*, that the statute evidently contemplates the case of a joint invention and a joint patent. *Second*, that although the statute does not expressly direct that the joint inventors shall all sign the application and make the oath,

quent application for a joint patent as a kind of surrender in law of their prior several patents. It is not easy to reconcile this decision with that in the subsequent case of Odiorne *v.* The Amesbury Nail Factory (2 Mason, 28), in which the same learned judge held that a prior patent, unrepealed, is an estoppel to any future patent for the same thing, unless we make an exception in the case of a joint invention, and treat the subsequent application for a joint patent as a renunciation of all right obtained by the inventors separately by prior separate patents. If such a case were to occur now, the remedy for a third person would apparently be, to bring a bill in equity for interfering patents, and have the one or the other declared void. See Act of 1836, § 16.

[1] Act of 1793, § 1.

it is quite capable of the construction that they may do so, especially if they apply by joint petition for a joint patent. *Third*, that in all applications, the truth of the case should be pursued, and the application of the statute to the facts should be carefully noted. *Fourth*, That while the terms of the statute do not seem positively to preclude an application by one for a joint patent on a joint invention, or for a patent to that one who has received an assignment from the other joint inventor, it would be most prudent to avoid raising the question of the effect of such an assignment, if it be practicable. The subsequent statute, which makes inventions assignable before application for a patent (act of 1837, § 6), seems to embrace the case of a several, and not the case of a joint invention. In the case, therefore, of a joint invention, where one inventor has assigned his interest to the other before application, the assignment would appear to rest upon common-law principles; and if so, the question how the patent should or may be applied for, under the statute, would depend upon the peculiar facts of the case.

§ 115 *a*. In the act of 1870, the language referring to the inventor, discoverer, and applicant, is used in a singular sense.

§ 116. As to what constitutes joint invention, it is obvious that the question may be to some extent different from what would arise where the issue is whether one of two persons is to be considered as the sole inventor. But perhaps the same leading principle is to be applied to ascertain whether A. is to be regarded as a part inventor with B., as to ascertain whether A. is to be regarded as sole inventor against B.

§ 117. This, too, may be an appropriate place to suggest a useful caution against covering by a subsequent patent what has already been described in a previous patent issued to the same inventor. In the first place, if the previous patent describes something which it does not claim as new, its actual novelty may not save it from the peril of having become dedicated to the public. It is a very strong, perhaps a conclusive, presumption, that what is described in a patent and not claimed is given up to public use.[1]

[1] It is not intended, in this passage of the text, to intimate that a technical "claim," or summary, is necessary to support a patent. A specification satisfies the requirements of the statute, if it points out in any manner what the inventor means to secure to himself by the grant of the patent. The summary, technically called a "claim," may or may not be a convenient mode of

Probably this presumption can be removed only by a surrender and reissue of the patent, under the statute which provides for *bonâ fide* inadvertency. At all events, it seems clear that the difficulty cannot be corrected by the issue of a second and independent patent, if the thing that is sought to be covered by the second was already covered by a valid claim in the first patent. But if the subject of a second patent was embraced in a claim of a previous patent, which turns out to have been more extensive than the patentee was entitled to make it, such second patent may be good. To this effect, the case of O'Reilly *v.* Morse is a direct decision. Morse, in the first patent issued for the electro-magnetic telegraph, had inserted, besides the special claims covering the particular machinery then invented by him for the recording or marking of intelligible signs at long distances, a claim of a broad and general character, for the use of the electro-magnetic current as a motive-power, in a printing or recording telegraph, without confining himself to the particular machinery described. Subsequently he invented and took a patent for the local circuits, — a combination of devices by which the message can be recorded at intermediate stations as well as at the terminus of the line. The Supreme Court of the United States held that the general claim of the first patent, if valid, would include the local circuits, but that it was not valid, because it attempted to embrace things not then invented, or at least not described; that this being so, the new patent for the local circuits, being for an invention not described in the first patent, and being a distinguishable improvement upon what was described in the first patent, was properly granted.[1]

§ 118. The several provisions of the patent acts not only require that the invention should possess the qualities of which we have treated in the last preceding chapter, but they also make it necessary that the patentee should be the actual inventor, or the assignee or legal representative of the actual inventor, of the thing

ascertaining what the party means to have the patent embrace. But whether this or some other mode of designating the subject of invention or discovery be employed, there is a necessary presumption that things described, and not represented to be part of the invention or discovery which the patentee intends to cover, are dedicated to the public, even if they are original. This presumption may be removed by a surrender and reissue.

[1] O'Reilly *v.* Morse, 15 Howard, 62.

patented. No person can take a patent for that which he did not invent, unless he derives a legal title from the true inventor, by assignment or by operation of law. In either case, therefore, whether the applicant claims as the inventor or as holding the title of the inventor, a question may arise as to the real authorship of the invention; because suggestions, hints, or conceptions, or practical assistance may have been derived from others, and if so derived, the fact of whether the invention was in truth made by the party claiming to be the inventor may require determination. But it is a presumption of law that the patentee was the inventor of that which he patented, and whoever alleges the contrary assumes the burden of proof.[1]

This is a mixed question of law and fact; or, in other words, it is one of those questions on which no precise and universal rule can be stated, but certain general principles of determination may be laid down, under the guidance of which the facts attending the process of forming or realizing the invention may be investigated. Generally speaking, the cases will divide themselves into two classes: in one of which the effort will be to show that the plan, conception, or suggestion of the thing patented came from some other person than the patentee, and that nothing more was done by him than to supply the mechanical details, or other practical means, of embodying or working the suggestion; while in the other class, it will be found that the patentee had conceived the plan or principle of the invention, but derived from others the practical knowledge or manual skill necessary to give it an operative and useful existence.

§ 119. With respect to the first of these two classes of cases, the general principle seems to be, that, in order to invalidate a patent upon the ground that the patentee received from another person the suggestion of the invention, it is not enough to show that the naked idea, or bare possibility of accomplishing the object, was suggested. On the other hand, it is not necessary that the mere *minutiæ* of the invention should have been communicated by another person. The true test to apply is, to ascertain whether the principle or plan of the invention was substantially communicated to the patentee by some one else, so that nothing remained for the former to do but to apply the skill of a constructor.[2] This

[1] Pitts *v.* Hall, 2 Blatchf. 229.

[2] Alden *v.* Dewey, 1 Story, 336.

test has been applied, with all the precision of which such a question admits, by Mr. Justice Nelson, in the following instruction to a jury: "There is no doubt that a person, to be entitled to the character of an inventor within the meaning of the act of Congress, must himself have conceived the idea embodied in his improvement. It must be the product of his own mind and genius, and not of another's. Thus, in this case, the arrangement patented must be the product of the mind and genius of C., and not of B. or F. This is obvious to the most common apprehension. At the same time it is equally true, that, in order to invalidate a patent on the ground that the patentee did not conceive the idea embodied in the improvement, it must appear that the suggestions, if any, made to him by others, would furnish *all* the information necessary to enable him to construct the improvement. In other words, the suggestions must have been sufficient to enable C. [the patentee], in this case, to construct a complete and perfect machine. If they simply aided him in arriving at the useful result, but fell short of suggesting an arrangement that would constitute a complete machine, and if, after all the suggestions, there was something left for him to devise and work out by his own skill or ingenuity, in order to complete the arrangement, then he is, in contemplation of law, to be regarded as the first and original discoverer. On the other hand, the converse of the proposition is equally true. If the suggestions or communications of another go to make up a complete and perfect machine, embodying all that is embraced in the patent subsequently issued to the party to whom the suggestions were made, the patent is invalid, because the real discovery belongs to another."[1]

§ 119 *a*. Where a master-workman has conceived the plan of an invention and is engaged in experiments to perfect it, suggestions from a person employed by him are not sufficient to deprive the employer of the exclusive property in the perfected improvement, unless such suggestions amount to a new method or arrangement, which in itself is a complete invention. This issue was presented in the case of the Agawam Company *v.* Jordan,[2] decided by the Supreme Court of the United States in 1868. One Goulding had

[1] Pitts *v.* Hall, 2 Blatchf. 229, 234. See also Sparkman *v.* Higgins, 1 Blatchf. 205.

[2] 7 Wall. 583.

invented an improved cording machine, consisting of a combination of known devices or machines. It was alleged by the defence, however, that Goulding had not bestowed any ingenuity upon the invention, but had derived his knowledge from Edward Winslow, who was employed by him. It appeared that Goulding, while experimenting, had adopted certain suggestions of Winslow, which had proved useful in the result.[1] As viewed by the court, they were of value only as an *auxiliary* part of Goulding's invention, and did not either form the entire invention or any one of its separate combinations. After a minute statement of the facts involved, Mr. Justice Clifford, who pronounced the opinion of the court, thus stated the principles of law applicable to the point in dispute: "Suggestions from another, made during the progress of such experiments, in order that they may be sufficient to defeat a patent subsequently issued, must have embraced the plan of the

[1] The following statement of facts is given in the report of the case: "Taken all together, this part of the case, on favorable assumption for the defendant, seemed somewhat thus: After Goulding came to Dedham, and had been experimenting there for a considerable time, one Edward Winslow, a blacksmith by trade, but, if the testimony in his favor was to be believed, an ingenious man, came into his service. Winslow professed no skill out of his business, but made himself useful generally in whatever Goulding found it most convenient to set him to do; working generally in iron. He had no charge of Goulding's machine-shop, but was not unfrequently in it. Goulding himself directed all that was done about machinery, whether as to making or to altering it. In 1824, Winslow having been to a neighbor's factory, where certain devices, meant to produce long or endless rolls, and to serve as receptacles for the rovings, had been introduced on machinery for spinning yarn, Goulding, who had now nearly completed his improvement, and while he was diligently prosecuting his experiments, asked him what he thought of them. Winslow replied that the principle of them was good, but that the agencies employed were bad, and suggested certain substitutes (a spool and drum) for them. 'You don't know any thing,' was Goulding's first reply. However, upon seeing an experiment, apparently at first successful, made at his own mill, on the basis of Winslow's idea, he exclaimed, 'Winslow, you have got it. I will give you $2500 and half of what we can make.' But the experiment broke down in the process of exhibiting it. Goulding then exclaiming, 'Your plan isn't worth a cent, I would not give a fig for it,' left the mill. Upon further conversation and consideration, Goulding saw merit in Winslow's suggestions, and having made them practicable by an addition of his own (the 'traverser,' whose effect was to wind the roving evenly on the spool), he adopted them (instead of cans, the far less convenient agency previously used), as two items of his far larger improvement. As it turned out in the result they proved useful."

improvement, and must have furnished such information to the person to whom the communication was made, that it would have enabled an ordinary mechanic, without the exercise of any ingenuity and special skill on his part, to construct and put the improvement in successful operation.

"Persons employed, as much as employers, are entitled to their own independent inventions, but where the employer has conceived the plan of an invention, and is engaged in experiments to perfect it, no suggestions from an employee, not amounting to a new method or arrangement, which in itself is a complete invention, is sufficient to deprive the employer of the exclusive property in the perfected improvement. But where the suggestions go to make up a complete and perfect machine, embracing the substance of all that is embodied in the patent subsequently issued to the party to whom the suggestions are made, the patent is invalid, because the real invention or discovery belonged to another."

§ 120. The other class of cases, namely, those in which the author of the plan or principle of an invention has availed himself of the suggestions or skill of workmen or other persons in giving practical embodiment to his ideas, depend upon the relative situations of the parties, the nature of the employment, the fact that the patentee had conceived the main idea of the invention, and the further fact that the suggestions made or the assistance afforded to him by another did not materially affect the result. The general rule being that the person who plans the invention is to be regarded as the inventor, it will make no difference that such person worked as a servant in the employment of another, provided the servant really conceived the improvement patented. Thus, Baron Alderson put this issue to a jury in the following terms: "If Sutton suggested the principle to Mr. Minter (the patentee), then he would be the inventor. If, on the other hand, Mr. Minter suggested the principle to Sutton, and Sutton was assisting him, then Mr. Minter would be the first and true inventor, and Sutton would be a machine, so to speak, which Mr. Minter uses for the purpose of enabling him to carry his orig nal conception into effect."[1] So, too, in Arkwright's case, with respect to a particular roller, part of the machinery, the evidence was that Arkwright had been told of it by one Kay; that, being

[1] Minter *v.* Wells, 1 Webs. Pat. Cas. 132.

satisfied of its value, he took Kay for a servant, kept him for two years, employed him to make models, and afterwards claiming it as his invention, made it the foundation of a patent. The same fact was proved concerning a crank, which had been discovered by a person of the name of Hargrave, and had been adopted by Arkwright. This evidence was fatal to the patentee's claim of invention in respect to both of these improvements.[1]

§ 121. But in these cases, the thing patented was a specific part, or instrument, in a complicated machine, constituting, if it had the merit of novelty, a special improvement. On the other hand, it is obvious that a person may be the real author of the plan of a complicated machine, or other invention, which requires for its perfection the skill, and to some extent the inventive faculties, of workmen or engineers, in adapting the best means to the successful application of the principle. Thus it was objected, at a trial in the King's Bench, that parts of the improvements in Foudrinier's paper machine were the inventions of one Donkin; but Donkin proved that when he made those improvements he was employed as an engineer, for the purpose of bringing the machine to perfection, and was paid for so doing, and that he was acting as the servant of the inventor of the machine, for the purpose of suggesting those improvements. He did not discover the principle of the machine, or invent the important movements of it. The objection did not prevail.[2] But perhaps the most striking case of this class is that of the invention of the electro-magnetic telegraph, by Professor Morse. His plan for combining two or more electric or galvanic circuits, with independent batteries, for the purpose of overcoming the diminished force of electro-magnetism in long circuits, was fully formed in the spring of 1837; and the process, combination, powers, and machinery appeared, on a judicial investigation, to have been then arranged in his own mind. But it could not be brought out without the highest order of mechanical skill; and the want of means to employ the services of workmen capable of affording him the necessary aid was proved to have been the cause for the non-production of his invention until a later period.

[1] The King *v.* Arkwright, Davies's Pat. Cas. 61, 1 Webs. Pat. Cas. 64. See also Barker *v.* Shaw, 1 Webs. 126.

[2] Bloxam *v.* Elsee, 1 Car. & P. 567; Davies's Pat. Cas. 132; Godson on Patents, 27, 28; Hindmarch on Patents, 26.

Upon this state of the case, Mr. Chief Justice Taney, delivering the judgment of the Supreme Court of the United States, said: "Neither can the inquiries he made, or the information or advice he received from men of science, in the course of his researches, impair his right to the character of an inventor. No invention can possibly be made, consisting of a combination of different elements of power, without a thorough knowledge of the properties of each of them, and of the mode in which they operate on each other; and it can make no difference, in this respect, whether he derives his information from books or from conversation with men skilled in the science. If it were otherwise, no patent in which a combination of different elements is used could ever be obtained. For no man ever made such an invention without having first obtained this information, unless it was discovered by some fortunate accident. And it is evident that such an invention as the electro-magnetic telegraph could never have been brought into action without it. For a very high degree of scientific knowledge and the nicest skill in the mechanic arts are combined in it, and were both necessary to bring it into successful operation. And the fact that Morse sought and obtained the necessary information and counsel from the best sources, and acted upon it, neither impairs his rights as an inventor, nor detracts from his merits."[1]

§ 121 *a*. In the case of Blandy *v*. Griffith,[2] it appeared that the complainant had suggested to a draughtsman in his employ the plan of a portable steam-engine substantially the same as that described in the patent, and had marked a diagram to illustrate his ideas, in the sand upon the floor. He then directed his draughtsman to prepare the drawings, and ordered the engine to be made. Mr. Justice Swayne thereupon stated the distinction between invention and mechanical skill in the following clear and concise language: "Invention is the work of the brain, and not of the hands. If the conception be practically complete, the artist who gives it reflex and embodiment in a machine is no more the inventor than the tools with which he wrought. Both are instruments in the hands of him who sets them in motion and prescribes the work to be done. Mere mechanical skill can never rise to the sphere of invention. The latter involves higher thought,

[1] O'Reilly *v*. Morse, 15 Howard, 62, 111.

[2] (1869), 3 Fisher's Pat. Cas. 609.

and brings into activity a different faculty. Their domains are distinct. The line which separates them is sometimes difficult to trace; nevertheless, in the eye of the law it always subsists. The mechanic may greatly aid the inventor, but he cannot usurp his place. As long as the root of the original conception remains in its completeness, the outgrowth — whatever shape it may take — belongs to him with whom the conception originated. In the case before us it does not seem to be any pretence for saying that Wedge invented any thing. He simply executed the design drawn by Blandy in the sand. All the engines since made have been substantially like the first one."

§ 122. In like manner it has been held, that, after the main principle of an invention has been discovered, the suggestion by a workman of subordinate improvements, accessory to the main principle of the invention, and tending to carry it out more conveniently, may be adopted by the patentee and embodied in his specification. The case in which this doctrine was very clearly applied was that of an improvement in the machinery for making cloth by felting, without spinning or weaving. The invention consisted in substituting a compound travelling apron, on which to form the bat, instead of the surface of a perforated cylinder; whereby certain important advantages were gained, and a material change in the process of the manufacture was introduced. A workman employed by the patentee suggested a modification of this principle by means of successive sets of aprons placed one above another, so that the machine might be used in less extensive premises than would be required if two long extended aprons were employed. Upon these facts, Mr. Justice Erle instructed the jury as follows: "I take the law to be, that, if a person has discovered an improved principle, and employs engineers or agents or other persons to assist him in carrying out that principle, and they, in the course of the experiments arising from that employment, make valuable discoveries accessory to the main principle, and tending to carry that out in a better manner, such improvements are the property of the inventor of the original improved principle, and may be embodied in his patent; and if so embodied, the patent is not avoided by evidence that the agent or servant made the suggestions of that subordinate improvement of the primary and improved principle. The improvement claimed by Shaw (the workman) is, that, after the bat has been formed upon a revolving apron, by successive folds or layers of sliver, three or more revolving aprons should be placed one above another, and connected with each other. That is but a more convenient mode of carrying out the principle of the patentee." This instruction was affirmed by all the judges of the Common Pleas, on a rule to show cause why a new trial should not be granted, Tindal, C. J., saying: "It would be difficult to define how far the suggestions of a workman employed in the construction of a machine are to be considered as distinct inventions by him, so as to avoid a patent incorporating them taken out by his employer. Each case must depend upon its own merits. But when we see that the principle and object of the invention are complete without it, I think it is too much that a suggestion of a workman, employed in the course of the experiments, of something calculated more easily to carry into effect the conceptions of the inventor, should render the whole patent void."[1]

§ 123. From the distinctions thus taken between the cases in which the employer is the real author of the principle or plan of the invention, and those in which the servant, workman, or agent is such real author, it follows that, where the relation between the two parties amounts to a contract, by which one agrees to employ his inventive faculties in the service of another, and the workman, in the course of the employment, makes a substantive invention, the question will arise whether the employer can become the patentee of that invention without a written assignment. In a case tried before Mr. Justice Washington (in 1821), under the statute of 1793, the defence was set up under a special notice authorized by the act, that the plaintiff surreptitiously obtained the patent for a discovery of one Wimbly, who worked as a journeyman in the plaintiff's shop. The learned judge gave the following instruction: "If the jury are satisfied that the discovery was in reality made by Wimbly, they must be also satisfied that the patent was obtained in fraud of any right which such discovery bestowed upon Wimbly. For if, upon the evidence, you should be of opinion that Wimbly gave up his right of discovery to the plaintiff, by expressly or impliedly permitting him to encounter the trouble and expense of obtaining a patent, it cannot

[1] Allen *v.* Rawson, 1 Man. Granger & Scott, 551. It was certainly worthy of consideration, whether this improvement amounted to a distinct patentable subject.

be affirmed that the plaintiff obtained the patent surreptitiously, or in fraud of Wimbly's discovery."[1] The authority of this instruction is not to be pressed beyond the precise issue in respect to which it was given. It was contended by the defendant, that, inasmuch as no assignment from Wimbly to the plaintiff appeared to have been made, the plaintiff's obtaining the patent must be deemed to have been surreptitious, in relation to Wimbly, and that the patent was therefore void, under the clause of the act which permitted the defendant to show that the patentee "had surreptitiously obtained a patent for the discovery of another person." But this allegation was obviously capable of being rebutted by evidence that Wimbly acquiesced in the plaintiff's application for the patent; and it was in reference to the evidence which tended to show such acquiescence, and to the special issue raised, that the learned judge gave the instruction above quoted. But where, under a plea of the general issue, evidence should be offered that the patentee was not, but that a workman was, the real inventor, could the action be maintained without showing a written assignment, or a written contract that would operate as an assignment, even if the real inventor had acquiesced in the plaintiff's application? This is a distinct question from that which arises under the clause of the statute against surreptitious applications in fraud of the rights of the true inventor. When it is considered that, by the sixth section of the act of 1836, the right to the patent is vested in the inventor, who must himself take the steps requisite to the grant of the patent, and that, by the sixth section of the act of 1837, it is made necessary to the grant of a patent to an assignee, that an assignment should be previously recorded, and that the inventor should make oath to the specification, it can scarcely be doubted that, where the real author of the invention is any other person than the patentee, it is necessary that some contract capable of operating as an assignment should precede the issuing of the patent. But such a case is distinguishable from that of a workman who is employed and paid by one who has conceived the principle or plan of an invention, and who relies on the ingenuity of another to enable him to perfect the details and realize his conception.

[1] Dixon *v.* Moyer, 4 Wash. 68, 71.

CHAPTER IV.

OF THE EXTENT TO WHICH THE PRINCIPLE OF AN INVENTION MAY BE CARRIED BY LETTERS-PATENT. — WHAT IS MEANT BY PATENTING A PRINCIPLE.

§ 124. NOTWITHSTANDING the ambiguity which of necessity attends the use of the term "principle," there is probably no other more convenient term with which to introduce the discussion to which the present chapter is to be devoted. I design to consider, as a branch of the general topic of what may be the subject-matter of a patent, that very difficult question, of how far a discovery or invention which may first disclose and practically embody some truth in physics or some law in the operation of the forces of nature, for a useful purpose, is capable of being carried in the exclusive privileges secured by the grant of letters-patent. The discussion of this question, when followed into some of the adjudicated cases, will be found to be connected with the construction of particular specifications. So, too, it enters into the whole subject of infringements, when the question is whether what the defendant has done is within the scope of the patent that may be before the court in a given case. But notwithstanding the necessity of anticipating, to some extent, what it may be necessary hereafter to say on the topics of construction and infringement, it may be useful to consider the special question, which can, perhaps, be best stated as follows: How far can the characteristic principle of a discovery or an invention be made to extend by letters-patent, when that principle consists in a novel and useful application of some physical law, property of matter, or natural force? [1]

Perhaps the best method for the treatment of this subject will

[1] Although the reader may object to the terms in which this question is propounded, it is believed that he will have no difficulty in discovering what it is that the writer means to discuss. Considerable difficulty must always attend the use of any terms by which we attempt to designate so abstract and abstruse a subject.

be to select some prominent and peculiar invention, as an illustration of the question, and group the general principles and the prior and subsequent cases around it. By this method it will be seen to what extent the doctrines of the law may be regarded as settled. A very apposite illustration for this purpose is afforded by the invention of the magnetic telegraph.

§ 125. Morse, availing himself of the fact that a current of electro-magnetic fluid may be transmitted from place to place, along a wire, and at the terminus opposite to that from which the fluid proceeds may be used as the means of moving a delicate instrument, adapted an apparatus for throwing a current of such fluid along the wire, and for recording certain signs or marks, according to a system invented by him, at the farther extremity of the wire, by means of the movements of a recording instrument there suspended, and operated upon by the electro-magnetic current. Adopting the results of an adjudication, I assume that he was the first person who, by means of newly invented machinery adapted to the purpose, embodied and made of practical utility the fact in nature that the electro-magnetic current may be used at long distances as a moving force, for the purpose of recording or marking at pleasure intelligible signs or marks. On this hypothesis, the scope of his invention was the application and use of the electro-magnetic fluid, by means of suitable machinery and a concerted system of signs or marks, to the recording of intelligible signs or marks at a long distance from the operator. How far could he make this characteristic or principle of his invention the subject of an exclusive privilege under letters-patent? Could he patent the application and use of the electro-magnetic current, for this purpose, by any and all machinery which would effect the end proposed? or could he patent only the machinery by which he himself effected this application and use, and all other means which were substantially the same?

§ 126. This very grave question arose upon a claim in the early patent obtained by Morse, which was in these words: "I do not propose to limit myself to the specific machinery, or parts of machinery, described in the foregoing specifications and claims; the essence of my invention being the use of the motive-power of the electric or galvanic current, which I call electro-magnetism, however developed, for marking or printing intelligible characters or signs at any distances, being a new application of that power, of which I claim to be the first inventor or discoverer." It was not denied by the Supreme Court of the United States that he was the first inventor or discoverer of this application and use of the electro-magnetic current; but a great difference of opinion arose among the judges on the validity of this claim; a majority of the court holding it to be invalid, as being a claim without any limitation in respect to the means by which the electro-magnetic current could be used for the purpose described.[1] It is not intended here to state the different views of the judges, or to comment upon the decision. The case is now referred to only as an illustration of the subject before us.

§ 127. It has often been laid down that a mere elementary principle cannot be made the subject of a patent. What has been meant by this, it is of course important to ascertain. One of the earliest cases in which this topic came into consideration was that which arose upon Watt's invention of a separate condenser for the steam-engine. In the engines which preceded Watt's, the steam was condensed in the body of the cylinder. He discovered that, by condensing the steam in a separate vessel, and keeping the cylinder from cooling down, a great saving of steam, and by consequence of the fuel used to produce it, would be effected. In the unskilful fashion of that age, his patent was taken for "a newly invented *method* of lessening the consumption of steam and fuel in fire-engines"; and his enrolled specification proceeded to state that this *method* consisted of certain *principles*, the chief of which consisted in certain modes of preventing the cylinder from being cooled down below the temperature of the steam which entered it, and in the introduction of a separate condensing vessel or vessels. He did not describe any particular engine built according to his method, but a special verdict found that the specification was sufficient to enable a mechanic acquainted with the old engines to build an engine that would operate upon his plan and produce the new proposed effect of saving steam and fuel. It so happened, that, at the time when the action was brought in which this special verdict was found, Watt was entitled to sue by virtue of a special act of Parliament which had extended his patent for twenty-five years, but which had described it as a patent for making and vending certain *engines*, and which vested in him the sole right to

[1] O'Reilly *v.* Morse, 15 Howard, 62.

make and vend the *engines* described therein. The special verdict also found that, at the time of making the letters-patent, the invention was new and useful, and that the defendants had infringed the privilege vested in Watt by the special act of Parliament, as the plaintiff's had declared, namely, by making and selling *engines* in imitation of the *engine* invented by Watt, and vested in him by the special act and the latters-patent.

§ 128. It is manifest that the real question in this case was, whether the patent could be construed as a patent for a machine embodying certain principles of construction and operation; for if the patent covered only a *process*, or a *method*, considered abstractly from a particular organization of machinery, the act of Parliament, which called the subject of the patent an *engine*, could not be regarded as having continued it. All that was said by the judges of the Common Pleas, therefore, on the subject of *principle*, must be taken with reference to this question of construction, on which it was said *arguendo*. Two views were taken of this patent in the Common Pleas. *First*, that it was a patent for a *principle;* and by this it would appear to have been meant that Watt had undertaken to patent the principle of condensing the steam, not in the cylinder, but out of the cylinder, without describing any newly invented machinery for this purpose. The judges, who took this view of it, held that the patent must be void, upon the ground that a principle abstracted from particular organization is not capable of being made the subject of a patent. *Secondly*, the patent was viewed as a new mode of working an old engine by a method pointed out. This would make the invention in effect a new engine, or an improved engine. But on this construction, Mr. Justice Buller held the patent void, upon the ground that the patentee had really claimed the whole of the old engine, without pointing out his own improvement in the mechanism. Lord Chief Justice Eyre, on the other hand, held that it was not a patent for a principle (in the above sense), but for a newly invented method of working with steam, which method was exhibited by, and embodied in, a new mode of constructing engines. By this reasoning he reconciled the patent and the act by which it was continued. No judgment, however, was given in the Common Pleas, and a case was stated to be carried by writ of error to the King's Bench.[1]

[1] Boulton & Watt *v.* Bull, 2 H. Blackst. 463.

§ 129. In the latter court, all difficulty vanished; and it appears somewhat remarkable that the view taken of the patent in that court should not have occurred to those who had to consider the case in the court below. Lord Kenyon, although professedly no friend to patents, proceeded with great directness to hold this to be a patent for a *manufacture*, consisting of an engine or machine composed of material parts, which were to produce the effect described, and the mode of producing which was so described as to enable mechanics to put it in operation.[1] The objection that, if it was a patent for an improved engine, the specification should have pointed out the improvement, whereas the patent embraced, if any thing material, the whole of the old engine, was answered by the very able judgment of Grose, J., by saying that it was not a patent for the old engine, but for the improvement on the old engine.

§ 130. This analysis of the case is sufficient to show that in truth it sheds but little light upon the question now under consideration. The validity of this patent depended upon the question whether the specification had described a thing that could be brought within the term "manufacture," in the statute of monopolies. So far as the case is an authority to the position that the discovery of a law, or truth, or fact, in nature, is not of itself a *manufacture*, — a position which was correctly assumed by all the judges, — so far it elucidates the nature of what may be a patentable subject. But it did not embrace the case of the new application of one of the forces of nature, or properties of matter, to the production of a particular mechanical effect, accompanied by some described mechanical means of producing that effect; or how far such application, when produced by one means, may be made to extend as a patent privilege. Without adverting for the present to any supposed embarrassment arising out of the term "manufacture" in the English law, and to the possibility of a broader scope that may be given to our term "art," there are some observations of Lord Chief Justice Eyre, in the case of Boulton *v.* Bull, which show that at that early period (1795) this distinction between an abstract or unembodied principle, and the application of a principle by a described means, was present to his mind. "Undoubtedly," he said, "there can be no patent for a mere principle; but for a principle, so far embodied and

[1] Hornblower *v.* Boulton, 8 Term R. 95.

connected with corporeal substances as to be in a condition to act, and to produce effects in any art, trade, mystery, or manual occupation, I think there may be a patent. Now this is, in my judgment, the thing for which the patent stated in the case was granted, and this is what the specification describes, though it *miscalls it a principle.* It is not that the patentee has conceived an abstract notion that the steam in fire-engines may be lessened, but he has discovered a *practical manner of doing it;* and for that practical manner of doing it he has taken his patent."[1]

§ 131. There is a case prior to this in point of time, which was adverted to by Lord Chief Justice Eyre, in his judgment above cited, as being a case of a valid patent. This was the case of Hartley's patent for "a particular method of securing buildings and ships against the calamities of fire."[2] It consisted in fastening plates of metal and wire to the structure to be protected, joining or overlapping the edges. It was granted in 1773. Lord Chief Justice Eyre considered that this invention consisted in a new method of disposing plates of iron so as to produce the negative effect of preventing combustion, and that as such the patent was properly granted. Mr. Webster regards it in the same light, and says that it satisfies the terms of the statute, "working or making any manner of new manufacture," because it is a new mode of building houses or ships with a view to a particular effect.[3] But it does not appear that this patent was subjected to litigation. It has been frequently referred to, however, as a valid patent. If it was so, it must have been upon the construction above suggested; under which it was simply a patent for a new

[1] 2 H. Blackst. 495.

[2] The specification (1 Webs. Pat. Cas. 54), was in the following terms: "A particular method of securing buildings and ships against the calamities of fire.

"My invention of a particular method of securing buildings and ships against the calamities of fire is described in the manner following: that is to say, by the application of plates of metal and wire, varnished and unvarnished, to the several parts of buildings and ships, so as to prevent the access of fire and the current of air, securing the several joints by doubling in, overlapping, soldering, riveting, or in any other manner closing them up; nailing, screwing, sewing, or in any other manner fastening the said plates of metal into and about the several parts of buildings and ships, as the case may require."

[3] 1 Webs. Pat. Cas. pp. 55, 56, *note.*

mode of building, and was not of the class of inventions in which a new discovery is made of the application of a force or property of matter never before used for the production of a positive effect, accompanied by some described means of making the application.

§ 132. The next case to be adverted to, after Watt's, is that of Forsyth's patent for a method of discharging cannon, fire-arms, mines, &c., by the application of detonating powder, the invention of which he did not claim. In his specification, he described the manner in which he introduced the detonating powder as priming, by a particular mechanical contrivance, and a mode of causing it to explode by a stroke, or sudden and strong pressure. It is stated by Mr. Webster, that he succeeded in an action of infringement against a party using a lock of a different construction to any shown in the drawing annexed to his patent.[1] Such a verdict must have been rendered upon the ground that this patent, like Hartley's, covered the new application of a known thing to produce a particular effect to which it had never been previously applied. Of the same class is the patent of Hall, for the application of the flame of gas to singe off the superfluous fibres of lace, in the place of a flame of oil or alcohol. This patentee made use of a chimney, above the lace, to create a current of air, which would force the flame of gas through the meshes of the lace; but he disclaimed "the exclusive use of any apparatus or combination of machinery, except in connection with, and in aid of, the application of the flame of inflammable gas to the purposes described." Lord Tenterden directed a verdict for the plaintiff, and it is said that the patentee enjoyed the benefit of his patent during the whole of its term.[2] It does not appear very distinctly how far the verdict depended upon evidence showing the use of the same apparatus as the plaintiff's; but Mr. Webster understands the effect of the case as establishing that the use of gas for singeing lace by any apparatus was within the patent.

§ 133. We now come, however, to a case which presents distinctly the question we are considering. Before the invention of Neilson (1828–29), furnaces for the manufacture of iron, &c., had been worked by a blast of cold air. He discovered that by heating the blast, and introducing it heated into the furnace, a

[1] Forsyth *v.* Riviere, cited 1 Webs. Pat. Cas. p. 97, note from Chit. Prerog. Crown, 182.

[2] Hall *v.* Jervis, 1 Webs. Pat. Cas. 97, 100.

great improvement would be effected in the quality of the manufacture. In other words, he discovered a new application of a natural agent, heated air, by using it as a blast for furnaces. This agent he did not and could not invent. At most, he could only construct an apparatus for heating the air; but he did not take his patent for any particular form of heating apparatus, but he took it for what he denominated "an improved application of air"; which, under the circumstances, was the same as an application of air *improved* by being hot instead of cold. So very general was his description of an apparatus for making the application, that he merely directed heating the air on its passage from the bellows or blowing apparatus, by passing it through a vessel or receptacle artificially heated, and introducing it thence into the furnace. He gave no particular directions as to temperature; left it to workmen to adapt the size of the air-vessel to the temperature desired; and went so far as to declare that "the form or shape of the vessel or receptacle is immaterial to the effect, and may be adapted to the local circumstances or situation. It is obvious that this patent laid claim to the use of air artificially heated between the blowing apparatus and the furnace, in any kind or shape of vessel interposed between those machines, and heated to any degree that would produce the improved effect of using heated air instead of cold. If it was true that the form or shape of the heating vessel was immaterial to the production of *some* effect, namely, the effect produced by blasting with heated air, — and if the specification was rightly to be construed to mean this, so that a workman or builder would understand that all he had to do was to make a vessel that would enable him to give some increased temperature to the air, — then the sole question that would remain would be whether the principle of using heated air as a blast for furnaces was capable of appropriation under a patent, by a party who had described *some* mode by which it could be so used to a beneficial effect.

§ 134. At the trial on this patent before Baron Parke, he construed it as being a claim to "the discovery of heating air in any vessel of any size, provided it is a close vessel, and exposed to heat between the blowing apparatus and the furnace." He did not say that such a patent would in his judgment be valid, if the patentee had not furnished any directions by which a workman of competent skill could apply the new discovery; but being of opinion that the specification contained directions which warranted such an issue, he put it to the jury to find whether a person of ordinary skill and knowledge in the construction of blowing apparatus would be able, from the specification alone, to construct an apparatus that would be productive of some beneficial effect; and he told the jury, if they found this issue affirmatively, the patent was, in his opinion, valid for the claim as he had described it. But being of opinion that the patentee had made an incorrect statement, in saying that the form and size of the heating vessel were immaterial to the effect, — assuming that this meant to the extent of effect, and not to some effect, — he directed the jury to find, upon the evidence before them, whether this statement would mislead a person of ordinary skill and knowledge. The jury found that a person of ordinary skill and knowledge could, from the specification alone, construct an apparatus that would produce some beneficial effect, by using any shape and form of heating vessel, but that the shape and form of the vessel were material to the extent of effect; and they also found that such a person would not be misled by the statement that the form and size of the vessel were immaterial in producing the effect. Thereupon, a verdict was entered for the plaintiff upon issues which assumed that the patent was valid in respect to the application of heated air in any vessel that would produce some beneficial effect; and for the defendant, upon the construction adopted by the court that the statement of the patent meant that form and shape were immaterial to the extent of effect, which the jury found not to be true.

§ 135. In this position, the findings of the jury came before the Court of Exchequer, on leave reserved to the parties to have the verdict entered according to the opinion of the court respecting the construction of the patent. Baron Parke himself pronounced the judgment of the court, in the course of which, speaking of the invention as disclosed by the specification, he said: "It is very difficult to distinguish it [the specification] from the specification of a patent for a principle, and this at first created in the minds of some of the court much difficulty; but after full consideration, we think that the plaintiff does not merely claim a principle, but a machine embodying a principle, and a very valuable one. We think the case must be considered as if the principle being well known [the principle of blowing furnaces with hot air], the plaintiff had first invented a mode of applying it by a mechanical apparatus to furnaces; and his invention then consists in this, — by interposing a receptacle for heated air between the blowing apparatus and the furnace. In this receptacle he directs the air to be heated by the application of heat externally to the receptacle, and thus he accomplishes the object of applying the blast, which was before of cold air, to the furnace." He concurred with the rest of the court in reversing the construction which he had given at the trial to that clause of the specification which stated that the shape and size of the receptacle were immaterial to the effect. It was construed to mean immaterial to the degree of effect; and the jury having found that any shape which a competent workman would be likely to adopt would produce a beneficial effect, the verdict was entered for the plaintiff.[1]

§ 136. It is quite apparent then, *first*, that in speaking of the specification of a patent for a principle, in reference to this case of the hot blast, the court had in view a specification stating in the abstract that the patentee had found out that furnaces could be advantageously worked with a blast of hot air instead of cold air, without describing any particular means of applying or working out this principle. Hence, it is to be inferred that there is a distinction between the principle itself and the application or working out of the principle, in arts or manufactures. The former cannot be the subject of a patent; the latter may be. *Secondly*, the case is an authority to show when and how the application of a principle may be made the subject of a patent; for it ascertains that if the specification discloses, by sufficient and clear directions, some practical means by which persons of competent skill in the art can apply the principle and work it, so as to produce the effect contemplated by the patentee, it discloses a patentable invention, that invention consisting in a machine or other thing embodying the principle; or, stated in the other way, the patentable invention consists in the practical application of the principle. *Thirdly*, the case is an authority to show that when a patent covers the application of a principle, in the above sense, it may be infringed by the use of machinery or apparatus

[1] Neilson *v.* Harford, 1 Webs. Pat. Cas. 273–373. After this judgment, an injunction was revived by Lord Chancellor Cottenham (which had been dissolved by his predecessor, pending an action at law), he holding that the construction given to the patent by the Court of Exchequer was a reasonable one. Ibid. 373.

differing as machinery or apparatus from that described by the patentee, provided it effects a practical application of the same principle embodied by the patentee by means of *his* machinery or apparatus.[1]

§ 137. That this is the correct legal result of this decision is apparent from what took place in the Court of Sessions in Scotland, and in the House of Lords, on the same patent. Neilson held a patent in Scotland, the specification of which was a verbal copy of that enrolled under his English patent. At the trial in Scotland, before Lord Justice Clerk Hope and a jury, the learned judge, with much more amplification, but substantially to the same effect, instructed the jury as Baron Parke had done before him, in respect to the invention which the patent was to be considered to embrace. He made it to consist altogether in the application of the principle of using a hot-air blast for furnaces, &c., by means of any form or size of apparatus in which the air could be heated beneficially on its passage from the blowing machinery to the furnace. The jury found the several issues put to them as follows: "That in respect of the matters proven before them, they find for the pursuer on all the issues; and further find, that by the description in the said specification, the patentee did not refer to any particular form, or shape, or mode of constructing the air-vessel or vessels, or receptacle or receptacles, in which the air under blast is to be heated; and further find, that by the use of the term 'effect' in the specification, the patentee did not state that the form and shape, &c., were immaterial for the purpose of heating the air in such vessel or vessels; and further find, that the terms of the specification respecting the air-vessels or receptacles, and the size and number thereof, are not such as to mislead persons acquainted with the process of heating air, &c.; and they assess the damages at £3,000."

§ 138. When this case came by appeal before the House of

[1] This case of Neilson *v.* Harford underwent great consideration. Four actions were consolidated in the Court of Exchequer, under a rule, and after the judgment in that court a perpetual injunction was granted against the four different defendants. In the case, on the facts of which the trial and judgment proceeded in the Court of Exchequer, the heating receptacle used by the defendants consisted of a coil or series of pipes; whereas the patent described the heating to be effected in "an air vessel, or receptacle," and different cubic contents were stated as suitable for different circumstances; but the specification did not undertake to enumerate all the sizes that would be suitable for all circumstances.

Lords, the whole of the charge to the jury appeared in the record, and was excepted to upon various grounds. The judgment was reversed upon one of these exceptions, which related to a point in the charge not involving the nature and scope of the patent, and it was affirmed upon all the other exceptions, thus affirming the construction and extent given to the patent. In delivering his opinion in the House of Lords, Lord Campbell said: "The other exceptions, till we come to the eleventh, turn upon the construction of the patent. Now, in one stage of these proceedings, I certainly did entertain some doubt on that subject.[1] But after the construction put upon it by the learned judges of the Court of Exchequer, sanctioned by the high authority of my noble and learned friend now upon the woolsack, when presiding in the Court of Chancery, I think the patent must be taken to extend to all machines, of whatever construction, whereby the air is heated intermediately between the blowing apparatus and the blast-furnace. That being so, the learned judge was perfectly justified in telling the jury that it was unnecessary for them to compare one apparatus with another, because, confessedly, that system of conduit pipes was a mode of heating air by an intermediate vessel between the blowing apparatus and the blast-furnace, and therefore it was an infraction of the patent."[2]

[1] His Lordship, while at the bar, had been leading counsel in the defence at the English trial of Neilson *v.* Harford, before Baron Parke, and perhaps alluded here to the views which he had then taken of the patent.

[2] The Househill Company *v.* Neilson, 1 Webs. Pat. Cas. 673–718. I insert here the most material parts of the charge thus sanctioned by Lord Campbell, because it contains a very elaborate statement of the doctrine: —

"It is quite true that a patent cannot be taken out solely for an abstract philosophical principle, — for instance, for any law of nature, or any property of matter, apart from any mode of turning it to account in the practical operations of manufacture, or the business and arts and utilities of life. The mere discovery of such a principle is not an invention, in the patent-law sense of the term. Stating such a principle in a patent may be a promulgation of the principle, but it is no application of the principle to any practical purpose. And without that application of the principle to a practical object and end, and without the application of it to human industry or to the purposes of human enjoyment, a person cannot in the abstract appropriate a principle to himself. But a patent will be good, though the subject of the patent consists in the discovery of a great, general, and most comprehensive principle in science or law of nature, if that principle is by the specification applied to any special purpose, so as thereby to effectuate a practical result and benefit not previously attained.

"The main merit, the most important part of the invention, may consist

§ 139. To the same effect are the observations made by Baron Alderson in a previous case: "You cannot take out a patent for

in the conception of the original idea, in the discovery of the principle in science, or of the law of nature, stated in the patent, and little or no pains may have been taken in working out the best manner and mode of the application of the principle to the purpose set forth in the patent. But still, if the principle is stated to be applicable to any special purpose, so as to produce any result previously unknown, in the way and for the objects described, the patent is good. It is no longer an abstract principle. It comes to be a principle turned to account, to a practical object, and applied to a special result. It becomes, then, not an abstract principle, which means a principle considered apart from any special purpose or practical operation, but the discovery and statement of a principle for a special purpose, that is a practical invention, a mode of carrying a principle into effect. That such is the law, if a well-known principle is applied for the first time to produce a practical result for a special purpose, has never been disputed. It would be very strange and unjust to refuse the same legal effect when the inventor has the additional merit of discovering the principle as well as its application to a practical object. The instant that the principle, although discovered for the first time, is stated, in actual application to, and as the agent of, producing a certain specified effect, it is no longer an abstract principle, it is then clothed with the language of practical application, and receives the impress of tangible direction to the actual business of human life. Is it any objection, then, in the next place, to such a patent that terms descriptive of the application to a certain specified result include every mode of applying the principle or agent so as to produce that specified result, although one mode may not be described more than another, — although one mode may be infinitely better than another, — although much greater benefit would result from the application of the principle by one method than by another, — although one method may be much less expensive than another? Is it, I next inquire, an objection to the patent, that, in its application of a new principle to a certain specified result, it includes every variety of mode of applying the principle according to the general statement of the object and benefit to be attained? You will observe that the greater part of the defenders' case is truly directed to this objection. This is a question of law, and I must tell you distinctly, that this generality of claim, that is, for all modes of applying the principle to the purpose specified, according to or within a general statement of the object to be attained, and of the use to be made of the agent to be so applied, is no objection whatever to the patent. That the application or use of the agent for the purpose specified may be carried out in a great variety of ways, only shows the beauty, and simplicity, and comprehensiveness of the invention. But the scientific and general utility of the proposed application of the principle, if directed to a specified purpose, is not an objection to its becoming the subject of a patent. That the proposed application may be very generally adopted in a great variety of ways is the merit of the invention, not a legal objection to the patent.

"The defenders say, you announce a principle, that hot air will produce

a principle; you may take out a patent for a principle, coupled with the mode of carrying the principle into effect, provided you

heat in the furnace; you direct us to take the blast without interrupting, or rather without stopping it, to take the current in blast, to heat it after it leaves the blast, and to throw it hot into the furnace. But you tell us no more; you do not tell us how we are to heat it. You say, you may heat in any way, in any sort of form of vessel. You say, — I leave you to do it how you best can. But my application of the discovered principle is, that if you heat the air, and heat it after it leaves the blowing engine (for it is plain you cannot do it before), you attain the result I state; that is the purpose to which I apply the principle. The benefit will be greater or less. I only say, benefit you will get, I have disclosed the principle; I so apply it to a specified purpose by a mechanical contrivance, viz., by getting the heat when in blast, after it leaves the furnace; but the mode and manner, and extent of heating, I leave to you, and the degree of benefit, on that very account, I do not state. The defenders say, the patent, on this account, is bad in law. I must tell you, that, taking the patent to be of this general character, it is good in law. I state to you the law to be, that you may obtain a patent for a mode of carrying a principle into effect; and if you suggest and discover, not only the principle, but suggest and invent how it may be applied to a practical result by mechanical contrivance and apparatus, and show that you are aware that no particular sort or modification or form of the apparatus is essential in order to obtain benefit from the principle, then you may take your patent for the mode of carrying it into effect, and are not under the necessity of describing and confining yourself to one form of apparatus. If that were necessary, you see what would be the result? Why, that a patent would hardly ever be obtained for any mode of carrying a newly discovered principle into practical results, though the most valuable of all discoveries. For the best form and shape or modification of apparatus cannot, in matters of such vast range, and requiring observation on such a great scale, be attained at once; and so the thing would become known, and so the right lost, long before all the various kinds of apparatus could be tried. Hence you may generally claim the mode of carrying the principle into effect by mechanical contrivance, so that any sort of apparatus applied in the way stated will, more or less, produce the benefit, and you are not tied down to any form.

"The best illustration I can give you, and I think it right to give you this, is from a case as to the application of that familiar principle, the lever, to the construction of chairs, or what is called the self-adjusting lever. This case, which afterwards came under the consideration of the whole court, was tried in the Court of Exchequer during the presidency of Lord Lyndhurst. The case was as to the patent reclining chair, the luxury of which some of you may have tried; it had a self-adjusting lever, so that a person sitting or reclining, — and I need not tell you what variety can be assumed by a person reclining in a chair, — in whatever situation he placed his back, there was sufficient resistance offered through means of the lever to preserve the equilibrium. Now any thing more general than that I cannot conceive; it was the

have not only discovered the principle, but invented some mode of carrying it into effect. But then you must start with some mode of carrying it into effect; if you have done that, then you are entitled to protect yourself from all other modes of carrying the same principle into effect, that being treated by the jury as piracy of your original invention."[1]

§ 140. It will now be sufficiently apparent what is meant in the English cases by patenting or not patenting a principle; and the question will recur to the reader, does Baron Alderson's language above quoted embrace a correct statement of what is held to be law in England? Of this it would seem there can be no doubt, both from the cases of which an analysis has now been given, and from a much more recent case. A patentee in his specification claimed as his invention exhausting from the cases of mill-stones the dusty air blown between the grinding surfaces by a blast of air, by using a combination of a blast and an exhaust, for the purpose of carrying off the dust which would otherwise be deposited in the meal. A blast had been used before, and an exhaust had been used before; but the combination of the blast and exhaust was new, and productive of great advantages. The claim was not restricted to any particular mode of creating or applying the blast, or the exhaust, but the patentee described a mode of working the exhaust in combination with the blast. The new principle, in this case, was the combined use of a blast and

application of a well-known principle, but for the first time applied to a chair. He made no claim to any particular parts of the chair, nor did he prescribe any precise mode in which they should be made; but what he claimed was a self-adjusting lever to be applied to the back of a chair, where the weight of a seat acts as a counterpoise to the back, in whatever posture the party might be sitting or reclining. Nothing could be more general. Well, a verdict passed for the patentee, with liberty to have it set aside; but Lord Lyndhurst and the rest of the court held, that this was not a claim to a principle, in whatever shape or form it may be constructed. Just so as to the hot blast, only the principle is also new. The patentee says: 'I find hot air will increase the heat in the furnace, that a blast of hot air is beneficial for that end.' Here is the way to attain it. 'Heat the air under blast, between the blowing apparatus and the furnace; if you do that, I care not how you may propose to do it, — I neither propose to you, nor claim any special mode of doing it; you may give the air more or less degrees of heat; but if you so heat it, you will get by that contrivance the benefit I have invented and disclosed, more or less, according to the degree of heat.' This is very simple, very general; but its simplicity is its beauty, and its practical value not an objection in law."

[1] Jupe *v.* Pratt, 1 Webs. Pat. Cas. 146.

an exhaust. The application consisted in working this principle by a described means. The patent was held to be valid, as a patent for the application of the principle, because the patentee had described an application of it, although he did not claim any novelty in the apparatus itself by which he produced either the exhaust or the blast. No attempt appears to have been made to establish a defence by showing that the defendant had used a different apparatus. The infringement turned upon the fact that the defendant had used an exhaust and a blast in combination.'[1]

[1] Bovil *v.* Keyworth, 7 Ell. & Bl. Q. B. 724. As the case is very instructive, I cite a portion of Lord Campbell's judgment relating to the validity of the patent: —

"We are of opinion that the objections to the validity of this patent cannot be supported.

"The whole of the plaintiff's process, if the combination be new, is certainly the subject of a patent; and so would the part No. 2, if taken separately, for 'exhausting the air from the cases of mill-stones, combined with the application of a blast to the grinding surfaces,' as they introduce very important 'improvements in manufacturing wheat and other grain into meal and flour.' The combination of the *exhaust* with the *blast*, so as to carry off the warm dusty air blown through between the stones to a chamber above, while the pure flour, in a dry condition, without the stive, descends into a chamber below, added to the quantity and improved the quality of the flour produced in grinding; and its effect was highly favorable to the health and comfort of the men employed in the operation.

"Still, if the specification does not point out the mode by which this part of the process (No. 2) is to be conducted, so as to accomplish the object in view, it would be the statement of a principle only, and the patent would be invalid. But we are of opinion that the specification, on the face of it, cannot (as contended) be pronounced, in point of law, to be bad in this respect; and we are of opinion that the evidence adduced at the trial shows it to be quite sufficient. The specification says: 'In carrying out the second part of my invention, when working mill-stones with a blast of air, I introduce a pipe to the mill-stone case from a fan or other exhausting machine, so as to carry off all the warm, dusty air blown through between the stones to a chamber, as hereafter described.' 'And this part of my invention relates only to sucking away the plenum of dusty air forced through the stones, and not to employing a sufficient exhausting power to induce a current of air between the mill-stones without a blast.' The *exhaust* produced by the pipe and fan is to be proportioned to the plenum caused by the *blast*, taking care not to produce the inconvenient current of air, against which a caution is given. How can a judge take upon himself to say that this may not be enough to enable a workman of competent skill to construct the machinery? According to the evidence, the specification was abundantly sufficient for this purpose; and, therefore, it could be no more necessary in the specification to explain the details, by which the pipe

§ 141. The next inquiry is, Does the doctrine on which these cases turned appear to have been impaired or changed by any thing that has since taken place in the English courts, under the same or other judges? It is to be observed that this doctrine embraces three requisites for a valid patent that is to comprehend the application of a principle, by means which are different from those used by the patentee. *First*, the principle itself must be new in respect to practical application; for as the principle constitutes the basis of the invention, which invention is the application of the principle to practical uses, novelty in the application is of course essential to such a patent as we are here considering. The principle itself, which may be an element, or truth, or force in nature, when abstracted from practical application, is not within the field of invention, in the sense of the patent law. It is brought within the field of invention by practical application. *Second*, the patentee must have invented and described some mode of carrying the principle into effect. He may or he may not have invented new devices, contrivances, or means, in order to give effect to the application of the principle. He has invented what he is required to invent when he has by any means, new or old, but by the use of means, for the first time given practical application to the principle; and he has described what he is required to describe, when he has shown a practical means of effecting the application. The means itself is in such cases new in its relation to the application of the principle, whether it be in other relations and for other uses new or old. It may, however, be a new device or instrument as to all relations or uses; in which case it may be, as an invention, quite distinct

and fan were to be employed to create and to regulate the *exhaust*, than to describe how the mill-stone case or the stones themselves were to be fashioned. The learned counsel for the defendants, after being familiarly acquainted with the manner in which this part of the process is conducted, being asked to suggest the fit language to be employed to instruct the workman how to adjust the *exhaust* so as properly to suck away the plenum, that the stive may be discharged into the chamber above, were unable to devise any improvement upon the specification.

"Therefore, the plaintiff being now allowed to be the inventor, the jury being, in our opinion, fully justified in finding that the process had not been publicly practised at Glasgow before the date of the patent, and the specification being sufficient, the patent is valid; and we have only to consider whether there has been an actionable infringement."

from the subject-matter which is to be embraced in a patent for the application of the principle, and may be of itself the subject of a distinct patent or claim. *Third*, the means described by the patentee must be so described as to enable competent persons skilled in the art to effect a practical application of the principle, or, in other words, to work or practise the invention. It will be found that in recent English cases, in which this subject of patenting or claiming a principle has been touched upon, the absence of one or more of these requisites has occasioned the difficulty that has attended the patents.

§ 142. Thus in a case tried before Pollock, C. B., in 1855, it appeared that, before the plaintiff's invention, vegetable gas had been made from the oil expressed from seeds and other vegetable matter containing oleaginous substance. The plaintiff discovered that such gas might be made direct from the seeds, &c., omitting the intermediate process of pressing out the oil. In his specification, he stated that his process of making gas from seed, &c., might be carried on by the apparatus ordinarily used for making gas from coal, but he preferred projecting the seed into a hot retort, &c., and gave for exemplification a plan of a retort. He then concluded with the following general claim: "I claim for making gas direct from seeds, and matters herein named, for practical illuminations, or other useful purposes, instead of making it from the oils, resins, or gums previously extracted from such substances." A verdict was found for the defendant, under the ruling of the court that the invention comprised in the patent was not a matter for which letters-patent could by law be granted. On error to the Exchequer Chamber, it was held that this direction was erroneous, and that the making gas directly from seeds and other oleaginous substances, instead of making it from oils, thus dispensing with one or two processes, was a patentable invention, if new. A new trial was therefore ordered.[1]

§ 143. On the second trial, a previous patent was read in the defence, which described a mode of making gas direct from seeds; and thereupon the Chief Baron directed the jury to find a verdict for the defendant, upon the ground that the previous patent had anticipated the plaintiff's discovery of the general principle that gas may be made direct from seeds, and upon the further ground

[1] Booth *v.* Kennard, 1 Hurlstone and Norman, 527.

that the plaintiff's claim, being merely for making gas direct from seeds, &c., without any reference to any method of doing it, was too large and general a claim, and could not be supported.

A rule *nisi* having been obtained, the Chief Baron, in delivering the judgment of the court, said: "It is a claim to make gas direct from seeds, not in any mode pointed out in the specification, but generally. After the publication of Heard's specification, no patent could be taken out for the process generally, though a patent might be taken out for a particular method of doing it. We think the plaintiff's patent was not for any particular method of doing it, but for the doing of it by any method; and we think if even it had been new (which it turns out not to be), such a mode of specifying and claiming the invention cannot be sustained as a good specification."[1]

§ 144. The next case to be examined in this connection was one tried before Lord Campbell in 1857, in which the patentee supposed himself, when he enrolled his specification, to have been the first to invent the application of the principle of centrifugal force in fliers employed in machinery for preparing, slubbing, and roving cotton, &c., for the purpose of producing a pressure upon the bobbin, in order to make a hard and evenly compressed bobbin. He described one mode of applying the centrifugal force to a flier employed in an ordinary roving machine, by written description and drawing, giving the devices he used. He then added: "I do not intend to confine myself to this particular method; but I claim as my invention the application of the law or principle of centrifugal force to the particular or special purpose above set forth; that is, to fliers used in machinery or apparatus for pre-

[1] Booth *v.* Kennard, 2 Hurl. & Norm. 84. Practitioners who have occasion to prepare specifications should take warning from this and other cases of a similar nature, to avoid falling into the error of summing up the claim of invention in such a way as to separate the principle supposed to have been for the first time discovered, from the means of applying the principle. However novel and meritorious the discovery, a specification which fails to describe definitely a means of applying and working the discovery cannot support a general claim for the principle itself; and the cases of Booth, Seed, and Morse, referred to in the text, have a strong tendency to show that, unless the general claim is so stated as to embrace directly or by implication the particular means described for the application of the principle, and all other means which will substantially perform the like office in the application, it will be in danger of failing.

paring, slubbing, or roving cotton and other fibrous materials, for the purpose of producing a hard and evenly compressed bobbin." Minute as this supposed invention was, it was of great practical utility; and had the patentee in fact been the first person to make a practical application of centrifugal force to the machinery and the special purpose referred to, he would have stood in a different position to that which he in fact occupied. It turned out, however, that an earlier patentee had, by a device or system of devices somewhat different in their operation, anticipated the plaintiff in the application of the principle of centrifugal force to this kind of machinery and for this special purpose. The patentee, after discovering this, filed a disclaimer, which, taken in connection with his original specification, was held by the court to have limited his claim to his *one* described means of using the centrifugal force; and the question tried was, whether the defendant had infringed the claim so limited. After a verdict for the plaintiff, the question came before the Court of Queen's Bench, *in banc*, whether the original specification did not claim something so different from that which was described as the subject of invention in the disclaimer, that the patentee had not properly specified his invention. But it was held that this objection was not tenable; that the patent as amended by the disclaimer was good for the plaintiff's one mode of using the centrifugal force, and that the defendant had infringed it.[1] On appeal to the Exchequer Chamber, this construction of the original specification was not disturbed; but it was held unanimously that there was no evidence of infringement which ought to have been left to the jury.[2] On a final appeal to the House of Lords, the judgment of the Exchequer Chamber was unanimously affirmed.[3] Now it will be found, by examining the opinions of the judges of the Exchequer Chamber, and of the Lords who sat in this case on the final appeal, that the evidence, which failed to show an infringement of the patent as narrowed by the disclaimer, would most probably have been held sufficient to establish an infringement, if the original specification had not been so narrowed, or if the proofs affecting the validity of the patent had left the patentee in a position to claim the application of the principle of centrifugal force by various

1 Seed *v.* Higgins, 8 Ell. & Bl. 755.
2 Higgins *v.* Seed, 8 Ell. & Bl. 771.
3 Seed *v.* Higgins, 3 Law Times R., N. S. 101.

means. It is quite true, undoubtedly, that the claim was a very general one, and may have needed amendment, if it had been adhered to, so as to have let in evidence that the means used by the defendant, although differing in form, performed the like office in the application of the principle as the means used and described by the patentee. But without turning aside to consider this, it may be useful on the topic now treated of, to note the observations of some of the judges upon the nature and position of this claim. Thus, Mr. Justice Williams, observing upon the original intention of the patentee to take out a patent for a principle comprehending every possible mode of applying it, said: "Having that intention, in order to comply with the terms on which the patent was granted, of specifying and describing how the work was to be performed, he attaches to his specification drawings showing *one way* of applying the principle to a roving-machine having a flier. . . . That is, he sets out one mode of application, yet wishes to state that his patent consists in applying the principle in any way. Then seeing that his claim is not good, *either as comprehending something not new, or as not explaining sufficiently so general a claim*, he enters a disclaimer." Willes, J., observed: "The patent was originally taken out generally for an application of centrifugal force to the proposed object. The patentee thought that this was his own discovery, *and did not know of Dyer's patent.* Then he discovered that Dyer had previously applied centrifugal force, and therefore that his own patent could not be sustained. Accordingly he lodged a disclaimer, abandoning his original claim except so far as he had described, in his drawing, *a machine* by which the application of centrifugal force could be effected." [1]

Lord Wensleydale said, in the House of Lords: "They" [the scientific witnesses] "prove — and indeed that is evident from the models — that in the plaintiff's machine the centrifugal force operates on a higher plane than the defendant's, and that in that respect the plaintiff's is a better invention than the defendant's. But that shows that the machines operate differently, although they both operate on the finger or presser by centrifugal force, and if the subject of the patent still were *any mode* of applying centrifugal force to the finger or presser, undoubtedly the defendant's machine would have been an infringement. But the disclaimer

[1] 8 Ellis & Bl. 773, 774.

puts an end to that argument; and the patent being for a particular machine only, which clearly operates differently, it seems, I own, to be very clear that one is not a piracy of the other. It is only by confounding the patent *as it was* with the patent *as it is*, that an infringement of the patent can be made out."[1]

§ 145. These citations are sufficient to show that there were two difficulties attending this original claim. *First*, it was not true that the patentee was the first to apply the principle of centrifugal force to the described purpose; he would have failed therefore in an attempt to enforce this claim, for want of the first requisite in a patent which is to lay claim to the new application of a principle. *Second*, his claim was perhaps too general for the purposes of such a claim; because it omitted to state that he claimed the application of the principle by the means he had described, and by all other means which would perform the like office in the application. This addition to it might or might not have brought the particular means of the defendant within the scope of the patent; but it would have been, apparently, the true way in which to have amended it, if the previous patent of Dyer had not stood in the way.

The facts of this case have been specially examined in this connection, because it does not appear that any thing took place in either of the three tribunals impugning the previously settled doctrine that, in certain conditions, there may be a patent for the application of a principle. I shall have occasion hereafter to point out some resemblances between this claim and that of Morse, and to trace the similarity between the inventions of Morse and Neilson. At present it will be worthy of the reader's notice that Neilson's specification did not contain what is technically called a "claim." But this omission does not effect the doctrine that is to govern the patentable extent of such inventions. If Neilson, after describing the nature of his invention, showing how it was to be performed, and stating that its performance was practicable by a great variety of contrivances of which he did not and could not give the shape or dimensions, had proceeded to sum up in a technical claim, he might have incurred the danger of separating his principle from *all* mechanical means, and thus have made it

[1] Seed *v.* Higgins, House of Lords (6 Jur. N. S. 1264); Law Times Reports, N. S. vol. 3, p. 101, 105.

too general. It will be suggested hereafter, that this may have been the error fallen into by Morse, as it probably was Seed's error. But it is also worthy of suggestion, whether a technical claim, that is apparently open to the criticism of being too general and abstract, ought not to be saved by a construction that will relieve it, if the intention of the patentee not to claim the principle abstractly from application by mechanical means can be fairly gathered from the whole specification.[1]

§ 146. We may now turn to the American cases, in order to ascertain whether there is a substantial difference between the English doctrine and our own. One of the first cases in which this subject appears to have been touched upon is that of Stone *v.* Sprague, tried before Mr. Justice Story in 1840. The patentee was the inventor of an improvement in looms, which consisted in communicating motion from the reed to the yarn-beam, and in the connection of one with the other, which was described as produced by a particular machinery; the invention being claimed as follows: "I claim as my invention the connection of the reed with the yarn-beam, and the communication of the motion from the one to the other, *which may be done as above specified.*" It was contended, in the defence, that this was a claim for an abstract principle, or all modes by which motion could be communicated from the reed to the yarn-beam, and therefore that the patent was void. But the court construed it as a patent for an invention limited to the specific machinery and mode of communicating the motion specially described; at the same time intimating a very decided opinion that, if construed to include all other modes of effecting the object, it would be void, as an attempt to maintain a patent for an abstract principle.[2]

[1] It will be readily understood, that, by a *technical claim*, I mean the summary in which, according to the general practice, the patentee states what he intends his patent shall secure to him.

[2] Stone *v.* Sprague, 1 Story, 270. Mr. Justice Story observed: "Upon the question of the true interpretation of the specification, the court entertain some doubt. But on the whole, *ut res magis valeat, quam pereat*, we decide, that, although the language is not without some ambiguity, the true interpretation of it is, that the patentee limits his invention to the specific machinery and mode of communication of the motion from the reel to the yarn-beam, set forth and specially described in the specification. We hold this opinion the more readily, because we are of opinion, that, if it be construed to include all other modes of communication of motion from the reed to the yarn-beam, and

As the observations made by the court in this case are exceedingly pointed, it may be worth while to inquire whether there was not an intermediate view of it that might have been taken. Was it in truth necessary, in order to support this patent, to construe it as limited to the precise method set forth? This would depend, in part, upon the answer to the further inquiry, whether there was no other construction than the one which would drive the patentee to the extreme consequences indicated by the court. It would scarcely seem that this patent was one covering an abstract principle. At least, the report does not sufficiently inform us what was the real novelty of the invention. If the patentee was the first person to discover and *apply* the principle of communicating motion from the reed to the yarn-beam (on which the case does not inform us), and if he described a means of doing it, then his patent did not claim an abstract principle, unless by his claim he had severed the principle from all mechanical means. By an abstract principle, in the sense of the patent law, I understand a law, or rule of action, or physical truth, disconnected from practical application by means necessary to its working. If this patentee had not pointed out, at the close of his claim, as he did, that the principle or rule of communicating motion from the reed to the yarn-beam might be effected in the mode "above specified," he would have been in the situation of claiming an abstraction. But it would seem that, having described a means of applying the principle, and having claimed its application by that means, the question would arise whether the proper scope of his patent did not embrace all analogous means which will perform the like office in applying the principle as *his* means. The learned judge hints at those considerations which we shall presently find have had great influence in the discussion of this subject; for he alludes to the consequence of making the patent

for the connection of the one to the other generally, it is utterly void, as being an attempt to maintain a patent for an abstract principle, or for all possible and probable modes whatever of such communication, although they may be invented by others, and substantially differ from the mode described by the plaintiff in his specification. A man might just as well claim a title to all possible or practicable modes of communicating motion from a steam-engine to a steamboat, although he had invented but one mode; or, indeed, of communicating motion from any one thing to all or any other things, simply because he had invented one mode of communicating motion from one machine to another in a particular case."

embrace other contrivances of future invention by others, and differing substantially from those described by the patentee. But it is to be observed that the question in all cases is, *first*, what is the invention; and, *secondly*, is that invention a patentable subject; and, if the invention really consists in the new application of a principle not before made use of, the future possible contrivances for applying the principle may stand in the relation of equivalents or substitutions, as means of working the invention, although they may in other senses differ substantially from the contrivances used by the patentee. The coil of pipes used by the defendant in Neilson's case was, in one sense, exceedingly unlike the heating vessel or receptacle which a mechanic would see described in his patent; yet, as the invention covered by the patent was held to consist in using air heated in any vessel capable of answering the purpose of producing a hot blast, the pipes, though of subsequent invention, were equivalent or substituted means in respect to the application of the principle.

§ 147. Upon the whole, the case of Stone *v.* Sprague, in respect to the limitation of the claim to the specific devices or contrivances described in the patent, is probably to be regarded as a case in which some one had preceded the plaintiff in communicating the described motion by another means. Without this hypothesis, it is not clear that the extreme alternative construction suggested by the court would be necessary; but the limited construction which confined the patentee to his device, as in the case of Seed *v.* Higgins, *ante*, would upon this hypothesis be the right one.

§ 148. Next in the order of time is the case of Wyeth *v.* Stone, tried before the same judge in the same year. The patent was granted "for a new and useful improvement in the manner of cutting ice, together with the machinery and apparatus therefor." After setting forth two machines, to be used separately or in combination, for the purpose of cutting ice, the patentee summed up his claim as follows: "It is claimed *as new*, to cut ice of a uniform size, by means of an apparatus worked by any other power than human. The invention of this art, as well as of the particular method of the application of the principle, are claimed by the subscriber." It was held that the first clause of this claim had undertaken to cover an art or principle in the abstract, namely, the cutting of ice of a uniform size by means of an apparatus worked by any other power than human; which would render the patent void, unless a disclaimer had been filed in season to save it as a patent for the machines or machine which constituted the particular method embraced by the second clause of the claim.[1] Certainly if it was necessary to construe this as a claim to the invention and appropriation of an art, being the art of cutting ice by any other than human power, it is an indisputable proposition that it covered no possible subject of a patent privilege. But the first clause of this claim was probably mere surplusage, intended only to state that the patentee was the first person who had invented an apparatus for cutting ice of a uniform size, and that it mattered not by what power the apparatus was moved along the ice. The second clause is the one in which the invention resided; and this appeared on the face of the claim to be a particular method of applying what the patentee miscalled an art or principle, it being in truth no art or principle whatever to cut ice by any other than human power. In other words, the patent was a patent for an apparatus to be used in cutting ice, and all beyond that, which did not mislead any one, might have been rejected as surplusage. The case is not one which belongs strictly to the class we are here considering. The patentee neither discovered nor applied any force, or truth, or element in nature, or any law or property of matter, never before discovered and applied to the same purpose. He merely invented a machine capable of doing what had before been done by hand.

§ 149. From this case we pass to that of Foote *v.* Silsby (1849–1853). The plaintiff claimed "the application of the expansive and contracting power of a metallic rod by different degrees of heat, to open and close a damper which governs the admission of air into a stove, in which such rod shall be acted upon directly by the heat of the stove or the fire which it contains." At the trial before Conkling, J., he ruled that this was a claim for the application of a natural property of metals to the purpose set forth, and was not the fit subject of a patent, although the specification described devices by which a metallic rod was to be made to work in the application of the expansive and contractile property by means of variation in the heat of the stove. Mr. Justice Nelson reversed this construction, on a motion for a new trial,

[1] Wyeth *v.* Stone, 1 Story, 273.

and held that the claim was not for a natural property of the metallic rod, but for a new application of it by means of mechanical contrivances; and it appeared on this trial that the patentee was the first to make this application to the regulation of the heat of a stove. The mechanical devices used by the defendant were, however, substantially the same as those of the plaintiff. Upon this the learned judge observed: "I am not sure that the plaintiff was bound to go to this length in making out a case of infringement. There is some ground for the position that the new application of the principle, by means of mechanical contrivances, constitutes of itself a part of his invention, and that any different or improved mode of application is but an improvement upon his discovery, and not available without his consent."[1] But the verdict that was affirmed by the refusal of a new trial rested on the validity of a claim which covered the particular combination only. In this *dictum* we reach, for the first time in any American case, the suggestion of a doctrine which, in reference to cases of this kind, must either be established in or rejected from the patent law. This doctrine treats the application of the principle, by some mechanical means, as being at least a part of the invention and of the subject-matter of the patent; and, as a corollary of this position, it regards a variation of the means, even if an improvement, as still an infringement, if used without the consent of the patentee. The opposite doctrine is that which is maintained by those who contend that the application of a principle in this sense is not capable of appropriation under a patent; that its appropriation can extend only to the application of the principle as effected by the particular means used by the patentee, and by such other means as may turn out to be colorable imitations, mechanical equivalents, or fraudulent evasions, to neither of which categories is a real improvement to be referred. We have seen what the weight of English authority is on this subject; and, having now contrasted the opposite doctrines, we may continue the investigation of the cases in our own courts.

§ 150. The same patent involved in the case of Foote *v.* Silsby subsequently came before the same court in a proceeding in equity, and feigned issues were ordered to try the question of novelty of the general claim, as well as of one other claim which

[1] Foote *v.* Silsby, 1 Blatchf. 445; s. c. 14 Howard, 218.

covered the particular mechanical combination used by the patentee. Mr. Justice Nelson instructed the jury that the general claim for the application of the principle of contraction and expansion in a metallic rod acted upon by the heat of the stove, to open and close a damper for the regulation of the draft, was valid, independently of the particular device used, provided the patentee was the first person to make the application of this principle to this purpose. In giving this instruction the learned judge followed what he understood to be the doctrine of Neilson *v.* Harford, and the interpretation which the present writer had given to that case in his former treatise. The jury found both the issues against the plaintiff, but on a final hearing in equity the court disregarded the findings, and made a decree for the plaintiff. This decree, however, rested on the validity of the claim which covered the particular combination used by the patentee, and not on the general claim for the application of the principle, the novelty of which was, in this proceeding, disproved.[1]

§ 151. This case of Foote *v.* Silsby reached the Supreme Court of the United States, but not in a position to present for revision the doctrine applied on the trial of the issues in respect to the general claim of the patent; and before it came there, Morse's case had been heard and decided. There is a case, however, which preceded Morse's in the Supreme Court, the history of which should now be stated, because it is supposed to have been decided upon the doctrine that governed the latter case, and was relied upon as a precedent by the majority of the court. This was the case of Le Roy *v.* Tatham. The Tathams were the proprietors of a patent for an invention by which lead pipe could be made by being wrought under heat, by pressure and constriction, from set metal, instead of being cast in a mould. It was conceded, substantially, in the specification itself, that the combination of devices used in the process was not new, excepting in their application for the working of a newly discovered property of lead, which consisted in its capacity to reunite, after separation, by being forced through a peculiar aperture, which admitted of pressing the previously separated particles together, provided the

[1] Foote *v.* Silsby, 2 Blatchf. 260; s. c. 20 Howard, 378. It will be seen, by examining the report in 20 Howard, that the basis of the decree in the court below was differently understood by the different judges; a majority, however, affirmed it, reducing the damages.

lead is worked under heat, although in what is called a set state. The employment of this property in the metal, which was a new discovery, made an essential difference in the character of the article manufactured. The patentees stated their claim thus: "We do not claim as our invention and improvement any of the parts of the above described machinery, independently of its arrangement and combination above set forth. What we do claim as our invention, and desire to secure, is the combination of the following parts above described, to wit, the core and bridge, or guide-piece, with the cylinder, the piston, the chamber, and the die, *when used to form pipes of metal, under heat and pressure, in the manner set forth, or in any other manner substantially the same.*"[1]

§ 152. So far as there is any distinction between this invention and Morse's, it consists in the fact that, in Tatham's case, the combination of machinery made use of is admitted to have substantially existed before, and to have been used in the manufacture of pipe, but not in the manner and for the purpose described in the patent; whereas, in Morse's case, the combination of machinery employed by him was his own invention. But in both cases the inventor effected the application and employment of a property of matter never before used for the production of the result at which he aimed; that result, in the one case, being the solid union of the particles of metal which had previously been out of contact; and, in the other, the recording or marking of intelligible signs at long distances. The decision in the case of Tatham turned upon a construction of the claim, by which it was held, contrary to the view of it taken in the Circuit Court, that it covered, not the practical application of the newly discovered property in the metal, but the combination of the machinery in part, putting the novelty of that combination in issue. The judgment below was reversed, because it was held that the novelty of the combination of machinery was, under the specification, a material fact for the jury; and the case was likened to that of Bean *v.* Smallwood (2 Story, 408), which was an application of an old contrivance to a new purpose. It was not denied that the practical application of a newly discovered property of matter is a patentable invention, if effected by a described process sufficiently

[1] Le Roy *v.* Tatham, 14 Howard, 156.

explained to enable an ordinary mechanic to construct and apply the necessary process. But it seems to have been considered by a majority of the judges, that, unless the machinery by which the process was to be worked was novel, the invention amounted only to the application of an old contrivance to a new purpose.[1]

§ 153. The view taken by the minority of the judges of this patent of Tatham's embraces two important topics: *first*, it was considered that, by the true construction of the claim, it did not put in issue the novelty of the combination of machinery made use of, but that it rested the invention on the new application of that machinery to the development and employment of the newly discovered property of the metal in the art of manufacturing lead pipe; *secondly*, it was deemed important to place upon record an assertion of the doctrine that the discovery and practical application of a new principle in the arts may become the subject of a patent, even where the patentee claims no other novelty in the mechanical means used, excepting the novelty which resides in the employment itself of those means for the working of the new principle. This explanation will be sufficient to show the judicial attitude of this subject at the time when the case of O'Reilly *v.* Morse came before the Supreme Court.[2]

[1] See the opinion delivered as that of a majority of the court, by Mr. Justice M'Lean, 14 Howard, 171, *et seq.* That the doctrine which denies patentability to the use of an old contrivance for a new purpose is not universally true, is established by numerous exceptions. In the previous chapters I have endeavored, as far as practicable, to define what are double or analogous uses; and it is quite well settled, that where the new use of an old contrivance or combination practically results in effects new in kind, as by the development and application of a new property of matter, or a new method of working in the arts, there is an invention which, when rightly stated, may be patented. The case of Le Roy *v.* Tatham (14 Howard) resulted unfavorably to the patentees, by a construction of the claim which, if correct, shows that the real invention was not duly described in the claim itself. But in a subsequent proceeding (in equity), this patent again came before the Supreme Court, and appears to have been construed and sustained as a patent for a new *process*, which it undoubtedly was. In coming to this result, the court necessarily discarded the idea that the patented subject consisted in the application of an old contrivance to a new use, which was merely a double use, and they supported the patent upon the ground that, although the machinery might be old, yet its application to the development and employment of a new property of lead made a new and patentable process. See Le Roy *v.* Tatham, 22 Howard, 132.

[2] The dissenting opinion delivered by Nelson, J., in Le Roy *v.* Tatham, and concurred in by Wayne, J., and Grier, J., is in part as follows:—

§ 153 *a.* In the case of Roberts *v.* Dickey, the invention claimed was a method of increasing the productiveness of oil wells by

"The patentees state, that they do not intend to confine themselves to the arrangement of the apparatus thus particularly specified, and point out several other modes by which the same result may be produced, all of which variations would readily suggest themselves, as they observe, to any practical engineer, without departing from the substantial originality of the invention, the remarkable feature of which, they say, is, that lead, when in a set state, being yet under heat, can be made, by extreme pressure, to reunite perfectly around a core after separation, and thus be formed into strong pipes or tubes. Pipes thus made are found to possess great solidity and unusual strength, and a fine uniformity, such as had never before been attained by any other mode. The essential difference in its character, and which distinguishes it from all other heretofore known, they add, is, that it is wrought under heat, by pressure and constriction, from set or solid metal.

"They do not claim, as their invention or improvement, any of the parts of the machinery independently of the arrangement and combination set forth.

"'What we claim as our invention,' they say, 'is the combination of the following parts above described, to wit, the core and bridge or guide-piece, with the cylinder, the piston, the chamber, and die, when used to form pipes of metal under heat and pressure, in the manner set forth, or in any other manner substantially the same.'

"It is supposed that the patentees claim, as the novelty of their invention, the arrangement and combination of the machinery which they have described, disconnected from the employment of the new property of lead, which they have discovered, and by the practical application and use of which they have succeeded in producing the new manufacture. And the general title or description of their invention, given in the body of their letters-patent, is referred to as evidence of such claim. But every patent, whatever may be the general heading or title by which the invention is designated, refers to the specification annexed for a more particular description; and hence this court has heretofore determined that the specification constitutes a part of the patent, and that they must be construed together when seeking to ascertain the discovery claimed. Hogg *et al.* *v.* Emerson, 6 How. 437.

"The same rule of construction was applied by the Court of Exchequer, in England, in the case of Neilson's patent for the hot-air blast. Webster's Cases, 373.

"Now, on looking into the specification, we see that the leading feature of the invention consists in the discovery of a new property in the article of lead, and in the employment and adaptation of it, by means of the machinery described, to the production of a new article, wrought pipe, never before successfully made. Without the discovery of this new property in the metal, the machinery and apparatus would be useless, and not the subject of a patent. It is in connection with this property and the embodiment and adaptation of it to practical use, that the machinery is described, and the arrangement

causing an explosion of gunpowder in the particular manner described. This invention was based upon the geological knowl-

claimed. The discovery of this new element or property led naturally to the apparatus, by which a new and most useful result is produced. The apparatus was but incidental, and subsidiary to the new and leading idea of the invention. And hence, the patentees set forth, as the leading feature of it, the discovery that lead, in a solid state, but under heat and extreme pressure in a close vessel, will reunite, after separation of its parts, as completely as though it had never been separated. It required very little ingenuity, after the experiments in a close vessel, by which this new property of the metal was first developed, to construct the necessary machinery for the formation of the pipe. The apparatus, essential to develop this property, would at once suggest the material parts, especially in the state of the art at the time. Any skilful mechanic, with Burr's machine before him, would readily construct the requisite machinery.

"The patentees, therefore, after describing their discovery of this property of lead, and the apparatus by means of which they apply the metal to the manufacture of pipe, claim the combination of the machinery only when used to form pipes under heat and pressure, in the manner set forth, or in any other manner substantially the same. They do not claim it as new separately, or when used for any other purpose, or in any other way; but claim it only when applied for the purpose and in the way pointed out in the specification. The combination, as machinery, may be old; may have been long used; of itself, what no one could claim as his invention, and may not be the subject of a patent. What is claimed is, that it never had been before applied or used in the way and for the purpose they have used and applied it, namely, in the embodiment and adaptation of a newly discovered property in lead, by means of which they are enabled to produce a new manufacture, wrought pipe, out of a mass of solid lead. Burr had attempted it, but failed. These patentees, after the lapse of seventeen years, having discovered this new property in the metal, succeeded by the use and employment of it, and since then none other than wrought lead pipe, made out of solid lead, has been found in the market, having superseded, on account of its superior quality and cheapness, all other modes of manufacture.

"Now the construction, which I understand a majority of my brethren are inclined to give to this patent, namely, that the patentees claim, as the originality of their invention, simply the combination of the machinery employed, with great deference, seems to me contrary to the fair and reasonable import of the language of the specification, and also of the summary of the claim. The tendency of modern discoveries is to construe specifications benignly, and to look through mere forms of expression, often inartificially used, to the substance, and to maintain the right of the patentee to the thing really invented, if ascertainable upon a liberal consideration of the language of the specification, when taken together. For this purpose, phrases, standing alone, are not to be singled out, but the whole are to be taken in connection. 1 Sumner, 482–485.

"Baron Parke observed, in delivering the opinion of the court in Neilson's

edge that petroleum, or other oil taken from oil wells, was contained in seams or crevices, usually in the second or third strata

patent, "that half a century ago, or even less, — within fifteen or twenty years, — there seems to have been very much a practice with both judges and juries to destroy the patent right, even of beneficial patents, by exercising great astuteness in taking objections, either as to the title of the patent, but more particularly as to the specifications, and many valuable patent rights have been destroyed in consequence of the objections so taken. Within the last ten years or more, the courts have not been so strict in taking objections to the specifications, and they have endeavored to hold a fair hand between the patentee and the public, willing to give the patentee the reward of his patent.'

"Construing the patent before us in this spirit, I cannot but think that the thing really discovered, and intended to be described, and claimed by these patentees, cannot well be mistaken. That they did not suppose the novelty of their invention consisted simply in the arrangement of the machinery described, is manifest. They state, distinctly, that the leading feature of their discovery consisted of this new property of lead, and some of its alloys; this, they say, is the remarkable feature of their invention; and the apparatus described is regarded by them as subordinate, and as important only as enabling them to give practical effect to this newly discovered property, by means of which they produce the new manufacture. If they have failed to describe and claim this, as belonging to their invention, it is manifest, upon the face of their specification, that they have failed to employ the proper words to describe and claim what they intended; and that the very case is presented, in which, if the court, in the language of Baron Parke, will endeavor to hold a fair hand between the patentee and the public, it will look through the forms of expression used, and discover, if it can, the thing really invented. Apply to the specification this rule of construction, and all difficulty at once disappears. The thing invented, and intended to be claimed, is too apparent to be mistaken.

"The patentees have certainly been unfortunate in the language of the specification, if, upon a fair and liberal interpretation, they have claimed only the simple apparatus employed; when they have not only set forth the discovery of this property in the metal, as the great feature in their invention, but, as is manifest, without it the apparatus would have been useless. Strike out this new property from their description and from their claim, and nothing valuable is left. All the rest would be worthless. This lies at the foundation upon which the great merit of the invention rests, and without a knowledge of which the new manufacture could not have been produced; and, for aught we know, the world would have been deprived of it down to this day.

"If the patentees had claimed the combination of the core and bridge or guide-piece, with the cylinder, the chambers, and the die, and stopped there, I admit the construction, now adopted by a majority of my brethren, could not be denied; although, even then, it would be obvious, from an examination of the specification as a whole, that the draughtsman had mistaken the thing

of sandstone, or other rock abounding in the oil regions; and that these seams, being of different dimensions and irregularly located,

really invented, and substituted in its place matters simply incidental, and of comparative insignificance. But the language of the claim does not stop here. The combination of these parts is claimed only when used to form pipes of lead, under heat and pressure, in the manner set forth, that is, when used for the embodiment and adaptation of this new property in the metal for making wrought pipe out of a solid mass of lead. This guarded limitation of the use excludes the idea of a claim to the combination for any other, and ties it down to the instance when the use incorporates within it the new idea or element which gives to it its value, and by means of which the new manufacture is produced. How, then, can it be consistently held, that here is a simple claim to the machinery and nothing more, when a reasonable interpretation of the words not only necessarily excludes any such claim, but in express terms sets forth a different one, — one not only different in the conception of the invention, but different in the practical working of the apparatus, to accomplish the purpose intended?

"I conclude, therefore, that the claim, in this case, is not simply for the apparatus employed by the patentees, but for the embodiment or employment of the newly discovered property in the metal, and the practical adaptation of it, by these means, to the production of a new result, namely, the manufacture of wrought pipe out of solid lead.

"Then is this the proper subject-matter of a patent?

"This question was first largely discussed by counsel and court in the celebrated case of Boulton *v.* Bull, 2 H. Black. 463, involving the validity of Watt's patent, which was for 'a new invented method for lessening the consumption of fuel and steam in fire-engines.' This was effected by enclosing the steam vessel or cylinder with wood or other material, which preserved the heat in the steam vessel, and by condensing the steam in separate vessels. It was admitted, on the argument, that there was no new mechanical construction invented by Watt, and the validity of the patent was placed on the ground that it was for well-known principles, practically applied, producing a new and useful result. On the other hand, it was conceded, that the application of the principles in the manner described was new, and produced the result claimed; but it was denied that this constituted the subject-matter of a patent. Heath and Buller, Justices, agreed with the counsel for the defendant. But Lord Chief Justice Eyre laid down the true doctrine, and which, I think, will be seen to be the admitted doctrine of the courts of England at this day. 'Undoubtedly,' he observed, 'there can be no patent for a mere principle; but for a principle, so far embodied and connected with corporeal substances as to be in a condition to act, and to produce effects in any art, trade, mystery, or manual occupation, I think there may be a patent. Now this,' he continues, 'is, in my judgment, the thing for which the patent stated in the case was granted; and this is what the specification describes, though it miscalls it a principle. It is not that the patentee conceived an abstract notion that the consumption of steam in fire-engines may be lessened, but he has dis-

were frequently not penetrated by the wells made for this purpose, which circumstance materially affected the supply of oil. Modes

covered a practical manner of doing it; and for that practical manner of doing it he has taken this patent. Surely,' he observes, 'this is a very different thing from taking a patent for a principle. The apparatus, as we have said, was not new. There is no new mechanical construction, said the counsel for the patentee, invented by Watt, capable of being the subject of a distinct specification ; but his discovery was of a principle, the method of applying which is clearly set forth.' Chief Justice Eyre admitted that the means used were not new, and that, if the patent had been taken out for the mechanism used, it must fail.

"He observed: 'When the effect produced is some new substance or composition of things, it should seem that the privilege of the sole working or making ought to be for such new substances or composition, without regard to the mechanism or process by which it has been produced, which, though perhaps also new, will be only useful as producing the new substance.' Again: 'When the effect produced is no new substance or composition of things, the patent can only be for the mechanism, if new mechanism is used; or for the process, if it be a new method of operating, with or without old mechanism, by which the effect is produced.' And again he observes: 'If we wanted an illustration of the possible merit of a new method of operating with old machinery, we might look to the identical case before the court.' Pages 493, 495, 496.

"This doctrine, in expounding the law of patents, was announced in 1795; and the subsequent adoption of it by the English courts shows that Chief Justice Eyre was considerably in advance of his associates upon this branch of the law. He had got rid, at an early day, of the prejudice against patents so feelingly referred to by Baron Parke in Neilson *v.* Harford, and comprehended the great advantages to his country if properly encouraged. He observed, in another part of his opinion, that 'the advantages to the public from improvements of this kind are beyond all calculation important to a commercial country; and the ingenuity of artists, who turn their thoughts towards such improvements, is, in itself, deserving of encouragement.'

"This doctrine was recognized by the Court of King's Bench in the King *v.* Wheeler, 2 B. & Ald. 350.

"It is there observed, that the word 'manufacturers,' in the Patent Act, may be extended to a mere process to be carried on by known implements or elements, acting upon known substances, and ultimately producing some other known substance, but producing it in a cheaper or more expeditious manner, or of a better or more useful kind.

"Now, if this process to be carried on by known implements acting upon known substances, and ultimately producing some other known substance of a better kind, is patentable, *à fortiori*, will it be patentable, if it ultimately produces not some other known substance, but an entirely new and useful substance?

"In Forsyth's patent, which consists of the application and use of detonat-

of overcoming this difficulty had been used, but with only partial success. The improvement of the patentee was to fracture the

ing powder as priming for the discharge of fire-arms, it was held that whatever might be the construction of the lock or contrivance by which the powder was to be discharged, the use of the detonating mixture as priming, which article of itself was not new, was an infringement. Webs. Pat. Cas. 94, 97 (*n*); Curtis on Pat. 230.

"This case is founded upon a doctrine which has been recognized in several subsequent cases in England, namely, that where a person discovers a principle or property of nature, or where he conceives of a new application of a well-known principle or property of nature, and also of some mode of carrying it out into practice, so as to produce or attain a new and useful effect or result, he is entitled to protection against all other modes of carrying the same principle or property into practice for obtaining the same effect or result.

"The novelty of the conception consists in the discovery and application in the one case, and of the application in the other, by which a new product in the arts or manufactures is the effect; and the question, in case of an infringement, is as to the substantial identity of the principle or property, and of the application of the same, and consequently the means or machinery made use of, material only so far as they effect the identity of the application.

"In the case of Jupe's patent for 'an improved expanding table,' Baron Alderson observed, speaking of this doctrine: 'You cannot take out a patent for a principle; you may take out a patent for a principle coupled with the mode of carrying the principle into effect. But then, you must start with having invented some mode of carrying the principle into effect; if you have done that, then you are entitled to protect yourself from all other modes of carrying the same principle into effect, that being treated by the jury as piracy of your original invention.' Webs. Pat. Cas. 146. The same doctrine was maintained also in the case of Neilson's patent for the hot-air blast, in the K. B. and Exchequer in England. Webs. Pat. Cas. 342, 371; Curtis, §§ 74, 148, 232; Webs. Pat. Cas. 310.

"This patent came also before the Court of Sessions in Scotland; and in submitting the case to the jury, the Lord Justice remarked: 'That the main merit, the most important part of the invention, may consist in the conception of the original idea, — in the discovery of the principle in science, or of the law of nature, stated in the patent; and little or no pains may have been taken in working out the best mode of the application of the principle to the purpose set forth in the patent. But still, if the principle is stated to be applicable to any special purpose, so as to produce any result previously unknown, in the way and for the objects described, the patent is good. It is no longer an abstract principle. It becomes to be a principle turned to account to a practical object, and applied to a special result. It becomes, then, not an abstract principle, which means a principle considered apart from any special purpose or practical operation, but the discovery and statement of a principle for a special purpose, that is, a practical invention, a mode of carrying a principle into effect. That such is the law,' he observes, 'if a well-known principle is

oil-bearing rock in proximity to the bore of the well, and for some distance around it, thus making artificial passages into seams or

applied for the first time to produce a practical result for a special purpose, has never been disputed; and it would be very strange and unjust to refuse the same legal effect when the inventor has the additional merit of discovering the principle as well as its application to a practical object.'

"Then he observes, again: 'Is it an objection to the patent, that, in its application of a new principle to a certain specified result, it includes every variety of mode of applying the principle according to the general statement of the object and benefit to be obtained? This,' he observes, 'is a question of law; and I must tell you distinctly that this generality of claim, that is, for all modes of applying the principle to the purpose specified, according to or within a general statement of the object to be attained, and of the use to be made of the agent to be so applied, is no objection to the patent. The application or use of the agent for the purpose specified may be carried out in a great variety of ways, and only shows the beauty and simplicity and comprehensiveness of the invention.'

"This case was carried up to the House of Lords on exceptions to the charge, and, among others, to this part of it, which was the sixth exception, and is as follows: 'In so far as he (the judge) did not direct the jury, that, on the construction of the patent and specification, the patentee cannot claim or maintain that his patent is one which applies to all the varieties in the apparatus which may be employed in heating air while under blast; but was limited to the particular described in the specification.' And, although the judgment of the court was reversed in the House of Lords on the eleventh exception, it was expressly affirmed as respects this one. Lord Campbell at first doubted, but, after the decision of the courts in England on this patent, he admitted that the instruction was right. Webs. Pat. Cas. 683, 684, 698, 717.

"I shall not pursue a reference to the authorities on this subject any further. The settled doctrine to be deduced from them, I think, is, that a person having discovered the application for the first time of a well-known law of nature, or well-known property of matter, by means of which a new result in the arts or in manufactures is produced, and has pointed out a mode by which it is produced, is entitled to a patent; and if he has not tied himself down in the specification to the particular mode described, he is entitled to be protected against all modes by which the same result is produced, by an application of the same law of nature or property of matter. And, *à fortiori*, if he has discovered the law of nature or property of matter, and applied it, is he entitled to the patent and aforesaid protection?

"And why should not this be the law? The original conception, — the novel idea in the one case is the new application of the principle or property of matter, and the new product in the arts or manufactures, — in the other, in the discovery of the principle or property, and application, with like result. The mode or means are but incidental, and flowing naturally from the original conception; and hence of inconsiderable merit. But it is said this is patenting a principle, or element of nature. The authorities to which I have referred

crevices containing oil, which, without such passages, would not communicate with the well, and also enlarging existing apertures

answer the objection. It was answered by Chief Justice Eyre, in the case of Watt's patent, in 1795, fifty-seven years ago; and more recently in still more explicit and authoritative terms. And what if the principle is incorporated in the invention, and the inventor protected in the enjoyment for the fourteen years? He is protected only in the enjoyment of the application for the special purpose and object to which it has been newly applied by his genius and skill. For every other purpose and end, the principle is free for all mankind to use. And, where it has been discovered as well as applied to this one purpose, and open to the world as to every other, the ground of complaint is certainly not very obvious. Undoubtedly, within the range of the purpose and object for which the principle has been for the first time applied, piracies are interfered with during the fourteen years. But anybody may take it up and give to it any other application to the enlargement of the arts and of manufactures, without restriction. He is only debarred from the use of the new application for the limited time, which the genius of others has already invented and put into successful practice. The protection does not go beyond the thing which, for the first time, has been discovered and brought into practical use, and is no broader than that extended to every other discoverer or inventor of a new art or manufacture.

"I own I am incapable of comprehending the detriment to the improvements in the country that may flow from this sort of protection to inventors.

"To hold, in the case of inventions of this character, that the novelty must consist of the mode or means of the new application producing the new result, would be holding against the facts of the case, as no one can but see that the original conception reaches far beyond these. It would be mistaking the skill of the mechanic for the genius of the inventor.

"Upon this doctrine, some of the most brilliant and useful inventions of the day, by men justly regarded as public benefactors, and whose names reflect honor upon their country, — the successful application of steam power to the propulsion of vessels and railroad cars, the application of the electric current for the instant communication of intelligence from one extremity of the country to the other, and the more recent but equally brilliant conception, the propulsion of vessels by the application of the expansibility of heated air, the air supplied from the atmosphere that surrounds them. It will be found, on consulting the system of laws established for their encouragement and protection, that the world had altogether mistaken the merit of their discovery; that, instead of the originality and brilliancy of the conception that had been unwittingly attributed to them, the whole of it consisted of some simple mechanical contrivances which a mechanician of ordinary skill could readily have devised. Even Franklin, if he had turned the lightning to account, in order to protect himself from piracies, must have patented the kite, and the thread, and the key, as his great original conception, which gave him a name throughout Europe, as well as at home, for bringing down this element from the heavens, and subjecting it to the service of man. And if these simple

into oil deposits, or clearing such apertures when they had become clogged. The method devised for accomplishing these objects was to sink into the well to the desired position a water-tight flask containing gunpowder or other powerful explosive material, then to fill the well with water and cause an explosion of the powder in the flask, which would open communication between the well and the oil-bearing crevices. "It has been further urged," said Mr. Justice Strong, "that all Roberts discovered was that the seams or rifts in oil-bearing rock would, if opened by a blast, yield oil, and that this was merely a discovery of a law of nature, a geological truth, and not the invention of a new art or manufacture. If this were all, doubtless it would not have been patentable. But it was not all. He devised a mode of turning to practical account this geological truth; and if the means thus devised were novel, if the process was the product of invention and was useful, it was a proper subject for a patent."

This combination, therefore, of instrumentalities before known to produce a new and useful result, was held to be patentable as an art.[1]

contrivances, taken together, and disconnected from the control and use of the element by which the new application and new and useful result may have been produced, happened to be old and well known, his patent would be void; or, if some follower in the track of genius, with just intellect enough to make a different mechanical device or contrivance, for the same control and application of the element, and produce the same result, he would, under this view of the patent law, entitle himself to the full enjoyment of the fruits of Franklin's discovery.

"If I rightly comprehend the ground upon which a majority of my brethren have placed the decision, they do not intend to controvert so much the doctrine which I have endeavored to maintain, and which, I think, rests upon settled authority, as the application of it to the particular case. They suppose that the patentees have claimed only the combination of the different parts of the machinery described in their specification, and therefore are tied down to the maintenance of that as the novelty of their invention. I have endeavored to show that this is a mistaken interpretation; and that they claim the combination only when used to embody and give a practical application to the newly discovered property in the lead, by means of which a new manufacture is produced, namely, wrought pipe out of a solid mass of lead; which, it is conceded, was never before successfully accomplished.

"For these reasons, I am constrained to differ with the judgment they have arrived at, and am in favor of affirming that of the court below."

[1] Roberts *v.* Dickey (1871), 4 Fisher's Pat. Cas. 532. "It was insisted in the argument," said Mr. Justice Strong, "that the claim of the patentee

§ 153 *b*. In the case of Piper *v*. Brown, decided in the Circuit Court for the District of Massachusetts in 1870, the invention consisted in a *method* of preserving fish and other articles by placing them within a chamber and cooling the latter by means of a freezing mixture so applied that no communication should exist between the interior of the preserving chamber and that of the vessels in which the freezing mixture was placed. The inventor did not claim to have invented the means of producing artificial congelation, or to have discovered the fact that no decay takes place in animal substances, so long as they are kept a few degrees below the freezing point of water. But his claim was for the practical application of these to the art of preserving fish and meats, and he described the apparatus for effecting successfully the objects of his invention. The court held this to be a new and valuable improvement, and patentable as an "art."[1]

is for that which is known and denominated as a double use, and it was urged that if Roberts was the first to use torpedoes in oil wells with success, it was only obtaining a different fluid from what had been obtained before by the same means. This argument proceeds under a misapprehension of the subject of the patent. It would be of weight, were the invention claimed only the application of an old and known process to a new use. But that is not what was patented. It has already been seen that the invention claimed is not the employment of explosive materials as a mechanical force, nor is it enclosing such materials in flasks of specified forms, or any particular mode of merely producing an explosion. Nor is it simply causing an explosion in a well or under water. Nor is it a result, — obtaining oil. It is doing these things under peculiar and novel arrangements. It is a process of which some or all these things are a part, instruments or agencies in the process. Until then, it is shown that the process, as described in the specification, was known as a process before this patent was issued, and that it had been applied in the same way to some use cognate to that to which this patent applied it, the argument of the defendant that the claim is only for a new use of an old thing, or, in other words, for a double use, must fail. It is an incorrect view of the patent to consider it as an attempt to secure the exclusive use of a well-known mechanical force operating in the usual manner, and applied by familiar mechanical devices, for a purpose existing in the mind of the operator, in the same way in which it had been applied for other purposes by other operators."

[1] 4 Fisher's Pat. Cas. 175. In delivering the judgment of the court, Judge Shepley said: "It is not that the patentee claims to have discovered the fact that no decay takes place in animal tissues, as long as they are kept a few degrees below the freezing point of water, nor does he claim to have invented any means of producing artificial congelation. The active agent for producing congelation, and the effect of congelation on animal substances, was

§ 154. To the case of O'Reilly *v.* Morse, therefore, we may now return; and there can be no doubt that it presented most of the important features involved in this much-controverted doctrine. *First*, it appeared on the evidence that Morse was the first person to make use of a current of the electro-magnetic fluid, as a moving force, to cause the vibration of an instrument suspended at the extremity of a long wire, for the purpose of recording or making intelligible signs or sounds. *Secondly*, that he had constructed, and described in his specification, an elaborate combination of machinery, by which the electro-magnetic fluid could be so used. *Thirdly*, that he not only claimed this machinery as a new invention, but that he also sought to claim the principle of using the motive power of the electro-magnetic fluid for this particular purpose generally. It was ascertained by the facts of the case that he had made a new application of the power which he employed; but a majority of the judges held that his general claim was void, because it was too sweeping and comprehensive.[1]

§ 155. The principal ground on which this decision was reached appears to have been that the eighth claim of the patent was virtually a claim for an abstraction; that to hold it valid it would be

well known. But he claims that he was the first to discover and reduce to practice an art of producing and continuing this artificial congelation upon animal substances, enclosed in a chamber with non-conducting walls, which chamber was a close chamber, that is, having no communication with the outer or surrounding atmosphere, and so constructed also that no communication shall exist between the interior of the preserving chamber and that of the vessels in which the freezing mixture is placed. This claim is not limited to a method of supplying and renewing the frigorific mixture without exposing the animal substances in the preserving chamber, and the atmosphere itself in the preserving chamber to change of temperature from contact with the outer atmosphere, while the active agent of congelation — the frigorific mixture — is being supplied. It proceeds upon the further and broader ground that an injurious effect upon the animal substances to be preserved results from the presence in the preserving chamber itself, of the salt and ice, or other freezing mixture, affecting the atmosphere of the preserving chamber. The patentee proposes to preserve animal substances in an atmosphere not materially affected by the temperature of the external atmosphere surrounding the chamber, because the atmosphere in which the animal substances are placed is confined by non-conducting walls in a *close* chamber, and what is more important in an atmosphere 'freezing,' because reduced to a low temperature by contact with the exteriors of the pipes containing the frigorific mixtures, and 'dry' because free from contact with the freezing mixture itself."

[1] O'Reilly *v.* Morse, 15 Howard, 62.

necessary to say that no specification of the means by which the patentee effected the use of the motive power was necessary, and that he had only to announce that by using that motive power he could print or mark intelligible characters or sounds at a distance. We have already seen that when the summary of a patent appears to have separated the principle of employing a natural agent for a new purpose from all means of giving it that employment, it becomes an abstraction, and is not within the scope of the patent law either in England or in this country. But we have also seen that, when to a claim of a discovery of this kind there is added a practical mode of effecting what is proposed, the question wears a different aspect. If the general claim of Morse's patent, fairly construed, separated the use of the galvanic fluid from all mechanical means of using it, it was clearly void. A minority of the judges strongly questioned the propriety of this construction, and pointed out, from other parts of his specification, that Morse had described a recording or printing telegraphic machinery, and that the use which he claimed of the motive power of the galvanic fluid was a use in a printing or recording telegraph. This characteristic of his invention, they said, should be taken into view in construing the claim in controversy; and, if taken into view, and if the fact is added that he described an appropriate apparatus to be used for this purpose, they held that the claim does not result in an abstraction.

§ 156. Another ground relied upon by the majority of the court consisted in a denial that Neilson's case, as decided in the Court of Exchequer, covered the case of Morse's claim. It is somewhat difficult to see that Neilson's claim, as allowed by the Court of Exchequer, was valid if Morse's claim was void; and if we take Mr. Chief Justice Taney's statement of the decision in Neilson's case, it leads to the same result in Morse's. In Neilson's case (to use the words of the Chief Justice in delivering the opinion of the Supreme Court upon Morse's claim), "it was finally decided that this principle [that hot air would promote the ignition of fuel better than cold] must be regarded as well known, and that the plaintiff had invented a mechanical mode of applying it to furnaces; and that his invention consisted in interposing a heated receptacle between the blower and the furnace, and by this means heating the air after it left the blower and before it was thrown into the fire. Whoever, therefore, used this method of throwing hot air into the furnace, used the process he had invented, and thereby infringed his patent, although the form of the receptacle or the mechanical arrangements for heating it might be different from those described by the patentee. For, whatever form was adopted for the receptacle, or whatever mechanical arrangements were made for heating it, the effect would be produced in a greater or less degree if the heated receptacle was placed between the blower and the furnace, and the current of air passed through it."[1] In like manner, *mutatis mutandis*, similar conditions are predicable of Morse's invention. The principle or truth, that the electro-magnetic fluid is a moving force, may, for the purposes of adjudicating a question of its appropriation under a patent, be assumed as known. The machinery then consists in connecting a galvanic battery, from which the fluid is to be generated, by means of a wire of indefinite length, with a recording instrument that is to be moved by that force. By this means the force is to be made to act upon the recording instrument. To this is added a contrivance for closing and breaking the circuit, in order that the force may not act continuously. Within the limits of these conditions, whatever form was adopted for the mechanical arrangements used, the effect of moving the recording instrument at the required intervals for marking intelligible characters or sounds would be produced. Although it is true that Morse had not discovered that the electric or galvanic current will always print at a distance under all conditions, he had discovered that under certain conditions it will do so; and the real inquiry was, whether he could not by a patent appropriate those conditions and all the variations of mechanical arrangements which are within those conditions. Just as in Neilson's case the discovery was that, under certain conditions, namely, of the interposition of a heating vessel of any form or size that would raise the temperature of the blast on its passage through that vessel, the effect of using a hot blast could be produced, and consequently his method could be used.

§ 157. Finally, the objection was much relied upon by the majority of the Supreme Court, that to allow this claim of Morse's as valid would be to stop the progress of invention. This objection deserves to be quoted in the words of the Chief Justice. "For aught that we now know, some future inventor, in the

[1] 15 Howard, 116.

onward march of science, may discover a mode of writing or printing at a distance by means of the electric or galvanic current, without using any part of the process or combination set forth in the plaintiff's specification. His invention may be less complicated, less liable to get out of order, less expensive in construction and in its operation. But yet, if it is covered by this patent, the inventor could not use it, nor the public have the benefit of it, without the permission of this patentee. Nor is this all: while he shuts the door against the inventions of other persons, the patentee would be able to avail himself of new discoveries in the properties and powers of electro-magnetism which scientific men might bring to light. For he says he does not confine himself to the machinery or parts of machinery which he specifies, but claims for himself a monopoly in its use, however developed, for the purpose of printing at a distance. New discoveries in physical science may enable him to combine it with new agents and new elements, and by that means attain the object in a manner superior to the present process, and altogether different from it. And if he can secure the exclusive use by his present patent, he may vary it with every new discovery and development of the science, and need place no description of the new manner, process, or machinery upon the records of the Patent Office. And when his patent expires, the public must apply to him to learn what it is. In fine, he claims an exclusive right to use a manner and process which he has not described, and, indeed, had not invented, and therefore could not describe when he obtained his patent. The court is of opinion that the claim is too broad, and not warranted by law."[1]

§ 158. Upon this it may be observed, *First*, that if the claim was rightfully to be construed as grasping at every improvement where the use of electro-magnetism is the moving force and the result is the marking of intelligible characters or signs, it would certainly be too broad and general. But if the claim, when compared with the scope of what the patentee established as his invention, should be construed as embracing the new application of the power which he had developed and described, and that application involved certain conditions, his pretensions did not go beyond, although they embraced all that might be within, those

[1] 15 Howard, 113.

conditions. *Secondly*, when the real subject and scope of any patented invention is ascertained, the author of any subsequent improvement may use it, if it is outside of that subject and scope of the patented invention, without the consent of the patentee, otherwise he may not. It has not yet appeared that this rule is to be varied when the patented invention is the new application of some principle which may be applied by various mechanical contrivances, any more than when the patented invention is restricted to narrower limits by being a particular device. No patent closes the progress of invention. It merely appropriates for a time what the patentee has invented to the extent to which the invention can be made the subject of a patent. Within those limits, he who makes an improvement is still subject to the claims of the prior inventor, although as an improvement his invention may be itself patentable. A mechanism may be an improvement upon the particular mechanism used by the prior patentee; but if that prior patentee has rights which extend to the application of a principle independently of the particular means by which the application is effected, the fact that the means are improved may not change at all that which is the real subject of the prior patent. *Thirdly*, the fact that the patentee has not described or invented all the means by which the same application of his newly discovered principle may be made, is, as we have seen from the English authorities, no answer to his claim for the application of the principle, if he can show that he has effected it by some means. When he has shown this, he has established the conditions which mark the patentable extent of his invention; and the inquiry must then be whether the future improvements which he has not described or invented are within or without those conditions.

§ 159. These are some of the chief considerations which will require attention when this subject again comes fully under judicial consideration. At present, however, it remains for me to state what I understand to be the judicial effect of the decision in O'Reilly *v.* Morse. It is commonly supposed to have been a decision establishing that a patent cannot extend to the application of a newly discovered truth in physics, or the operation of a newly discovered element or property of matter by mechanical or other means that are so different from those used by the patentee as not to be equivalent and obvious substitutions or fraudulent evasions in relation to the particular means used by the patentee. But in truth the decision turned entirely upon a view taken of the general claim, which gave it an extent that divested it of all conditions and made it an abstraction. "It is impossible," said the learned Chief Justice, "to misunderstand the extent of this claim. He claims the exclusive right to every improvement where the *motive-power* is the electric or galvanic current, and the *result* is the marking or printing intelligible characters, signs, or letters at a distance. If this claim can be maintained, it matters not by what process or machinery the result is accomplished." Having laid down this construction of the claim, the judgment proceeds with many illustrations to show that such a claim is void.

§ 159 *a.* In the case of Morton *v.* The New York Eye Infirmary,[1] one of the grandest and most useful discoveries of modern times was held not to be patentable, on the ground that it did not fall within the principles of law relating to the application of discoveries to practical uses. The invention claimed consisted in the discovery, by Drs. Jackson and Morton, of ether as an anæsthetic and its application in surgical operations to alleviate pain. The distinction between the legal purport of the words "discovery" and "invention" was thus stated by the court:[2] "In its naked, ordinary sense, a discovery is not patentable. A discovery of a new principle, force, or law, operating, or which can be made to operate on matter, will not entitle the discoverer to a patent. It is only where the explorer has gone beyond the mere domain of discovery, and has laid hold of the new principle, force, or law, and connected it with some particular medium or mechanical contrivance by which, or through which, it acts on the material world, that he can secure the exclusive control of it under the patent laws. He then controls his discovery through the means by which he has brought it into practical action, or their equivalent, and only through them. It is then an invention, although it embraces a discovery. Sever the force or principle discovered from the means or mechanism through which he has brought it into the domain of invention, and it immediately falls out of that domain and eludes his grasp. It is then a naked discovery, and not an invention.

Every invention may, in a certain sense, embrace more or less of discovery, for it must always include something that is new;

[1] (1862), 5 Blatchf. 116; s. c. 2 Fisher's Pat. Cas. 320.

[2] Judge Shipman.

but it by no means follows that every discovery is an invention. It may be the *soul* of an invention, but it cannot be the subject of the exclusive control of the patentee, or the patent law, until it inhabits a *body*, no more than can a disembodied spirit be subjected to the control of human laws.

It is important here to ascertain precisely what the discovery was as viewed by the court. It was described in the specification as "a new and useful improvement in surgical operations on animals." The discovery of the origin and existence of ethers was not claimed, as it was admitted in the specification to be "well known to chemists that, when alcohol is submitted to distillation with certain acids, peculiar compounds, termed *ethers*, are formed, each of which is usually distinguished by the name of the acid employed in its preparation." It was further conceded that "it has also been known that the vapors of some, if not all, of these chemical distillations, particularly those of sulphuric ether, when breathed or introduced into the lungs of an animal, have produced a *peculiar effect* on the nervous system, one of which has been supposed to be analogous to what is usually termed intoxication"; also that narcotics had been administered to patients undergoing surgical operations by introducing them into the *stomach*, but not into the *lungs* or *air passages*. It had not, however, until this discovery, been known that the inhalation of such vapors, particularly those of sulphuric ether, would produce insensibility to pain, or such a state of quiet of nervous action as to render a person or animal incapable to a great extent, if not entirely, of experiencing pain while under the action of the knife or other surgical instrument. This was the real discovery; and the invention, as claimed on behalf of the complainant, consisted in the application of the discovery to surgical operations by the means described, viz., "the process of rendering the system insensible to pain by the inhalation of ether. Directions for administering the ether were given, and an apparatus adapted to that purpose was described.

The court construed the claim in this case to be one for a new *effect* "produced by old agents, operating by old means upon old subjects," and therefore not patentable. "This new or additional effect," says Mr. Justice Shipman, "is not produced by any new instrument by which the agent is administered, nor by any different application of it to the body of the patient. It is simply produced by increasing the *quantity* of the vapor inhaled, and even this quantity is to be regulated by the discretion of the operator, and may vary with the susceptibilities of the patient to its influence. It is nothing more in the eye of the law than the application of a well-known agent, by well-known means, to a new or more perfect use, which is not sufficient to support a patent." The same judge, in criticising the claim as one for a *process*, continues: "What is the *process* which is here set forth? The process of inhalation of the vapor, and nothing else. To couple with it the *effect* produced by calling it a process of rendering the system insensible to pain is merely to connect the results with the means. The *means*, that is, the process of inhalation of vapors, existed among the animals of the geologic ages preceding the creation of our race. That process, in connection with these vapors, is as old as the vapors themselves. We come, therefore, to the same point only by a different road. We have, after all, only a new or more perfect effect of a well-known chemical agent, operating through one of the ordinary functions of animal life."

§ 160. It has been attempted more than once, in this discussion, to show that wherever a claim does in truth sever the use of a motive-power or other elemental agency from all conditions of its application in the arts, and presents *it only* as a *causa causans* of a result, it is void; because some practical means of producing the result is the necessary link between cause and effect. It follows, however, from this established doctrine, that when the conditions of the application are given, and means of making it are furnished, the claim is not necessarily void; for the reason ceasing which has made it void, the rule which rests upon that reason ceases also. It then becomes a case in which it is necessary to define the conditions which form the limits of the asserted invention; and when those conditions are ascertained, it may be found that they embrace many devices or forms differing from those used by the patentee. Such was Neilson's case, which appears to have been decided strictly in accordance with the principles of the patent law.

§ 161. I do not understand the Supreme Court of the United States to have denied that there may be such a case. On the contrary, it appears to have been admitted that Neilson not only discovered a new principle or method of blasting a furnace, but that he gave the conditions which admitted of its application, and that within these conditions there were many forms of apparatus capable of being used. But it was held that Morse's general claim did not correspond to the scope of Neilson's patent, because it was considered to be unlimited in respect to the conditions under which the application of the newly discovered power could be effected.

§ 162. It is somewhat unfortunate that it became necessary to consider the validity of this claim upon a mere question of costs. The mechanical apparatus used by the defendant was substantially like that described by Morse, so that the court held it to be an infringement of that part of Morse's patent which covered the apparatus invented by him. But the questions being made, whether, in consequence of the asserted invalidity of the general claim, the whole patent was not void, no disclaimer having been filed, and, if the general claim only was void, whether the plaintiff could have costs, the character and operation of that claim were necessarily considered without applying to the determination any particular form of apparatus supposed to be within its scope, and yet differing from the particular apparatus described in the patent. It is apparent that, when a claim of this general character is adjudicated under circumstances like these, the subject of the extent to which a principle may be appropriated is presented under a great disadvantage ; for it becomes necessary, perhaps, to go into the field of conjecture respecting those possible future improvements which have not yet been developed, and respecting which it must be uncertain whether they would be within or without the conditions under which the patentee seeks to appropriate the application of a broad and comprehensive principle. Reasoning upon such conjectural elements, the tendency of the judicial mind would probably be to generalize the claim of the inventor more than he himself had done, and to disregard the conditions by which he had in truth limited the extent of his supposed right. This disadvantage did not attend the adjudication of Neilson's case ; for that adjudication having ascertained that his application of the principle of using the hot blast was limited by certain conditions, the very apparatus used by the defendant was found to be within those conditions, and to be at the same time quite different from his own in shape and dimensions.

§ 163. For these and other reasons it is probable that, when a case shall arise in which a claim to the application of a principle by various means appears to be attended by novelty in the application, and by the description of some appropriate means, and the supposed infringement involves the operation of such a claim, by the presentation of improved or different devices, or mechanical or other means, the whole subject ought to be re-examined. Such cases are, of course, rare. But they have risen heretofore, and will arise again. No one acquainted with the difficulties attending the investigation of questions of infringement can doubt that they sometimes open a great field of controversy. It is only necessary to cite the well-known *dictum* in which Mr. Chief Justice Taney has summed up the operation of the patent laws, to be sensible that, however tersely and with whatever general accuracy he has expressed himself, there remains, as to the class of cases treated of in this chapter, the very serious inquiry, what the patented invention is in relation to which a substantial difference or a substantial identity of means is to be predicated. "Whoever," said the learned Chief Justice, "discovers that a certain useful result will be produced in any art, machine, manufacture, or composition of matter by the use of certain means, is entitled to a patent for it; provided he specifies the means he uses in a manner so full and exact, that any one skilled in the science to which it appertains can, by using the means he specifies, without any addition to or subtraction from them, produce precisely the result he describes. And if this cannot be done by the means he describes, the patent is void; and if it can be done, then the patent confers on him the exclusive right to use the means he specifies to produce the result or effect he describes, and nothing more. And it makes no difference, in this respect, whether the effect is produced by chemical agency or combination, or by the application of discoveries or principles in natural philosophy known or unknown before his invention, or by machinery acting altogether upon mechanical principles. In either case he must describe the manner and process as above mentioned, and the end it accomplishes. And any one may lawfully accomplish the same end without infringing the patent, if he uses means substantially different from those described."[1]

§ 164. It is plain that it could not have been the intention of

[1] O'Reilly *v.* Morse, 15 Howard, 119.

the Chief Justice to embrace within the limits of such a paragraph a statement of the whole doctrines of the patent law in respect to patentability and infringement. What was thus said was of necessity general, intended to illustrate the most familiar principles of the subject, but leaving much, as every such *dictum* must, for qualification and discrimination. Thus we are led at once to the inquiry, *for what* is the discoverer of a useful result entitled to a patent? Is it for the result? Certainly not; the patentable subject is the result or effect as produced by applying a method or rule of action, whether the invention is of an art, machine, manufacture, or composition of matter. Then, again, what is meant by using *the means* specified by the patentee? In some cases the means specified will be a single device, or a special combination of mechanical or chemical agents, because the method or rule of action resides in, or can be effected by, them alone or their equivalents. In other cases the method or rule of action may be followed out by using a great variety of agents. Inasmuch, therefore, as, in the first class of cases, the question of substantial difference of means must be tested by first ascertaining what is the method or rule of action embodied by the invention, and thence determining what means are equivalents of each other in relation thereto; so, in the other class, when the method or rule of action is ascertained, the question of substantial difference or identity of means relates to the function discharged by those means in the performance of that method or rule of action. In neither class of cases, according to the principles of the patent law, does substantial difference of means depend upon differences of form, structure, composition, or other external variations, so long as the method or rule of action embraced by the patent remains unchanged.

§ 165. Thus, to illustrate these principles by two of the cases already cited, we may refer first to that of Seed *v.* Higgins. As limited by the disclaimer, this patent was confined to a particular mechanism for using the action of centrifugal force in a cotton-roving machine for the purpose of producing pressure upon the bobbin as it was wound; the patentee renouncing all claim to the application of centrifugal force by other means than the one described, he not being the first in the order of invention to apply centrifugal force to this purpose. Under his patent so limited, therefore, the method or rule of action which he claimed resided solely in the mode of operation of the device or devices he had described; and the device or devices of the defendant, although still using centrifugal force, being found to be clearly without the limits of this mode of operation, the court said that there was not even evidence of the infringement to be submitted to the jury. But if we suppose that this patent could have been rightfully so drawn as to present a broader claim, namely, for the first employment of centrifugal force, by certain means described, and by such other means as would still effect that employment of centrifugal force, then the method or rule of action would have had wider limits, because it would have resided in the use of centrifugal force by various means, each of which would effect what was proposed. So, too, in Neilson's case, the method or rule of action did not consist in using air heated in an apparatus of any particular shape or dimensions, but in one of any shape or dimensions that would admit of heating the air; and Neilson stood in such a position in the order of invention that he was entitled to make this claim: and it comprehended the defendant's coil of pipes, although such a heating apparatus was not described in Neilson's specification, or used by him, but it fell within the conditions he had given in respect to the use of heated air.

§ 166. But this subject should not be left in its present state without again laying down a certain caution to be observed by those who undertake the duty of preparing specifications. We have seen that it is possible to destroy a claim to a very important and easily understood invention, by separating the principle from its application by the necessary means; and the more striking and comprehensive the discovery of the principle, the greater will be the tendency, perhaps, to fall into this error. Although there are grounds for contending that Morse's specification furnished the materials for saving his eighth claim from this fatal defect, it cannot be denied that it was so drawn as to expose it to the force of this objection. What, then, is the proper mode, or one of the proper modes, of avoiding this peril? The danger of claiming an abstract principle will be avoided by the use of appropriate terms, signifying that the application of the principle is claimed as effected by the means used and described by the patentee, and by all other means which, when applied within the just scope of his conditions, will perform, for the purpose of the application, the like office. No particular form of words can be suggested capable of general use as a formula. Indeed, formularies are of very little use in this branch of the law ; for, to use an expression of Lord Kenyon's, " there is no magic in words," as mere words. Words which mean things, and which relate to things, are the important matters of judicial cognizance in determining the meaning and operation of these instruments.

CHAPTER V.

OF WHAT RELATES TO THE TITLE IN OR UNDER LETTERS-PATENT.

§ 167. The grant of letters-patent for an invention creates a legal estate of a peculiar nature, consisting of the exclusive right to make, vend, or use the subject of the grant for a specified period. It has many of the incidents of other legal estates, and among these are the equitable interests which may spring out of it either by contract or by operation of law. These various interests, legal and equitable, will now be considered.

§ 168. The person to whom the grant is made, by name called the patentee, is, of course, the holder of the legal title, which, like other legal estates, descends to representatives. But the patentee is not necessarily the inventor; for, whether an invention is or is not assignable at common law before any patent for it has been obtained, it has been deemed expedient to make it so assignable by statute. Accordingly provision has been made for the issuing of a patent to an assignee of the inventor, provided the application is made and the specification duly sworn to by the inventor himself, and the assignment is duly recorded.[1] When so granted, the exclusive interest is vested as a legal estate in the assignee, who thus becomes the patentee of the invention, and the inventor himself is divested of the legal title.

§ 169. But although the assignee of an inventor, who has become such before the patent has issued, does not become the holder of the legal title to the patent until it has issued, he becomes the holder of a right to obtain the patent and to pursue certain remedies, both against his assignor and against third persons. Thus, where an inventor had made an application for a patent in his own name, which had been rejected, and a patent had been granted to a competing inventor, and after his rejection

[1] Act of March 3, 1837, § 6; Act of March 3, 1839, § 7; Act of July 8, 1870, § 33; Herbert *v.* Adams, 4 Mason, 15; Dixon *v.* Moyer, 4 Wash. 71, 72.

he had assigned his invention to the plaintiff, as set forth in his specification on file in the Patent Office, and the plaintiff was authorized by the assignment to obtain the patent for himself, it was held that the plaintiff was entitled, even before recording his assignment, to pursue the remedy provided by statute for annulling the competing patent, given by the acts of July 4, 1836, § 16, and March 3, 1839, § 10.[1]

§ 170. The statutes, however, which authorize the assignment of an invention before the patent has been obtained, appear to embrace only the cases of perfected or completed inventions. There can, properly speaking, be no assignment of an inchoate or incomplete invention, although a contract to convey a future invention may be valid, and may be enforced by a bill for a specific performance.[2] But the legal title to an invention can pass to another only by a conveyance which operates upon the thing invented after it has become capable of being made the subject of an application for a patent. This is apparent from the provisions of the statute which require the specification and the application to be made in the name of the inventor. A contract to convey a future invention, or an improvement to be made upon a past invention, cannot alone authorize a patent to be taken by the party in whose favor such contract was intended to operate.

§ 171. With respect to the legal formalities to be observed in conveying inventions before an application for a patent, it is apparent that, as the statute authorizing this to be done prescribes no particular form of instrument, any instrument in writing which evinces an intention to vest the whole interest in the assignee, and to authorize him to take the patent in his own name, is a sufficient conveyance. Two requisites are however fixed by the act of March 3, 1837, § 6.[3] These are, that the assignment shall be "first entered of record," and that the "application" shall be "duly made and the specification duly sworn to by the inventor." The first of these requisites, the registration, is of course to be regarded as speaking of the Patent Office as the place of registration, that being the place contemplated by all the statutes *in pari materia*. The time relates to any time before the patent issues, although, for obvious reasons, the recording should be

[1] Gay *v.* Cornell, 1 Blatchf. 506.

[2] Nesmith *v.* Calvert, 1 Wood. & M. 34.

[3] The same requirements are contained in the act of 1870, § 33.

before or at the time of the application. But, as we have seen, such an assignment, before a patent has been issued, may, it has been held, be made after the inventor has applied for a patent and been refused; that is to say, it may be made while proceedings to obtain the patent are pending in the name of the inventor; and if recorded at any time before the patent issues, the patent will rightfully issue to the assignee.[1]

§ 172. Very nice questions may arise upon particular instruments, executed by inventors before an application for a patent, as to whether they do or do not amount to assignments of the legal title to the invention, or whether they are mere contracts or covenants to convey after the patent has been issued to the inventor. Thus, where an inventor, who had perfected a machine and was contemplating to make improvements thereon, and to take out letters-patent for the machine and the improvements, covenanted that he would assign the patents when obtained to the covenantees, and afterwards, in 1841, he obtained a patent for the machine, and in 1843 obtained a further patent for the improvements, a bill in equity was sustained to compel him to make the conveyances.[2] In this case the instrument was manifestly a mere covenant for future conveyances, the parties not contemplating that the patents were not to issue to the inventor; and, although the defence was set up that the patent for the improvements obtained in 1843 was for a subject-matter not contemplated by the covenant, the instrument and the surrounding facts were not held to warrant that construction. But where any doubt arises on the true meaning and operation of such instruments, such doubts may be solved, in respect to the question whether they are to operate as assignments before the patent, or only as covenants to assign after the patent, by attending to the following considerations.[3] That an inchoate right to obtain a

[1] Gay *v.* Cornell, *ut supra.*

[2] Nesmith *v.* Calvert, 1 Wood. & M. 34.

[3] I have endeavored to invent a phrase which, without circumlocution, shall sufficiently describe these assignments before a patent. But although in another branch of the law it is easy to speak of *ante* and *post* nuptial contracts, — and other similar phrases will occur to the reader, — yet our language is not flexible enough, even with the aid of a Latin preposition, to describe these *ante*-patent assignments. I forbear, therefore, from attempting to introduce such an expression into my text, and leave my readers to use it, or to avoid it, as they best can, informing them at the same time that I do not

patent on a perfected invention may be the subject of bargain and sale; but as the method of making such a sale available to vest the legal title in the invention as the subject of a patent in the purchaser has been regulated by statute, it is necessary to look into the instrument to see whether it contemplates that the patent shall issue to the supposed assignee or to the inventor. However absolute may be the words of bargain and sale of the invention, if the instrument contemplates that the patent shall issue to the inventor, it would seem that it must operate, as respects the legal title to the patent when obtained, as a contract to convey, and the party holding such an instrument will hold an equitable and not a legal title, until he has converted the former into the latter.[1] If the instrument is executed and recorded before the patent issues, but it appears to have been intended that the patent shall issue to the inventor, and it does so issue, then I conceive that the holder of the instrument is the holder of an equitable and not a legal title. But if the instrument intends that the patent shall issue to the holder of the instrument, and it does so issue, the instrument is an assignment of the legal title under the act of 1837, as it is, if executed and recorded after the patent has issued to the inventor, under the act of 1836.

§ 173. There is, however, one class of instruments which, even if executed before the patent issues, will pass the legal title to

make myself responsible for the correlative term of a *post*-patent assignment. Both are awkward enough.

[1] Clum *v.* Brewer, 2 Curtis Circ. C. R. 506. This was a case which arose upon an instrument executed by an inventor before a patent had been obtained, whereby he conveyed an undivided fourth part of his "invention," as described in his *caveat* then filed. But the instrument clearly contemplated the issuing of the patent to the inventor, and it was so issued. There was a covenant in the instrument for future conveyances. Now, although it was intimated in this case that the covenantee might possibly be regarded, after the patent had issued, as having a legal title to one undivided fourth part of the patent, yet as the case only called for the decision of the point that he had an equitable title, which clearly appeared, I think it proper to leave the position stated in the text as it stands. For, inasmuch as the statute regulating conveyances before a patent has issued contemplates an application by the patentee, and justifies an issue of the patent to another person only when such person records an instrument authorizing this to be done, I do not understand how a previous instrument can operate as a legal assignment of a patent which issues to the inventor, unless it appears to have been intended, by the terms of the conveyance, that the monopoly when obtained shall vest in the assignee. (See the note, *infra*.)

the monopoly, although the patent itself happens to issue to the inventor; and these instruments, according to a decision of the Supreme Court of the United States, operate as assignments of the patent under the act of 1836. This will be the case where the invention is perfected and a specification prepared, and the assignment, being made and recorded in the Patent Office before the patent issues, requests that the patent may issue to the assignee, and otherwise evinces the intention of the assignor to make the assignee the owner of the legal estate or monopoly, when it has become perfect and absolute, even if the patent should issue in the name of the inventor. The effect of this decision is, that when parties undertake to act under the sixth section of the act of 1837, which directs the mode of procuring a patent in the name and for the benefit of an assignee, and the requisite steps have been taken for that purpose, but the patent, contrary to the intent of the conveyance, has issued to the inventor, the conveyance, being recorded before the patent issues, will operate as an assignment of the patent interest under the act of 1836, and a subsequent conveyance is not necessary to enable the assignee to sue in his own name. This decision was made apparently with a view to quiet titles, which had been taken and acted upon under the supposition that such was the law. It gives a somewhat broader operation to the act of 1836, § 11, than its terms appear to embrace; for whereas that act would seem to have contemplated only assignments after a patent has issued, the act of 1837 was passed to enable assignments to be made before the patent issues. But the construction is beneficial; and if the conditions stated by the court are observed, no injury can result from it.[1]

[1] Gaylor *v.* Wilder, 10 Howard, 477. The following is the reasoning of the court, as contained in the opinion pronounced by Taney, C. J.:—

"The first question arises upon the assignment of Fitzgerald to Enos Wilder. The assignment was made and recorded in the Patent Office before the patent issued. It afterwards issued to Fitzgerald. And the plaintiffs in error insist that this assignment did not convey to Wilder the legal right to the monopoly subsequently conferred by the patent, and that the plaintiff who claims under him cannot therefore maintain this action.

"The inventor of a new and useful improvement certainly has no exclusive right to it until he obtains a patent. This right is created by the patent, and no suit can be maintained by the inventor against any one for using before the patent is issued. But the discoverer of a new and useful invention is vested

§ 174. Assignment by act or operation of law is where the title passes without any conveyance by the patentee or other person holding the legal title; as where a bankruptcy divests a person of all his property of every kind, a patent interest passes with the rest of his estate. This is certainly true of a patent already issued before the assignment in bankruptcy; and in England it has been held that a patent issued after an act of bankruptcy and an assignment by the commissioners, but before the bankrupt had obtained his certificate, passes to the assignees.[1] It is necessary,

by law with an inchoate right to its exclusive use, which he may perfect and make absolute by proceeding in the manner which the law requires. Fitzgerald possessed this inchoate right at the time of the assignment. The discovery had been made, and the specification prepared to obtain a patent. And it appears by the language of the assignment that it was intended to operate upon the perfect legal title which Fitzgerald then had a lawful right to obtain, as well as upon the imperfect and inchoate interest which he actually possessed. The assignment requests that the patent may issue to the assignee. And there would seem to be no sound reason for defeating the intention of the parties by restraining the assignment to the latter interest, and compelling them to execute another transfer, unless the act of Congress makes it necessary. The court think it does not. The act of 1836 declares that every patent shall be assignable in law, and that the assignment must be in writing, and recorded within the time specified. But the thing to be assigned is not the mere parchment on which the grant is written: it is the monopoly which the grant confers, the right of property which it creates. And when the party has acquired an inchoate right to it, and the power to make that right perfect and absolute at his pleasure, the assignment of his whole interest, whether executed before or after the patent issued, is equally within the provisions of the act of Congress.

"And we are the less disposed to give it a different construction, because no purpose of justice would be answered by it, and the one we now give was the received construction of the act of 1793 in several of the circuits, and there is no material difference in this respect between the two acts. As long ago as 1825, it was held by Mr. Justice Story, that, in a case of this kind, an action could not be maintained in the name of the patentee, but must be brought by the assignee. 4 Mason, 15. We understand the same rule has prevailed in other circuits; and if it were now changed, it would produce much injustice to assignees who have relied on such assignments, and defeat pending suits brought upon the faith of long-established judicial practice and judicial decision. Fitzgerald sets up no claim against the assignment, and to require another to complete the transfer would be mere form. We do not think the act of Congress requires it; but that, when the patent issued to him, the legal right to the monopoly and property it created was, by operation of the assignment then on record, vested in Enos Wilder."

[1] Hesse v. Stevenson, 3 Bos. & Pul. 565.

however, that the invention should have been perfected, and, at least, that the bankrupt inventor should have applied for a patent. It was said in this case (Hesse *v.* Stevenson), that the schemes which a man has in his head, or the fruits which he may make of them, do not pass; but if he has carried his schemes into effect, and thereby acquired a beneficial interest, that interest is of a nature to be affected by an assignment in bankruptcy. The party has then done all that the law requires for the creation of the interest, and the issue of the patent furnishes him with the evidence of his exclusive right.

§ 175. I am not aware that the effect of an assignment in bankruptcy upon a patentable invention, on which no application has been made for a patent, has been adjudicated in this country. The statute which provides for assignments before a patent issues contemplates only voluntary assignments; or, at least, it is capable of being executed only when the inventor applies for the patent and makes oath to the specification. According to the provisions of most bankrupt or insolvent laws, the bankrupt may be compelled to do various acts necessary to preserve, collect, or render effectual his various claims to property of all kinds. But an invention, although perfected and reduced to practice, on which no application has been made for a patent, is such a peculiar kind of property that it may well be doubted whether the bankrupt inventor could be compelled to take the steps which our law makes necessary to the vesting of the patent in another person. If indeed the invention has taken a concrete form, as if a newly invented machine is built before the assignment in bankruptcy, the machine itself, or the materials of which it was composed, would perhaps pass to the assignees. But if this is so, it would not determine the question of the right to use the machine, as against the inventor who might have taken a patent for it thereafter. The mere property in a patented machine, as distinguished from the right to use it, has been recognized as an interest on which a sheriff can levy an execution, and sell, by virtue of such a levy, without subjecting himself to an action of infringement for selling.[1] In the case in which this distinction was drawn, it was not held that the right to use the machine had passed by the levy and sale. In the case of a machine passing by assignment

[1] Sawin *v.* Guild, 1 Gallis. 485.

in bankruptcy before the patent has been applied for, and a subsequent grant of the patent to the bankrupt inventor, the same distinction would seem to be applicable. With respect to the interest in the patent itself, when so obtained, the question whether the patentee could be compelled to convey it to his assignee in bankruptcy, must depend in no inconsiderable degree upon the provisions of the bankrupt law and the methods provided for making it effectual. If the bankrupt law, *proprio vigore*, vests a granted patent in the assignee in bankruptcy, no special conveyance by the bankrupt patentee can be necessary.

§ 176. As to the interest which the creditors in bankruptcy take under an assignment by operation of the law of bankruptcy, it has been suggested by an English writer, that they do not acquire any right to use or exercise the patent privilege, but are only entitled to the proceeds to arise from a sale of the patent.[1] Whether this suggestion was founded on any thing peculiar to the English bankrupt laws, which might render it improper or impracticable for assignees in bankruptcy to engage in the working of a patent, there can be no reason, in principle, if the title to a patent is cast upon any person by operation of law for the benefit of third persons, why the holder should not exercise the patent privilege. Prudential reasons may make it proper for the assignee in bankruptcy to sell the patent; but if it is for the interest of the creditors that he should exercise the rights granted by the patent, there seems to be nothing in his situation or the nature of his title to prevent it, unless the law under which he acts requires the immediate sale and conversion into money of all the bankrupt's effects.

§ 177. One other instance only of assignment by act or operation of law, before a patent has been applied for, needs to be mentioned in this connection. This relates to the vesting of the right to take a patent in the legal representatives of a deceased inventor. A special provision of the statute regulates this right. It is the tenth section of the act of 1836. It contemplates a perfected invention or discovery, for which the inventor, if living, could have taken a patent under the other provisions of the act. The right to apply for and obtain the patent is made to devolve on the executor or administrator of the deceased inventor in trust

[1] Hindmarch on Patents, p. 67.

for his heirs or devisees, and the oath or affirmation of invention is to be varied accordingly. The right to take and hold the patent is vested in the executor or administrator, "in as full and ample manner, and under the same conditions, limitations, and restrictions, as the same was held, or might have been claimed or enjoyed, by such person [the inventor] in his or her lifetime."[1]

§ 178. We now come to the consideration of assignments, after a patent has been obtained, and their various incidents and effects. Although the kind of legal estate created by a patent would perhaps be assignable at common law, yet, as its transfer has been regulated by statute, it is necessary to examine the several interests therein, as if the statute alone were the source of the authority for such transfers of the legal title. In truth, as the statute has regulated the whole subject of transferring or subdividing the exclusive right vested by the patent in the patentee, we can only look to the statute for the conditions and modes in which the legal estate may be transferred. The provision is as follows: "That every patent shall be assignable in law, either as to the whole interest or any undivided part thereof, by any instrument in writing; which assignment, and also every grant and conveyance of the exclusive right, under any patent, to make and use, and to grant to others to make and use, the thing patented, within and throughout any specified part or portion of the United States, shall be recorded in the Patent Office within three months from the execution thereof, for which the assignee or grantee shall pay to the commissioner the sum of three dollars."[2]

§ 179. It is obvious that this statute undertakes to deal with the legal estate vested (or to be vested) in the patentee by the grant of the patent, and with that alone. It makes the interest so vested "assignable in law"; or, in other words, it recognizes the exclusive right vested in the patentee, as a legal estate, capable of being conveyed to another by a written instrument, which shall vest in that other a complete title, either to the whole of that exclusive right, or to some part of it in some specified portion of the United States. Mere licenses, therefore,

[1] The Act of 1870, § 34, contains a similar provision.

[2] Act of July 4, 1836, § 11.

or contracts conferring the limited and not the exclusive right to exercise some of the privileges secured by the patent, are not the subjects of regulation in this statute. It relates solely to grants or conveyances of the exclusive right, or legal estate, vested in the patentee, which leave no interest in the patentee for the particular territory and the particular right to which they relate.

§ 180. As to the formalities for such a grant or conveyance, it is to be observed, in the first place, that such an assignment may be by "any instrument in writing." It need not therefore be an instrument under seal. But in order to operate as an assignment, it must, to the full extent of the territory to which it relates, convey absolutely to the grantee the exclusive interest vested in the patentee with which it undertakes to deal. And here it will be noticed that the statute makes that interest divisible in two aspects: first, because it makes the patent assignable either as to "the whole interest," which it secures, or as to "any undivided part" of that interest;[1] and, secondly, because it enables the patentee to grant the exclusive right under his patent "within and throughout any specified part or portion of the United States." These various subdivisions, and the rights and interests which spring from them, will be considered hereafter.

§ 180 *a*. In this connection the language of the recent patent law (1870, ch. 230, § 36) requires to be carefully noted. It is as follows: "That every patent, or any interest therein, shall be assignable in law, by an instrument in writing; and the patentee, or his assigns or legal representatives, may, in like manner, grant and convey an exclusive right under his patent to the whole or any specified part of the United States; and said assignment, grant, or conveyance shall be void as against any subsequent purchaser or mortgagee for a valuable consideration, without notice, unless it is recorded in the Patent Office within three months from the date thereof."

§ 181. The provisions of the statute in respect to recording the conveyances by which an interest in a patent is transferred bring into view some of the distinctions between an assignment and a license. The conveyances required to be recorded are of

[1] It further separates the right "to make and use" from the right "to grant to others to make and use the thing patented."

three classes: *first*, an assignment of the whole patent; *second*, an assignment of an undivided part of the patent; and *third*, a grant or conveyance of the exclusive right to make and use, and the exclusive right to grant to others to make and use, the thing patented, within and throughout any specified part of the United States. This description of the kind of conveyances required to be recorded shows very clearly that the instrument must be one which divests the patentee of all interest in that part of the patent, or in that particular territory, which the instrument affects. If it vests in the grantee an exclusive interest, so that thereafter the patentee can exercise no control over that interest, it is such an instrument as is required by the statute to be recorded. If it be not a grant of an exclusive interest, but at most the grant of a right or privilege to make or vend or use the subject of the patent concurrently with the patentee, or with other grantees under him, it is in the nature of a license, and is not required to be recorded by the statute above cited.[1] Further illustrations of the distinctive character of licenses, as distinguished from assignments, will be presented hereafter. But, having laid down the rule which determines the character of an instrument which is within this provision of the statute, the next inquiry is as to the force and effect of the clause which declares that it "shall be recorded in the Patent Office within three months from the execution thereof." Is such recording requisite to vest the title in the assignee, as against the grantor himself, or as against third persons, or is the provision merely directory, and intended to protect subsequent *bonâ fide* purchasers without notice? And if not recorded within three months, what are the rights of the assignee in respect to suits for infringement?

§ 182. These questions, which were originally not without difficulty, have been settled by decisions in which there has been a general acquiescence. In 1843, Mr. Justice Story held that "the recording within three months is merely directory, and that, excepting as to intermediate *bonâ fide* purchasers, without notice, any subsequent recording of an assignment will be sufficient to pass the title to the assignee."[2] What he intended to say, it is presumed, was that an assignment, if not recorded within

[1] Brooks *v.* Byam, 2 Story, 526; Pitts *v.* Whitman, ibid. 609.

[2] Brooks *v.* Byam, 2 Story, 542.

three months from the date of its execution, vests in the assignee a good title as against his grantor, and a title as against third persons, which he can make effectual by recording at any time. This meaning he made more distinct in a subsequent case, adjudicated in the same year, in which he made a more elaborate examination of the subject, and gave to the statute the construction which has since been generally acted upon.[1] Mr. Justice

[1] Pitts *v.* Whitman, 2 Story, 609, 614. The following is the reasoning on which this construction was based:—

"The first objection, taken upon the motion for a new trial, is, that the deed of assignment from John A. Pitts to the plaintiff, dated on the 17th of April, 1838, was not recorded in the Patent Office until the 19th of April, 1841, after the present suit was commenced; whereas it ought to have been recorded within three months after the execution thereof. By the Patent Act of 1793, ch. 55, § 4, every assignment, when recorded in the office of the Secretary of State, was good to the title of the inventor, both as to right and responsibility; but no time whatever was prescribed within which the assignment was required to be made. By the eleventh section of the act of 1836, ch. 357, it is provided, 'That every patent shall be assignable in law, either as to the whole interest or any undivided part thereof.' Now, it is observable, that there are no words in this enactment which declare that the assignment, if not recorded, shall be utterly void; and the question, therefore, is, whether it is to be construed as indispensable to the validity of an assignment, that it should be recorded within the three months, as a *sine qua non*, or whether the statute is merely directory for the protection of purchasers. Upon the best reflection which I have been able to bestow upon the subject, my opinion is, that the latter is the true interpretation and object of the provision. My reasons for this opinion are the inconvenience and difficulty and mischiefs which would arise upon any other construction. In the first place, it is difficult to say why, as between the patentee and the assignee, the assignment ought not to be held good as a subsisting contract and conveyance, although it is never recorded, by accident, or mistake, or design. Suppose the patentee has assigned his whole right to the assignee for a full and adequate consideration, and the assignment is not recorded within the three months, and the assignee should make and use the patented machine afterwards, could the patentee maintain a suit against the assignee for such making or use as a breach of the patent, as if he had never parted with his right? This would seem to be most inequitable and unjust; and yet if the assignment became a nullity and utterly void by the non-recording within the three months, it would seem to follow as a legitimate consequence that such suit would be maintainable. So strong is the objection to such a conclusion, that the learned counsel for the defendant admitted at the argument, that, as between the patentee and the assignee, the assignment would be good, notwithstanding the omission to record it. If so, then it would seem difficult to see why the assignment ought not to be held equally valid against a mere wrong-doer, piratically invading the patent right.

"Let us take another case. Could the patentee maintain a suit against a

McLean, at about the same period, adopted the same view of the statute.[1]

mere wrong-doer, after the assignment was made, and he had thereby parted with all his interest, if the assignment was not duly recorded? Certainly it must be conceded that he could not, if the assignment did not thereby become a mere nullity, but was valid as between himself and the assignee; for then there could accrue no damage to the patentee, and no infringement of his rights under the patent. Then could the assignee, in such a case, maintain a suit for the infringement of his rights under the assignment? If he could not, then he would have rights without any remedy. Nay, as upon this supposition, neither the patentee nor the assignee could maintain any suit for an infringement of the patent; the patent right itself would be utterly extinguished, in point of law, for all transferable purposes. Again, could the assignee, in such a case, maintain a suit for a subsequent infringement against the patentee? If he could, then the patentee would be in a worse predicament than a mere wrong-doer. If he could not, then the assignment would become, in his hands, in a practical sense, worthless, as it would be open to depredations on all sides.

"On the contrary, if we construe the tenth section of the act to be merely directory, full effect is given to the apparent object of the provision, the protection of purchasers. Why should an assignment be required to be recorded at all? Certainly not for the benefit of the parties, or their privies; but solely for the protection of purchasers, who should become such, *bonâ fide*, for a valuable consideration, without notice of any prior assignment. By requiring the recording to be within three months, the act, in effect, allows that full period for the benefit of the assignee, without any imputation or impeachment of his title for *laches* in the intermediate time. If he fails to record the assignment within the three months, then every subsequent *bonâ fide* purchaser has a right to presume that no assignment has been made within that period. If the assignment has not been recorded until after the three months, a prior purchaser ought, upon the ground of *laches*, to be preferred to the assignee. If he purchases after the assignment has been recorded, although not within the three months, the purchaser may justly be postponed, upon the ground of *mala fides*, or constructive notice of the assignment. In this way, as it seems to me, the true object of the provision is obtained, and no injustice is done to any party. In respect to mere wrong-doers, who have no pretence of right or title, it is difficult to see what ground of policy or principle there can be in giving them the benefit of the objection of the non-recording of the assignment. They violate the patent-right with their eyes open; and as they choose to act *in fraudem legis*, it ought to be no defence that they meant to defraud or injure the patentee, and not the assignee. Indeed, if the defence were maintainable, it would seem to be wholly immaterial whether they knew of the assignment or not.

---

[1] Boyd *v.* McAlpin, 3 McLean, 427. See also Case *v.* Redfield, 4 McLean, 526.

§ 183. The law on this subject of recording, therefore, may be thus stated. As against the patentee himself, an assignment vests a good title in the assignee from the time of its execution, and recording within the three months is not necessary to its validity. As against third persons, a suit may be maintained in law or equity, by an assignee, provided he records his title at any time before the trial or hearing.[1] But as respects subsequent purchasers without notice and for a valuable consideration, the prior assignment must be recorded within the three months. In order to guard against an outstanding title of over three months' duration, a purchaser need only look to the records of the Patent Office. Within that period he must protect himself in the best way he can, as an unrecorded prior assignment would prevail; but it must be an assignment in writing that might have been recorded within three months.

"In furtherance, then, of right and justice, and the apparent policy of the act, *ut res magis valeat, quam pereat*, and in the absence of all language importing that the assignment, if unrecorded, shall be deemed void, I construe the provision as to recording to be merely directory, for the protection of *bonâ fide* purchasers without notice. And assuming that the recording within the three months is not a prerequisite to the validity of the assignment, it seems to me immaterial (even admitting that a recording at some time is necessary) that it is not made until after the suit is brought. It is like the common case of a deed required by law to be registered, on which the plaintiff founds his title, where it is sufficient, if it be registered before the trial, although after the suit is brought, for it is still admissible in evidence as a deed duly registered."

[1] In the case of Wyeth *v.* Stone, 1 Story, 273.

[2] Gibson *v.* Cook, 2 Blatchf. 144; Perry *v.* Corning, 7 Blatchf. 195. Probably it has occurred within the professional experience of many of my readers to be called upon to consider the operation of contracts, sometimes made by inventors, by which they have obligated themselves to convey inventions not *in esse*; and the question may arise whether the recording of such contracts in the Patent Office, within three months from the time of their execution, will operate as notice of title, so as to prevent the acquisition of a title by another purchaser after a patent has been obtained. We have seen that a contract of sale of a future invention, although in terms an absolute sale, can operate only as a contract to convey; and there is no statute which contemplates or requires the recording of any conveyances excepting assignments of existing patents after patents have been obtained, or assignments of inventions made and perfected, when it is intended to have the patent issue to the assignee. It has always been assumed that the object for which the act of 1836, § 11, requiring the recording of assignments of existing patents within three months, is the protection of subsequent *bonâ fide* purchasers; although this object is not specially declared. Assuming, then, that the recording of such

§ 184. We may now pass to the consideration of the relations which an assignment establishes between the assignor and the assignee, assuming it to have all the requisites of an assignment, as well as the nature and extent of the interest which it passes. And, in the first place, it has been held, in England, that a mere naked assignment of an interest in a patent does not import a warranty by the assignor of the validity of the patent.[1] A

an assignment operates as notice to everybody of the title of the assignee, can such an effect be attributed to the recording of a contract to convey an invention that is not only not patented, but has not yet been made? With respect to patents already issued, an assignment necessarily points to the patent conveyed, and the public records afford to every one the means of ascertaining what has passed by the assignment. But a contract to convey an invention not *in esse*, although recorded, affords a subsequent purchaser of an interest in a patent no means of ascertaining what the inventor had bound himself to convey to another person, It is true there might be cases where it could be made certain by inquiry whether the invention contemplated by the contract was the same as that subsequently patented. But is the subsequent purchaser bound to institute such an inquiry? We are considering a question of notice of title; and if the instrument supposed to operate as a notice could not, in the nature of things, give the information, can the subsequent purchaser be bound to look elsewhere? This difficulty, as well as the further consideration that the statute does not contemplate the recording of such contracts, should, perhaps, lead parties to understand that contracts for the conveyance of future inventions are really of no greater force than as the personal covenants of the inventor, to be specifically enforced against him; and that to record them will not necessarily operate as notice of title, so as to defeat a title made by the inventor to another person after he has perfected the invention and applied for or obtained a patent. At the same time, there may, in some cases, be a practical benefit to be derived from recording such contracts.

[1] Hall *v.* Condor, 38 Law & Eq. R. 253; Smith *v.* Neale, 40 Law & Eq. R. 244. In the first of these cases, Mr. Justice Williams, delivering the judgment of the court, said: "With regard to the sale of ascertained chattels, it has been held that there is not any implied warranty of either title or quality, unless there are some circumstances, beyond the mere fact of a sale, from which it may be implied. The law on this subject was fully explained by Parke, B., in giving the judgment of the Court of Exchequer in Morely *v.* Attenborough, 3 Exch. 500, which, as far as title is concerned, he thus sums up: 'From the authorities in our law, to which may be added the opinion of the late Sir N. Tindal, C. J., in Ormrod *v.* Huth, it would seem that there is no implied warranty of title on sale of goods; and that if there be no fraud, a vendor is not liable for a bad title, unless there is an express warranty, or an equivalent to it, by declarations or conduct; and the question in each case, where there is no warranty in express terms, will be, whether there are such circumstances as to be equivalent to such a warranty.' And the law is quite

mere assignment, without words which imply an undertaking that the patent is valid, is to be regarded as a sale of an ascer-

as firmly established, that on the sale of a known ascertained article, there is no implied warranty of its quality. Chanter *v.* Hopkins, 4 M. & W. 399. But there is another class of cases in which it has been held that a party is not bound to accept and pay for chattels unless they are really such as the vendor professed to sell and the vendee intended to buy; of which Young *v.* Cole, 3 N. C. 724; 4 Scott, 489; and Gompertz *v.* Bartlett, 2 El. & Bl. 849; s. c. 24 Eng. Rep. 156, are strong instances. In the latter case Lord Campbell says, it is precisely as if an article was sold as gold, which was, in fact, brass, the vendor being innocent. In this case the thing sold was ascertained, viz., a moiety of a patent granted by her Majesty. There was no express warranty, and whether it be said that the question raised on this plea impeaches the plaintiff's title to the thing sold or its quality, no warranty can be implied. But did the plaintiff profess to sell, and the defendants to buy a good and indefeasible patent right, or was the contract merely to place the defendants in the same situation as the plaintiff was in with reference to the alleged patent? In which case his position would be similar to that of the plaintiff in Kintrea *v.* Preston, 25 Law J. Rep. (N. S.) Exch. 287; s. c. 37 Eng. Rep. 556. The plaintiff professed to have invented a method for the prevention of boiler explosions. It is not alleged that he was guilty of any fraud; he must, therefore, have been an inventor, for if he was not, he must have known it, and would have been guilty of fraud in pretending to have invented. Whether he was the first and true inventor within the meaning of the statute of James I. is another question. The first material allegation in the plea is, that the alleged invention was wholly worthless, and of no utility to the public. Now that was a matter as much within the knowledge of the defendants as of the plaintiff. The next allegation, viz. that it was not new as to the public use thereof in England, and that the plaintiff was not the first and true inventor, was also a matter as much within the knowledge of the defendants as of the plaintiff. They had the same means of inquiry into the fact, and of learning whether it had been in use, or the invention had been previously made known in England. Why, therefore, should we assume that the plaintiff meant to assert that the patent was indefeasible, and that the defendants purchased on that understanding, rather than that each, knowing what the invention was, and having equal means of ascertaining its value, they contracted for the patent, such as it was, each acting on his own judgment?

"We think that the latter was the true nature of the contract, and that there was no warranty, expressed or implied; and that the case does not fall within Young *v.* Cole, or Gompertz *v.* Bartlett, which proceeded on the somewhat nice distinction before pointed out; nor is it within the principle upon which the case of Chanter *v.* Leese, 4 M. & W. 295; 5 M. & W. 698, was decided, for there the plaintiff contracted that the defendants should have the exclusive right to sell certain things for which patents had been obtained. There was no doubt as to what the parties contracted for; and as the plaintiff,

tained chattel, viz., the patent issued, in respect to the validity of which the parties have an equal opportunity to inform themselves; and, therefore, in an action for a breach of such a contract, brought by the assignor against the assignee, a plea of *non-concessit* puts in issue the granting only of the patent, and not its novelty or utility. But the necessary limitations of this doctrine imply that words may be used which do import a warranty extending to the validity of the patent. The consideration of the effect of recitals or other clauses which may be held to import a warranty of title has most frequently arisen under licenses. But no reason is perceived why the principles which have governed the operation of licenses in this respect should not be applied to assignments or to contracts to assign.

§ 185. In the next place, the nature of the relations between the assignor and the assignee of a part of a patent, in respect to their rights as against each other, is a subject involved in no inconsiderable obscurity. We have seen that the true characteristic of an assignment under our law is, that it is an instrument which vests in the grantee an indefeasible title to the whole or some part of the entire interest of the patentee. It is clear, then, that an assignment of part of a patent constitutes the assignee a joint owner with the assignor, in whom the residue of the interest remains. But are the joint owners of a patent to be regarded in the light of copartners? And if they are not copartners by the mere fact of joint ownership, may they under any and what circumstances become so? And if, in any given case, they are not found to be copartners, what are their relative rights and interests in the working of the patent, and what is their accountability to each other?

§ 186. With respect to the mere relation of joint ownership, it appears to be considered, both in England and in this country,

if one of the patents contracted for was invalid, could not confer the privilege which he agreed to confer, and for which the defendants contracted to pay, the consideration for the defendants' promise failed; and (to use the language of Lord Abinger) the whole resting in contract, and nothing having been done under it, the contract was at an end. Here the plaintiff was capable of fulfilling all that he contracted to do; he had already done it in equity. The defendants might have had all that they contracted to receive, and were therefore bound to pay."

that the joint proprietors are not partners.[1] The reason is chiefly that no mere proprietor of a share in a patent can be compelled to become jointly concerned in the profit or loss of working the patent, or to concur with his co-proprietors in granting licenses to others to use it, nor be prevented from working the invention himself.[2] But it is equally true that the relation of partners may subsist between the joint proprietors of a patent, in respect to the working of the invention, if they agree to work it together. In such a case the relations of the parties will be governed by the law of partnership. If the contract ascertains the proportions in which they are to share the profits of working the patent, a court of equity can enforce it like any other contract of partnership.[3] If the contract merely shows that the joint proprietors agreed to work the patent on joint account, it would seem that the accounting is to be regulated by their proportionate interests in the patent.[4]

§ 187. Thus far the general principles of the law of partnership, when there is a partnership, will regulate the rights of joint proprietors of a patent without difficulty. But a far more embarrassing question arises when there is no partnership, and when one of several proprietors of a patent, holding an interest which makes him a tenant in common with another owner or owners, undertakes to work the patent on his own account. Is he accountable to his co-proprietors, and if accountable, in what proportion, and in respect to what profits, and how can he be reached?

§ 188. It has been held on one occasion — and upon one only, so far as I am informed — that a part owner of a patent can maintain an action of infringement against his co-proprietor, and recover therein as damages "a proportionate share of the value of the property appropriated," which share will be measured by

[1] Hindmarch on Patents, p. 67; Parkhurst *v.* Kinsman, 2 Blatchf. 72; Kinsman *v.* Parkhurst, 18 Howard, 289.

[2] Ibid.

[3] Parkhurst *v.* Kinsman, and Kinsman *v.* Parkhurst, *ut supra.* See further what agreements may or may not constitute partnership in a patent. Elgie *v.* Webster, 5 Mees. & Welsb. 518. See also a question of fact, as to the existence of a partnership. Ridgeway *v.* Phillips, 1 Cromp., Mees. & Rosc. 415.

[4] Ibid.

the interest of the plaintiff in the patent.[1] The ground on which this conclusion was rested by the learned judge who so ruled,

[1] Pitts *v.* Hall, 3 Blatchf. 201, 206. The following is the very ingenious and able reasoning of the learned Judge Hall, on which I have undertaken in the text to offer some comments: "But I am inclined to think that the plea is bad upon another ground, and that the plaintiffs would be entitled to judgment, even if the undivided one-fourth interest in the extended patent had actually vested in the defendant. The rights of joint patentees, or of assignees of undivided interests in a patent, as against each other, in respect to the making, using, and vending the patented invention, have not, so far as I have been able to discover, been discussed by any elementary writer or in any reported case. The counsel, on the argument of the demurrer in this case, declared the question to be an embarrassing one, which had never been decided; and, without intending now to express an opinion by which I shall feel bound, if, upon a further discussion of the question, a different conclusion shall be reached, I propose to put upon paper for further use the result of my reflections upon it, in the hope that the attention of parties interested may be attracted to the subject, and that the question may be brought before the Supreme Court of the United States for adjudication.

"In the case of joint patentees, where no agreement of copartnership exists, the relation of copartners certainly does not result from their connection as joint patentees; and when one joint owner of a patent transfers his undivided interest to a stranger, the assignee does not become the partner of his co-proprietor. In both cases the parties interested in the patent are simply joint owners, or tenants in common, of the rights and property secured by the patent; and their rights, powers, and duties, as respects each other, must be substantially those of the joint owners of a chattel.

"Part owners of goods and chattels are either joint owners or tenants in common, each having a distinct, or at least an independent, although an undivided interest in the property. Neither can transfer or dispose of the whole property; nor can one act for the other in relation thereto, but merely for his own share, and to the extent of his own several right and interest; and, at common law, the one had no action of account against the other for his share of the profits derived from the common property. Story on Partnership, § 89.

"A personal chattel vested in several different proprietors cannot possibly be enjoyed advantageously by all without a common consent and agreement among them. To regulate their enjoyment, in case of disagreement, is one of the hardest tasks of legislation; and it is not without wisdom that the law of England and of this country in general declines to interfere in their disputes, leaving it to themselves either to enjoy their common property by agreement, or to suffer it to remain unenjoyed, or to perish by their dissension, as the best method of forcing them to a common consent for their common benefit. Abbott on Shipping, 98.

"It is well settled that a destruction or sale of the joint property by one of the part owners authorizes his co-proprietor to maintain trover for the conver-

was, that, in the case of personal chattels vested in different proprietors, a destruction or sale of the joint property by one of

sion. 2 Kent's Comm. 8th ed. 351, note. But, on such a sale, only the right of the party who makes the sale passes to the purchaser; and the purchaser becomes a tenant in common with the owner of the remaining interest, unless and until the latter confirms the sale, or recovers the value of his share from the wrong-doer.

"The principles of these doctrines are, it strikes me, applicable to the case of the joint ownership of patent rights. The grant of the exclusive right to make, use, and vend to others to be used, is to the patentees jointly, and not to either severally. The right, the property secured by the patent, may be granted to others by license or assignment, or by the sale of machines by the patentees jointly; and a license or assignment or sale of a machine by them is a transfer, *pro tanto*, of the property secured by the patent. One joint owner can legally grant, assign, license, or sell only in respect to his own share or right. He cannot sell and give a good title to his co-owner's right, for the same reason that one joint owner of a chattel cannot transfer the share of his co-proprietor. And if he appropriates any portion of the exclusive right or common property to his separate use or benefit, by either the use or the sale of the patented machine, he does what is in principle the same as the conversion, by destruction or sale of the joint property by a tenant in common, which authorizes his co-tenant to maintain trover.

"I can see no objection in principle to the doctrine, that the joint owner of a patent can sustain his action for an infringement against his co-owner, in which he can recover his actual damages, according to his interest in the patent. His rights are invaded by the act of his co-proprietor, and he is entitled to his legal remedy. This invasion is tortious, and no action founded upon a contract can be sustained, unless this tort is waived, and the tortious act confirmed; for no contract exists upon which such an action can be founded, without such waiver and confirmation. The injury is a violation of the exclusive right secured by the patent; and for this injury the action for an infringement is the appropriate remedy, and one which enables the court, without the violation of legal principles, and in the most direct and convenient mode, to do justice between the parties. In such an action the plaintiff may recover, as he should, his actual and proper damages, proportioned to the value and extent of his undivided interest in the exclusive right, without regard to the amount which his co-proprietor has received by means of the infringement. And there is certainly nothing in the language of the statute which authorizes this form of action, — or rather recognizes it, for this form of action was given by the Common Law, — (Curtis on Patents, §§ 257, 258), to prevent the action from being sustained in such a case; for the action on the case, under the fourteenth section of the act of 1836, may be brought in the name or names of the person or persons interested, whether as patentees, assigns, or grantees of the exclusive right within and throughout a specified part of the United States. Indeed, no satisfactory reason is perceived for holding that the part owner of a patent right cannot, like the part owner of a chat-

them authorizes the other to maintain trover for the conversion; that a similar wrongful appropriation takes place when one of the proprietors of a patent undertakes to appropriate to himself the entire property; and that the action of infringement may in such a case be regarded as analogous to the action of trover, and be regulated by the same principles. The action in which this doctrine was propounded was the ordinary action of infringement, in which the defendant was charged by the declaration with making, using, and vending to others to be used, without the consent of the plaintiff, numbers of a machine patented to the plaintiff. The defendant set up a title in himself to one undivided half of the patent for certain States: so that, if the action of infringement could be maintained at all, it must be maintained by one part owner against another part owner, in respect to the rights granted by the patent, and vested by the assignments (pleaded) in the defendant and the plaintiff, in equal, undivided moieties. There was a question raised by a demurrer to the plea, whether the interest set up had actually vested in the defendant, but after finding that it had not, the learned judge held that, even if it had vested, the action could be maintained.

§ 189. It would seem that there is no inconsiderable difficulty in maintaining this view. The analogy drawn from the action of trover, in the case of a wrongful conversion of a chattel by one part owner, would extend, in the case of a patent, only to a sim-

tel, have his remedy, by an action on the case, against his co-proprietor, for the exclusive appropriation of the joint property, in the same form as though the plaintiff were the sole owner, and the defendant a stranger; the reduction of the amount of damages to be recovered to a proportionate share of the value of the property appropriated being, in both cases, the natural and necessary consequence of the partial ownership by the wrong-doer.

"In the case of the joint owners of a patent right, the ordinary action for an infringement is, it appears to me, the most appropriate and simple remedy, even if an action of account could be sustained. In an action of account, the amount of profits received by the joint owner would ordinarily determine the aggregate sum of which the plaintiff would recover his just proportion. And it might well happen, indeed it would most usually be the case, that the sums received by the joint owner would be either much more or much less than the actual damages sustained by the injured party. The party selling territorial rights, or granting licenses, or selling machines, might wilfully or systematically sell the right at an insignificant price; and certainly this conduct on the part of the wrong-doer should not, and, in the appropriate form of action, would not, reduce the recovery of the party injured."

ilar conversion, namely, a tortious sale of the whole patent itself by one part owner, to the injury of another, if such a case can be supposed. But in the case of an exercise of the right of making, using, or vending to others the machine, or other thing that is the subject of a patent, — a right vested, for example, in undivided moieties in two parties, — how can there be any wrongful conversion? As tenants in common of that right, the one is as much entitled to exercise it as the other. The very nature of the right, and the manner in which it may be held and exercised, presuppose that both parties have an equal title to the exercise of the peculiar privileges which the patent secures. When either undertakes to sell the right itself, that is, to convey to another the undivided share of the patent privilege vested in him, he deals with a subject which is analogous to a similar share in other chattel interests, and he can of course make a title to no more than his share of the joint property. But in respect to the *user* of the exclusive privileges granted by the patent, each tenant in common holds an equal right with the others to exercise those privileges. If A., by exercising those privileges, gains more than B., or if B. chooses to remain inactive and not to exercise his rights under the patent, how can A. be made accountable to B. in respect to the gains which have resulted from the exercise of a right which is vested in him as much as it is in B.? The action of infringement necessarily implies that the defendant has, without right and against the plaintiff's consent, made, used, or sold to others, a thing, in respect to which the right of making, using, or selling was vested solely in the plaintiff. This averment cannot be made in an action of infringement by one part owner of a patent against another, and if made, it would seem to be successfully met by a plea which shows title to an undivided part of the patent in the defendant; for the law would annex the consent of the plaintiff to the title of the defendant.

§ 190. These considerations seem to me to dispose of the subtle distinctions suggested in the case referred to respecting the measure of the plaintiff's damages, namely, that their reduction to "a proportionate share of the value of the property appropriated" is "the natural consequence of the partial ownership of the wrong-doer." If the partial owner is not a wrong-doer in exercising the rights secured by the patent, no property has been appropriated which belonged to the other proprietor of the patent, and the ground of damages fails. That this is the real relation of the parties would seem to follow from their situation as tenants in common of a right to exercise the patent privileges. In respect to the disposal of the title to those privileges, they stand upon the same footing as tenants in common or joint owners of other chattels, namely, each can dispose of his own share only. But in respect to the right of exercising the patent privileges, they stand upon a different footing. It has been held that a court of equity will not enjoin one part owner of a patent, at the suit of another part owner, from using the thing patented, even though the plaintiff may hold the legal, and the defendant only an equitable, title. In such a case, the equitable is treated by a court of equity as if it were a legal title, if the holder has a right to convert it into a legal title. This decision was put expressly upon the ground that "one tenant in common has as good right to use and to license third persons to use the thing patented as the other tenant in common has. Neither can come into a court of equity and assert a superior equity, unless it has been created by some contract modifying the rights which belong to them as tenants in common."[1]

§ 191. It may then, it seems, be assumed, that, in the case of a naked assignment, vesting in the assignee an undivided interest in a patent, and in the absence of any contract creating a relation in the nature of partnership, or otherwise establishing an express accountability, one part owner cannot be enjoined by another, or sued in an action of infringement, for exercising the rights secured by the patent.

§ 192. With respect to the suggestion that a right of action might exist in favor of one part owner against another, who wilfully and systematically exercises the patent privileges to the injury of the plaintiff by taking an insignificant price for the thing patented, it would seem that the appropriate remedy is not an action of infringement, but a special action on the case. In such an action, the plaintiff must aver and show that he exercised, or endeavored to exercise, the patent privileges himself, and that he sustained special damage by the course of the defendant, who wilfully prevented him from reaping profits that would otherwise have accrued to him.

[1] Clum *v.* Brewer, 2 Curtis, Cir. C. R. 506, 524.

§ 193. Instruments which undertake to deal with an interest under a patent may be either assignments, or contracts to assign, or licenses. The distinction between an assignment and a contract to assign presents the question, whether the holder of the instrument has, by force of it, a legal or an equitable title. As we have seen, in order to constitute an assignment, there must be a grant which vests in the grantee the exclusive right to the whole patent, or some undivided part of it, or to the whole or an undivided part of some territorial interest. It is a question of construction on the instrument, whether it is to operate as such a present grant, or as a contract for a future conveyance of the interest; and one of the elements which enter into this question is, whether the interest on which the instrument operates has a present existence, or is merely contemplated to exist *in futuro*.

§ 194. And first, as to patents which are already granted. There is an early English case in which an absolute grant of certain patents, excepting some then in litigation, the legal title to which was reserved by the grantor until the determination of the suit, operated to vest the legal interest in the grantee after the determination of the suit, without any further conveyance.[1] Under our law it has been held that a contract by a patentee, who is about to apply for a renewal, that he will assign the renewed patent to A., vests in A. an equitable title, which he can convert into a legal title by paying, or offering to pay, the stipulated consideration. And where, after such a contract, and after the renewal, the patentee executed an instrument from which the court inferred the intent to make B. a trustee for the benefit of A., it was held that the entire interest, legal and equitable, was vested in B.[2]

§ 195. But in respect to interests not *in esse* at the time of the contract, it has been held that a contract to convey a future interest in a term not yet obtained is not an assignment.[3] The future interests, in reference to which this distinction was taken, were interests under renewals or extensions not obtained at the time of the contracts; and in one of the cases it was considered that the offer to perform a condition precedent, which was to be performed before the vesting of the interest, did not give effect

1 Cartwright *v.* Amalt, 2 Bos. & Pul. 43.

2 Hartshorn *v.* Day, 19 Howard, 211.

3 Gibson *v.* Cook, 2 Blatchf. 144; Pitts *v.* Hall, 3 Blatchf. 201.

to the instrument as a grant.[1] But in this connection the case of Gaylor *v.* Wilder, which involved a contract of assignment of a patent then applied for but not issued, must not be overlooked, since it appears to establish a peculiar exception to the general rule which governs contracts respecting future interests. What that exception is has already been pointed out.

§ 196. The question may arise, however, whether there are some incidental interests in future terms of an existing patent, to which assignees under the original patent may become entitled, by force of their assignments; and these, in their various aspects, are now to be examined.

§ 197. There is a well-defined distinction between the operation of assignments (made during and concerning the original term of the patent) upon the reissue of the original patent, and their operation upon the extension or renewal of the patent.[2] An assignment vests in the assignee an interest in the existing patent, indefeasible by the act of the patentee. The statute which authorizes a surrender and reissue of a patent, in order to correct a defective specification (act of 1836, § 13),[3] has always been construed, not as creating a new interest, but as amending the original patent from its commencement, although suits can be maintained for such infringements only as have taken place after the reissue. When, therefore, a patentee has by an assignment vested in an assignee a portion of the monopoly which he holds, he cannot affect the rights of such assignee by a surrender and reissue without his consent. In fact, the statute itself saves the rights of assignees who held a legal title at the time of the surrender and reissue by the following clause: "And in case of his (the patentee's) death, or any assignment by him made of the original patent, a similar right [surrender and issue] shall vest in his executors, administrators, or assignees." The proper effect to be given to this clause requires that, where the whole patent has been vested in an assignee, he should make the surrender,

[1] Pitts *v.* Hall, *ubi supra.*

[2] The term "renewal" is often erroneously used to describe the "reissue" of a patent. Its true signification is, the further or enlarged term which is added by an extension of the monopoly beyond the term originally granted. A "reissue" signifies the residue of the term which was running at the time when the patent was surrendered for correction, whether that existing term was the original or an extended one.

[3] The act now in force is that of 1870.

and where a part only has been assigned, the assignee should unite with the patentee in the surrender. But if the surrender is made by the patentee alone, and the patent is reissued to him, previous assignments are not vacated, but the reissued term enures to the benefit of the assignee without any new assignment.[1] And if the assignee has consented to the surrender, although he is not a party on the record of the application for a reissue, it enures to his benefit and becomes his act, and he is properly a party in any suits brought for infringement within the territory covered by the assignment.[2] In respect, therefore, to reissues, it is not necessary to insert any special clause in an assignment to protect the interest of the assignee, as his interest by operation of law remains the same.

§ 198. But in respect to what are called "renewals" or "extensions," assignees who became such during the term preceding the new grant stand upon a different footing. It was held in 1844 by Mr. Justice Story, upon a full consideration of the eighteenth section of the act of 1836, which authorized the extension of patents by the Patent Office, that an assignee under the original term acquires no right at all under the extended term, *unless such right be expressly conveyed to him by the patentee.*[3] Mr. Justice McLean at about the same time held the same view of the statute.[4] But soon afterwards this question came before the Supreme Court, involving the inquiry into the true construction of the clause in which, after providing for an extension or renewal, it is declared that "the benefit of such renewal shall extend to assignees and grantees of the right to use the thing patented to the extent of their respective interests therein." A majority of the court held that this clause was not to be construed as saving the rights of previous assignees to make and vend the thing patented, but that it is to be regarded as saving the rights of those who were in the use of the patented article at the time of the renewal.[5] Subse-

[1] Wyeth *v.* Stone, 1 Story, 273; Brooks *v.* Bicknell, 4 McLean, 64, 353, 526; Woodworth *v.* Stone, 3 Story, 749; Woodworth *v.* Hall, 1 Woodb. & M. 248.

[2] Woodworth *v.* Stone, 3 Story, 749.

[3] Woodworth *v.* Sherman, 3 Story, 171.

[4] Brooks *v.* Bicknell, 4 McLean, 64.

[5] Wilson *v.* Rousseau, 4 Howard, 646. The following is the reasoning of the majority of the court, as embraced in the opinion pronounced by Mr. Justice Nelson:—

quently, the same doctrine was held in relation to a second extension granted by special act of Congress after the first exten-

" The second question is, whether, by force and operation of the eighteenth section, already referred to, the extension granted to W. W. Woodworth, as administrator, on the 16th day of November, 1842, enured to the benefit of assignees under the original patent granted to William Woodworth on the 27th day of December, 1828, or whether said extension enured to the benefit of the administrator only in his said capacity.

" The most of this section has already been recited in the consideration of the first question, and it will be unnecessary to repeat it. It provides for the application of the patentee to the commissioner for an extension of the patent for seven years; constitutes a board to hear and decide upon the application; and if his receipts and expenditures, showing the loss and profits accruing to him from and on account of his invention, shall establish to the satisfaction of the board that the patent should be extended, by reason of the patentee, without any fault on his part, having failed to obtain from the use and sale of his invention a reasonable remuneration for his time, ingenuity, and expense bestowed upon the same, and the introduction of it into use, it shall be the duty of the commissioners to extend the same by making a certificate thereon of such extension for the term of seven years from and after the first term; 'and thereupon the said patent shall have the same effect in law as though it had been originally granted for the term of twenty-one years.' And then comes the clause in question: 'And the benefit of such renewal shall extend to assignees and grantees of the right to use the thing patented to the extent of their respective rights therein.'

" The answer to the second question certified depends upon the true construction of the above clause respecting the rights of assignees and grantees.

" Various and conflicting interpretations have been given to it by the learned counsel, on the argument, leading to different and opposite results, which it will be necessary to examine.

" On one side it has been strongly argued, that the legal operation and effect of the clause save and protect all the rights and interests of assignees and grantees in the patent existing at the time of the extension; and thus secure and continue the exclusive use and enjoyment of these rights and interests for the seven years, to the same extent, and in as ample a manner, as held and enjoyed under the first term. That if A. holds an assignment of a moiety of the patent, he will hold the same for the new term of seven years; if of the whole patent, then the whole interest for that period. And that as soon as the new grant is made to the patentee, the interest therein passes, by operation of this clause, to the assignees of the old term, in proportion to their respective shares.

" On the other side it has been argued, with equal earnestness, that, according to the true construction and legal effect of the clause, protection is given, and intended to be given, only to the rights and interests of assignees and grantees acquired and held by assignments and grants from the patentee in and under the second or new term; and that it does not refer to, or em-

sion granted by the Patent Office; for it was held that a special act in favor of a patentee, extending the time beyond that orig-

brace, or in any way affect the rights and interests of assignees or grantees holding under the old.

"In connection with this view, it is said that the rights thus protected in the new term may be acquired by means of the legal operation of the clause, either from a direct assignment or grant after the extension of the patent, or by an appropriate provision for that purpose, looking to an extension, contained in the assignment or grant under the old.

"It is not to be denied but that, upon any view that has been taken or that may be taken of the clause, its true meaning and legal effect cannot be asserted with entire confidence; and, after all, must depend upon such construction as the court can best give to doubtful phraseology and obscure legislation, having a due regard to the great object and intent of Congress, as collected from the context and general provisions and policy of the patent law.

"The rule is familiar and well settled, that, in case of obscure and doubtful words or phraseology, the intention of the law-makers is to be resorted to, if discoverable from the context, in order to fix and control their meaning, so as to reconcile it, if possible, with the general policy of the law.

"Now, the serious difficulty in the way, and which renders the first interpretation inadmissible, except upon the most explicit and positive words, is, that it subverts at once the whole object and purpose of the enactment, as is plainly written in every line of the previous part of the section. It gives to the assignees and grantees of the patent, as far as assigned under the old term, the exclusive right and enjoyment of the invention, — the monopoly, — in the extended term for the seven years; when, by the same provision, it clearly appears that it was intended to be secured to the patentee as an additional remuneration for his time, ingenuity, and expense in bringing out the discovery, and in introducing it into public use. It gives this remuneration to parties that have no peculiar claims upon the government or the public, and takes it from those who confessedly have.

"The whole structure of the eighteenth section turns upon the idea of affording this additional protection and compensation to the patentee, and to the patentee alone, and hence the reason for instituting the inquiry before the grant of the extension, to ascertain whether or not he has failed to realize a reasonable remuneration from the sale and use of the discovery, — the production of an account of profit and loss to enable the board to determine the question; and as it comes to the one or the other conclusion, to grant the extended term or not.

"It is obvious, therefore, that Congress had not at all in view protection to assignees. That their condition on account of dealing in the subject of the invention, whether successful or otherwise, was not in the mind of that body, nor can any good reason be given why it should have been.

"They had purchased portions of the interest in the invention, and dealt with the patent rights as a matter of business and speculation, and stood in no different relation to the government or the public than other citizens engaged in the common affairs of life.

inally limited, must be considered as ingrafted on the general patent law; that the general patent law, in force at the time of

"Nothing short of the most fixed and positive terms of a statute could justify an interpretation so repugnant to the whole scope and policy of it, and to wise and judicious legislation.

"We think this construction not necessarily required by the language of the clause, and is altogether inadmissible.

"Then as to the second interpretation, namely, that the clause refers to and includes assignees and grantees of interests acquired in the new term, either by an assignment or grant from the patentee after the extension, or by virtue of a proper clause for that purpose in the assignment under the old term.

"The difficulty attending this construction lies in the uselessness of the clause upon the hypothesis, — the failure to discover any subject-matter upon which to give reasonable operation and effect to it, — and hence to adopt the construction is to make the clause virtually a dead letter, the grounds for which conclusion we will proceed to state.

"The eleventh section of the Patent Act provides that every patent shall be assignable in law, either as to the whole interest or any undivided part thereof, by an instrument in writing; which assignment, and also every grant and conveyance of the exclusive right under any patent, &c., shall be recorded in the Patent Office. And the fourteenth section authorizes suits to be brought in the name of the assignee or grantee, for an infringement of his rights, in a court of law.

"One object of these provisions found in the general patent system is to separate the interest of the assignee and grantee from that which may be held by the patentee, and to make each fractional interest held under the patent distinct and separate; in other words, to change a mere equitable into a legal title and interest, so that it may be dealt with in a court of law.

"Now, in view of these provisions, it is difficult to perceive the materiality of the clause in question, as it respects the rights of assignees and grantees, held by an assignment or grant in and under the new term, any more than in respect to like rights and interests in and under the old.

"The eleventh and fourteenth sections embrace every assignment or grant of a part or the whole of the interest in the invention, and enable these parties to deal with it, in all respects, the same as the patentee. They stand upon the same footing under the new term as in the case of former assignments under the old. Nothing can be clearer. It is impossible to satisfy the clause by referring it to these assignments and grants; or to see how Congress could, for a moment, have imagined that there would be any necessity for the clause, in this aspect of it. It would have been as clear a work of supererogation as can be stated.

"The only color for the argument in favor of the necessity of this clause, in the aspect in which we are viewing it, is, as respects the contingent interest in the new term, derived from a provision in an assignment under the old one, looking to the extension. As the right necessarily rested on contract, at least

the special act, permitted a party who had purchased a patented machine during the period to which the patent was first limited

till the contingency occurred, there may be some doubt whether, even after its occurrence, the eleventh and fourteenth sections had the effect to change it into a vested legal interest, so that it could be dealt with at law; and that a new assignment or grant from the patentee would be required, which could be enforced only in a court of equity. To this extent there may be some color for the argument, some supposed matter to give operation and effect to the clause.

"But what is the amount of it? Not that the clause creates or secures this contingent interest in the new term, for that depends upon the contract between the parties, and the contract alone, and which, even if the general provisions of the law respecting the rights of assignees and grantees could not have the effect to change into a legal right, might be enforced in a court of equity.

"The only effect, therefore, of the provision in respect to assignees and grantees of this description would be to change the nature of the contingent interest, after the event happened, from a right resting in contract to a vested legal interest; or, to speak with more precision, to remove a doubt about the nature of the interest in the new term, after the happening of a certain contingency, which event, in itself, was quite remote. This seems to be the whole amount of the effect that even ingenious and able counsel have succeeded in finding to satisfy the clause. It presupposes that Congress looked to this scintilla of interest in the new term, which might or might not occur, and cast about to provide for it, for fear of doubts as to its true nature and legal character, and the effect of the general system upon it.

"We cannot but think a court should hesitate before giving a construction to the clause so deeply harsh and unjust in its consequences, both as it respects the public and individual rights and interests, upon so narrow a foundation.

"But there are other difficulties in the way of this construction.

"The eleventh section, regulating the rights of assignees and grantees, provides: 'That every patent shall be assignable at law,' &c., 'which assignment, and also every grant and conveyance of the exclusive right under any patent to make and use, and to grant to others to make and use, the thing patented within and throughout any specified part or portion of the United States,' &c., 'shall be recorded.'

"Now it will be apparent, we think, from a very slight examination of the clause in question, that it does not embrace assignees or grantees, in the sense of the eleventh section, at all; nor in the sense in which they are referred to when speaking of these interests generally under the patent law, without interpolating words or giving a very forced construction to those composing it.

"The clause is as follows: 'And the benefit of such renewal shall extend to assignees and grantees of the right to use the thing patented, to the extent of their respective interests therein.'

"It will be seen that the word 'exclusive,' used to qualify the right of a grantee in the eleventh section, and, indeed, always when referred to in the

to continue to use it during the further extension; and that there was nothing in the special act to take the case out of the operation of this rule.[1]

patent law (§ 14), and also the words 'to make,' 'and to grant to others to make and use,' are dropped, so that there is not only no exclusive right in the grantee, in terms, granted or secured by the clause, but no right at all, no right whatever, to make or to grant to others to make and use the thing patented; in other words, no exclusive right to make or vend. And it is, we think, quite obvious, from the connection and phraseology, that assignees and grantees are placed, and were intended to be placed, in this respect, upon the same footing. We should scarcely be justified in giving to this term a more enlarged meaning as to the right to make and sell, as it respects the one class, than is given to the others, as they are always used as correlative, in the patent laws, to the extent of the interests held by them. The clause, therefore, in terms, seems to limit studiously the benefit or reservation, or whatever it may be called, under or from the new grant, to the naked right to use the thing patented; not an exclusive right even for that, which might denote monopoly, nor any right at all, much less exclusive, to make and vend. That seems to have been guardedly omitted. We do not forget the remaining part of the sentence, 'to the extent of their respective interests therein,' which is relied on to help out the difficulty. But we see nothing in the phrase giving full effect to it, necessarily inconsistent with the plain meaning of the previous words. The exact idea intended to be expressed may be open to observation; but we think it far from justifying the court in holding that the grant or reservation of a right to use a thing patented, well known and in general use at the time, means an exclusive right to make and use it; and not only this, but an exclusive right to grant to others the right to make and use it, meaning an exclusive right to vend it.

"The court is asked to build up a complete monopoly in the hands of assignees and grantees in the thing patented, by judicial construction, founded upon the grant of a simple right to use it to the extent of the interest possessed; for the argument comes to this complexion. A simple right to use is given, and we are asked to read it an exclusive right, and not only to read it an exclusive right to use, but an exclusive right to make and vend the patented article.

"Recurring to the patent law, it will be seen that Congress, in granting monopolies of this description, have deemed it necessary to use very different language. The grant in the patent must be in express terms, for 'the full and exclusive right and liberty of making, using, and vending,' in order to confer exclusive privileges. The same language is also used in the act when speaking of portions of the monopoly in the hands of assignees and grantees (§§ 11, 14).

"We cannot but think, therefore, if Congress had intended to confer a monopoly in the patented article upon the assignees and grantees by the clause

[1] Bloomer *v.* McQuewan, 14 Howard, 539.

§ 199. Two other cases in the Supreme Court have involved a further application of the same doctrine. In one it was held, that

in question, the usual formula in all such grants would have been observed, and that we should be defeating their understanding and intent, as well as doing violence to the language, to sanction or uphold rights and privileges of such magnitude by the mere force of judicial construction.

"We conclude, therefore, that the clause has no reference to the rights or interests of assignees and grantees under the new and extended term, upon the ground, —

"1. Because, in that view, giving to the words the widest construction, there is nothing to satisfy the clause, or upon which any substantial effect and operation can be given to it; it becomes virtually a dead letter, and work of legislative superfluity; and,

"2. Because the clause in question, upon a true and reasonable interpretation, does not operate to vest the assignees and grantees named therein with any exclusive privileges whatever, in the extended term, and therefore cannot be construed as relating to or embracing such interests in the sense of the law.

"The extension of the patent, under the eighteenth section, is a new grant of the exclusive right or monopoly in the subject of the invention for the seven years. All the rights of assignees or grantees, whether in a share of the patent, or to a specified portion of the territory held under it, terminate at the end of the fourteen years, and become reinvested in the patentee by the new grant.

"From that date he is again possessed of 'the full and exclusive right and liberty of making, using, and vending to others the invention,' whatever it may be. Not only portions of the monopoly held by assignees and grantees as subjects of trade and commerce, but the patented articles or machines throughout the country, purchased for practical use in the business affairs of life, are embraced within the operation of the extension. This latter class of assignees and grantees are reached by the new grant of the exclusive right to use the thing patented. Purchasers of the machines, and who were in the use of them at the time, are disabled from further use immediately, as that right became vested exclusively in the patentee. Making and vending the invention are prohibited by the corresponding terms of his grant.

"Now, if we read the clause in question with reference to this state of things, we think that much of the difficulty attending it will disappear. By the previous part of the section, the patentee would become reinvested with the exclusive right to make, use, and vend the thing patented; and the clause in question follows, and was so intended as a qualification. To what extent, is the question. The language is: 'And the benefit of such renewal shall extend to assignees and grantees of the right to use the thing patented to the extent of their respective interest therein'; naturally, we think, pointing to those who were in the use of the patented article at the time of the renewal, and intended to restore or save to them that right which, without the clause, would have been vested again exclusively in the patentee. The previous part of the section operating in terms to vest him with the exclusive right to use, as

a party, who claims a right so to continue in the use of a patented machine after an extension, must show a continuous chain of title

well as to make and vend, there is nothing very remarkable in the words, the legislature intending thereby to qualify the right in respect to a certain class only, leaving the right as to all others in the patentee, in speaking of the benefit of the renewal extending to this class. The renewal vested him with the whole right to use, and therefore there is no great impropriety of language, if intended to protect this class, by giving them in terms the benefit of the renewal. Against this view it may be said that 'the thing patented' means the invention or discovery, as held in M'Clurg *v.* Kingsland, 1 How. 202; and that the right to use 'the thing patented' is what, in terms, is provided for in the clause. That is admitted, but the words, as used in the connection here found, with the right simply to use the thing patented, — not the exclusive right, which would be a monopoly, — necessarily refer to the patented machine, and not to the invention; and, indeed, it is in that sense that the expression is to be understood generally throughout the patent law, when taken in connection with the right to use, in contradistinction to the right to make and sell.

"The 'thing patented' is the invention; so the machine is the thing patented; and to use the machine is to use the invention, because it is the thing invented, and in respect to which the exclusive right is secured, as is also held in M'Clurg *v.* Kingsland. The patented machine is frequently used as equivalent for the 'thing patented,' as well as for the invention or discovery, and, no doubt, when found in connection with the exclusive right to make and vend, always means the right of property in the invention, the monopoly. But when in connection with the simple right to use, — the exclusive right to make and vend being in another, — the right to use the thing patented necessarily results in a right to use the machine, and nothing more. Then as to the phrase 'to the extent of their respective interests therein,' that obviously enough refers to their interests in the thing patented, and, in connection with the right simply to use, means their interests in the patented machines, be that interest in one or more at the time of the extension.

"This view of the clause, which brings it down in practical effect and operation to the persons in the use of the patented machine or machines at the time of the new grant, is strengthened by the clause immediately following, which is, 'that no extension of the patent shall be granted after the expiration of the term for which it was originally issued. What is the object of this provision? Obviously, to guard against the injustice which might otherwise occur to a person who had gone to the expense of procuring the patented article, or changed his business upon the faith of using or dealing with it, after the monopoly had expired, which would be arrested by the operation of the new grant. To avoid this consequence, it is provided that the extension must take place before the expiration of the patent, if at all. Now it would be somewhat remarkable if Congress should have been thus careful of a class of persons who had merely gone to the expense of providing themselves with the patented article for use or a matter of trade, after the monop-

back to some one who could lawfully sell it to him for use during the former term.[1] In the other it was held that, if he does show a right to use the machine, derived during the original term from some one who could then lawfully impart to him that right, he may continue to use it after any and every extension of the

oly had ceased, and would be disappointed and exposed to loss if it was again renewed, and at the same time had overlooked the class who, in addition to the expense and change of business, had bought the right from the patentee, and were in the use and enjoyment of the machine, or whatever it might be, at the time of the renewal. These provisions are in juxtaposition, and we think are but parts of the same policy, looking to the protection of individual citizens from any wrong and injustice on account of the operation of the new grant.

"The consequences of any different construction than the one proposed to be given are always to be regarded by courts, when dealing with a statute of doubtful meaning. For between two different interpretations, resting upon judicial expositions of ambiguous and involved phraseology, that which will result in what may be regarded as coming nearest to the intention of the legislature should be preferred.

"We must remember, too, that we are not dealing with the decision of the particular case before us, though that is involved in the inquiry, but with a general system of great practical interest to the country; and it is the effect of our decision upon the operation of the system that gives to it its chief importance.

"The eighteenth section authorizes the renewal of patents in all cases where the board of commissioners is satisfied of the usefulness of the invention, and of the inadequacy of remuneration to the patentee. Inventions of merit only are the subject of the new grant, — such as have had the public confidence, and which it may be presumed have entered largely, in one way and another, into the business affairs of life.

"By the report of the commissioner of patents, it appears that five hundred and two patents were issued in the year 1844, — for the last fourteen years the average issue yearly exceeded this number, — and embrace articles to be found in common use in every department of labor or art, on the farm, in the workshop and factory. These articles have been purchased from the patentee, and have gone into common use. But if the construction against which we have been contending should prevail, the moment the patent of either article is renewed, the common use is arrested by the exclusive grant to the patentee. It is true the owner may repurchase the right to use, and doubtless would be compelled from necessity; but he is left to the discretion or caprice of the patentee. A construction leading to such consequences, and fraught with such unmixed evil, we must be satisfied was never contemplated by Congress, and should not be adopted unless compelled by the most express and positive language of the statute."

[1] Chaffee *v.* Boston Belting Co., 22 How. 217.

patent subsequently obtained, as long as it lasts, and may even repair it.[1]

§ 199 *a*. This doctrine has been confirmed by recent decisions, in which it has been held that the right to use the specific machine is guaranteed by section eighteen of the act of 1836. A purchaser may use the identical machine as long as it lasts, and may repair it after an extension of the patent.[2]

§ 200. This course of decisions, then, establishes a distinction, in respect to the right of previous assignees, between the right to *make and vend* the patented article, and the right to *use* it, after an extension. The former, it is held, is a part of the franchise which the patent confers, and the right to exercise that franchise after an extension ceases in the previous assignee, unless there is a stipulation to the contrary. The latter, it is said, is the acquisition of a right which takes the patented article out of the monopoly of the patent, makes it the property of the individual purchaser, and removes it from the protection of the patent laws.

§ 201. It may be observed, here, that four of the cases above cited related to *machines* licensed or authorized under a former term of the patent. A difficulty will be experienced when it becomes necessary to apply the same doctrines to patents embracing other subjects; for the question will then arise whether the clause in the act of 1836, saving the rights of assignees, applies at all to

[1] Bloomer *v.* Millingen, 1 Wallace, 340. There is a case, decided on the circuit by Mr. Justice Nelson, in 1855 (prior to Chaffee *v.* Bost. Belt. Co., *ante*), in which a distinction is drawn between the rights of a purchaser who bought a machine from the patentee himself, who had built it for him, and the case of a purchaser of a machine from one holding a license to make and sell under the first term of the patent; and it is intimated that, in the former case, a special act of Congress extending the patent could not take away the right to use the machine sold by the patentee, even if it should undertake to do so. Without going into the consideration of this last suggestion, it may be observed that the course of decisions in the Supreme Court makes no such distinction as to the source from which the right to use was derived during a former term, but merely requires that the use in its inception should be lawful, or be conferred by some one who then had the right to confer it. The case referred to is Blanchard *v.* Whitney, 3 Blatchf. 307. The effect of the eighteenth section of the statute of 1836 is not adverted to in this case, and the right of the vendee of the machine is put upon the ground that by the sale the patentee conveyed an unlimited right to use it until worn out.

[2] Farrington *v.* Board of Water Commissioners, 4 Fisher's Pat. Cas. 216; Hawley *v.* Mitchell, ibid. 388; Tilghman *v.* Mitchell, ibid. 615.

such patents, and if so, in what way. Thus, for example, to take the case of a patented process of manufacture, resulting in a new article of commerce, such as that suggested by Mr. Webster, of a patent starch. The patent monopoly, in such a case, embraces the right to make, the right to use, and the right to vend to others to use. While, then, it may be conceded that the sale of the particular kind of starch by the patentee, during a former term, carries to the purchaser of the starch the right to consume it or to vend it as an article of commerce after an extension, is this all the application of the clause protecting the rights of assignees or grantees that can be given to such a case? Is the former assignee or grantee of a right to practise the patented process excluded from the clause? What is "the extent of his interest therein," in relation to the extended term of the monopoly? What, in other words, is "the right to use the thing patented," which the statute saves to an assignee after an extension, according to the extent of "his interest therein," in a case of this description?

§ 202. It has been suggested that this clause in the statute applies only to patented machines. But there appears to be nothing in the terms or nature of the provision which limits it to patents of a particular class. All that can be said at present is, that the Supreme Court have been called upon, as yet, to apply it only to patents for machines, and that they have given it a construction which cuts the knot of certain difficulties which arise in that direction. If, in so doing, embarrassments have been created in its application to patents of another kind, they can be solved only when the cases arise.[1]

§ 203. The doctrine, then, as it now stands, in relation to the rights of assignees, or purchasers under a former term, is that, in the absence of an express stipulation, mere assignees of the right to make and vend (a patented machine), who acquired their right under a former term, take nothing under an extension, whether the extension was obtained under the standing law or under a special law; but that purchasers of the patented machine, who derived from a competent source a lawful right to use it, can con-

[1] See the close of the opinion of the court in Chaffee *v.* Bost. Belt. Co., 22 Howard. See also the case of Day *v.* The Union India-Rubber Company, 3 Blatchf. 488; and Wood *v.* Michigan Southern R.R. (1868), 3 Fisher's Pat. Cas. 464.

tinue to use it until it is worn out, or as long as it can be repaired.[1] It becomes important, then, to know what will operate as a stipu-

[1] The point still remains undecided by the Supreme Court whether an assignee or licensee of the right to use the thing patented is confined, after an extension, to the use of the identical machine or apparatus which was in existence in his hands at the time of the extension. All the decisions, thus far, involved as the point for judicial determination the right to use a machine constructed before the extension of the patent; and in dealing with these cases, the Supreme Court has been led (as in Wilson *v.* Simpson, 9 How. 109) into some rather subtle distinctions between repairs or reconstructions which do not, and those which do, change the identity of the machine which had become the property of the assignee or grantee before the extension. It will be seen, on examining these cases, that the construction given to the clause of the eighteenth section of the act of 1836 rests mainly upon the position that a sale of a patented machine takes *that machine* out of the monopoly, and puts it upon the same footing in the hands of the purchaser with all other property. But this carries no right to construct another machine like it; and hence, so long as the operation of the clause in question is governed by the unquestionable truth that the *machine sold* became the absolute property of the grantee, it may be necessary to go into nice inquiries respecting the identity of the machine which the grantee is using and the machine which was sold or licensed to him. But there may be cases where this basis of the construction of the statute will furnish no guide whatever. Take the case of a mixed patent, where the thing patented embraces a process which can be exercised only by machinery described in or perhaps covered by the patent. Or take the case of a patent for a process alone, but one requiring the use of a peculiar apparatus, which may not itself be covered by the patent. Is the grantee of "the thing patented" confined in such cases to the use of the identical apparatus which he was using at the time of the extension? Or is the grantee of "the thing patented," where that thing is nothing but a machine, confined to the identical machine which he had bought or been licensed to use before the extension? These inquiries show that the construction heretofore given to the statute has, perhaps, been narrowed rather more than was needful, and that the fact that a particular structure has become the property of the grantee is not alone a sufficient basis for the construction, as it obviously will not satisfy all cases. The necessity for a broader construction of the statute will be seen by examining the case of Day *v.* The Union India-Rubber Company, 3 Blatchf. 488, decided by Judge Hall, in which he entered into an elaborate examination of all the cases that had been decided by the Supreme Court, and held, that whatever was the tendency of the reasonings employed in them, they had judicially decided nothing more than the point, that where the defendant is using the same machine which he was licensed to use before the extension, he may continue to use and even repair *that machine.* The learned judge, therefore, felt himself at liberty to examine and decide the further case of the use of a thing patented, whether the particular apparatus was or was not in existence prior to the extension. The thing patented in this case was a subject in which a process

lation *inter partes*, that assignees or grantees of the right to exercise the patent monopoly shall continue to have the same right in future terms ; and what, if any, are the rules of construction applicable to such instruments in the determination of this question ?

§ 204. In the case of Wilson *v.* Rousseau, there was a covenant that any " renewal " of the patent should " enure to the benefit " of the assignee. At the time of making this covenant, there was no standing law of the United States providing for an extension of the term beyond the fourteen years expressed in the patent. Nor was there, at that time, any law providing for a surrender and reissue, on account of a defective specification ; but a decision had been made in the Circuit Court for the New York circuit, to the effect that, upon general principles, such a surrender and reissue might be made. This was the state of the law, statutory or declared, at the time of this covenant respecting " any renewal." A majority of the Supreme Court held that the parties to the covenant were to be presumed to have made it " with a reference to the known and existing rights and privileges secured to patentees under the general system of the government established for that purpose " ; that this, at the time, embraced a right to take out a new patent for the residue of the unexpired term

and machinery for working the process were so blended that it was doubtful whether the patent covered the one or the other, or both. The learned judge held, that whether the patent covered a process or a machine, or both, and whether the machinery used by the defendant was or was not in existence prior to the extension of the patent, the eighteenth section of the statute gave him, as grantee " of the right to use the thing patented," the same rights of use after the extension that he held before. The opinion pronounced is highly instructive and able. The case was taken to the Supreme Court, but was decided there upon other grounds. See Day *v.* Union India-Rub. Co., 20 How. 216. It was followed by the cases of Chaffee *v.* Bost. Belt. Co., and Bloomer *v.* Millingen; but these did not involve any thing beyond the points previously decided as to the use of the identical machine sold or licensed before the extension. The whole subject needs further examination. For the convenience of the reader the cases are here cited in their chronological order: Wilson *v.* Rousseau, 4 How. 646 (1845); Simpson *v.* Wilson, 4 How. 709 (1845); Wilson *v.* Simpson, 9 How. 109 (1849); Bloomer *v.* McQuewan, 14 How. 539 (1852); Day *v.* The Union India-Rub. Co., 3 Blatchf. 488 (1856); Hartshorn *v.* Day, 19 How. 211 (1856); Day *v.* Union India-Rub. Co., 20 How. 216 (1857); Chaffee *v.* Bost. Belt. Co., 22 How. 217 (1859); Bloomer *v.* Millingen, 1 Wallace, 340 (1863).

of fourteen years; and that the term "renewal" was to be satisfied with reference to this new patent so to be obtained, and was not to be construed to embrace a renewal to be created by further legislation of Congress.[1] It may admit of some question whether a narrower construction of the term "renewal," than it might have received under the principle of construction adopted, was not resorted to in this case. Assuming the correctness of the principle, that parties, in making such a covenant, are presumed to contemplate such rights and privileges as the existing patent system itself contemplates, it is to be observed, that, at the time of this covenant, the practice of obtaining extensions by special act of Congress had long been known; and that, although there was no standing law for that purpose, there was also no standing law for obtaining what the court called a new patent, by surrender and reissue of the old one.

§ 205. The utmost that existed on this subject was embraced in a decision of a Circuit Court that a patent might be surrendered and reissued, and the possibility that the Supreme Court might, as they afterwards did, sanction this ruling. So far, therefore, as the meaning of the term "renewal" could be gathered from what might be brought into existence thereafter, it would seem that a future extension by subsequent legislation was as fairly within that meaning as the new patent to be obtained for the residue of fourteen years, by a surrender and reissue under the sanction of a judicial decision. But the principle of construction appears of itself to have been sound, namely, that when parties use such a term as the "renewal" of the patent, they are to be supposed to embrace what the law provides as a "renewal." Fortunately, the subsequent legislation fixes the meaning of this term as referring to what is also called an "extension." Thus, while the thirteenth section of the act of 1836 speaks of a reissued patent as a "*new* patent," it does not denominate the term a "renewal"; but the eighteenth section, which provided for extensions by the commissioner, describes the further term so obtained by both the terms "extension" and "renewal." Accordingly, it has been held, that where the term "renewal" or "renewed letters-patent" was used in an agreement made while the eighteenth section of the

[1] Wilson *v.* Rousseau, 4 How. 646.

act of 1836 was in force, the parties are to be deemed to have had in view an extension under that section.[1]

§ 206. What then, it may be asked, will be the rights of an assignee or covenantee, under the use of the term "renewal" or "renewed letters-patent," in respect to the new patent obtained by a surrender and reissue, or in respect to an extension obtained by a special law, and not under a standing law? Are these to be excluded by construction from the operation of the covenant? To this it may be answered, in the first place, that, in respect to a patent reissued on account of a defective specification, the question may be practically unimportant, if the contract is a clear assignment of an interest in the existing patent; because the reissued patent, being, in contemplation of law, the same as the original, the law annexes the right to it to the interest obtained by the assignee under the original. But in respect to extended terms that may be obtained by special laws, aside from, or in the absence of, any standing law providing for such further grants, the context of the instrument under which the assignee or covenantee claims, construed by the application of certain established principles respecting this species of property, must determine what the party is to take. The question is chiefly, if not solely, a question of intent. These instruments are, of course, framed in a great variety of forms, and the language used is to be applied to the subject-matter about which the parties appear to have dealt.

§ 207. There is nothing in the nature of a future contingent interest in a patent, whether it may be obtained under a standing or under a special law, to prevent it from being a subject of bargain and sale. It is clear that the inchoate right to obtain an extension under a standing law may be conveyed or controlled in advance by the party who has the power to obtain and make it perfect; and it seems to be equally clear that an inventor, either before or after he has obtained one patent, may so deal with the possibility of obtaining future patents on his invention, as to vest an interest in such future patents in his assignee or grantee. The question in either case will be, whether he has conveyed or covenanted to convey a future contingent interest.

§ 208. In deciding such a question, it has been considered that a sale of the "invention" does not necessarily carry with it the ex-

[1] Pitts *v.* Hall, 3 Blatchf. 201.

clusive right for an extended term, obtained under the standing law; for this right is not a mere incident to the invention, but its existence is made to depend, not only on matter subsequent to the invention, but exclusively personal to the inventor himself, and only he or his personal representatives can obtain it.[1] But is there, then, any presumption capable of being applied to such a sale, which should exert a controlling influence upon the operation that is to be given to it? It is, on the one hand, the well-settled doctrine in relation to the act of 1836, that the extended term therein provided for was intended as a reward to an inventor who had failed to obtain an adequate remuneration for his invention during the first term; that the right to obtain it is an inchoate right, which belongs solely to the inventor or to his personal representatives; and these considerations undoubtedly had a large influence in causing the strict construction that was given in the case of Wilson *v.* Rousseau, to the clause in that act which concerned the rights of assignees. So far, therefore, as the legitimate influence of this policy of the law can extend, in the construction of a contract of sale of the invention, it should undoubtedly be held, that unless an intention to convey something beyond the first term can be found in the instrument, the assignee should not be held to take any thing beyond that term. On the other hand, while a sale of the "invention," made during or before the first or original term, may not of itself evince an intention to convey more than that term, it is quite consistent with such an intention; and if that intention can be gathered from the whole instrument, it will operate, not so much by reason of any superior force in the term "invention," as by other clauses which point to the extent and duration of the interest which was designed to be vested in the grantee.[2]

§ 208 *a*. Where a license was granted "for and during the term for which said letters-patent are or may be granted," it was held that there was nothing in this language to indicate that the parties had in view a continuance of the license during any extended term of the patent, but that it applied only to a reissue."[3]

[1] Clum *v.* Brewer, 2 Curtis, C. C. R. 506.

[2] Ibid.

[3] Hodge *v.* Hudson River & Harlem R.R. Cos. (1868), 3 Fisher's Pat. Cas. 410; S. C. 6 Blatchf. 85; also, 165. In this case Judge Blatchford said: "As to the duration of the license, nothing is said in the license about

§ 208 *b*. And so where the assignment granted all the right, title, and interest of the patentee to be held and enjoyed by the assignee

an extension of the patent. The license is to continue 'for and during the term for which said letters-patent are or may be granted.' The first question that arises is as to the meaning of these words 'may be'; and whether they refer to or can be construed to include an extended term of the patent. I do not think there is any thing in the license to indicate that the parties to it had at all in view a continuance of the license during any extended term of the patent. The provision that the license is to continue 'during the term for which said letters-patent are or may be granted,' is satisfied by holding it to apply exclusively to a reissue of the patent. There is nothing in the language which makes it exclusively or even necessarily applicable to an extension. The presumption of law in regard to every license under a patent is that the parties deal in regard only to the term existing when the license is given, unless an express provision is inserted, looking to a further interest. Wilson *v.* Rousseau, 4 How. 646, 685, 686. Unless there be such a stipulation showing that the parties contemplated an extension, the court is bound to construe the instrument, and each and all of its provisions, as relating to the existing term only. Gibson *v.* Cook, 2 Blatchf. C. C. R. 144, 146. The language of the license in the present case is very different from the language of the instrument in the case of Phelps *v.* Comstock, 4 McLean, 353. In that case, the language was: 'to the full end of the term or terms for which letters-patent are or may be granted for said improvements.' The court held that that language embraced any subsequent extension of the patent. So, also, in Case *v.* Redfield, 4 McLean, 526, where the court held that the language of the instrument embraced an extension, the language was, 'all the right, title, and interest . . . in said invention and improvement, as secured . . . by said letters-patent for the whole of the United States . . . for which letters-patent were or may be granted for said improvement.' In Clum *v.* Brewer, 2 Curtis, C. C. R. 506, 508, where the court held that the parties intended to cover an interest in an extension, the language was, 'one undivided fourth part of my said invention, and of all my right and property therein, secured by my said *caveat* or otherwise, that I have or may have from any letters-patent for the same, granted by the government of the United States, and within the limits thereof.' In Pitts *v.* Hall, 3 Blatchf. C. C. R. 201, where the court held that there was no doubt that the parties intended, by the language used, to refer to and provide for an extension, the language to that effect was clear and unambiguous. In all forms of the cases referred to, the instrument under consideration was one purporting to convey, by assignment or grant, an interest in the invention patented, and an interest in the entire right granted by the existing patent to make and use, and vend to others to be used, the invention patented. As Mr. Justice Curtis says, in Clum *v.* Brewer, p. 521: 'Where the invention is the subject sold, it would be natural to expect to find in the instrument of sale something showing an intention that the purchaser should be interested not merely in the original letters-patent, but in any extension thereof securing the exclusive right to the same invention which was the sub-

"to the full end of the term for which the said letters-patent are or may be granted," it was held that the words "may be granted" might pass a subsequent reissue of the patent for the residue of the original term, but could not be construed as including an extended term. In this case the court remarked that "the words 'may be granted' are the only ones in the whole instrument that can possibly be thought to point to an extension that might subsequently be acquired. But they must be read in connection with, and subordination to the rest of the instrument; and this very clause refers to 'the term for which the said letters-patent,' &c.; a single term is referred to, and the said letters-patent. The reference is in terms to the term and the letters-patent already mentioned. The phrase 'may be granted' seems to be an expression loosely used, and without any definite meaning in the connection in which it is found, unless it refers to other reissues of patents covering the remainder of said term. There had already been one reissue, and the facts show that a second reissue was had for the remainder of the term after this assignment, doubtless to cover some defect. These reissues are authorized by the act of Congress, and often occur. In a certain sense, when the patents thus originally issued are surrendered and others issued in their place, the whole may be regarded as the same letters-patent: they cover the same term. The reissued patent covers no improvement or extension, but is intended to rectify some error, or remedy some defect, and accomplish the

ject of the sale.' In the present case, neither the invention nor any interest in it, nor any interest in the entire right covered by the patent, was granted, but merely a license to use the invention, and to construct brakes containing it for such use, on certain cars on a certain railroad, and such license is to continue during the term for which said letters-patent are or may be granted.' The term for which said letters-patent, that is, the letters-patent granted October 2, 1849, and reissued March 1, 1853, were granted or might be granted, was a term ending October 2, 1863. It is impossible, on any fair construction of the language, and in view of the adjudged cases, to hold that the license was intended by the parties to cover an extended term of the patent. There being, then, in this case, no express stipulation, carrying the license into the extended term, the only right which the Hudson River Railroad Company possesses, under the extended term, is that which is given to it by the clause of section 18 of the act of July 4, 1836, 5 U. S. Stat. at Large, 125, which provides that the benefit of the extension of a patent shall 'extend to assignees and grantees of the right to use the thing patented to the extent of their respective interest therein.'"

identical object intended to be accomplished by the letters originally issued. In this sense, they are substantially the same letters-patent. In this view, the words 'may be granted' may have some significance as used in this instrument, and they are satisfied by applying them to any further letters-patent that might be issued for the same term, and to accomplish the same objects intended by those already issued. And in this instance there was a subsequent reissue for the remainder of the term to which they might in fact apply. But upon a view of the whole instrument, to construe them as referring to a new term, and letters-patent not yet *in esse*, would be doing great violence to the language. I have found no authority to justify such a construction."[1]

§ 208 *c*. In the case of Railroad Company *v.* Trimble,[2] decided by the Supreme Court of the United States in 1870, it appeared that one Howe, having obtained in 1840 letters-patent for an improvement in the manner of constructing the truss frame of bridges, granted all his interest therein for certain States to Isaac R. Trimble, by a deed dated July 9, 1844, which was duly recorded. This assignment conveyed the rights of Howe in these words: "All the right, title, and interest which I have in said invention, as secured to me by said letters-patent; and also all right, title, and interest which may be secured to me for alterations and improvements in the same from time to time; . . . the same to be held and enjoyed by the said Trimble, &c., to the full end of the term for which said letters-patent are or may be granted, as fully and entirely as the same would have been held and enjoyed by me, had this assignment and sale not have been made."

On the 28th of August, 1846, another patent was granted to Howe for an improvement in the manner of constructing these truss frames; and on the 18th of September, 1854, after the death of Howe, his administrator, in order to "secure to I. R. Trimble more perfectly his legal rights, and tend to a more speedy adjustment of any disputed claim," executed in favor of Trimble an assignment of the same interest in the patent of 1846 that he held in the others. On the application of the same administrator, the patent of 1846 was extended for seven years from August 28th, 1860. The Philadelphia, Wilmington, and Baltimore Railroad

[1] Jenkins *v.* Nicolson Pavement Co. (1870), 1 Abbott's U. S. Reports, 567, Sawyer, J.

[2] 10 Wall. 367.

Company having infringed the patent for this improvement, during the term of the extension, a suit for damages was brought, and the issue was raised whether the assignment of July 9, 1844, from Howe to Trimble, vested in the latter an interest in the extension of the patent of 1846.

In passing upon this question, the Supreme Court held that the language employed in the assignment included alike all the patents which had been issued, and all which might be issued to the patentee for the inventions referred to, whether reissues, renewals, or extensions. "The language employed," said Mr. Justice Swayne, "is very broad. It includes alike the patents which *had been* issued, and all which might be issued thereafter. No discrimination is made between those for the original inventions and those for alterations and improvements, nor between those which were first issues and those which were reissues or renewals and extensions. The entire inventions and all alterations and improvements, and all patents relating thereto, whensoever issued, to the extent of the territory specified, are within the scope of the terms employed. No other construction will satisfy them. Upon the fullest consideration we have no doubt such was the meaning and intent of the parties."

The judges were further of opinion that this case came directly within the principles of law laid down in Gaylor *v.* Wilder, and that the assignment by Howe of the extension of his patent, before any extension had issued, vested in the assignee, Trimble, the legal as well as the equitable title in both the original patent and the extension. In the language of the court: "The rule laid down [in Gaylor *v.* Wilder] is the law of this tribunal upon the subject. There the patent was an original one, here it is an extension. The question before us arises under the eleventh and eighteenth sections of the act of 1836. But the arguments which controlled the decision in that case apply in this with equal force. The same considerations are involved in both. There is no substantial ground of distinction. The application of the same principle to the assignment of an extended patent, made before the extension, is an inevitable corollary, from the reasoning and ruling of the court. Without, in effect, overruling that adjudication, we cannot hold that Trimble had not a legal title under the extended as well as under the original patent. In our judgment he had such a title.

"In this connection our attention has been called by the counsel for the plaintiffs in error to Wilson *v.* Rousseau, and several other cases. None of them turned upon the question we have been considering, and neither of them contains any thing in conflict with the proposition established by Gaylor *v.* Wilder."[1]

§ 208 *d.* Prior to the statute of 1870, it seems to have been the practice of the Patent Office to grant reissues to assignees of the whole patent, without requiring the original patentee to join in the surrender of the patent and the application for a reissue; and

[1] Railroad Company *v.* Trimble, 10 Wall. 367. Mr. Justice Bradley dissented, on the ground that the language in the assignment by Howe to Trimble was not sufficient to show that a transfer of the extension was intended.

In applying the principles of Gaylor *v.* Wilder to this case, Mr. Justice Swayne, who delivered the judgment of the court, said: "The effect of such a contract, we think, has been settled by this court in Gaylor *v.* Wilder and others. Fitzgerald, the inventor, before the patent was issued, assigned his entire right to Enos Wilder. The assignment contained a request that the patent should be issued to the assignee, and was duly recorded in the Patent Office. This brought the case within the terms of the sixth section of the act of 1836. Fitzgerald made no assignment after the patent was issued to him. Enos Wilder, his assignee, assigned to Benjamin Wilder, who was the plaintiff in the action. The defendants insisted that Enos Wilder had not the legal, but only an equitable title. Upon the question, whether an assignment subsequent to the issuing of the patent was necessary to pass the former to the assignee, this court said: 'We do not think the act of Congress requires it, but that when the patent issued to Fitzgerald, the legal right to the monopoly and the property it created was, by the operation of the assignment then on record, vested in Wilder.' The argument which controlled the judgment of the court may be thus stated: Fitzgerald had an inchoate right at the time of the assignment, the invention being then complete and the specification prepared. It appeared, by the language of the assignment, that it was intended to operate upon the perfect legal title, which he then had a lawful right to obtain, as well as upon the inchoate right which he then possessed. There was no sound reason for defeating the intention of the parties by restricting the assignment to the latter interest, and compelling the parties to execute another transfer, unless the act of Congress required it, which, in the opinion of the court, it did not. The act of 1836 declares that every patent shall be assignable to law. The thing to be assigned is not the mere parchment on which the grant is written, but the monopoly which the grant confers, — the right of property which it creates. And when the party has acquired an inchoate right to it, and the power to make that right perfect and absolute at his pleasure, the assignment of his whole interest, whether executed before or after the patent issued, is equally within the provisions of the act of Congress. We concur in these views. The rule laid down is the law of this tribunal upon the subject."

the courts have held such reissues to be valid. When this point was under consideration in the case of Swift *v.* Whisen,[1] Judge Leavitt remarked that "until the Supreme Court of the United States shall have had this point before them, and shall have decided adversely to the usage and practice of the Patent Office, and the views to which I have referred, I shall feel compelled to regard the statute as authorizing a reissue to an assignee of an assignee, and that without the consent, or approbation, or knowledge of the original patentee. . . . There does seem to me some inconsistency in requiring the assignee, in sustaining his application for a reissue, to go before the commissioner and to make oath in regard to the invention covered by the reissue, and to show that it is the same invention covered by the original patent. But, as I said before, there is no prohibition in the statute to this effect, and as there are no judicial decisions to the contrary, and as it has been the uniform usage of the Patent Office to grant reissues under these circumstances, the court would not now feel authorized to say that the patent in question, the patent upon which you are to pass, is invalid upon the ground referred to."

§ 208 *e*. The law on this point, however, has been regulated by the statute of 1870.[2] Section thirty-three of that act provides "that patents may be granted and issued or reissued to the assignee of the inventor or discoverer, the assignment thereof being first entered of record in the Patent Office; but in such case the applicant for the patent shall be made, and the specification sworn to, by the inventor or discoverer; and also, if he be living, in case of an application for reissue." By a subsequent act[3] it was declared that the provisions of this section should not be construed to apply to patents issued and assigned prior to July 8, 1870.

§ 208 *f*. In the case of the Commissioner of Patents *v.* Whiteley,[4] decided by the Supreme Court of the United States in 1866, the very important question was raised, whether the grantee of an exclusive territorial interest in a patent has the legal right to apply for a reissue. The defendant in error, in this case, was the assignee of the entire rights of the patentee in all the territory embraced in the patent, except the State of Ohio and a portion of Illinois; and without joining the other assignees

[1] (1867), 3 Fisher's Pat. Cas. 343.

[2] See Appendix.

[3] March 3, 1871.

[4] 4 Wall. 522.

in the application, applied to the commissioner of patents for a reissue, according to the thirteenth section of the act of 1836. The commissioner refused to consider this application, on the ground, that the applicant, not being the assignee of the whole interest in the patent, was not entitled to the reissue asked for. It is to be regretted that this important question, thus passed upon by the commissioner, was not determined by the highest judicial tribunal known to our law. The court only remarked, that it was not before them for consideration, and added: "If it were, as at present advised, we are not prepared to say that the decision of the commissioner was not correct."

§ 209. The conclusion to which the cases as well as sound principle leads is this, that the only presumption applicable to contracts for the sale of a patent interest is that the parties dealt for the existing term, unless a provision was inserted in the grant or assignment looking to a further interest.[1]

§ 210. There is one other mode in which the interests of an assignee may be affected by the act of the patentee, and that is by a disclaimer. When a disclaimer is filed under the seventh and ninth sections of the act of 1837, an assignee of the whole patent is the proper party to file it; and it has been held, that, if the patent had been previously assigned in part, the disclaimer will not operate to the benefit of the assignee, in any suit brought by him, either at law or in equity, unless he joined in the disclaimer.[2]

§ 211. We now come to that other class of contracts made by patentees, which, not being assignments, confer upon another the right to exercise in some way the privileges secured by the patent, — contracts which are popularly as well as technically known as licenses. The distinction between an assignment and a license, under our patent laws, relates to the interest in the patent, as distinguished from a mere right to use the thing patented or to practise the invention. An assignment, whether of the whole or of an undivided part of the whole patent, of the exclusive right within a particular district, necessarily operates to diminish *pro tanto* the interest of the patentee. But a license is a grant or permission to practise the invention or to use the thing patented,

1 Gibson *v.* Cooke, 2 Blatchf. 144.
2 Wyeth *v.* Stone, 1 Story's R. 273.

which leaves the interest of the patentee just as extensive as it was before. Thus, when a patentee sells to another a patented machine made by himself, or permits another to make the machine, without making the permission exclusive as to any particular territory, the party thus authorized becomes a licensee, and does not acquire the rights and position of an assignee. Such a party has no part of the legal estate; he cannot authorize others to make the machine; nor does the permission extended to him diminish in any degree the power of the patentee to make, or to authorize others to make, the patented machine. So, also, where the subject of the patent is a compound or composition of matter, if the patentee authorizes another to make and sell the article, the party so authorized becomes a licensee, but he has no interest in the patent, and no power to grant to others any portion of the exclusive right of making the thing, which is vested in the patentee.[1] Upon this distinction it follows that a license does not require to be recorded, and that suits for infringement cannot be brought in the name of the licensee, but must be brought in the name of the patentee or other person holding the legal title; for an assignee may sue in his own name, because he holds the entire and unqualified interest which the suit is to vindicate.[2]

§ 212. If, then, an instrument vests in the grantee the exclusive right, either for the whole country, or for a particular district, of making and using the thing patented, and of granting that right to others, it is an assignment. The entire monopoly secured by the patent, for the whole country or for a particular district, must be embraced by an instrument which is to operate as an assignment. Any conveyance short of this is a license.[3] If the patentee has seen fit to limit the extent of the monopoly, as by limiting the number of machines which his grantee may build and use in the particular district, the instrument may still be an assignment, provided it vests in the assignee the whole of the exclusive right so limited, including the right to grant to others the right to build and use any of the limited number of machines. But an exclusive license is no more than a common license, unless it vests

[1] Brooks *v.* Byam, 2 Story's R. 525, 538, 539, 542.

[2] Gaylor *v.* Wilder, 10 How. 477.

[3] Ibid.; Blanchard *v.* Eldredge, 1 J. W. Wallace, 337; Brooks *v.* Byam, 2 Story, 525; Protheroe *v.* May, 1 Webs. Pat. Cas. 445; s. c. 5 Mees. & Welsb. 675; Woodworth *v.* Wilson, 4 How. 712.

in the licensee a right to grant to others the right to make and use the thing patented.[1]

§ 212 *a*. Where the patentee had transferred all his right, title, and interest in certain letters-patent, embracing all future terms and improvements, to the assignee "to manufacture and sell the same within the States of New York and Connecticut," it was contended on behalf of the defendants that this instrument was not an assignment of the whole or of an undivided part of the patent.[2] It was held by the court, however, that such an instrument, if not technically an assignment of the patent, or an undivided part thereof, was a grant of the exclusive right under the patent to use, and to grant to others to make and use, the thing patented within the limits specified, and was sufficient to warrant a suit in the name of the assignee for an infringement within the territory named. The effect of this instrument was thus discussed by Mr. Justice Woodruff, who delivered the opinion of the court: "Although the instrument does not employ the terms 'to grant to others to make and use' the invention, &c., I think its just construction fully excludes the patentee from all interest in, or control over, the invention, or the manufacture or use of the thing patented, within the specified territory, and so excludes him from any right to confer the privilege upon any others. He assigns all his right, title, and interest in the invention, improvement, or patent, within and throughout the two States mentioned, for the term of the patent, and the terms of any patent for the same or other improvements thereof, or any extensions for or of either thereof, which might be granted to the assignor, or his heirs, executors, administrators, or assigns, to manufacture and sell the same within the States of New York and Connecticut. This transfers the whole interest of the patentee in those States; and the concluding words of the granting clause do not restrict the grantees to the manufacture in their own persons. They are descriptive of the future and other improvements and extensions which might thereafter be granted to the patentee, to manufacture and sell in New York and Connecticut, and are not limitations or qualifications of the full right, title, and interest in the invention and its use, previously therein granted. That the as-

[1] Gaylor *v.* Wilder, 10 How. 477; Woodworth *v.* Wilson, 4 How. 712; Protheroe *v.* May, 1 Webs. Pat. Cas. 445; Ritter *v.* Serrell, 2 Blatchf. 379.

[2] Perry *v.* Corning (1870), 7 Blatchf. 195.

signment gave to Treadwell and Perry the entire monopoly which the patentee had in those States, and to the exclusion of the patentee himself, is, I think, quite certain; and this is made the test of the right to sue, in Gaylor *v.* Wilder, by Chief Justice Taney."

§ 212 *b.* In Hussey *v.* Whitely it appeared that the complainant by a written instrument had granted the exclusive right to make and sell his improved reaping and mowing machine during the continuance of his patent in twenty-three counties of Ohio, including that in which the defendant's factory was carried on. The consideration was to be ten dollars for each machine made and sold by the licensees; but the plaintiff expressly reserved the right of sending machines of his own manufacture into the territory embraced in the contract. This was held to be not an assignment of the interest of Hussey in the patent within the territory named, but a mere license; and the complainant, as a "party aggrieved," under section seventeen of the act of 1836, had a remedy in chancery for infringement without joining the licensees above-mentioned as parties complainant.[1]

§ 213. A license, being an authority to exercise some of the privileges secured by the patent, but which still leaves an interest in the monopoly in the patentee, the first question that arises is, whether it is assignable. This quality is inherent in an assignment, but whether it belongs to a license depends on the terms of the instrument. A mere license to a party, without mentioning his *assigns*, is a grant of a power, or a dispensation with a right or a remedy, and confers a personal right upon the licensee, which is not transmissible to another person. It seems, however, that the use of the word "assigns" in the granting part of a license will not necessarily operate to make it assignable, when, from the tenor of the whole instrument, it appears to have been intended as a personal privilege.[2] But whether a license is assignable or not, as to the entirety of the privilege, it is still more questionable whether it is apportionable, so as to permit the licensee to grant to others rights to work the patent, by subdividing the rights that may have been granted to himself.

§ 214. This question arose in a case where the patentee of friction matches granted to another the right to make, use, and sell

[1] Hussey *v.* Whitely (1860), 2 Fisher's Pat. Cas. 120.
[2] Brooks *v.* Byam, 2 Story's R. 525.

the friction matches, and "to have and to hold the right and privilege of manufacturing the said matches, and *to employ in and about the same six persons and no more*, and to vend the said matches in the United States." The licensee afterwards undertook to sell and convey to a third person "a right of manufacturing friction matches, according to letters-patent, &c., in said town of A., to the amount of *one right*, embracing one person only, so denominated, in as full and ample a manner to the extension (extent) of the said one right, as the original patentee." Mr. Justice Story held that every conveyance of this sort must be construed according to its own terms and objects, in order to ascertain the true intent and meaning of the parties; and that, in this case, the interest under the license was an entirety, incapable of being split up into distinct rights, each of which could be assigned to different persons in severalty.[1]

§ 215. The relations of a licensee to the patentee, in respect to the validity and scope of the patent, involve an inquiry into the terms of the license. The taking of a naked license, or permission to work under a patent, does not, without some recitals or covenants amounting to an admission, estop the licensee from denying the validity of the patent, or the fact that he has used the patented thing or process, if he is subsequently proceeded against for infringement. It is necessary to look into the instrument, and to ascertain that there are recitals or covenants which will deprive a licensee of the defences to which all other persons may resort. If, by his agreement, the licensee has admitted that the process or thing which he uses is the patented process or thing, and he is afterwards proceeded against for not complying with the terms of his agreement, he will not be permitted to show that he did not use that patented thing or process.[2] So, too, if the deed contain recitals or statements amounting to an admission of the validity of the patent, either as to the novelty or utility of the supposed invention, or the sufficiency of the specification, the licensee will be estopped in an action of covenant for the rent or license dues, to deny the validity of the patent, by setting up any thing contrary to the admissions in the deed.[3] But if the

[1] Brooks *v.* Byam, 2 Story's R. 525.

[2] Baird *v.* Neilson, 8 Cl. & Fin. 726.

[3] Bowman *v.* Taylor, 2 Ad. & El. 278; Jones *v.* Lees, 38 Eng. L. & Eq. R. 318.

patentee join issue upon an allegation made by a licensee contrary to an admission in his deed, instead of pleading the estoppel, the deed will be evidence for the patentee, but will not, as evidence, be conclusive.[1]

§ 216. It has also been held that a licensee, who has paid an annuity in consideration of a license to use a patent privilege, which he has had the benefit of, cannot recover back the money he has paid, upon the ground of the invalidity of the patent, in an action for money had and received.[2] This is upon the ground that the licensee has had the benefit of what he stipulated for, and also upon the ground that the consideration is not divisible. But another question arises where there are periodical payments reserved by a license, and after some payments have been made, and while others remain to be made, the patent turns out to be invalid. In such a case, is there an estoppel growing out of the mere fact that the licensee has dealt with the patentee as if the patent were valid, and has paid some of the license dues? It would appear from the case of Hayne *v.* Maltby, and from the mode in which that case has been subsequently understood, that the estoppel must arise out of recitals or admissions of the defendant in his contract, and that it does not arise out of the mere circumstance of having worked under a license. In Hayne *v.* Maltby there was no recital of the plaintiff's title, but an agreement to use a machine according to the specification, and a covenant to pay. A plea that the invention was not new was sustained, and it was held that the doctrine of estoppel did not apply.[3] The effect of this case has been thus explained by Lord Cottenham: "That although a party has dealt with the patentee, and has carried on business, yet that he may stop, and then the party who claims to be patentee cannot recover without giving the other party the opportunity of disputing his right, and if the defendant successfully dispute his right, that notwithstanding he has been dealing under a contract, it is competent to the defendant to do so. That is exactly coming to the point which I put,

[1] Bowman *v.* Rostrom, 2 Ad. & El. 295.

[2] Taylor *v.* Hare, 1 N. R. 260; s. c. 1 Webs. Pat. Cas. 292. Where the contract between patentee and licensee has been executed, and is not still executory, a plea by the licensee that the patent is invalid, in an action for the license money, is bad. Lawes *v.* Purser, 38 Law & Eq. R. 48.

[3] Hayne *v.* Maltby, 3 T. R. 438.

whether, at law, the party was estopped from disputing the patentee's right, after having once dealt with him as the proprietor of that right; and it appears from the authority of that case, and from the other cases, that from the time of the last payment, if the manufacturer can successfully resist the patent right of the party claiming the rent, that he may do so in answer to an action for the rent for the use of the patent during that year." [1]

§ 217. Where there has been no enjoyment by the licensee, and there is no covenant or recital admitting the validity of the patent, its invalidity may be set up as a failure of consideration, in an action upon an agreement to pay a certain sum for the right to use the patent privilege.[2] The competency of a licensee to dispute the validity of the patent is a question which may also arise where the licensee is proceeded against for an infringement, upon the ground that he is using the patent contrary to the conditions in his license. If, for example, one receive a license to use a patented machine on condition that he pay a stipulated sum on all the articles which he may make by it, and, after having begun to use the machine, he refuses or neglects to pay the license dues, or to comply with any other condition of the license, he may be enjoined in equity for an infringement like any other person unlawfully using the machine.[3] Whether, in such a case, the licensee can set up the invalidity of the patent, as any other party could, must depend on the terms and operation of his contract, and upon what he himself claims under it. Merely taking a license, without any covenants or recitals admitting the validity of the patent, does not, as we have already seen, estop the licensee. But if there are such admissions in the contract, and the licensee has worked under it, and has paid the license dues for a time, and then stops, or if he still continues to claim under the license, and excuses his non-payment by reason of the non-performance of some agreement on the part of the patentee, he will still remain bound by his relation as licensee to admit the validity of the patent, and the sole question will be whether he is liable for an infringement; which will depend upon the validity of his excuses for not paying on account of a breach of

[1] Neilson *v.* Fothergill, 1 Webs. Pat. Cas. 290.

[2] Chauter *v.* Leese, 4 M. & W. 295; affirmed on error, 5 M. & W. 698.

[3] Brooks *v.* Stolley, 3 M'Lean, 523; Neilson *v.* Fothergill, Webs. Pat. Cas. 287, 290; Woodworth *v.* Cooke, 2 Blatchf. 151.

the agreement by the patentee. But a different question arises where the licensee undertakes to repudiate the contract of license altogether, and to stand upon the right of every person to use the alleged invention because it is not new, or because the patent is void for some other reason. In such a case he foregoes all benefit of the license as a permission to use the alleged invention; but having taken the license, he is estopped by any admissions which it contains, unless he can avoid their effect by showing that he was deceived and misled.

§ 218. The situation of a licensee where the patentee undertakes to treat the license as forfeited for non-performance or violation of the conditions of the license, also presents several important subjects of inquiry. In the first place, it has been held, that a clause in a license, making it void on non-payment of the money consideration stipulated, is to be regarded as giving the patentee a double remedy; that is to say, he may enforce the collection of what is due to him, or he may treat the license as forfeited, and proceed to enjoin the licensee as infringer.[1] So, too, a breach of a condition in a license, under which the licensee was bound not to sell the manufactured products of a machine to be carried for consumption out of the territory embraced by the license, works a forfeiture, and the licensee may be enjoined.[2] In the next place, it has been held, that where the proprietor of the patent elects to treat a license as forfeited for breach of a condition, and to proceed against the licensee as against any other person using the patented thing without right, and to have the license declared void, the defendant is remitted to any rights he had anterior to the license, so that he may set up in his answer (in equity) a right which he had derived from the original patentee under a former term of the patent, and which in con-

[1] Woodworth *v.* Weed, 1 Blatchf. 165.

[2] Wilson *v.* Sherman, 1 Blatchf. 536. In this case the condition on which a license was granted to use a machine for planing lumber was, that the licensee should not sell to others the manufactured products of the machine to be carried out of the territory or sold as an article of merchandise, or dress lumber for other persons to be carried out of the territory and resold as an article of merchandise. It was held that the true meaning and operation of this restriction was, that the manufactured product should not, with the privity or consent of the licensee, be sold out of the territory as an article of merchandise, or with his privity and consent be sold within the territory, to be carried out and resold as merchandise.

templation of law survived into the existing term.[1] How far the principle of this decision would extend, to permit the defendant to avoid any admissions contained in the license respecting the validity of the patent, is, of course, questionable. It is to be observed that what was held in this case was that, where the plaintiff undertook to avoid the license by reason of a breach of a condition on the part of the licensee, or, in other words, to proceed against the licensee as a person without a title to use the invention, the latter could be permitted to show a prior title devolved upon him before the license, and still existing. But it may be questioned whether, in such a case, the defendant, as against admissions made by him in his contract of license respecting the validity of the patent, would be remitted to *all* the rights which he had anterior to the license, one of which would have been the right to dispute the patent itself. The decision above cited does not extend to this point.

§ 218 *a*. A license to a person to use an invention "at his own establishment, but not to be disposed of to others for that purpose," simply authorizes the licensee to use it himself at his own establishment, and does not confer upon him the right to authorize others to use it in conjunction with himself, or otherwise; nor is he entitled to use it at another establishment owned by himself and others.[2] And so where a railroad company was licensed to use a patented improvement, and subsequently by consolidation and change of name greatly extended their lines, it was held that the license extended no further than the road in use at the time of granting the license, or which the company was then authorized to construct, and did not therefore entitle the company to use the improvement on the newly acquired portion.[3] So also a license to use vulcanized India rubber for coating cloths for the purpose of japanning, marbling and variegated japanning, restricted the licensee to the manufacture of the particular kind of goods therein specified, and conveys no authority to use the rubber for coating cloths for any other purpose.[4]

[1] Woodworth *v.* Cook, 2 Blatchf. 151.

[2] Rubber Company *v.* Goodyear (1869), 9 Wall. 788.

[3] Emigle *v.* Chicago, Burlington, & Quincy R.R. Co. (1863), 2 Fisher's Pat. Cas. 387.

[4] Goodyear *v.* Providence Rubber Co. (R. I. 1864), 2 Fisher's Pat. Cas. 499.

CHAPTER VI.

THE SPECIFICATION.

§ 219. Having ascertained the kinds of subjects for which letters-patent may be obtained, and the parties entitled to take, renew, or extend them, we have now to state the proceedings requisite to the issuing, renewal, and extension of patents, and the principles which govern their construction. As the first step to be taken, in making application for a patent, is to prepare a written description of the invention or discovery, the requisites for this instrument, called the specification, and the rules for its construction, will first engage our attention.

§ 220. The act of Congress of July 4, 1836, c. 357, § 6, contained the following enactment: —

"But before any inventor shall receive a patent for any such new invention or discovery, he shall deliver a written description of his invention or discovery, and of the manner and process of making, constructing, using, and compounding the same, in such full, clear, and exact terms, avoiding unnecessary prolixity, as to enable any person skilled in the art or science to which it appertains, or with which it is most nearly connected, to make, construct, compound, and use the same; and in case of any machine, he shall fully explain the principle and the several modes in which he has contemplated the application of that principle or character by which it may be distinguished from other inventions; and shall particularly specify and point out the part, improvement, or combination, which he claims as his own invention or discovery. He shall, furthermore, accompany the whole with a drawing or drawings, and written references, where the nature of the case admits of drawings, or with specimens of ingredients, and of the composition of matter, sufficient in quantity for the purpose of experiment, where the invention or discovery is of a composition of matter; which descriptions and drawings, signed by the inventor and attested by two witnesses, shall be filed in the Patent Office; and he shall, moreover, furnish a model of his invention, in all cases which admit of a representation by model, of a convenient size to exhibit advantageously its several parts." [1]

These provisions were substantially re-enacted in the law of 1870.[2]

§ 221. The specification, under our law, occupies a relation to the patent somewhat different from the rule in England. In England the specification does not form part of the patent, so as to control its construction; but the rights of the inventor are made to depend on the description of his invention, inserted in the title of the patent, and cannot be helped by the specification, the office of which is to describe the mode of constructing, using, or compounding the invention mentioned in the patent.[3] But in the United States the specification is drawn up and filed before the patent is granted, and is referred to in the patent itself, a copy being annexed. It is therefore the settled rule in this

[1] The act of 1793, c. 55, § 3, sets forth the requisites of a specification as follows: "And be it further enacted, that every inventor, before he can receive a patent, shall swear or affirm, that *he does verily believe, that he is the true inventor or discoverer of the art, machine, or improvement, for which he solicits a patent;* which oath or affirmation may be made before any person authorized to administer oaths, and shall deliver a written description of his invention, and of the manner of using or process of compounding the same, in such full, clear, and exact terms as to distinguish the same from all other things before known, and to enable any person skilled in the art or science of which it is a branch, or with which it is most nearly connected, to make, compound, and use the same. And in the case of any machine, he shall fully explain the principle, and the several modes in which he has contemplated the application of that principle or character, by which it may be distinguished from other inventions; and he shall accompany the whole with drawings and written references, where the nature of the case admits of drawings, or with specimens of the ingredients, and of the composition of matter, sufficient in quantity for the purpose of experiment, where the invention is of a composition of matter; which description, signed by himself and attested by two witnesses, shall be filed in the office of the Secretary of State, and certified copies thereof shall be competent evidence, in all courts, where any matter or thing, touching such patent right, shall come in question. And such inventor shall, moreover, deliver a model of his machine, provided the Secretary shall deem such model to be necessary."

[2] See *post*, §§ 275 *a* and 275 *b*, also appendix.

[3] Phillips on Patents, p. 223; Godson on Patents, p. 108, 117; Hogg *v.* Emerson, 6 How. 437, 479.

country that the patent and the specification are to be construed together, in order to ascertain the subject-matter of the invention, and that the specification may control the generality of the terms of the patent, of which it forms a part.[1] In like manner drawings annexed to a specification, in compliance with the statute, are held to form a part of it, and are to be regarded in the construction of the whole instrument.[2] Where the term "patent," therefore, is used in the following discussion of the rules of construction, it will be understood to include the specification and drawings annexed to it.[3]

§ 222. In construing patents, it is the province of the court to determine what it is that is intended to be patented, and whether the patent is valid in point of law. Whether the invention itself be specifically described with reasonable certainty is a question of law upon the construction of the terms of the patent; so that it is for the court to determine whether the invention is so vague and incomprehensible as in point of law not to be patentable, whether it is a claim for an improved machine, for a combination, or a single invention; and, in short, to determine what the subject-matter is, upon the whole face of the specification and the accompanying drawings.[4] It is, therefore, the duty of the jury

[1] Whittemore *v.* Cutter, 1 Gallis. 429, 437; Barrett *v.* Hall, 1 Mas. 447, 477; Pitts *v.* Whitman, 2 Story's R. 609, 621. So, too, the specification may enlarge the recitals of the invention in the letters. Hogg *v.* Emerson, *ut supra.*

[2] Earle *v.* Sawyer, 4 Mas. 9. It seems, too, that drawings not *referred to* in the specification may be used to explain it. Washburn *v.* Gould, 3 Story's R. 122, 133; Brooks *v.* Bicknell, 3 M'Lean's R. 250, 261. But they must be drawings accompanying the specification, otherwise they do not form a part of it.

[3] The fifth section of the act of 1836 declares that "every patent shall contain a short description or title of the invention or discovery, correctly indicating its nature and design," and "referring to the specification for the particulars thereof, a copy of which shall be annexed to the patent, specifying what the patentee claims as his invention or discovery." The Supreme Court of the United States, in a recent case, have held that wherever this form of letters, with a specification annexed and referred to, has been adopted, either before or since the act of 1836, the specification is to be considered as part of the letters in construing them. Hogg *v.* Emerson, 6 How. 437, 482.

[4] Davis *v.* Palmer, 2 Brock. 298; Lowell *v.* Lewis, 1 Mas. 189; Carver *v.* Braintree Manuf. Co., 2 Story, 434, 437, 441; Washburn *v.* Gould, 3 Story, 122, 130, 137, 138, 140, 141; Davoll *v.* Brown, 1 Woodbury & Minot, 53, 56; Emerson *v.* Hogg, 2 Blatchf. 1.

to take the construction of the patent from the court, absolutely, where there are no terms of art made use of which require to be explained by evidence, and no surrounding circumstances to be ascertained as matter of fact, before a construction can be put upon the instrument. But where terms of art requiring explanation are made use of, or where the surrounding circumstances affect the meaning of the specification, these terms and circumstances are necessarily referred to the jury, who must take the construction from the court, conditionally, and determine it according as they find the facts thus put to them.[1]

Where, however, it becomes necessary to compare two specifications, e. g. where the defendant, in an action for infringement, controverts the novelty of plaintiff's invention by producing a patent previously granted to some third party, several questions arise, which have recently received in England an elaborate discussion. One is, whether the *court alone* can, on a mere comparison of the two specifications, decide that the inventions therein described are in fact identical.[2] The other is, whether the prior specification, which is relied upon to defeat the claim of a subsequent patentee, must be in itself so clear and complete as to sustain a patent therefor, or whether it is enough if it contain

[1] Washburn *v.* Gould, *ut supra.* In Neilson *v.* Harford, Webs. Pat. Cas. 370, in the Exchequer, Parke, B., delivering the judgment of the court, said: "Then we come to the question itself, which depends on the proper construction to be put on the specification itself. It was contended, that of this construction the jury were to judge. We are clearly of a different opinion. The construction of all written instruments belongs to the court alone, whose duty it is to construe all written instruments as soon as the true meaning of the words in which they are couched and the surrounding circumstances, if any, have been ascertained by the jury; and it is the duty of the jury to take the construction from the court, either absolutely, if there be no words to be construed as words of art, or phrases used in commerce, and the surrounding circumstances to be ascertained, or conditionally, where those words or circumstances are necessarily referred to them. Unless this were so, there would be no certainty in the law, for a misconstruction by the court is the proper subject, by means of a bill of exceptions, of redress in a court of error, but a misconstruction by the jury cannot be set right at all effectually. Then, taking the construction of this specification upon ourselves, as we are bound to do, it becomes necessary to examine what the nature of the invention is which the plaintiff has disclosed by this instrument."

[2] On this point consult the chapter on Questions of Law and of Fact.

a mere hint of the process or other invention underlying the subsequent patent.[1]

§ 223. It is, however, the province of the jury to decide, on the evidence of experts, whether the invention is described in such full, clear, and exact terms as to enable a skilful person to put it in practice, from the specification itself.[2] As specifications are drawn by persons more conversant with the subject than juries, who are selected indiscriminately from the public, and as they are addressed to competent workmen, familiar with the science or branch of industry to which the subject belongs, the evidence of those persons must be resorted to who are able to tell the jury that they see enough on the face of the specification to enable them to make the article, or reproduce the subject of the patent, without difficulty.[3]

§ 224. The rule of our law, that the specification may control the generality of the terms of the patent, must be subject to this qualification. If there is a clear repugnancy between the description of the invention as given in the specification, and the invention stated in the letters-patent, the patent will be void; for if the letters are issued for an invention that is not described in the specification, the statute is not complied with. The rule which allows the letters-patent to be controlled by the specification cannot extend to a case where the terms of the former are inconsistent with those of the latter.[4]

[1] As to this, see Chapter on Action at Law. The leading cases on the subject are Bovill *v.* Pimm, 36 E. L. & Eq. 441; Bush *v.* Fox, 38 E. L. & Eq. 1; Betts *v.* Menzies, 7 Law Times, N. S. 110, or 4 Best & Smith, Q. B. 996, overruling same case in 8 Ell. & Blackb. 923; Hill *v.* Evans, 6 Law Times, N. S. 90.

[2] Davis *v.* Palmer, 2 Brock. 298; Lowell *v.* Lewis, 1 Mas. 182, 190; Carver *v.* Braintree Manf. Co., 2 Story's R. 432, 437, 441; Washburn *v.* Gould, 3 Story's R. 122, 138; Davoll *v.* Brown, 1 Woodbury & Minot, 53, 57; Walton *v.* Potter, Webs. Pat. Cas. 585, 595.

[3] Walton *v.* Potter, Webs. Pat. Cas. 585, 595.

[4] The case of the King *v.* Wheeler, 2 Barn. & Ald. 345, presents an instance of the invention stated in the patent remaining wholly undescribed by the specification, which described something else. In the recent case of Cook *v.* Pearce, 8 Ad. & Ell. N. S. 1044, where the patent was taken out "for improvement in *carriages*," and the invention was in fact an improvement in *German shutters*, which were used only in some kinds of carriages, the Exchequer Chamber, reversing the opinion of the Q. B., held that where the title is not inconsistent with the specification, and no fraud is practised on the crown or the

§ 225. The general rule for the construction of patents in this country is that they are to be construed liberally, and not to be subjected to a rigid interpretation. The nature and extent of the invention claimed by the patentee is the thing to be ascertained; and this is to be arrived at through the fair sense of the words which he has employed to describe his invention.[1]

subject, it is not a fatal objection that the title is so general as to be capable of comprising a different invention from that which is claimed; and that the title in question did not necessarily imply any untrue assertion, and the patent was valid.

[1] Ames *v.* Howard, 1 Sumner, 482, 485. Mr. Justice Story said: "Patents for inventions are not to be treated as mere monopolies, odious in the eyes of the law, and therefore not to be favored; nor are they to be construed with the utmost rigor, as *strictissimi juris*. The Constitution of the United States, in giving authority to Congress to grant such patents for a limited period, declares the object to be to promote the progress of science and useful arts, an object as truly national and meritorious and well founded in public policy as any which can possibly be within the scope of national protection. Hence, it has always been the course of the American courts (and it has latterly become that of the English courts also) to construe these patents fairly and liberally, and not to subject them to any over-nice and critical refinements. The object is to ascertain what, from the fair sense of the words of the specification, is the nature and extent of the invention claimed by the party; and when the nature and extent of that claim are apparent, not to fritter away his rights upon formal or subtle objections of a purely technical character."

In Blanchard *v.* Sprague, 3 Sumner, 535, 539, the same learned judge said: "Formerly, in England, courts of law were disposed to indulge in a very close and strict construction of the specifications accompanying patents, and expressing the nature and extent of the invention. This construction seems to have been adopted upon the notion, that patent rights were in the nature of monopolies, and therefore were to be narrowly watched, and construed with a rigid adherence to their terms, as being in derogation of the general rights of the community. At present a far more liberal and expanded view of the subject is taken. Patents for inventions are now treated as a just reward for ingenious men, and as highly beneficial to the public, not only by holding out suitable encouragements to genius and talents and enterprise, but as ultimately securing to the whole community great advantages from the free communication of secrets, and processes, and machinery, which may be most important to all the great interests of society, to agriculture, to commerce, and to manufactures, as well as to the cause of science and art. In America this liberal view of the subject has always been taken; and indeed it is a natural, if not a necessary result, from the very language and intent of the power given to Congress by the Constitution, on this subject. Congress (says the Constitution) shall have power to promote the progress of science and useful arts, by securing for limited times to authors and inventors the exclu-

Patents for inventions are not to be treated as mere monopolies, and therefore as odious in the law, but are to receive a liberal construction, and under a fair application of the rule that they be construed *ut res magis valeat quam pereat.* Hence where the claim immediately follows the description, it may be construed in connection with the explanations contained in the specification, and be restricted accordingly.[1]

§ 226. But at the same time it is to be observed, that the statute prescribes certain requisites for this description of an invention which are of long standing; and the decisions of the courts, explaining and enforcing these requisites, have established certain rules of construction, intended to guard the public against defective or insufficient descriptions, on the one hand, and to guard inventors, on the other hand, against the acuteness and ingenuity and captious objections of rivals and pirates. The foundation of all these rules of construction is to be found in the object of the specification, which may be thus stated, in the language of the Supreme Court of the United States.

§ 227. The specification has two objects: one is to make known the manner of constructing the machine (if the invention is of a machine) so as to enable artisans to make and use it, and thus to give the public the full benefit of the discovery after the expiration of the patent; the other object of the specification is, to put the public in possession of what the party claims as his own invention, so as to ascertain if he claim any thing that is in common use or is already known, and to guard against prejudice or injury from the use of an invention which the party may otherwise innocently suppose not to be patented. It is, therefore, for the purpose of warning an innocent purchaser or other person using a machine of his infringement of the patent, and at the same time of taking

sive right of their respective writings and discoveries." Patents, then, are clearly entitled to a liberal construction, since they are not granted as restrictions upon the rights of the community, but are granted "to promote science and useful arts."

See, also, Ryan *v.* Goodwin, 3 Sumner, 514, where it is said that if the court can perceive, on the whole instrument, the exact nature and extent of the claim made by the inventor, it is bound to adopt that interpretation, and to give it full effect. See also Wyeth *v.* Stone, 1 Story's R. 270, 286; Davoll *v.* Brown, 1 Woodbury & Minot, 53, 57.

[1] Turrill *v.* Michigan Southern, &c. R.R., 1 Wall. 491. See Turrill *v.* Illinois Central R.R. Co., 3 Fisher's Pat. Cas. 330.

from the inventor the means of practising upon the credulity or the fears of other persons, by pretending that his invention is more than what it really is, or different from its ostensible objects, that the patentee is required to distinguish his invention in his specification.[1]

The claim is not intended to be any description of the means by which the invention is to be performed, but is introduced for the security of the patentee, that he may not be supposed to claim more than he can support as an invention. It is introduced, lest in describing and ascertaining the nature of his invention, and by what means the same is to be performed (particularly in the case of a patent for an improvement), the patentee should have inadvertently described something which is not new, in order to render his description of the improvement intelligible. The claim *is not intended to aid the description, but to ascertain the extent of what is claimed as new.* It is not to be looked to as the means of making a machine according to the patentee's improvements.[2]

§ 228. It has been justly remarked, by a learned writer, that the statute requisites for a good specification run so much into each other, in their nature and character, and are so blended together, that it is difficult to treat of them separately.[3] But the leading purposes of the whole of the statute directions are two: *first*, to inform the public what the thing is of which the patentee claims to be the inventor, and therefore the exclusive proprietor during the existence of his patent; *second*, to enable the public, from the specification itself, to practise the invention thus described, after the expiration of the patent. The principles of construction, and the authorities from which they are drawn, may therefore be discussed with reference to these two objects.

§ 229. I. The first rule for preparing a specification is, —

To describe the subject-matter, or what the patentee claims to have invented, so as to enable the public to know what his claim is.

Whether the patentee has done this, in a given case, is, as we have seen, generally a question of law for the court, on the construction of the patent. It is not necessary that the language employed should be technical, or scientific, although at the same time it must not mislead. If the terms made use of will enable

[1] Evans *v.* Eaton, 7 Wheaton, 356, 433.

[2] Per Lord Cottenham, L. C., in Kay *v.* Marshall, 2 Webs. Pat. Cas. 39.

[3] Phillips on Patents, p. 237.

the court to ascertain clearly, by fair interpretation, what the party intends to claim, an inaccuracy or imperfection in the language will not vitiate the specification.[1] But it must appear with reasonable certainty what the party intends to claim; for it is not to be left to minute references and conjectures, as to what was previously known or unknown; since the question is not what was before known, but what the patentee claims as new.[2] If the patentee has left it wholly ambiguous and uncertain, so loosely defined, and so inaccurately expressed, that the court cannot, upon fair interpretation of the words, and without resorting to mere vague conjecture of invention, gather what the invention is, then the patent is void for this defect. But if the court can clearly see what is the nature and extent of the claim, by a reasonable use of the means of interpretation of the language used, then, it is said, the patentee is entitled to the benefit of it, however imperfectly and inartificially he may have expressed himself. For this purpose, phrases standing alone are not to be singled out, but the whole is to be taken in connection.[3]

§ 230. The statute requires the patentee to give "a written description of his invention or discovery." This involves the necessity, in all cases where the patentee makes use of what is old, of distinguishing between what is old and what is new. He is required to point out in what his invention or discovery consists;

[1] Wyeth *v.* Stone, 1 Story's R. 271, 286; Carver *v.* The Braintree Manf. Co., 2 Story's R. 408, 446; Neilson *v.* Harford, Webs. Pat. Cas. 331, 369; Bloxam *v.* Elsee, 1 Car. & P. 558; Blake *v.* Stafford, 3 Fisher's Pat. Cas. 294.

[2] Lowell *v.* Lewis, 1 Mas. 182, 188. A general statement that the patented machine is, in all material respects (without stating what respects), an improvement on an old machine, is no specification at all. Ib. See also Kneass *v.* The Schuylkill Bank, 4 Wash. 9. If the patent be for an improved machine, or for an improvement of a machine (the meaning of the terms is the same), it must state in what the improvement specifically consists, and it must be limited to such improvement. If, therefore, the terms be so obscure or doubtful that the court cannot say which is the particular improvement which the patentee claims, and to what it is limited, the patent is void for ambiguity; and if it covers more than the improvement, it is void, because it is broader than the invention. Barrett *v.* Hall, 1 Mas. 447.

[3] Ames *v.* Howard, 1 Sumner, 482, 485. The drawings are to be taken in connection with the words, and if, by a comparison of the words and the drawings, the one would explain the other sufficiently to enable a skilful mechanic to perform the work, the specification is sufficient. Bloxam *v.* Elsee, 1 Car. & P. 558.

and if he includes in his description what has been invented before, without showing that he does not claim to have invented that, his patent will be broader than his invention, and therefore void.[1] Whatever appears to be covered by the claim of the patentee, as his own invention, must be taken as part of the claim, for courts of law are not at liberty to reject any part of the claim; and therefore if it turns out that any thing claimed is not new, the patent is void, however small or unimportant such asserted invention may be.[2]

[1] Dixon *v.* Moyer, 4 Wash. 68, 73. In this case, Mr. Justice Washington said: "It was insisted by the plaintiff's counsel, that this specification is perfectly intelligible to an artist, who could experience no difficulty in making such a saddle as is there described; and that if it be not so, still the defendant cannot avail himself of the defect, unless he had stated it in his notice, and also proved at the trial an intention in the plaintiff to deceive the public. But these observations are all wide of the objection, which is not that the specification does not contain the whole truth relative to the discovery, or that it contains more than is necessary. It is admitted that the specification does not offend in either of these particulars. But the objection is, that throughout the whole of a very intelligible description of the mode of making the saddle, the patentee has not distinguished what was new from what was old and before in use, nor pointed out in what particulars his improvement consisted." See also Carpenter *v.* Smith, Webs. Pat. Cas. 530, 532, where Lord Abinger, C. B., said: "It is required as a condition of every patent, that the patentee shall set forth in his specification a true account and description of his patent or invention, and it is necessary in that specification that he should state what his invention is, what he claims to be new, and what he admits to be old; for if the specification states simply the whole machinery which he uses, and which he wishes to introduce into use, and claims the whole of that as new, and does not state that he claims either any particular part, or the combination of the whole as new, why then his patent must be taken to be a patent for the whole, and for each particular part, and his patent will be void if any particular part turns out to be old, or the combination itself not new." See also Davis *v.* Palmer, 2 Brock. 298; Wyeth *v.* Stone, 1 Story's R. 273; Lowell *v.* Lewis, 1 Mas. 188, where Mr. Justice Story said: "The patentee is clearly not entitled to include in his patent the exclusive use of any machinery already known; and if he does, his patent will be broader than his invention, and consequently void. If, therefore, the description in the patent mixes up the old and the new, and does not distinctly ascertain for which, in particular, the patent is claimed, it must be void; since if it covers the whole, it covers too much, and if not intended to cover the whole, it is impossible for the court to say what, in particular, is covered as the new invention."

[2] Moody *v.* Fiske, 2 Mas. 112, 118. In this case, Mr. Justice Story said: "Where the patentee claims any thing as his own invention, in his specifica-

§ 231. But there is a very important rule to be attended to, in this connection, which has been laid down by the Court of Common Pleas in England, viz., that a specification should be so construed, as, consistently with the fair import of language, will make the claim coextensive with the actual discovery. So that a patentee, unless his language necessarily imports a claim of things in use, will be presumed not to intend to claim things which he must know to be in use.[1]

tion, courts of law cannot reject the claim ; and if included in the patent, and found not to be new, the patent is void."

In the case of Campion *v.* Benyon, 3 Brod. & B. 5, the patent was taken out for " an improved method of making sail-cloth, without any starch whatever." The real improvement consisted in a new mode of texture, and not in the exclusion of starch, the advantage of excluding that substance having been discovered and made public before. Park, J., said : " In the patentee's process he tells us that the necessity of using starch is superseded, and mildew thereby entirely prevented ; but if he meant to claim as his own an improved method of texture or twisting the thread to be applied to the making of unstarched cloth, he might have guarded himself against ambiguity, *by disclaiming* as his own discovery the advantage of excluding starch." In this case, the specification itself furnished no means by which the generality of its expressions could be restrained. But there is a case where the literal meaning of terms which would have covered too much ground was limited by other phrases used in the context. The specification stated the invention to be an improved apparatus for " extracting inflammable gas by heat, from pit-coal, tar, or *any other substance* from which gas or gases, capable of being employed for illumination, can be extracted by heat." Lord Tenterden held that the words " any other substance " must mean other substances *ejusdem generis ;* and therefore that it was not a fatal defect that the apparatus would not extract gas from oil ; and that oil was not meant to be included, it being at that time considered too expensive for the making of gas for purposes of illumination, though it was known to be capable of being so used. Crossley *v.* Beverly, 3 Car. & P. 513 ; Webs. Pat. Cas. 106. Upon this distinction, Mr. Webster remarks that " the true principle would appear to be the intention of the party at the time, first, as expressed distinctly on the face of the specification ; and secondly, as may be inferred therefrom, according to the state of knowledge at the time, and other circumstances." Webs. Pat. Cas. 110, note. Where the patentee in his specification claimed " an improvement in the construction of the axles or bearings of railway or *other wheeled carriages,*" and it appeared that the improvement, though it had never before been applied to railway carriages, was well known as applied to other carriages, it was held that the patent was not good. Winans *v.* Providence Railroad Company, 2 Story's R. 412.

[1] Haworth *v.* Hardcastle, Webs. Pat. Cas. 480, 484. In this case, Sir N. C. Tindal, C. J., said : " As to the second ground upon which the motion for a

§ 232. The object of the distinction between what is new and what is old is to show distinctly what the patentee claims as his invention. But it has been said that the mere discrimination between what is old and what is new will not, in all cases, show this, for perhaps the patentee does not claim all that is new.[1] But the meaning of the authorities, as well as the purpose of the statute, shows that the object of the specification is to state distinctly what the patentee claims as the subject-matter of his invention or discovery; and the discrimination commonly made between what is new and what is old is one of the means necessary to present clearly the subject-matter of the invention or discovery.[2] In order to make this discrimination, the patentee is not confined to any precise form of words.[3] The more usual

nonsuit proceeded, we think, upon the fair construction of the specification itself, the patentee does not claim, as part of his invention, either the rails or staves over which the calicoes and other cloths are to be hung, or the placing them at the upper part of the building. The use of rails and staves for this purpose was proved to have been so general before the granting of this patent, that it would be almost impossible *à priori* to suppose that the patentee intended to claim what he could not but know would have avoided his patent, and the express statement that he makes, 'that he constructs the stove or drying house in a manner nearly similar to those which are at present in use, and that he arranges the rails or staves on which the cloth or fabric is intended to be hung or suspended near to the upper part of the said stove or drying house,' shows clearly that he is speaking of those rails or staves as of things then known and in common use, for he begins with describing the drying house as nearly similar to those in common use; he gives no dimensions of the rails or staves, no exact position of them, nor any particular description by reference, as he invariably does when he comes to that part of the machinery which is peculiarly his own invention. There can be no rule of law which requires the court to make any forced construction of the specification, so as to extend the claim of the patentee *to a wider range than the facts would warrant; on the contrary, such construction ought to be* made as will, consistently with the fair import of the language used, make the claim of invention coextensive with *the new discovery* of the grantee of the patent. And we see no reason to believe that he intended under this specification to claim either the staves, or the position of the staves as to their height in the drying house, as a part of his own invention."

[1] Phillips on Patents, 270.

[2] See Barrett *v.* Hall, 1 Mas. 475; Woodcock *v.* Parker, 1 Gallis. 438; Whittemore *v.* Cutter, ibid. 478; Odiorne *v.* Winkley, 2 Gallis. 51; Evans *v.* Eaton, 3 Wheat. 454; 7 ibid. 356; Wyeth *v.* Stone, 1 Story's R. 273; Ames *v.* Howard, 1 Sumner, 482.

[3] Wyeth *v.* Stone, 1 Story's R. 273.

form is to state affirmatively what the patentee claims as new, and if he makes use of any thing old, to state negatively that he does not claim that thing.[1] It is not enough that the thing designed to be embraced by the patent should be made apparent on the trial, by a comparison of the new with the old machine. The specification must distinguish the new from the old, so as to point out in what the improvement consists.[2]

§ 233. In describing what is old, it is not always necessary to enter into detail. Things generally known, or in common use, may be referred to in general terms, provided they create no ambiguity or uncertainty, and provided such reference is accompanied by an intelligible description of what is new.[3] In describing an improvement of a machine, or, what is the same thing, an improved machine, great care must be taken not to describe the whole in such a way as to make it appear to be

[1] If a specification truly sums up and distinguishes the invention of the patentee, it will not be open to the objection of being too broad, although it describes with unnecessary minuteness a process well known to those conversant with the art. Kneass *v.* The Schuylkill Bank, 4 Wash. 9, 14. See also Ames *v.* Howard, 1 Sumner, 482, 485. Mr. Godson gives the following directions for drawing specifications: "That the new parts of the subject may be more clearly seen and easily known, the patentee must not only claim neither more nor less than his own invention, but he must *not appear* even unintentionally to appropriate to himself any part which is old, or has been used in other manufactures. (Huddart *v.* Grimshaw, Dav. Pat. Cas. 295; 1 Webs. Pat. Cas. 85.) Those parts that are old and immaterial, or are not of the essence of the invention, should either not be mentioned, or should be named only to be designated as old. The patentee is not required to say that a screw or bobbin, or any thing in common use, is not part of his discovery; yet he must not adopt the invention of another person, however insignificant it may appear to be, without a remark. If any parts are described as essential without a protest against any novelty being attached to them, it will seem, though they are old, that they are claimed as new. (Bovill *v.* Moore, Dav. Pat. Cas. 404; Manton *v.* Parker, Dav. Pat. Cas. 329.) The construction will be against the patentee that he seeks to monopolize more than he has invented, or that, by dwelling in his description on things that are immaterial or known, he endeavors to deceive the public, who are not to be deterred from using any thing that is old by its appearing in the specification as newly invented. They are to be warned against infringing on the rights of the patentee, but are not to be deprived of a manufacture which they before possessed. (Dav. Pat. Cas. 279; and 3 Meriv. 629.) It seems, therefore, to be the safest way in the specification to describe the whole subject, and then to point out all the parts which are old and well known." Godson on Patents, 128.

[2] Dixon *v.* Moyer, 4 Wash. R. 68.

[3] Davis *v.* Palmer, 2 Brock. 298.

claimed as the invention of the patentee. The former machine, or other thing, should be set forth in the patent sufficiently to make known, according to the nature of the case, what it is that the patentee engrafts his improvement upon; he should then disclaim the invention of the thing thus referred to or described, and state distinctly his improvement as the thing which he claims to have invented.[1]

§ 233 *a*. Thus in Nichols *v*. Ross,[2] the specification described the patented process as follows: "The table *a* moves on a *hollow spindle*, which is *fixed* in the framing of the machine by screw and nut at *b*; through the tube *b*, the strand or thread of india-rubber, or cotton, or other fibrous material which is to form one of the longitudinal elastic or non-elastic threads of the fabric, passes; the upper part of the tube *b* rising to such a position amongst the braiding threads that in the evolution of those threads from one selvage of the fabric to the other they pass under and over (and lie at the back and front of the fabric) each of the longitudinal threads or yarns." The jury found that the plaintiff's machine was new, but that the use of a *revolving* hollow tube was *not* new. It was held that, as the plaintiff's claim was for the hollow spindle, not *general* but *fixed*, this finding did not negative the novelty of the plaintiff's invention.

In Holmes *v*. Lond. & N. W. R. W.,[3] Jervis, C.J., in rendering the decision of the court, says: "It is impossible for any one to read this specification without seeing that it claims what one would naturally have expected to be claimed. Harrison did not know at the time his specification was drawn what had been invented by Hancock; therefore he claims the whole as new. He takes out his patent for 'an improved turning-table for railway purposes.' The surface rails and catches are old; but Harrison, by applying certain supporting rods or arms in a new way, constructs what he describes as an improved turning-table. He goes

[1] In Hill *v*. Thompson, 8 Taunt. 375, Lord Ch. J. Dallas said: "This, like every other patent, must undoubtedly stand on the ground of improvement or discovery. If of improvement, it must stand on the ground of improvement invented; if of discovery, it must stand on the ground of the discovery of something altogether new; and the patent must distinguish and adapt itself accordingly." See also Bovill *v*. Moore, Dav. Pat. Cas. 398.

[2] Nichols *v*. Ross, 8 Mann., Gr. & Scott, 679.

[3] Holmes *v*. Lond. & N. W. R. W., 12 Com. Ben. 831; 16 E. L. & Eq. 409.

on in his specification to announce the general principle of his invention to consist 'in supporting the revolving plate or upper platform of the turning-table, as also its stays, braces, arms, and supports on the top of a fixed post, well braced, and resting on or planted in the ground; the top of which post forms a pivot for the table to turn on, while support arms radiating from the framework (the weight of which is also sustained on the post), moving round the bottom part of the post with friction rollers, and fastened to the outer edges of the plate, stay the plate on all sides, and keep it steady to receive the superincumbent weight of carriages or whatsoever is to be turned upon it.' He then goes on to describe how he does it. He does it by taking the old revolving plate or platform, with its rails and catches, and supporting it on a post, the top of which forms a pivot, which, for aught that appears, may be new, with support arms radiating from a framework moving round the bottom of the post, with friction rollers, and fastened to the outer edges of the plate; each of these being described as new, or at least not being stated to be old. The jury found that the post, the arms, and every thing except the suspending rods, were old. In order to make his specification good, either for an improvement of an old machine or for a new combination, Harrison should have said, 'My principle is to suspend the revolving plate or platform on a post, with arms, braces, and supports'; and then, going through Hancock's patent and describing all that as old, he should have gone on to say, 'To this I add suspending rods, for the purpose of bringing the bearing on the centre of the table.' No one can read this specification without seeing that this is in truth the meaning of it, and that the patentee supposes the arms to be new as well as the suspending rods, — in short, that all is new except the table, the rails, and the catches, which, by means of the suspending rods, he converts into a new and improved suspended turn-table. That being so, he clearly does not, in my opinion, comply with the rule which requires the patentee distinctly to state what is new and what is old."[1]

In Hullett *v.* Hague,[2] Lord Tenterden says: "The specification continues: 'and I further declare that my said invention

[1] See also Tetley *v.* Easton, 22 E. L. & Eq. 321; Allen *v.* Rawson, 1 Mann., Gr. & Scott, 551.

[2] Hullett *v.* Hague, 2 B. & Ad. 370.

and improvement consists in forcing, by means of bellows or any other blowing apparatus, atmospheric or any other air, either in a hot or cold state, through the liquid or solution subjected to evaporation.' Now it was said that the words which immediately follow, 'and this I do by means of pipes,' constituted a separate and distinct sentence from those which immediately preceded them, and that the patentee had stated his invention in the preceding sentence, and had claimed (by implication) the same invention as that described by Knight and Kirk in their specification. But we think that the words, 'and this I do by means of pipes,' must, in conjunction with those which immediately precede them, be taken to form one entire sentence, and that they amount altogether to an allegation, on the part of the patentee, that his invention consisted of the method or process of forcing, by means of bellows or any other blowing apparatus, hot or cold air through the liquid subjected to evaporation, this being effected by means of pipes placed as directed in the specification. Now the method described in Knight and Kirk's patent appears to us entirely different."

In Hastings *v.* Brown,[1] the specification was held bad for leaving it uncertain whether the claim was for an invention of a cable-holder to hold one cable of whatever size, or for one to hold cables of different sizes.

In Gamble *v.* Kurtz,[2] the court say: "The other question depends upon what is the true nature of the plaintiff's claim as an inventor. If he claimed the use of two chambers with separate furnaces, as part of his invention, the jury have said it was not new, and the verdict should be entered for the defendant; otherwise, for the plaintiff. It seems to us that no reasonable doubt can be entertained as to the claim made by the plaintiff. After describing, by words and drawings, the apparatus which he used, he claimed as his invention 'iron retorts worked in connection *with each other*, as above described.' It was contended, on behalf of the plaintiff, that the meaning was that he claimed the use of two retorts worked in connection with the whole of the apparatus for condensing the muriatic gas. But the words of the specification are 'in connection with each other,' not in connection with the condensing apparatus; and he after-

[1] Hastings *v.* Brown, 16 E. L. & Eq. 172; s. c.

[2] Gamble *v.* Kurtz, 3 Mann., Gr. & Scott, 425.

wards goes on to claim as his the particular arrangement of receivers, which he had previously described. We can give no other meaning to this than that the plaintiff claimed, as part of his invention, the use of two chambers with separate furnaces, worked in connection with each other, so that the materials might be decomposed in one, and roasted or finished in the other; and that the plaintiff understood such to be the nature of his claim, appears clearly from the disclaimer he has entered in this case; in which, after disclaiming certain words in his description of his claim, he says: 'I further declare that, though I did not intend the words to extend to any other retorts than the iron retorts described in my specification, viz., iron retorts worked in connection with each other, in which the process is commenced in one retort and finished in the other, yet I have been informed the words may be construed to extend to any iron retorts; for which reason I am anxious to disclaim.' And this was the nature of the claim which the plaintiff endeavored at the trial to establish by evidence. The jury having found that the evidence did not establish it, the verdict on that special finding must be entered for the defendant."

In Elliott *v.* Turner,[1] the patentee described the invention to consist in the application of a warp of *soft or organzine* silk. The jury, having asked how they were to understand the word "or" in the specification, i. e. whether it was to be considered as having been used disjunctively, or whether the word "organzine" was to be regarded as the construction of the word "soft," the judge told them that unless the silk (used by the defendants) were *organzine*, it did not fall under the description of the patent. In the Exchequer Chamber this charge was overruled, the court deciding that the judge should not have told the jury that, in his opinion, soft and organzine silk were absolutely the same, but that the words were *capable* of being so construed, if the jury were satisfied that at the date of the patent there was only one description of soft silk, and that organzine, used in satin weaving; but otherwise, that the proper and ordinary sense of the word "or" was to be adopted, and the patent held to apply to every species of soft silk as well as to organzine silk.

§ 234. One of the most common defects in a specification con-

[1] Elliott *v.* Turner, 2 Mann., Gr. & Scott, 446.

sists in that sort of vagueness and ambiguity in the manner of describing the invention which makes it difficult or impossible to determine what the invention is. This is an objection distinct from an ambiguity in the terms made use of. Thus, where the directions contained in a specification were "to take any quantity of lead and calcine it, or minium, or red-lead," the objection was that it was uncertain whether the minium and red-lead were to be calcined, or only the lead.[1] So, too, if it be stated that a whole class of substances may be used to produce a given effect, when, in fact, only one is capable of being so used successfully, an ambiguity is at once produced, and the public are misled;[2] but if the patentee states the substances which he makes use of himself, and there are still other substances which will produce the effect, and he claims them, by a generic description, as comprehended within his invention, his claim will not be void for ambiguity, or too broad for his invention, provided the combination is new in respect to all the substances thus referred to.[3]

[1] Turner *v.* Winter, Webs. Pat. Cas. 80. Another objection taken was as to the white-lead which the patent professed to make by the same process by which it made something else; to which it was answered, that the invention did not profess to make common white-lead. Ashurst, J., said: "But that is no answer; for if the patentee had intended to produce something only like white-lead, or answering some of the purposes of common white-lead, it should have been so expressed in the specification. But, in truth, the patent is for making white-lead and two other things by one process. Therefore, if the process, as directed by the specification, does not produce that which the patent professes to do, the patent itself is void."

[2] Bickford *v.* Skewes, Webs. Pat. Cas. 218. If more parts be inserted than are necessary, as ten, where four are sufficient, the specification is void. The King *v.* Arkwright, Webs. Pat. Cas. 70.

[3] Ryan *v.* Goodwin, 3 Sumner, 514, 519. In this case, Mr. Justice Story said: "Then as to the third point. This turns upon the supposed vagueness and ambiguity and uncertainty of the specification and claim of the invention thereby. The specification, after adverting to the fact, that the *loco-foco* matches, so called, are a compound of phosphorus, chlorate of potash, sulphuret of antimony, and gum arabic or glue, proceeds to state that the compound which he (Phillips) uses 'consists simply of phosphorus, chalk, and glue'; and he then states the mode of preparing the compound and the proportions of the ingredients; so that, as here stated, the essential difference between his own matches and those called *loco-foco* consists in the omission of chlorate of potash and sulphuret of antimony, and using in lieu thereof chalk. He then goes on to state, that 'the proportions of the ingredients may be varied, and that gum arabic, or other gum, may be substituted for glue; and other absorbent earths or materials may be used instead of carbonate of lime.'

§ 234 *a*. In like manner, where a particular effect or purpose in machinery is a part of the invention, and that effect may be pro-

He afterwards sums up his invention in the following terms: 'What I claim as my invention is the using of a paste or composition to ignite by friction, consisting of phosphorus, and [an] earthly material, and a glutinous substance only, without the addition of chlorate of potash, or of any other highly combustible material, such as sulphuret of antimony, in addition to the phosphorus. I also claim the mode herein described, of putting up the matches in paper, so as to secure them from accidental friction.' Upon this last claim I need say nothing, as it is not in controversy, as a part of the infringement of the patent, upon the present trial. Now, I take it to be the clear rule of our law in favor of inventors, and to carry into effect the obvious object of the Constitution and laws in granting patents, 'to promote the progress of science and useful arts,' to give a liberal construction to the language of all patents and specifications (*ut res magis valeat, quam pereat*), so as to protect and not to destroy the rights of real inventors. If, therefore, there be any ambiguity or uncertainty in any part of the specification, yet if, taking the whole together, the court can perceive the exact nature and extent of the claim made by the inventor, it is bound to adopt that interpretation, and to give it full effect. I confess that I do not perceive any ground for real doubt in the present specification. The inventor claims as his invention the combination of phosphorus with chalk or any other absorbent earth or earthy material, and glue, or any other glutinous substance; in making matches, using the ingredients in the proportions substantially as set forth in the specification. Now, the question is, whether such a claim is good, or whether it is void, as being too broad and comprehensive. The argument seems to be, that the inventor has not confined his claim to the use of chalk, but has extended it to the use of any other absorbent earths or earthy materials, which is too general. So he has not confined it to the use of glue, or even of gum arabic, but has extended it also to any other gum or glutinous substance, which is also too general. Now, it is observable that the Patent Act of 1793, c. 55, does not limit the inventor to one single mode, or one single set of ingredients, to carry into effect his invention. He may claim as many modes as he pleases, provided always that the claim is limited to such as he has invented, and as are substantially new. Indeed, in one section (§ 3) the act requires, in the case of a machine, that the inventor shall fully explain the principle, and the several modes in which he has contemplated the application of that principle or character, by which it may be distinguished from other inventions. The same enactment exists in the Patent Act of 1836, c. 357, § 6. I do not know of any principle of law which declares, that, if a man makes a new compound, wholly unknown before for a useful and valuable purpose, he is limited to the use of the same precise ingredients in making that compound; and that, if the same purpose can be accomplished by him by the substitution in part of other ingredients in the composition, he is not at liberty to extend his patent so as to embrace them also. It is true that, in such a case, he runs the risk of having his patent avoided, if either of the combinations, the original or the substituted, have been known or used before in the like combination.

duced in several modes, it is sufficient for the patentee to state the modes which he contemplates as best, and his claim will not be void, as too vague or comprehensive, although he claims the variations from those modes as being equally his invention, without describing the manner of producing those variations.[1]

But, if all the various combinations are equally new, I do not perceive how his claim can be said to be too broad. It is not more broad than his invention. There is no proof, in the present case, that the ingredients enumerated in this specification, whether chalk, or any other absorbent earth or earthy substance, were ever before combined with phosphorus and glue, or any gum or other glutinous substance, to produce a compound for matches. The objection, so far as it here applies, is not that these gums or earths have been before so combined with phosphorus, but that the inventor extends his claim so as to include all such combinations. There is no pretence to say, upon the evidence, that the specification was intended to deceive the public, or that it included other earthy materials than chalk, or other glutinous substances than glue, for the very purpose of misleading the public. The party has stated frankly what he deems the best materials, phosphorus, chalk, and glue, and the proportions and mode of combining them. But because he says that there may be substitutes of the same general character, which may serve the same purpose, thereby to exclude other persons from evading his patent and depriving him of his invention, by using one or more of the substitutes, if the patent had been confined to the combination solely of phosphorus, chalk, and glue, I cannot hold that his claim is too broad, or that it is void. My present impression is, that the objection is not well founded. Suppose the invention had been of a machine, and the inventor had said, I use a wheel in a certain part of the machine for a certain purpose, but the same effect may be produced by a crank, or a lever, or a toggle-joint, and therefore I claim these modes also ; it would hardly be contended that such a claim would avoid his patent. I do not know that it has ever been decided, that, if the claim of an inventor for an invention of a compound states the ingredients truly which the inventor uses to produce the intended effect, the suggestion that other ingredients of a kindred nature may be substituted for some part of them, has been held to avoid the patent *in toto*, so as to make it bad, for what is specifically stated. In the present case it is not necessary to consider that point. My opinion is, that the specification is not, in point of law, void from its vagueness, or generality, or uncertainty."

[1] Carver *v.* Braintree Manf. Co., 2 Story's R. 432, 440. "Another objection is, that the plaintiff, in his claim, has stated that the desired distance or space between the upper and the lower surfaces of the rib, whether it 'be done by making the ribs thicker at that part, or by a fork or division of the rib, or by any other variation of the particular form,' is a part of his invention. It is said, that the modes of forking and dividing are not specified, nor the variations of the particular form given. This is true; but then the Patent Act requires the patentee to specify the several modes 'in which he has contemplated the application of the distinguishing principle or character of his

§ 235. This kind of ambiguity is also distinguishable from the want of clear or specific directions, which will enable a mechanic to make the thing described. A specification may be perfectly sufficient, as to the point of stating what the invention is, and yet the directions for making the thing may be so vague and indefinite, as not to enable a skilful mechanic to accomplish the object.[1] It is for this reason, as we have seen, that the question, whether the specification discloses what the invention is, is a question for the court on construction of the patent; while the question, whether it sufficiently describes the mode of carrying the invention into practice, is a question for the jury.[2]

invention.' (Act of 1836, c. 357, § 6.) Now, we all know that a mere difference of form will not entitle the party to a patent. What the patentee here says in effect is : One important part of my invention consists in the space or distance between the upper and lower surfaces of the ribs, and whether this is obtained by making the rib solid, or by a fork, or division of the rib, or by any other variation of the form of the rib, I equally claim it as my invention. The end to be obtained is the space or distance equal to the fibre of the cotton to be ginned; and you may make the rib solid, or fork it, or divide it, or vary its form in any other manner, so as that the purpose is obtained. The patentee, therefore, guards himself against the suggestion, that his invention consists solely in a particular form, solid, or forked, or divided ; and claims the invention to be his, whether the exact form is preserved or not, if its proportions are kept so as to be adapted to the fibre of the cotton which is to be ginned. In all this I can perceive no want of accuracy or sufficiency of description, at least so far as it is a matter of law, nor any claim broader than the invention, which is either so vague or so comprehensive as in point of law not to be patentable. It was not incumbent upon the patentee to suggest all the possible modes by which the rib might be varied, and yet the effect produced. It is sufficient for him to state the modes which he contemplates to be best, and to add, that other mere formal variations from these modes he does not deem to be unprotected by his patent."

[1] "It may not, perhaps, be easy to draw a precise line of distinction between a specification so uncertain as to claim no particular improvement, and a specification so uncertain as not to enable a skilful workman to understand the improvement, and to construct it. Yet we think the distinction exists. If it does, it is within the province of the jury to decide whether a skilful workman can carry into execution the plan of the inventor. In deciding this question, the jury will give a liberal common-sense construction to the directions of the specification." Per Marshall, C. J., in Davis v. Palmer, 2 Brock. 298, 308.

[2] Thus, in the case of a patent for "a new and useful improvement in the ribs of the cotton-gin," Mr. Justice Story said : "It is true, that the plaintiff in his specification, in describing the thickness of the rib in his machine, declares that it should be so thick, that the distance or depth between the upper

§ 235 *a*. Where ambiguity exists in the specification to such a degree that it cannot be elucidated, it is immaterial whether it had its origin in the *mala fides* of the patentee, or in the haste or incompetency of the draftsman. Whether the claim, which is invalid, was introduced purposely or by mistake is not taken into consideration by the court. The fact that the patent is ambiguous, or claims too much, is the vital test of its validity, and not the motive or circumstance in which such ambiguity or excessive claim originated.[1]

§ 236. The ambiguity produced by a too great fulness of detail in the specification is likely to mislead both in determining what the invention claimed is, and in determining whether it is described with such accuracy as will enable a competent workman to put it in practice. We shall have occasion hereafter to state the rule, that the patentee is bound to disclose the most advantageous mode known to him, and any circumstance conducive to the advantageous operation of his invention; and it is a correlative

and the lower surface should be 'so great as to be equal to the length of the fibre to be ginned,' which, it is said, is too ambiguous and indefinite a description to enable a mechanic to make it, because it is notorious that not only the fibres of different kinds of cotton are of different lengths, long staple and short staple, but that the different fibres in the same kind of cotton are of unequal lengths. And it is asked, what then is to be the distance or depth or thickness of the rib? Whether a skilful mechanic could from this description make a proper rib for any particular kind of cotton is a matter of fact which those only who are acquainted with the structure of cotton gins can properly answer. If they could, then the description is sufficient, although it may require some niceties in adjusting the different thicknesses to the different kinds of cotton. If they could not, then the specification is obviously defective. But I should suppose that the inequalities of the different fibres of the same kind of cotton would not necessarily present an insurmountable difficulty. It may be, that the adjustment should be to be made according to the average length of the fibres, or varied in some other way. But this is for a practical mechanic to say, and not for the court. What I mean, therefore, to say on this point is, that, as a matter of law, I cannot say that this description is so ambiguous that the patent is upon its face void. It may be less perfect and complete than would be desirable, but still it may be sufficient to enable a skilful mechanic to attain the end. In point of fact, is it not actually attained by the mechanics employed by Carver, without the application of any new inventive power, or experiments? If so, then the objection could be answered as a matter of fact or a practical result." Carver *v.* The Braintree Manf. Co., 2 Story's R. 432, 437.

[1] Blake *v.* Stafford (1867), 6 Blatchf. 195; s. c. 3 Fisher's Pat. Cas. 294.

of this rule, that if things wholly useless and unnecessary are introduced into the specification, as if they were essential, although the terms are perfectly intelligible, and every necessary description has been introduced, and the parts claimed are all newly invented, the patent may be declared void. The presumption, in such cases, according to the English authorities, is, that the useless and unnecessary descriptions were introduced for the purpose of overloading the subject and clouding the description, in order to mislead the public and conceal the real invention.[1]

§ 237. There is one case where it seems to have been held that an improved mode of working his machine by the patentee, different from the specification of his patent, casts upon him the burden of showing that he made the improvement subsequently to the issuing of his patent, otherwise it will be presumed that he did not disclose in his specification the best method known to him.[2] But where a patentee of an improved machine claimed as his invention a part of it which turned out to be useless, it was held that this did not vitiate the patent, the specification not

[1] In Arkwright's case, several things were introduced into the specification, of which he did not make use. Buller, J., said: "Wood put No. 4, 5, 6, and 7 together, and that machine he has worked ever since; he don't recollect that the defendant used any thing else. If that be true, it will blow up the patent at once; he says he believes nobody that ever practised would find any thing necessary upon this paper but the No. 4, 5, 6, and 7; he should look after no others. Now if four things only were necessary instead of ten, the specification does not contain a good account of the invention." The King *v.* Arkwright, Webs. Pat. Cas. 70.

In Turner's patent for producing a yellow color, minium was directed to be used among other things, but it appeared that it would not produce the desired effect. The same learned judge said: "Now in this case no evidence was offered by the plaintiff to show that he had ever made use of the several different ingredients mentioned in the specification, as for instance minium, which he had nevertheless inserted in the patent; nor did he give any evidence to show *how* the yellow color was produced. If he could make it with two or three of the ingredients specified, and he has inserted others which will not answer the purpose, that will avoid the patent. So, if he makes the article, for which the patent is granted, with cheaper materials than those which he has enumerated, although the latter will answer the purpose equally well, the patent is void, because he does not put the public in possession of his invention, or enable them to derive the same benefit which he himself does." Turner *v.* Winter, Webs. Pat. Cas. 80. See also Savory *v.* Price, R. & M. 1; Webs. Pat. Cas. 83.

[2] Bovill *v.* Moore, Dav. Pat. Cas. 361, 401.

describing it as essential to the machine.[1] At the same time, it is necessary that the specification should be full and explicit enough to prevent the public from infringing the right of the patentee. An infringement will not have taken place, unless the invention can be practised completely by following the specification; otherwise, it has been said, it would be an infringement to do that perfectly, which, according to the specification, requires something else to be done to make it perfect. An infringement is a copy made after and agreeing with the principle laid down in the patent;[2] and if the patent does not fully describe any thing essential to the making or doing of the thing patented, there will be no infringement by the fresh invention of processes which the patentee has withheld from the public.[3]

[1] Lewis *v.* Marling, 10 B. & Cress. 22.

[2] Per Sir N. Tindal, C. J., in Galloway *v.* Bleaden, Webs. Pat. Cas. 521.

[3] This doctrine was very clearly laid down by Alderson, B., in Morgan *v.* Seaward, Webs. Pat. Cas. 167, 181. " Then Henry Mornay, a young gentleman in Mr. Morgan's employment, where he has been apparently studying the construction of engines, speaks of a circumstance which does appear to me to be material. He says, Mr. Morgan in practice makes his rods of different lengths. He must necessarily do so, in order that the floats may follow at the same angle as that at which the driving float enters the water. The problem which Mr. Park solved is a problem applying to three floats only; but it appears that the other floats will not follow in the same order, unless some adjustment of the rods is made. Now, suppose it was to be desired that the floats should all enter the water at the given or required angle, if one should go in at one angle, and one at another, the operation of the machine would not be uniform; and the specification means that the party constructing a wheel should be able to make a wheel, the floats of which shall all enter at the same angle, and all go out at the same angle. Now in order in practice to carry that into effect, if there are more than three floats, something more than Mr. Park's problem would be required; and Mr. Mornay says actually, that Mr. Morgan in practice makes his rods of different lengths, and he must necessarily do that in order that the floats may follow at the same angle as the driving float enters the water. If so, he should have said in his specification, ' I make my rods of different lengths, in order that the rest of my floats may enter at the same angle; and the way to do that is so and so.' Or he might have said, ' it may be determined so and so.' But the specification is totally silent on the subject; therefore, a person reading the specification would never dream that the other floats must be governed by rods of unequal length; and least of all could he ascertain what their lengths should be, until he had made experiments. Therefore it is contended that the specification does not state, as it should have stated, the proper manner of doing it. He says, if they are made of equal lengths, though the governing rod would be vertical at the time of entering, and three would be so when they arrived at

It is the duty of an inventor to describe in his specification each substantially different modification of his invention which he has made.[1]

§ 238. The ambiguity produced by a misuse of terms, so as to render the specification unintelligible, will be as fatal as any

the same spot, by reason of the operation Mr. Park suggests, yet the fourth would not come vertical at the proper point, nor would the fifth, sixth, or seventh. Then they would not accomplish that advantage which professes to be acquired. The patentee ought to state in his specification the precise way of doing it. If it cannot completely be done by following the specification, then a person will not infringe the patent by doing it. If this were an infringement, it would be an infringement to do that perfectly, which, according to the specification, requires something else to be done to make it perfect. If that be correct, you would prevent a man from having a perfect engine. He says, practically speaking, the difference in the length of the rods would not be very material, the difference being small. But the whole question is small, therefore it ought to have been specified; and if it could not be ascertained fully, it should have been so stated. Now this is the part to which I was referring, when, in the preliminary observations I addressed to you, I cited the case before Lord Mansfield, on the subject of the introduction of tallow to enable the machine to work more smoothly. There it was held that the use of tallow ought to have been stated in the specification. This small adjustment of these different lengths may have been made for the purpose of making the machine work more smoothly ; if so, it is just as much necessary that it should be so stated in the specification, as it was that the tallow should be mentioned. The true criterion is this, has the specification substantially complied with that which the public has a right to require? Has the patentee communicated to the public the manner of carrying his invention into effect? If he has, and if he has given to the public all the knowledge he had himself, he has done that which he ought to have done, and which the public has a right to require from him."

[1] Sargent *et al.* *v.* Carter, 21 Mon. Law Rep. 651. "He (the defendant in his own patent) describes two devices. If he was then possessed of a third, he was bound to describe that also. Having failed to do so, though I do not doubt he had made machines with a flexible arm before he applied for his first patent, I have strong reason to doubt whether it was capable of effecting the object proposed. It is a circumstance, also, that in the machines now built by the defendant, he has used, not the flexible arm, but a movable or rotating arm. If he first invented a flexible arm, as appears from the evidence in this case, and it accomplished the desired end, why does he not continue to use it? The other modification relied on is placing one end of the arm in a loose socket, where it is held by a pin, which being smaller than the aperture through the arm in which the pin is inserted, allows some play of the arm. But this modification was tried before he took his original patent, and not being therein alluded to or described and claimed in the reissued patent, the same observation applies to this as to the flexible knife-arm."

other defect. Thus, where the directions were to use "sea-salt, or sal-gem, or fossil-salt, or any marine salt," and it appeared that "sal-gem" was the only thing that could be used, and that "fossil-salt" was a generic term, including "sal-gem," as well as other species of salt, it was held that the use of the term "fossil-salt" could only tend to mislead and to create unnecessary experiments, and therefore that the specification was in that respect defective.[1] In like manner, where the specification directed the use of "the finest and purest chemical white-lead," and it appeared that no such substance was known in the trade by that name, but that white-lead only was known, the specification was held defective.[2] But a mere mistake of one word for another in writing or printing, if explained by other parts of the patent and specification, as the use of the word "painting" for "printing," is immaterial.[3]

§ 239. The description of an improvement, when an improvement is the real subject-matter of the patent, should be made in such a manner as will clearly show that the improvement only is claimed by the patentee. If a machine substantially existed before, and the patentee makes an improvement therein, his patent should not comprehend the whole machine in its improved state, but should be confined to his improvement;[4] and this is true, although the invention of the patentee consists of an addition to the old machine, by which the same effects are to be produced in a better manner, or some new combinations are added, in order to produce new effects.[5] But if well-known effects are produced by machinery which in all its combinations is entirely new, the subject-matter will be a new machine, and of course the patent will cover the whole machine.[6]

§ 239 *a*. Where the invention embraces only one or more parts of a machine, as the coulter of a plough, or the divider or sweep-rake of a reaping-machine, the part or parts claimed must be specified and pointed out, so that constructors, other inventors, and the public may know how to make the invention, and what

[1] Turner *v.* Winter, 1 T. R. 606; Webs. Pat. Cas. 77.

[2] Sturz *v.* De La Rue, Webs. Pat. Cas. 83.

[3] Kneass *v.* The Schuylkill Bank, 4 Wash. 9.

[4] Woodcock *v.* Parker, 1 Gallis. 438; Odiorne *v.* Winkley, 2 Gallis. 51; Barrett *v.* Hall, 1 Mas. 447, 476.

[5] Whittemore *v.* Cutter, 1 Gallis. 478.

[6] Ibid.

is withdrawn from general use. But where both a new ingredient and a combination of old ingredients, embodied in the same machine, are claimed, greater particularity is required, as the property of the patentee consists not only in the new ingredient, but also in the new combination; and it is essential that the invention shall be so fully described that its precise nature may be known to the public.

In case of a claim for a combination, where all the ingredients of the invention are old, and where the invention consists entirely in a new combination of old ingredients, whereby a new and useful result is obtained, "such combination is sufficiently described, if the ingredients of which it is composed are named, their mode of operation given, and the new and useful result to be accomplished pointed out, so that those skilled in the art, and the public, may know the extent and nature of the claim, and what the parts are which co-operate to produce the described new and useful result."[1]

§ 240. If the invention be an improvement, and be claimed as such, but nothing is said of any previous use, of which the use proposed is averred to be an improvement, the patent may incur the risk of being construed as a claim of entire and original discovery. Hence arises the necessity for reciting what had formerly been done, and describing a different mode as the improvement claimed.[2]

[1] Seymour *v.* Osborne, 11 Wall. 516.

[2] In Hill *v.* Thompson, Webs. Pat. Cas. 226, 228, 229, the specification contained among other things the following claim: "And that my said improvements do further consist in the use and application of lime to iron subsequently to the operations of the blast furnace, whereby that quality in iron from which the iron is called 'cold short,' howsoever and from whatever substance such iron be obtained, is sufficiently prevented or remedied, and by which such iron is rendered more tough when cold. . . . And I do further declare, that I have discovered that the addition of lime or limestone, or other substances consisting chiefly of lime, and free or nearly free from any ingredient known to be hurtful to the quality of iron, will sufficiently prevent or remedy that quality in iron from which the iron is called 'cold short,' and will render such iron more tough when cold; and I do, for this purpose, if the iron, howsoever and from whatever substance the same may have been obtained, be expected to prove 'cold short,' add a portion of lime or limestone, or of the other said substances, of which the quantity must be regulated by the quality of the iron to be operated upon, and by the quality of the iron wished to be produced; and further, that the said lime or limestone, or other aforesaid sub-

§ 241. But in describing the improvement of a machine in use and well known, it is not necessary to state in detail the structure of the entire and improved machine. It is only necessary to describe the improvement, by showing the parts of which it consists, and the effects which it produces.[1] In the case of machinery there is a particular requisition in the statute, designed to insure fulness and clearness in the specification. "And in

stances, may be added to the iron at any time subsequently to the reduction thereof, in the blast furnace, and prior to the iron becoming clotted, or coming into nature, whether the same be added to the iron while it is in the refining or in the puddling furnace, or in both of them, or previous to the said iron being put into either of the said furnaces." It appeared that "cold short" had been prevented by the use of lime before; and Dallas, J., said: "The purpose is to render bar iron more tough, by preventing that brittleness which is called 'cold short,' and which renders bar iron less valuable; the means of prevention stated are the application of lime. In what way, then, is lime mentioned in the patent? The first part of the specification, in terms, alleges certain improvements in the smelting and working of iron, during the operations of the blast furnace; and then, introducing the mention of lime, it states, that the application of it to iron, subsequently to the operation of the blast furnace, will prevent the quality called 'cold short.' So far, therefore, the application of lime is in terms claimed as an improvement, and nothing is said of any previous use, of which the use proposed is averred to be an improvement; it is, therefore, in substance a claim of entire and original discovery. The recital should have stated, supposing a previous use to be proved in the case, that, 'whereas lime has been in part, but improperly, made use of,' &c., and then a different mode of application and use should have been suggested as the improvement claimed. But the whole of the patent must be taken together, and this objection will appear to be stronger as we proceed. And here again, looking through the patent, in a subsequent part of the specification, the word 'discovery' first occurs, and I will state the terms made use of in this respect. 'And I do further declare, that I have discovered that the addition of lime will prevent that quality in iron from which the iron is called "cold short," and will render such iron more tough when cold; and that for this purpose I do add a portion of lime or limestone, to be regulated by the quantity of iron to be operated upon, and by the quality of the iron to be produced, to be added at any time subsequently to the reduction in the blast furnace, and this from whatever substance the iron may be produced, if expected to prove "cold short."' Now this appears to be nothing short of a claim of discovery, in the most extensive sense, of the effect of lime applied to iron to prevent brittleness, not qualified and restrained by what follows, as to the preferable mode of applying it under various circumstances, and therefore rendering the patent void, if lime had been made use of for this purpose before, subject to the qualification only of applying it subsequently to the operation in the blast furnace."

[1] Brooks *v.* Bicknell, 3 M'Lean's R. 250, 261.

case of any machine, he (the patentee) shall fully explain the principle and the several modes in which he has contemplated the application of that principle or character by which it may be distinguished from other inventions; and shall particularly specify and point out the part, improvement, or combination, which he claims as his own invention or discovery."[1] By the principle of a machine, as used in this clause of the statute, is to be understood the peculiar structure and mode of operation of such machine;[2] or, as the statute itself explains it, the character by which it may be distinguished from other inventions. By explaining "the several modes in which he has contemplated the application of that principle," the statute is presumed to direct the patentee to point out all the modes of applying the principle, which he claims to be his own invention, and which he means to have covered by his patent, whether they are those which he deems the best, or are mere formal variations from the modes which he prefers. In other words, he is to state not only the peculiar device or construction which he deems the best for producing the new effect, exhibited in his machine, but also all the other modes of producing the same effect, which he means to claim as being substantially applications of the same principle. But in doing this, it is not, as we have seen, necessary for him to enter into a minute description of the mode of producing those variations of structure which he thus claims, in addition to the structure which he prefers. It is sufficient, if he indicates what variations of the application of the principle he claims beyond those which he deems the best.[3]

§ 242. The duty of determining what the claim of the patentee is involves the necessity of determining whether the description in the specification discloses a patentable subject. The real invention may be a patentable subject; but at the same time it may be claimed in such a way as to appear to be a mere function, or abstract principle, which it will be the duty of the court to declare is not patentable; whereas, if it had been described differently, it would have been seen to be a claim for a principle or

[1] Act of July 4, 1836, § 6.

[2] Whittemore *v.* Cutter, 1 Gallis. 478, 480; Barrett *v.* Hall, 1 Mas. 447, 470.

[3] See the observations of Mr. Justice Story, cited *ante*, from the case of Carver *v.* The Braintree Manuf. Company, 2 Story's R. 432, 440.

function embodied in a particular organization of matter for a particular purpose, which is patentable. The patentee may have been engaged in investigations into the principles of science or the laws of nature. He may have attained a result, which constitutes a most important and valuable discovery, and he may desire to protect that discovery by a patent; but he cannot do so by merely stating his discovery in a specification. He must give it a practical application to some useful purpose, to attain a result in arts or manufactures not before attained, and his specification must show the application of the principle to such a special purpose, by its incorporation with matter in such a way as to be in a condition to produce a practical result.[1] Care should be taken,

[1] In the Househill Company *v.* Neilson, Webs. Pat. Cas. 673, 683, Lord Justice Clerk Hope, in the Court of Sessions, made the following clear observations to the jury: "It is quite true that a patent cannot be taken out solely for an abstract philosophical principle, — for instance, for any law of nature, or any property of matter, apart from any mode of turning it to account in the practical operations of manufacture, or the business and arts and utilities of life. The mere discovery of such a principle is not an invention in the patent-law sense of the term. Stating such a principle in a patent may be a prolongation of the principle, but it is no application of the principle to any practical purpose. And without that application of the principle to a practical object and end, and without the application of it to human industry, or to the purposes of human enjoyment, a person cannot in the abstract appropriate a principle to himself. But a patent will be good, though the subject of the patent consists in the discovery of a great, general, and most comprehensive principle in science or law of nature, if that principle is by the specification applied to any special purpose, so as thereby to effectuate a practical result and benefit not previously attained.

"The main merit, the most important part of the invention, may consist in the conception of the original idea, — in the discovery of the principle in science, or of the law of nature stated in the patent, and little or no pains may have been taken in working out the best manner and mode of the application of the principle to the purpose set forth in the patent. But still, if the principle is stated to be applicable to any special purpose, so as to produce any result previously unknown, in the way and for the objects described, the patent is good. It is no longer an abstract principle. It comes to be a principle turned to account to a practical object, and applied to a special result. It becomes, then, not an abstract principle, which means a principle considered apart from any special purpose or practical operation, but the discovery and statement of a principle for a special purpose, that is, a practical invention, a mode of carrying a principle into effect. That such is the law, if a well-known principle is applied for the first time to produce a practical result for a special purpose, has never been disputed. It would be very strange and unjust to refuse the

therefore, in drawing specifications, not to describe the invention as a mode or device for producing an effect, detached from machinery, or from the particular combination or use of matter, by which the effect is produced.[1] The danger in such cases is, that the claim will appear to be a claim for an abstract principle, or for all possible modes of producing the effect in question, instead of being, what alone it should be, a claim for the particular application of the principle which the patentee professes to have made.

Where a party has discovered a new application of some property in nature never before known or in use, by which he has produced a new and useful result, the discovery is the subject of a patent, independent of any peculiar or new arrangement of machinery for the purpose of applying the new property.[2]

same legal effect, when the inventor has the additional merit of discovering the principle as well as its application to a practical object. The instant that the principle, although discovered for the first time, is stated, in actual application to, and as the agent of, producing a certain specified effect, it is no longer an abstract principle, it is then clothed with the language of practical application, and receives the impress of tangible direction to the actual business of human life."

[1] Barrett *v.* Hall, 1 Mas. 476.

[2] Foote *v.* Silsby, 2 Blatchf. 260. "There has been some difference of opinion as regards the true construction to be given to the first claim, and it will therefore be necessary for the court to call your attention particularly to this branch of the case. It will be seen that the patentee, after he has set forth, in general terms, that he has made a new and useful improvement in regulating the heat of stoves, has set forth with great particularity two modes by which he adapts this improvement to use, through the arrangement of various machinery; and that then, in this first claim, he claims the application of the expansive and contracting power of a metallic rod, by different degrees of heat, to open and close a damper which governs the admission of air into a stove in which it may be used, by which a more perfect control over the heat is obtained than can be by a damper in the flue. Now, it is the application of the expansive and contracting power of the metallic rod to regulate the heat of the stove by opening and closing the damper, the whole being self-acting in the admission or exclusion of air, that is specifically claimed in this part of the patent; and, according to the construction I give to it and have always given to it, it is a claim independent of any particular arrangement or combination of machinery or contrivance for the purpose of applying the principle to the regulation of the heat of stoves. I have always supposed, therefore, that the peculiar arrangement or construction of machinery did not enter into this branch of the claim. Where a party has described a new application of some property in nature, never before known or in use, by which he has produced

A claim for a combination of several devices, so combined as to produce a particular result, is not good as a claim for any mode of combining such devices.[1]

a new and useful result, the discovery is the subject of a patent, independent of any new or peculiar arrangement of machinery for the purpose of applying the new property in nature ; and hence the inventor has a right to use any means, old or new, in the application of the new property to produce the new and useful result, to the exclusion of all other means. Otherwise a patent would afford no protection to an inventor in cases of this description ; because, if the means used by him for applying his new idea must necessarily be new, then, in all such cases, the novelty of the arrangement used for the purpose of effecting the application would be involved in every instance of infringement, and the patentee would be bound to make out, not only the novelty in the new application, but also the novelty in the machinery employed by him in making the application. (Then citing from Neilson *v.* Harford, the judge (Nelson) continues) : Now in this case, as I understand the claim of the patentee, he claims the application of the principle of expansion and contraction in a metallic rod to the purpose of regulating the heat of a stove. This is the new conception which he claims to have struck out; and, although the mere abstract conception would not have constituted the subject-matter of a patent, yet when it is reduced to practice by any means, old or new, resulting usefully, it is the subject of a patent, independently of the machinery by which the application is made. I think, therefore, that in examining the first question presented to you, you may lay altogether out of view the contrivance by which the application of the principle is made, and confine yourselves to the original conception of the idea carried into practice by some means ; but whether the means be old or new is immaterial, for although old means be used for giving application to the new conception, yet the patent excludes all persons other than the patentee from the use of those means and of all other means in a similar application." This opinion was sustained on appeal to the Supreme Court, in Silsby *v.* Foote, 20 How. 378, where, however, Judge Grier delivered a strong dissenting opinion, based on the grounds of the decision rendered under the eighth claim of Morse's patent. O'Reilly *v.* Morse, 15 How. 62. Judge Taney, in giving that decision, says : "The difficulty arises on the eighth (claim). It is in the following words : '*Eighth.* I do not propose to limit myself to the specific machinery or parts of machinery described in the specification ; the essence of my invention being the use of the motive-power of the electric or galvanic current, which I called electro-magnetism, however developed, for marking or printing intelligible characters, signs, or letters, at any distances, being a new application of that power of which I claim to be first inventor or discoverer.' Now, the provisions of the acts of Congress in relation to patents may be summed up in a few words. Whoever discovers that a certain useful result will be produced in any art, machine,

[1] Case *v.* Brown, 2 Wall. 320.

§ 242 *a*. A claim for a result will not be sustained; it must be for the means or apparatus by which such result is produced. And where such claim was, "in effect, a claim to the use of the proper chemicals to precipitate the metal from the liquid waste solution, by putting such chemicals into any proper vessel containing the solution," it was held to be too general and vague, and therefore invalid.[1]

A claim which might otherwise be held to be bad as covering a function, or result, when containing the words "substantially as described," or "substantially as set forth," must be construed in connection with the specification, and may be held valid. Where the claim immediately follows the description of the invention, it may be construed in connection with the explanations contained in the specifications, and where it contains words referring back to the specifications, it cannot properly be construed in any other way.[2]

§ 243. According to the terms of the Patent Act, in cases

manufacture, or composition of matter, by the use of certain means, is entitled to a patent for it; provided he specifies the means used in a manner so full and exact that any one skilled in the science to which it appertains can, by using the means he specifies, without any addition to or subtraction from them, produce precisely the result he describes. And if this cannot be done by the means he describes, the patent is void. And if it can be done, then the patent confers on him the exclusive right to use the means he specifies to produce the result or effect he describes, and nothing more. And it makes no difference, in this respect, whether the effect is produced by chemical agency or combination, or by the application of discoveries or principles in natural philosophy known or unknown before his invention, or by machinery acting altogether on mechanical principles. In either case, he must describe the manner and process as above-mentioned, and the end it accomplishes. And any one may lawfully accomplish the same end without infringing the patent, if he uses means substantially different from those described. Indeed, if the eighth claim of the patentee can be maintained, there was no necessity for any specification further than to say that he had discovered that, by using the motive power of electro-magnetism, he could print intelligible characters at any distance. We presume it will be admitted on all hands that no patent could have issued on such a specification. Yet this claim can derive no aid from the specification filed. It is outside of it, and the patentee claims beyond it. And if it stands, it must stand simply on the ground that the broad terms above-mentioned were a sufficient description, and entitled him to a patent in terms equally broad. In our judgment, the act of Congress cannot be so construed."

[1] The Shaw & Wilcox Company *v.* Lovejoy (1870), 7 Blatchf. 232.

[2] Seymour *v.* Osborne, 11 Wall. 516.

where the invention falls within the category of machines, a patent must be granted for it (the machine) and not for a "mode of operation," "principle," "idea," or other abstraction.[1]

This is well illustrated by several cases. In one, the invention claimed was "the communication of motion from the reed to the yarn-beam, in the connection of the one with the other, which is produced as follows," describing the mode. The patent was sustained, only by construing it as a claim for the specific machinery invented by the patentee for the communication of motion from the reed to the yarn-beam, specially described in the specification. As a claim for all possible modes of communicating the motion, &c., it would have been utterly void.[2] In another case, a patent "for an improvement in the art of making nails, by means of a machine which cuts and heads the nails at one operation," was seen at once not to be a grant of an abstract principle, but of a combination of mechanical contrivances operating to produce a new effect, and constituting an improvement in the art of making nails.[3] So, too, where the patentee, in a patent for a machine for turning irregular forms, claimed "the method or mode of operation in the abstract explained in the second article, whereby the infinite variety of forms, described in general terms in this article, may be turned or wrought," and the second article in his specification explained the structure of a machine by which that mode of operation was carried into effect, and the mode of constructing such a machine so as to effect the different objects to be accomplished, it was held that the specification did not claim an abstract principle or function, but a machine.[2] So,

[1] Burr *v.* Duryea, 1 Wall. 531, *vide infra*, p. 264.

[2] Stone *v.* Sprague, 1 Story's R. 270.

[3] Gray *v.* James, Peters's C. C. R. 394.

[4] Blanchard *v.* Sprague, 2 Story's R. 164, 170. In this case, Mr. Justice Story said: "Looking at the present specification, and construing all its terms together, I am clearly of opinion, that it is not a patent claimed for a mere function; but it is claimed for the machine specially described in the specification; that is, for a function as embodied in a particular machine, whose mode of operation and general structure are pointed out. In the close of his specification, the patentee explicitly states that his 'invention is described and explained in the second article of his specification, to which reference is made for information of that which constitutes the principle or character of his machine or invention, and distinguishes it, as he verily believes, from all other machines, discoveries, or inventions known or used

also, it has been held that the making of wheels on a particular principle which is described in the specification is the subject of a patent;[1] and where the plaintiff claimed as his invention "the application of a self-adjusting leverage to the back and seat of a chair, whereby the weight on the seat acts as a counterbalance to the pressure against the back of such chair, as above described," it was held not to be a claim to a principle, but to an application to a certain purpose and by certain means.[2]

before." Now, when we turn to the second article, we find there described, not a mere function, but a machine of a particular structure, whose modes of operation are pointed out, to accomplish a particular purpose, function, or end. This seems to me sufficiently expressive to define and ascertain what his invention is. It is a particular machine, constituted in the way pointed out, for the accomplishment of a particular end or object. The patent is for a machine, and not for a principle or function detached from machinery." Blanchard's Gunstock Turning Factory *v.* Warner, 1 Blatchf. 259.

[1] Jones *v.* Pearce, Webs. Pat. Cas. 123.

[2] Minter *v.* Wells, Webs. Pat. Cas. 135. "Godson, in pursuance of leave reserved, moved for a nonsuit, on the ground that the specification is for a principle, the plaintiff having summed up the whole of his patent in his claim to the principle, and not to any particular means. Either the plaintiff claims a principle, or he does not; to the former he is not entitled; and as to the latter, the defendant has not used the mechanical means of the plaintiff." [Lord Lyndhurst, C. B.: He says, "What I claim as my invention is the application of a self-adjusting leverage to the back and seat of a chair, whereby the weight on the seat acts as a counterbalance to the pressure against the back of such chair, as above described." This is what he claims, a self-adjusting leverage acting in that way. Then he points out the particular mode in which that is effected. The question, therefore, is, whether you have infringed that particular method.] [Alderson, B.: All the witnesses proved that there never had been a self-adjusting leverage in a chair before.] That I admit, and contend that this case is nearly the same as K. *v.* Cutler, (1 Stark. 354; Webs. Pat. Cas. 76, n.) [Lord Lyndhurst, C. B.: He says, "I claim the application of a self-adjusting leverage to the back and seat of a chair," so as to produce such an effect.] Yes, my lord, that effect being nothing more than the motion of a lever backwards and forwards, producing such an effect. [Lord Lyndhurst, C. B.: It is the application of a self-adjusting leverage to the back and seat of a chair, he having described what that self-adjusting leverage was before. Any application of a self-adjusting leverage to the back and seat of a chair producing this effect, that the one acts as a counterbalance to the pressure against the other, would be an infringement of this patent, but nothing short of that.] [Alderson, B.: The difference between this chair and all others, as it appeared in evidence, was very well described by Mr. Brunton; he says, this chair acts (looking at the one you produced), — this chair acts, but not by a self-adjusting leverage.

§ 244. But, on the other hand, a claim to a principle, to be carried into effect by any means, without describing an application of the principle by some means, is a claim to the abstract principle. As, where a specification stated that "it is claimed as new, to cut ice of a uniform size by means of an apparatus worked by any other power than human," it was held that this claim to the art of cutting ice by means of any other power than human was utterly void.[1] It is, therefore, essential that the specification should describe some practical mode of carrying the principle into effect; and then the subject-matter will be patentable, because it will be, not the principle itself, but the mode of carrying it into effect; and on the question of infringement it will be for the jury to say whether another mode of carrying it into

By pressing on the back the seat rises, and *vice versa*, by pressing on the seat the back rises; that is what he calls a self-adjusting leverage. In the other case, you might sit for ever, and the back would never rise.] The plaintiff, by his specification, has appropriated to himself a first principle in mechanics, viz., the lever, and therefore nobody else may use it. [Lord Lyndhurst, C. B.: It is not a leverage only, but the application of a self-adjusting leverage; and it is not a self-adjusting leverage only, but it is a self-adjusting leverage producing a particular effect, by the means of which the weight on the seat counterbalances the pressure against the back.] This is nothing more than one of the first principles of mechanics. [Parke, B.: But that, not being in combination before, can that not be patented? It is only for the application of a self-adjusting leverage to a chair, — cannot he patent that? He claims the combination of the two, no matter in what shapes or way you combine them; but if you combine the self-adjusting leverage, which he thus applies to the subject of a chair, that is an infringement of his patent.] What is the combination? [Lord Lyndhurst, C. B.: Why the application of a self-adjusting leverage producing a particular effect. He says, I do not confine myself to the particular shape of this lever.] If your lordships translate this to mean machine, of course I have no further argument to urge. [Lord Lyndhurst, C. B.: It is every machine consisting of a self-adjusting leverage producing that particular effect in a chair.] That is the extent to which I am putting it. If your lordships say you can, in favor of the patentee, so read it, that it is the machine and the combination only that the plaintiff has claimed, then I should be wasting your lordships' time if I argued the matter further. [Lord Lyndhurst, C. B.: Substantially that combination.] [Parke, B.: Therefore a chair made upon that principle which you have directed to be constructed here, would be an infringement of his patent, that is, the application of a self-adjusting leverage to a chair, such a one as you have produced here to-day.] [Lord Lyndhurst, C. B.: It has the particular effect.] Rule refused.

[1] Wyeth *v.* Stone, 1 Story's R. 273, 285.

effect is not a colorable imitation of the mode invented by the patentee.[1] Hence a claim, construed to include every improvement in which the motive-power is the electric or galvanic current, and the result is the marking or printing of intelligible characters at a distance, is broader than the patent laws allow, and invalid.[2]

§ 245. This being the case, the question next arises whether it is necessary, after having described the application of the principle by some mechanical contrivance, or other arrangement of matter, to claim in the specification all the other forms of apparatus, or modifications of matter, by which the principle may also be applied in order to produce the same beneficial effect, or whether the patent does not cover all these, without particular description, by covering the application of the principle. When we consider that the subject-matter of such a patent is the application of the principle effected by means of some machinery, or other arrangement, it will be apparent that the reason why the patentee is bound to describe some machinery or practical method of making the application, is in order to show that he has actually applied the principle, and to enable others to do so after him. But the real subject of the patent is the practical application of the principle; and hence, although the means by which the patentee has made that application must be described, in order to

[1] In Neilson *v.* Harford, Webs. Pat. Cas. 342, Alderson, B., said : "I take the distinction between a patent for a principle and a patent which can be supported, is, that you must have an embodiment of the principle in some practical mode described in the specification of carrying the principle into actual effect, and then you take out your patent, not for the principle, but for the mode of carrying the principle into effect. In Watt's patent, which comes the nearest to the present of any you can suggest, the real invention of Watt was, that he discovered that by condensing steam in a separate vessel a great saving of fuel would be effected by keeping the steam cylinder as hot as possible, and applying the cooling process to the separate vessel, and keeping it as cool as possible, whereas, before, the steam was condensed in the same vessel ; but then Mr. Watt carried that practically into effect by describing a mode which would effect the object. The difficulty which presses on my mind here is, that this party has taken out a patent, in substance like Watt's, for a principle, that is, the application of hot air to furnaces, but he has not practically described any mode of carrying it into effect. If he had, perhaps he might have covered all other modes, as being a variation."

[2] O'Reilly *v.* Morse, 15 How. 62. For an elaborate discussion of this claim, see chapter on Extent of Principle.

show that he has done what he says he has done, and to enable others to do what he says can be done, yet a variation of the means and machinery, if it produces the same beneficial effect, that is, is the same application of the same principle, does not show that the party making such variation has not infringed the patent, by making use of that which exclusively belonged to another, viz., the application of the principle to produce a particular effect.

§ 246. Examples will best illustrate this distinction. Minter's patent, for a self-adjusting chair, which has been already referred to, was a case of the application of a well-known principle, that of the lever, for the first time applied to a chair. He made no particular claim of shape or form for the construction of the chair, but showed that if a lever was applied to the back of the chair, so that the weight of the seat would act as a counterpoise to the back, in whatever posture the occupant might be sitting or reclining, a self-adjusting chair would be obtained. Now, there might be various modes of constructing a chair on this principle; but as the constructing of chairs on this principle was the true subject of the patent, the court held the making of any chair upon the same principle of a self-adjusting leverage was an infringement.[1]

§ 247. Neilson's patent involved the principle of blowing furnaces, for the smelting of iron, with a blast of hot air, instead of cold, and he applied that principle by finding out a mode by which air may be introduced in a heated state into the furnace, viz., by heating the air in a closed vessel between the blowing apparatus and the furnace. The specification, after stating that the air, heated up to red heat, may be used, but that it is not necessary to go so far to produce a beneficial effect, proceeded to state that the size of the receptacle would depend on the blast necessary for the furnace, and gave directions as to that. It then added, "The shape of the receptacle is immaterial to the effect, and may be adapted to local circumstances." After great consideration, it was held that the word "effect" was not meant to apply to the degree of heat to be given to the air in the heating receptacle, but that any shape of the heating receptacle would produce the beneficial effect of passing heated air into the fur-

[1] Minter *v.* Wells, Webs. Pat. Cas. 134.

nace. This construction settled what the patent was for, viz., the application of the principle of blowing with hot air, by means of a vessel in which the air should be heated on its passage from the blowing apparatus to the furnace. Consequently the subject-matter embraced all the forms of apparatus by which the application of the same principle could be effected.[1]

[1] Neilson *v.* Harford, Webs. Pat. Cas. 295, 369. The same patent was litigated in Scotland, and, upon the point of the generality of the claim as regards the forms of the apparatus, Lord Justice Clerk Hope made the following observations to the jury: "Is it any objection, then, in the next place, to such a patent, that terms descriptive of the application to a certain specified result include every mode of applying the principle or agent so as to produce that specified result, although one mode may not be described more than another,—although one mode may be infinitely better than another,—although much greater benefit would result from the application of the principle by one method than by another,—although one method may be less expensive than another? Is it, I next inquire, an objection to the patent, that, in its application of a new principle to a certain specified result, it includes every variety of mode of applying the principle according to the general statement of the object and benefit to be attained? You will observe, that the greater part of the defenders' case is truly directed to this objection. This is a question of law, and I must tell you distinctly, that this generality of claim, that is, for all modes of applying the principle to the purpose specified, according to or within a general statement of the object to be attained, and of the use to be made of the agent to be so applied, is no objection whatever to the patent. That the application or use of the agent for the purpose specified may be carried out in a great variety of ways, only shows the beauty and simplicity and comprehensiveness of the invention. But the scientific and general utility of the proposed application of the principle, if directed to a specified purpose, is not an objection to its becoming the subject of a patent. That the proposed applications may be very generally adopted in a great variety of ways, is the merit of the invention, not a legal objection to the patent.

"The defenders say, you announce a principle that hot air will produce heat in the furnace; you direct us to take the blast without interrupting, or rather without stopping it, to take the current in blast, to heat it after it leaves the blast, and to throw it hot into the furnace. But you tell us no more,—you do not tell us how we are to heat it. You say you may heat in any way, in any sort of form of vessel. You say, I leave you to do it how you best can. But my application of the discovered principle is, that if you heat the air, and heat it after it leaves the blowing engine (for it is plain you cannot do it before), you attain the result I state: that is the purpose to which I apply the principle. The benefit will be greater or less; I only say, benefit you will get, I have disclosed the principle; I so apply it to a specified purpose by a mechanical contrivance, viz., by getting the heat when in blast, after it leaves the furnace; but the mode and manner and extent of heating I leave to you, and the degree of benefit, on that very account, I do not state. The defenders say,

§ 248. In this case, it was also laid down by Parke, B., to the jury, that the omission to mention in the specification any thing

the patent, on this account, is bad in law. I must tell you, that taking the patent to be of this general character, it is good in law. I state to you the law to be, that you may obtain a patent for a mode of carrying a principle into effect; and if you suggest and discover, not only the principle, but suggest and invent how it may be applied to a practical result by mechanical contrivance and apparatus, and show that you are aware that no particular sort or modification or form of the apparatus is essential in order to obtain benefit from the principle, then you may take your patent for the mode of carrying it into effect, and you are not under the necessity of describing and confining yourself to one form of apparatus. If that were necessary, you see, what would be the result? Why, that a patent could hardly ever be obtained for any mode of carrying a newly discovered principle into practical results, though the most valuable of all discoveries. For the best form and shape or modification of apparatus cannot, in matters of such vast range, and requiring observation on such a great scale, be attained at once; and so the thing would become known, and so the right lost, long before all the various kinds of apparatus could be tried. Hence you may generally claim the mode of carrying the principle into effect by mechanical contrivance, so that any sort of apparatus applied in the way stated will, more or less, produce the benefit, and you are not tied down to any form.

"The best illustration I can give you — and I think it right to give you this illustration — is from a case as to the application of that familiar principle, the lever, to the construction of chairs, or what is called the self-adjusting lever. (Minter's Patent, Webs. Pat. Cas. 126 and 134.) This case, which afterwards came under the consideration of the whole court, was tried in the Court of Exchequer during the presidency of Lord Lyndhurst. The case was as to the patent reclining chair, the luxury of which some of you may have tried; it had a self-adjusting lever, so that a person sitting or reclining, — and I need not tell you what variety of postures can be assumed by a person reclining in a chair, — in whatever situation he placed his back, there was sufficient resistance offered through means of the lever to preserve the equilibrium. Now any thing more general than that I cannot conceive; it was the application of a well-known principle, but for the first time applied to a chair. He made no claim to any particular parts of the chair, nor did he prescribe any precise mode in which they should be made; but what he claimed was a self-adjusting lever to be applied to the back of a chair, where the weight of the seat acts as a counterpoise to the back, in whatever posture the party might be sitting or reclining. Nothing could be more general. Well, a verdict passed for the patentee, with liberty to have it set aside; but Lord Lyndhurst and the rest of the court held, that this was not a claim to a principle, but to the construction of a chair on this principle, in whatever shape or form it may be constructed. (Minter *v.* Wells, Webs. Pat. Cas. 134.) Just so as to the hot blast, only the principle is also new. The patentee says, 'I find hot air will increase the heat in the furnace, that a blast of hot air is beneficial for that end.' Here is the

which the patentee knows to be necessary for the beneficial enjoyment of the invention is a fatal defect; but the omission to mention something which contributes only to the degree of benefit, provided the apparatus would work beneficially and be worth adopting, is not a fatal defect.[1]

§ 249. As it is the duty of the court to determine on the construction of the patent, what the subject-matter is, it is often necessary to decide whether the patentee claims a combination of several things, or the distinct invention of several things or both. General principles cannot be laid down for the determination of questions of this kind, depending exclusively on the particular facts. There is, however, one circumstance that will always be decisive in construing a patent against a claim for the several things described in the specification, and that is, that one or more of them is not new. If this turns out to be the case, the question may then be, whether the patent can be sustained for the combination.[2] In determining this question it is to be observed, that a patent for a combination of three things cannot at the same time be a patent for a combination of any two of them. If the subject-matter is the combination of any given number of things, or processes, or parts, no portion of the combination less than the whole can be considered at the same time as being also the subject-matter.[3]

For instance, where letters-patent were granted for "improve-

way to attain it, 'heat the air under blast, between the blowing apparatus and the furnace; if you do that, I care not how you may propose to do it, I neither propose to you nor claim any special mode of doing it; you may give the air more or less degrees of heat, but if you so heat it, you will get by that contrivance the benefit I have invented and disclosed, more or less, according to the degree of heat.' This is very simple, very general, but its simplicity is its beauty and its practical value, — not an objection in law." The Househill Company *v.* Neilson, Webs. Pat. Cas. 684, 686.

1 Neilson *v.* Harford, Webs. Pat. Cas. 317.

2 For some of the cases where the question has been between a combination or a claim for several distinct things, see Howe *v.* Abbott, 2 Story's R. 190; Ames *v.* Howard, 1 Sumner, 482; Prouty *v.* Ruggles, 16 Peters, 336; s. c. Prouty *v*, Draper, 1 Story, 568; Pitts *v.* Whitman, 2 Story's R. 609; Carver *v.* Braintree Manuf. Company, 2 Story's R. 432; Buck *v.* Hermance, 1 Blatchf. 398.

3 Prouty *v.* Draper, 1 Story, 568, 572; s. c. Prouty *v.* Ruggles, 16 Peters, 336; Winans *v.* Schenectady & Troy R.R., 2 Blatchf. 279.

ments in agricultural machines," and the specification described them as for "the constructing and placing of holding fingers, cutting blades, and gathering reels respectively, in a manner described, and the embodiment of these parts so constructed and placed, all or any of them, in machines for reaping purposes," it was held that the patent was for the combination, and that the use of a knife alone, similar to that described in the patented machine, was not an infringement.[1]

§ 249 *a*. In the case of Blake *v*. Stafford, the specification in the original patent contained the following general description of the mechanism: —

"My stone-breaker, so far as respects its principle, or its essential characteristics, consists of a pair of jaws, one fixed and the other movable, between which the stones are to be broken, having their acting faces nearly in an upright position, and convergent downward one toward the other, in such manner that while the space at the top is such as to receive the stones that are to be broken, that at the bottom is only sufficient to allow the fragments to pass when broken to the required size, and giving to the movable jaw a short and powerful vibration through a small space, say one-fourth of an inch, more or less. By means of this form and arrangement of the jaws, and this motion of the movable jaw, when a stone is dropped into the space between them, it falls down until its further descent is arrested between their convergent faces; the movable jaw, advancing, crushes it, then receding liberates the fragments, and they again descend, and, if too large, are again crushed, and so on until all the fragments, having been sufficiently reduced, have passed out through the narrow space at the bottom. The details of the structure of the machine, other than those already specified, relating to the manner of supporting the jaws in their proper relative position, and giving motion with the required power to the movable jaw, may be varied indefinitely without affecting its principle of operation."

In the reissue, dated January 9, 1866, this general description was enlarged so as to include a revolving shaft, and the claim was as follows: "1. The combination in a stone-breaking machine of the upright, convergent jaws with a revolving shaft

[1] McCormick *v*. Gray, 4 Law Times, N. S. 832.

and mechanism for imparting a definite reciprocating movement to one of the jaws from the revolving shaft, the whole being and operating substantially as set forth; 2. The combination in a stone-breaking machine of the upright movable jaw with the revolving shaft and fly-wheel, the whole being and operating substantially as set forth; 3. In combination with the upright, converging jaws and revolving shaft, imparting a definitely limited vibration to the movable jaw, so arranging the jaws that they can be set at different distances from each other at the bottom, so as to produce fragments of any desired size."

This specification was objected to by the defendant as being "vague, ambiguous, and uncertain," and as not describing with sufficient certainty the invention claimed or the manner of making the machine.

In pronouncing in favor of the validity of this specification, Judge Shipman said: "The whole claim, when read in the light of the specification and drawings, discloses plainly the organized mechanism which the inventor has patented. It consists of two strong, upright, or nearly upright, convergent jaws, fixed in a suitable frame, one of the jaws being stationary, and the other movable, the movable jaw being connected with a revolving shaft and mechanism, whereby, when the motive power is applied, a definite reciprocating and vibratory movement is imparted to the movable jaw by which it alternately advances and recedes from the fixed jaw, crushing the stones as it advances and liberating them as it recedes, so that they drop out from between the bottom of the jaws of a size substantially determined by the distance by which they are separated when the movable jaw is drawn back. This distance, and consequently the size of the fragments, may be varied by adjusting the machine as described in the specification." [1]

§ 249 *b*. In the case of Railroad Company *v*. Dubois, the issue was whether the patent was for a process or a device. The invention consisted of "a new and useful improvement in the mode of building piers for bridges and other structures and setting the same." To enable his invention to be practised, the patentee gave a full description of a floating caisson, or coffer-dam, with all the details of its construction, and also of guide-

[1] Blake *v*. Stafford, 6 Blatchf. 195; s. c. 3 Fisher's Pat. Cas. 294.

piles, with a mode for their use in directing the coffer-dam in its descent with the pier to the foundation. He then added, "I have given a minute description of means for carrying out my invention, but I do not wish to be confined to those means, but desire to be protected in the principle of operation embodied in a floating coffer-dam, substantially as described, for building and setting piers for bridges and other structures."

The patentee then claimed: "1st, Building and setting piers by means of a floating coffer-dam, substantially as set forth; 2d, The use of the tube which constitutes the dam for incasing and strengthening the pier, substantially as set forth; 3d, the guide-piles (AA) in combination with a floating coffer-dam, substantially as and for the purpose set forth."

At the trial it became material to determine for what invention the patent was granted, and especially what construction should be given to the first claim. The defendant asked the court to rule that the first claim was for a *process* of building and setting piers, and that unless the defendants had used that *process* the complainants could not recover. The court construed the claim to be, not for a process, but for a device or instrument to be employed in a process, the instrument being a floating coffer-dam, constructed as described in the specification, in which the masonry of the pier might be laid and sunk to the foundation by its own gravity; and therefore refused to give the instruction. This construction was held to be correct by the Supreme Court of the United States, when the matter came before them on appeal.[1]

[1] Railroad Company *v.* Dubois, 12 Wall. 47. In construing the second and third claims, the court below thus charged, which was held to be correct by the Supreme Court: "The second claim of the plaintiff's patent is for the use of the tube or material of which the dam is made for incasing and strengthening the pier; that is, it shall be so constructed that it can be used for the casing and strengthening the pier, no matter whether it be first placed in position entire, or be built in sections as the masonry progresses.

"The third claim of the plaintiff's patent is for a combination of a floating coffer-dam, as claimed in the first claim, with guide-piles, which are driven into the bottom of the river, around the site of the proposed pier, and reach above the surface of the water, and pass through holes in the platform, and have their tops framed together with ties; when the pier is building, they are to sustain and keep upright the tube with its pier inside, and to guide it down to its foundation prepared at the bottom of the river; when the pier is finished,

§ 249 *c*. In the case of Coffin *v*. Ogden,[1] the invention consisted in an improvement in locks and knob latches. The claims of the patent were two in number: 1. So dividing the hub or follower, and so combining the same with a reversible latch, that the arms, or their equivalents, of the divided hub or follower, may be released, for the purpose of allowing the latch to be reversed or turned. This was held to be not a claim for a result, and therefore bad, but "a claim to dividing the hub or follower in substantially the manner described by the patentee, and to combining the hub so divided with a reversible latch in substantially the manner described by the patentee, the arms of the hub being released in substantially the manner described by the patentee for the purpose of allowing the latch to be reversed." 2. So constructing and arranging the individual parts of a divided hub or follower, that the reversal or turning of the latch is prevented only by the presence of the spindle within the lock. This was held to be a "claim to constructing and arranging the individual parts of the divided hub in substantially the manner described by the patentee, the reversal of the latch being prevented only by the presence of the spindle in the lock in substantially the manner described by the patentee."

§ 249 *d*. In the case of Clark *v*. Bousfield, letters-patent had been granted for a new and useful improvement in machines for graining pails, and other analogous uses. The invention consisted in constructing an elastic bed, containing the impression of the device to be grained upon the pail, in separate panels, each of different design, so that by moving the pail over it the various designs would be stamped upon the staves, thus giving them the appearance of different kinds of wood. The instrument or machine described for this purpose was a box or bed, which might be constructed of wood or iron, or other suitable material, and the office of which was to hold the elastic material, whether of rubber or leather, or the compound of glue and molasses, such as is used for printers' rollers, which was preferred.

Having described the apparatus and the process, the patentees set forth their claims, the first two of which were: —

they are then to be cut off just above the top of the platform, and their stumps left to prevent any lateral movement of the platform and pier on its foundation."

[1] (1869), 3 Fisher's Pat. Cas. 640.

"First. We claim constructing the bed of the elastic material used in graining machines, in the form herein shown, substantially as and for the purposes specified.

"Second. We claim arranging the elastic material aforesaid, whether curved or rectangular in form, in a series of distinct staves or designs, substantially as and for the purposes herein shown and set forth."

On behalf of the defendant, it was maintained that the second claim was for a *design* to be impressed on the bed, and was therefore patentable under the eleventh section of the act of 1861, and not under that of 1836. The patent was therefore void, as containing a claim for a machine and a claim for a design, which two things were patentable under different acts, and for different terms of time. Upon this question, whether the second claim was for any thing more than a design, the judges of the Circuit Court were divided in opinion, and the issue was carried to the Supreme Court of the United States. In affirming the validity of the patent, Mr. Justice Nelson, who delivered the opinion of the court, said: "The learned counsel for the defendants below insist that this second claim is only an arrangement of designs, and in a limited sense he is no doubt right; but in its connection with the first claim, and with the machine for transferring designs to pails, it is more: it is a part of the machine or instrument, and an indispensable part; it is the elastic bed of rubber or of leather, or compound of glue and molasses, of any arranged figure or design, that constitutes an element in the machine, and which, with the curved box and contrivances for working the instrument, produces the desired result. The figure or design is but incidental, and, as such, has no other protection than that which the patent secures to the inventor of the machine. The right to the use of the machine carries along with it the right to use the designs."[1]

[1] Clark *v.* Bousfield (1869), 10 Wall. 133. Mr. Justice Nelson further said: "In order to understand the full meaning of this second claim, it will be useful to settle the meaning of the first, as the two are intimately connected.

"The first, as we have seen, is for constructing the bed for the elastic material used in graining machines in the form shown, and for the purposes specified. The patentees describe it as a box or bed, and which may be constructed of wood or iron, or of any other suitable material. This box or bed is made for the purpose of holding the elastic material, whether of rubber or

§ 249 *e*. In a recent English case,[1] the complainant having taken out a patent for "certain improvements in the construction of ships, and other vessels, navigating on water," by his specification claimed, among other things, as his invention, "first, the combination of an iron frame with an external covering of timber planking for the sides, bilges, and bottoms"; and 'sixthly, the construction of iron frames for ships, or other vessels, navigating on water, adapted to an external covering of timber planking for the sides, bilges, and bottoms, as described." On a careful consideration of the specification, the court held that the expression "iron frame," in the first claim, was not confined to an iron frame, such as that specified in the sixth claim, "but comprehended whatever might, according to the ordinary use of language, be called 'an iron frame' for a ship," and was therefore "a claim for planking with timber any iron frame of a ship."

§ 249 *f*. In the case of Arnold *v*. Bradbury,[2] recently decided in England, the invention related to an improved ruffle-frill, or gathered fabric, and to the machinery for making the same. The patentee, after fully describing an improved ruffle or frill, and the machinery by which he proposed to make such improved ruffle, and to fasten it to a plain fabric by a single series of stitches, claimed, among other things, "the production, by machinery, of ruffles, frills, and gathered work, and the simul-

leather, or the compound of glue and molasses, which is preferred. Now, the second claim is for arranging the elastic material, when placed in this box or bed, whether curved or rectangular in form, '*in a series of distinct staves or designs*,' for the purpose specified; that is, for the purpose of graining pails in the variety of colors or figures described. The elastic bed may be arranged, as is stated in the specification, so as to present one continuous or uniform design, or it may be arranged in blocks or staves, each of different designs, so that the vessel shall present the appearance of different kinds of wood, as rosewood, oak, walnut, and others. It may also be constructed of separate pieces or blocks, as shown in the drawing, or the material may be a single united mass, impressed by different designs arranged in staves, so as to produce the same effect as when constructed in separate blocks. The two claims, as we see, are closely connected, and each essential to the complete construction of the instrument or apparatus, which, when put into practical operation by the contrivances pointed out in the specification, can accomplish the desired result, which result is the graining of the exterior body of the pail with a variety of colors and figures."

[1] Jordan *v*. Moore (1866), L. R. 1 C. P. 624.

[2] (1871), Law Rep. 6 Chan. Ap. 706.

taneous attachment of the same to a plain fabric, by means of a single series of stiches, which serve both to confine and stitch the gathers, and also to secure one fabric to the other."

It was contended, on the part of the defendants, that the above claim was bad, because there was nothing to limit the patent to any particular process, and that a proper construction of the expression "by machinery" would embrace all machinery for making ruffles and fastening them to the fabric by a series of single stitches. The claim was, therefore, too large, and consequently invalid. This construction, however, was not accepted by the court, who, interpreting the claim in the light of the preceding description, sustained the validity of the patent. In considering this point, Lord Hatherly said: "I do not think that the proper way of dealing with this question is to look first at the claims, and then see what the full description of the invention is; but rather first to read the description of the invention, in order that your mind may be prepared for what it is the inventor is about to claim. He tells you that he has now described and particularly ascertained the nature of his invention and the manner in which it is to be performed; and then, in the claim, we do not find any thing asserted or claimed as his invention beyond what is found in the previous part. And it is to be observed that he reserves to himself the right of making modifications in the machinery to produce similar results. . . . I do not deny that this case might be brought, by evidence, within the case of Jordan *v.* Moore.[1] If it were proved to be the case that this, after all, was only one of a series of inventions, and that as numbers of machines had been made anterior to this gentleman's machine, although not precisely the same, for effecting this very object, then the court might have reason to say, "You fail, not because you are claiming too much, but because your claim takes in that which has already been invented," just as occurred in the case with regard to iron framing for ships. But when an inventor says he is describing a new thing, and gives very full details, and says he will not exclude himself from making modifications which are substantially the same as his present invention, and then says that the object of his claim is simply to point out what he considers to be novel in what he has already stated, I think in such

[1] Law Rep. 1 C. P. 624.

a case it would be a strange perversion of the construction of the instrument to hold that he is intending to shut everybody out from any conceivable machinery which may subsequently be invented."

§ 250. The rule which we have thus endeavored to illustrate, which requires the patentee so to describe his invention as to enable the public to know what his claim is, of course imposes upon him the duty of not misleading the public, either by concealing any thing material to the invention, or by adding any thing not necessary to be introduced. The ambiguity which we have been considering in the preceding pages may be produced involuntarily; but there is a special provision of the statute aimed at the voluntary concealment or addition of any thing material. The statute enacts it as one of the defences to an action on a patent, that the specification "does not contain the whole truth relative to his invention or discovery, or that it contains more than is necessary to produce the described effect; which concealment or addition shall fully appear to have been made for the purpose of deceiving the public."[1] This defence will be made good, when it appears that the patentee fradulently concealed something that he knew to be material to the practice of his invention, or fraudulently added something which he knew was not useful, material, or necessary, at the time when he prepared his specification. If it was subsequently discovered not to be useful, material, or necessary, his patent will not be affected by it.[2]

§ 251. II. The second rule for preparing a specification is,

To describe the invention in such a manner as to enable the public to practise it, from the specification alone.

§ 252. The statute requires the patentee to describe "the manner and process of making, constructing, using, and compounding his invention or discovery, in such full, clear, and exact terms, avoiding unnecessary prolixity, as to enable any person skilled in the art or science to which it appertains, or with which it is most nearly connected, to make, construct, compound, and use the same; and in case of any machine, he shall fully explain the principle and the several modes in which he has contemplated the application of that principle or character by which it may be

[1] Act of July 4, 1836, § 15.

[2] See *post*, chapter on Infringement, and also chapter on Action at Law.

distinguished from other inventions; and shall particularly specify and point out the part, improvement, or combination which he claims as his own invention or discovery."

§ 253. We have seen that the question whether a specification answers this requisite of the statute, is a question of fact for the jury; and although it is not necessary that technical terms should be made use of in a specification, they often are made use of and often require to be explained by evidence. In judging of a specification, therefore, a distinction must be taken between that sort of ambiguity which a person unacquainted with technical terms would encounter, and the ambiguity which might appear to a person skilled in the particular art. It is not necessary that the specification should contain an explanation level with the capacity of every person, which would often be impossible.[1] The statute allows the patentee to address himself to persons of competent skill in the art, and it requires him to use such full, clear, and exact terms as will enable that class of persons to reproduce the thing described from the description itself. It is, therefore, important to ascertain what the rules of construction are, which define what will constitute an ambiguity or uncertainty to artists and persons skilled in the subject.

§ 254. And, *first*, with regard to the persons whose judgment and apprehension are thus appealed to: they are not those who possess the highest degree of skill or knowledge in the particular art or science to which the subject-matter belongs, nor are they day-laborers; they are practical workmen, or persons of reasonably competent skill in the particular art, science, or branch of industry. If persons of the highest skill were those whom the law has in contemplation, the object of a specification which is to enable competent persons to reproduce the thing patented, without making experiments, inventions, or additions of their own, could not generally be answered.[2]

§ 255. *Secondly*, as to the application of their knowledge and skill, by such persons, to the understanding and carrying out of the description given by the patentee. The description must be such as will enable persons of competent skill and knowledge to

[1] Per Story, J., in Lowell *v.* Lewis, 1 Mas. 182.

[2] The King *v.* Arkwright, Dav. Pat. Cas. 106; Webs. Pat. Cas. 64; Lowell *v.* Lewis, 1 Mas. 182; Harmar *v.* Playne, 11 East, 101. And see particularly the observations of M. Baron Parke, cited *post*, from Neilson *v.* Harford.

construct or reproduce the thing described, without invention or addition of their own, and without repeated experiments.[1] Thus, it has been held, that any material alteration to be made in existing apparatus or machinery must be stated, and not left to be supplied by the workman; as, with reference to the materials employed, or their form, or the speed of the parts, or their relative dimensions, where these are material.[2] So, too, the specification is insufficient, if information must be derived from experiments, or from seeing others make the thing described;[3] or as it

[1] The King *v.* Arkwright, Webs. Pat. Cas. 66, 67, 69, 70. It will not do to rely for the correction of errors on the ordinary knowledge of competent workmen. In Neilson *v.* Harford, the specification contained a particular passage, which the jury found to be untrue; but they also found that any workman of competent knowledge of the subject would correct the statement. Parke, B.: "Nor do we think that the point contended for by Sir William Follett, that if a man acquainted well with the process of heating air were employed, this misstatement would not mislead him, would at all relieve the plaintiffs from the difficulty; for this would be to support the specification by a fresh invention and correction by a scientific person, and no authority can be found that in such a case a specification would be good. To be valid, we think it should be such as, if fairly followed out by a competent workman, without invention or addition, would produce the machine for which the patent is taken out, and that such machine so constructed must be one beneficial to the public." Webs. Pat. Cas. 37.

[2] Ibid. p. 67.

[3] Ibid. p. 67, 70, 71. Upon this point, Buller, J., said: "Immison says, that from the specification he should have made a parallel cylinder, and not a spiral one, but this is the one used by the defendant. As to the rollers, it does not appear from the specification some were to go faster than others; from the specification, without other sources, it is impossible to say how they should be made, as there is no scale or plan to work by. A roller is necessary to the feeder to give regular direction to the work; it will not answer without it. From the knowledge he has now, he should add a roller if he was directed to make the machine. But that does not prove the specification to be sufficient, because, if a man, from the knowledge he has got from three trials, and seeing people immediately employed about it, is able to make use of it, it is his ideas improve the plan, and not the merit of the specification; if he makes it complete, it is his ingenuity, and not the specification of the inventor. . . . Upon the other hand, several respectable people are called, upon the part of the defendant, who say they could do it, but there is this difference in their description; most, if not every one of them, have looked at and seen how the machines were worked by the defendant, and have got their knowledge by other means, and not from the specification and plan alone; besides, they admit the manner the defendant works it is not consistent with the plan laid

has also been said, if it requires the solution of a problem.[1] And, generally, a specification, to be valid, must be such as, when fairly

down, particularly as to the cylinder, a particular part of the business, for Moore says, this upon the face of it must be taken to be a parallel, whereas that which plainly appears to be used is a spiral ; besides, after all this, they have spoken most of them in a very doubtful way, particularly Mr. Moore, who qualified his expression in the way which I have stated to you, and the others qualifying their expressions, saying they think upon the whole they could do it. Suppose it perfectly clear they could with the subsequent knowledge they had acquired, yet, if it be true that sensible men, that know something of this particular business, and mechanics in general, cannot do it, it is not so described as is sufficient to support this patent."

[1] In Morgan *v.* Seaward, Webs. Pat. Cas. 170, 174, Alderson, B., said : "If the invention can only be carried into effect by persons setting themselves a problem to solve, then they who solve the problem become the inventors of the method of solving it ; and he who leaves persons to carry out his invention by means of that application of their understanding, does not teach them in his specification, that which, in order to entitle him to maintain his patent, he should teach them, the way of doing the thing, but sets them a problem, which being suggested to persons of skill, they may be able to solve. That is not the way in which a specification ought to be framed. It ought to be framed so as not to call on a person to have recourse to more than those ordinary means of knowledge (not invention) which a workman of competent skill in his art and trade may be presumed to have. You may call upon him to exercise all the actual existing knowledge common to the trade, but you cannot call upon him to exercise any thing more. You have no right to call upon him to tax his ingenuity or invention. Those are the criteria by which you ought to be governed, and you ought to decide this question according to those criteria. You are to apply those criteria to the case now under consideration, and you should apply them without prejudice, either one way or the other, for it is a fair observation to make, that both parties here stand, so far as this observation is concerned, on a footing of perfect equality. The public, on the one hand, have a right to expect and require that the specification shall be fair, honest, open, and sufficient ; and, on the other hand, the patentee should not be tripped up by captious objections, which do not go to the merits of the specification. Now, applying those criteria to the evidence in the cause, if you shall think that this invention has been so specified that any competent engineer, having the ordinary knowledge which competent engineers possess, could carry it into effect by the application of his skill, and the use of his previous knowledge, without any inventions on his part, and that he could do it in the manner described by the specification, and from the information disclosed in the specification, then the specification would be sufficient. If, on the other hand, you think that engineers of ordinary and competent skill would have to set themselves a problem to solve, and would have to solve that problem before they could do it, then the specification would be bad." See also Gray *v.* James, 1 Pet. C. C. R. 394, 476.

followed out by a competent workman, without invention or addition, the object of the patent may be obtained.[1]

[1] In Neilson *v.* Harford, Webs. Pat. Cas. 295, 313, Parke, B., instructed the jury as follows: "Now, then, understanding the meaning of this specification to be the sense I have given to it, that he claims as his invention a mode of heating the blast between the blowing apparatus and the furnace, in a vessel exposed to the fire, and kept to a red heat, or nearly (and which description I think sufficient), of the size of a cubic foot for a smith's forge, or the other size mentioned, or of any shape, these questions will arise for your decision. It is said that, understanding it in that sense, the patent is void, because there are no directions given for any mode of constructing the instrument. But understanding the patent in that sense, it seems to me, that if you should be of opinion that a person of competent skill (and I will explain to you what I mean by that) would nevertheless construct such a vessel as would be productive of some useful and beneficial purpose in the working of iron, that the patent nevertheless is good, though no particular form of vessel is given. Then it is to be recollected that this claim is a patent right, — a right of heating in any description of vessel; and in order to maintain that right, it is essential that the heating in any description of vessel, either the common form, the smith's forge, the cupola, or the blast furnace, that it should be beneficial in any shape you may choose for all those three purposes. Now, then, I think therefore that this is correctly described in the patent; and if any man of common understanding and ordinary skill and knowledge of the subject, and I should say in this case that the subject is the construction of the blowing apparatus, such a person as that is the person you would most naturally apply to in order to make an alteration of this kind, if you are of opinion, on the evidence, that such a person as that, of ordinary skill and knowledge of the subject (that is, the construction of the old blowing apparatus), would be able to construct, according to the specification alone, such an apparatus as would be an improvement, that is, would be productive practically of some beneficial result, no matter how great, provided it is sufficient to make it worth while (the expense being taken into consideration) to adapt such an apparatus to the ordinary machinery in all cases of forges, cupolas, and furnaces, where the blast is used; in that case, I think the specification sufficiently describes the invention, leaving out the other objection (to which I need not any further direct your attention) that there is not merely a defective statement in the specification, unless those conditions were complied with, but there is a wrong statement. But leaving out the wrong statement for the present, and supposing that it was not introduced, then if, in your opinion, such a person as I have described — a man of ordinary and competent skill — would erect a machine which would be beneficial in all those cases, and be worth while to erect; in that case it seems to me that this specification is good, and the patent, so far as relates to this objection, will be good. It is to be a person only of ordinary skill and ordinary knowledge. You are not to ask yourselves the question, whether persons of great skill, — a first-rate engineer, or a second-class engineer, as described by Mr.

For example, a specification which states that part of the process consists in cutting hides into thin slices, is valid, although it does not state whether the hides should be wet or dry.[1]

§ 256. But slight defects in a specification will sometimes prevent the object of the patent from being obtained by any competent person who may undertake to apply it, and will therefore render the patent void, because they create a necessity for the exercise of inventive power on the part of the person who thus undertakes to apply the description. As the omitting to state the use of tallow, which the patentee employed for facilitating the manufacture of steel trusses;[2] or, in a patent medicine, stating the ingredients without stating the proportions.[3] If any thing be omitted which gives an advantageous operation to the thing invented, it will vitiate the patent; as the omission to state the use of a material, *aquafortis*, which the patentee used himself for obtaining the effect more rapidly;[4] for the patentee is bound to give the most advantageous mode known to him, and any circumstance conducive to the advantageous operation; otherwise he does not pay the price for his monopoly, because he does not give the public the benefit of all that he knows himself.[5]

Farey, — whether they would do it; because generally those persons are men of great science and philosophical knowledge, and they would upon a mere hint in the specification probably invent a machine which should answer the purpose extremely well; but that is not the description of persons to whom this specification may be supposed to be addressed, — it is supposed to be addressed to a practical workman, who brings the ordinary degree of knowledge and the ordinary degree of capacity to the subject; and if such a person would construct an apparatus that would answer some beneficial purpose, whatever its shape was, according to the terms of this specification, then I think that this specification is good, and the patent may be supported so far as relates to that."

[1] Wallington *v.* Dale, 16 E. L. & Eq 584.

[2] Liardet *v.* Johnson, Webs. Pat. Cas. 53.

[3] Ibid. 54, note.

[4] Wood *v.* Zimmer, Webs. Pat. Cas. 82.

[5] Morgan *v.* Seaward, Webs. Pat. Cas. 175, 182. See the remarks of Alderson, B., cited *ante.* See also The King *v.* Arkwright, Webs. Pat. Cas. 66; Walton *v.* Bateman, ibid. 622; Turner *v.* Winter, ibid. 81, where the employment of cheaper materials than those mentioned in the specification, or the insertion of materials which would not answer, were said to be sufficient to avoid a patent.

§ 257. So, too, if a specification directs the use of a substance, which, as generally known, contains foreign matter, the presence of which is positively injurious, and does not show any method of removing that foreign matter, or refer to any method generally known, or state how the substance in a proper state can be procured, the specification will be defective.[1]

[1] Derosne *v.* Fairie, Webs. Pat. Cas. 154, 162. In this very instructive case, Lord Abinger, C. B., said: "Upon the main point, however, that respecting the bituminous schistus, nothing that I have heard has removed my original impression, that there was no evidence to show that this process, carried on with bituminous schistus, combined with any iron whatsoever, would answer at all. The plaintiff himself has declared, that in that bituminous schistus, which he himself furnished, the whole of the iron was extracted; and it appears, that it was admitted by the counsel, that the presence of iron would not only be disadvantageous, but injurious. Thus, then, it appearing by the evidence, that in all the various forms in which the article exists in this country, sulphuret of iron is found, and the witnesses not describing any known process by which it can be extracted, it appears to me that the plaintiff ought to prove one of two things, — either that the sulphuret of iron in bituminous schistus is not so absolutely detrimental as to make its presence disadvantageous to the process (in which case this patent would be good), or that the process of extracting the iron from it is so simple and well known that a man may be able to accomplish it with ease. As the bituminous schistus which was procured and used was exclusively that which was furnished by the plaintiff, not in its original state, but after it had undergone distillation, and had been made into charcoal in a foreign country, and as in that stage of its preparation it could not be discovered, by examining it, whether it was made from one substance or another (the residuum, after distillation, of almost every matter, vegetable as well as animal, being a charcoal mixed more or less with other things), then there is only the plaintiff's statement to prove that the substance which was furnished by him and used was charcoal of bituminous schistus. It appeared, also, that he had declared to one of the witnesses that he had extracted all the iron from the substance so sent, and that it also underwent another process. I am, therefore, of opinion, that without considering whether or not the patent would be avoided by the process requiring the use of means to extract the iron from the bituminous schistus, which were kept secret by the patentee, he has not shown in this case, that what he has described in the patent could be used as so described, without injury to the matter going through the process. Under all these circumstances, I think that the plaintiff ought to have given some evidence to show that bituminous schistus, in the state in which it is found and known in England, could be used in this process with advantage, and as he has not done that, the defendants are entitled to a nonsuit; but, at the same time, as it is alleged that the plaintiff may supply the defect of proof as to the schistus on a new trial by other evidence, we are desirous that the patent, if a good one, should not be affected by our judgment, and think it right to direct a new trial on the terms which have been stated."

§ 258. In like manner, a specification will be defective if an article be described by a particular name, the patentee knowing that the requisite article cannot ordinarily be procured under the name by which it is described in the specification, and it be not stated where it may be procured; because the public have not that full and precise information which they have a right to require.[1] A specification will also be defective which states that the manner in which a power is to be applied varies with the circumstances in some measure, without showing in what the improvement consists, as distinguished from all former modes of doing the same thing.[2] If obscure terms be employed for the sake of concealment, so as to induce the belief that elaborate processes are necessary, when the simplest will succeed, the specification is bad;[3] and if a patentee states that he prefers a certain material, having ascertained that no other will answer, he misleads the public.[4]

Where a general term, acids, is used, and evidence shows that some of the varieties of that class will not answer, the specification is faulty. Such term will however be understood as embracing only such acids as are generally known and used, and not obscure acids, existing only in the chemist's laboratory. The inventor should confine his specification to substances which he *knows* will answer, leaving the question of infringement by substances impliedly contained in the description or subsequently discovered as one of colorable imitation, to be passed upon by a jury.

Thus, where the patentee in his description said: "Dissolve one pound of strong alkali (for instance, American potash) in one gallon of water; this solution is to be neutralized with *acid* (sulphuric is *best* for the purpose), &c., and on the trial it was proved that a well-known acid, nitric, would not answer, the specification was held insufficient.[5]

§ 259. The rule, however, which forbids a patentee to leave the public to find out by experiment how to apply his discovery or invention, is subject to one important limitation. If, for instance, the specification of a patent for a composition of matter

1 Sturz *v.* De La Rue, Webs. Pat. Cas. 83.
2 Sullivan *v.* Redfield, Paine's C. C. R. 441, 450, 451.
3 Savory *v.* Price, Webs. Pat. Cas. 83.
4 Crompton *v.* Ibbotson, ibid. 83.
5 Stevens *v.* Keating, 2 Webs. Pat. Cas. 172.

is so drawn, that no one can use the invention without first ascertaining by experiment the exact proportion of the different ingredients required to produce the intended result, the patent will be void. But it has been determined by the Supreme Court of the United States, that if, in such a specification, the patentee gives a certain proportion as the general rule applicable to the ordinary state of the ingredients, he may, without the risk of having his patent declared void by the court, for vagueness and uncertainty, state other and variable proportions as exceptions to the rule, applicable to the varying states of the ingredients, although the precise proportion adapted to a given state of the ingredients, other than the usual state, can only be ascertained by computing it from the general rule, after the particular state of the ingredients is ascertained. In such cases it is for the jury to decide, on the evidence of experts, whether the general rule given is susceptible of application, and whether it furnishes the means of determining the proportions to be used, in the excepted cases, by the exercise of the ordinary knowledge and skill of the workman.[1] A specification which intentionally creates in the

[1] Wood *v.* Underhill, 5 How. S. C. R. 1, 3, 4. The specification in this case was as follows : " Be it known that I, the said James Wood, have invented a new and useful improvement in the art of manufacturing bricks and tiles. The process is as follows : take of common anthracite coal, unburnt, such quantity as will best suit the kind of clay to be made into brick or tile, and mix the same, when well pulverized, with the clay before (it) is moulded ; that clay which requires the most burning will require the greatest proportion of coal dust ; the exact proportion, therefore, cannot be specified, but, in general, three-fourths of a bushel of coal dust to one thousand brick will be correct. Some clay may require one-eighth more, and some not exceeding a half bushel. The benefits resulting from this composition are the saving of fuel and the more general diffusion of heat through the kiln, by which the contents are more equally burned. If the heat is raised too high, the brick will swell, and be injured in their form. If the heat is too moderate, the coal dust will be consumed before the desired effect is produced. Extremes are therefore to be avoided. I claim as my invention the using of fine anthracite coal or coal dust with clay, for the purpose of making brick and tile as aforesaid, and for that only claim letters-patent from the United States." Mr. Chief Justice Taney, delivering the judgment of the court, said : " The plaintiff claims that he has invented a new and useful improvement in the art of manufacturing bricks and tiles, and states his invention to consist in using fine anthracite coal or coal dust with clay, for the purpose of making brick or tile, and for that only he claims a patent. And the only question presented by the record is, whether his description of the relative proportions of coal

mind of one applying it any doubt as to the relative proportions of the ingredients is defective, for the public are to rely on an

dust and clay, as given in his specification, is upon the face of it too vague and uncertain to support a patent. The degree of certainty which the law requires is set forth in the act of Congress. The specification must be in such full, clear, and exact terms as to enable any one skilled in the art to which it appertains to compound and use it without making any experiments of his own. In patents for machines the sufficiency of the description must, in general, be a question of fact to be determined by the jury. And this must also be the case in compositions of matter where any of the ingredients mentioned in the specification do not always possess exactly the same properties in the same degree. But when the specification of a new composition of matter gives only the names of the substances which are to be mixed together, without stating any relative proportion, undoubtedly it would be the duty of the court to declare the patent to be void. And the same rule would prevail where it was apparent that the proportions were stated ambiguously and vaguely. For in such cases it would be evident, on the face of the specification, that no one could use the invention without first ascertaining by experiment the exact proportion of the different ingredients required to produce the result intended to be obtained. And if the specification before us was liable to either of these objections, the patent would be void, and the instruction given by the Circuit Court undoubtedly right. But we do not think this degree of vagueness and uncertainty exists. The patentee gives a certain proportion as a general rule, that is, three-fourths of a bushel of coal dust to one thousand bricks. It is true, he also states that clay which requires the most burning will require the greatest proportion of coal dust; and that some clay may require one-eighth more than the proportions given, and some not more than half a bushel instead of three-fourths. The two last-mentioned proportions may, however, be justly considered as exceptions to the rule he has stated, and as applicable to those cases only where the clay has some peculiarity and differs in quality from that ordinarily employed in making bricks. Indeed, in most compositions of matter, some small difference in the proportions must occasionally be required, since the ingredients proposed to be compounded must sometimes be in some degree superior or inferior to those most commonly used. In this case, however, the general rule is given with entire exactness in its terms; and the notice of the variations mentioned in the specification would seem to be designed to guard the brick-maker against mistakes, into which he might fall if his clay was more or less hard to burn than the kind ordinarily employed in the manufacture. It may be, indeed, that the qualities of clay generally differ so widely, that the specification of the proportions stated in this case is of no value, and that the improvement cannot be used with advantage in any case, or with any clay, without first ascertaining by experiment the proportion to be employed. If that be the case, then the invention is not patentable. Because, by the terms of the act of Congress, the inventor is not entitled to a patent. But this does not appear to be the case on the face of this specification. And whether the

honest, open, and candid exposition by the patentee of every thing that is necessary for the easy and certain procurement of that for which the patent is granted.[1]

fact is so or not, is a question to be decided by a jury, upon the evidence of persons skilled in the art to which the patent appertains. The Circuit Court, therefore, erred in instructing the jury that the specification was too vague and uncertain to support the patent, and its judgment must be reversed."

[1] Muntz *v.* Foster *et al.*, 2 Webs. Pat. Cas. 85, 96. The patentee had worded his description thus: "I take that quality of copper known in the trade by the appellation of 'best selected copper,' and that quality of zinc known in England as 'foreign zinc,' and melt them together in the usual manner in any proportions between 50 per cent of copper to 50 per cent of zinc, and 63 per cent of copper to 37 per cent of zinc; both *of which extremes*, and *all intermediate proportions*, *will roll at a red heat.*" Then he goes on to say: "but as too large a proportion of copper increases the difficulty of working the metal, and too large a proportion of zinc renders the metal too hard when cold, and not sufficiently liable to oxidation to effect in the best manner the intended purpose, I prefer the alloy to consist of about 60 per cent of copper to 40 per cent of zinc," &c. The court said: "There have been several questions asked of witnesses; they have had the specification put into their hands, and the usual question in these cases has been asked them, whether a competent workman, looking at this specification, could by his own skill and understanding of it produce the result which is the subject of the patent. I do not find any person who has been called, on the part of the defendants, distinctly say that he cannot make the compound here described from the specification. And, therefore, that which is generally the objection which is made would not prevail here. But there is a further objection made, pointed to one particular part of the specification, and that is, that the plaintiff has given certain limits within which he says the patent can be carried into effect. The invention may be made by different proportions, within certain limits, to which I shall now call your attention. And they (defendants) say, upon the evidence of Mr. Prosser, one of the witnesses called by the plaintiff, that the invention cannot be made in one or two of the different proportions of zinc and copper which are here specified. If such be the fact, if, upon reading this, what the witness has said has shown that the specification is not only difficult to understand, but is actually false and incorrect in that particular, there would be an end at once of the patent; because, when the plaintiff takes upon him to say that he melts copper and zinc of the qualities referred to in the usual manner, 'in any proportions between 50 per cent of copper to 50 per cent of zinc, and 63 per cent of copper to 37 per cent of zinc, both of which extremes and all intermediate proportions will roll at a red heat,' if it is found out that the two extremes would not do that which he here specifies they will do, that would be a statement of a property belonging to his discovery which it did not really possess. That would only have the effect of forcing persons to make different experiments in a way in which they must afterwards be defeated, and would, in short, be a contradiction to that object

§ 260. But although it is necessary that a specification should clearly and fully describe the invention, and should give the best process, materials, and methods known to the inventor, yet it is not necessary for the patentee to describe the mode of making every thing which he uses, or detail known processes, or explain the terms appropriate to the particular art, or science, or branch

and intention of the condition, which was that all should be certain, true, and intelligible.

"Prosser underwent a long examination and stated, you know, that he made a scale in which 40 was the fixed quantity of zinc he employed, and then he varies the quantity of copper in which, when reduced to the hundredth scale in which the plaintiff has framed his specification, agrees in the limits with those terms. When he comes to the last one, I think he was asked this question, 'I should say the experiment 40 to 50 copper with my scale, — which was 55½ to 44½ according to the plaintiff's scale, — I would say it is of no use at all for sheathing. It is perfectly useless in more respects than one. It does not corrode enough, it is too hard, too brittle, it would roll at a red heat and at a cold heat.' Then he goes to some others, '47 of zinc, 53 of copper, this would corrode less than the last mentioned, and be more brittle; 48 zinc and 52 copper still more, quite useless for sheathing. I do not think it could be put on a ship on account of its being brittle.' What he says of all this is that it would roll at a red heat. Now the question is, whether, looking at this specification, more is meant or intended by the expression in it, when the patentee is giving these quantities, than that it shall be a metal which will roll at a red heat. This is what he (the patentee) says: 'I melt them together in the usual manner in any proportions between 50 per cent copper to 50 per cent zinc, and 63 per cent copper to 37 per cent zinc, both of which extremes and all intermediate proportions' — he does not say will oxidize sufficiently, or will make sheathing for a ship, but — 'will roll at a red heat'; and then he goes on to say, as to the other quality which this is to possess, 'but as too large a proportion of copper increases the difficulty of working the metal, and too large a proportion of zinc renders the metal too hard when cold, and not sufficiently liable to oxidation to effect in the best manner the intended purpose, I prefer the alloy to consist of about 60 per cent of copper to 40 per cent of zinc.'

"Therefore, understanding the specification in that way, the question (the only question of fact that you can determine upon this) is, whether this account, which his own witness has given of it, has falsified the statement in the specification. If that statement had been distinctly that the lower mixture of the lower compound, the extreme, would have been sufficient for the sheathing of ships, both in respect of oxidation and of rolling hot, I should have thought the specification bad and avoided the patent. But you must say for yourselves whether you are satisfied that all that was described here was, that it would roll at a red heat and at the intermediate states; whether, in point of fact, it would roll at a red heat."

of industry to which his invention belongs.[1] The specification is, as we have seen, addressed to persons acquainted with the nature of the business; some technical knowledge is presumed on the part of those who will undertake, after the patent is expired, to carry out the invention; and such persons are to be called as witnesses to explain the language to the jury, while the patent is in force, and to show that it is capable of being understood by those to whom it is addressed. Accordingly it has been said, that a specification containing scientific terms, which are not understood, except by persons acquainted with the nature of the business, is not bad because an ordinary person does not understand it, provided a scientific person does; but a specification using common language, and stating that by which a common man may be misled, though a scientific man would not, when it does not profess to use scientific terms, and an ordinary man is misled by it, would not be good.[2] And it has been held that if a specification contain an untrue statement in a material circumstance, of such a nature that, if literally acted upon by a competent workman, it would mislead him, and cause the experiment to fail, the specification is therefore bad, and the patent invalidated, although the jury, on the trial of an action for the infringement of the patent, find that a competent workman, acquainted with the subject, would not be misled by the error, but would correct it in practice.[3] This rule, however, must not, we apprehend, be applied too rigorously. Where the specification contains the description of a long and complicated process, consisting of several operations following one another in regular order, and the description as a whole is clear and sufficient, the court will not pronounce it invalid because of a slight obscurity of language in describing one of the operations, especially where such obscurity is rather grammatical than real, and would not seriously mislead a competent workman.[4]

[1] Per Lord Abinger, C. B., in Neilson *v.* Harford, Webs. Pat. Cas. 341. See also Derosne *v.* Fairie, ibid. 154, 167.

[2] Ibid.

[3] Neilson *v.* Harford, 8 M. & W. 806; s. c. Webs. Pat. Cas. 328.

[4] Beard *v.* Egerton, 8 Mann., Gr. & Scott, 165, overruling s. c. 2 Carr. & Kirw. 667. "Applying the same principle of construction to the specification before us, we think it is free from any such mistake or obscurity as would mislead a person of fair intelligence. The specification states that the

§ 261. The specification need not describe that which is within the ordinary knowledge of any workman who would be employed

process is divided into five operations. 'The first consists in polishing and cleaning the silver surface of the plate, in order to properly prepare or qualify it for receiving the sensitive layer or coating upon which the action of the light traces the design. The second operation is the applying that sensitive layer or coating to the surface. The third, in submitting in the camera obscura the prepared surface or plate to the action of the light, so that it may receive the images. The fourth, in bringing out or making appear the image, picture, or representation which is not visible when the plate is first taken out of the camera obscura. The fifth and last operation is that of removing the sensitive layer,' &c. It then gives a description of the first operation, — preparing the silver surface of the plate; the concluding part of which directs that nitric acid dissolved in water is to be applied three different times, care being taken to sprinkle, each time, the plate with powder, and rub it dry and very lightly with clean cotton; and this concludes the description of the first operation, viz., the preparing the silver surface of the plate, when it is intended for immediate use; and to this part of the specification no objection was or could be made. But then some further information is given in respect to the preparation of the plate, in these words: 'When the plate is not intended for immediate use or operation, the acid may be used only twice upon its surface, after being exposed to heat. The first part of the operation, that is, the preparation as far as the second application of the acid, may be done at any time; this will allow of a number of plates being kept prepared up to the last slight operation. It is, however, considered indispensable, that just before the moment of *using the plates in the camera*, or the reproducing the design, to put at least once more some acid on the plate, and to rub it lightly with pounce, as before stated; finally, the plate must be cleaned with cotton from all pounce-dust which may be on the surface or its edges.' Upon this part of the specification it was contended that the direction to apply acid just before the moment of using plates in the camera (which is the third operation) was a direction to use it after the second operation, viz., the coating the plate with iodine; and that using the acid at that period would entirely spoil the whole process. But it must be remembered that the passage in question is part of the direction given for performing the first operation, viz., preparing the plate to receive the iodine. It is to be observed when the plate is not intended to be used immediately, and where it has previously been *partially* but not *entirely* prepared for the iodine, this last application of acid is still *to precede the second operation*. The whole passage may be considered as in a parenthesis, and the expression 'just before the moment of using the plate in the camera' is put in opposition to the time of partially preparing the plate; after which it is supposed to have been laid by for future use. That this is the real meaning of the passage is further manifested by what follows in a subsequent part of the printed specification: 'After this second operation, viz., application of the iodine, the plate is to be passed to the third operation, or that of the *camera obscura*. Wherever it is possible, the one operation should immedi-

to put up the apparatus; as, a condenser in constructing a gas apparatus.[1] So, too, a deviation from the precise dimensions shown by the specification and model, so as to make different parts work together, is within the knowledge of any workman.[2] But if the practical application of the invention involves a particular kind of knowledge on the part of a workman, requiring him to do that which a person of ordinary engineering skill ought to know how to do, it must at least suggest to him that that thing is to be done, if it does not specifically point out the mode of doing it.[3] In like manner it is not necessary, in the descrip-

ately follow the other.' It is plain, therefore, that the patentee did not intend any separate operation to intervene between the application of iodine and the introduction of the plate into the camera obscura. The last application of acid, therefore, must have been intended to precede the second operation.

"This, we think, is the fair construction of the language of the specification. And although there may be at first sight some appearance of obscurity in it, we think that it is cleared away by a consideration of the whole, and that it is sufficiently plain to be understood by an operator of fair intelligence." Wilde, C. J.

[1] Crossley *v.* Beverley, Webs. Pat. Cas. 110, note.

[2] Morgan *v.* Seaward, Webs. Pat. Cas. 176. In this case, Alderson, B., said to the jury: "In the case of the steam engine, there was put in, on the part of the defendants, a model made, as it was said, according to the specification, which model would not work. The model was a copy of the drawing and would not work, because one part happened to be a little too small, whereas if it had been a little larger, it would have worked. Now, a workman of ordinary skill, when told to put two things together, so that they should move, would, of course, by the ordinary knowledge and skill he possesses, make them of sufficient size to move. There he would have to bring to his assistance his knowledge that the size of the parts is material to the working of the machine. That is within the ordinary knowledge of every workman. He says: 'I see this will not work, because it is too small,' and then he makes it a little larger, and finds it will work; what is required is, that the specification should be such as to enable a workman of ordinary skill to make the machine; with respect to that, therefore, I do not apprehend you will feel much difficulty."

[3] In the case last cited, the same learned judge further instructed the jury as follows: "Mr. George Cottam says: 'It is a common problem to find a centre from three given points, and a person of ordinary engineering skill ought to be able to do that.' The question is, whether it ought not to be suggested to him by the specification, that that is the problem to be solved. Then Mr. Curtis says: 'I have made wheels on this plan.' You see he made the two wheels which were sent to the Venice and Trieste Company, but those were made under the direction of Mr. Galloway, the inventor. Now, it some-

tion of a machine, to state of what material every part should be made, where the principle of operation and the effect are the same, whether the parts be made of one material or another;[1] but if a particular material be essential to the successful operation of the machine, as the patentee uses it, he must direct the use of that material.

Thus, where the invention was the formation of grinding chambers by the combination of movable conical rings with stationary cylinders, and the particular description in the specification showed a mill with three grinding chambers, but the claim was to the combination of stationary *cylinders* with *one or more* movable conical rings, so that both cylinders and rings might be multiplied to any extent, or the mill limited to two cylinders and one ring, it was ruled by the court that the description was sufficient to enable a mechanic of ordinary skill to make a mill with more chambers than three.[2]

§ 261 *a*. In Tyler *v*. Boston, the patent was for a new burning fluid, compounded of fusel oil with the mineral and earthy oils. The patentee claimed "the compound produced by the combination of the mineral or earthy oils with fusel oil, in the manner and for the purpose substantially as herein set forth; said compound constituting a new manufacture." The component parts of this new manufacture were described as, "by measure, crude fusel oil one part, kerosene one part." This combination, the patent stated, might be varied by the substitution of naphtha, or crude petroleum, in place of kerosene, or a part of the kerosene by an *equal* quantity of naphtha or crude petroleum; the

what detracts from the weight due to his testimony, not as to respectability, but as to the value of his evidence to you, that he had received the verbal instructions of Mr. Galloway. It may be, that he could do it because of his practice under Mr. Galloway; and it must be recollected that people in other places would not have that advantage. He says, he would not have any difficulty in doing it; and he says: 'I should not consider my foreman a competent workman unless he were able to make the wheel from the specification and drawings.' He says: 'I could alter the angle by altering the cranks.' The question is not, whether he could do that, but whether he could alter the angle to a particular angle by altering the cranks in a particular way, that is, whether, having the angle given to him, he could make the alteration that was desired."

[1] Brooks *v*. Bicknell, 3 McLean's R. 250, 261.

[2] Wilbur *v*. Beecher, 2 Blatchf. 132.

exact quantity of fusel oil which is necessary, to produce the most desirable compound, must be determined by experiment."

The defendants used a burning fluid, composed of naphtha seventy-two and fusel oil twenty-eight parts; and expert chemists proved that seventy-two parts *in bulk* of naphtha was the *substantial equivalent* of twenty-eight parts of kerosene. The court below charged the jury, "that the patentee, in suggesting that naphtha might be substituted for kerosene, intended to describe the same proportion in the combination," and "that the jury should understand the construction of the suggested substitution, to wit, naphtha for kerosene, as contemplating the same proportion of the two ingredients, that is, one and one, or fifty per cent of one, and fifty per cent of the other; and, further, that "whether one compound of given proportions is substantially the same as another compound varying in the proportions — whether they are substantially the same or substantially different — is a question of fact, and for the jury." Under this charge the jury found for the defendant, and the ruling was affirmed by the Supreme Court of the United States. "While the specification of the patent," said Mr. Justice Grier, "suggests the substitution of naphtha for crude petroleum, it prescribes no other proportion than that of equal parts by measure. The explanation, that the kerosene must be replaced by an *equal quantity* of naphtha, does not alter the case." [1]

§ 261 *b*. Where the invention consisted of an improved process in annealing car wheels, the description directed that "the temperature of the furnace or chamber, and its contents, be gradually raised to a point a little below that at which fusion commences," and these words were substantially repeated in the claim. The court held, that the inventor, in referring to a degree of heat a little below the point of fusion, indicated the degree which, in the hands of an operator of skill and judgment, would effect practically and successfully the object of his invention. "He avoids the point of incipient or actual fusion, but requires the heat to be a *little* below that point. This expression clearly imports some latitude of discretion in the operator. It clearly does not require that the temperature of the wheels shall be raised to the precise point above which fusion would commence. It

[1] Tyler *v.* Boston (1868), 7 Wall. 327.

must be presumed that the inventor knew, that if wheels were heated to incipient infusion, or to the degree immediately below, they would be so soft as not to retain their shape or symmetry, in their position in the chamber or furnace, and that thus their utility would be destroyed. "It is not supposable that the inventor intended what would destroy the very object he had in view, namely, to make a wheel in which the drill of the periphery should be preserved, and the inherent strain, from unequal contraction, avoided. I am clear that the patent may be regarded as claiming, by the fair import of the words, 'a little below the point of fusion,' such a degree of heat as is necessary to effectuate the intention of the inventor. His object was to guard against the point of fusion, and also against a temperature so low that an inherent strain would be produced between the thin and the thick parts of the wheel. He says expressly, 'they must not be allowed to cool, after removal from the mould, to a degree which will cause this strain.'"[1]

And so, where the invention consisted in a process for manufacturing free fat acids and glycerine from fatty bodies or substances, by the action of water at a high temperature and pressure, the "melting point of lead" was given as the proper degree of heat to be used in the operation, and it was added that "the change of fatty matter into fat acid and glycerine takes place with some materials (such as palm oil), at or below the melting point of bismuth." This was regarded by the court as a precise degree of heat, it being well known that lead melts at 612° Fahrenheit and bismuth at about 510°.

The specification further stated that "the heat has been carried considerably above the melting point of lead, without any apparent injury, and the decomposing action of water becomes more powerful as the heat is increased." The fact that the degree of heat might be thus varied without injury did not render the specification liable to objection, for want of certainty and clearness. In the language of the court, "There is a fixed rule given, which may be safely followed, while it is made known that the manufacturer may safely depart, to some extent, from this rule, if, from experiment and a just exercise of discretion, it should be expedient to do so."[1]

[1] Leavitt, J., Whitney *v.* Mowry (1867), 3 Fisher's Pat. Cas. 157.

[2] Tilghman *v.* Werk (1862), 2 Fisher's Pat. Cas. 229.

§ 261 *c*. Where the invention consisted in producing hard rubber by "thoroughly mixing India rubber, or other vulcanizable gum, with sulphur, whether with or without auxiliary ingredients, in the proportion of about four ounces to a pound of sulphur, to a pound of the gum, and then subjecting the same to a high degree of artificial heat, as in the vulcanizing process of Charles Goodyear, until the compound shall have acquired the required hard and tough property," &c., the range of heat given being not less than 260° or 275° Fahrenheit, it was held that the descriptions in the patents, both as respects the proportion of sulphur and rubber, and as to the degree of heat, necessary to produce the new substance, was sufficiently full and certain within the requirements of the patent law."[1] "The proportions of the mixture," said Mr. Justice Nelson, in Goodyear *v.* Wait, "is about from four ounces to a pound of sulphur, to a pound of rubber, which we understand as meaning any proportion of sulphur between four ounces and a pound to a pound of rubber, properly mixed and subjected to the required heat, will produce the substance. What uncertainty is there in this, or necessity of experimenting, on the part of a person of ordinary skill in the art, to make the compound? The inventive faculty is exhausted in the directions given to make the article. All the work that remains to be done is that by the hand of the skilful workman. We agree, if it could be shown that the mixture, as described, when properly reduced to practice, failed to produce the article, the patent could not be upheld. But that is a different question from the one here presented, namely, whether the description is sufficiently clear and certain."

§ 262. In the case of machinery, the statute directs the patentee to accompany his specification with "a drawing or drawings, and written references, where the nature of the case admits of drawings." The object of annexing drawings is both to distinguish the thing patented from other things known before, and to explain the mode of constructing the subject of the patent. It has been settled, that the drawings constitute a part of the specification, when annexed thereto, and may be used to explain or help out the otherwise imperfect description in the specification. So that it is not necessary that the description should be wholly

[1] Goodyear *v.* Wait (1867), 3 Fisher's Pat. Cas. 242; Goodyear *v.* N. Y. Gutta Percha Co. (1862), 2 Fisher's Pat. Cas. 312.

in writing, but it may be partly in writing and partly in drawing; and if, by a comparison of the words and the drawings, the one will explain the other sufficiently to enable a skilful mechanic to perform the work, and to show what is the invention claimed, the specification will be sufficient.[1] And it has been held, that in order to make a drawing, when annexed to or accompanying a specification, part of the specification, so that the written description may be read by it, it is not necessary that the written description should contain references to the drawing; that the direction in the statute, to annex "drawings and written references," means that where references from the writing to the drawing are necessary to the understanding of the machine or improvement, they are to be made; but that the description of many machines or improvements, when accompanied by a drawing, may be perfectly understood without references in the description itself.[2]

The entire specification and drawings are to be examined together, and an error in one place to be corrected by the aid of the residue.[3] The drawings need not be mentioned in the specification, but it is sufficient if the patentee puts them and written references on file with the specification.[4]

A drawing filed some time after the recording anew of a patent, under section one, act March, 1837, is admissible in evidence, but is not to be deemed and taken as part of the specification, nor to be used for correcting any material defect therein.[5]

§ 263. It was formerly held in England that the drawings annexed to specifications ought to be drawn on a scale; so that the relation and proportion of the parts to each other, and the dimensions of the different parts, might appear in due ratio to each other.[6] But this rule has been modified; and it seems now to be considered that if a mechanic can make the subject of the patent from the drawing in perspective, it is not necessary that

[1] Earle *v.* Sawyer, 4 Mas. 1, 9; Bloxam *v.* Elsee, 1 Car. & P. 558; Brunton *v.* Hawkes, 4 B. & Ald. 540; Swift *v.* Whisen, 3 Fisher's Pat. Cas. 343.

[2] Brooks *v.* Bicknell, 3 McLean's R. 250, 261; Washburn *v.* Gould, 3 Story's R. 122, 133.

[3] Hogg *et al.* *v.* Emerson, 11 How. 587; affirming and explaining, 6 How. 437; Kittle *v.* Merriam, 2 Curtis, C. C. 475.

[4] Emmerson *v.* Hogg, 2 Blatchf. 1.

[5] Winans *v.* Schenectady & Troy R.R., 2 Blatchf. 279.

[6] The King *v.* Arkwright, Dav. Pat. Cas. 114.

there should be a scale.[1] Indeed, it is a necessary consequence of the rule which makes the written description open to explanation by the drawing, to hold that the drawing is open to explanation by the written description. So long as both together enable the public to know and practise the invention, it must be immaterial whether the drawing is made upon a scale or not. But if the subject of the patent could not be made without many experiments, unless the drawing is upon a scale, then undoubtedly the whole specification taken together, being the written description and the drawing, would be defective.

§ 264. It should not be forgotten, that the statute requires a formal attestation of the specification and drawings. They must be signed by the inventor and by two witnesses.[2] It has been suggested, that the signing of the specification referring to the drawings is in effect attesting the drawings.[3] But whether the statute is to be so construed as to require both the specification and the drawings to be signed has not been decided.

§ 264 *a*. The act of 1870 provides that the "specification and claim shall be signed by the inventor, and attested by two witnesses"; and the following section requires that a copy of the drawings "shall be attached to the patent, as part of the specification."

§ 265. Provision was made by the thirteenth section of the act of 1836 for the amendment of the specification by the addition of new improvements made after the patent has issued. The description of any such new improvement may be filed in the Patent Office, and is directed to be annexed by the commissioner to the original specification, with a certificate of the time of its being so annexed; and thereafter it is to have the same effect as if it had been embraced in the original specification. This provision was, however, repealed by the act of 1861, c. 88, § 9, which enacted: "and that so much of the 13th section of the act of Congress, approved July 4, 1836, as authorizes the annexing to letters-patent of the description and specification of additional improvements, is hereby repealed, and in a'l cases where additional improvements would now be admissible, independent

[1] Godson on Patents, p. 137.

[2] Act of July 4, 1836, § 6, "which description and drawings, signed by the inventor and attested by two witnesses, shall be filed in the Patent Office."

[3] Phillips on Patents, p. 302, 303.

patents must be applied for." (See chapter on Proceedings at Patent Office.) Improvements made and entered before the passage of this repealing clause are not, of course, affected by it, but are still valid under the act of 1836.

§ 266. A still further provision is made for the amendment of a redundant specification, by the filing of a *disclaimer*. The act of 1837, c. 45, § 7, provided that, "whenever any patentee shall have, through inadvertence, accident, or mistake, made his specification of claim too broad, claiming more than that of which he was the original or first inventor, some material and substantial part of the thing patented being truly and justly his own, any such patentee, his administrators, executors, and assigns, whether of the whole or of a sectional interest therein, may make disclaimer of such parts of the thing patented as the disclaimant shall not claim to hold by virtue of the patent or assignment, stating therein the extent of his interest in such patent, which disclaimer shall be in writing, attested by one or more witnesses, and recorded in the Patent Office, on payment by the person disclaiming, in manner as other patent duties are required by law to be paid, of the sum of ten dollars. And such disclaimer shall thereafter be taken and considered as part of the original specification, to the extent of the interest which shall be possessed in the patent or right secured thereby, by the disclaimant, and by those claiming by or under him subsequent to the record thereof. But no such disclaimer shall affect any action pending at the time of its being filed, except so far as may relate to the question of unreasonable neglect or delay in filing the same."

§ 267. The ninth section of the same act provided as follows: ("Any thing in the fifteenth section of the act to which this is additional to the contrary notwithstanding) that, whenever by mistake, accident, or inadvertence, and without any wilful default or intent to defraud or mislead the public, any patentee shall have in his specification claimed to be the original and first inventor or discoverer of any material or substantial part of the thing patented, of which he was not the first and original inventor, and shall have no legal or just right to claim the same, in every such case the patent shall be deemed good and valid for so much of the invention or discovery as shall be truly and *bona fide* his own: *Provided*, it shall be a material and substantial part of the thing patented, and be definitely distinguishable from the other parts so claimed without right as aforesaid. And every such patentee, his executors, administrators, and assigns, whether of a whole or a sectional interest therein, shall be entitled to maintain a suit at law or in equity on such patent for any infringement of such part of the invention or discovery as shall be *bona fide* his own as aforesaid, notwithstanding the specification may embrace more than he shall have any legal right to claim. But, in every such case in which a judgment or verdict shall be rendered for the plaintiff, he shall not be entitled to recover costs against the defendant, unless he shall have entered at the Patent Office, prior to the commencement of the suit, a disclaimer of all that part of the thing patented which was so claimed without right: *Provided, however*, that no person bringing any such suit shall be entitled to the benefit of the provisions contained in this section, who shall have unreasonably neglected or delayed to enter at the Patent Office a disclaimer as aforesaid."

This subject is now regulated by the statute of 1870. The fifty-fourth section of that act provides: "That whenever, through inadvertence, accident, or mistake, and without any fraudulent or deceptive intention, a patentee has claimed more than that of which he was the original or first inventor or discoverer, his patent shall be valid for all that part which is truly and justly his own, provided the same is a material or substantial part of the thing patented; and any such patentee, his heirs or assigns, whether of the whole or any sectional interest therein, may, on payment of the duty required by law, make disclaimer of such parts of the thing patented as he shall not choose to claim or to hold by virtue of the patent or assignment, stating therein the extent of his interest in such patent; said disclaimer shall be in writing, attested by one or more witnesses, and recorded in the Patent Office, and it shall thereafter be considered as part of the original specification to the extent of the interest possessed by the claimant and by those claiming under him after the record thereof. But no such disclaimer shall effect any action pending at the time of its being filed, except so far as may relate to the question of unreasonable neglect or delay in filing it."

The following cases, although occurring under the provisions of the English statute of Disclaimer (5 & 6 Will. IV. c. 83), may be cited as illustrative of the general principles applicable to this topic.

Thus, in Seed *v.* Higgins,[1] the patentee, in his specification, states his invention to consist in the application of the principle of centrifugal force in the fliers employed in the above-mentioned machinery, for the purpose of producing the required elasticity or pressure upon the bobbin, by causing the small spur or lever which conducts the sliver of cotton or other fibrous material on to the bobbin, to press or bear against the same simply by the action of such force, — and adds, that he has attached a drawing to the specification, minutely describing by reference to such drawing a machine, — and then continues: "I do not confine myself to this particular method, but claim as my invention the application of the law or principle of centrifugal force to the particular purpose set forth, i. e. to fliers used in machinery or apparatus for preparing, slubbing, and roving cotton for the purpose of producing a hard and evenly compressed bobbin."

Afterwards, he entered a disclaimer, declaring, "For the reason aforesaid, I do hereby disclaim all application of the law or principle of centrifugal force as being part of my invention or comprised in my claim, except only the application of centrifugal force by means of a weight acting upon a presser, so as to cause it to press against the bobbin, as described in said specification."

It was held by the Court of Queen's Bench, and affirmed by the Exchequer Chamber, that this disclaimer was valid, and that, the original specification being read in connection with it, the result was a claim for only the machine particularly described.

In Tetley *v.* Easton,[2] it was held by Creswell, J., that the effect of a disclaimer was merely to strike out from the specification those parts of the machinery which are disclaimed, and that it cannot be read as explanatory of what remains.

In Ralston *v.* Smith,[3] the invention of "improvements in embossing and finishing woven fabrics, and in the machinery or apparatus employed therein," as described in the specification, consisted in the use of rollers having "any design grooved, fluted, engraved, milled, or otherwise indented upon them." A disclaimer was afterwards entered, by the statements wherein it appeared that the desired effect could *only* be produced by the use of a certain

[1] 8 Ell. & Blackb. 755, 771.

[2] Tetley *v.* Easton, 2 Com. Ben. N. S. 706.

[3] Ralston *v.* Smith, 11 Com. Ben. N. S. 471, affirming 9 Com. Ben. N. S. 117.

species of roller not particularly described in the specification, namely, a roller having circular grooves round its surface. All other rollers were expressly disclaimed. The Exchequer Chamber, affirming the judgment of the Court of Common Pleas, held that such a disclaimer was merely an attempt to turn a specification for an impracticable generality into a claim for a specific process, which was in one sense comprised under the generality, but which could not be discovered there without going through the same course of experiment as that which led to the discovery of the specific process mentioned in the disclaimer. Consequently the disclaimer was void as an attempt to extend the patent.

By the statute 16 & 17 Vict. c. 115, an inventor is allowed to make a provisional specification, pending the proceedings for obtaining letters-patent. In Mackelcan *v.* Rennie,[1] it was held that such provisional specification is not to be admitted in explanation or enlargement of the complete specification.

§ 268. The disclaimer mentioned in the seventh section has been held to apply solely to suits pending when the disclaimer was filed in the Patent Office ; and that mentioned in the ninth section, to suits brought after the disclaimer is so filed.[2]

[1] 13 C. B. N. S. 50.

[2] Wyeth *v.* Stone, 1 Story's R. 273, 293. In this case, Mr. Justice Story thus expounded the statute: " We come, then, to the remaining point, whether, although under the Patent Act of 1793, ch. 55, the patent is absolutely void, because the claim includes an abstract principle, and is broader than the invention ; or, whether that objection is cured by the disclaimer made by the patentee (Wyeth), under the act of 1837, c. 45. The seventh section of that act provides, ' That whenever any patentee shall have, through inadvertence, accident, or mistake, made his specification too broad, claiming more than that of which he was the original or first inventor, some material and substantial part of the thing patented being truly or justly his own, any such patentee, his administrators, executors, or assigns, whether of the whole or a sectional part thereof, may make disclaimer of such parts of the thing patented as the disclaimant shall not claim to hold by virtue of the patent or assignment, &c. And such disclaimer shall be thereafter taken and considered as a part of the original specification, to the extent of the interest which shall be possessed in the patent or right secured thereby by the disclaimant,' &c. Then follows a proviso, that ' no such disclaimer shall affect any action pending at the time of its being filed, except so far as may relate to the question of unreasonable neglect or delay in filing the same.' The ninth section provides, ' That whenever, by mistake, accident, or inadvertence, and without any wilful default or intent to defraud or mislead the public, any patentee shall have, in his specification, claimed to be the first and original inventor or discoverer of any mate-

The disclaimer, however, mentioned in section nine, which provides that the suit shall not be defeated where the patentee claims

rial or substantial part of the thing patented, of which he was not the first and original inventor, and shall have no legal or just right to claim the same, in every such case the patent shall be deemed good and valid for so much of the invention or discovery, as shall be truly and *bonâ fide his own;* provided it shall be a material and substantial part of the thing patented, and shall be definitely distinguishable from the other parts so claimed without right as aforesaid.' Then follows a clause, that in every such case, if the plaintiff recovers in any suit, he shall not be entitled to costs, 'unless he shall have entered at the Patent Office, prior to the commencement of the suit, a disclaimer of all that part of the thing patented, which was so claimed without right'; with a proviso, 'That no person bringing any such suit shall be entitled to the benefits of the provisions contained in this section, who shall have unreasonably neglected or delayed to enter at the Patent Office a disclaimer as aforesaid.'

"Now, it seems to me, that upon the true construction of this statute, the disclaimer mentioned in the seventh section must be interpreted to apply solely to suits pending when the disclaimer is filed in the Patent Office; and the disclaimer mentioned in the ninth section to apply solely to suits brought after the disclaimer is so filed. In this way the provisions harmonize with each other; upon any other construction they would seem, to some extent, to clash with each other, so far as the legal effect and operation of the disclaimer is concerned.

"In the present case, the suit was brought on the 1st of January, 1840, and the disclaimer was not filed until the 24th of October, of the same year. The proviso, then, of the seventh section would seem to prevent the disclaimer from affecting the present suit in any manner whatsoever. The disclaimer, for another reason, is also utterly without effect in the present case; for it is not a joint disclaimer by the patentee and his assignee, Tudor, who are both plaintiffs in this suit, but by Wyeth alone. The disclaimer cannot, therefore, operate in favor of Tudor, without his having joined in it, in any suit, either at law or in equity. The case, then, must stand upon the other clauses of the ninth section, independent of the disclaimer.

"This leads me to say, that I cannot but consider that the claim made in the patent for the abstract principle or art of cutting ice by means of an apparatus worked by any other power than human, is a claim founded in inadvertence and mistake of the law, and, without any wilful default or intent to defraud or mislead the public, within the proviso of the ninth section. That section, it appears to me, was intended to cover inadvertences and mistakes of the law, as well as inadvertences and mistakes of fact; and, therefore, without any disclaimer, the plaintiffs might avail themselves of this part of the section to the extent of maintaining the present suit for the other parts of the invention claimed, that is, for the saw and for the cutter, and thereby protect themselves against any violation of their rights, unless there has been an unreasonable neglect or delay to file the disclaimer in the office. Still, however, it does not seem to me, that a court of equity ought to interfere to grant a perpetual

more than he has invented, applies only to cases where the part invented can be clearly distinguished from that claimed but not invented.[1]

§ 269. In this section it is intended to give a condensed statement of the constructions given by the courts to the specifications of some of the leading patents litigated in this country and in England.

The distinction between an improvement in a machine and a novel result attained by a mere alteration in an old machine is abundantly illustrated by the course of decision upon Kay's patent, in the case of Kay *v.* Marshall.[2] The patentee, after describing his improved machinery for *macerating* flax, goes on to describe his *improved machinery* for *spinning* such macerated flax: "I place the drawing rollers only two and a half inches from the retaining rollers, and this constitutes the *principal improvement in said spinning machinery;* . . . and that which I claim as my invention in respect of improved machinery, is (the wooden or other trough marked D, for holding the rovings when taken from the macerating vessels, and) the placing of the retaining rollers and the drawing rollers nearer to each other than they have ever before been placed, say within two and a half inches of each other, for the purpose aforesaid." After an extensive course of litigation before the Vice Chancellor, Baron Parke, on trial of a feigned issue, and the Court of Common Pleas on issue of law, the case was finally decided by the House of Lords. It was there held, Lord Cottenham rendering the decision, that the processes of maceration and of spinning were entirely distinct, and conse-

injunction in a case of this sort, whatever might be the right and remedy at law, unless a disclaimer has been in fact filed at the Patent Office before the suit is brought. The granting of such an injunction is a matter resting in the sound discretion of the court; and if the court should grant a perpetual injunction before any disclaimer is filed, it may be, that the patentee may never afterwards, within a reasonable time, file any disclaimer, although the act certainly contemplates the neglect or delay to do so to be a good defence, both at law and in equity, in every suit brought upon the patent, to secure the rights granted thereby. However, it is not indispensable in this case to dispose of this point, or of the question of unreasonable neglect or delay, as there is another objection, which in my judgment is fatal, in every view, to the maintenance of the suit in its present form."

[1] Vance *v.* Campbell, 1 Black. 427; *vide* Peterson *v.* Wooden, 3 M'Lean, 248.

[2] Kay *v.* M., 2 W. P. C. 34.

quently that the patent was for two inventions, and not for one alone; also that the patentee's claim must be construed as one for a machine, and not for a process or a result; that as the jury, on the feigned issue, had found that parties other than the patentee had previously placed the rollers at varying distances apart, therefore the patentee's claim was void for want of novelty.[1]

In McCormick's patent of October 23, 1847, for improvements in reaping-machines, the patentee says: "I also claim, as my invention, the arrangement of the *seat* of the raker over the end of the finger-piece which projects beyond the range of fingers, and just back of the driving-wheel, *as described*, in combination with and placed at the end of the reel." This was construed not to be a claim for the seat, as *a seat*, or for its peculiar mode and form of construction, but a claim for the arrangement and combination of machinery described, by which the benefit of a seat or position

[1] "The *invention* was not of macerating flax or of machinery, but of treating flax in a certain manner, i. e. spinning macerated flax at a short ratch; the doing that was a new manufacture of flax; the result, as evidence by the effects on trade, was of national importance. Such was Kay's invention in fact.

"Kay's patent, i. e. title (claim), was for 'new and improved machinery for preparing and spinning flax,' &c. The spinning machine thus described was old; upon this ground, therefore, the patent was invalid, and in this ground of invalidity all the judgments concur.

"The judgments also concur in this, that the fixing at a given distance, as two and a half inches, the rollers of spinning machinery adapted to work at greater or less distances, is not *per se* any manufacture, or the subject of letters-patent.

"But the judgment of the Court of Common Pleas has been supposed to go further, and has applied to sustain propositions to the following effect: first, that the use of such old machinery for the special purpose of spinning macerated flax could not be the subject of a valid patent; secondly, if a specification contains a claim to any matter which is not *per se* the subject of letters-patent, though in fact new, and there being no false suggestion, i. e. the title being supported by other matters contained in the specification, that such letters-patent are invalid. The following paragraph in the judgment of the House of Lords, 'If he has discovered any means of using the machine which the world had not known before the benefit of, that he has a right to secure to himself by means of a patent' (p. 82), is an authority against the former proposition, and an authority to show that the spinning of macerated flax by known machinery would have been the subject-matter of letters-patent, if the title and specification had properly been adapted thereto. . . . The flax so spun would be a new manufacture, both in respect of the method and result." Note by Mr. Webster, p. 84.

for the raker on the machine is obtained.[1] In a subsequent action arising under the same patent,[2] it was held that claims No. 2 and No. 3 of the specification, "(2) I claim the reversed angle of the teeth of the blade, in manner described; (3) I claim the arrangement and construction of the fingers or teeth for supporting the grain so as to form the angular places in front of the blade, as and for the purpose described," were not to be read in connection with each other, but separately.

Goodyear, in describing the nature of his invention,[3] says in his specification: "The nature of the first part of my invention consists in curing caoutchouc or india-rubber, when combined with or in the presence of sulphur, by submitting the same to the action of a high degree of artificial heat, at a temperature say from 212 to 350 or thereabouts. . . . And the second part of my invention consists in preparing and curing the triple compound of caoutchouc, or india-rubber, sulphur, and a carbonate or other salt or oxide of lead, for the purpose above described." He then proceeds to describe the process and relative proportions of the ingredients; and after stating the leading features of his invention to be the effects produced by heat on the rubber thus combined, he concludes: "What I claim as my invention and desire to secure by letters-patent is the curing of caoutchouc, or india-rubber, by submitting it to the action of a high degree of artificial heat, substantially as herein described and for the purposes specified. And I also claim the preparing and curing the compound of india-rubber, sulphur, and a carbonate or other salt or oxide of lead, by subjecting the same to the action of artificial heat, substantially as herein described."

In the construction of this specification, it was held that the patentee had claimed not merely the process of preparing vulcanized india-rubber, but the product itself, as a new manufacture or composition of matter. Mr. Justice Grier in this case observed: "On account of the vagueness and indefiniteness of the language used in describing the various arts, machines, manufactures, and compositions of matter, it is impossible to

[1] McCormick *v.* Seymour, 2 Blatchf. 240. Affirmed (except as to rule of damages) in Seymour *v.* McCormick, 16 How. 480.

[2] Seymour *v.* McCormick, 19 How. 96. See also an English case under the same patent in 4 Law Times, N. S. 832.

[3] Goodyear *v.* The R.R., 2 Wallace, C. C. 356.

describe the real nature of many discoveries or processes in language absolutely free from all ambiguity and all misconstruction. Different persons, looking at it from different points of view, would describe it in different terms. In the present case, one might describe it as 'the art of curing india-rubber'; another, as 'a new and useful improvement in the process of curing india-rubber'; another, as 'the art of rendering caoutchouc and manufactures in which it is used insensible to heat or cold, or the action of most of its known solvents'; another, as 'a fabric, manufacture, or new composition of matter, having qualities never before combined in any other known substance, being elastic, water-proof, insensible to acids, to heat, or to cold.' Still, call it what you will, if the patentee has set forth fully the materials, their various proportions, and the processes necessary to the production of this composition of matter, he has done all that the law requires, and should be entitled to its protection. The patent should be carefully examined to find the thing discovered, and if it be clearly set forth, the patentee should not suffer for the imperfection or vagueness of the language used in describing its true extent and nature. The description ought not to be repugnant to the specification; but, provided it honestly sets forth in few words the nature and design of the patent, it is sufficient. It should show what the patentee claims to have discovered or invented, wherein it differs from what was heretofore known, and by what combinations or processes the new material may be compounded. . . . It is essentially proper, in patents for complicated machines, that the specification should clearly set forth what the patentee admits to be old and what he claims to be of his invention. In anomalous cases like the present, when a new product has been discovered, and the process of compounding it or obtaining it is disclosed, the patentee, by stating his discovery and revealing his process, has done all that he is required to do or can do. The careful separation of new from old, the limitation of claims to particular parts or combinations, cannot be required as a substantial part of the specification. If the specification sets forth a discovery, a new composition of matter, and the process for compounding it, that should be taken as the extent of his claim and the measure of his franchise. Now, what is this india-rubber, cured substantially as described in Mr. Goodyear's description? It is clearly not merely an improved method or process of producing an old and well-known composition or material, but it is a new product, fabric, manufacture, or composition of matter, having qualities possessed by no other known material. This is what is described and claimed in the patent, — a new product as well as a new process."

In Howe's sewing-machine patent, the first claim of the specification was worded thus: "The forming of the seam by carrying a thread through the cloth, by means of a curved needle on the end of a vibrating arm, and the passing of a shuttle, furnished with its bobbin, in the manner set forth, between the needle and the thread which it carries, under a combination and arrangement of parts substantially the same with that described."[1] This was construed to be in words a claim for the result, but in reality for the means or mechanism by which that result was to be attained; also, that too much stress should not be laid upon the distinction between a machine and a combination; also, that the patentee's claim was for a general combination, consisting of several sub-combinations, viz., a mechanism for forming the stitch, a mechanism for holding the cloth to be sewed, and a mechanism for feeding the cloth, and that all these general elements in combination and arrangement were set forth in the specification.

Winans' patent for an "improvement in the construction of cars or carriages intended to run on railroads" claimed "the before described manner of arranging and connecting the eight wheels, which constitute the two bearing carriages, with a railroad car, so as to accomplish the end proposed by the means set forth, or by any others which are analogous and dependent upon the same principles." This claim was construed to be one for the car itself, constructed and arranged as in the patent; consequently, the novelty of the invention was not impeached by evidence showing that parts of the invention had been in use previously.[2]

The case of Burr *v.* Duryee,[3] decided in the United States Supreme Court, on appeal from the Circuit Court of New Jersey, presents an exhaustive discussion of the principles distinguishing an invention for a *machine* from one for a *process*. Burr, the

[1] Howe *v.* Morton *et al.*; Howe *v.* Williams, per Sprague, J., MS.

[2] Ross Winans *v.* Schenectady & Troy R.R., 2 Blatchf. 279.

[3] Burr *v.* Duryee, 1 Wallace, 531.

complainant, was assignee of the Wells patent for hat-making; the original patent therefor was granted in 1846, but in 1856 it was surrendered and a reissue obtained. In the spring of 1860 an extension was granted. In January, 1860, a patent was granted to Boyden for improved machinery in hat-making, of which Duryee and others became the assignees. This machinery the complainants, by permission of the defendants, examined. Afterwards, in December, 1860, they surrendered their extended patent and obtained a second reissue, upon the construction of which the decision of the matter in controversy turned. It was held to be an attempt to convert an improved machine into an abstraction, a principle, or mode of operation; a use of general and abstract terms, by which the specification was made so elastic that it might be construed to claim only the machine, or to exclude all previous and future inventions for the same purpose.

Wells, in his original specification, says: "What I claim, &c., is *the arrangement of the two feeding belts (bb′) with their planes inclined to each other*, and passing around the lips (dd′) formed substantially as described, the better to prevent *the fibres to the action of the rotating brush* (F), as described in combination with the rotating brush and tunnel or chamber (M), which *conducts* the fibres to the perforated cone or other 'former' placed in front of *the aperture* or *mouth thereof*, substantially as herein described. I claim the *chamber* (M) into which the fibres are thrown by the brush, in combination with the perforated cone or other former, *placed in front of the delivery aperture thereof* for the purpose and in the manner substantially as herein described, the said chamber being provided with an aperture (N) below and back of the brush, for the admission of a current of air to aid in throwing and directing the fibres on to the cone or other former, as described. I also claim the employment of the *hinged hood (s) to regulate the distribution of the fibres on the perforated cone or other former as described.* And I also claim providing the *lower part or delivery aperture of the tunnel or chamber with a hinged flap* (9), *for the purpose of regulating the delivery of the fibres to increase the thickness of the hat where more strength is required, as herein described, in combination with the hood as herein described.*" This claim was decided to be a valid one for an improved machine.

The reissue of 1860 ran thus: "The mode of operation of the

said invention of the said Henry Wells is such, that the fur fibres are directed and controlled so as to travel from the picking and disintegrating brush (F) towards the surface of the previous cone, &c., that they may be deposited thereon to the thickness required to make a hat of uniform thickness all the way around, and of the required varying thickness from brim to top; and this *mode of operation* results from combining with a rotary picking and disintegrating brush and a pervious cone or equivalent former, connected with an exhausting apparatus, *suitable means* for directing and controlling the fur-bearing currents. The *said mode of operation invented by the said Henry A. Wells is embodied in the following description of the mode of application*, reference being had to the accompanying drawings, &c. . . . What I claim as the invention of the said Henry A. Wells, &c., is the *mode of operation substantially as herein described*, &c., which *mode of operation* results from the combination of the rotating picking mechanism or the *equivalent* thereof, the pervious former and its exhausting mechanism or the *equivalent* thereof, and the *means* for directing the fur-bearing current or the *equivalent* thereof, as set forth."

Judge Grier, in giving the decision of the Supreme Court, said: "The surrender of valid patents and the granting of reissued patents thereon, with expanded or equivocal claims, where the original was clearly neither 'inoperative nor invalid,' and whose specification is neither 'defective nor insufficient,' is a great abuse of the privilege granted by the statute, and productive of great injury to the public. We concur, therefore, in the decision of the Circuit Court, that the machine of Boyden is not an infringement of the invention of Wells, and if it be an infringement of the reissued patent, that patent is void." (p. 577.)

Many *v.* Jagger *et al.*[1] was a suit brought for infringement of the Wolf patent for improvement in cast-iron wheels for railroads and other purposes. The specification was in these words: "We give to the rim of our wheels the same form in all respects as is now given to the rims of car-wheels; but instead of arms, we cast our wheels with two parallel or nearly parallel plates, which plates are convex on one side and concave on the other. The hub, or

[1] Many *v.* Jagger, 1 Blatchf. 372.

nave, which is to receive the axle, is cast in the centre of these plates, extending from one to the other. . . . We are aware that car-wheels have been made with plates as a substitute for arms, but such plates have been made separate from the wheels and united together by screwed bolts, embracing the hub in a distinct piece between them. The difference between such wheels and those constructed by us is so obvious as not to need pointing out. *What we claim* as our invention, &c., is the manner of constructing wheels for railroad cars, or for other purposes to which they may be applied, with double convex plates, one convex outwards and the other inwards, and an undivided hub, the whole cast in one piece as herein fully set forth."

In construing this patent, the court held that the claim was not for the mode of constructing the wheel as distinct from the wheel itself, but was for the car-wheel after it was constructed. Also, that the claim was not for any separate part of the wheel, but for the entire wheel, and that it sufficiently distinguished between the new and the old.

In Buck *v.* Hermance,[1] the words of the claim for a patent in cooking-stoves, "the extending of the oven under the apron or open hearth of the stove, and in combination with the flues constructed as above specified," were held to be a claim for a *combination* of the extension of the oven under the hearth of the stove *with* the flues, as described.

Booth *v.* Garelly.[2] Here, a patent for a *new and ornamental design for figured silk buttons*, under act, August 29, 1842, where the specification claimed *the radially formed ornaments on the face of the mould of the button, combined with the mode of winding the covering of the same, substantially as set forth*, and described the configuration of the mould and the winding it with various colored threads, but did not describe the process of winding the silk, was construed not to cover that process, but merely the arrangement of the different colored threads in the process, so as to produce the described ornaments.

In Oxley *v.* Holden,[3] the words of the claim for the second part of the invention were: "I claim the metal fixings and the mode

[1] Buck *v.* Hermance, 1 Blatchf. 398.
[2] Booth *v.* Garelly, 1 Blatchf. 247.
[3] Oxley *v.* Holden, 8 C. B. N. S. 666.

of applying the same, described herein as the second part of my invention." The claim was construed not to apply to the metal fixings (which were notoriously old and well known) apart from their application.[1]

[1] Oxley *v.* Holden, 8 C. B. N. S. 705.

CHAPTER VII.

PROCEEDINGS AT THE PATENT OFFICE.

I. Caveat for incomplete Invention.
II. The Petition, Oath, Payment of Fees.
III. Signatures of the Secretary of the Interior and Commissioner.
IV. Interfering Applications.
V. Reissue and Amendment of Patents.

CAVEAT FOR INCOMPLETE INVENTION.

§ 270. THE twelfth section of the act of July 4, 1836, provided that any citizen of the United States, or alien who shall have been resident in the United States one year next preceding, and who shall have made oath of his intention to become a citizen thereof, who shall have invented any new art, machine, or improvement thereof, and shall desire further time to mature the same, may, on payment of the sum of twenty dollars, file in the Patent Office a *caveat*, setting forth the design and purpose thereof, and its principal and distinguishing characteristics, and praying protection of his right till he shall have matured his invention; which sum of twenty dollars, in case the person filing such caveat shall afterwards take out a patent for the invention therein mentioned, shall be considered a part of the sum required for the same. And such caveat shall be filed in the confidential archives of the office, and preserved in secrecy. And if application shall be made by any other person within one year from the time of filing such a caveat, for a patent of any invention with which it may in any respect interfere, it shall be the duty of the commissioner to deposit the description, specifications, drawings, and model in the confidential archives of the office, and to give notice, by mail, to the person filing the caveat, of such application, who shall, within three months after receiving the notice, if he would avail himself of the benefit of his caveat, file his description, specifications, drawings, and model; and if, in the opinion of the commissioner, the specifications of claim interfere with each other, like proceedings may be had in all respects as are provided in the case of interfering applications.

These provisions were somewhat modified by the Patent Act of 1861 (Laws 1861, c. 88, § 9), which declared, "*And be it further enacted*, That no money paid as a fee on any application for a patent after the passage of this act shall be withdrawn or refunded, nor shall the fee paid on filing a caveat be considered as part of the sum required to be paid on filing a subsequent application for a patent for the same invention. That the three months' notice given to any caveator, in pursuance of the requirements of section twelve, act of July 4th, 1836, shall be computed from the day on which such notice is deposited in the post-office at Washington, with the regular time for the transmission of the same added thereto, which time shall be indorsed in the notice." Section ten of this act of 1861 also abolishes the laws regulating the fees at the Patent Office, and discriminating between citizens of the United States and that of other countries, and provides that the fee for filing each caveat shall be *ten* instead of *twenty* dollars. As to the effect of a caveat upon a subsequent patent, see the ruling of Sprague, J., in Johnson *v.* Root,[1] MS.: "It is contended, on the part of the defendant, that the caveat itself is conclusive evidence that the invention was not perfected. You will observe that the application, which is in the caveat before you, made to the Patent Office by Mr. Johnson for leave to file a caveat, sets forth that he has made a certain new and useful improvement in the sewing-machine, and that he is then making experiments to perfect it, and he asks leave to file a caveat to secure it. The defendant insists that that application is of itself conclusive evidence that he has not perfected it. We will look at it, gentlemen, and see. I do not instruct you that it is conclusive evidence; but it is evidence for you to take into view in connection with the other evidence, and in connection with the other parts of the same instrument, in which he begins by saying that he has made a new and useful invention in the sewing-machine. Now, gentlemen, although a caveat is understood to be, and in this instance is, filed in order to allow the party to perfect his machine, yet if, in point of fact, the invention had been perfected

[1] See also Johnson *v.* Root, 2 Fisher's Pat. Cas. 291.

in the eye of the law, as I have explained to you, then, if you are satisfied of that from the evidence, you may deem it, for the purposes of this trial, as perfected. Or it may happen that a person may choose to file a caveat while he is going on and making improvements upon an invention which he has already completed, so as to be of practical utility. Therefore, gentlemen, I would say to you that you will take into consideration the declaration of the plaintiff himself in the application, that he had made a new and useful improvement in sewing-machines, and the further declaration that he is making experiments in order to perfect his invention, and the subsequent declaration that he has made a new and useful improvement, and the other evidence in relation to the case, — that is, what is described in the caveat and the model made in 1848, — and see if that exhibits to you a perfected machine; and then such further evidence as you have as of the actual operation of the machine that will be before you.

"Now, gentlemen, if he had perfected it, then he had a right to embrace it in a patent that he should afterwards take out. If he had not perfected it, then another question will arise, and that is, had he invented the feeding mechanism at that time, and did he use due diligence to perfect that and put it into a perfect machine so as to make it of some practical utility. . . . If the invention was perfected, as I have already said, or, if not perfected, if Mr. Johnson used reasonable diligence to perfect it, then he had a right to have it incorporated into his patent, and to supersede those that had intervened between his first discovery and his subsequent taking out of the patent. If he had not perfected it, and did not use due diligence to carry it into effect, and in the mean time, before he got his patent, some one else had invented and used and incorporated into a practical, useful machine that mode of feeding, then he could not, by subsequent patent, appropriate to himself what was embraced in the former machine, between his caveat and the obtaining of his patent."

§ 270 *a*. The law on this subject is now regulated by the act of 1870, section forty of which provides: "That any citizen of the United States who shall have made any new invention or discovery, and shall desire further time to mature the same, may, on payment of the duty required by law, file in the Patent Office a caveat setting forth the design thereof, and of its distinguishing characteristics, and praying protection of his right until he shall have matured his invention ; and such caveat shall be filed in the confidential archives of the office and preserved in secrecy, and shall be operative for the term of one year from the filing thereof; and if application shall be made within the year by any other person for a patent with which such caveat would in any manner interfere, the commissioner shall deposit the description, specification, drawings, and model of such application in like manner in the confidential archives of the office, and give notice thereof, by mail, to the person filing the caveat, who, if he would avail himself of his caveat, shall file his description, specifications, drawings, and model within three months from the time of placing said notice in the post-office in Washington, with the usual time required for transmitting it to the caveator added thereto, which time shall be indorsed on the notice. And an alien shall have the privilege herein granted, if he shall have resided in the United States one year next preceding the filing of his caveat, and made oath of his intention to become a citizen."

THE PETITION, OATH, PAYMENT OF FEES, ETC.

§ 271. The act of 1836, § 6, required an inventor who desired to obtain a patent to "*make application in writing* to the Commissioner of Patents," &c. This application in writing has, from the origin of the government, been by way of petition, generally with the specification annexed and referred to, or accompanied by the specification, filed at the same time. The form of the petition is not material, provided it set forth the facts to which the applicant is required to make oath. When filed, it is to be presumed to adopt the specification, or schedule, filed at the same time, and to ask for a patent for the invention therein described.[1]

If a party chooses to withdraw his application for a patent and pay the forfeit, intending at the time of such withdrawal to file a new petition, and he accordingly does so, the two petitions are to be considered as parts of the same transaction and as constituting a continuous application, within the meaning of the law. The question of the continuity of the application should be submitted to the jury.[2] Where an inventor, having made application for a

[1] Hogg *v.* Emerson, 6 How. 437, 480. The rules of the Patent Office give a form of petition which it is advisable to adopt in all cases. See Appendix.

[2] Godfrey *v.* Eames, 1 Wall. 317.

patent for certain improvements, afterwards, with his claim still on file, makes application for another but distinct improvement in the same branch of art, describing therein the former application, but not claiming it as original, such description and non-claim is not to be considered a dedication of the prior invention.[1]

§ 272. The applicant is also required to make oath or affirmation that he does verily believe that he is "the original and first inventor," &c., "and that he does not know or believe that the same was ever before known or used," and also of what country he is a citizen; which oath or affirmation may be made before any person authorized by law to administer oaths.[2]

§ 273. The applicant is required to make oath or affirmation, not that he is the original and first inventor or discoverer, but that he believes himself to be so. He cannot know absolutely whether he first invented or discovered the thing for which he claims a patent, but he may believe that he did; and it is only when he is willing to make oath that he so believes, that the law grants him the patent. A subsequent section of the same statute provides for one case in which a patent shall still be valid, if issued to an applicant who believed himself to be the first inventor or discoverer, although he was not so, in point of fact. This case is where the invention or discovery had been previously known or used in a foreign country, but had not been patented or described in any public work, and the patentee was ignorant of that fact. If the patentee, before making his application, had learned that the thing had been known or used in a foreign country, although not patented or described in any foreign work, he cannot have believed himself to be the first inventor or discoverer. But if he learn the fact after he has taken the oath, it will not invalidate his patent.[3]

§ 274. An irregularity in the form of the oath will be cured by the issuing of the patent, and it seems that a patent would be valid, when issued, although the oath might not have been taken at all. It has been held that the taking of the oath is only a prerequisite to the granting of the patent, and in no degree

[1] Suffolk Co. *v.* Hayden, 3 Wall. 315.

[2] Act of July 4, 1836, § 6. The oath extends to all described in the schedule filed with the petition, as well as to the title or description of the invention contained in the petition itself. Hogg *v.* Emerson, 6 How. 437, 482.

[3] Act 4th July, 1836, § 15.

essential to its validity; so that if the proper authorities, from inadvertence or any other cause, should grant a patent, where the applicant had not made oath according to the requisitions of the statute, the patent would still be valid. But where the oath has been taken and is recited in the patent, it is the foundation of the *onus probandi* thrown on the party who alleges that the patentee was not the original and first inventor.[1]

§ 274 *a*. The taking of the oath, though to be done prior to the granting of the patent, is not a *condition precedent*, in the absence of which the patent will become void. It is the evidence required to be furnished to the Patent Office, that the applicant verily believes he is the original and first inventor.[2]

§ 275. The ninth section of the Act of 1836 provided, that before any application for a patent shall be considered by the commissioner, the applicant shall pay into the treasury of the United States, or into any of the deposit banks to the credit of the Treasury, if he be a citizen of the United States, or an alien, and shall have been resident in the United States for one year next preceding, and shall have made oath of his intention to become a citizen thereof, the sum of thirty dollars; if a subject of the King of Great Britain, the sum of five hundred dollars.[3]

These provisions were superseded by the fee-bill contained in the act of March 2, 1861, § 10. *And be it further enacted*, That all laws now in force fixing the rates of the Patent Office fees to be paid, and discriminating between the inhabitants of the United States and those of other countries, which shall not discriminate against the inhabitants of the United States, are hereby repealed, and in their stead the following rates are established: —

On filing each caveat, ten dollars.

On filing each original application for a patent, except for a design, fifteen dollars.

On issuing each original patent, twenty dollars.

On every appeal from the examiner in chief to the commissioner, twenty dollars.

On every application for the reissue of a patent, thirty dollars.

[1] Alden *v*. Dewey, 1 Story's R. 336, 341.

[2] Crompton *v*. Belknap Mills (1869), 3 Fisher's Pat. Cas. 536. See, also, Whittemore *v*. Cutter, 1 Gal. 429.

[3] Act 4th July, 1836, § 9.

On every application for the extension of a patent, fifty dollars; and fifty dollars in addition, on the granting of every extension.

On filing each disclaimer, ten dollars.

For certified copies of patents and other papers, ten cents per hundred words.

For recording every assignment, agreement, power of attorney, and other papers of three hundred words or under, one dollar.

For recording every assignment and other papers over three hundred and under one thousand words, two dollars.

For recording every assignment or other writing, if over one thousand words, three dollars.

For copies of drawings, the reasonable cost of making the same.

§ 275 *a*. The proceedings relating to the application, payment of fees, &c., are now regulated by the act of 1870.[1] Section twenty-six of that act provides: "That before any inventor or discoverer shall receive a patent for his invention or discovery, he shall make application therefor, in writing, to the commissioner, and shall file in the Patent Office a written description of the same, and of the manner and process of making, constructing, compounding, and using it, in such full, clear, concise, and exact terms as to enable any person skilled in the art or science to which it appertains, or with which it is most nearly connected, to make, construct, compound, and use the same; and in case of a machine, he shall explain the principle thereof, and the best mode in which he has contemplated applying that principle so as to distinguish it from other inventions; and he shall particularly point out and distinctly claim the part, improvement, or combination which he claims as his invention or discovery; and said specification and claim shall be signed by the inventor and attested by two witnesses."

§ 275 *b*. When the nature of the case admits of drawings, the applicant is required to furnish one copy signed by the inventor or his attorney in fact, and attested by two witnesses, which shall be filed in the Patent Office; and a copy of the drawings, to be furnished by the Patent Office, is to be attached to the patent as part of the specification.[2] When the invention or discovery is of a composition of matter, the applicant, if required by the commissioner, must furnish specimens of ingredients and of the

[1] See Appendix.

[2] § 27.

composition sufficient in quantity for the purpose of experiment.[1] And in all cases which admit of representation by model, the applicant, if required by the commissioner, must furnish one of convenient size to exhibit advantageously the several parts of his invention or discovery.[2]

§ 275 *c*. Section thirty provides: "That the applicant shall make oath or affirmation that he does verily believe himself to be the original and first inventor or discoverer of the art, machine, manufacture, composition, or improvement for which he solicits a patent; that he does not know and does not believe that the same was ever before known or used; and shall state of what country he is a citizen. And said oath or affirmation may be made before any person within the United States authorized by law to administer oaths, or, when the applicant resides in a foreign country, before any minister, *chargé d'affaires*, consul, or commercial agent holding commission under the Government o the United States, or before any notary public of the foreign country in which the applicant may be."

On the filing of any such application and the payment of the duty required by law, the commissioner is required to cause an examination to be made of the alleged new invention or discovery; and if it appear on such examination that the claimant is justly entitled to a patent under the law, and that the same is sufficiently useful and important, it is made the duty of the commissioner to issue a patent therefor.[3]

§ 275 *d*. All applications for patents must be completed and prepared for examination within two years after the filing of the petition, and in default thereof, or upon failure of the applicant to prosecute the same within two years after any action therein, of which notice shall have been given to the applicant, they shall be regarded as abandoned by the parties thereto, unless it be shown to the satisfaction of the commissioner that such delay was unavoidable.[4]

§ 275 *e*. Where the assignee of the inventor or discoverer, having recorded the assignment in the Patent Office, seeks to obtain letters-patent, the application for the patent must be made and the specification sworn to by the inventor or discoverer; and also, if he be living, in case of an application for reissue.[5] It was

[1] § 28. [2] § 29. [3] § 31.
[4] § 32. [5] § 33.

subsequently enacted that this provision "shall not be construed to apply to patents issued and assigned prior to July 8, 1870." [1]

In case of the death of the inventor or discoverer before a patent is granted, the right of applying for and obtaining the patent devolves on his executor or administrator, in trust for the heirs-at-law of the deceased, in case he shall have died intestate; or if he shall have left a will disposing of the same, then in trust for his devisees; and when the application shall be made by such legal representatives, the oath or affirmation required shall be so varied in form that it can be made by them.[2]

§ 275 *f.* Section thirty-five of the act of 1870 provides: "That any person who has an interest in an invention or discovery, whether as inventor, discoverer, or assignee, for which a patent was ordered to issue upon the payment of the final fee, but who has failed to make payment thereof within six months from the time at which it was passed and allowed, and notice thereof was sent to the applicant or his agent, shall have a right to make an application for a patent for such invention or discovery the same as in the case of an original application: *Provided*, that the second application be made within two years after the allowance of the original application. But no person shall be held responsible in damages for the manufacture or use of any article or thing for which a patent, as aforesaid, was ordered to issue, prior to the issue thereof: *And provided further*, that when an application for a patent has been rejected or withdrawn, prior to the passage of this act, the applicant shall have six months from the date of such passage to renew his application, or to file a new one; and if he omit to do either, his application shall be held to have been abandoned. Upon the hearing of such renewed applications, abandonment shall be considered as a question of fact."

§ 275 *g.* Whenever, on examination, any claim for a patent is rejected for any reason whatever, the commissioner is required to notify the applicant thereof, giving him briefly the reasons for such rejection, together with such information and references as may be useful in judging of the propriety of renewing his application or of altering his specification. If the applicant, after receiving such notice, persist in his claim for a patent with or

[1] Act of March 3, 1871.
[2] § 34.

without altering his specifications, the commissioner is required to order a re-examination of the case.[1]

Section forty-two of the act of 1870 provides: "That whenever an application is made for a patent which, in the opinion of the commissioner, would interfere with any pending application, or with any unexpired patent, he shall give notice thereof to the applicants, or applicant and patentee, as the case may be, and shall direct the primary examiner to proceed to determine the question of priority of invention. And the commissioner may issue a patent to the party who shall be adjudged the prior inventor, unless the adverse party shall appeal from the decision of the primary examiner, or of the board of examiners-in-chief, as the case may be, within such time not less than twenty days, as the commissioner shall prescribe."

§ 275 *h*. The fees established by the act of 1870 are as follows:[2]

On filing each original application for a patent, fifteen dollars.

On issuing each original patent, twenty dollars.

On filing each caveat, ten dollars.

On every application for the reissue of a patent, thirty dollars.

On filing each disclaimer, ten dollars.

On every application for the extension of a patent, fifty dollars.

On the granting of every extension of a patent, fifty dollars.

On an appeal for the first time from the primary examiners to the examiners-in-chief, ten dollars.

On every appeal from the examiners-in-chief to the commissioner, twenty dollars.

For certified copies of patents and other papers, ten cents per hundred words.

For recording every assignment, agreement, power of attorney, or other paper, of three hundred words or under, one dollar; of over three hundred and under one thousand words, two dollars; of over one thousand words, three dollars.

For copies of drawings, the reasonable cost of making them.

In design cases the rate of fees is as follows:[3] —

For three years and six months, ten dollars.

For seven years, fifteen dollars.

For fourteen years, thirty dollars.

For all other cases in which fees are required, the same rates as in cases of inventions or discoveries.

[1] Act of 1870, § 41. [2] § 68. [3] § 75.

SIGNATURES OF THE SECRETARY OF THE INTERIOR AND OF THE COMMISSIONER OF PATENTS.

§ 276. The act of July 4, 1836, c. 357, § 5, provided that patents should be issued from the Patent Office "in the name of the United States, and under the seal of said office, and be signed by the Secretary of State, and countersigned by the commissioner of said office."

The act of 1849, c. 108, § 2, required the Secretary of the Interior to "exercise and perform all the acts of supervision and appeal in regard to the office of Commissioner of Patents, now exercised by the Secretary of State," and so according to the act of 1870, § 21, all patents "shall be signed by the Secretary of the Interior and countersigned by the commissioner."

§ 277. It has been held that the sanction of the Secretary of State (now of the Interior) to a correction of a clerical mistake in letters-patent may be given in writing afterwards; and that he need not re-sign the letters themselves. But the commissioner, if he be the same officer who countersigned the letters originally, may make the correction without re-signing or resealing. If the mistake occurs in the copy of the patent, and not in the record or enrolment, it may be corrected by the commissioner and made to conform to the original. If the mistake in the enrolled patent be a material one, the letters cannot operate except on cases arising after the correction is made; but if the correction be of a clerical mistake only, it operates back to the original date of the letters, unless, perhaps, as to third persons, who have acquired intervening rights to be affected by the alteration.[1]

§ 278. It has also been held, that a signature to the patent, and a certificate of copies by a person calling himself "acting commissioner," is sufficient on its face in controversies between the patentee and third persons, as the law recognizes an acting commissioner.[2]

[1] Woodworth *v.* Hall, 1 Woodb. & M. 248; S. C. Ibid. 389.

[2] Woodworth *v.* Hall, 1 Woodb. & M. 248. Where evidence is offered to prove that the "acting commissioner" who signs a patent was not appointed by the President, it is doubtful whether it is competent in controversies where he is not a party. S. C. 1 Woodb. & M. 389.

REISSUE OR AMENDMENT OF A PATENT.

§ 279. The act of July 4, 1836, § 13, made the following provision in case of a defective or insufficient specification, or of the subsequent invention of something which the patentee wishes to add to his specification.

§ 280. "And be it further enacted: That whenever any patent which has heretofore been granted, or which shall hereafter be granted, shall be inoperative or invalid, by reason of a defective or insufficient description or specification, or by reason of the patentee claiming in his specification, as his own invention, more than he had or shall have a right to claim as new; if the error has or shall have arisen by inadvertency, accident, or mistake, and without any fraudulent or deceptive intention, it shall be lawful for the commissioner, upon the surrender to him of such patent, and the payment of the further duty of fifteen dollars, to cause a new patent to be issued to the said inventor, for the same invention, for the residue of the period then unexpired for which the original patent was granted, in accordance with the patentee's corrected description and specification. And in case of his death, or any assignment by him made of the original patent, a similar right shall vest in his executors, administrators, or assignees. And the patent so reissued, together with the corrected description and specification, shall have the same effect and operation in law, on the trial of all actions hereafter commenced for causes subsequently accruing, as though the same had been originally filed in such corrected form, before the issuing out of the original patent. [And whenever the original patentee shall be desirous of adding the description and specification of any new improvement of the original invention or discovery which shall have been invented or discovered by him subsequent to the date of his patent, he may, like proceedings being had in all respects as in the case of original applications, and on the payment of fifteen dollars, as hereinbefore provided, have the same annexed to the original description and specification; and the commissioner shall certify, on the margin of such annexed description and specification, the time of its being annexed and recorded; and the same shall thereafter have the same effect in law, to all intents and purposes, as though it had been embraced in the original description and specification."[1]]

That provision of the section in brackets was abolished by the act of 1861, c. 88, § 9, which provided "that so much of the thirteenth section of the act of Congress, approved July 4, 1836, as authorizes the annexing to letters-patent of the description and specification of additional improvements is hereby repealed. And in all cases where additional improvements would now be admissible, independent patents must be applied for."

§ 280 *a*. The law on this subject is now regulated by section fifty-three of the act of 1870, which provides: "That whenever any patent is inoperative or invalid, by reason of a defective or insufficient specification, or by reason of the patentee claiming as his own invention or discovery more than he had a right to claim as new, if the error has arisen by inadvertence, accident, or mistake, and without any fraudulent or deceptive intention, the commissioner shall, on the surrender of such patent and the payment of the duty required by law, cause a new patent for the same invention, and in accordance with the corrected specifications, to be issued to the patentee, or, in the case of his death or assignment of the whole or any undivided part of the original patent, to his executors, administrators, or assigns for the unexpired part of the term of the original patent, the surrender of which shall take effect upon the issue of the amended patent; and the commissioner may, in his discretion, cause several patents to be issued for distinct and separate parts of the thing patented, upon demand of the applicant, and upon

[1] The act of March 3, 1837, § 8, made a further provision on this subject: —

"And be it further enacted, That, [whenever application shall be made to the commissioner for any addition of a newly discovered improvement to be made to an existing patent, or] whenever a patent shall be returned for correction and reissue, the specification of claim annexed to every such patent shall be subject to revision and restriction, in the same manner as are original applications for patents; the commissioner shall not [add any such improvement to the patent in the one case, nor] grant the reissue in the other case, until the applicant shall have entered a disclaimer, or altered his specification of claim in accordance with the decision of the commissioner; and in all such cases the applicant, if dissatisfied with such decision, shall have the same remedy and be entitled to the benefit of the same privileges and proceedings as are provided by law in the case of original applications for patents." The parts in brackets are repealed by act of 1861, c. 88, § 9.

payment of the required fee for a reissue for each of such reissued letters-patent. And the specification and claim in every such case shall be subject to revision and restriction in the same manner as original applications are. And the patent so reissued, together with the corrected specification, shall have the effect and operation in law, on the trial of all actions for causes thereafter arising, as though the same had been originally filed in such corrected form; but no new matter shall be introduced into the specification, nor in case of a machine patent shall the model or drawings be amended, except each by the other; but when there is neither model nor drawing, amendments may be made upon proof satisfactory to the commissioner that such new matter or amendment was a part of the original invention, and was omitted from the specification by inadvertence, accident, or mistake, as aforesaid."

In the cases of patents issued and assigned prior to the act of July 8, 1870, the application for reissue may be made by the assignee; but in the case of patents issued or assigned since that date the application must be made and the specification sworn to by the inventor, if he be living.[1]

§ 281. The object of conferring this power of surrender and reissue is to enable patentees to remedy accidental mistakes. In a recent case the court took the opportunity of pointedly condemning a practice which had sprung up of late, and which consists in surrendering valid patents and obtaining reissues for the purpose of inserting therein expanded and equivocal claims.[2]

[1] See section 275 *e*.

[2] Burr *v.* Duryee, 1 Wallace, 531. "Since the date of this act, not only the Patent Office, but the bar can furnish gentlemen fully competent to the task of drawing up proper specifications, and but little liable to commit blunders from inadvertency. Specifications now seldom issue from the Patent Office to which such an imputation can be made. Nevertheless, this privilege of surrender and reissue is resorted to more frequently than ever. Formerly, when in course of investigation in a court of justice it was discovered that a patent was invalid, for any of the reasons mentioned in the act, it was resorted to. *Now*, after a patent has been declared to be valid, the specification without defect, and the claim for nothing more than the invention, after it has undergone examination for many years, and courts and juries have decided that the patent is *not* invalid through inadvertency, accident, or mistake, the assignees come forward and make oath that the inventor's original patent is 'unavailable' for some purpose unnecessary to be divulged. In the present case, the purpose is transparent. The specification of this reissued patent,

Inasmuch as it is the duty of the commissioner of patents to see that a reissue does not cover more than the original, the reissue is to be presumed to be for the same invention until the contrary be shown. Variations in the two patents do not necessarily imply that the subsequent one is for a different discovery. The right to surrender the old patent and receive another in its place was given for the purpose of enabling the patentee to give a more perfect description of his invention, when any mistake or oversight was committed in the first. If a separate invention is covered by one of the claims in a surrendered patent, and that claim, as there made, is void, the patentee may take a distinct patent therefor.[1]

Whether the defect be in the description or the claim, the patentee may surrender his patent, and, by an amended specification, cure the defect. A substantially new and different invention cannot be claimed; but where the specification or claim is made so vaguely as to be inoperative or invalid, yet an amendment may give to it validity. The patentee has a right to restrict or enlarge his claim so as to give it validity and effectuate his invention.[2]

A patent which is extended by a special act of Congress becomes thereby a patent for the period of twenty-eight years from its original date, and a surrender and reissue thereof after such extension stand on the same footing as if they had been made in the case of a patent for twenty-one years.[3]

§ 282. The question has been raised, how far the decision of the commissioner of patents upon the existence of a defect in

instead of describing first the *machine* and the several devices which exhibit its peculiar mode of operation in order to produce the desired effect, and stating what the patentee claims as his peculiar invention, commences by describing ' a *mode of operation* ' as the thing intended to be patented, and uses these words: The said *mode of operation* invented by the said Henry A. Wells is embodied in the following description of the mode of application. The claim is for the mode of operation substantially as herein described.

"We have no leisure for a further development of this novel form of patent, or how, by the use of general and abstract terms, the specification is made so elastic that it may be construed to claim only the machine, or so expanded as to include all previous or future inventions for the same purpose."

[1] O'Reilly *v.* Morse, 15 How. 62.

[2] Battin *v.* Taggert, 17 How. 74. Reversing the same case in 2 Wallace, C. C. R. 101.

[3] Gibson *v.* Harris, 1 Blatchf. 167. (1846.)

the specification, arising from inadvertence, accident, or mistake, is re-examinable elsewhere. It becomes important when, in an action under the reissued patent, the defence is set up that the reissue is for a different invention from that described in the surrendered patent. Inasmuch as the descriptions in the two patents necessarily differ, it follows that if the commissioner's decision is open to re-examination, so that the fact of the existence of defects in the former patent can be inquired into, the defendant is at liberty to show that the reissued patent is not for the same invention as that covered by the surrendered one. But if, on the other hand, the commissioner's action in the matter of surrender and reissue is conclusive, then the granting of a new patent, as provided by statute, precludes all inquiry into the fact whether it was or was not rightly granted, and makes the new patent of necessity applicable to the same invention as the old.

Under the act of 1832 the Supreme Court held that the reissue of a patent by the commissioner was *primâ facie* evidence that the proofs of defect required by the statute had been regularly furnished and were satisfactory.[1] Subsequently, under the act of 1836, the same court appears to have considered the granting of the renewed patent as so far conclusive upon the question of the existence of error in the original patent arising from inadvertency, accident, or mistake, that nothing remained open but the fairness of the transaction; that the question of fraud might be raised, and that this was for the jury; but that, unless the surrender and renewal were impeached by showing fraud, the reissue must be deemed conclusive proof that the case provided for by the statute existed.[2]

This view is also taken in Woodworth *v.* Stone, Allen *v.* Blunt, incidentally affirmed in O'Reilly *v.* Morse, and expressly affirmed in Potter *v.* Holland.[3]

[1] The Philadelphia and Trenton R.R. Co. *v.* Stimpson, 14 Pet. 448.

[2] Stimpson *v.* Westchester R.R. Co., 4 How. 380.

[3] Woodworth *v.* Stone, 3 Story's R. 749, 753. In this case, which was in equity, the learned judge said: "But the most material objection taken is, that the new patent is not for the same invention as that which has been surrendered. And certainly, if this be correct, there is a fatal objection to the prolongation of the injunction. But is the objection well founded, in point of fact? It is said, that the present patent is for a combination only, and that the old patent was for a combination and something more, or different. But

§ 282 *a*. In the case of Jordan *v.* Dobson,[1] decided by the Circuit Court of Pennsylvania in 1870, it appeared that in 1863

I apprehend that, upon the face of the present patent, the question is scarcely open for the consideration of the court; and, at all events, certainly not open in this stage of the cause. I have already, in another cause, had occasion to decide, that where the commissioner of patents accepts a surrender of an old patent and grants a new one, under the act of 1836, c. 357, his decision, being an act expressly confided to him by law, and dependent upon his judgment, is not re-examinable elsewhere; and that the court must take it to be a lawful exercise of his authority, unless it is apparent, upon the very face of the patent, that he has exceeded his authority, and there is a clear repugnancy between the old and the new patent, or the new one has been obtained by collusion between the commissioner and the patentee. Now, upon the face of it, the new patent, in the present case, purports to be for the same invention and none other, that is contained in the old patent. The avowed difference between the new and the old is, that the specification in the old is defective, and that the defect is intended to be remedied in the new patent. It is upon this very ground that the old patent was surrendered and the new patent was granted. The claim in the new patent is not of any new invention, but of the old invention more perfectly described and ascertained. It is manifest that, in the first instance, the commissioner was the proper judge whether the invention was the same or not, and whether there was any deficit in the specification or not, by inadvertence, accident, or mistake; and consequently he must have decided that the combination of machinery claimed in the old patent was, in substance, the same combination and invention claimed and described in the new. My impression is, that at the former trial of the old patent before me, I held the claim substantially (although obscurely worded) to be a claim for the invention of a particular combination of machinery, for planing, tongueing, and grooving, and dressing boards, &c.; or, in other words, that it was the claim of an invention of a planing-machine or planing apparatus such as he had described in his specification.

"It appears to me, therefore, that *primâ facie*, and at all events in this stage of the cause, it must be taken to be true, that the new patent is for the same invention as the old patent; and that the only difference is, not in the invention itself, but in the specification of it. In the old, it was defectively described and claimed. In the new, the defects are intended to be remedied. Whether they are effectually remedied is a point not now properly before the court. But as the commissioner of patents has granted the new patent as for the same invention as the old, it does not appear to me that this court is now at liberty to reverse his judgment, or to say that he has been guilty of an excess of authority, at least (as has been already suggested) not in this stage of the cause; for that would be for the court of itself to assume to decide many matters of fact as to the specification and the combination of machinery in both patents, without any adequate means of knowledge or of guarding

[1] 2 Abbott's U. S. Rep. 398.

the complainant had become the owner by assignment of a patent for a new and useful improvement in machinery for the

itself from gross error. For the purpose of the injunction, if for nothing else, I must take the invention to be the same in both patents, after the commissioner of patents has so decided, by granting the new patent."

In Allen *v.* Blunt, 3 Story's R. 742, 743, which was an action at law, the same judge observed: "The thirteenth section of the Patent Act of 1836, c. 357, enacts, that whenever any patent shall be inoperative or invalid, by reason of a defective or insufficient description or specification, or by reason of the patentee claiming in his specification, as his own invention, more than he had, or shall have a right to claim as new, if the error has or shall have arisen by inadvertency, accident, or mistake, and without any fraudulent or deceptive intention, it shall be lawful for the commissioner, upon the surrender to him of such patent, and the payment of the further duty of fifteen dollars, to cause a new patent to be issued for the same invention for the residue of the term then unexpired, for which the original patent was granted, in accordance with the patentee's corrected description and specification. Now, the specification may be defective or insufficient, either by a mistake of law, as to what is required to be stated therein in respect to the claim of the inventor, or by a mistake of fact, in omitting things which are indispensable to the completeness and exactness of the description of the invention, or of the mode of constructing, or making, or using the same. Whether the invention claimed in the original patent, and that claimed in the new amended patent, is substantially the same, is and must be in many cases a matter of great nicety and difficulty to decide. It may involve consideration of fact as well as of law. Who is to decide the question? The true answer is, the commissioner of patents; for the law intrusts him with the authority, not only to accept the surrender, but to grant the new amended patent. He is bound, therefore, by the very nature of his duties to inquire into and ascertain whether the specification is sufficient or insufficient, in point of law or fact, and whether the inventor has claimed more than he has invented, and in such case whether the error has arisen from inadvertency, accident, or mistake, or with a fraudulent or deceptive intention. No one can well doubt, that in the first instance, therefore, he is bound to decide the whole law and facts arising under the application for the new patent. *Primâ facie*, therefore, it must be presumed that the new amended patent has been properly and rightfully granted by him. I very much doubt whether his decision is or can be re-examinable in any other place, or in any other tribunal, at least, unless his decision is impeached on account of gross fraud or connivance between him and the patentee; or unless his excess of authority is manifest upon the very face of the papers; as, for example, if the original patent were for a chemical combination, and the new amended patent were for a machine. In other cases, it seems to me, that the law, having intrusted him with authority to ascertain the facts, and to grant the patent, his decision, *bonâ fide* made, is conclusive. It is like many other cases, where the law has referred the decision of a matter to the sound discretion of a public officer, whose adjudication becomes conclusive. Suppose the Secretary of the Treas-

manufacture of wool and other fibrous material originally granted to John Goulding. The patent was first issued in 1826, and in 1836 was surrendered, and a reissue obtained. An extension of the patent was not obtained by the patentee before the expiration of the time for which it was originally issued, but under the act of Congress of May 30, 1862, empowering the commissioner of patents to grant renewals and extensions for the term of seven

ury should remit a penalty or forfeiture incurred by a breach of the laws of the United States, would his decision be re-examinable in any court of law upon a suit for the penalty or forfeiture? The President of the United States is by law invested with authority to call forth the militia to suppress insurrections, to repel invasions, and to execute the laws of the Union; and it has been held by the Supreme Court of the United States, that his decision as to the occurrence of the exigency is conclusive. Martin *v.* Mott, 12 Wheat. R. 19. In short, it may be laid down as a general rule, that, where a particular authority is confided to a public officer, to be exercised by him in his discretion upon the examination of facts, of which he is made the appropriate judge, his decision upon these facts is, in the absence of any controlling provisions, absolutely conclusive as to the existence of those facts. My opinion, therefore, is, that the grant of the present amended patent by the commissioner of patents *is conclusive as to the existence of all the facts, which were by law necessary to entitle him to issue it;* at least, unless it was apparent on the very face of the patent itself, without any auxiliary evidence, that he was guilty of a clear excess of authority, or that the patent was procured by a fraud between him and the patentee, which is not pretended in the present case."

Potter *et al.* *v.* Holland. "The power and duty of granting a new patent for the original invention, when a lawful surrender of the old patent has been made, are by law expressly confided to the commissioner. The decision made by him in this case is that the reissued patents are for the same invention originally discovered and intended by the patentee to be secured by the original patent. That decision the law has confided to his judgment. The court must take that decision as a lawful exercise of his authority. It is not re-examinable here, unless it is apparent upon the face of the patent that the commissioner has exceeded his authority, or unless there is a clear repugnancy between the old and the new patents, or unless the new one has been obtained by collusion between the commissioner and the patentee. Woodworth *v.* Stone, 3 Story, 749. It is not apparent upon the face of either of the reissued patents that the commissioner, in granting the same, has exceeded his authority; neither does there appear to be any clear repugnancy between the old and the new patents; nor is there any satisfactory evidence to show that either of the new patents was obtained by collusion between the commissioner and patentee. The exception, therefore, taken by the defendant, that the invention secured by the reissued patents was not the invention of the patentee when the original patent was granted, and was not intended by him to be secured by that patent, must fail." 4 Blatchf. 206. See also Blake *v.* Stafford, 3 Fisher's Pat. Cas. 294.

years, the patent was extended by the commissioner for seven years from August 20, 1862. In the following year the complainant became the owner, and on June 28, 1864, this extended patent was surrendered and reissued to the complainant for the remainder of the seven years.

Upon this state of facts, in a suit brought by the complainant for infringement, it was contended, on behalf of the defendant, that when the reissue was granted, in 1836, the surrender was not made, as alleged, because the original patent was inoperative and invalid by reason of a defective specification, without any fraudulent or deceptive intention, but that the surrender was made and the reissued letters-patent were obtained with a fraudulent and deceptive intention of including important changes not a part of the invention of the patentee. The same allegation was made respecting the surrender of the extended patent and its reissue to the complainant in 1864. It was thereupon contended that, by reason of such fraudulent and deceptive intention, the reissued patents were void.

The court, however, held that as it was the duty of the commissioner, before granting a reissue, to determine whether the defect or insufficiency of the original specification arose from inadvertence, accident, or mistake, or originated in a fraudulent intention, his decision was conclusive, and "not re-examinable, except, perhaps, so far as he decided there was no fraud." In a suit, therefore, founded upon a reissued patent, the courts must presume that the commissioner duly performed his duty of ascertaining that the defect in the original specification was owing to inadvertence, accident, or mistake; and that the amended description is of the same invention as was covered by the original patent.

§ 282 *b*. In a very recent case[1] the Supreme Court of the United States fully considered the question, how far it was competent to go behind the action of the commissioner in extending a patent, and inquire into the frauds by which the extension was alleged to have been procured. It was there definitely settled that in a suit for infringement, whether of a reissued or an extended patent, the defendant is not at liberty to question the decision of the commissioner in granting such reissue or surrender

[1] Rubber Company *v.* Goodyear (December, 1869), 9 Wall. 788; s. c. 2 Clifford, 375.

upon the ground of fraud. By this decision the door has been closed against showing fraud in procuring reissued or extended patents as a defence in a suit for infringement of such reissued or extended patent; but it decides nothing as to whether the patent may be impeached on the ground of fraud in a proceeding had directly for that purpose.

In giving the reasons by which the court was led to this conclusion, Mr. Justice Swayne said: "The extension was granted by the commissioner pursuant to the first section of the act of 1848 and the eighteenth section of the act of 1836. The latter declares that upon the making and recording of the certificate of extension 'the said patent shall have the same effect in law as though it had been originally granted for the term of twenty-one years.' The law made it the duty of the commissioner to examine and decide. He had full jurisdiction. The function he performed was judicial in its character. No provision is made for appeal or review.[1] His decision must be held conclusive until the patent is impeached in a proceeding had directly for that purpose according to the rules which define the remedy, as shown by the precedents and authorities upon the subject. We are not, therefore, at liberty to enter upon the examination of the evidences of fraud to which we have been invited by the counsel for the appellants. The door to that inquiry in this case is closed upon us by the hand of the law. The rule which we have thus laid down is intended to be limited to the class of cases to which, as respects the point in question, the one before us belongs. We decide nothing beyond this."

This ruling was approved and applied by the same court in the subsequent cases of Eureka Company *v.* Bailey Company,[2] and Seymour *v.* Osborne.[3] In the latter the law was stated in the following language: "Where the commissioner accepts a surrender of an original patent, and grants a new patent, his decision in the premises, in a suit for infringement, is final and conclusive, and is not re-examinable in such a suit in the Circuit Court, unless it is apparent upon the face of the patent that he has exceeded his authority; that there is such a repugnancy between the old and the new patent that it must be held, as matter of

[1] Foley *v.* Harrison, 15 How. 448.

[2] 11 Wall. 488.

[3] Ibid. 516.

legal construction, that the new patent is not for the same invention as that embraced and secured in the original patent."[1]

Since the announcement of the doctrine by the Supreme Court that a person sued as an infringer cannot abrogate a reissued or

[1] Seymour *v.* Osborne, 11 Wall. 516. See also Battin *v.* Taggert, 17 How. 83; O'Reilly *v.* Morse, 15 How. 111, 112; Sickles *v.* Evans, 2 Clifford, 222; Allen *v.* Brunt, 3 Story, 744. In the Rubber Company *v.* Goodyear, the court said: "Can we go behind the action of the commissioner in extending the patent, and inquire into the frauds by which it is alleged that the extension was procured? The fifth section of the act of 1790 provided for the repeal of patents under the circumstances and in the manner specified. This act was repealed by the act of 1793. The tenth section of that act re-enacted the fifth section of the act of 1790. The fifth section of the latter act authorized substantially the same defences in suits upon patents which are allowed by the fifteenth section of the act of 1836, with the further provision, that if the facts touching either defence were established, 'judgment shall be rendered for the defendant with costs, and the patent shall be declared void.' This act continued in force until it was repealed by the act of 1836. These provisions were not then, and they have not since been re-enacted. The sixteenth section of the act of 1836 authorizes a court of equity, in cases of interference, to take jurisdiction and annul the patent issued to the party in the wrong. Beyond this the patent laws are silent upon the subject of the exercise of such authority. This review furnishes a strong implication that it was the intention of Congress not to allow a patent to be abrogated in any collateral proceeding, except in the particular instance mentioned, but to leave the remedy in all other cases to be regulated by the principles of general jurisprudence. To those principles we must look for the solution of the question before us. The subject was examined by Chancellor Kent with his accustomed fulness of research and ability, in Jackson *v.* Lawton (10 Johnson, 23). He there said: 'Unless letters-patent are absolutely void on the face of them, or the issuing of them was without authority, or was prohibited by statute, they can only be avoided in a regular course of pleading, in which the fraud, irregularity, or mistake is regularly put in issue. The principle has been frequently admitted, that the fraud must appear on the face of the patent to render it void in a court of law, and that when the fraud or other defect arises on circumstances, *dehors* the grant, the grant is voidable only by suit (1 Hening and Munford, 19, 187; 1 Munford, 134). The regular tribunal is chancery, founded on a proceeding by *scire facias* or by bill or information.' The patent in that case was for land, but, as regards the point here under consideration, there is no distinction between such a patent and one for an invention or discovery. If there be, the case is stronger as to the latter. In the case of Field *v.* Seabury, the patent was also for land. This court ruled the point in like manner, and the same remarks apply. Viewing the subject in the light of the principle involved, we can see no defect in the parallelism between that case and the one before us."

extended patent by showing that it had been obtained by fraud, it has come to be regarded as the better opinion that all matters of fact connected with the surrender and reissue of a patent are conclusively settled by the decision of the commissioner granting the reissued patent. Matters of construction, however, arising upon the face of the instrument, are still open to examination.[1]

§ 282 *c*. It is clearly settled, both by the statute authorizing reissues and by the construction put upon it by the courts, that the reissued letters-patent must be for the same invention as that embraced in the original patent. Consequently where it appears by a comparison of the two instruments, as matter of law, that the invention covered by the reissued patent is substantially different from that embodied in the original, the former must be held to be invalid, because no jurisdiction to grant such a patent is vested in the commissioner.

It is not disputed that the commissioner is authorized to allow the patentee, if his patent is inoperative or invalid, to redescribe his invention in an amended specification. In so doing the patentee is not rigidly confined to what was described before, but he may include in the new description whatever else was suggested or substantially indicated in the old, provided it was properly embraced in the invention as actually made and

[1] Seymour *v.* Osborne, 11 Wall. 516; Rubber Co. *v.* Goodyear, 9 Wall. 796. See also American Wood Paper Co. *v.* Glen's Falls Paper Co., 8 Blatchf. 513; s. c. 4 Fisher's Pat. Cas. 324; and Parkham *v.* The American Buttonhole, Overseaming, and Sewing-Machine Co., 4 Fisher's Pat. Cas. 468. In the last-named case Mr. Justice McKennan said: "The only ground, then, on which the allowance of a reissued patent is open to objection is that the commissioner has exceeded his authority in granting a reissue for an invention different from the one embraced in the original patent. If both are for the same invention, the decision of the commissioner is unimpeachable, and the reissued patent, with the new specification, is to be substituted for the old as the evidence of the patentee's title and of the nature and object of his invention. Differences in the description and claims of the old and the new specifications are not the tests of substantial diversity, but the description may be varied, and the claim restricted or enlarged, provided the identity of the subject-matter of the original patent is preserved. Within this range, whatever change is required to protect and effectuate the invention is allowable. Battin *v.* Taggert, 17 How. 84. Nor is the alleged discrepancy to be determined by a reference exclusively to the two specifications; the drawings and model filed with the original specification are also proper subjects of consideration and are often of decisive weight. Seymour *v.* Osborne, 11 Wall. 516."

perfected. But interpolations of new features, ingredients, or devices which were neither described, suggested, nor indicated in the original patent, and which would make the reissued patent for a substantially different invention from that embraced in the original, are not allowed, and will render the reissued patent void. If the patentee has claimed as new more than he was entitled to claim, or if the description, specification, or claim is defective or insufficient, he is accorded the privilege of correcting such description, specification, or claim; but he cannot, under such an application, make material additions to the invention which were not substantially embraced in the letters-patent surrendered.

Whether a reissued patent is for the same invention as that embodied in the original patent, or for a different one, is a question of construction for the court, to be determined by a comparison of the two instruments. In performing this duty the court will be aided by the testimony of expert witnesses, if either or both of the instruments contain technical terms requiring such assistance in ascertaining the true meaning of the language employed.[1] The rule on this point has been clearly stated by Mr. Justice Clifford: "Where the specification and claim, both in the original and reissued patents, are expressed in ordinary language, without employing any technical terms or terms of art, the question whether the reissued patent is for the same invention as that described in the original patent or for a different one is purely a question of construction; but where both or either contain technical terms or terms of art the court may hear the testimony of scientific witnesses to aid the court in coming to a correct conclusion. Cases doubtless arise where the language of the specification and claim, both of the surrendered and reissued patents, is so interspersed with technical terms and terms of art that the testimony of scientific witnesses is indispensable to a correct understanding of its meaning. Both parties in such a case would have a right to examine such witnesses, and it would undoubtedly be error in the court to reject the testimony, but the case before the court is not of a character to render it expedient to pursue the inquiry.[2]

[1] Seymour *v.* Osborne, 11 Wall. 516; Sickles *v.* Evans, 2 Clifford, 203.

[2] Bischoff *v.* Wethered, 9 Wall. 814; Betts *v.* Menzies, 4 Best & Smith, Q. B. 999.

"Apply the rule to the present case, that the question is one of construction, and it is clear that the defence under consideration is not open to the respondents, as they did not introduce in evidence the original letters-patent from which the reissued patents were derived." [1]

In a very recent case it was held that a principle, although known to the patentee when he made his invention, could not be incorporated in a reissue, if it was not described in the original patent.[2]

§ 282 *d.* There is a recent case where the reissued patent contained a broader claim and invention than was embraced in the original, but under the following circumstances. Herman E. and Charles H. Davidson, inventors of a new and useful syringe, having applied for a patent therefor in the proper form, the commissioner of patents refused to grant the patent except upon a limited claim, which he suggested, narrowing the invention. This decision of the commissioner was based upon the ground that a prominent feature of the invention, as claimed by the Davidsons, had been anticipated by prior improvements made by other parties. The applicants acquiesced in the rejection, and, having submitted an amended and restricted claim, received a patent in accordance therewith. Subsequently it was discovered that the invention, supposed by the commissioner to have anticipated that of the Davidsons, presented no legal objection to the claim as first presented by them to the Patent Office. Accordingly a surrender and amendment of the claim restoring it to its original form were allowed, and a reissue was granted coextensive with the invention as originally claimed.

On this state of facts it was contended, on the part of the defendants (the appellants), that the original patent not being either "inoperative or invalid," and the specification not being "defective or insufficient," the case did not come within the provisions of the thirteenth section of the act of 1836, and the reissue therefore was without authority of law. The court, however, did not accept this construction, but held that, the error or mistake having been made by the commissioner himself, he not only had full authority to grant the amendment and thus correct

[1] Seymour *v.* Osborne, 11 Wall. 516.

[2] Dyson *v.* Danforth, 4 Fisher's Pat. Cas. 133.

his own error, but, "under the special circumstances of the case, it would seem to have been a duty, as the inventors were led into the error by himself." [1]

In the case of Bennet *v.* Fowler,[2] "the invention had been originally covered by one patent, but in the reissue was separated and embodied in two reissues; and the reissue in the twofold form was held valid by the court. It is true that both reissued patents related to lifting and depositing a load of hay in the mow of a barn or in a rick or shed; but in one of the reissues the lifter was somewhat differently constructed, so as to adapt it specially to the stacking of hay. In this case the court referred to the difficulty of laying down any general rule by which to determine whether a given invention or improvements shall be embraced in one or more patents, and said, "Some discretion must necessarily be left on this subject to the head of the Patent Office. It is often a nice and perplexing question."

§ 282 *e*. Under the acts of 1836 and 1837, it was made the duty of the commissioner, on the filing of an application for a patent, or a reissue, and the payment of the duty required, to make or cause to be made an examination of the alleged new invention, or the amended specification and claim accompanying the application for a reissue, and to grant such patent or reissue, if all the statutory requirements had been complied with. If the commissioner refuse to receive such application, a *mandamus* will lie to compel him to do so. If the application is in proper form, and the requirements of the statute regulating applications have been complied with, the commissioner is bound to consider the case and render a decision. If, having investigated the subject, the commissioner decides that the claimant is not entitled to a patent or a reissue, such claimant has a remedy by appeal from this decision. A *mandamus*, however, will only lie in case of refusal by the commissioner to act, and cannot be made to perform the functions of a writ of error.

An important case, involving the points under consideration, was decided by the Supreme Court of the United States in 1866.[3] Whiteley, the defendant in error, was the assignee of an exclusive sectional interest in a patent granted in 1855, for an

[1] Morey *v.* Lockwood (1868), 8 Wall. 230.

[2] 8 Wall. 445.

[3] Commissioner of Patents *v.* Whiteley, 4 Wall. 522.

improvement in mowing-machines. In 1863, he applied to the commissioner of patents for a reissue of the patent, without joining the other assignees of interests in the same patent in the application. On the ground that the applicant was not the assignee of the whole interest in the patent, the commissioner declined to entertain the application. He also declined to allow an appeal to be taken from this decision. A writ of *mandamus* was thereupon obtained from the Supreme Court of the District of Columbia, commanding the commissioner "to refer said application to the proper examiner, or otherwise examine or cause the same to be examined according to law." A writ of error was now brought in the Supreme Court of the United States to reverse that order.

Among other things it was contended on the part of the commissioner that no application had been filed in the Patent Office. This position, however, was held by the court to be untenable, as it appeared that the application had been filed with the acting commissioner, and the requisite fees had been paid by the relator; although it further appeared that such fees had not been placed to the credit of the Patent Office, but were in the hands of the chief clerk subject to the relator's order. The court was of the opinion that the relator, by taking these steps, "had done all in his power to make his application effectual, and had a right to consider it properly before the commissioner." It was therefore the duty of the commissioner to examine into the merits of the question, and the status of the applicant. It was his duty to decide whether the applicant was an assignee at all, and, if so, whether he was an assignee with such an interest as entitled him to a reissue within the meaning of the statutory provision upon the subject. The law regulating the action of the commissioner was thus stated by Mr. Justice Swayne, who pronounced the judgment of the court: "It was his first duty to receive the application, whatever he might do subsequently. Without this initial step there could be no examination, and indeed no rightful knowledge of the subject on his part. Examination and the exercise of judgment, with their proper fruit, were to follow, and they did follow.

"The commissioner found the question, whether the assignee was such a one as the law entitled to a reissue, lying at the threshold of his duties. It required an answer before he could proceed further. His decision was against the appellant. His examination of the subject was thorough, and his conclusion is supported by an able and elaborate argument. It was made a part of his reply to the rule, and is found in the record.

"From this decision, whether right or wrong, the relator had a right, under the statute, to appeal.

"If the *mandamus* had ordered the commissioner to allow the appeal, we should have held the order under which it was issued to be correct. But the order was that he should proceed to examine the application. That he had already done. The preliminary question which he decided was as much within the scope of his authority as any other which could arise. Having resolved it in the negative, there was no necessity for him to look further into the case. Entertaining such views, it would have been idle to do so. *The question* was vital to the application, and its resolution was fatal, so far as he was concerned. Only a reversal by the tribunal of appeal could revive it, and cast upon him the duty of further examination."

§ 282 *f*. In the case of Potter *v.* Braunsdorf,[1] it appeared that letters-patent for an improvement in sewing-machines had been granted to John Bachelder, May 8, 1849, for fourteen years. Subsequently Singer and Clark, while owners of the original patent by assignment, surrendered it, and obtained a reissue on the 2d of November, 1858, the specification of such reissue being signed by themselves, but not by Bachelder. This reissue was not assigned to Bachelder. After such assignment and reissue, an application for the extension of the original patent was made by Bachelder, and such extension was granted to him by the commissioner of patents for the term of seven years from May 8, 1863. The original patent, so extended, was reissued to Bachelder, September 22, 1863, and was again reissued to him December 12, 1865.

On this state of facts, it was contended on the part of the defendants that the original patent ceased to exist by the surrender of November 2, 1858, and that, therefore, and until the 8th of May, 1863, only the reissue of the former date was in existence. The extension, therefore, it was asserted, was made after the term of the original patent had expired by such surrender, and was null and void under the eighteenth section of the act of 1836, which provided that "no extension of a patent shall be granted after the expiration of the term for which it was originally issued."

[1] (1869) 7 Blatchf. 97.

This view of the law, however, was not accepted by the court, and the extension was declared to be valid. The court considered that the question had been disposed of by the decision in the case of Potter *v.* Holland.[1] After quoting from the opinion in that case, Mr. Justice Blatchford thus stated the law governing the point under consideration: "These principles and views apply, with especial force, to the case in hand. Where a patentee, having secured his invention by a patent with a specification in such form as he regards to be most proper, assigns the entire patent for the original term only, reserving his right, under the eighteenth section of the act of 1836, to apply for and obtain an extension, it ought not to be, and it is not, in the power of the assignee, by surrendering the patent and obtaining a reissue of it, on a specification not signed, assented to, or adopted by the patentee, and which perhaps the patentee may regard as rendering the reissued patent invalid, or as securing, by new and different claims, rights of little value, to affect, without his consent, the statutory right conferred on the patentee to apply for and obtain an extension of the only patent which he has ever adopted or assented to. The point taken that such right is thus affected is not made with any grace, nor is it entitled to any favor. It is not made in the interest of the assignees, Singer and Clark, who obtained the reissue. They have no interest whatever in the extended term. Their rights expired with the first term. The point is taken in the interest of the infringers, to whom it must be a matter of indifference whether the certificate of extension was made on the original patent, or on the reissue granted to Singer and Clark. As Bachelder did not choose to take advantage of the surrender and reissue, or to ratify or adopt them, he had, after such surrender and reissue, the same rights, in respect to obtaining an extension or prolongation of the original term of fourteen years, under the original patent, that he had before such surrender and reissue. The fact that his assignment to Singer and Clark was of the whole original patent, and not of an undivided part thereof, or of his interest in the same within and throughout a specified part of the United States, can make no difference. He still retained his right to apply for an extension of the original patent, as fully as he would have done if he had conveyed away less than the whole of his interest in the original term. The extended term did not come

[1] 4 Blatchf. 206.

into being until the term granted by the reissue expired, so that the apparent objection does not obtain that there were two patents in existence at the same time for one and the same invention. The inhibition, in the eighteenth section of the act of 1836, against granting an extension after the expiration of the term for which a patent was originally issued, was intended to close the door absolutely, after the fourteen years have expired, against the issuing then of a further seven years' grant. The mischief to be guarded against was, that after the fourteen years had expired, individuals who had relied on such expiration should not be surprised by a grant thereafter of a new term of seven years. In the present case, the fourteen years had not expired when the extension was granted by the certificate referred to. The case of Moffitt *v.* Garr has no application to the present case. There, the patentee himself had surrendered his patent, and the question was whether, after such surrender, he could maintain a suit at law to recover damages for an infringement of the surrendered patent."

§ 283. Mr. Justice Story has held that the statutes which authorize the reissue of a patent because of a defective or redundant specification, without fraud or for the purpose of adding thereto an improvement, do not require the patentee to claim in his renewed patent all things which were claimed in his original patent, but give him the privilege of retaining whatever he deems proper.[1]

[1] Carver *v.* The Braintree Manuf. Co., 2 Story, 438. "The next objection is, that the patentee has omitted some things in his renewed patent which he claimed in his original patent as a part of his invention, viz., the knob, the ridge, and the flaring of the lateral surface of the rib above the saw, and that he claims in his renewed patent the combination of the thickness and the slope of the front and back surfaces of the rib. Now by § 13 of act 1836, c. 357, it is provided, that whenever any patent which is granted 'shall be inoperative or invalid by reason of a defective or insufficient description or specification, or by reason of the patentee claiming in his specification, as his own invention, more than he had or shall have a right to claim as new, if the error shall have arisen by inadvertency, mistake, or accident, and without any fraudulent or deceptive intention, it shall be lawful for the commissioner, upon the surrender to him of such patent, and the payment of the further sum of fifteen dollars, to cause a new patent to be issued to the inventor for the same invention for the residue of the period then unexpired for which the original patent was granted, in accordance with the patentee's corrected description and specification.' And it is afterwards added, that, 'whenever the original patentee shall be desirous of adding the description of any new im-

§ 284. When a patent is thus reissued, it is granted for the unexpired term, commencing from the date of the original patent,

provement of the original invention or discovery which shall have been invented or discovered by him subsequent to the date of his patent, he may, like proceedings being had in all respects as in the case of original applications, and on the payment of fifteen dollars, as hereinbefore provided, have the same annexed to the original description and specification.' Abrogated by act 1861, c. 88, § 9. The act of 1837, c. 45, § 8, further provides, 'that whenever any application shall be made to the commissioner for any addition of a newly discovered improvement to be made to an existing patent, or whenever a patent shall be returned for correction and reissue, the specification annexed to every such patent shall be subject to revision and restriction in the same manner as original applications for patents; the commissioner shall not add any such improvements to the patent in the one case, nor grant the reissue in the other case, until the applicant shall have entered a disclaimer, or altered his specification of claim, in accordance with the decision of the commissioner. Act 1836, c. 357, § 15.

"Now I see nothing in these provisions which, upon a reissue of a patent, requires the patentee to claim all things in the renewed patent which were claimed as his original invention or part of his invention in his original patent. On the contrary, if his original patent claimed too much, or if the commissioner deemed it right to restrict the specification, and the patentee acquiesced therein, it seems to me that in each case the renewed patent, if it claimed less than the original, would be equally valid. A specification may be invalid and unmaintainable under the Patent Act, as well by an excess of claim as by a defect in the mode of stating it. How can the court, in this case, judicially know whether the patentee left out the knob and ridge and flaring of the lateral surface of the rib, in the renewed patent, because he thought they might have a tendency to mislead the public by introducing what, upon further reflection, he deemed immaterial or unessential, and that the patent would thus contain more than was necessary to produce the described effect, and be open to an objection which might be fatal to his right, if it was done to deceive the public. Act 1836, c. 357, § 15. Or, how can the court judicially know that the commissioner did not positively require this very omission? It is certain that he might have given it his sanction. But I incline very strongly to hold a much broader opinion; and that is, that an inventor is always at liberty in a renewed patent to omit a part of his original invention, if he deems it expedient, and to retain that part only of his original invention which he deems fit to retain. No harm is done to the public by giving up a part of what he has actually invented, for the public may then use it; and there is nothing in the policy or terms of the Patent Act which prohibits such a restriction.

"The other part of the objection seems to me equally untenable. If the description of the combination of the thickness and the slope of the front and back surfaces of the rib were a part of the plaintiff's original invention (as the objection itself supposes), and were not fully stated in the original speci-

which is surrendered. Consequently, it operates from the commencement of the original, and will enure to the benefit of assignees who became such before the reissue, although no assignment is made to them after the reissue.[1]

fication, that is exactly such a defect as the Patent Acts allow to be remedied. A specification may be defective, not only in omitting to give a full description of the mode of constructing a machine, but also in omitting to describe fully in the claim the nature and extent and character of the invention itself. Indeed, this latter is the common defect, for which most renewed patents are granted."

[1] Woodworth *v.* Stone, 3 Story, 749; Woodworth *v.* Hall, 1 Woodb. & Minot, 248. Both of these cases related to the same patent. In the first, Mr. Justice Story said: "If the present case had stood merely upon the original bill, it appears to me clear, that the motion to dissolve the injunction granted upon that bill, ought to prevail, because, by the surrender of the patent, upon which that bill is founded, the right to maintain the same would be entirely gone. I agree that it is not in the power of the patentee, by a surrender of his patent, to affect the rights of third persons, to whom he has previously, by assignment, passed his interest in the whole or a part of the patent, without the consent of such assignees. But here the supplemental bill admits that the assignees, who are parties to the original and supplemental bill, have consented to such a surrender. They have, therefore, adopted it; and it became theirs in the same manner as if it had been their personal act, and done by their authority.

"The question, then, is precisely the same as if the suit were now solely in behalf of the patentee. In order to understand with clearness and accuracy some of the objections to the continuance of the injunction, it may be necessary to state, that the original patent to William Woodworth (the inventor), who is since deceased, was granted on the 27th of December, 1838. Subsequently, under the eighteenth section of the act of 1836, c. 357, the commissioner of patents, on the 16th of November, 1842, recorded the patent in favor of William W. Woodworth, the administrator of William Woodworth (the inventor), for seven years, from the 27th of December, 1842. Congress, by an act passed at the last session (act of 26th of February, c. 27), extended the time of the patent for seven years, from and after the 27th of December, 1849 (to which time the renewed patent extended); and the commissioner of patents was directed to make a certificate of such extension in the name of the administrator of William Woodworth (the inventor), and to append an authenticated copy thereof to the original letters-patent, whenever the same shall be requested by the said administrator or his assigns. The commissioner of patents, accordingly, on the 3d of March, 1845, at the request of the administrator, made such certificate on the original patent. On the 8th day of July, 1845, the administrator surrendered the renewed patent granted to him, 'on account of a defect in the specification.' The surrender was accepted, and a new patent was granted on the same day to the administrator, reciting the preceding facts, and that the surrender was 'on account of a defective specification,' and declaring that the

When a patentee is about to apply for a renewal of his patent, and agrees with another person that, in case of success, he will

new patent was extended for fourteen years, from the 27th December, 1826, 'in trust for the heirs at law of the said W. Woodworth (the inventor), their heirs, administrators, or assigns.'

"Now, one of the objections taken to the new patent is, that it is for the term of fourteen years, and not for the term of seven years, or for two successive terms of seven years. But it appears to me that this objection is not well founded, and stands *inter Apices juris;* for the new patent should be granted for the whole term of fourteen years, from the 27th of December, and the legal effect is the same as it would be if the patent was specifically renewed for two successive terms of seven years. The new patent is granted for the unexpired term only, from the date of the grant, viz., for the unexpired period existing on the 8th of July, 1845, by reference to the original grant in December, 1828. It is also suggested, that the patent ought not to have been in trust for the heirs at law of the said W. Woodworth, their heirs, administrators, or assigns. But this is, at most, a mere verbal error, if indeed it has any validity whatsoever; for the new patent will, by operation of law, enure to the sole benefit of the parties in whose favor the law designed it should operate, and not otherwise. It seems to me that the case is directly within the purview of the tenth and thirteenth sections of the act of 1836, c. 357, taking into consideration their true intent and objects.

"Another objection urged against the continuation of the injunction is, that the breach of the patent assigned in the original bill can have no application to the new patent, and there is no ground to suggest, that, since the injunction was granted, there has been any new breach of the old patent, or any breach of the new patent. But it is by no means necessary that any such new breach should exist. The case is not like that of an action at law for the breach of a patent, to support which it is indispensable to establish a breach before the suit was brought. But in a suit in equity the doctrine is far otherwise. A bill will lie for an injunction, if the patent right is admitted, or has been established upon well-grounded proof of an apprehended intention of the defendant to violate the patent-right. A bill, *quia timet*, is an ordinary remedial process in equity. Now, the injunction already granted (supposing both patents to be for the same invention) is *primâ facie* evidence of an intended violation, if not of an actual violation."

In the last case, Mr. Justice Woodbury said: "The original patent for fourteen years, given in December, 1828, expired in 1842, and though it was extended by the board for seven years more, which would last till 1849, and by Congress for seven more, which would not expire till 1856, yet all of these patents were surrendered July 8th, 1845, and a new one taken out for the whole twenty-eight years from December, 1828. This was done, also, with some small amendments or corrections in the old specification of 1828. After these new letters-patent for the whole term, no assignment having been made to Washburn and Brown, but only one previously on the 2d of January, 1843, the plaintiffs contend that all the previous letters being surrendered, and a new specification filed, and new letters issued, any conveyance of any interest

assign to him the renewed patent; and the patent is renewed, such an agreement is valid, and conveys to the assignee an equitable title, which can be converted into a legal title by paying or offering to pay the stipulated consideration.[1]

§ 285. The Supreme Court of the United States have decided, upon great consideration, that the commissioner of patents can lawfully receive a surrender of letters-patent for a defective specification, and issue new letters-patent upon an amended specification, after the expiration of the term for which the original term was granted, and pending the existence of an extended term of seven years. Such surrender and renewal may be made at any time during such extended term.[2]

§ 286. Specifications may also be amended by another process, that of filing a disclaimer, whenever through inadvertency, accident, or mistake, the original claim was too broad, claiming more than that of which the patentee was the original or first inventor, provided some material and substantial part of the thing patented is justly and truly his own. Such a disclaimer may be filed in

under the old letters is inoperative and void under the new ones; and hence that Washburn and Brown possess no interest in these last, and are improperly joined in the bill.

"But my impression, as at present advised, is, that when a patent has been surrendered, and new letters are taken out with an amended specification, the patent has been always considered to operate, except as to suits for violations committed before the amendment, from the commencement of the original term. The amendment is not because the former patent or specification was utterly void, as seems to be the argument, but was defective or doubtful in some particular, which it was expedient to make more clear. But it is still a patent for the same invention. It can by law include no new one, and it covers only the same term of time which the former patent and its extensions did.

"In the present case, these are conceded to have been the facts; and it is an error to suppose that on such facts the new letters ought to operate only from their date. By the very words of those letters, no less than by the reasons of the case as just explained, they relate back to the commencement of the original term, and for many purposes should operate from that time."

[1] Hartshorn *et al.* *v.* Day, 19 How. 211.

[2] Wilson *v.* Rousseau, 4 How. 646. See also Gibson *v.* Harris, 1 Blatchf. 167; Woodworth *v.* Edwards, 3 Woodb. & Minot, 120. If a new patent, issued on surrender of an old one, be void for any cause connected with the acts of public officers, it is questionable whether the original patent must not be considered in force till its term had expired. Woodworth *v.* Hall, 1 Woodb. & Minot, 389.

the Patent Office by the patentee, his administrators, executors, and assigns, whether of the whole or of a sectional interest in the patent; and it will thereafter be taken and considered as part of the original specification, to the extent of the interest of the disclaimant in the patent, and by those claiming by or under him, subsequent to the record thereof.[1]

§ 287. Patents are sometimes extended by special acts of Congress, passed upon the application of the patentees. By the act of July 4, 1836, c. 357, § 18, the Secretary of State, the Commissioner of the Patent Office, and the Solicitor of the Treasury were constituted a board of commissioners to hear evidence for and against the extension prayed for, and to decide whether, having due regard to the public interest therein, it is just and proper that the term of the patent should be extended, because the patentee has failed to obtain a reasonable remuneration. The commissioners being satisfied that the patent ought to be renewed, it was m de the duty of the commissioner of patents to make a certificate on the original patent, showing that it is extended for a further term of seven years from the expiration of the first term.

By the act of 1848, c. 47, § 1, this power was vested solely in the commissioner of patents, who was thereby required to refer the appl cation to the principal examiner, having charge of the class of inventions to wh ch the case belongs, and, upon his report, to grant or refuse the patent, upon the same principles and rules that had governed the board provided by the former act.

But the act of 1861, c. 88, § 16, enacted, "That all patents *hereafter* granted shall remain in force for the term of *seventeen* years from the date of issue; and all extension of such patents is hereby prohibited." The operation of the statute is that all patents granted after the passage of the act of 1861 are incapable of being extended, except by special act of Congress, while patents granted before that date may still be extended on application to the commissioner. It therefore remains of importance to ascer-

[1] Act of 1837, c. 45, § 7; act of 1870, § 54; Tuck *v.* Bramhill (1868), 3 Fisher's Pat. Cas. 400; Aiken *v.* Dolan, ibid. 197. As to the effect of a disclaimer, see chapter on Action at Law.

"A disclaimer cannot work in favor of an assignee, without his having joined in it, in any suit, either at law or in equity." Per Story, J., in Wyeth *v.* Stone, 1 Story, 273.

tain the construction passed by the courts upon the action of the commissioner in granting an extension, whether and to what extent the same is examinable elsewhere.

Upon this point Judge Curtis, in Clum *v*. Brewer, ruled as follows: "Of all matters necessary to an extension there is not only a strong presumption arising from the act of extension, but in respect to the entire merits of the patentee, and the existence of the legal grounds for an extension, the law makes the commissioner the judge, and in the absence of fraud his adjudication is conclusive."[1] Similar language is employed by Judge Nelson in his decision in the case of Colt *v*. Young.[2] In an earlier case it was held that the decision of the Board of Commissioners of Extension, while conclusive as to the matter of expense, the payment of the money required, and the notice, was not conclusive as to the question of law, whether or not an administrator had a right under the act of 1836 to apply for an extension.[3]

§ 287 *a*. Section sixty-three of the act of 1870 provides: "That where the patentee of any invention or discovery, the patent for which was granted prior to the second day of March, eighteen hundred and sixty-one, shall desire an extension of his patent beyond the original term of its limitation, he shall make application therefor, in writing, to the commissioner, setting forth the reasons why such extension should be granted; and he shall also furnish a written statement under oath of the ascertained value of the invention or discovery, and of his receipts and expenditures on account thereof, sufficiently in detail to exhibit a true and faithful account of the loss and profit in any manner accruing to him by reason of said invention or discovery. And said application shall be filed not more than six months nor less than ninety days before the expiration of the original term of the patent, and no extension shall be granted after the expiration of said original term."

Upon the receipt of such application, and the payment of the duty required by law, it is made the duty of the commissioner to "cause to be published in one newspaper in the city of Washington, and in such other papers published in the section of the

[1] Clum *v*. Brewer, 2 Curtis, C. C. 506.

[2] Colt *v*. Young, 2 Blatchf. 471.

[3] Brooks *et al*. *v*. Bicknell *et al*., 3 M'Lean, 250; Crompton *v*. Belknap Mills, 3 Fisher's Pat. Cas. 536. See *supra*, § 282 *a*.

country most interested adversely to the extension of the patent as he may deem proper, for at least sixty days prior to the day set for hearing the case, a notice of such application, and of the time and place when and where the same will be considered, that any person may appear and show cause why the extension should not be granted." [1]

On the publication of such notice, the commissioner is required to refer the case to the principal examiner having charge of the class of inventions to which it belongs, who shall make to said commissioner a full report of the case, and particularly whether the invention or discovery was new and patentable when the original patent was granted.

It then becomes the duty of the commissioner to "hear and decide upon the evidence produced, both for and against the extension; and if it shall appear to his satisfaction that the patentee, without neglect or fault on his part, has failed to obtain from the use and sale of his invention or discovery a reasonable remuneration for the time, ingenuity, and expense bestowed upon it, and the introduction of it into use, and that it is just and proper, having due regard to the public interest, that the term of the patent should be extended, the said commissioner shall make a certificate thereon, renewing and extending the said patent for the term of seven years, from the expiration of the first term, which certificate shall be recorded in the Patent Office, and thereupon the said patent shall have the same effect in law as though it had been originally granted for twenty-one years."

By section sixty-seven the benefit of the extension of a patent is extended to the assignees and grantees of the right to use the thing patented, to the extent of their interest therein.

In Jordan *v.* Dobson,[2] it was held that Congress has power to authorize, by special act, the extension of a patent, notwithstanding the fact that the original patent has previously expired, and the invention has been introduced to public use.

[1] § 64. [2] 2 Abbott's U. S. Rep. § 398.

CHAPTER VIII.

INFRINGEMENT.

§ 288. THE statute grants to the patentee, for a term not exceeding fourteen years, "the full and exclusive right and liberty of making, using, and vending to others to be used, the invention or discovery";[1] and it gives a right of action for damages, in case of "making, using, or selling" the thing patented.[2] No definition of what is to constitute an infringement is given in the statute; but, of course, there is an infringement of the right, when one "makes, uses, or sells a thing" which another has the exclusive right of "making, using, and vending to others to be used." But what constitutes making, using, and selling, with reference to the various things that may be the subjects of patents, so as to interfere with the exclusive right of the patentee, is left by the statute for judicial interpretation.

§ 289. An infringement takes place whenever a party avails himself of the invention of the patentee, without such variation as will constitute a new discovery;[3] or, as it has also been stated,

[1] Act of July 4, 1836, c. 357, § 5.

[2] Ibid. § 14.

[3] In Walton *v.* Potter, Webs. Pat. Cas. 585, 586, Sir N. C. Tindall, C. J., said to the jury: "Now, according to the general rule upon this subject, that is a mere question of fact, and peculiarity for the consideration of a jury, and it will be for you to say, under the circumstances that have been brought in review before you, whether that which has been done by the defendants amounts to such an infringement or not. Where a party has obtained a patent for a new invention or a discovery he has made by his own ingenuity, it is not in the power of any other person, simply by varying in form or in immaterial circumstances the nature or subject-matter of that discovery, to obtain either a patent for it himself, or to use it without the leave of the patentee, because that would be in effect and in substance an invasion of the right; and therefore, what you have to look at upon the present occasion, is not simply whether, in form or in circumstances that may be more or less

an infringement is a copy made after and agreeing with the principle laid down in the specification.[1] There will be therefore different modes in which patents may be infringed, according to their subject-matter. Our statute has made use of the phrases "making, using, and vending to others to be used," to comprehend the exclusive right of the patentee; and consequently the making, using, or selling are the modes in which that right may be infringed, according to the nature of the subject-matter. We are now, therefore, to consider the meaning of these phrases, as applied to the infringement of the several classes of things which may be the subjects of letters-patent.

In a recent case it was held, after an elaborate discussion, "That the rights of property and exclusive use granted to a patentee do not extend to a foreign vessel lawfully entering one of our ports; and that the use of such improvement in the construction, fitting out, or equipment of such vessel, while she is coming into or going out of a port of the United States, is not an infringement of the rights of an American patentee, provided it

immaterial, that which has been done by the defendants varies from the specification of the plaintiff's patent, but to see whether in reality, in substance, and in effect, the defendants have availed themselves of the plaintiff's invention in order to make that fabric, or to make that article which they have sold in the way of their trade; whether, in order to make that, they have availed themselves of the invention of the plaintiff. The course which the evidence has taken has made it not an immaterial, but, on the contrary, a very necessary inquiry for you upon this first head of investigation, to determine whether the defendant's patent, which they have taken out, is in effect borrowed from the plaintiff's or not, because there can be no doubt whatever that all the defendants have done they have endeavored to clothe themselves with the right of doing by taking out the subsequent patent of 1839. The only evidence of infringement we have had before us is the purchase at the manufactory of the defendants of that little piece of card which was marked with the initials S. G., and there can be no doubt but that that fabric, which was so produced in evidence before us, is made on the plan and according to the specification of their own patent, and therefore it will be not immaterial to call to your attention upon this first head of inquiry the specification of the plaintiff's, and next that of the defendant's patent, in order that we may compare them together, and see whether there really is that variation in substance so as to give the denomination of a new discovery to what the defendants have done, or whether they are not following out the invention of the plaintiff, with some variation in the description, which may not allow it the name of a new discovery."

[1] Galloway *v.* Bleaden, Webs. Pat. Cas. 523.

was placed upon her in a foreign port and authorized by the laws of the country to which she belongs."[1]

§ 290. 1. *As to a Machine.*—When a machine is the subject of a patent, the patent covers both the machine itself, the thing invented, and the mode or process of making it. The statute vests in the patentee the exclusive right of making it, the exclusive right of using it, and the exclusive right of vending it to others to be used. It is, therefore, an infringement to make a patented machine, for use or for sale, though in fact it is neither used nor sold;[2] it is an infringement to use it, though made by

[1] Browne *v.* Duchesne, 19 How. 183, per Taney, C. J.; affirming the previous opinion of Curtis, J., in same case, 2 Curtis, C. C. 371. This opinion is directly opposed to that laid down in the English case of Caldwell *v.* Van Vliessingen, 9 E. L. & Eq. 51, which however, according to Taney, C. J., turned upon the construction given to 32 Hen. VIII. c. 16, § 9.

[2] Whittemore *v.* Cutter, 1 Gallis. 429, 433. In this case, Mr. Justice Story said: "Another objection is to the direction that the making of a machine fit for use, and with a design to use it for profit, was an infringement of the patent right, for which an action was given by the statute. This limitation of the making was certainly favorable to the defendant, and it was adopted by the court, from the consideration that it never could have been the intention of the legislature to punish a man who constructed such a machine merely for philosophical experiments, or for the purpose of ascertaining the sufficiency of the machine to produce its described effects. It is now contended by the defendant's counsel, that the making of a machine is, under no circumstances, an infringement of the patent. The first section of the act of 1793 expressly gives to the patentee, &c., 'the full and exclusive right and liberty of making, constructing, using, and vending to others to be used,' the invention or discovery. The fifth section of the same act gives an action against any person who 'shall make, devise, and use *or* sell,' the same. From some doubt whether the language of the section did not couple the making and *using* together to constitute an offence, so that making without using, or using without making, was not an infringement, the legislature saw fit to repeal that section; and by the third section of the act of 17th April, 1800, c. 25, gave the action against any person who should "make, devise, use, or sell" the invention. We are not called upon to examine the correctness of the original doubt, but the very change in the structure of the sentence affords a strong presumption that the legislature intended to make every one of the enumerated acts a substantive ground of action. It is argued, however, that the words are to be construed distributively, and that 'making' is meant to be applied to the case of a *composition* of matter, and not to the case of a machine. That it is clear that the use of certain compositions (as patented pills) could not be an infringement, and unless making were so, there would be no remedy in such cases. We cannot feel the force of this distinction. The word 'making' is equally as applicable to machines as to compositions

another; and it is an infringement to sell it, whether made by one's self or by another; because the statute vests the exclusive right of doing all these things in the patentee.

A mere workman, however, employed by one who is not the patentee to make parts of the patented machine, is not liable for damages.[1]

§ 291. The doctrine suggested by Mr. Justice Story, that the making of a machine for philosophical experiment, or for the purpose of ascertaining its sufficiency to produce the described effect, would not be an infringement, is founded in the supposition that such a making is not injurious to the patentee. It is true, that the making for the purpose of using becomes directly injurious to the patentee, because it deprives him of a purchaser of that which he alone is authorized to construct and sell; and it is also true, that when the machine is made by one not the patentee, for the mere purpose of experimenting on the sufficiency of the specification, no profits are taken away from the patentee. There is therefore a difference, undoubtedly, in the tendency of the two acts; but it is not quite clear, that the legislature meant to recognize this difference, or that they used the words "make, use," &c., in any other than their ordinary sense. The prohibition is express, that no other person shall "make"; and that no other person shall "use"; and Mr. Justice Washington held that the motive of testing the practical utility of a machine was no answer to a charge of infringement by having "used" it.[2] But it was held by Mr. Justice Story that the making of a patented machine is an infringement only when it is made for use or for sale, and the doctrine seems to be the same in England.[3]

of matter; and we see no difficulty in holding that the using or vending of a patented composition is a violation of the right of the proprietor. It is further argued, that the making of a machine cannot be an offence, because no action lies, except for *actual damage*, and there can be no actual damages, or even a rule for damages, for an infringement by making a machine. We are, however, of opinion, that where the law gives an action for a particular act, the doing of that act imports of itself a damage to the party. Every violation of a right imports some damage, and if none other be proved, the law allows a nominal damage."

[1] Delano *v.* Scott, 1 Gilpin, 489.

[2] Watson *v.* Bladen, 4 Wash. 583.

[3] In Jones *v.* Pearce, Webs. Pat. Cas. 125, Patteson, J., said, in reply to a question by the jury whether there was any evidence of the defendant having

The test is, whether the party made the machine with an intent to infringe the patent right, and deprive the owner of the lawful rewards of his discovery.[1]

§ 292. It is said that there may be a constructive using of a patented machine: as, if a person were to make a machine, in violation of the right of the patentee, or purchase it of one who had so made it, and then hire it out to another person for use, he might, under some circumstances, be held responsible for using it. There is a case, where the plaintiff was the patentee of a machine for making watch-chains, and it appeared that the defendant had made an agreement with one C. to purchase of him all the watch-chains, not exceeding five gross a week, which C. might be able to manufacture within six months, and C. had agreed to devote his whole time and attention to the manufacture of watch-chains, and not to sell or dispose of any of them, so as to interfere with the exclusive privilege secured to the defendant of purchasing the whole quantity which it might be practicable for C. to make; and it was proved that the machine used by C., with the knowledge and consent of the defendant, in the manufacture, was the same with that invented by the plaintiff, and that all the watch-chains thus made by C. were delivered to the defendant according to the contract; the Supreme Court of the United States held, that if the contract were real and not colorable, and if the defendant had no other connection with C. than that which grew out of the contract, it did not amount to a "using" by him of the plaintiff's machine; but that such a contract, connected with evidence from which the jury might legally infer, either that the machine which was to be employed in the manufacture of the patented article was owned wholly or in part by the defendant, or that it was hired by the defendant for six months, under color of a sale of the articles to be manufactured with it, and with intent to invade the plaintiff's patent right, would amount to a breach of his right.[2]

used or sold the wheels: "The terms of the patent are, 'without leave or license make,' &c. Now if he did actually make these wheels, his making them would be a sufficient infringement of the patent, unless he merely made them for his own amusement, or as a model."

[1] Sawin *v.* Guild, 1 Gallis. 485, 487.

[2] Keplinger *v.* De Young, 10 Wheaton, 358, 363. Washington, J., delivring the judgment of the court, said: "The only question which is pre-

§ 293. It seems to be in accordance with the doctrine of this case, to consider that a using of a machine is to be taken as

sented by the bill of exceptions to the consideration of this court, is, whether the court below erred in the instruction given to the jury; and this must depend upon the correct construction of the third section of the act of Congress, of the 17th of April, 1800, c. 179, which enacts, 'that where any patent shall be granted, pursuant to the act of the 21st of February, 1793, c. 156, any person without the consent of the patentee, his executors, &c., first obtained in writing, shall make, devise, use, or sell the thing whereof the exclusive right is secured to the said patentee, by such patent, such person so offending shall forfeit and pay to the said patentee a sum equal to three times the actual damage sustained by such patentee,' &c.

"The contract, taken in connection with the whole of the evidence stated in the bill of exceptions, if the same were believed by the jury, formed most certainly a strong case against the defendant, sufficient to have warranted the jury in inferring either that the machine which was to be employed in the manufacture of watch-chains was owned in whole or in part by the defendant, or that it was hired to the defendant for six months under color of a sale of the articles which might be manufactured with it, and with intent to invade the plaintiff's patent right. Whether the contract, taken in connection with the whole of the evidence, does or does not amount to a hiring by the defendant of the machine, or the use of it for six months, is a point which is not to be considered as being decided either way by the court. The bill of exceptions does not call for an opinion upon it.

"But the contract taken by itself amounted to no more than an agreement by the defendant to purchase at a fixed price all the watch-chains, not exceeding five gross a week, which Hatch and Kirkner might be able to manufacture in the course of six months, with any machine they might choose to employ; and an agreement on the part of Hatch and Kirkner, to devote their whole time and attention to the manufacture of the chains, and not to sell or dispose of any of them, so as to interfere with the exclusive privilege secured to the defendant, of purchasing the whole quantity which it might be practicable for them to make.

"If this contract was real, and not colorable, which is the obvious meaning of the instruction, and the defendant had no other connection with H. & K. in regard to these chains than what grew out of it, it would, in the opinion of the court, be an extravagant construction of the patent law, to pronounce that it amounted to a breach of the plaintiff's patent right, by fixing upon the defendant the charge of having used the plaintiff's machine. Such a construction would be highly inconvenient and unjust to the rest of the community, since it might subject any man who might innocently contract with a manufacturer to purchase all the articles which he might be able to make within a limited period, to the heavy penalty inflicted by the act, although he might have been ignorant of the plaintiff's patent, or that a violation of it would be the necessary consequence of the contract. It might possibly extend further, and affect contracts express or implied, though of a more limited

proved, either when the party charged has used it himself or has employed others to use it for him, or has profited by the use of it.[1]

character, but equally innocent, as to which, however, it is not the intention of the court to express any opinion, as this case does not call for it.

"This cause was argued by the plaintiff's counsel, as if the opinion of the court below had been given upon the whole of the evidence. But this was not the case. No instruction was asked for but by the defendant's counsel, and that was confined to a single part of the case, the connection between the defendant and H. & K. in regard to the watch-chains which the latter bound themselves, by their contract, to manufacture and deliver to the former. If the jury had been of opinion, upon the whole of the evidence, that the contract was not a real one, or that that instrument did not constitute the sole connection between those parties, or that the transaction was merely colorable, with a view to evade the law, the jury were not precluded by the instruction from considering the plaintiff's patent right as violated, and finding a verdict accordingly.

"Had the plaintiff's counsel thought proper to call upon the court for an opinion and instruction to the jury, upon any points arising out of the whole or any part of the evidence, it would have been their duty to give an opinion upon such points, leaving the conclusion of fact from the evidence to be drawn by the jury. But this course not having been pursued, this court can take no notice of the evidence, although spread upon the record, except so far as it is connected with the single point upon which the opinion, which is excepted to, was given. As to the residue of that opinion, that 'the legal aspect of the case would not be changed, although the defendant might, on any occasion, have supplied, at the cost of H. & K., the wire from which the chains so manufactured were made,' it is quite as free from objection as the preceding part of it, since it stands on precisely the same principle."

[1] Woodworth *v.* Hall, 1 Woodb. & M. 248, 251. In this case Mr. Justice Woodbury said: "There has been no evidence whatever offered in this case of any use of the planing-machine by Isaac Hall since his license expired, except what is contained in the affidavit of Aaron Pratt. This witness did not see him use it; but made a bargain with him, about the 15th of July, 1845, to plane for the witness certain boards at the ordinary price, intending to set off the amount against rent due from said Isaac.

"Clement Hall, however, was present, and said, 'we can plane them for you,' and the work was done; but the witness does not say by whom, nor whether in fact the compensation for it was made to Isaac.

"Against this is the answer of Isaac, responsive to the bill, and sworn to, denying that he had ever used the machine since his license expired; and this agrees with Clement's assertion in his answer, that the machine was used by him alone. The facts testified by Pratt might, standing alone, be sufficient to justify an inference that Isaac had planed the boards and used the machine.

"In such cases it may be that any workman on the machine, though not interested in it, is liable to be restrained in order to prevent evasions, by treating all as principals who are aiding.

§ 294. As to the sale of a patented machine, in order to be an infringement of the right, it must be something more than a sale of the materials, either separate or combined; it must be a sale of a complete machine, for use as a machine, which is patented, in order to render the vendor liable for an infringement of the patent by a "sale." [1]

"It is a common case, also, that if one does not in person perform the work, but procures another to do it for his advantage on a machine owned by himself, he can still be restrained, and is estopped from denying, *qui facit per alium, facit per se.* Possibly, too, if one hires another to do work on such a machine, he may be restrained. 4 Mann. & Gran. 179. But it is not necessary to give a decisive opinion on this, after comparing the evidence with the denial in Isaac's sworn answer.

"After that answer thus testified to as true, the probability is, and it is a construction not inconsistent with the veracity of both Pratt and Isaac, that the boards were planed by Clement alone, and on his own contract, or his own assent to the arrangement, and for his own profit. It would seem also very easy to produce further evidence of the fact of Isaac's using the machine, or receiving the profits from it, if such was the truth. Until it is produced, the fairest construction of the affidavits and answer are, that Isaac did not work the machine or profit by it. If this construction were not the most reasonable, and did not reconcile what is sworn to in the affidavit and answers, the court would still be compelled to refuse to issue an injunction against Isaac, on the affidavit of Pratt alone, for the want of evidence in it to overcome Isaac's answer. Because something more must be produced than the evidence of a single witness to overcome an answer under oath, and responsive to the bill. Carpenter *v.* Prov. Wash. Ins. Co., 4 How. 185. Certainly something more than the evidence of one witness, and he not testifying explicitly that Isaac either owned or worked the machine, or received any of its profits.

"But in respect to the liability of Clement to an injunction, the testimony is very different; and notwithstanding the several ingenious objections that have been urged, I have come to the conclusion that one ought to be issued against him."

[1] A sale of the materials of a patented machine by a sheriff, on execution, is not an infringement. Sawin *v.* Guild, 1 Gallis. 485. In this case, Mr. Justice Story said: "This is an action on the case for the infringement of a patent right of the plaintiffs, obtained in February, 1811, for a machine for cutting brad nails. From the statement of facts agreed by the parties, it appears that defendant is a deputy-sheriff of the county of *Norfolk*, and having an execution in his hands against the plaintiffs for the sum of $567.27 debt, and costs, by virtue of his office seized and sold on said execution the *materials* of three of said patented machines, which were at the time complete and fit for operation, and belonged to the plaintiffs. The purchaser, at the sheriff's sale, has not, at any time since, put either of the said machines in operation; and the whole infringement of the patent consists in the seizure and sale by the defendant as aforesaid. The question submitted to the court

§ 295. The sale of the articles produced by a patented machine, or by a process which is patented, is not an infringement.[1]

is, whether the complete materials, of which a patented machine is composed, can, while such machine is in operation by the legal owner, be seized and sold on an execution against him?

"The plaintiffs contend that it cannot be so seized and sold, and they rely on the language of the third section of the act of the 17th of April, 1800, c. 25, which declares that if 'any person, without the consent of the patentee, his or her executors, &c., first obtained in writing, shall make, devise, use, or *sell* the thing, whereof the exclusive right is secured to the said patentee, such person, so offending, shall forfeit,' &c.

"It is a sound rule of law, that every statute is to have a sensible construction; and its language is not to be interpreted so as to introduce public mischiefs, or manifest incongruities, unless the conclusion be unavoidable. If the plaintiffs are right in their construction of the section above stated, it is practicable for a party to lock up his whole property, however great, from the grasp of his creditors, by investing it in profitable patented machines. This would undoubtedly be a great public mischief, and against the whole policy of the law, as to the levy of personal property in execution. And upon the same construction this consequence would follow, that every part of the materials of the machine might, when separated, be seized in execution, and yet the whole could not be, when united; for the exemption from seizure is claimed only when the whole is combined and in actual operation under the patent.

"We should not incline to adopt such a construction unless we could give no other reasonable meaning to the statute. By the laws of *Massachusetts*, property like this is not exempted from seizure in execution; and an officer, who neglected to seize, would expose himself to an action for damages, unless some statute of the *United States* should contain a clear exception. No such express exception can be found; and it is inferred to exist only by supposing that the officer would, by *the sale*, make himself a wrong-doer, within the clause of the statute above recited. But, within the very words of that clause, it would be no offence to *seize* the machine in execution. The whole offence must consist in a *sale*. It would therefore follow, that the officer might lawfully seize; and if so, it would be somewhat strange if he could not proceed to do those acts which alone by law could make his seizure effectual.

"This court has already had occasion to consider the clause in question, and upon mature deliberation it has held, that *the making* of a patented machine, to be an offence within the purview of it, must be the making with an intent to use for profit, and not for the mere purpose of philosophical experiment, or to ascertain the verity and exactness of the specification. Whittemore *v.* Cutter, 1 Gallis. p. 429. In other words, that the making must be

---

[1] Boyd *v.* Brown, 3 McLean's R. 295. "The complainant filed his bill, representing that he is the legal owner of a certain patent right, within the

But where the specification, although clumsily worded, still contains in substance and intendment a claim for both process

with an intent to infringe the patent right, and deprive the owner of the lawful rewards of his discovery.

"In the present case, we think that a sale of a patented machine, within the prohibitions of the same clause, must be a sale, not of the materials of a machine, either separate or combined, but of a complete machine, with the right, express or implied, of using the same in the manner secured by the patent. It must be a tortious sale, not for the purpose merely of depriving the owner of the materials, but of the use and benefit of his patent. There is no pretence, in the case before us, that the officer had either sold or guaranteed a right to use the machine in the manner pointed out in the patent right. He sold the *materials* as such, to be applied by the purchaser as he should by law have a right to apply them. The purchaser must therefore act at his own peril, but in no respect can the officer be responsible for his conduct."

---

county of Hamilton, in Ohio, for making bedsteads of a particular construction, which is of great value to him ; that the defendant, professing to have a right under the same patent, to make and vend bedsteads in Dearborn County, Indiana, which the complainant does not admit, but denies ; that the defendant sends the bedsteads he manufactures to Hamilton County to sell, in violation of the complainant's patent ; and he prays that the defendant may be enjoined from manufacturing the article, and vending it within Hamilton County, &c.

"The defendant sets up in his answer a right duly assigned to him to make and vend the article in Indiana, and that he is also possessed of an improvement on the same ; and he denies that the sales in Hamilton County, complained of by the complainant, are made at his instance or for his benefit. A motion is now made for an injunction, before the case is prepared for a final hearing.

"On the part of the complainant, it is contended that, by his purchase of the right to make and vend the article within Hamilton County, he has an exclusive right to vend as well as to make, and that his right is infringed by the sales complained of ; that his right is notorious, and is not only known to the defendant, but to all those who are engaged in the sales stated. If the defendant, who manufactures the bedsteads in Indiana, be actually engaged in the sale of them in Hamilton County, it might be necessary to inquire whether this is a violation of the complainant's right. But, as this fact is denied in the defendant's answer, for the purposes of this motion, the answer must be taken as true, and that question is not necessarily involved.

"The point for consideration is, whether the right of the complainant is infringed by a sale of the article within the limits of the territory claimed by the complainant. It is not difficult to answer this question. We think that the article may be sold at any and every place, by any one who has purchased it for speculation or otherwise.

"There can be no doubt that the original patentee, in selling rights for

and product, the sale or use of the manufactured article will constitute *per se* an infringement. Thus it was held by Mr. Justice Grier, that "the sale or use of the product of a patented machine is no violation of the exclusive right to use, construct, or sell the machine itself; and the patent for a discovery of a new and improved process, by which any product or manufacture before known in commerce may be made in a better and cheaper manner, grants nothing but the exclusive right to use the process. Where a known manufacture or product is in the market, purchasers are not bound to inquire whether it was made on a patented machine or by a patented process. But if the patentee be the inventor or discoverer of a "new manufacture or composition of matter not known or used by others before his discovery or invention," it is clear that his franchise or sole right to use and vend to others to be used is the new composition or substance itself. The product and the process constitute one discovery, the exclusive right to vend which, for a limited term, is secured to the inventor or discoverer. Now, what is this India-rubber, cured substantially as described in Mr. Goodyear's description? It is clearly not merely an improved method or process of producing an old and well-known composition or material, but it is a new product, fabric, manufacture, or composition of matter, having qualities possessed by no other known material. This is

counties or states, might, by a special covenant, prohibit the assignee from vending the article beyond the limits of his own exclusive right. But in such a case, the remedy would be on contract, and not under the patent law. For that law protects the thing patented, and not the product. The exclusive right to make and use the instruments for the construction of this bedstead in Hamilton County is what the law secures, under his assignment, to the complainant. Any one violates this right who either makes, uses, or sells these instruments within the above limits. But the bedstead, which is the product, so soon as it is sold, mingles with the common mass of property, and is only subject to the general laws of property.

"An individual has a patent right for constructing and using a certain flouring-mill. Now, his exclusive right consists in the construction and use of the mill; the same as the right of the complainant to construct and use the instruments in Hamilton County, by which the bedstead is made. But can the patentee of the mill prohibit others from selling flour in his district? Certainly he could not. The advantage derived from his right is, or may be, the superior quality of the flour, and the facility with which it is manufactured. And this sufficiently illustrates the principle involved in this motion." See, further, Simpson *v.* Wilson, 4 How. 709.

what is described and claimed in the patent, — a new product as well as a new process. The product and process being both new and proper subjects of a patent, the patentee has a right to prohibit the sale or use of the composition, unless when purchased from persons licensed by him to use the process and vend the product."[1]

§ 296. But if the person who sells is connected with the use of the machine, he is responsible as for an infringement; and if a court of equity have jurisdiction of the person, such a vendor may be enjoined, although the machine may be used beyond the jurisdiction of the court.[2]

[1] Goodyear *v.* R. R., 2 Wallace, C. C. R. 356. As to the specification in question, and its construction, see *supra*, chapter on Specification. With regard to the matter of infringement of the process claimed in this patent, see *infra*.

[2] Boyd *v.* McAlpin, 3 McLean, 427, 429. In this case the same learned judge said: "It is insisted that the sale of the thing manufactured by the patented machine is a violation of the patent. But this position is wholly unsustainable. The patent gives 'the exclusive right and liberty of making, constructing, using, and vending to others to be used, the said improvement.' A sale of the product of the machine is no violation of the exclusive right to use, construct, or sell the machine itself. If, therefore, the defendant has done nothing more than purchase the bedsteads from Brown, who may manufacture them by an unjustifiable use of the patented machine, still the person who may make the purchase from him has a right to sell. The product cannot be reached, except in the hands of one who is in some manner connected with the use of the patented machine.

"There are several patents of mills for the manufacture of flour. Now, to construct a mill patented, or to use one, would be an infringement of the patent. But to sell a barrel of flour manufactured at such mill, by one who had purchased it at the mill, could be no infringement of the patent. And the same may be said of a patented stove, used for baking bread. The purchaser of the bread is guilty of no infringement; but the person who constructed the stove, or who uses it, may be enjoined, and is liable to damages. These cases show that it is not the product, but the thing patented, which may not be constructed, sold, or used. This doctrine is laid down in Keplinger *v.* De Young, 10 Wheat. 358. In that case watch-chains were manufactured by the use of a patented machine, in violation of the right of the patentee; the defendant, by contract, purchased all the chains so manufactured, and the court held, that, as the defendant was only the purchaser of the manufactured article, and had no connection in the use of the machine, that he had not infringed the right of the patentee.

"But in the case under consideration, the bill charges that the defendant, in connection with Brown, constructed the machine patented; and that they

§ 297. The Supreme Court of the United States have decided that an assignment of an exclusive right to use a machine, and to vend the same to others for use, within a specified territory, authorizes the assignee to vend elsewhere, out of that territory, articles manufactured by such machine.[1]

Also, that one who is in the lawful use and enjoyment of a patented machine at the time of the expiration of letters-patent, may lawfully continue to use that identical machine, although the term of the letters-patent has been still further extended by a *special act* of Congress, there being nothing in the act to deprive him of that right.[2] Where a patent is extended under the *general provisions* of the act of 1836, c. 357, § 18, the assignees and grantees of the right *to use the thing patented* have, by the terms of that act, the right to continue such use to the extent of their respective interests therein.[3] The assignee of a right to use a patented planing-machine, having the right to continue the use of a particular machine after an extension of the letters-patent, may repair the same, e. g. by replacing the knives when worn out, without destroying the identity of the particular machine and

use the same in making the bedsteads which the defendant is now selling in the city of Cincinnati. If this allegation of the bill be true, the defendant is so connected with the machine in its construction and use as to make him responsible to the plaintiff. The structure and use of the machine are charged as being done beyond the jurisdiction of the court; but having jurisdiction of the person of the defendant, the court may restrain him from using the machine and selling the product. When the sale of the product is thus connected with the illegal use of the machine patented, the individual is responsible in damages, and the amount of his sales will, in a considerable degree, regulate the extent of his liability.

"Whether, if the defendant acts as a mere agent of Brown, who constructed the patented machine, and uses it in Indiana, in making bedsteads, is responsible in damages for an infringement of the patent and may be enjoined, is a question which need not now be determined. Such a rule would undoubtedly be for the benefit of Brown, who, according to the bill, had openly and continually violated the patent in the construction and use of the machine. There are strong reasons why the interest of the principal should, by an action at law, and also by a bill in chancery, be reached through his agent. Injunction allowed."

[1] Simpson *v.* Wilson, 4 How. 709.

[2] Bloomer *v.* McQuewan, 14 How. 539, per Taney, C.J.; reasserted in Bloomer *v.* Millinger, 1 Wall. 340; McLean and Nelson, JJ., strongly dissenting.

[3] Cf. Wilson *v.* Rousseau, 4 How. 646.

infringing the patentee's right.[1] If a license to use be conditioned on the payment of money, the use without such payment will be an infringement of the patent, giving the United States courts jurisdiction, and may be enjoined.[2]

§ 298. 2. *As to a Manufacture or Composition of Matter.* — Assuming that the word is used in our statute to describe the vendible and tangible product of any branch of industry, a patent for a "manufacture" will be infringed by the same acts as a patent for a composition of matter, that is, by making, using, or selling the thing itself, or by importing it from a foreign country where it has been made.[3]

§ 299. In cases of this kind, however, some difficulty may arise as to what constitutes a using. When the subject-matter is the thing produced, the patent will generally also cover the process of making it; as in the case of a paint, a medicine, a stove, or a fabric of cloth. In these cases, a using of the invention would, in one sense, consist in putting it in practice. But the statute vests the exclusive right to use the thing itself in the patentee, because it is the thing produced which is the subject of the patent. Strictly speaking, therefore, the use of the thing at all, in any form of consumption or application, would be an infringement. But as the purpose of the law is to prevent acts injurious to the patentee, with as little restraint on the public as possible,[4] it may be necessary to consider whether the word "using" is employed in a limited or an unlimited sense.

§ 300. Whether the dictum of Mr. Justice Story that "the using or vending of a patented composition is a violation of the right of the proprietor,"[5] can be considered to extend to every form of use, so as to give the proprietor a right to maintain an action, is worthy of consideration. If a patented medicine is made by one not authorized to make it, and is sold to a person who consumes it, it would be a somewhat inconvenient restraint upon the public to hold that the latter is to be considered as using the invention in the sense of the statute. He cannot know that the article is not made by the true proprietor; the probability is

[1] Wilson *v.* Simpson, 9 How. 109.
[2] Brooks *v.* Stolley, 3 McLean, 523.
[3] Walton *v.* Lavater, 8 C. B. N. S. 162.
[4] Per Coleridge, J., in Minter *v.* Williams, Webs. Pat. Cas. 135, 138.
[5] Whittemore *v.* Cutter, 1 Gallis. 429.

that he intends to purchase the genuine composition, and that he is deceived into supposing that he does purchase it. Still, in strictness, he may be held liable to an action for using the thing itself by consuming it.

The sale of a patented article to an agent of the patentee employed to make the purchase on account of the patentee, is not in itself an infringement; but, when accompanied by other circumstances, may be submitted to the jury as evidence of infringement.[1] In a recent English case, where the plaintiff claimed, under a patent for "treating chemically the collected contents of sewers and drains in cities, towns, and villages, so that the same may be applied to agricultural and other purposes," by precipitating the animal and vegetable matter in sewage water by hydrate of lime, it was held that the defendants, the Board of Health, had not infringed by applying the process to the deodorization of sewage water, where some precipitate of animal and vegetable matter was produced, which, however, was not used as an article of value, but *bonâ fide* rejected as an accidental product.[2]

§ 301. It would seem, in regard to all those classes of things which perish in the using, that the use by which they are consumed may be regarded as a violation of the patent right; and that the party may be held responsible for using, who sells, or gives to others to be consumed, the article that is the subject of the patent; because both make use of the invention to the injury of the patentee. In such cases, it matters not whether the party makes the article himself, in violation of a patented process, or procures it to be made by others.[3]

§ 302. Where the subject of the patent is a machine, the using

[1] Byam *v.* Bullard, 1 Curtis, C. C. 100.

[2] Higgs *v.* Goodwin, 1 Ell., Blackb. & Ell. 529.

[3] Gibson *v.* Brand, 4 Man. & Gr. 179, 196. Tindal, C. J.: "The breach alleged in the declaration is, that the defendant had 'directly and indirectly made, used, and put in practice the said invention, and every part thereof, and counterfeited, imitated, and resembled the same.' The proof in support of the breach was, that an order had been given by the defendant, in England, for the making of silk by the same process as the plaintiffs; which order had been executed in England; and that is enough to satisfy the allegation in the declaration, that the defendant made, used, and put in practice the plaintiff's invention, though the silk was, in fact, made by the agency of others." For the converse of this case, where the defendant infringes by executing an order for another person, see §§ 292, 303.

it is altogether prohibited by the statute, because it intends to vest in the patentee the full enjoyment of the fruits of his invention, both in the practice of making the machine, and of producing the effect or result intended to be produced by it.

§ 303. Where an order was given to the defendants by a third person to manufacture a patented article, on a model furnished by him, and the order was executed, it was held that the defendants were guilty of an infringement, although, when they began to execute the order, they had no knowledge of the plaintiff's patent.[1]

§ 304. 3. *An Art.* — Where an art is the subject-matter of a patent, the patent will be infringed by exercising or practising the same art, which will constitute a "using" of the invention or discovery.

It may, however, be doubted whether the mere using of the art or process, especially for a different purpose, and with rejection of the valuable result of that process, is to be considered as an infringement. Thus, in a recent English case, the patent stated that the invention consisted in the use and application of a certain chemical agent for the purpose of precipitating the solid animal and vegetable matter contained in sewage water. The Board of Health used the process for the purpose of disinfecting and deodorizing sewage water, whereby some precipitate of animal and vegetable matter appeared, which, however, was not used, but rejected as an accidental result. The Queen's Bench held that there was no evidence of an infringement.[2]

§ 305. But the great question that arises when an infringement is charged to have taken place, is, whether the two things, one of which is said to be an infringement upon the other, are the same, or different. If they are the same, there is an infringement. If they are different, there is not. But what kind and what degree of resemblance constitute the identity which the patent law designates as an infringement, and what kind and what degree of difference will relieve from this charge, are the difficult and metaphysical questions to be determined in each particular case.[3]

[1] Bryce *v.* Dorr, 3 McLean, 582. Two of the articles were made after notice of the patent.

[2] Higgs *v.* Goodwin, 1 Ell., Bl. & Ell. 529.

[3] There is a very great dearth of reported cases in our own books, giving with any detail the facts brought out at the trial, on which the infringement

§ 306. Learned judges have often laid it down that where two things are the same in principle, the one is an infringement upon the other. This mode of stating the general doctrine on which the fact of infringement depends is not quite satisfactory, because that which constitutes the principle of an invention is very likely to be regarded differently by different minds. Still, there is a sense in which the principle of an invention is undoubtedly to be considered in determining whether an infringement has taken place; because we cannot determine whether there is a substantial identity between two things, without first observing the distinguishing characteristics of the one which is taken as the subject of comparison. But I propose, without rejecting the light of any of the cases in which this language is employed, to inquire whether the fact of an infringement may not be tried by a test more definite, precise, and practical.[1]

depended. The reporters of the Circuit Courts of the United States seem to have acted on the idea that there is nothing to be reported in a patent cause, unless some question of law is raised on motion for a new trial, or for arrest of judgment, &c.; and then we get the facts, only so far as it is convenient for the court to state them, in deciding the questions raised. This is a great mistake. A careful summary of the evidence given on every important trial for infringement of a patent, including the professional characters and qualifications of the witnesses, together with an accurate description of the plaintiff's and defendant's inventions, the rulings of the court in the progress of the trial, and the charge to the jury, would be of great value.

[1] The meaning to be ascribed to the term *principle* of an *invention* or *discovery* has been thus commented on by different judges. Mr. Justice Washington, in Treadwell *v.* Bladen, 4 Wash. 706, said: "What constitutes form, and what principle, is often a nice question to decide; and upon none are the witnesses who are examined in patent causes, even those who are skilled in the particular art, more apt to disagree. It seems to me that the safest guide to accuracy in making the distinction is, first, to ascertain what is the result to be obtained by the discovery; and whatever is essential to that object, independent of the mere form and proportions of the thing used for the purpose, may generally, if not universally, be considered as the principles of the invention."

In Whittemore *v.* Cutter, 1 Gallis. 478, 480, Mr. Justice Story said: "By the principles of a machine (as these words are used in the statute) is not meant the original elementary principles of motion, which philosophy and science have discovered, but the *modus operandi*, the peculiar device or manner of producing any given effect. The expansive powers of steam, and the mechanical powers of wheels, have been understood for many ages; yet a machine may well employ either the one or the other, and yet be so entirely new, in its mode of applying these elements, as to entitle the party to a patent

§ 306 *a*. *Designs*. — What constitutes infringement in the case of designs has been the subject of recent judicial discussion. The Circuit Court held,[1] that the proper test on the question of infringement is substantial identity, as in the case of machinery, not

for his whole combination. The intrinsic difficulty is to ascertain, in complicated cases like the present, the exact boundaries between what was known and used before, and what is new, in the *mode of operation*." In Barrett *v.* Hall, 1 Mas. 447, 470, the same learned judge said: "As to the opinion of skilful witnesses, whether the principles of two machines are the same, no person doubts that it is competent evidence to be introduced into a patent cause. But care should be taken to distinguish what is meant by a principle. In the minds of some men a principle means an elementary truth, or power, so that, in the view of such men, all machines which perform their appropriate functions by motion, in whatever way produced, are alike in principle, since motion is the element employed. No one, however, in the least acquainted with law would for a moment contend that a principle in this sense is the subject of a patent; and if it were otherwise, it would put an end to all patents for all machines which employed motion, for this has been known as a principle or elementary power from the beginning of time. The true legal meaning of the principle of a machine, with reference to the Patent Act, is the peculiar structure or constituent parts of such machine. And in this view the question may be very properly asked, in cases of doubt and complexity, of skilful persons, whether the principles of two machines be the same or different. Now the principles of two machines may be the same, although the form or proportions may be different. They may substantially employ the same power in the same way, though the external mechanism be apparently different. On the other hand, the principles of two machines may be very different, although their external structure may have great similarity in many respects. It would be exceedingly difficult to contend, that a machine, which raised water by a lever, was the same in principle with a machine which raised it by a screw, a pulley, or a wedge, whatever, in other respects, might be the similarity of the apparatus." See note on the "Principle of an Invention," at the end of this chapter.

[1] The Gorham Manufacturing Co. *v.* White, 7 Blatchf. 513.

"The same principles," said Mr. Justice Blatchford, "which govern in determining the question of infringement in respect to a patent for an invention connected with the operation of machinery must govern in determining the question of infringement in respect to a patent for a design. A design for a configuration of an article of manufacture is embraced within the statute, as a patentable design, as well as a design for an ornament to be placed on an article of manufacture. The object of the former may solely be increased utility, while the object of the latter may solely be increased gratification to a cultivated taste, addressed through the eye. It would be as reasonable to say that equal utility should be the test of infringement in the first case, as to say that equal appreciation by the eye should be the test of infringement in the latter case. There must be a uniform test, and that test can only be,

in view of the observation of a casual observer, but of a person versed in the business of designs in the particular trade in question, and who is accustomed to compare such designs intelligently one with the other; and that the mere fact that the resemblance between two designs, which are substantially different, is such as to mislead ordinary purchasers and casual observers, and to induce them to mistake one for the other, is not sufficient to constitute an infringement.

These views, however, were not concurred in by the Supreme Court of the United States. It was the opinion of that court,[1] that the acts of Congress which authorize the grant of patents for designs were plainly intended to give encouragement to the decorative arts. "They contemplate not so much utility as ap-

as in the case of a patent in respect to machinery, substantial identity, not in view of the observation of a person whose observation is worthless, because it is casual, heedless, and unintelligent, and who sees one of the articles in question at one time and place, and the other of such articles at another time and place, but in view of the observation of a person versed in the business of designs in the particular trade in question — of a person engaged in the manufacture or sale of articles containing such designs — of a person accustomed to compare such designs one with another, and who sees and examines the articles containing them, side by side. The question is not, whether one design will be mistaken for the other by a person who examines the two so carelessly as to be sure to be deceived, but whether the two designs can be said to be substantially the same, when examined intelligently side by side. There must be such a comparison of the features which make up the two designs. As against an existing patented design, a patent for another design cannot be withheld because, to a casual observer, the general appearance of the later design is so like that of the earlier one as to lead him, without proper attention, to mistake the one for the other. The same test must be applied on the question of infringement. . . . A patent for a design, like a patent for an improvement in machinery, must be for the means of producing a certain result or appearance, and not for the result or appearance itself. The plaintiffs' patent is for their described means of producing a certain appearance in the completed handle. Even if the same appearance is produced by another design, if the means used in such other design to produce the appearance are substantially different from the means used in the prior patented design to produce such appearance, the later design is not an infringement of the patented one. It is quite clear, on a consideration of the points of difference before enumerated between the plaintiffs' design and the designs of White, that each of the latter is substantially different from the former in the means it employs to produce the appearance. Such is the undoubted weight of the evidence, and such is the judgment of the court."

[1] Gorham Co. *v.* White, 14 Wall. 511.

pearance, and that not an abstract, impression, or picture, but an aspect given to those objects mentioned in the acts." It is the appearance itself which makes the article salable, and therefore valuable to the inventor; and the object of the law is to secure for a limited time to the ingenious producer of these appearances the advantages flowing from them. "Manifestly the mode in which these appearances are produced has very little, if any thing, to do with giving increased salableness to the article. It is the appearance itself which attracts attention, and calls out favor or dislike. It is the appearance itself, therefore, no matter by what agency caused, that constitutes mainly, if not entirely, the contribution to the public which the law deems worthy of recompense. The appearance may be the result of peculiarity of configuration, or of ornament alone, or of both conjointly; but, in whatever way produced, it is the new thing, or product, which the patent law regards. . . . We do not say that, in determining whether two designs are substantially the same, differences in the lines, the configuration, or the modes by which the aspects they exhibit, are not to be considered; but we think the controlling consideration is the resultant effect."

In laying down rules governing the test of infringement, Mr. Justice Strong, who delivered the opinion of the court, said: "We are now prepared to inquire what is the true test of identity of design. Plainly, it must be sameness of appearance; and mere difference of lines in the drawing or sketch, a greater or smaller number of lines, or slight variances in configuration, if sufficient to change the effect upon the eye, will not destroy the substantial identity. An engraving which has many lines may present to the eye the same picture, and to the mind the same idea or conception, as another with much fewer lines. The design, however, would be the same. So a pattern for a carpet or a print may be made up of wreaths of flowers arranged in a particular manner. Another carpet may have similar wreaths, arranged in a like manner, so that none but very acute observers could detect a difference. Yet in the wreaths upon one there may be fewer flowers, and the wreaths may be placed at wider distances from each other. Surely in such a case the designs are alike. The same conception was in the mind of the designer, and to that conception he gave expression.

"If, then, identity of appearance, or (as expressed in McCrea *v.*

Holdsworth) sameness of effect upon the eye, is the main test of substantial identity of design, the only remaining question upon this part of the case is whether it is essential that the appearance should be the same to the eye of an expert. The court below was of opinion that the test of a patent for a design is not the eye of an ordinary observer. The learned judge thought there could be no infringement unless there was "substantial identity," in view of the observation of a person versed in designs in the particular trade in question — of a person engaged in the manufacture or sale of articles containing such designs — of a person accustomed to compare such designs one with another, and who sees and examines the articles containing them, side by side. There must, he thought, be a comparison of the features which make up the two designs. With this we cannot concur. Such a test would destroy all the protection which the act of Congress intended to give. There never could be piracy of a patented design, for human ingenuity has never yet produced a design, in all its details, exactly like another, so like that an expert could not distinguish them. No counterfeit bank-note is so identical in appearance with the true, that an experienced artist cannot discern a difference. It is said an engraver distingishes impressions made by the same plate. Experts, therefore, are not the persons to be deceived. Much less than that which would be substantial identity in their eyes would be undistinguishable in the eyes of men generally, of observers of ordinary acuteness, bringing to the examination of the article upon which the design has been placed that degree of observation which men of ordinary intelligence give. It is persons of the latter class who are the principal purchasers of the articles to which designs have given novel appearances, and if they are misled, and induced to purchase what is not the article they supposed it to be, if, for example, they are led to purchase forks or spoons, deceived by an apparent resemblance into the belief that they bear the "cottage" design, and therefore are the production of the holders of the Gorham, Thurber, and Dexter patent, when in fact they are not, the patentees are injured, and that advantage of a market which the patent was granted to secure is destroyed. The purpose of the law must be effected if possible; but, plainly, it cannot be if, while the general appearance of the design is preserved, minor differences of detail in the manner in which the appearance is produced, observable by experts, but not noticed by ordinary observers, by those who buy and use, are sufficient to relieve an imitating design from condemnation as an infringement.

"We hold, therefore, that if, in the eye of an ordinary observer, giving such attention as a purchaser usually gives, two designs are substantially the same, if the resemblance is such as to deceive such an observer, inducing him to purchase one supposing it to be the other, the first one patented is infringed by the other."

Applying the above rules to the facts of the case at bar, the court held that there was an infringement, and reversed the decree of the court below. Justices Miller, Field, and Bradley dissented; but whether their dissent had reference to the principles of law enunciated by the court, or simply to the question whether there was an infringement in the case before the court, does not appear from the report.

§ 307. An infringement involves substantial identity, whether that identity is described by the terms, "same principle," "same *modus operandi*," or any other. It is a copy of the thing described in the specification of the patentee, either without variation, or with only such variations as are consistent with its being in substance the same thing.[1] What will amount to such a substantial identity cannot be stated in general terms; we can only look to individual cases for illustrations and applications of the general doctrine.

[1] In Walton *v.* Potter, Webs. Pat. Cas. 586, Sir N. C. Tindal, Ch. J., said: "Where a party has obtained a patent for a new invention or a discovery he has made by his own ingenuity, it is not in the power of any other person, simply by varying in form or in immaterial circumstances the nature or subject-matter of that discovery, to obtain either a patent for it himself, or to use it without the leave of the patentee, because that would be in effect and in substance an invasion of the right; and, therefore, what you have to look at upon the present occasion is not simply whether in form or in circumstances, that may be more or less immaterial, that which has been done by the defendants varies from the specification of the plaintiff's patent, but to see whether, in reality, in substance, and in effect, the defendants have availed themselves of the plaintiff's invention in order to make that fabric, or to make that article which they have sold in the way of their trade; whether, in order to make that, they have availed themselves of the invention of the plaintiff."

Thus, in Aiken *v.* Bemis,[1] Woodbury, J., uses the following language: "The present was a case of the former character, for a combination, and the difference in the patent from the instrument here consists in this, that the hammer of the saw-set was all made of steel by Bemis, and that all but the point was made of wrought-iron in the patent. This looks, at first blush, as not a very material difference, and one rather colorable or accidental than designed. But when we advert to the evidence in the case, it appears that the use of wrought-iron was found by experiment to be much better than steel, and was hence patented, and this without making the specification in terms broad enough to cover steel also. It is a matter of doubt, therefore, whether the use of an inferior material for the hammer of the saw-set, when the patent covers only a superior one, is a legal violation of it. Why should the plaintiff complain of what he had tried, but deemed too useless or valueless to be adopted? Had the patent extended only to the form or parts of the saw-set, combined as set out and made of any kind of materials, or saying nothing of the materials, the right would be violated by a machine of like form, as the form would be the sole matter patented. But when the patentee chooses to go further, and cover, with his patent, the material of which a part of his machine is composed, he entirely endangers his right to prosecute when a different and inferior material is employed, especially one which he himself, after repeated experiments, had rejected."

§ 308. If the invention of the patentee be a machine, it will be infringed by a machine which incorporates in its structure and operation the substance of the invention; that is, by an arrangement of mechanism which performs the same service or produces the same effect in the same way, or substantially the same way. But perhaps the only method of satisfactorily explaining what is meant by operating in the same or substantially the same way is to cite from the instructions of the courts on this question in several of the leading patent cases. Thus, in Wyeth *v.* Stone,[2] Mr. Justice Story charged as follows: "It (the defendant's machine) is substantially, in its mode of operation, the same as Wyeth's machine; and it copies his entire cutter; the only important difference seems to be that Wyeth's machine has a double

[1] 3 Woodb. & Minot, 348.

[2] Wyeth *v.* Stone, 1 Story's R. 273.

series of cutters on parallel planes, and the machine of the defendant's has a single series of chisels in one plane. Both machines have a succession of chisels, each of which is progressively below the other, with a proper guide placed at such a distance as the party may choose, to regulate the movement; and in this succession of chisels, one below the other, on one plate or frame, consists the substance of Wyeth's invention. The guide in Wyeth's machine is the duplicate of his chisel plate or frame; the guide in the defendant's machine is simply a smooth iron on a level with the cutting-chisel frame or plate. Each performs the same service substantially in the same way." In Odiorne *v.* Winkley,[1] the same learned judge said: "It is often a point of intrinsic difficulty to decide whether one machine operates upon the same principles as another. In the present improved state of mechanics, the same elements of motion and the same powers must be employed in almost all machines. The level, the wheel, and the screw are powers well known; and if no person could be entitled to a patent who used them in his machine, it would be in vain to seek for a patent. The material question, therefore, is not whether the same elements of motion or the same component parts are used, but whether the given effect is produced substantially by the same mode of operation and the same combination of powers in both machines. Mere colorable differences or slight improvements cannot shake the right of the original inventor. To illustrate these positions, suppose a watch was first invented by a person so as to mark the *hours* only, and a second person added the work to mark the *minutes*, and a third the *seconds;* each of them using the same combinations and mode of operation to mark the hours as the first. In such a case the inventor of the second-hand could not have entitled himself to a patent embracing the inventions of the other parties. Each inventor would undoubtedly be entitled to his own invention and no more. In the machines before the court, there are three great stages in the operation, each producing a given and distinct effect: (1) The cutting of the nail for the head; (2) The griping of the nail; (3) The heading of the nail. If one person had invented the cutting, a second the griping, and a third the heading, it is clear that neither could entitle himself to a patent for the whole

[1] Odiorne *v.* Winkley, 2 Gallis. 51.

of a machine which embraced the inventions of the other two, and by the same mode of operation produced the same effect; and if he did, his patent would be void. Some machines are too simple to be thus separately considered; others, again, are so complex as to be invented by a succession of improvements, each added to the other. And on the whole, in the present case, the question for the jury is, whether, taking Reed's machine and Perkins's machine together, and considering them in their various combinations, they are machines constructed substantially upon the same principles and upon the same mode of operation."

One machine is the same in substance as another, if the principle be the same in effect, though the form of the machine be different. Thus in Boville *v.* Moore,[1] Gibbs, C. J., said: "I remember that was the expedient used by a man in Cornwall, who endeavored to pirate the steam-engine. He produced an engine which, on the first view of it, had not the least resemblance to Boulton and Watt's engine; where you looked for the head you found the feet, and where you looked for the feet you found the head; but it turned out that he had taken the principle of Boulton and Watt's; it acted as well one way as the other; but if you set it upright, it was exactly Boulton and Watt's engine. So here I make the same observation, because I observe it is stated that one acts upwards and the other downwards; one commences from the bottom and produces the lace by an upward operation, the other acts from above and produces it by an operation downwards; but that, if the principle be the same, must be considered as the same in point of invention." [2]

In McCormick *v.* Seymour,[3] Nelson, J., gave the following instructions: "The next objection taken by the defendants is that, assuming the divider of the plaintiff to be new and useful and patentable, and that he is entitled to the enjoyment of it free from any interference, still he is not entitled to recover, because the defendants have not used his separator, but a different contrivance. In order to take the separator of the defendants out of the charge of infringement, it is necessary that they should satisfy you that it is substantially and materially different from the plaintiff's; in other words, that it involves some new idea

[1] Boville *v.* Moore, Dav. Pat. Cas. 361, 402.

[2] Compare Buck *v.* Hermance, 2 Blatchf. 398.

[3] McCormick *v.* Seymour, 2 Blatchf. 240.

in its construction not to be found in the plaintiff's. If it is found there, of course it is an appropriation of his invention. If not, then it is an independent improvement and no violation of the plaintiff's right. It is proper to observe, in respect to this particular question, that whether the separator of the defendants be or be not an interference with that of the patentee, will depend upon this, whether the plan which the defendants have employed, in constructing their separator and dividing the grain, is or is not in substance the same as the plaintiff's, and whether or not the differences that have been introduced by the defendants in their form of construction and in accomplishing the design which all these separators seek to accomplish, are merely differences in things not material or important; in other words, whether their plan is, in substance and effect, a colorable evasion of the plaintiff's contrivance, or whether it is new, and substantially a different thing. If the defendants have taken the same general plan and applied it for the same purpose, although they may have varied the mode of construction, it will still be, substantially and in the eye of the patent law, the same thing. Otherwise it will not."

To the same effect, in Blanchard *v.* Beers,[1] the same judge said: "It is material, at this stage of the case, to recall your attention to a principle already stated, namely, that whether or not the one machine is an infringement of the other, does not necessarily depend upon whether their mechanical structures are different. But the question is, whether (whatever may be the mechanical construction) the later machine contains the means or combination found in the previous machine, — whether, taking the structure as you find it, you see the new idea embodied in it. If the combination of Blanchard is found substantially incorporated in the defendant's machine, then its mechanical construction, whatever it may be, is, as matter of law, but an equivalent for the mechanical construction of Blanchard's machine. No man can appropriate the benefit of the new ideas which another has originated and put into practical use, because he may have been enabled by superior mechanical skill to embody them in a form different in appearance or different in reality. For although

[1] Blanchard *v.* Beers, 2 Blatchf. 418. Compare McCormick *v.* Talcott, 20 How. 402; Winans *v.* Denmead, 15 How. 332; Sickels *v.* Borden, 3 Blatchf. 535; Dobbs *v.* Penn, 3 Wels., Hurls. & Gord. 427.

he may not have preserved the exterior appearance of the previous machine, he may have appropriated the ideas which gave to it all its value. . . . It is unfair, when the question is between Blanchard's machine thus organized and a machine organized for one particular purpose and to produce one particular result of Blanchard's machine, such as the wagon-spoke, to hold that, because the machine organized for that specific purpose is differently constructed and dissimilar in appearance, and can produce the particular thing more rapidly, it therefore necessarily fails to embody the same idea or combination. We know that any machine constructed to accomplish a particular object or purpose may be often materially changed from the original construction, and yet do the work very well. There are mechanical equivalents, by the use of which the whole features may be changed, and a great departure made from the apparent principle and combination of the machine, and yet it may operate well. In view of this consideration, it should be particularly noticed, in this case, that the defendant's machine has been constructed for one object, — for the purpose of turning wagon-spokes of slight irregularity of form, — and therefore, as is obvious, may admit of very material changes from the original machine. It will be proper, therefore, for you to look into these two machines and see whether or not the change in the organization of the defendant's machine from the plaintiff's might not have been the production of the skill of a mechanic examining and studying the Blanchard machine with a view to reorganize it and adapt it to the performance of one of its functions, namely, producing an axe-handle or a wagon-spoke. Because, whenever a defendant sets up that he has substantially departed from the existing machine, so as to avoid the consequences of an infringement, it is necessary that he should satisfy the court and jury that his departure has been such as involves invention, and not mere mechanical skill, in order to entitle him to a patent for the discovery. There must be mind and inventive genius involved in it, and not the mere skill of the workman. . . .

"These views present all that I mean to trouble you with upon the main question in the case. As to the fact that the defendant's machine can cut a greater number of spokes in a given time than the plaintiff's, the law is as stated by the counsel on both sides. The fact may be taken into consideration in examining into the question whether or not the principle or combination of the two machines is substantially the same. If it is, then, without regard to the result, and although a greater number of spokes can be made by the defendant's machine in a given time, that machine would still be an infringement. This superiority is sometimes produced by a superior construction of the machine; or it may, in this case, be the result of making one adapted exclusively to the accomplishment of one of the purposes of Blanchard's; or it may be the result of an improvement on his; but this will not entitle its author to use the principle or combination of Blanchard's."

To the same effect are the instructions of Sprague, J., in Howe *v.* Morton and Howe *v.* Williams, MS.: "We find, then, to look at the Williams machine, in the first place, that it has two holding surfaces, between which the cloth is fed by mechanism, — a piece of metal taking hold of the cloth and carrying it along between these two surfaces. That is the sub-combination of Howe's, so far. And that is one material part of the defendant's machine, and found in no machine prior to Howe's; the presser-foot is divided into two parts, operating alternately, one of which is always upon the cloth and pressing it down upon the table; one part presses the cloth down upon the roughened feeding surface below; the feeding is done by advancing the roughened surface and then withdrawing it in the same plane; one part of the presser-foot being raised, that it may not press the cloth down while the roughened surface is retreating; the other part, in the mean time, being down, holds the cloth in position while the first is up; these opposing surfaces are holding the cloth all the time between them for the operation of tightening the stitch and for resisting the thrust and retraction of the needle, and keeping the cloth in place while it is fed along. We find, in the next place, that it has two threads, and forms the stitch by the interlocking of these two threads; and so far, — without speaking of the minor mechanism by which this is accomplished, — so far it is like Howe's; and Howe's was not anticipated in that respect by any machine prior to his. These sub-combinations are like Howe's. The general combination and arrangement are like Howe's. It is testified by the experts that they are identical; and I see no reason to doubt that statement.

"We find, then, that the Williams machine has adopted the general combination and arrangement of Howe's, and some at least of the sub-combinations of Howe's, in which that machine differs from others. Without undertaking, therefore, to go into the minutiæ of the mechanism, the Williams machine, in my judgment, contains so much of Howe's sub-combinations and of his general combination and arrangement, that it is an infringement of his patent.

"The Sloat machine differs not substantially or scarcely at all from Howe's, in the holding apparatus. It has two surfaces, the table, and the presser-foot. The foot presses on the material which is between that and the table, and which is there fed along by the four-motion-feed, as it is sometimes called, not requiring the presser-foot to rise to enable the roughened surface to return. And the same remark applies here as to the Williams machine, that it has these surfaces holding the material for the same operations, — the tightening of the stitch, resisting the thrust and retraction of the needle, and keeping the cloth in its proper place when it is fed.

"As regards the formation of the stitch, the Sloat machine also uses two threads and makes the interlocking stitch. The shuttle is not carried between the needle and its thread, but the thread of the needle is carried around the shuttle, thus producing the interlocking, — the stitch being substantially the same as Howe's and produced by these instruments, — the needle and the shuttle having each its thread, one carried through the loop of the other, in the manner I have described. It is my opinion that the Sloat machine also contains so much of Howe's sub-combination or subordinate parts and of his general combination and arrangement, that it is an infringement of his patent."

§ 308 *a*. Where the patent was for an "improvement in springs for hoop-skirts" it was held to be an infringement to sell "an article of dress called a bustle, containing hoop-skirt wire made in substantially the same manner described in the patent, "the bustle referred to being," in the language of the court, "substantially a hoop-skirt of a diminished size." [1]

§ 309. But if the difference between the two machines is not a mere difference of form, if there is a material alteration of structure, if they are substantially different combinations of mechanism, to effect the same purpose by means which are really not the same

[1] Young *v.* Lippman, 9 Blatchf. 277.

in substance, then the one will not be an infringement of the other.[1]

[1] Lowell *v.* Lewis, 1 Mas. 182, 191. In this case Mr. Justice Story said: "The manner in which Mr. *Perkins's* invention is, in his specification, proposed to be used, is in a square pump, with triangular valves, connected in the centre, and resting without any box on the sides of the pump, at such an angle as exactly to fit the four sides. The pump of Mr. *Baker*, on the other hand, is fitted only for a circular tube, with butterfly valves of an oval shape, connected in the centre, and resting, not on the sides of the pump, but on a metal rim, at a given angle, so that the rim may not be exactly in contact with the sides, but the valves may be. If from the whole evidence the jury is satisfied that these differences are mere changes of form, without any material alteration in real structure, then the plaintiff is entitled to recover; if they are substantially different combinations of mechanical parts to effect the same purposes, then the defendant is entitled to a verdict. This is a question of fact, which I leave entirely to the sound judgment of the jury."

In Gray *v.* James, Peters's C. C. R. 394, 397, Mr. Justice Washington said: "What constitutes a difference in principle between two machines is frequently a question of difficulty, more especially if the difference in form is considerable, and the machinery complicated. But we think it may safely be laid down, as a general rule, that where the machines are substantially the same, and operate in the same manner, to produce the same result, they must be in principle the same. I say *substantially*, in order to exclude all formal differences; and when I speak of the same result, I must be understood as meaning *the same kind of result, though it may differ in extent. So that the result is the same, according to this definition, whether the one produce more nails, for instance, in a given space of time, than the other, if the operation is to make nails.*"

The American Pin Co. *v.* The Oakville Co., 3 Blatchf. 190. "Neither of these operations can be found, either in form or in substance, in the Crosby machine (defendant's). There is no hopper in Crosby's machine, unless the inclined channel-way in which the pins hang by their heads in a vertical position may be considered a hopper. That, if it be considered as a hopper, does not move. It is stationary. Of course it neither slides nor passes over any thing. From the lower extremity of the channel-way, the pins are taken, one by one, by the thread of a screw, while it is revolving and while the pin is vertical, and, by force of mechanical power, the pin is carried in the thread of the screw to the other end of the screw, and is there deposited by the screw, in a horizontal position, in a groove channel. The screw, while operating, has no motion but a revolving motion. During the whole time it remains in the same space. It neither moves forward nor back. There is, then, nothing in the machine which, either in form or in substance, has any resemblance to a sliding hopper, sliding or passing over recesses in a plate to receive the pins as they drop from a hopper, or to recesses for receiving pins sliding or passing under a hopper. In Slocum's machine, one of these processes must take place; and, without one of them, a machine for this purpose cannot be

Thus, in a recent English case, the *plaintiff's* invention consisted in the application of ventilating vanes or screws at the centre of the stones for supplying the air between the grinding surfaces; a portable ventilating machine, blowing by a screw vane which caused a current of air parallel to the axis of the vane, being attached externally to the eye of the upper mill-stone, and thus the screw vane being set in rapid motion, the air was compelled to pass through the eye into the centre of the stones and so find its way out again; the *defendant's* plan was to remove from the centre of both stones a large circular portion of each, and in this space, opposite to the opening between the two stones to place a fan or blower, by the rapid rotation of which a centrifugal motion was given to the air, and it was driven between the stones. It was held that the one invention was not an infringement of the other, but that each was a new method of accomplishing a well-known object, on the common principle of obtaining a current of air by means of a rotating-vane.[1]

§ 309 *a.* The question of what constitutes an infringement in case of a combination has been discussed in several recent American cases. The law on this subject was thus stated by the Supreme Court of the United States in the recent case of Seymour *v.* Osborne:[2] "Actual inventors of a combination of two or more ingredients in a machine, secured by letters-patent in due form, are entitled, even though the ingredients are old, if the

a Slocum machine. In the Slocum machine, the recess in the plate which receives the pin from the hopper must be of the exact size of the barrel of the pin. In the Crosby machine, the recess in the thread of the screw which receives the pin, and by which it is transported to the other end of the screw, and which, it is claimed, is a mechanical equivalent for the recess in the plate with grooves in Slocum's machine, need not be of the exact depth or breadth of the barrel of the pin. It may be of any size, provided it is not sufficiently large to permit the head of the pin to fall through. The essential means used in Crosby's machine to bring about the result, to wit, a separation of the pins from the pile or column, are, therefore, substantially different from the means used in Slocum's machine to produce the same result. In this respect the two machines operate differently and depend upon distinct organizations. The same substantial means are not used in each." Per Ingersoll, J.

[1] Bovill *v.* Pimm, 36 E. L. & Eq. 441. Compare also Seed *v.* Higgings, 8 Ell. & Blackb. 755.

[2] 11 Wall. 516. The opinion of the court was delivered by Mr. Justice Clifford.

combination produces a new and useful result, to treat every one as an infringer who makes and uses or vends the machine to others to be used without their authority or license.

They cannot suppress subsequent improvements which are substantially different, whether the new improvements consist in a new combination of the same ingredients, or of the substitution of some newly discovered ingredient, or of some old one, performing some new function not known at the date of the letters-patent, as a proper substitute for the ingredient withdrawn from the combination constituting their invention. Mere formal alterations in a combination in letters-patent, however, are no defence to the charge of infringement, and the withdrawal of one ingredient from the same, and the substitution of another which was well known at the date of the patent as a proper substitute for the one withdrawn, is a mere formal alteration of the combination if the ingredient substituted performs substantially the same function as the one withdrawn.

Patentees, therefore, are entitled in all cases to invoke to some extent the doctrine of equivalents, but they are never entitled to do so in any case to suppress all other substantial improvements; and the rule which disallows such pretensions, if properly understood and limited, is as applicable to the inventor of a device, or even of an entire machine, as to the inventor of a mere combination, except that the inventor of the latter cannot treat any one as an infringer whose machine does not contain all of the material ingredients of the prior combination, as in that state of the case the subsequent invention is regarded as substantially different from the former one, unless the latter machine employs as a substitute for the ingredient left out to perform the same function some other ingredient which was well known as a proper substitute for the same when the former invention was patented.

Bonâ fide inventors of a combination are as much entitled to suppress every other combination of the same ingredients to produce the same result, not substantially different from what they have invented and caused to be patented, as any other class of inventors. All alike have the right to suppress every colorable invasion of that which is secured to them by their letters-patent, and it is a mistake to suppose that this court ever intended to lay down any different rule of decision."

A patent for a combination of several elements is not infringed by a combination which dispenses with one of the elements, and substitutes therefor another substantially different in construction and operation, but serving the same purpose.[1]

§ 309 *b*. It has been held to be an infringement to manufacture and sell without authority some of the parts of a patented combination, provided such parts are useless without the remaining parts, and they are sold with the understanding and intention that such remaining parts shall be supplied by another, and the whole be combined for use. This question arose in the case of Wallace *v.* Holmes,[2] wherein the complainant's patent was for an improvement in lamps, and embraced the combination of the chimney and the burner. It appeared that the defendant had manufactured and sold the burner, which was useless without the chimney, it being necessary for purchasers, before using the burner, to obtain the chimney and use both in combination. According to the construction given by the court to the specification and claim, the complainant's patent did not claim the burner as new, but the combination of the burner with the chimney. Upon these facts the court held that there had been an infringement of the plaintiff's patent by the defendant. The grounds upon which this decision was based are thus given by Mr. Justice Woodruff, who delivered the judgment of the court: "The rule of law invoked by the defendants is this, — that, where a patent is for a combination merely, it is not infringed by one who uses one or more of the parts, but not all, to produce the same results, either by themselves or by the aid of other devices. This rule is well settled, and is not questioned on this trial. The rule is fully stated by Chief Justice Taney, in Prouty *v.* Ruggles (16 Peters, 336, 341), and in other cases cited by the counsel. (Byam *v.* Farr, 1 Curtis's C. C. R. 260, 265; Foster *v.* Moore, ibid. 279, 292; Vance *v.* Campbell, 1 Black, 427; Eames *v.* Godfrey, 1 Wallace, 78, 79.) But I am not satisfied that this rule will protect these defendants. If, in actual concert with a third party, with a view to the actual production of the patented improvement

[1] Crompton *v.* Belknap Mills, 3 Fisher's Pat. Cas. 536; Eames *v.* Godfrey, 1 Wall. 79; Vance *v.* Campbell, 1 Black, 427. See also Waterbury Brass Co. *v.* Miller, 9 Blatchf. 77; Nicholson Pavement Co. *v.* Hatch, 3 Fisher's Pat. Cas. 432; Sayles *v.* Chicago and Northwestern R.R. Co., 4 Fisher's Pat. Cas. 584; Densmore *v.* Schofield, ibid. 148; Carter *v.* Baker, ibid. 404.

[2] 9 Blatchf. 65.

in lamps, and the sale and use thereof, they consented to manufacture the burner, and such other party to make the chimney, and, in such concert, they actually make and sell the burner, and he the chimney, each utterly useless without the other, and each intended to be used, and actually sold to be used, with the other, it cannot be doubtful that they must be deemed to be joint infringers of the complainant's patent. It cannot be that, where a useful machine is patented as a combination of parts, two or more can engage in its construction and sale, and protect themselves by showing that, though united in an effort to produce the same machine, and sell it, and bring it into extensive use, each makes and sells one part only, which is useless without the others, and still another person, in precise conformity with the purpose in view, puts them together for use. If it were so, such patents would, indeed, be of little value. In such case, all are tort-feasors, engaged in a common purpose to infringe the patent, and actually, by their concerted action, producing that result. In a suit brought against such party or parties, a question might be raised, whether all the actors in the wrong should be made parties defendant; but I apprehend that, even at law and certainly when non-joinder was not pleaded, the want of all the parties would be no defence. Each is liable for all the damages.

"Here the actual concert with others is a certain inference from the nature of the case, and the distinct efforts of the defendants to bring the burner in question into use, which can only be done by adding the chimney. The defendants have not, perhaps, made an actual prearrangement with any particular person to supply the chimney to be added to the burner; but every sale they make is a proposal to the purchaser to do this, and his purchase is a consent with the defendants that he will do it, or cause it to be done. The defendants are, therefore, active parties to the whole infringement, consenting and acting to that end, manufacturing and selling for that purpose. If the want of joinder of other parties could avail them for any purpose (which is not to be conceded), they must set it up as a defence, and point out the parties who are acting in express or implied concert with them. Nor is it any excuse that parties desiring to use the burner have all the glass manufacturers in the world from whom to procure the chimneys. The question may be novel, but, in my judgment, upon these proofs, the defendants have no protection in the rule upon which alone they rely as a defence against the charge of infringement."

§ 309 c. Where the patent was for a combination of three distinct devices forming an improved water-wheel, none of which was claimed as new, it was held that the use of two of the devices without the other was not an infringement. The omission of immaterial parts or the substitution of equivalents will not constitute a valid defence. The question is whether the machines are substantially the same. "But here," says Mr. Justice Woodruff,[1] "the patentee claims to combine a wheel and a spiral conductor, neither of which he claims to have invented, with a tube (F) to carry off the water from the surface of the wheel. Now, if the defendant had substituted an equivalent device for the tube (F), he might be an infringer, but he was not, by this patent, prevented from using the other two without any such device. His using them in a location, in reference to the flume, which rendered the tube unnecessary and useless, was not substituting an equivalent device, but was only using them without any device of any kind for the purpose indicated. The case falls, therefore, within the rule stated, namely, that when a combination of known elements or devices is patented, and the combination only, the use of any of the devices less than all is no infringement. This rule is not to be construed so strictly as to conflict with the other rule above stated, and to permit the substitution of equivalent devices where the combination is substantially the same. But here the tube (F) is a distinct member of the combination for a specific useful purpose; and it cannot be rejected in determining what is, in law and fact, the subject of the patent. If the wheel had been claimed, or the combination of the wheel and the spiral conductor, the defendant could not have protected himself by dispensing with the tube (F), although the plaintiff had also patented the three in combination; but, as the case stands, I see no alternative but to hold the ruling on the trial correct."

§ 310. But, in cases where the patent is not for a combination, if the principle is applied in the same way as the patentee has applied it, then the absence of two or three things in the defendant's machine, which are mentioned in the specification, will not

[1] Rich *v.* Close, 8 Blatchf. 41. See also Crompton *v.* Belknap Mills, 3 Fisher's Pat. Cas. 536.

prevent the patentee from recovering for an infringement.[1] It is in relation to this question of substantial identity, that the doctrine

[1] Jones *v.* Pearce, Webs. Pat. Cas. 122, 124. And if the imitation be so nearly exact as to satisfy the jury that the imitator attempted to copy the model, and to make some almost imperceptible variation, for the purpose of evading the right of the patentee, it may be considered a fraud upon the law, and such slight variation will be disregarded. Davis *v.* Palmer, 2 Brock. 298, 309.

Winans *v.* Denmead, 15 How. 330. In this case, the claim of the patentee was in the following words: "What I claim as my invention and desire to secure by letters-patent is making the body of a car for the transportation of coal, &c., in the form of a frustum of a cone, substantially as herein described, whereby the force exerted by the weight of the load presses equally in all directions, and does not tend to change the form thereof, so that every part resists its equal proportion, and by which also the lower part is so reduced as to pass down within the truck-frame and between the axles, to lower the centre of gravity of the load without diminishing the capacity of the car as described. I also claim extending the body of the car below the connecting piece of the truck-frame and the line of draft, by passing the connecting bars of the truck-frame and the draft-bar through the body of the car, substantially as described."

The testimony showed that the defendants had made cars similar to the plaintiffs', except that the form was octagonal instead of circular. There was evidence tending to prove that, considered in reference to the practical uses of such a car, the octagonal car was substantially the same as the circular. Among others, James Millholland, called by the defendants, testified, "that the advantage of a reduced bottom of the car was obtained, whether the car was octagonal or conical; that the strengthening of the bottom due to the adoption of a conical form was the same when the octagonal form was adopted or the circular; that the circular form was the best to resist the pressure, as e. g. in a steam-boiler, and an octagonal one better than the square form; that the octagonal car was not better than the conical; that for practical purposes one was as good as the other; that a polygon of many sides would be equivalent to a circle; that the octagon car, practically, was as good as the conical one; and that, substantially, the witness saw no difference between the two." Curtis, J., in reversing the charge of the circuit judge, said: "Undoubtedly there may be cases in which the letters-patent do include only the particular form described and claimed. Davis *v.* Palmer, 2 Brock. 309, seems to have been one of those cases. But they are in entire accordance with what is above stated. The reason why such a patent covers only one geometrical form is not that the patentee has described and claimed that form only; it is because that form only is capable of embodying his invention; and consequently, if the form is not copied, the invention is not used. Where form and substance are inseparable, it is enough to look at the form only. Where they are separable, where the whole substance of the invention may be copied in a different form, it is the duty of courts and juries to look through the form for the substance, —

of mechanical equivalents becomes practically applicable. This doctrine depends upon the truth that the identity of purpose, and not of form or name, is the true criterion in judging of the similarity or dissimilarity of two pieces of mechanism. The question whether one thing is a mechanical equivalent for another is a question of fact for the jury, on the testimony of experts, or an inspection of the machines; and it is an inference to be drawn from all the circumstances of the case, by attending to the consideration, whether the contrivance used by the defendant is used for the same purpose, performs the same duties, or is applicable to the same object, as the contrivance used by the patentee.[1] Hence, two things may be mechanical equivalents

for that which entitled the inventor to his patent, and which the patent was designed to secure. Where that is found, there is an infringement; and it is not a defence that it is embodied in a form not described and in terms claimed by the patentee. Patentees sometimes add to their claims an express declaration to the effect that the claim extends to the thing patented, however its form or proportions may be varied. But this is unnecessary. The law so interprets the claim without the addition of these words. The exclusive right to the thing patented is not secured if the public are at liberty to make substantial copies of it, varying its form or proportions. . . . How is a question of infringement of this patent to be tried? It may safely be assumed that neither the patentee nor any other constructor has made or will make a car exactly circular. In practice deviations from a true circle will always occur. How near to a circle, then, must a car be to a circle, in order to infringe? May it be slightly elliptical or otherwise depart from a true circle, and if so, how far? In our judgment, the only answer that can be given to these questions is, that it must be so near a true circle as substantially to embody the patentee's mode of operation, and thereby attain the same kind of result as was reached by his invention. It is not necessary that the defendant's car should employ the plaintiff's invention to as good advantage as he employed it, or that the result should be precisely the same in degree. It must be the same in kind, and effected by his mode of operation in substance." See also dissenting opinion of Campbell, J.

[1] In Morgan *v.* Seaward, Webs. Pat. Cas. 170, Alderson, B., instructed the jury as follows: "The first defence is, that they did not infringe the patent. That is a question of fact, with regard to which I do not think it is at all material to recapitulate the evidence, for I understand from an intimation you have thrown out, that you entertain no doubt of it, that is, that the one is an infringement of the other. Upon that subject, the question would be, simply, whether the defendants' machine was only colorably different, that is, whether it differed merely in the substitution of what are called mechanical equivalents for the contrivances which are resorted to by the patentee. I think, when you are told what the invention of the plaintiffs' really is, you will see that those

for each other under some circumstances, which would not be so under different circumstances. Hence, also, the names as well as the forms of things are of comparatively little importance. The question to be determined is, whether, under a variation of form, or by the use of a thing which bears a different name, the defendant accomplishes in his machine the same purpose, object,

differences which Mr. Donkin and others point out as existing between the one machine and the other, are in truth differences which do not affect the principle of the invention. Therefore, the two machines are alike in principle, one man was the first inventor of the principle, and the other has adopted it; and though he may have carried it into effect, by substituting one mechanical equivalent for another, still you are to look to the substance, and not to the mere form, and if it is in substance an infringement, you ought to find that it is so. If in principle it is not the same, but really different, then the defendants cannot be said to have infringed the patent. You will, however, when you are considering that subject, remember, that when the model of Mr. Stevens's paddles was put into the hands of Mr. Donkin, he said, at first sight, that it was exactly like the plaintiffs'; and so like was it as to induce him to say that it was precisely the same in principle, till I pointed out to him a material difference in it, and then it appeared, that though there was a similarity of execution, there was a real difference in principle, therefore it was not similar to the plaintiffs' wheel, though at first sight it had the appearance of being similar. So you see you ought to look always to the substance, and not to the form." In Webster *v.* Lowther, before Lord Tenterden, the jury, upon the evidence of *sportsmen* that the lock with a sliding bolt was more readily used in the field, particularly in wet weather, than the screw and washer, found that the alteration was a material and useful improvement; and upon evidence *by mechanics*, that a spring in a bolt was the same thing as a bolt sliding in a groove, they found that the defendant had infringed the patent of the plaintiff. Godson on Patents, 232, 233. Here an important advantage was gained, but it was gained by the use of a mechanical equivalent, and consequently the new advantage did not prevent the defendants' lock being an infringement on the plaintiffs'.

The term mechanical equivalent, or mechanical substitute, was thus defined by Mr. Justice Sawyer, in Carter *v.* Baker, 4 Fisher's Pat. Cas. 404: "When in mechanics one device does a particular thing, or accomplishes a particular result, every other device *known* and *used* in mechanics, which skilful and experienced workmen know will produce the same result, or do the same particular thing, is a known mechanical substitute for the first device mentioned for doing the same thing, or accomplishing the same result, although the first device may never have been detached from its work, and the second one put in its place. It is sufficient to constitute known mechanical substitutes that when a skilful mechanic sees one device doing a particular thing, that he knows the other devices, whose uses he is acquainted with, will do the same thing."

or effect as that accomplished by the patentee; or whether there is a real change of structure and purpose.[1]

[1] Thus, in the old mode of making chains, the different parts of the chain were held together by one branch of the chain being linked within another, or else the different branches were connected together by holes perforated through each, and connected by a pin or screw. Subsequently, a party united these two modes, by inserting one link within the other, and perforating both by a pin. A second inventor then made a chain which united both these principles of support, but in a different manner, by using a piece of metal, *called* a pin, for a totally different purpose, not performing the same duties, or applicable to the same object; and it was held that he was well entitled to a patent for his invention. In the Matter of Cutler's patent, Caveat at the Great Seal, Webs. Pat. Cas. 418, 430. In Morgan *v.* Seaward, Webs. Pat. Cas. 167, Sir L. Shadwell, V. C., said: "The question in the case is simply whether the eccentric motion is produced by the adoption of the same combination of machinery by the defendants as the plaintiffs are entitled exclusively to use. Upon reading the specification, it appears that a particular combination, insisted on, is described under the item rods, bent rods, disk, and crank. If Mr. Galloway had been asked, at the time he gave this description, whether he meant the disk should revolve on a crank only, or that it should be made to revolve by any other suitable means, his reply might have been general; but as he has thought proper to specify a crank, the question to determine is, whether the eccentric axis, with a collar in the defendants' contrivance, is the same as a crank in that of the plaintiffs'. The term "crank" is a relative term, and might have reference to some particular piece of machinery. The arrangement adopted by the defendants is a most important variation from the invention; for instead of weakening the action of the paddle wheel, that is preserved entire, unbroken, and unincumbered. That perpetual vibration or destroying power, as it might be termed, on the outer part of the frame work that supports the wheel, is entirely avoided, and the vibration at the centre of the disk within the wheel is transferred from a part of the machinery least able to bear it to the side of the vessel, that is made strong for the purpose; and although it might be said the action of the rods on one side of the float boards might distort them a little, that inconvenience might be more than counterbalanced by other advantages. The alteration is, therefore, not merely colorable, but *primâ facie* a decided improvement by the introduction into a combination of three things of that which is not noticed at all in the specification."

In Gray *v.* Osgood, Peters's C. C. R. 394, 398, may be found a clear illustration of the doctrine of mechanical equivalents. Washington, J., said: "In the former [the plaintiff's machine] we find the two jaws of a vice, the one fixed, and the one movable on a pivot at the top, which connects them together. In each of these jaws is fixed a cutter, the use of which is to cut off from the bar of iron as much as will be necessary to form the nail, which, being separated, falls by its own gravity into a die, which holds it by a firm gripe until the head is formed, by what is called the set, or heading die. The

Thus, the substitution by defendants of a cylinder having a domed or spherical top, for the cone or the cone with the conoidal open in the plaintiff's apparatus, — both the defendant's and the plaintiff's apparatus being used for the same purpose and in

power which produces this double operation is a lever of the first order, acting upon a toggle-joint, which compresses the two jaws, and consequently the cutters together, and also the set in such a manner as to head the nail. But the whole is performed by the same movement of the lever.

"It is impossible to describe the parts of the defendant's machine, and its operation, without using the same expressions, except that his is inverted, the pivot of the vice being below, and a lever of the second order embracing the jaws with a friction-roller, acting on an inclined plane made on the moving jaw of the vice, instead of the lever of the first order, and the toggle-joint. But it is in full proof that these differences as to the lever and the friction-roller are the necessary consequences of the machine being inverted. After having made this comparison, and ascertained the mode of operation by each machine, connected with the result of each, the jury can find little difficulty in deciding whether they are the same in principle or not.

"The witnesses have differed in opinion as to the comparative merit of the toggle-joint in Perkins's machine, and the friction-roller in Read's. If their operation is precisely the same, the difference in form does not amount to an invention of any kind.

"If the friction-roller is better than the toggle-joint, which seems to be the opinion of some of the defendant's witnesses, then Read has the merit of having discovered an improvement on Perkins's machine, and no more.

"If the jury should be of opinion that the parts of the two machines which I have noticed are the same in principle, and that each will by the same operation cut and head nails; then it would follow, that the forcing-slide, the proximity of the cutters and dies to each other, the balance wheel, and some other additional parts in Read's machine, which give it a great and acknowledged preference over Perkins's, are merely improvements, but do not change the principle of the machine. If improvements only, what is the legal consequence? Most clearly this, and no more: that Perkins, and those claiming under his patent, have no right to use those improvements, without a license from the inventor. But, on the other hand, neither Read nor any other person can lawfully use the discovery of Perkins of the principal machine without a license from him. The law, wisely and with justice, discriminates between them, and rewards the merit of each by granting an exclusive property to each in his discovery, but prevents either from invading the rights of the other. If then the jury should be of opinion that the two machines are the same in principle, it is no defence for the defendant's, for using Perkins's discovery, that they have improved it, no matter to what extent." So, too, it is wholly immaterial that the defendant's invention is better than that of the plaintiff, unless there is a substantial difference in principle. Alden *v.* Dewy, 1 Story's R. 336, 337.

very nearly the same way, — was held to be strong evidence of infringement.[1]

§ 311. If the change introduced by the defendant constitutes a mechanical equivalent, in reference to the means used by the patentee, and, besides being such an equivalent, it accomplishes some other advantage beyond the effect or purpose accomplished by the patentee, it will still be an infringement, as respects what is covered by the patent, although the further advantage may be a patentable subject as an improvement upon the former invention.

Thus, in Electric Telegraph Co. *v.* Brett,[2] where the patentee's invention was described as an invention of "improvements in giving signals and sounding alarms in distant places, by means of electric currents transmitted through *metallic circuits;* and the defendant's plan was to use the *earth* as a return circuit by plunging the two ends of the wire into it, it was held that such a circuit would, if used in connection with the machinery for signals, be an infringement. In other words, the earth was, as far as the alarm-machinery was concerned, a mere equivalent for the former return wire. Such a circuit might of itself constitute an improvement in telegraphing, which would warrant a separate patent, but no one could use even this or any other circuit in connection with the patented machinery for giving signals, without infringing the same. In this particular case the discovery that the earth would form a return circuit was made after the patentees had obtained their letters-patent.

§ 312. Where the subject-matter of the patent is a manufacture, the same test of substantial identity is to be applied. In many cases of this kind, it will not be by varying in form, or in immaterial circumstances, the nature of the article, or the process by which it is produced, that a party can escape the penalties of infringement. The question will be, whether in reality and in substance the defendant has availed himself of the invention of the patentee, in order to make the fabric or article which he has made. If he has taken the same plan and applied it to the same purpose, notwithstanding he may have varied the pro-

[1] *In re* Newall and Elliot, 4 C. B. N. S. 269.

[2] 10 C. B. 838 (a fuller report than that contained in 4 E. L. & Eq. 348).

cess of the application, his manufacture will be substantially identical with that of the patentee.[1]

[1] Walton *v.* Potter, Webs. Pat. Cas. 585, 607. In this case Erskine, J., said: "Then there remains the first plea, by which it is denied that the defendants had infringed the patent of the plaintiff, and that depends upon whether the plan which the defendants have employed is in substance the same as the plaintiff's, and whether all the differences which have been introduced by them in the manner of making their cards are not merely differences in circumstances not material, and whether it is not in substance and effect a mere colorable evasion of the plaintiff's patent. The jury, it appears to me, have come to the right conclusion, that this was in effect and substance the same as the plan of the plaintiff. The plaintiff's plan is, the insertion of the teeth through india-rubber, giving to the teeth the additional elasticity of the india-rubber, beyond what the wire had of itself. The defendant's plan is for the same purpose. The only difference is, that the plaintiff, in employing the india-rubber, takes a slice either from the original block, as it is imported into this country, or from the improved block, as it is used after it has been compressed, and places it upon a piece of holland, for the purpose of keeping the teeth more firmly in their places, and then afterwards placing it on the engine, by nailing that holland on the engine, or taking away the holland, and cementing the india-rubber to the cylinder, giving an elasticity to the teeth of the card by the india-rubber, which is next to them. The defendant's plan is to saturate a piece of cloth with india-rubber dissolved, and then to lay upon the surface a further layer of india-rubber on both sides, and then to insert the teeth through the substance of the cloth and the india-rubber. But what is the principle upon which this becomes useful to the card, and the person who employs those cards in the carding of wool? Why it is, that there is upon the surface and the substance of the cloth the elasticity of the india-rubber; that the india-rubber is there in its natural state, having been brought back into its natural state by the evaporation of the material in which it had been first dissolved, for the purpose of first laying it on. The only difference, therefore, is in the mode of laying on the india-rubber for the purpose of having it pierced by the teeth. That appears to me not to be a difference in principle, or a matter which so varies the plan of the defendants from the plan of the plaintiff as to entitle them to call it a new invention, or different from the plaintiff's. It seems to me a mere difference in circumstances not material, and therefore it is an infringement of the plaintiff's right, and the verdict of the jury ought to stand."

Goodyear *v.* The R. R., 2 Wallace, C. C. 356. "Even assuming this patent to be merely for a process and not for a product or fabric, still, in a question of infringement, the inquiry is, what is the essential or substantial agent in the patentee's process or discovery? The specification affirms it to be a high degree of artificial heat, and that no commixture or combination of substances with caoutchouc will give it these qualities, unless the composition be exposed for a length of time to such high degree of heat. It is clear that the plaintiff claims the vulcanization of rubber and sulphur by

§ 312 *a.* The discovery by Charles Goodyear of the process of preparing india-rubber, and Nelson Goodyear's improvement, by which hard rubber or vulcanite is produced, has given rise to much litigation, one phase of which may be here noticed.

The process of Nelson Goodyear consisted in mixing the rubber as produced by the process of Charles Goodyear with sulphur, in the proportion of about four ounces to a pound of sulphur to a pound of rubber, and subjecting this mixture to not less than from 260° to 275° Fahrenheit. This process produced, under the prescribed conditions of time and place, the compound or substance known as vulcanite, which has the hard and tough qualities found in ivory, bone, tortoise-shell, and horn, and the spring-like property under flexure belonging to whalebone. These qualities gave to vulcanite great value as a material for use in the mechanic arts, where it is applied to a great variety of uses.

Chief among the preparations decided to infringe the rights of the Goodyears was the hard rubber or compound made under the patent granted to Edward L. Simpson, October 16, 1866, and intended primarily for dental purposes. In his specification, Simpson says: "The rubber now used for dental purposes has incorporated in it large proportions of free sulphur, for the purpose of vulcanizing the rubber after it is formed. . . . The odor and taste occasioned by the presence of this sulphur is extremely obnoxious to many persons, and occasions the principal, if not the only, objection to the use of rubber for dental purposes. To overcome this objection, and produce vulcanized rubber for dental purposes, without the actual or apparent presence of sulphur, is the object of my invention, and consists in preparing the

artificial heat however produced. The modes of producing heat are very numerous and extremely different. But the result is the same. Heat is heat, however produced, or by whatsoever agent. The method of communicating heat is not the thing patented; and even if it were the thing, and steam were a patented invention or discovery, made since the patent of Goodyear, while Goodyear could not use it, still the defendant could not, by applying this new form of heat to the curing of india-rubber, go on and destroy all Goodyear's patent rights. But steam is not patented by Goodyear nor by anybody to cure rubber. On the contrary, it is curing rubber by artificial heat that is patented. Steam is indeed an effect of heat on water, but it is also heat itself. We have therefore no doubt that the use of steam in place of heated air, in the manufacture of India-rubber, is an infringement of the patent of Goodyear."

rubber for vulcanizing by the introduction of a peculiar vulcanizing compound."

In describing the mode by which this object may be effected, the patentee says: "I first boil linseed or other vegetable oil to the consistency of honey (this I do to facilitate the preparation); thoroughly mix two ounces of benzoin gum with one pound of pulverized sulphur; then to each quart of the boiled oil add one pound of the prepared sulphur, carefully subjecting this mixture to a moderate heat, sufficient only to cause the two substances to react upon each other, until they pass from a semi-fluid to a semi-hard state, having a honey-comb or spongy appearance." He adds that benzoin gum "by its vaporizing qualities more perfectly expels the fumes of the sulphur, as well as the odor from the oil, and renders the compound nearly, if not perfectly, odorless, and when combined with india-rubber or similar gum, and subjected to a regulated heat, will cause the same to undergo the change known as vulcanization." To make hard rubber or vulcanite for dental purposes, from ten to fourteen ounces of this vulcanizing compound is mixed with one pound of rubber by being ground between warm rollers. This mixture of rubber and vulcanizing compound is then subjected to a heat of 320° Fahrenheit for about four hours; or, if the heat is above 320°, for a less time. The result is a vulcanite "as tasteless and odorless as a metal plate."

In the several cases wherein the Simpson patent was in controversy, it was held that the process of vulcanizing there described was substantially the same as that described in the Nelson Goodyear patent, and that the product was the same, excepting that it was tasteless and odorless; and that while these qualities may have rendered the Simpson vulcanite an improvement for dental purposes over that of Goodyear, Simpson was not entitled to use without authority the process described in the Goodyear patents, or produce the product in substantially the same way, and therefore his patent was an infringement of the Goodyear patents.[1]

In discussing the question of infringement in the case of Goodyear *v.* Rust,[1] Mr. Justice Shipman said: "We have, then, Good-

[1] Goodyear *v.* Rust, 6 Blatchf. 229; Goodyear *v.* Evans, ibid. 121; Goodyear *v.* Berry, 3 Fisher's Pat. Cas. 439. See also Goodyear *v.* Mullee, 5 Blatchf. 429; Goodyear *v.* Wait, 5 Blatchf. 468.

year's invention, which consists in combining not much less than four ounces of sulphur with one pound of rubber, and submitting the same to not much less than 260° to 275° of heat, Fahrenheit's scale. We have Simpson's process, which consists in combining not much less than four ounces of sulphur with one pound of rubber, and subjecting the same to a heat of 320° Fahrenheit's scale. The distinction which is sought to be made between these two compositions, or processes, is founded upon the claim that, in Simpson's, one-half of the sulphur is first chemically combined with oil, forming a new substance termed vulcanized oil, and, while there, though acting in the same mass with the remaining half of the sulphur, as an auxiliary vulcanizing agent, acts in a free way from the free sulphur itself. In other words, half the quantity of sulphur necessary to vulcanize Goodyear's process has disappeared, and exists no longer, except as it is represented in a new chemical substance called vulcanized oil. The other half remains. But neither the half that remains nor any quantity of the new agent can alone vulcanize. Yet the two, acting together, at once perform this important office and produce the same result as Goodyear's combination."[1]

[1] Continuing the discussion, Mr. Justice Shipman said: "I have said that it appears from the evidence that the *chemically combined* elements of the compound of Simpson will not alone, when mixed with rubber, and heated, produce vulcanite. I infer this from the language already cited from Professor Seely's affidavit, where he says: 'A quantity of vulcanized oil, containing four or even sixteen ounces of sulphur may be mixed and heated with one pound of rubber, and not an atom of Goodyear's hard rubber can be produced. Simpson's compound is composed of vulcanized oil and free sulphur.' I have not failed to notice that the language is, that the vulcanized oil, in combination with the rubber, will not produce 'an atom of *Goodyear's* hard rubber.' But as the whole scope and direction of the defence are aimed at establishing a distinction between the *processes*, and not between the *products*, I can come to no other conclusion than that the compound alone, if destitute of free sulphur, would not, when mixed with rubber, perform the office of vulcanization. It is true that the compound, when made according to the patent of Simpson, always contains one-half of the sulphur in a free state, but it is agreed, on all hands, that this amount of free sulphur alone will not vulcanize. So the evidence, in whatever light we view it, proves that that portion of the compound which contains the elements in chemical combination is powerless, without the aid of the uncombined free sulphur, which is scattered through the pores of the combined mass.

"Now, it may be asked, how do these two agents, namely, vulcanized oil and free sulphur, perform by their united forces the work of vulcanization?

§ 313. But in regard to another class of cases, it not infrequently happens that the sole evidence of infringement consists in the similarity of the articles, without any direct evidence of their having been made by the same process. Similarity in appearance and structure will not of itself always establish an infringement; because the patent, though it covers the manufactured article itself, may be for the process of the manufacture. In such cases, the inference that the same process was used must be drawn from the evidence; and the rule was laid down by Lord Ellenborough, that the similarity of structure of two things is presumptive evidence of their being made in the same way.[1]

No part of this work is assigned, by the evidence, to the benzoin. It cannot be done by the chemically combined oil and sulphur alone. It cannot be done by the free sulphur alone. The latter, to the extent of its effective power, for all that appears in this case, works in the same way that it does in Goodyear's process. The effect of the former (oil and sulphur chemically combined), Professor Seely says, is not chemical, but 'must be done wholly to physical and molecular causes.' But, whether the auxiliary vulcanizing force, whatever it is, exerted by the chemically combined oil and sulphur, is supplied by the latter or not, does not appear by the proof. From what has long been known, however, of the vulcanizing power of sulphur, when mixed with rubber, and heated, that agent, though combined with another substance, would naturally be looked to as the seat of this force. It may be true that, as Professor Seely says, the effect of vulcanized oil, in hardening rubber, is due not to chemical, but 'to physical and molecular causes.' Of the nature or significance of this distinction, in the scientific sense, I do not presume to speak. But I do not see how this fact avoids Goodyear's patent. I do not find, in his specification, any evidence that he rested his invention upon any such nice scientific distinction, or that he limited his claim to sulphur, when working through chemical, as distinguished from physical or molecular laws. If the validity of his patent rests upon such a scientific problem as this, I think its solution should, in the present case, be left to final hearing. The suggestion of such a problem, in *ex parte* affidavits, at a very late stage of a series of protracted litigations, in which every other defence has thus far failed, is not a valid answer to this motion.

"There can be no question that Simpson uses a degree of heat within the scope of Goodyear's patent."

[1] Huddart *v.* Grimshaw, Webs. Pat. Cas. 85, 91. This is a very instructive case. The plaintiff's patent was for "a new mode of making great cables and other cordage, so as to attain a greater degree of strength therein, by a more equal distribution of the strain upon the yarns." Pieces of cordage made by the defendant were put into the hands of the plaintiff's witnesses, and from the fact that the same effect was produced in them, and from the similarity of structure, they gave the opinion that they were made by the same process as the plaintiff's. This was the question at issue, on the point of in-

§ 314. In such cases, where the object to be accomplished is open to the public, notwithstanding the patent, provided it can be accomplished in several modes, which, as processes, are substantially different, an infringement must be in respect of the process used by the patentee. But unless it appears that the article itself could be produced by another process, constituting an independent discovery, then an infringement may be proved by the making of the article. The burden of proof is always on the plaintiff, to show that his process has been infringed; and in the absence of direct evidence, the similarity of the effect produced will generally be sufficient to establish an infringement, and if this is aided by evidence of the use of similar apparatus, the presumption of a use of the same process will be still stronger.[1] Or, to state this in other words, where the invention, or subject-matter of the patent, is an entirely new manufacture, it is immaterial by what process it is produced, since the infringement must consist in making the same thing, whether by one process or another. But where the invention or subject-matter is the process of making a particular thing, which may be made by more than one process, the inquiry will be whether it has been made by the use of the process covered by the patent. In such cases, the identity of the manufactured article is, with all the other circumstances, competent evidence, from which the jury are to infer that it was made by the process of the patentee; although there may be cases, where, from the nature of the

fringement. The object to be accomplished, the making a stronger rope, was clearly open to the public. Lord Ellenborough said that it had happened to him in the same morning, to give, as far as he was concerned, his consent to the granting of three different patents for the same thing; but the modes of attaining it were all different. But it did not follow that the plaintiff's *method of attaining the object* was open to the public; and therefore the question for the jury was, whether the defendant had used the plaintiff's method, or some other.

[1] See the preceding note and the case there cited. See also the more recent case of Hall *v.* Boot, Webs. Pat. Cas. 100, 102. Hall's patent was for a new method of singeing off the superfluous fibres upon lace, by means of the flame of gas. The evidence to show the infringement consisted of proof that the defendant had secretly prepared a gas apparatus similar to that used by the plaintiff, and *that lace left with the defendant to be dressed had been returned in the state to which it would have been brought by the plaintiff's process, and that similar lace had been offered for sale by the defendant.* The plaintiff had a verdict.

article, this proof would be less strong, according as it appeared to be possible or probable that the article could be made by more than one process. The burden of proof of the infringement is upon the plaintiff throughout; and although it does not appear that the article could be made by another process, the jury must still draw the inference, from the identity of the manufacture, if that is all the evidence, or from that and the other evidence, that it was made by the patentee's process.

However, in a subsequent case it was held, *per totam curiam*, that where the specification stated the invention to relate to "a mode of manufacturing candles by the application of two or more plaited wicks in each candle," and set out at length the mode of so placing the wicks, that in burning the ends always turned outwards, — the mere production of a candle, made at defendant's factory, in which the wicks turned outward in burning, was no evidence of infringement.[1]

§ 315. But a much more difficult class of cases arises under those patents where the subject-matter is the application of a principle, by means of a process or method, in order to produce a particular effect. We have already had occasion to consider when such an invention or discovery is the proper subject-matter of a patent. We have seen that, under some circumstances, the discovery of a principle may, by application in the arts, be protected by a patent; and we have now to consider how far the proprietor of such a patent may protect himself against the use of the same principle by others; or, in other words, what will constitute an infringement of his right.

§ 316. In this inquiry, the first thing to be attended to is the subject-matter of the patent. A clear idea is to be formed of the object of the patent; and provided the specification properly points out what the claim of the patentee is, it is not material in what form his claim is presented, or whether, in form, the patent purports to be for a process or a manufacture. Wherever the real subject covered by the patent is the application of a principle, in arts or manufactures, the question, on an infringement, will be as to the substantial identity of the principle, and of the application of the principle; and consequently the means, machinery, forms, or modifications of matter made use of will be material, only so far as they affect the identity of the application.

[1] Palmer *v.* Wagstaffe, 25 E. L. & Eq. 535.

§ 317. Thus in Forsyth's patent, the subject-matter was the use and application of detonating powder as priming, for the explosion of gunpowder; and it was held that whatever the construction of the lock by which the powder was to be discharged, the use of detonating mixture as priming was an infringement.[1] So, too, where the claim of the patentee was for "the application of a self-adjusting leverage to the back and seat of a chair, whereby the weight and the seat act as a counterbalance to the pressure against the back of such chair," it was held, that a chair made in any way upon this principle was an infringement.[2] In like manner, where the principle of the invention was the welding of iron tubes by pressure of the edges of the iron, when heated, without the use of a mandril, or other internal support, it was held that a variation from the plaintiff's mode of applying the pressure, the application of the principle being the same, was still an infringement.[3]

§ 318. Clegg's patent was for the application of a law of natural science respecting the motion of fluids and solids, and the alternate filling and discharging of a vessel of gas, by means of that application; the object being to obtain an instrument for measuring the quantity of gas supplied to the consumer. The scientific witnesses said, that the moment a practical scientific man had got that principle, he could multiply without end the forms in which it could be made to operate. The instrument used by the defendant was different in form and construction from that used by the patentee; but the application of the principle, by means of a varied apparatus, was the same in both; and it was held to be an infringement.[4]

[1] Forsyth's patent, Webs. Pat. Cas. 95; Forsyth *v.* Riviere, ibid. 97, note.

[2] Minter *v.* Wells, Webs. Pat. Cas. 127, 134.

[3] Russell *v.* Cowley, Webs. Pat. Cas. 459, 462. See the extracts in the note, *ante*, § 79, p. 69.

[4] Cited in Jupe *v.* Pratt, Webs. Pat. Cas. 146. Alderson, B., said: "It was for measuring the quantity of gas that was supplied to every individual, in order that they might not take it without being known. There never was a more instructive case than that; I remember very well the argument put by the Lord Chief Baron, who led that case for the plaintiff, and succeeded. There never were two things to the eye more different than the plaintiff's invention and what the defendant had done in contravention of his patent right. The plaintiff's invention was different in form, different in construction; it agreed with it only in one thing, and that was, by moving in the water,

§ 319. In Neilson's patent, the invention consisted in the application of hot air to the blowing of furnaces by heating the air between its leaving the blowing apparatus and its introduction into the furnace, in any way, in a close vessel, exposed to the action of heat. The defendant's apparatus for this purpose was confessedly superior to what would be constructed according to the directions in the plaintiff's specification; but it was held to be an infringement.[1]

In a recent case, where the patentee claimed as his invention the combination of a blast and an exhaust in ventilating the grinding surfaces of mill-stones, it was held that such combination might be made the subject of a patent, although both blast and exhaust had been previously used separately, and also that it

a certain point was made to open, either before or after, so as to shut up another, and the gas was made to pass through this opening. Passing through it, it was made to revolve it; the scientific men, all of them, said, the moment a practical scientific man has got that principle in his head, he can multiply without end the forms in which that principle can be made to operate. The difficulty which will press on you, and to which your attention will be called in the present case, is this: you cannot take out a patent for a principle; you may take out a patent for a principle coupled with the mode of carrying the principle into effect, provided you have not only discovered the principle, but invented some mode of carrying it into effect. But then you must start with having invented some mode of carrying the principle into effect. If you have done that, then you are entitled to protect yourself from all other modes of carrying the same principle into effect, that being treated by the jury as piracy of your original invention. But then the difficulty that will press on you here is, that on the evidence there does not appear to have been any mode of carrying the principle into effect at all invented by you."

[1] Neilson *v.* Harford, Webs. Pat. Cas. 310. Parke, B., said to the jury: "If the specification is to be understood in the sense claimed by the plaintiffs, the invention of heating the air between its leaving the blowing apparatus and its introduction into the furnace, in any way, in any close vessel, which is exposed to the action of heat, there is no doubt that the defendant's machinery is an infringement of that patent, because it is the use of air which is heated much more beneficially, and a great improvement upon what would probably be the machine constructed by looking at the specification alone; but still it is the application of heated air, heated in one or more vessels between the blowing apparatus and the furnace; and, therefore, if it should turn out that the patent is good, and the specification is good, though unquestionably what the defendants have done is a great improvement upon what would be the machinery or apparatus constructed under this patent, it appears to me that it would be an infringement of it." See also the observations of the Lord Justice Clerk Hope, cited *ante*.

was valid independent of all claim for any particular mode of creating the blast or the exhaust. The patentee having described the upper stone as fixed, and the lower as revolving, and pointed out some advantages arising from such an arrangement, it was also held, that even if he had thereby limited his claim to the combination of blast and exhaust as applied to a mill where only the lower stone revolved, still the use of the combination of draught and exhaust in a mill where the upper stone rotates would be an infringement.[1]

§ 319 *a*. An important case illustrating the point under consideration was that of Mowry *v*. Whitney,[2] decided by the Supreme Court of the United States in December, 1871. The invention consisted of an improvement in the process of making cast-iron wheels for railroad cars. In a wheel for this purpose it is necessary to have the "tread," or the surface which runs over the rail, very hard, to prevent rapid wearing, while the hub against which there is no friction but which is subjected to great strain, need not be so hard, but must be very tough. It was found that the former quality was given to the periphery of the wheel by rapidly cooling the melted mass of iron after it had been run into the mould; while the latter quality could be imparted to the hub by the process of slow cooling. But there were great difficulties in the way of accomplishing these results, which, however, were successfully overcome by Whitney, who obtained letters-patent dated April 25, 1848, for "a new and useful improvement in the process of manufacturing cast-iron railroad wheels." In his specification he said: —

"My improvement consists in taking railroad wheels from the moulds in which they are ordinarily cast, as soon after being cast as they are sufficiently cool to be strong enough to move with safety, or before they have become so much cooled as to produce any considerable inherent strain between the thin and thick parts, and putting them in this state into a furnace or chamber that has been previously heated to a temperature as high as that of the wheels when taken from the moulds. As soon as they are deposited in this furnace or chamber, the opening through which they have been passed is closed, and the temperature of the furnace or chamber, and its contents, gradually raised to a point *a*

[1] Bovill *v*. Keyworth, 7 Ell. & Blackb. 725.
[2] 14 Wal. 620.

little below that at which fusion commences, when all the avenues to and from the interior are closed, and the whole mass left to cool no faster than the heat it contains permeates through, and radiates from the exterior surface of the materials of which it is composed. By this process all parts of each wheel are raised to the same temperature, and the heat they contain can only pass off through the medium of the confined atmosphere that intervenes between them and the walls of the furnace or chamber; consequently, the thinnest and thickest parts cool and shrink simultaneously together, which relieves them from all inherent strain whatever when cold."

Whitney did not claim to be the inventor of annealing castings made of iron or other metal, when done in the ordinary way; nor to have invented any particular form or kind of furnace in which to perform the process. But he claimed as his invention "the process of prolonging the time of cooling, in connection with annealing railroad wheels in the manner above described."

Mowry claimed to have made an improvement in the same process for which he obtained letters-patent, and which was thus described in his specification: "My invention consists in the use of charcoal or other equivalent substance, interlaid with the wheels in the annealing pits, in connection with the regulated admission of air, for the purpose of heating the wheels up to a proper temperature, prolonging the heat, and permitting them to cool in the course of a given time, gradually, as will be more particularly explained below.

"The operation of my invention is as follows: A layer of charcoal having been laid on the perforated bottom of the annealing pit, the wheels, as they are turned out of the moulds red-hot, are placed in the pits, with a layer of charcoal between each wheel, a layer of charcoal being laid on the uppermost wheel, and on this a perforated metal plate is laid.

"The charcoal, becoming now ignited by the hot wheels, the cover of pit is then laid on, and the damper opened so as to admit just sufficient air to effect the combustion of the contained charcoal, in the space of seventy-two hours, less or more, as may be found necessary for the annealing operation. The draft of air in the apparatus shown on drawings is from above downwards, but it may, without affecting my invention, be from below upwards, by conveying the air from the horizontal flue up through the pits, and through the aperture in cover, and from thence through flues, into the main shaft or chimney (C); the result will be the same in both cases, and the adoption of one or the other plan will be dictated by convenience."

A bill was filed by Whitney, charging Mowry with infringement, which was denied by the latter. In holding Mowry's process to be an infringement of the patent of Whitney, Mr. Justice Strong, who delivered the judgment of the Supreme Court of the United States, said: "What the process of the defendant was is clearly set out in a patent which he obtained on the 7th of May, 1861. It consists in placing in a pit the wheels as they are turned out of the moulds red-hot, with a layer of charcoal beneath the lowest wheel, and a layer between each wheel as well as above the uppermost, and covering the pit with a perforated metal plate. The charcoal is ignited by the hot wheels, and just sufficient air is admitted to effect combustion of the coal. Thus the wheels are reheated and permitted gradually to cool. There are some minor details which it is unnecessary to mention. So far as relates to reheating the wheels and retarding the cooling by the application of additional heat, it is obvious that the process is substantially the same. The purpose of the charcoal interlaid with the wheels is avowed to be to heat them in the pit to a proper temperature, prolonging the heat, and permitting them to cool gradually in a given time, said to be seventy-two hours, more or less, as may be found necessary for the annealing operation. The rapidity of combustion of the charcoal is regulated by a damper in the flue; and this process is followed, as the specification explains, that the different parts of the wheels may adjust themselves to each other, and accommodate the unequal contraction which results from the process of chilling. It is under this patent, and in accordance with its directions, that the defendant has prepared his car-wheels for market. As the object of the patentees is the same, — relief from the strain incident to unequal contraction, — the only inquiry is whether the object is attained by substantially the same means. The idea of Whitney was undoubtedly arresting contraction before any remediless strain had commenced, and regulating the progress of cooling so that all parts of the wheel may maintain an equal temperature at all stages of cooling. Manifestly the process of the defendant embodied the same idea, and carried it out by means identical in principle. It reheats the wheels when removed from the moulds to the chamber or pit. It prolongs the cooling in connection with the reheating, and it subjects the rapidity of cooling to control of the operator. The form or structure of the furnace chamber or pit is not claimed by either patentee.

"It hardly seems necessary to resort to the opinions of experts in order to reach the conclusion that the process of the defendant is only formally different from that of Whitney, while the essential element of the two processes is the same. But the testimony of the experts examined, taken as a whole, clearly supports such a conclusion."

§ 320. These cases show that when a party has invented some mode of carrying into effect a law of natural science, or a rule of practice, it is the application of that law or rule which constitutes the peculiar feature of his invention; that he is entitled to protect himself from all other modes of making the same application; and consequently that every question of infringement will present the question, whether the different mode, be it better or worse, is in substance an application of the same principle. The substantial identity, therefore, that is to be looked to, in cases of this kind, respects that which constitutes the essence of the invention, viz., the application of the principle. If the mode of carrying the same principle into effect, adopted by the defendant, still shows only that the principle admits of the same application in a variety of forms, or by a variety of apparatus, the jury will be authorized to treat such mode as a piracy of the original invention. But of course where the variations adopted by the defendant show that the application of the principle is varied, that some other law or rule of science, or of practice, is made to take the place of that which the patentee claims as the essence of his invention, then there will be no infringement, but a substantial invention.[1]

§ 321. And this brings us to the consideration of another test of the fact of infringement, viz., that which shows on the part of the defendant a substantive invention sufficient to support a patent, as for a new thing.

[1] In Barber *v.* Grace, 1 Wells., Hurlst. & Gord. 340, the process patented consisted in laying articles of hosiery in a box heated by steam and pressing them by means of a similar box heated by steam and applied by hydraulic pressure or by screws. It was held, that a process of finishing by means of iron rollers heated by steam was no infringement.

§ 322. There may be many different modes of obtaining the same object; and consequently if, after a patent has been obtained for a particular thing, another party, without borrowing from that patent, has invented a new mode of accomplishing the same object, he will be entitled to a patent for his discovery.[1] The fact that a party is entitled to a patent for a substantive invention becomes a test of his infringement of a prior patent in this way. He cannot have become entitled to a patent without the invention of something material and new, that goes to the essence and substance of the subject-matter. If what he has done is only to make a variation in certain particulars, which do not affect the principle of the invention, the subject-matter remains the same, notwithstanding such variation. But if he has produced a new subject-matter, whether it be in the mode of accomplishing a common object, or in the object itself, he has not infringed upon the subject-matter of another which was materially and essentially different.

§ 323. The application of this test is seen in a striking manner in the facts of a recent English case. The plaintiff had obtained a patent for "an invention of improvements in cards, for carding wool, cotton, silk, and other fibrous substances, and for raising the pile of woollen cloths." In his specification, he stated his invention to consist in "the application and adaptation of caoutchouc or india-rubber as a substitute for the fillets or sheets of leather that were commonly used in the construction of ordinary cards, and thus giving a superior elasticity and dura-

[1] Sir N. C. Tindal, Chief Justice, in Walton *v.* Potter, Webs. Pat. Cas. 590, thus states the general principle: "Now there can be no doubt whatever that, although one man has obtained a patent for a given object, there are many modes still open for other men of ingenuity to obtain a patent for the same object; there may be many roads leading to one place, and if a man has, by dint of his own genius and discovery, after a patent has been obtained, been able to give the public, without reference to the former one, or borrowing from the former one, a new and superior mode of arriving at the same end, there can be no objection to his taking out a patent for that purpose. But he has no right whatever to take, if I may so say, a leaf out of his neighbor's book, for he must be contented to rest upon his own skill and labor for the discovery, and he must not avail himself of that which had before been granted exclusively to another; and, therefore, the question again comes round to this, whether you are of opinion that the subject-matter of this second patent is perfectly distinct from the former, or whether it is virtually bottomed upon the former, varying only in certain circumstances, which are not material to the principle and substance of the invention."

bility to cards"; and in describing the mode of preparing the article, he stated that "the regularity of distance and uniformity of the dents or teeth of the cards were found to be better preserved by a piece of linen commonly called brown holland, or other like cloth, well glazed and cemented on to the back of the caoutchouc or india-rubber"; that the cloth so placed rendered the action of the dents or teeth less uncertain in their elastic movements; that the cloth so cemented to the india-rubber or caoutchouc was to be affixed to the cylinder or board of the ordinary carding engine by nails, but if it was to be affixed by cementing (which he recommended as the best mode of applying the cards), then it was desirable to remove the cloth"; and he then proceeded to show the ordinary mode of pricking or piercing holes for the reception of the dents or teeth, the mode of cutting the india-rubber, &c. The defendants subsequently obtained a patent also for "an improvement or improvements in cards for carding various fibrous substances, part of which improvements may be used as a substitute for leather"; and in their specification they stated their invention to consist in the manufacture of a new material or substance for receiving the wire teeth, which they described to be a woven fabric of a peculiar construction, soft and porous, saturated with a solution of india-rubber by being repeatedly passed through it, and then dried and submitted to pressure; the object being to render the fabric so dealt with "extremely elastic in the direction of the thickness of the fabric, so as to impart, as it were, elasticity to the wire teeth when set."

§ 324. The question as to the infringement was, whether the defendants had added any thing material, not covered by the plaintiff's patent, which could be considered as constituting a subject-matter distinct from that of the plaintiff's. It appeared that the difference between the article manufactured under the plaintiff's patent, and that under the defendant's patent, which was complained of as an infringement, was, that in the former the caoutchouc or india-rubber was cemented in slices cut from the solid block to linen cloth, or cloth made of linen and cotton, in the manner described in the plaintiff's specification, and that the latter consisted of cloth of a peculiar fabric saturated or impregnated by passing it through a liquid composed of caoutchouc or india-rubber dissolved in naphtha or oil of turpentine and highly rectified coal-tar oil, and afterwards drying and submitting it to pressure. The plaintiff's evidence tended to show that the article made by the defendants was a colorable imitation of that made under the plaintiff's patent; the cloth being merely placed in the centre between two strata of india-rubber or caoutchouc, instead of at the back, and the india-rubber, though applied in solution or in the form of a cement, being capable of being reproduced by evaporation of the solvent, and the principle and the result of both methods being the same, viz., the acquisition of an increased elasticity, though the modes of attaining that result were somewhat different. It was also sworn that, for the purpose of the plaintiff's patent, caoutchouc or india-rubber might be used either in the state in which it is imported, or in a manufactured state, that is, dissolved by certain known solvents, and afterwards, by evaporation of the solvents, restored to solid blocks; but that, if free from air-holes (in which state it was *possible* to obtain it), it was more desirable to have it in its natural state, its elasticity being somewhat diminished by the artificial process.

§ 325. On the part of the defendants, several witnesses, as well practical as scientific, were called, who stated that the principle of the manufactures respectively described in the specifications of the plaintiff and defendants was essentially different, as well in the materials used and the mode in which they were put together, as in the operation or result of their combination; the one process being wholly mechanical, the other strictly chemical, and the effect of the former being to give *elasticity*, and of the latter to give strength and *flexibility* or *pliancy*, but imparting only a very slight additional elasticity to the card; that the proportion which the india-rubber bore to the cloth, as used by the plaintiff, was generally about three to one, whereas the proportion of india-rubber solution used by the defendants was from twenty to forty per cent only; and that india-rubber as imported was wholly unfit for the purpose described in the plaintiff's specification, never being sufficiently free from imperfection.

§ 326. Upon the issue of not guilty, the jury found a verdict for the plaintiff, thereby establishing that the defendant's card was an infringement of the plaintiff's, both employing the elasticity of caoutchouc next the teeth, and the defendant's practising by a circuitous mode that which falls within the claim of the plaintiff's patent.[1]

§ 327. But if the defendants, in this case, could have succeeded in showing that the materials of which they made their cards, and the mode in which they were put together, were different from the materials and method of construction used by the plaintiff; if they could have satisfied the jury that the difference

[1] Walton *v.* Potter, Webs. Pat. Cas. 585, 597; 4 Scott's N. R. 91. On the application for a new trial, Maule, J., said: "With respect to the issue of not guilty, in order to determine whether or not the verdict has been correctly found for the plaintiff on that issue, it is necessary to consider what is the subject of the defendant's patent; for it is quite clear that what the defendants have done they claim to do under their patent. By their specification the defendants claim to be the inventors of a new material for forming the backs of cards; and they describe the mode of preparing it thus, viz.: 'by repeatedly passing a woven fabric of a peculiar construction through, and saturating it with, a solution of caoutchouc or india-rubber, and then drying it in order to evaporate the solvents, and leave the fabric impregnated and coated with caoutchouc or india-rubber, and afterwards submitting it to pressure'; and the object they describe as being to render the fabric so dealt with 'extremely elastic in the direction of the thickness of the fabric, so as to impart, as it were, elasticity to the wire teeth when set.' That is, in effect, producing by a circuitous process a cloth with a layer of caoutchouc or india-rubber on each side of it, so as to give a great degree of elasticity to the basis of the dents or teeth of the card. The plaintiff, by his specification, claims the exclusive right of making cards with caoutchouc or india-rubber, as the fillet, or sheet, or medium in which the dents or teeth are to be set; the object being, like that of the defendants, the attainment of a superior degree of elasticity and durability; and in describing his mode of attaining that object, he states that he inserts the wire dents or teeth in a foundation or fillet of caoutchouc or india-rubber, — a slice of india-rubber in its natural state, — and that with a view to preserve the regularity of distance and uniformity of the dents or teeth, and to render their action less uncertain, he cements to the back of the caoutchouc or india-rubber a piece of brown holland or other like cloth. The plaintiff does not confine his claim to using india-rubber by means of slicing it; he claims the exclusive right of making cards, by fixing the dents or teeth in india-rubber, using for that purpose cloth, some texture of linen or cotton. In some instances, he says, the cloth may be removed. That does not, in point of fact, make it less a part of the process, by which he applies cloth for the putting the dents into the layer of india-rubber. If that be so, I think it is evident the defendants claim to do a thing falling within the generality of the plaintiff's claim. Taking that to be so, the evidence is abundant to justify the jury in finding; and it seems to me to require them to find for the plaintiff." See also the observations of Erskine, J., cited *ante*.

expressed by saying that the one process was mechanical and the other chemical was a real and substantial, and not a colorable difference; then they would, notwithstanding the former patent of the plaintiff, and notwithstanding that the objects of both were the same, have appeared to be the authors of a substantive invention, because they would have produced a distinct subject-matter, new in all material respects, of a useful character, and therefore capable of supporting an independent patent. But it appeared that the plaintiff's patent covered the use of india-rubber combined with cloth, as a fillet or sheet, for the backs of cards, in which to insert the teeth, in order to accomplish certain purposes; and that the mode in which the defendants brought these same materials into combination, for the same purposes, was only a circuitous mode of doing what the plaintiff had done, and therefore that they had produced nothing new, material to the principle and substance of the invention.

§ 328. On the other hand, where the plaintiff had a patent for producing an effect in the manufacture of iron, said to be altogether new, by a mode or process, or series of processes unknown before, it being for a combination of processes altogether new, leading to one end; and the defendants had used the same ingredients, but in different proportions, which constituted a mode of working essentially different from that pointed out in the specification, it was held that there was no infringement. The plaintiff's invention in this case consisted in rendering available the slags or cinders produced in the manufacture of iron; and also in the use and application of lime, subsequent to the blast furnace, in order to prevent the quality called "cold short"; and his specification pointed out the proportion of slags, mine rubbish, coke, and limestone, to be used for the production of the effect. To prove the infringement, a witness in the employ of the defendants was called, who stated that he had seen the plaintiff's specification; that since the date of the patent the defendants preserved cinders, which they had not done before, and produced pig-iron, by mixing them with mine rubbish, and that in the subsequent processes they applied quicklime to prevent the iron from being "cold short." But he stated that the defendants did not work by the plaintiff's specification, but used very different proportions, viz., lime in the refinery furnace in about the proportion of one hundred and twentieth part of the whole charge of pig-iron, and that they used none in the puddling furnace, and that the defendants had used slags in the puddling furnace for years before the date of the patent. He also proved that the proportions of mine rubbish, as laid down in the specification, were not essential to the success of the process; that the defendants had been in the habit of varying those proportions; and that they once entirely omitted mine rubbish, when the result was most successful.[1]

§ 329. Now this patent was one of that class in which proportions or degrees, when specified as the mode in which a particular effect is to be produced, make a part of the essence of the invention. A discovery may consist in the effect produced by the union of certain ingredients or agents; but if a particular proportion is supposed to be necessary to the effect, and is claimed as entering into the production of that effect, the subject-matter of the patent will be the use of the particular ingredients in that particular proportion; and if the same ingredients in different proportions, or a part of the same ingredients in other proportions, are used by another person to produce a similar beneficial effect, more or less advantageous, that person will have discovered a new subject-matter, and consequently will not have infringed the right of a patentee, whose invention depends on the proportions which he has specified. Accordingly it was held in this case that the defendants' mode of working being essentially different from the specification of the plaintiff, they had not infringed his patent; and if we apply to the reasoning of the court the test of a sufficiency of invention on the part of the defendants to support a patent, as for a new discovery, it will be seen that the same facts will lead to that result, which show that the plaintiff's patent had not been infringed.[2]

[1] Hill *v.* Thompson, Webs. Pat. Cas. 225, 232, 233.

[2] Dallas, J., delivering the judgment of the court, said: "To prove the infringement, one witness only was called; and this part of the case depends, therefore, entirely upon his testimony. And, before adverting to the evidence in question, it will be necessary to look to the patent, as far as it relates to this part of the subject. It has not been contended that it is a patent introducing into use any one of the articles mentioned, singly and separately taken; nor could it be so contended, for the patent itself shows the controversy; and if it had been a patent of such a description, it would have been impossible to support it; for slags had undoubtedly been made use of previously to the patent, so had mine rubbish, and so had lime. But it is said, it is a patent

§ 330. The superior utility of one thing over another will sometimes furnish an important test upon this question of identity. It

for combinations and proportions, producing an effect altogether new, by a mode and process, or series of processes, unknown before; or, to adopt the language made use of at the bar, it is a patent for a combination of processes altogether new, leading to one end; and this being the nature of the alleged discovery, any use made of any of the ingredients singly, or any use made of such ingredients in partial combination, some of them being omitted, or any use of all or some of such ingredients, in proportions essentially different from those specified, and yet producing a result equally beneficial (if not more so) with the result obtained by the proportions specified, will not constitute an infringement of the patent.

"It is scarcely necessary here to observe, that a slight departure from the specification, for the purpose of evasion only, would of course be a fraud upon the patent, and therefore the question will be, whether the mode of working by the defendant has or has not been essentially or substantially different. For this we must look to the evidence of E. Forman; and he being the single witness to the point, by his testimony this part of the case must stand or fall. It may be difficult entirely to reconcile different parts of his evidence with each other, if his answers to the several questions be taken separately and detached; but looking to the result, it seems to be clear. On the part of the plaintiff he proves, that, before the patent was taken out, the defendants were not in the habit of making use of slags, and that his attention being called to the subject by the patentee in the first instance, and then by the patent itself, he has made use of them uniformly since; he has since also, at times, used mine rubbish, and also lime, which last, he also admits, was used to prevent the 'cold short,' which defect he allows was and is thereby prevented. So far, therefore, he proves separate use and occasional combination. He is next asked as to the proportions mentioned in the patent: 'Did you apply the lime in these proportions?' His answer is, 'I say no, to that.' 'Have you worked by the specification?' 'No, we did not.' He then explains in what respects they departed from the specification. This is his evidence on the examination in chief. On the cross-examination he says that the proportions used were very materially different, and that the proportions in the patent are not essential; that it would make no difference to him if he were to be restrained from using these proportions, and that the result would be better obtained by materially departing from them; indeed, by almost losing sight of them altogether. With respect to slags, on reconsideration, he states that the defendant had used slags previously to the patent, in the puddling furnace, for months together. As to mine rubbish, he says, we varied the proportions, and we found, in experience, that the use of it was best without reference to the preparations and restrictions pointed out in the specification, and when omitted the result was best of all. It is true, he afterwards states, that this omission took place when he was absent from home, and that, on his return, he ordered the mine rubbish to be restored; and in this respect, and going to this single point, there appears to be an incon-

is not always true that one machine, for instance, is not an infringement upon another, because it is better than the other; for it may contain the whole substance of that other machine, and something in addition which makes it better; or the patent may have been taken for an entire machine, substantially new in its structure, and the machine complained of may contain some substantial operating part of the machine patented, and so infringe. But where the patent is for some one operating part of a machine, designed to effect a particular end, and the machine complained of effects that end materially better, by the use of means which are in point of fact different, then the two modes of operation are not the same under the patent law. In other words, when the means employed are, in point of fact, not the same, or a known mechanical equivalent, and the question to be determined is, whether they are, under the patent law, the same in substance, or, as it is usually called, the same in principle, superior utility settles that

sistency. But still, as the case stands on his single evidence, if, in substance and result, it proves a mode of working essentially different from the specification, the foundation of the plaintiff's case is altogether gone. And the rule is, in this respect, strict, as stated by Mr. Justice Buller, in the case of Turner *v.* Winter (Webs. Pat. Cas. 77). In that case, the learned judge expressed himself in these words: 'Whenever the patentee brings an action on his patent, if the novelty or effect of the invention be disputed, he must show in what his invention consists, and that he procured the effect proposed, in the manner specified (Webs. Pat. Cas. 81)'; and in another part of the same case, he adds: 'Slight defects in the specification will be sufficient to vacate the patent (Webs. Pat. Cas. 82)'; and speaking of degree and proportion, he says: 'The specification should have shown by what degree of heat the effect was to be produced.' In that case, as in a great variety of others, instances may be found to show the strictness of the law, as bearing upon this point, either in regard of omission or of superfluous addition, or of uncertainty or insufficiency in quantities proposed. But, further, the evidence so applied does not confine itself to this point only; for it disproves also utility, as far as it depends on combination and proportion, leading and conducing to a specific result. Neither can it be justly said, that the use of the separate ingredients, or some of them partially combined, is a use made of the invention in part, so as to support the counts adapted to such partial use; because, as it has been already observed, and will more particularly be adverted to hereafter, each of the ingredients had before been separately used, and had been used, more or less, in partial combination.

"On the whole, our opinion is, as to this part of the case, that, considering the evidence of Forman, in its substance and result, and with reference to the peculiar nature of the patent, an infringement of the patent is not thereby proved." Hill *v.* Thompson, Webs. Pat. Cas. 242, 245, 246.

question. Two things are not the same under the patent law, when one is practically substantially better than the other, and this improvement is not gained by the use of known mechanical equivalents.

§ 331. This view of the patent law relieves it in a great degree from the uncertainties which have arisen from the loose and indeterminate sense in which the word "principle" has been employed; and, at the same time, it is in exact accordance with the great purposes, as well as with the particular provisions, of that system of law. Its leading purpose was to encourage *useful* inventions. Practical utility was its object; and it would be strange, if, with such object in view, it should consider two things as substantially the same, which, practically and in reference to their respective utility, are substantially different. And although this test has not seldom been lost sight of in the trial of patent causes, yet there is nowhere any authority opposed to it, and there is certainly much in its favor.[1]

[1] Thus, in Davis *v.* Palmer, 2 Brock. 310, Mr. Chief Justice Marshal states the principle clearly. He was commenting on the clause in the old patent law, that "simply changing the form or the proportion of any machine shall not be deemed a discovery"; and he says, "In construing this provision, the word 'simply' has, we think, great influence; it is not every change of form and proportion which is declared to be no discovery, but that which is simply a change of form and proportion, and nothing more. If by changing the form and proportion a *new effect* is produced, there is not simply a change of form and proportion, but *a change of principle also.*" To the same effect are the following cases: Earle *v.* Sawyer, 4 Mas. 1, where the substitution of a circular saw, in place of a reciprocating saw, in a shingle machine, was held to be a patentable improvement. — Davol *v.* Brown, 1 Woodb. & M. 53, where the arrangement of bowed fliers, in a fly-frame, in two rows, was held to be patentable, although open-bottomed fliers had previously been arranged in two rows, and geered in the same way, and bowed fliers had been arranged in the one row with like geering. — Russell *v.* Cowley, Webs. Pat. Cas. 464, where it was held, that tubes having been welded by grooved rollers on a mandril, it was a patentable improvement to weld them by grooved rollers without a mandril; and Lord Lyndhurst puts the case of welding them by *fixed dies* instead of *rollers*. See also Kneass *v.* The Bank, 4 Wash. 9; Crane *v.* Price, 1 Webs. Pat. Cas. 409; 1 Webs. Pat. Cas. 95.

In these cases the principle is necessarily involved, and in some of them distinctly announced, that any change in the instruments employed, by which a new result is produced, or an old result produced in a more economical or beneficial manner, is the subject of a patent. It is the invention of a *new* thing under the patent law. The same test is proposed by Mr. Webster in his

§ 332. Every patent stands upon its subject-matter, and accordingly the question of infringement depends upon the use of that which is covered by the patent. Where a patent is for the combination alone, it is no infringement to use any of the parts or things which go to make up the combination, provided the combination itself be not used.[1] In a recent English case, however, it has been decided that a valid patent for an entire combination for a process gives protection to each part thereof that is new and material to that process, without any express claim of particular parts, and notwithstanding that some parts of the combination are old.[2]

In Smith *v.* London & N. W. R. W.,[3] Lord Campbell observed: "The patent was for an improved wheel for carriages of different descriptions, and the patentee stated in his specification that 'the said improved wheel is manufactured wholly of bar-iron, by welding wrought-iron bars together into the form of a wheel, whereof the nave and spokes and rim, when finished, will consist of one solid piece of malleable iron, and the mode whereby the said bars of malleable iron are fashioned and united into the shape of a wheel is as follows.' The specification then showed, by the aid of drawings, how the nave and spokes and rim were formed and afterwards welded so as to make a wheel of one piece of malleable iron. In the claim, the patentee stated that the new invention consisted in the circumstance of the centre boss or nave, arms, and rim of the wheel being wholly composed of wrought or malleable iron welded into one solid mass in manner hereinbefore described. The evidence showed a clear imitation and infringement of the manner of forming the boss or nave into one piece of malleable iron with the rest of the wheel, but it was stated that the mode which the defendants had used of forming

very able dissertation on the Subject-Matter of Patents. He says, in substance, that the question is, whether the change be colorable and formal, or substantial and essential, that is, whether it be such as would of itself support a patent. The jury must find whether what is new is essential or useless, and a colorable evasion; whether, by reason of the change, the thing has acquired a new and distinct character.

[1] Barrett *v.* Hall, 1 Mas. 447. See observations of Mr. Justice Story cited from this case, *ante*. Evans *v.* Eaton, 1 Pet. C. C. 343.

[2] Lister *v.* Leather, 8 Ell. & Blackb. 1004; Bovill *v.* Keyworth, 7 Ell. & Blackb. 725; Smith *v.* London & N. W. R. W., 20 E. L. & Eq. 94.

[3] Smith *v.* London & N. W. R. W., 20 E. L. & Eq. 94.

and welding the spokes and rim did not amount to any infringement.

Mr. Atherton (defendant's counsel) contended that the words of the claim restricted the patent to the invention of a wheel made in every respect "in the manner aforesaid," and that as the defendants had not used the same mode with regard to the spokes and rim as the patentee had specified, there could be no infringement of the patent. My brother Martin, who tried the cause, intimated his opinion that the claim was for the invention of a wheel as described in the claim, but that if the defendants had imitated or pirated the mode of welding the nave, and that were a material part of the invention, there was an infringement of part of the patent for which the action was maintainable.

"We are of opinion that this ruling was quite correct, and that there was ample evidence to support the action. Where a patent is for the combination of two, three, or more old inventions, a user of any of them would not be an infringement of the patent; but where there is an invention consisting of several parts, the imitation or pirating of any part of the invention is an infringement of the patent. Suppose that a man invents a machine consisting of three parts, of which one is a very useful invention, and the two others are found to be of less practical use, surely it could not be said that it was free to any person to use the useful part so long as he took care to substitute some other mode of carrying out the less useful parts of the invention. We should be sorry to throw any doubt upon the question of an infringement of a material part of such an invention, being an infringement upon which an action is maintainable, by granting a rule to show cause upon such a point."

In Prouty *v.* Ruggles,[1] Mr. Chief Justice Taney said: "The patent is for a combination, and the improvement consists in arranging different portions of the plough, and combining them together in the manner stated in the specification, for the purpose of producing a certain effect. None of the parts referred to are new and none are claimed as new; nor is any portion of the combination, less than the whole, claimed as new, or stated to produce any given result. The end in view is proposed to be accomplished by the union of all, arranged and combined together in the manner described. And this combination, composed of

[1] Prouty *v.* Ruggles, 16 Peters, 336.

all the parts mentioned in the specification, and arranged with reference to each other and to other parts of the plough in the manner therein described, is stated to be the improvement, and is the thing patented. The use of any two of these parts only, or of two combined with a third, which is substantially different in form or in the manner of its arrangement and connection with the others, is therefore not the thing patented. It is not the same combination if it substantially differs from it in any of its parts. The jogging of the standard into the beam, and its extension backward from the bolt, are both treated by the plaintiffs as essential parts of their combination for the purpose of brace and draft. Consequently, the use of either alone, by the defendants, would not be the same improvement nor infringe the patent of the plaintiffs."

But in order to determine in those cases where the patent is for the combination alone whether the combination is used or whether there is an infringement, it may be necessary to inquire whether the defendant has employed a mechanical equivalent as a substitute for some material element of the plaintiff's combination. If so, it will be an infringement. Thus, in the specification of a patent for "improvements in looms for weaving," the plaintiff declared that his improvement applied to that class of machinery called power-looms, and consisted "in a novel arrangement of mechanism, designed for the purpose of instantly stopping the whole of the working parts of the loom whenever the shuttle stops in the shed." After describing the manner in which that was done in ordinary looms, the specification proceeded thus: "The principal defect in this arrangement, and which my improvement is intended to obviate, is the frequent breakage of the different parts of the loom, occasioned by the shock of the lathe or sley striking against the 'frog,' which is fixed to the framing. In my improved arrangement, the loom is stopped in the following manner: I make use of the 'swell' and the 'stop-rod finger' as usual. The construction of the latter, however, is somewhat modified, being of one piece with the small lever which bears against the 'swell'; but instead of striking a stop or 'frog' fixed to the framing of the loom, it strikes against a stop or notch upon the upper end of a vertical lever vibrating upon a pin or shed. The lever is furnished with a small roller or bowl, which acts against a projection on a horizontal lever, causing it to vibrate upon its centre and throw a clutch-box (which connects the main driving pulley to the driving shaft) out of gear, and allows the main driving pulley to revolve loosely upon the driving shaft, at the same time that a projection on the lever strikes against the 'spring handle' and shifts the strap; simultaneously with these two movements, the lower end of the vertical beam causes a break to be brought in contact with the fly-wheel of the loom, thus instantaneously stopping every motion of the loom without the slightest shock." After the date of the plaintiff's patent, the defendant obtained a patent for "improvements in, and applicable to, looms for weaving," and amongst them he claimed a novel arrangement of apparatus for throwing the loom out of gear when the shuttle failed to complete its course. In the defendant's apparatus the "clutch-box" was not used, but instead of it the "stop-rod finger" acted on a loose piece or sliding frog; but, instead of a rigid vertical lever, as in the plaintiff's machine, the defendant used an elastic horizontal lever, and, by reason of the pin travelling on an inclined plane, the brake was applied to the wheel gradually and not simultaneously. The jury found that the plaintiff's arrangement of machinery for stopping looms, by means of the action of the "clutch-box" in combination with the action of the brake, was new and useful; and that the defendant's arrangement of machinery for the latter purpose was substantially the same as the plaintiff's: held, upon these findings, that the specification was good; secondly, that the defendant had infringed the patent. A rule was entered for a new trial on the ground of misdirection, but was discharged. Pollock, C. B., in rendering the decision of the court, observed: "The second question is, whether the patent has been infringed. It was argued that there can be no infringement of a patent for a combination, unless the defendant has used the whole combination. But that is not so, for there may be an infringement by using so much of a combination as is material, and it would be a question for the jury, whether that used was not substantially the same thing. I recollect a patent for an invention, a part of which, supposed at first to be useful, turned out to be prejudicial, and was afterwards omitted, but the patent was nevertheless sustained. If that had been a combination of matters, each of them old, but entirely new as a combination, and the jury had found that the substantial parts of the combination were used, that, I think, would have been an infringement of the patent. Looking at this patent fairly, what is it for? It is for a mode to separate the machine from the source of power, and at the same time to stop the momentum which has already accumulated, and to do this by one and the same operation; in fact, to make the machinery itself do it. Whenever the shuttle remains among the sheds, and does not arrive at the shuttle-box, the machine is so constructed that, by one operation, it is thrown out of gear, and at the same time a brake is applied to the fly-wheel so as to stop the momentum. The defendant has substituted for the clutch-box the old plan of the frog, and instead of separating the power and the machine by a clutch-box, and so throwing the machine out of gear, he has used the old method of throwing off the strap, but he has adopted the brake, which the jury have found is, in itself, an arrangement of machinery new and useful. We are not now to decide what would have been the plaintiff's right if the clutch-box had been entirely new, and the plaintiff had complained of its use; but I think it may be laid down as a general proposition (if a general proposition can be laid down on a subject applicable to such a variety of matters, indeed incommensurable with each other, for the same doctrine would scarcely apply to a new medicine and a new material or new metal), that, if a portion of a patent for a new arrangement of machinery is in itself new and useful, and another person, for the purpose of producing the same effect, uses that portion of the arrangement, and substitutes for the other matters combined with it another mechanical equivalent, that would be an infringement. It appears to me, therefore, with reference to the facts found by the jury, that the specification is good, and that the defendant has infringed the patent." [1]

Mr. Justice Curtis has held that the doctrine of mechanical equivalents, in connection with such a use of a material part of a combination, is not confined by the patent law to those elements which are strictly known as such in the science of mechanics, but that it embraces those substitutions, which, as a matter of judgment in construction, may be employed to accomplish the same end.[2]

[1] Sellers *v.* Dickinson, 6 E. L. & Eq. 544.

[2] Foster *v.* Moore, 1 Curtis, C. C. 279. Compare Newton *v.* Grand Junction R. W., 6 E. L. & Eq. 557. Also Johnson *v.* Root, MS. per Sprague, J.

§ 333. But, on the other hand, where the patent is for several distinct improvements or things, and does not stand upon the com-

"The term 'equivalent,' gentlemen, has two meanings, as used in this class of cases. The one relates to the results that are produced; and the other in the mechanism by which those results are produced. Two things may be equivalent, that is, the one equivalent to the other, as producing the same result, when they are not the same mechanical means. Mechanical equivalents are spoken of as different from equivalents that merely produce the same result. A mechanical equivalent, I suppose, as generally understood, is where the one may be adopted instead of the other, by a person skilled in the art, from his knowledge of the art. Thus an instrumentality is used as a mechanism: you wish to produce a pressure downward; well, it can be done by a spring, or it can be done by a weight. A machine is presented to a person conversant with machines. He sees that the force applied downward in the one before him is by a weight; from a knowledge of his art he can pass at once to another force, the spring, to press it downward; and these are mechanical equivalents. But, gentlemen, there may be equivalents as producing the same results, each of which is an independent matter of invention, and in that sense they are not mechanical equivalents. To illustrate my meaning, suppose, in early days, the problem was to get water from a well to the surface of the earth. One man takes a rope made of grass and draws up a pail of water; another would see that, as a mechanical equivalent, a rope of hemp would accomplish the same result. But suppose another person comes, and for the first time invents a pump. That is equivalent in the result of bringing the water to the surface of the ground; in that respect it is equivalent, as producing that result, to hauling it up by a rope; but it is not mechanically equivalent; it brings into operation, as you know, very different powers and forces, and would require invention to introduce it.

"Now, gentlemen, however the appearances of a thing may be altered, if the aspect, the form, the appearances presented are changed only by the use of mechanical equivalents, then it is substantially the same thing, I suppose. That is to say, if a person has an invention, in which he is called upon, by the patent law, to make a full and clear description of the thing he has invented, if another person, looking at that, can from his knowledge of the subject pass to the other thing that is used, without any invention, then the one is substantially the same as the other. It is not that every unskilled person shall see how they pass; but what is required is, that it shall be so described that those skilled and competent in the art, those who understand it, shall be able (not that an ingenious man can, seeing the new machine, sit down and find something else afterwards, perhaps aided in some degree by that in inventing something that is not there, but whether, with a competent knowledge of his art, he will be able), by looking at that with care, and examining it, to see that it may be done in a different mode, in a different manner, and it is done in that different mode or different manner by the knowledge which he has in the art. That would not be a new invention, or substantially differing from the original. But if he is obliged to go to invention, then he has a right to

bination of such things, then the use of any one of them will be an infringement.[1] But in order to succeed in an action for the infringement of any one of such improvements, it was formerly necessary among us, as in England, that the whole of the improvements claimed as such should be new; and if the novelty of any one of them failed, though it might not be the one used by the defendant, the action could not be sustained. The reason for this was, not that the right of the patentee would not have been infringed if he had had a valid patent, but that his patent was void, on account of a partial failure of the whole consideration on which it was granted; the consideration on which a patent was granted being the novelty of all the things represented to be new, regarded as an entirety; and the consideration being entire, if it failed in part, it failed as to the whole. The government was, in such a case, deceived in its grant; the whole patent was therefore inoperative, and no action could be maintained upon it.[2]

the benefits of whatever he thus invents ; and if his invention is a substitution for the original invention, then it is not substantially the same, and he does not use it. But if he merely invents something to be added to it, then he cannot take the original invention, because he has made something distinct to add to it as a new improvement."

[1] Moody *v.* Fiske, 2 Mas. 115 ; Emerson *v.* Hogg, 2 Blatchf. 1 ; Hogg *v.* Emerson, 6 How. 437 ; Ibid. 11 How. 587.

[2] In Moody *v.* Fiske, 2 Mas. 112, 115, Mr. Justice Story hinted at this doctrine, when he said that, "In such a case, the patent goes for the whole of the improvements, *and if each be new and be claimed distinctly in the patent*, there does not seem to be any good reason why the party who pirates any part of the invention should not be liable in damages." The subsequent cases in England, of Hill *v.* Thompson, 8 Taunt. 382; 2 B. Moore, 433; Webs. Pat. Cas. 239; Brunton *v.* Hawkes, 4 B. & Ald. 541; and Morgan *v.* Seaward, 2 M. & W. 544; Webs. 187; have fully established this doctrine. In the last of these cases, Mr. Baron Parke, delivering the judgment of the court, said: "This brings me to the question whether this patent, which suggests that certain inventions are improvements, is avoided if there be one which is not so; and upon the authorities we feel obliged to hold that the patent is void, upon the ground of fraud on the crown, without entering into the question whether the utility of each and every part of the invention is essential to a patent, where such utility is not suggested in the patent itself as the ground of the grant. That a false suggestion of the grantee avoids an ordinary grant of lands and tenements from the crown, is a maxim of the common law, and such a grant is void, not against the crown merely, but in a suit against a third person. It is on the same principle that a patent for two or more inventions, when one is not new, is void altogether, as was held in Hill *v.* Thompson, 2 Moore, 421; 8 Taunt. 375; and Brunton *v.* Hawkes, 4 B. & Ald. 542.

§ 334. The statute of July 4, 1836, § 15, recognizes this doctrine, by establishing as a defence that the patentee was not the first inventor of the thing patented, "or of a substantial and material part thereof claimed as new." But a more recent statute has provided that the patent shall be deemed good and valid for so much of the invention or discovery as shall be truly and *bonâ fide* the invention or discovery of the patentee, if it is a material and substantial part of the thing patented, and is definitely distinguishable from the other parts which the patentee had no right to claim, notwithstanding the specification may be too broad, if it was so made by mistake, accident, or inadvertence, and without any wilful default or intent to defraud or mislead the public."[1] This leaves the former doctrine, by which a failure of novelty in any part vitiated the whole patent, still applicable to cases where the claim was made too broad, wilfully and knowingly, or with intent to defraud or deceive the public.

§ 335. The effect of a failure, in point of utility, of one or more of several parts or things claimed as distinct inventions, is held in England to be the same as a failure in point of novelty. If any thing claimed as essential turn out to be useless, the patent is voidable, provided it was known to the patentee, at the time of enrolling his specification, to be useless, because he misleads the

For although the statute invalidates a patent for want of novelty, and consequently by force of the statute the patent would be void so far as related to that which was old, yet the principle on which the patent has been held to be void altogether is, that the consideration for the grant is the novelty of all, and the consideration failing, or, in other words, the crown being deceived in its grant, the patent is void, and no action maintainable upon it. We cannot help seeing, on the face of this patent, as set out in the record, that an improvement in steam-engines is suggested by the patentee, and is part of the consideration for the grant; and we must reluctantly hold that the patent is void, for the falsity of that suggestion. In the case of Lewis *v.* Marling (10 B. & C. 22; 5 M. & Ry. 66), this view of the case, that the patent was void for a false suggestion, does not appear by the report to have been pressed on the attention of the court, or been considered by it. The decision went upon the ground that the brush was not an essential part of the machine, and that want of utility did not vitiate the patent; and, besides, the improvement by the introduction of the brush is not recited in the patent itself as one of the subjects of it, which may make a difference. We are, therefore, of opinion, that the defendants are entitled to our judgment on the third issue." See also the elaborate judgments in Brunton *v.* Hawkes.

[1] Act of 1837, § 9.

public by representing it to be useful; but if it was subsequently discovered not to be useful, material, or necessary, it forms no ground of objection to the patent.[1] A patent for an entire machine or other subject which is, taken altogether, useful, though a part or parts may be useless, will be valid, provided there is no false suggestion.[2] So, too, a finding of the jury, that the invention is useful on the whole, but fails or is not useful in some cases, is not a ground of nonsuit.[3] But these cases are entirely distinguished from those where the purpose wholly fails,

[1] Lewis *v.* Marling, 10 B. & C. 22; 4 Car. & P. 57; Webs. Pat. Cas. 493.

[2] Morgan *v.* Seaward, Webs. Pat. Cas. 187.

[3] Haworth *v.* Hardcastle, Webs. Pat. Cas. 480, 483. In this case, Sir N. C. Tindal, C. J., said: "The motion for entering a nonsuit was grounded on two points: first, that the jury had, by their special finding, negatived the usefulness of the invention to the full extent of what the patent and specification had held out to the public; secondly, that the patentee had claimed in his specification the invention of the rails or staves over which the cloths were hung, or, at all events, the placing them in a tier at the upper part of the drying-room. As to the finding of the jury, it was in these words: 'The jury find the invention is new and useful upon the whole; and that the specification is sufficient for a mechanic, properly instructed, to make a machine, and that there has been an infringement of the patent; but they also find that the machine is not useful in some cases for taking off goods.' The specification must be admitted, as it appears to us, to describe the invention to be adapted to perform the operation of removing the calicoes and other cloths from off the rails or staves after they have been sufficiently dried. But we think we are not warranted in drawing so strict a conclusion from this finding of the jury as to hold that they have intended to negative, or that they have thereby negatived, that the machine was useful in the generality of the cases which occur for that purpose. After stating that the machine was useful on the whole, the expression that, 'in some cases, it is not useful to take up the cloths,' appears to us to lead rather to the inference that in the generality of cases it is found useful. And if the jury think it useful in the general, because some cases occur in which it does not answer, we think it would be much too strong a conclusion to hold the patent void. How many cases occur, what proportion they bear to those in which the machine is useful, whether the instances in which it is found not to answer are to be referred to the species of cloth hung out, to the mode of dressing the cloths, to the thickness of them, or to any other cause distinct and different from the defective structure or want of power in the machine, this finding of the jury gives us no information whatever. Upon such a finding, therefore, in a case where the jury have given their general verdict for the plaintiff, we think that we should act with great hazard and precipitation, if we were to hold that the plaintiff ought to be nonsuited upon the ground that his machine was altogether useless for one of the purposes described in his specification."

and the invention described does not accomplish the effect that is claimed for it. On a patent of this description, of course, no action whatever can be maintained.[1]

§ 336. The principles of our law would apparently lead to the same conclusions upon this subject; for, although it is not material whether the subject-matter of a patent is more or less useful, it must possess some utility; and if the subject-matter consists of several things, all included in one patent, but claimed as the distinct inventions of the patentee, a failure of any one of them, in point of utility, must vitiate the patent, if it was represented to be useful, when it was known not to be so, for the same reasons which are applicable in England. Our statute, moreover, has expressly provided, as one of the defences to an action on a patent, "that it contains more than is necessary to produce the described effect," when such addition "shall fully appear to have been made for the purpose of deceiving the public"; that is to say, when it appears that the patentee was aware that he was introducing something not useful, material, or necessary, at the time of preparing his specification.[2]

§ 336 *a*. The topic of infringement by means of chemical equivalents has lately received in England an elaborate and almost exhaustive discussion, so elaborate, indeed, that we can hope to give in the present volume nothing more than a general outline and abstract. The reported *American* cases on the subject are but few.

In Byam *v*. Farr,[3] the patentee's claim was as follows: "What I claim as my invention is the using of a paste or composition to ignite by friction, consisting of phosphorus and earthy material and a glutinous substance only, without the addition of chlorate of potash, or of any highly combustible material, such as sulphuret of antimony, in addition to the phosphorus." In construing this specification, Judge Curtis says: "The old method of making

[1] Manton *v*. Parker, Dav. Pat. Cas. 327. This was a patent for "a hammer on an improved construction, for the locks of all kinds of fowling-pieces and small arms"; and a material part of the invention consisted in a means of letting out the air from the barrel, and causing a communication between the powder in the pan and in the barrel, without, at the same time, letting out the powder. The witnesses for the defendant having proved that the powder passed through the same hole as the air, the plaintiff was nonsuited.

[2] Act of July 4, 1836, § 15.

[3] Byam *v*. Farr, 1 Curtis, C. C. 260.

friction matches was to use a composition consisting of phosphorus, chlorate of potash, sulphuret of antimony, and glue; so that the invention claimed by the plaintiff consists in rejecting two of the elements, viz., chlorate of potash and sulphuret of antimony, and substituting in their place chalk or some earthy matter. To compare the methods of the patentee and of the defendant, it may be said that the patentee has improved on the known compound, by omitting two substances previously used, and introducing one not used; while the defendants have merely omitted one substance previously used. It is insisted, however, that the sulphuret of antimony, used by the defendants, has, in point of fact, the same effect in their composition as the chalk or other earthy substance has in the plaintiff's composition; that both act mechanically only, and not chemically: the office of each being to surround the particles of phosphorus, and, aided by the glue, to retain them and protect them from the air and from the action of caloric, until the phosphorus is ignited by friction, and then to convey the heat to the sulphur, and thus cause the match to burn. In other words, that in this compound and for this manufacture, sulphuret of antimony is a mere equivalent for the earthy matter employed by the patentee; and that though it is not technically, in the nomenclature of chemistry, an earthy matter, yet that the claim is not to be limited to substances strictly so termed; because, while the specification declares chalk or Spanish white to be the best material, it also makes known that the ingredients may be varied, 'and other absorbent earths or materials may be used instead of the carbonate of lime.' And it is urged that the substance of this invention does not consist in the use of carbonate of lime in this composition, but in the use of a material suitable to surround and protect the phosphorus, and convey its heat to the sulphur when ignited, and that the defendant uses such a material. There is certainly much force in this argument; but it is encountered by difficulties which I think insuperable. To substitute in place of some one element in a composition of matter a mere known equivalent, is an infringement; because, although the patentee has not expressly mentioned such equivalent in his claim, he is understood to embrace it, and in contemplation of law does embrace it, without an express mention of it. But he is not obliged to embrace equivalents in his claim. He may, if he choose, confine himself to the specific ingredients mentioned, and expressly exclude all others ; or he may expressly exclude some one or other. If he does so, it cannot be maintained that what he has expressly disclaimed is in point of law claimed. Now this patentee declares, in terms, that his composition is to be without the addition of sulphuret of antimony. It is said that he meant to exclude it, because he considered it, as he says in the claim, a highly combustible substance, and that he was under a mistake, as it is not. This may be true ; but the question is not what induced the patentee to exclude it, but whether he has in fact excluded it. If he made a mistake, the patent law affords means of correcting it ; but until corrected, it must be taken as it stands, whatever error may have led to it.

"It is also argued that it was the intention of the patentee to exclude sulphuret of antimony only when used with chlorate of potash. But this is not consistent with the plain meaning of the words, which are, 'without the addition of chlorate of potash, or any highly combustible material, such as sulphuret of antimony.' And when it is borne in mind what the composition previously known was, and how the patentee has described his invention, I think it cannot be admitted that the patentee really intended to cover the composition used by the defendants. As already stated, the old method was to combine phosphorus, glue, sulphuret of antimony, and chlorate of potash. If the patentee intended to cover an improvement consisting only in the omission of the chlorate of potash, as is now said, he might reasonably have been expected so to declare. But instead of this he, in terms, declared that his invention did not extend to the use of this substance. So far as respects his own intent, there can be no question it was to make a claim which excluded the composition used by defendants ; and this is decisive. It must be remembered that one object of the patent law in requiring the inventor to put on the public records a description of his invention is to inform the public what may safely be done during the existence of the patent, without interfering with his claims ; and, upon the soundest principles, the patentee must be held to be estopped from asserting a claim which is expressly waived on the record."

In a subsequent case arising under the same patent,[1] the court gave the following opinion : "The invention claimed in the spe-

[1] Byam *v.* Eddy, 2 Blatchf. 521.

cification is not a compound of new ingredients before unused in making matches, but simply and only a new combination of old materials before in use for that purpose. It purports to consist in a composition producing ignition and combustion by friction, formed of phosphorus with the earthy materials and the glutinous substance only, without the presence of chlorate of potash or any other like objectionable ingredient, thus avoiding the danger supposed to exist in the combination of substances of such a nature with phosphorus. This, as I understand the specification, is the 'new composition of matter,' or new combination of materials for producing ignition, claimed and patented as an improvement; and it seems quite clear that any person may use any one or all of the materials forming the composition, provided he does not use them in the combination patented. Certainly any one may lawfully use them for that purpose in combination with chlorate of potash, as they were formerly used, for that is a combination recognized as essential, different, and as being known and in use anterior to the patent. The question, therefore, is, whether the defendant, in manufacturing and dealing in friction matches, has used the plaintiff's combination, or made matches substantially according to their patent. . . . The only difference, aside from the relative proportions of the ingredients, between the composition patented and that claimed to have been used by the defendant, consists, as appears from the formula given by each, in the one being made *with* and the other *without* chlorate of potash; the question in the case is accordingly reduced to the simple inquiry, whether the matches manufactured by the defendant contain that substance as a principal ingredient, in conformity with the prescribed formula, or whether they are made without it or with so inconsiderable a portion of it as to be substantially according to plaintiff's patent." Thereupon the court decided, as a matter of fact, that the evidence was not sufficient to show that the defendants had departed from their own formula, and accordingly discharged the rule and refused an attachment.

With this may be compared the language of Grier, J., in Goodyear *v.* R. R.[1] "Although partaking somewhat of the nature of an *obiter dictum*, inasmuch as the specification was decided to be a claim for both the process and the *product*, and the patentee's

[1] 2 Wallace, C. C. 356.

patent consequently to be infringed by any one using the article alone, independent of the manner in which it might have been made, still it may serve as an expression of judicial opinion.

"What forms the essence or substance of this discovery? What is the *sine qua non*, or that without which this composition of matter cannot be produced? The specification says, it is the application of a high degree of heat between 212° and 350° Fahrenheit. You may vary the proportions of sulphur or change the metallic oxides, and succeed more or less, if the exposure to heat between these points be continued for a sufficient time. But no mere changes in the combined materials will have a beneficial effect without this application of a high degree of artificial heat. Now it must be evident that any person having the benefit of plaintiff's discovery, starting from the platform erected by him, may possibly vary the process and obtain the same result. He may use *salts of zinc* for *salts of lead*, *arsenic*, or magnesia for *sulphur*, or heat by steam instead of air; and many other variances of the relative proportions of the materials might be discovered to be as good as those patented. Yet it must be equally evident that such person is pirating the plaintiff's invention. Suppose that, before Goodyear's discovery, a manufacturer had taken to a chemist's laboratory some india-rubber, sulphur, and white lead, and asked him to make a compound, having the qualities now exhibited by the substance known as 'vulcanized rubber.' He would have received an answer denying the possibility of making such a compound by any process known to scientific men. Now suppose he had put into the same person's hand the specification of plaintiff's patent, and asked him to discover some means by which the same result might be produced in mode or proportions different from that set forth in the patent. What science was before incapable of producing by synthesis or any reasoning *à priori* can now be improved by valuable hints derived from analysis. The chemist can now immediately suggest many changes in the process which may produce equivalent or better results. He could at once suggest that a carbonate of zinc or some other metallic oxide could probably perform the office of white lead; that probably arsenic or magnesia or some other metal might be substituted for sulphur; that sulphur might perhaps be used better in a gaseous form; that the high degree of heat so necessary to the process could be as well or better applied by means of steam than dry heated air. Yet no one whose perceptions are not perverted can fail to see that all such changes, such interposition of chem'cal equivalents, though possibly improvements on the original process patented, have their foundation on the patentee's first discovery, and start by appropriating or pirating it."

On turning to the *English* cases on this subject, we find, first, the discussion of the infringement of Martin's patent for artificial cement.[1] This patent has already been treated of in the chapter on Specification. In substance, it was a claim for the production of hard cement by the use of gypsum, *alkali*, and *acid*. The defendant claimed also under a patent for combining gypsum, sulphate of lime, or other calcareous substance with *borax*. Application was made to the vice-chancellor for an injunction, which was granted, and on appeal affirmed by the chancellor, Lord Cottenham, who uses the following language: "Now the defendant says, 'My invention consists in combining gypsum, sulphate of lime, or other calcareous substance with borax, and subjecting them to heat.' *Primâ facie* that may appear to be a very different thing, because, till you come to examine what borax is, it may appear that borax is some substance totally different, and not within what the plaintiff discovered; that borax is a substance of itself which is capable, by combination with gypsum, of very hard cement; and that the patentee has no right to say, I am entitled to the exclusive privilege, because I claim the invention of uniting gypsum with acid and an alkali. But then, when we find that borax itself is composed of an acid and an alkali, where is the difference? If borax is an article used in the trade found in a natural state, but used as an artificial composition composed and compounded of an alkali and an acid, is it not exactly the same thing as if the plaintiff had said, I claim my invention to be the uniting of gypsum with the acid and alkali found in borax? It is hardly a different mode of describing the same thing. He has adopted different language, but if the language conveys the same meaning, it is the same thing."

A temporary injunction was accordingly granted, with an order to have the validity of the specification tried in a court of law. First, before Pollock, C. B., and a jury, then before Pollock, C. B.,

[1] 2 Webs. Pat. Cas. 172, 178, 179.

Parke, Alderson, and Platt, BB., it was held that the plaintiff's specification was bad on account of uncertainty, inasmuch as it claimed *any* acid, while in reality there were several well-known acids of commerce which would not answer. But with regard to the alleged infringement, the jury found, in accordance with the suggestion of Pollock, C. B., that the use of borax *was* an infringement of plaintiff's patent. The chief baron says in his charge: "Gentlemen of the jury, the only point that I have to leave to you is, whether you think the defendant has infringed the first patent of the plaintiff by using boracic acid and soda, that is, in the shape of borax, instead of the pearlash, which is potash and sulphuric acid, the only alkalis and only acid mentioned in the specification. . . . It has been said that this borax which the defendant uses is a chemical equivalent. I may say that I do not quite go along with the doctrine of equivalents in chemistry applied in the same way as in mechanics and those matters in which you can apply the principles of the exact sciences. . . . There you can frequently predict the results without the slightest difficulty, and with the same certainty as that with which a skilful arithmetician can tell you what will be the amount of certain numbers added together, and that a certain other set of numbers, apparently differing from them altogether, will, when added together, produce the same result. With precisely the same certainty a skilful mechanic will tell you that such and such a combination will produce a result, and that such and such another combination, to the ordinary eye apparently totally different, will produce precisely the same result; but looked at with the experienced eye of a mechanic, he would say, yes, there appears to be a great difference; here is a lever instead of an inclined plane, a pulley instead of two wheels to change the motion, and so on; but a skilful mechanic will say, the general expression in all these might be put down as exactly the same; so that, however different they may appear to the eye, they are to the mind precisely the same. I do not think that doctrine applies altogether to the case of chemistry, because, although you can predict with confidence in mechanics, in some instances, and in some cases where mathematics can be applied, in chemistry you almost entirely fail. You cannot — because sulphuric acid will succeed — tell at all that nitric acid will succeed, or any other acid, till it has been tried. They do not exist in any relation to each other as numbers do, or as mechanical science presents to you the different mechanical powers. You cannot anticipate the result; it is a mere question of result upon experiment. Still, there may be a probable anticipation of a result, which may be treated, and properly, by a jury, as merely a servile imitation or else a colorable evasion of the patent. That may occur in chemistry; and when one of the witnesses (Mr. Redwood) stated that he thought borax was a salt that would most probably suggest itself to anybody as likely to answer where sulphate of potash had succeeded, I must own that I heard it with great surprise; but when explained, it was perfectly true and intelligible. In reply to the question, 'If you wished to make a cement similar to the plaintiff's, without using sulphuric acid and potash, what would you suggest?' he replied, 'I should give the preference to borax.' Now I could not conceive why, sulphuric acid being a very strong acid, boracic acid a very weak one, and potash and soda being very analogous as the two fixed alkalies, why any one's attention as a chemist should be directed to borax more than to any other salt. Then it is explained. He says, 'Sulphate of potash acts as a flux. Borax is a salt that also acts as a flux. This opinion I obtained, for I examined the substance with a microscope, and I observed that particles of the plaintiff's cement presented to the microscope the appearance of having melted; I therefore thought that any salt that would operate as a flux would probably answer better than any other salt, therefore I should have used borax.' But if borax is used merely as a flux, and not because it is a mixture of an alkali and an acid, I should say that really has nothing to do with the infringement of the patent, any more than if they had used some totally foreign material that might be suggested, for instance, some one of the fifty odd metals that exist; if any one of these could be used as a flux, being neither an acid nor an alkali, he might have used that flux metal, and that could not be an infringement of the patent. The use of borax merely as a flux, and not as an alkali and an acid, would probably be considered no evasion of the patent. . . . Then, if sulphate of potash so used (i. e. used instead of its ingredients) would be an infringement, would borax, which is the boreate of soda, be an infringement? Why, soda is an alkali, and boracic acid is an acid, which exists in a separate form; it might be used, it has been used; and the question is, is that within the scope and compass, in point of fact, of the plaintiff's specification, assuming that the plaintiff claims acids and alkalies beyond those specifically named. The true construction, in point of law, of the specification, is, in my judgment, that he does claim acids and alkalies beyond those that he mentions. You will have to say whether, in your judgment, that which the defendant has done has been within the scope of the plaintiff's invention, or whether it is in imitation of it."

Munz's patent for improved metal plates for sheathing the bottoms of ships was called in question chiefly on the ground of want of novelty and want of sufficient directions in the specification as to the proportions and qualities of the ingredients. However, in the trial at law before the Court of Common Pleas, the subject of infringement came up for discussion among the other issues. Tindal, C. J., in his charge to the jury,[1] remarked upon that plea: "Further, the plaintiff says (and that evidence is before you) that in the month of April, when the mode of making it and the materials were somewhat altered, i. e. when, according to the testimony of defendant's witnesses, they used nothing but cake copper, and not the purest copper obtained from the regule of the copper, as the witnesses have stated, yet still it would be for you to say whether, if the very same effect and result is produced, it could have been produced in any other way than by some mode of altering the properties of the common cake copper; because there has been evidence brought before you that the cake copper would not produce the result and be attended with those properties which the plaintiff has taken out his patent for; and therefore, upon that second branch, you will have to ask yourselves whether, seeing that which has been used, and the analysis of it, and the result of such analysis, and the mode in which the witness on the part of the defendants explained that it was carried on, stating certainly that nothing was used but the cake copper for that purpose, whether, in the mode of using that cake copper, which before did not produce the result of the plaintiff's discovery, something or other must not have been managed or contrived, on the part of the defendants, to give it that purity, which, if you are satisfied upon the evidence it did not possess, it must have had through their instrumentality. If it were so, that would be a contrivance and an evasion of the

[1] 2 Webs. Pat. Cas. 101.

direct letter and description in the patent. Although the patent describes the copper must be of the purest quality (and that seems to me to be the sense of the specification), yet, if persons could take an inferior kind of copper, and by dressing it up, and by some particular way of melting and refining it, give it exactly the same effect as the best kind of copper would have done, it must be for you to say whether, in that case, they intended to imitate (as one branch of the declaration states) and to evade the patent which the other party had granted to him."

But the most interesting case, or rather series of cases, — both as regards the magnitude of the pecuniary interests at stake, and the elaborate discussions and decisions which it called forth, — is that arising under the celebrated Heath patent for making cast-steel.

In 1839, a patent was granted to Heath "for certain improvements in the manufacture of iron and steel." That part of the specification which immediately concerns us is contained in the following words: "Lastly, I propose to make an improved quality of cast-steel, by introducing into a crucible bars of common blistered steel broken as usual into fragments, or mixtures of cast and malleable iron, or malleable iron and carbonaceous matters, *along with from one to three per cent of their weight of carburet of manganese*, and exposing the crucible to the proper heat for melting the materials, which are when fluid to be poured into an ingot mould in the usual manner; but I do not claim the use of any such mixture of cast and malleable iron, or malleable iron and carbonaceous matter, as any part of my invention, but *only the use of carburet of manganese in any process for the conversion of iron into cast-steel.*"[1]

In 1843, the suit of Heath *v.* Unwin was brought in the Exchequer before Lord Abinger, C. B.[2] Heath, after enrolling his patent, discovered that the same effect might be produced by using coal-tar and black oxide of manganese, the ingredients of the carburet of manganese, as by the use of the carburet itself. This he communicated to the defendant Unwin, who was at that time in his employ as agent, and furnished him with parcels of these materials to sell instead of the compound, at the same time reducing the royalty. Unwin shortly afterwards ceased to be

[1] 2 Webs. Pat. Cas. 216.
[2] Heath *v.* Unwin, 2 Webs. Pat. Cas. 216.

patentee's agent, and commenced the manufacture of cast-steel by the use of coal-tar and manganese, without paying any license fee. For this infringement the action was brought. Lord Abinger nonsuited the plaintiff, ruling that the use of the materials, being out of all proportion cheaper than that of the carburet, was a new discovery, and that there was no evidence of the formation of carburet of manganese during defendant's process, and therefore no evidence of an infringement of plaintiff's patent. The Court of Exchequer refused to set aside the nonsuit.

In 1844, another action was brought in the Exchequer before Baron Parke.[1] The learned Baron, in his charge to the jury, said: "The next point for your consideration is, has the infringement taken place? Which depends on the fact, whether the use of the elements by the defendant is, in fact, a use of the compound, — whether the elements really form a carburet before the union with the steel takes place in the crucible. . . . If you are not satisfied of this, you will find for the defendant; if you find that there is carburet formed, I shall reserve the point. You will also say whether the defendant ever uses one per cent of this substance in his manufacture." The jury found that the defendant had infringed; and that though he might not have used *one per cent* of carburet, the words in the specification *from one to three per cent*, give a latitude as to the quantity to be used. Leave was then given the defendant to move to enter a verdict on the plea of not guilty. A motion before the Court of Exchequer for a rule to show cause why such verdict should not be entered for defendant[2] was granted and subsequently argued. The rule was made absolute, Baron Parke rendering the judgment as follows: "In order to decide this (the infringement), we must first determine for what invention the patent, as explained by the specification, is taken out. It is not for the use of oxide of manganese in the melting of cast-steel, for carburet of manganese is expressly mentioned and distinguished from oxide of manganese; nor could the patent for the use of the oxide have been supported, as that substance had been used long before in steel-making; nor is it for the use of oxide of manganese in any mode of combination with carbon generally. If it had it would have been liable to a similar objection, as oxide of manganese had been used in cruci-

[1] Heath *v.* Unwin, 2 Webs. Pat. Cas. 218.

[2] 2 Webs. Pat. Cas. 221; argued, p. 223.

bles containing in their construction a quantity of carbonaceous matter, with a portion of which it would necessarily combine during the process; nor is it for the use of the oxide with such a quantity of carbon as would deoxidize it and leave the manganese alone to operate upon the steel, so that neither the quantity of the steel be altered nor the crucible destroyed by the oxide of manganese abstracting, as it otherwise would do, some quantity of carbon from them. The patent is obtained for the use of one particular combination of carbon and manganese, the metallic substance called carburet of manganese, and for the use of it in that state. The specification is expressly for the employment of carburet of manganese, and the mode of using it is by putting a certain quantity by weight of that substance in an unmelted state into the crucible. This being, in our opinion, the true construction of the specification, it is clear that the defendant has not directly infringed the plaintiff's patent, for he has never used that substance in the mode described in the specification. Then comes the question whether he has indirectly infringed the patent by imitating and using the same patent substantially, but making a colorable variation. Now there is no doubt, we think, that if a defendant substitutes for a part of a plaintiff's invention some well-known equivalent, whether chemical or mechanical, he would probably be considered as only making a colorable variation. But here he has not done so. It is quite clear, upon the evidence, that the defendant never meant to use the carburet of manganese at all; he certainly never knew, and there is no reason to suppose that, prior to this investigation, any one else knew, that the substance would be formed in a state of fusion; and it is mere matter of speculative opinion (though after the verdict we must assume it to be a correct opinion among men of science) that it would, but it was clearly not ascertained, and still less was it a known fact. There was, therefore, no intention to imitate the patented invention, and we do not think the defendant can be considered guilty of any direct imitation if he did not intend to imitate at all."

Mr. Webster, in his note (p. 227) to this passage, says, "The doctrine of intention as here expressed has been dissented from by the learned judges who concurred in the judgment, as well as by all other judges whose attention has been called to it. Evidence of intention to imitate may be material for the consideration of the jury; but if the invention be in point of fact adopted or imitated, whether in ignorance or intention, the infringement is just the same."[1]

On the strength of the verdict given by the jury in the case tried before Baron Parke alone (p. 220, Webster), the patentee commenced proceedings in chancery for an injunction and account, but in consequence of the overruling of the verdict, as above stated, these proceedings were suspended. After an interval of two years the case of Stevens *v.* Keating occurred. The Vice-Chancellor and Lord Chancellor both dissenting here from the doctrine of intention as expressed by the Court of Exchequer, Mr. Heath was advised to renew his application to the Court of Chancery. Thereupon the Vice-Chancellor ordered an action to be brought in the Common Pleas, to try the questions of infringement and validity of the patent. Cresswell, J., in giving the ruling, said: "I feel fettered by the decision of the Court of Exchequer. My ruling is simply this, that the use of the ingredients, oxide of manganese and carbonaceous matter, is not an infringement of the patent, although these ingredients form a carburet of manganese before it enters into combination with the steel."

On appeal to the Exchequer Chamber by writ of error, this ruling was reversed and a new trial granted,[2] each of the judges giving an elaborate opinion. Crompton, Platt, Erle, and Wightman, *pro;* Coleridge and Alderson, *contra.* In 1853 the patent was extended for seven years by the Privy Council, on application of Charlotte Heath, executrix of the patentee.

The matter was then brought up before the House of Lords by writ of error upon this judgment of the Exchequer Chamber. (1854.)[3] The following question was proposed to the judges: "Whether, looking at the record as set forth in the joint appendix to the printed cases, there was evidence for the jury that the plaintiff in error (the former defendant Unwin) was guilty of an infringement of the patent stated in the declaration, by using oxide of manganese and carbonaceous matter in the manufacture of cast-steel, in the manner in which, according to his admission at the trial, he did use them." In reply, Crowder, J., Crompton, J., Williams, J., Platt, B., Erle, J., Cresswell, J., and Wightman,

[1] See also Stead *v.* Anderson, 2 Webs. Pat. Cas. 156.

[2] 2 Webs. Pat. Cas. 236.

[3] Unwin *v.* Heath, 32 E. L. & Eq. 45.

J., gave their opinion, that there *was* evidence of infringement; Maule, J., Parke, B., Alderson, B., and Pollock, C. B., that there was *not*.

The Lord Chancellor (Lord Cranworth) and Lord Brougham thereupon gave long and elaborate judgments in behalf of the plaintiff in error to establish that there was no evidence of infringement, and the House voted judgment accordingly, thereby sustaining the ruling of Cresswell, J., at the jury trial, and overruling the reversal of the Exchequer Chamber.

It would be impossible to give, within the limits of the present treatise, even a selection from the mass of adjudication which this celebrated case has elicited. For, as will appear from the foregoing synopsis of the course of litigation, nearly every leading judge in England was called upon to pronounce on the merits of the patent. The reader, however, is referred to the 32 E. L. & Eq. as containing a careful summary of the leading principles at issue.

The doctrines of Heath *v.* Unwin and Unwin *v.* Heath have been subsequently reaffirmed and applied in a very recent case.[1] Here, the plaintiff was the patentee of an invention for the purification of gas by means of precipitated oxides of iron, and also of a process by which the materials used could be revivified and again adapted for the same purifying process. It was held by the Lord Chancellor (Westbury) that the right of the patentee was restricted to the use of artificial precipitated oxides of iron, and that the user by defendants of a natural product known as bog ochre in its natural state, which answered the same purpose as the plaintiff's invention, was no infringement of the patent; but that so far as the revivification of the natural product was concerned, it was an infringement.

§ 336 *b*. In the case of Tyler *v.* Boston,[2] it appeared that the defendants had used a burning fluid composed of naphtha seventy-two and fusel oil twenty-eight parts; and expert chemists proved that seventy-two parts *in bulk* of naphtha was the *substantial equivalent* of twenty-eight parts of kerosene. The meaning of the term "equivalent" was thus defined in the opinion of the court. "This term 'equivalent,' when speaking of machines, has a certain definite meaning; but when used with regard to

[1] Hills *v.* Liverpool Gas. Co., 7 Law Times, N. S. 537.

[2] 7 Wall. 327.

the chemical action of such fluids as can be discovered only by experiment, it only means *equally good.* But while the specification of the patent suggests the substitution of naphtha for crude petroleum, it prescribes no other proportion than that of equal parts by measure."

§ 337. The rule of damages for the infringement of a patent is provided by statute in the following terms: "that, whenever in any action for damages for using or selling the thing whereof the exclusive right is secured by any patent heretofore granted, or which shall hereafter be granted, a verdict shall be rendered for the plaintiff in such action, it shall be in the power of the court to render judgment for any sum above the amount found by such verdict as the actual damages sustained by the plaintiff, not exceeding three times the amount thereof, according to the circumstances of the case."[1] By the terms "actual damages, sustained by the plaintiff," are meant such damages as he can actually prove, and has in fact sustained, as contra-distinguished from mere imaginary or vindictive damages, which are sometimes given in personal torts.[2] These damages will be trebled by the court, according to the statute.[3]

§ 338. In estimating the "actual damages" the rule is, in cases of infringement by an actual use of the plaintiff's invention, — as by making and using a patented machine, — to give the value of such use during the time of the illegal user, that is to say, the amount of profits actually received by the defendant,[4] but not the profits which he might have made by reasonable diligence.[5]

To this, it seems, there should be added all the losses to which the plaintiff has been subjected by the piracy.[6]

[1] Act of July 4, 1836, § 14.

[2] Whittemore *v.* Cutter, 1 Gallis. 478. It seems, however, that if the defendant is sued a second time for an infringement, exemplary damages may be given. Alden *v.* Dewey, 1 Story's R. 336, 339; Hall *v.* Wiles, 2 Blatchf. 194.

[3] Lowell *v.* Lewis, 1 Mas. 184, 185; Gray *v.* James, Peters's C. C. R. 394.

[4] Lowell *v.* Lewis, 1 Mas. 184; Whittemore *v.* Cutter, 1 Gall. 429.

[5] Dean *v.* Mason, 20 How. 198.

[6] Earle *v.* Sawyer, 4 Mas. 1. Story, J., said: "But I wish to say a few words in relation to the point of law which the objection suggests, and which is founded upon the decision of this court in Whittemore *v.* Cutter, 1 Gall. 479. To that decision, as founded in just principle, I still adhere, although, I confess, with subdued confidence, since I have reason to believe that it has not

Where there is no established patent or license-fee, general evidence of the utility and superiority of the invention may be

met the concurrence of other and abler judicial minds. It has been maintained by some learned persons, that the price of the invented machine is a proper measure of damages, in cases where there has been a piracy by making and using the machine, because, in such cases, the verdict for the plaintiff entitles the defendant to use the machine subsequently, and, in short, transfers the right to him in the fullest manner, and in the same way, that a recovery in trover or trespass, for a machine, by operation of law, transfers the right to such machine to the trespasser, for he has paid for it. If I thought such was the legal operation of a verdict for the plaintiff, in an action for making and using a machine, no objection could very forcibly occur to my mind against the rule. But my difficulty lies here. The Patent Act gives to the inventor the exclusive right of making and using his invention during the period of fourteen years. But this construction of the law enables any person to acquire that right, by a forced sale, against the patentee, and compels him to sell, as to persons or places, when it may interfere essentially with his permanent interest, and involve him in the breach of prior contracts. Thus, the right would not remain exclusive; but the very attempt to enforce it would involve the patentee in the necessity of parting with it. The rule itself, too, has no merit from its universality of application. How could it apply, when the patentee had never sold the right to any one? How, when the value of the right depended upon the circumstance of the right being confined to a few persons? Where would be the justice of its application, if the invention were of enormous value and profit, if confined to one or two persons, and of very small value if used by the public at large, for the result of the principle would be, that all the public might purchase and use it by a forced judicial sale. On the other hand, cases may occur, where the wrong done to the patentee may very far exceed the price which he would be willing to take for a limited use by a limited number of persons. These, among others, are difficulties which press on my mind against the adoption of the rule; and where the declaration goes for a user during a limited period, and afterwards the party sues for a user during another and subsequent period, I am unable to perceive how a verdict and judgment in the former case is a legal bar to a recovery in the second action. The piracy is not the same, nor is the gravamen the same. If, indeed, the plaintiff, at the trial, consents that the defendant shall have the full benefit of the machine forever, upon the ground of receiving the full price in damages, and the defendant is content with this arrangement, there may be no solid objection to it in such a case. But I do not yet perceive how the court can force the defendant to purchase, any more than the plaintiff to sell, the patent right for the whole period it has to run. The defendant may be an innocent violator of the plaintiff's right; or he may have ceased to use, or to have employment for such a machine. There are other objections alluded to in the case in 1 Gall. 434. Struck with similar difficulties in establishing any general rule to govern cases upon patents, some learned judges have refused to lay down any particular rule of damages, and have left the jury at large to esti-

submitted to the jury, who are therefrom to estimate the damages, not for the whole term of the patent, but only during the continuance of the infringement. A recovery of such damages does not vest in the infringer the right to continue the use.[1]

The difference between the actual cost of making a patented machine and its sale price is not all profit; but the jury must take into account the interest on the capital, the risk of bad debts, and the expenses of selling, in order to arrive at the defendant's real profits.[2]

In Pitts *v.* Hall,[3] the following rule has been given by Mr. Justice Nelson: "One mode of arriving at the actual damages is

mate the actual damages according to the circumstances of each particular case. I rather incline to believe this to be the true course. There is a great difference between laying down a special and limited rule as a true measure of damages, and leaving the subject entirely open, upon the proofs in the cause, for the consideration of the jury. The price of the machine, the nature, actual state and extent of the use of the plaintiff's invention, and the particular losses to which he may have been subjected by the piracy, are all proper ingredients, to be weighed by the jury in estimating the damages, *valere quantum valeant.*"

See also the observations of L. J. Clerk Hope, in Househill Co. *v.* Neilson, 1 Webs. Pat. Cas. 697, note. In Pierson *v.* Eagle Screw Co., 3 Story's R. 410, Story, J., again said: "But, upon the question of damages, I would upon this occasion state (what I have often ruled before), that if the plaintiff has established the validity of his patent, and that the defendants have violated it, he is entitled to such reasonable damages as shall vindicate his right and reimburse him for all such expenditures as have been necessarily incurred by him beyond what the taxable costs will repay, in order to establish that right. It might otherwise happen that he would go out of court with a verdict in his favor, and yet have received no compensation for the loss and wrong sustained by him. Indeed, he might be ruined by a succession of suits, in each of which he might, notwithstanding, be the successful party, so far as the verdict and judgment should go. My understanding of the law is that the jury are at liberty, in the exercise of a sound discretion if they see fit (I do not say that they are positively and absolutely bound under all circumstances) to give the plaintiff such damages, not in their nature vindictive, as shall compensate the plaintiff fully for all his actual losses and injuries occasioned by the violation of the patent by the defendants."

And yet, in Elwood *v.* Christy, 18 C. B. N. S. 494, the Court of Common Pleas, sitting in Chancery (under 15 & 16 Vict.), refused to order an account to be taken of *the loss which the plaintiff had sustained by the infringement*, and substituted, on motion, an account of *the profits which had been actually made by the defendants.*

[1] The Suffolk Co. *v.* Hayden, 3 Wall. 315.

[2] Wilbur *v.* Beecher, 2 Blatchf. 132.

[3] Pitts *v.* Hall, 2 Blatchf. 229.

to ascertain the profits which the plaintiff derives from the machines which he manufactures and sells, and which have been made and sold by the defendant. Another mode . . . is to ascertain the profits which the party infringing has derived from the use of the invention or the construction of the machine. . . . This measure of damages, however, is not controlling, and ought not to be; because a party concerned in infringing a patent stands in a different position from the patentee, not having been previously subjected to the expense and labor to which the latter is frequently exposed in the process of invention and experiment. Hence the person who enters upon the business without previous expense may very well afford to sell machines at a less profit than the patentee. . . . Profits which the party infringing might be satisfied with, and which would afford him compensation, would not afford indemnity to the patentee. If, therefore, on looking into the profits made by the defendant, the jury shall be of the opinion that they do not correspond with the fair profits which the plaintiff, if left alone, would have realized, they are not bound by the measure of the defendant's profits, but have a right to look to the profits which the patentee would have made under the circumstances, if not interfered with."

Still, where a plaintiff is allowed to recover "actual damages," he is bound to furnish evidence by which the jury may assess them. If he rest his case after merely proving an infringement, he is entitled to nominal damages, but no more. He cannot call on a jury to guess out his case without evidence. Actual damages must be calculated, not imagined, and an arithmetical calculation cannot be made without certain data.[1]

Where part of an invention is not original (e. g. where the patent is for an improvement), that part cannot, in estimating the damages of an infringement, be so mixed up with those which are original, that the jury may regard the whole as a unit.[2]

[1] City of New York *v.* Ransom, 23 How. 487. Here it was proved, on trial, that the corporation of New York had applied the patentee's invention to fifty steam fire-engines, but no information whatever was given of the price or value of a single license. The Supreme Court, on appeal, held that the jury had had no evidence to sustain a verdict for $20,000 damages.

[2] Jones *v.* Moorehead, 1 Wall. 155. In this case, the patentee's invention consisted in improving the casing of locks so as to make them double-faced. The jury at the circuit trial estimated the damages by taking the profits made

By way of conclusion, we quote *in extenso* from the decision of the Supreme Court, in Seymour *v.* McCormick,[1] as containing the

by the defendants on the sale of the entire lock as thus improved. The Supreme Court set aside the verdict, with costs.

[1] Seymour *v.* McCormick, 16 How. 480. "It must be apparent to the most superficial observer, that there cannot, in the nature of things, be any one rule of damages which will equally apply to all cases. The mode of ascertaining actual damages must necessarily depend on the peculiar nature of the monopoly granted. A man who invents or discovers a new composition of matter, such as vulcanized india-rubber, or a valuable medicine, may find his profit to consist in a close monopoly, forbidding any one to compete with him in the market, the patentee himself being able to supply the whole demand at his own price. If he should grant licenses to all who might desire to manufacture his composition, mutual competition might destroy the value of each license. . . . If any person could use the invention or discovery by paying what a jury might suppose to be the fair value of a license, it is plain that competition would destroy the whole value of the monopoly. In such cases the profits of the infringer may be the only criterion of the actual damage of the patentee. But one who invents some improvement in the machinery of a mill cannot claim that the profits of the whole mill should be the measure of damages. And where the profit of the patentee consists neither in the exclusive use of the thing invented or discovered, nor in the monopoly of making it for others to use, it is evident that this rule cannot apply. The case of Stimpson's patent for a turn-out in a railroad is an example. It was the interest of the patentee that all railroads should use his invention, provided that they paid him the price of his license. He could not make his profit by selling it as a complete and separate machine. An infringer of such a patent could not be liable to damages to the amount of the profits of the railroad, nor could the actual damages to the patentee be measured by any known ratio of the profits on the road. The only actual damage which the patentee has suffered is the non-payment of the price which he has put upon his license, with interest, and no more. There may be cases, as where the thing has been used but for a short time, in which the jury should find for less than that sum; and there may be cases where, from some peculiar circumstances, the patentee may show actual damages to a larger amount. Of this a jury must judge from the evidence, under instructions from the court that they can find only such damages as have been actually sustained. Where the inventor finds it profitable to exercise his monopoly by selling licenses to make or use his improvement, he has himself fixed the average of his actual damage when the invention is used without his license. If he claims any thing above that amount, he is bound to substantiate his claim by clear and distinct evidence. Where he has himself established the market value of his improvement as separate and distinct from the other machinery with which it is connected, he can have no claim in justice and equity to make the profits of the whole machine the measure of his demand. It is only where, from the peculiar circumstances of the case, no other rule can be found, that the

most recent enunciation of some of the principles applicable to this difficult question of estimating the damages in patent suits.

defendant's profits become the criterion of the plaintiff's loss. Actual damages must be actually proved, and cannot be assumed as a legal inference from any facts which amount not to actual proof of the fact. What a patentee 'would have made if the infringer had not interfered with his rights,' is a question of fact and not 'a judgment of law.' The question is not what speculatively he may have lost, but what he actually did lose. It is not a 'judgment of law' or necessary legal inference, that if all the manufactures of locomotives and steam-engines who have built and sold engines with a patented cut-off or steam-whistle had not made such engines, that therefore all the purchasers of engines would have employed the patentee of the cut-off or whistle; and that consequently such patentee is entitled to all the profits made in the manufacture of such steam-engines by those who may have used his improvement without his license. Such a rule of damages would be better entitled to the epithets of 'speculative,' 'fanciful,' 'imaginary,' than that of 'actual.'

"If the measure of damages be the same, whether the patent be for an entire machine or for some improvement in some part of it, then it follows that each one who has patented an improvement in any portion of a steam-engine or other complex machine may recover the whole profits arising from the skill, labor, material, and capital employed in making the whole machine; and the unfortunate mechanic may be compelled to pay treble his whole profits to each of a dozen or more several inventors of some small improvement in the engine he has built. By this doctrine, even the smallest part is made equal to the whole, and 'actual damages' to the plaintiff may be converted into an unlimited series of penalties on the defendant.

"We think, therefore, that it is a very grave error to instruct a jury 'that as to the measure of damages, the same rule is to govern, whether the patent covers an entire machine or an improvement on a machine.'

"It appears, from the evidence in this case, that McCormick sold licenses to use his original patent of 1834 for twenty dollars ($20) each. He sold licenses to the defendants to make and vend machines containing all his improvements to any extent for thirty ($30) dollars for each machine, or at an average of ten ($10) for each of his three patents. The defendants made and sold many hundred machines for that price, and no more. They refused to pay for the last three hundred machines, under a belief that the plaintiff was not the original inventor of this last improvement, whereby a seat for the raker was provided on the machine, so that he could ride and not be compelled to walk as before. Beyond the refusal to pay the usual license price, the plaintiff showed no actual damage. The jury gave a verdict for nearly double the amount demanded for the use of three several patents, in a suit where the defendant was charged with violating one only, and that for an improvement of small importance when compared with the whole machine. This enormous and ruinous verdict is but a corollary or necessary consequence of the instructions given in that part of the charge of the court on which we

§ 339. But where merely the making of a patented machine is proved, and no actual damages have been sustained, nominal damages only should be given.[1]

§ 340. Where patented articles (cast-iron water-wheels) were manufactured by the defendants on an order given by a third person, and the order was partially executed before the defendants had notice of the patent, and two wheels only were cast after notice, it was held that nominal damages only were proper.[2]

§ 341. After considerable fluctuation of opinion, it has been decided by the Supreme Court that counsel fees are not a proper element for the consideration of the jury in the estimation of damages in actions for the infringement of a patent right.[3]

§ 341 *a*. Prior to the act of 1870, two remedies were open to a patentee whose rights had been infringed, and he had his election between the two. He might proceed in equity against the infringer and recover the profits which had been made by an illegal use of the patentee's invention, in which case, if no profit had been realized, there would be no recovery. On the other hand, the injured party might sue at law for the damages he had sustained on account of the infringement, in which case he would be entitled to recover damages without regard to whether the defendant had profited by the infringement or not. The legal measure of the damages to be awarded in such a case was not what the defendant had gained, but what the plaintiff had lost.

But by the act of 1870,[4] this rule has been changed, and both profits and damages may now be recovered in equity.[5] Section fifty-five of that act provides: "That all actions, suits, controversies, and cases arising under the patent laws of the United States, shall be originally cognizable as well in equity as at law,

have been commenting and of the doctrines therein asserted, and to which this court cannot give their consent or concurrence." Per Grier, J. Compare McCormick *v.* Seymour, 2 Blatchf. 240, the case reversed.

[1] Whittemore *v.* Cutter, *supra.*

[2] Bryce *v.* Dorr, 3 McLean, 582.

[3] Day *v.* Woodworth, 13 How. 363; Teese *v.* Huntingdon, 23 How. 2; affirming the doctrine of Whittemore *v.* Cutter, 1 Gall. 429, and Stimpson *v.* The R. R., 1 Wall. C. C. R. 164, and overruling that of Boston Manuf. Co. *v.* Fiske, 2 Mason, 119; and Allen *v.* Blunt, 3 Story, 742. Cf. Blanchard's, &c. *v.* Warner, 1 Blatchf. 258, reporter's note to p. 272.

[4] Act of July 8, 1870, § 55, 16 U. S. Stat. at Large, 206. See appendix.

[5] Williams *v.* Leonard, 9 Blatchf. 476; Cowing *v.* Rumsey, 8 Blatchf. 36.

by the circuit courts of the United States, or any district court having the powers and jurisdiction of a circuit court, or by the Supreme Court of the District of Columbia, or of any territory; and the court shall have power, upon bill in equity filed by any party aggrieved, to grant injunctions according to the course and principles of courts of equity, to prevent the violation of any right secured by patent, on such terms as the court may deem reasonable, and upon a decree being rendered in any such case for an infringement, the complainant shall be entitled to recover, in addition to the profits to be accounted for by the defendant, the damages the *claimant* [complainant] has sustained thereby, and the court shall assess the same or cause the same to be assessed under its direction, and the court shall have the same powers to increase the same in its discretion that are given by this act to increase the damages found by verdicts in actions upon the case; but all actions shall be brought during the term for which the letters-patent shall be granted or extended, or within six years after the expiration thereof."

It is further provided by section fifty-nine, "That damages for the infringement of any patent may be recovered by action on the case in any circuit court of the United States, or district court exercising the jurisdiction of a circuit court, or in the Supreme Court of the District of Columbia, or of any territory, in the name of the party interested, either as patentee, assignee, or grantee. And whenever in any such action a verdict shall be rendered for the plaintiff, the court may enter judgment thereon for any sum above the amount found by the verdict as the actual damages sustained, according to the circumstances of the case, not exceeding three times the amount of such verdict, together with the costs."

When the injured party proceeds for the recovery of damages, the question to be determined is not the amount of profits realized by the defendant, for this sum may be greatly inferior to the complainant's loss; but what loss has the complainant sustained by reason of the defendant's infringement. It may be necessary, however, to prove the profits made by the infringer in order to determine the extent of the plaintiff's loss.[1]

The power given by the statute to increase the damages returned by the jury to a sum "not exceeding three times the

[1] Cowing *v.* Rumsey, 8 Blatchf. 36.

amount of such verdict," is vested in the discretion of the court, which will be governed by the circumstances of the case. "Cases may be readily conceived," said Mr. Justice Leavitt,[1] "in which it would be the imperative duty of a court to exercise the discretion given by the statute, by increasing the damages. It has happened, and may occur again, that a meritorious inventor of a valuable improvement, after spending years of patient thought and toil in making it practically useful, and obtaining a patent for it, has been wantonly and unjustly pirated upon, and compelled, for the establishment of his rights, to engage in long, vexatious, and expensive litigation, in which at last the sum that may be awarded by the verdict of a jury may be wholly inadequate as a compensation for the wrongs and injuries he has sustained. In such a case the instincts of justice would demand of a judge that he should exercise the discretion vested in him by law, by trebling the damages, and thus, as far as practicable, doing justice to one who, from the great utility of his invention, may be entitled to the name of a public benefactor. But clearly there is no such feature in the present case. The plaintiff has no claim or merit as an inventor, but is the mere assignee of a patented machine, the right to which he has purchased on speculation. The law under such circumstances will give him the actual damages which his evidence shows he has sustained, but will give him nothing more."

It has been held that in an accounting for profits the defendant cannot be credited with a sum of money as a salary earned by and paid to himself while engaged in the business producing the profits.[2]

[1] Schwarzel *v.* Holenshade, 3 Fisher's Pat. Cas. 116.

[2] Williams *v.* Leonard, 9 Blatchf. 476. Mr. Justice Woodruff in this case said: "As to the 'salaries' of the defendants, during the period in which they have been engaged in infringing, they have no title, as against the complainant. It would be very great injustice, if the *quantum* of gains and profits recoverable by a complainant depended on the question, how much of such gains and profits the defendants used for their own support, or the support of their families, or, as even more broadly claimed here by the defendants, how much they saw fit to appropriate to their own use. Infringers would rarely be required to pay over any thing, if they could divide the gains and profits among themselves, under the name of salary, wages, or any other designation. Men work for gains and profits, but they are gains and profits still. Men support themselves and their families out of their gains and profits, but that

§ 341 *b*. In the case of the Rubber Company *v*. Goodyear,[1] the circuit court having decreed that the Providence Company was liable "for all the profits made in violation of the rights of the complainants, under the patent aforesaid, by respondents, by the mnnufacture, use, or sale of any of the articles named in said bill," the Supreme Court held this to be "in accordance with the rule in equity cases established by this court." [2]

In making up the account, the master had allowed deductions from profits, for bad debts, for rents and interest paid, debiting rents and interest received; and allowance was made for the market value of the materials on hand when the infringement began, for the cost of those subsequently acquired to carry on the business, and for the usual salaries of the managing officers; also for the amounts expended in repairs of building and machinery, and in the purchase of new machinery, tools and fixtures; but no further allowance was made for "wear and tear, and depreciation." The master, being satisfied that the extraordinary salaries which it appeared by the books had been paid were dividends of profits represented as salaries for concealment and delusion, refused to make allowance therefor. He also refused to allow the value, at the time they were used, of materials bought for the purposes of infringement; also, for profits due to elements not patented, which entered into the composition of the patented articles.

This report was approved by the Supreme Court. In holding that the master had correctly refused to allow manufacturers profits and interest on the capital stock, Mr. Justice Swayne, who delivered the judgment of the court, said: "The profits made in violation of the rights of the complainants in this class of cases, within the meaning of the law, are to be computed and ascer-

does not change their nature. If it were not so, inventors might, by reason of infringements, fail to obtain any thing, and the infringers obtain what they see fit to term adequate salaries out of their piracy. What, in good faith, the defendants pay to others, as expenses, may be taken as the cost, to them, of their manufacture. What they take to themselves are gains. They might perhaps have earned and gained as much, or perhaps more, by laboring in some other business, in no violation of the rights of their neighbor; but they cannot be permitted to gain either wages or salary by a violation of such rights."

[1] 9 Wall. 788.

[2] Livingston *v*. Woodworth, 15 How. 546; Dean *v*. Mason, 20 ibid. 198.

tained by finding the difference between cost and yield. In estimating the cost, the elements of price of materials, interest, expenses of manufacture and sale, and other necessary expenditures, if there be any, and bad debts, are to be taken into the account, and nothing else. The calculation is to be made as a manufacturer calculates the profits of his business. 'Profit' is the gain made upon any business or investment, when both the receipts and payments are taken into the account. The rule is founded in reason and justice. It compensates one party and punishes the other. It makes the wrong-doer liable for actual, not possible, gains. The controlling consideration is that he shall not profit by his wrong. A more favorable rule would offer a premium for dishonesty, and invite to aggression."

§ 341 *c*. In the case of Mowry *v*. Whitney,[1] where the patent infringed was for an improved process of annealing car-wheels,[2] the court below, upon the report of the master, decreed against the defendant, the entire profits made by him in the manufacture and sale of the wheels, instead of those resulting from the use of Whitney's invention in a part of the manufacture; the amount of such profits being the difference between the cost of the wheels and the price for which they were sold.

This decree was reversed by the Supreme Court, which was of opinion that, in the case of an improved process in a manufacture as well as an improvement in a machine, an infringer is not liable to the extent of his entire profits in the manufacture.[3] In the language of the opinion, "The question to be determined in this case is, what advantage did the defendant derive from using the complainant's invention over what he had in using other processes then open to the public, and adequate to enable him to obtain an equally beneficial result? The fruits of that advantage are his profits. They are all the benefits he derived from the existence of the Whitney invention. It is found that there were other processes by which the inherent strain caused by unequal cooling could be and was prevented, counteracting which strain was the sole object of the complainant's invention, and a car-wheel could be prepared for similar service, valuable in the market and sal-

[1] 14 Wall. 620. [2] See *ante*, p. 419.

[3] Jones *v*. Morehead, 1 Wall. 155; Seymour *v*. McCormick, 16 How. 480. See also Cowing *v*. Rumsey, 8 Blatchf. 36; and Troy Iron and Nail Factory *v*. Corning, 3 Fisher's Pat. Cas. 497.

able at a price not less than was obtained for those which the defendant manufactured. The inquiry then is, what was the advantage in cost, in skill required, in convenience of operation, or marketability, in bringing car-wheels by Whitney's process from the condition in which they are when taken hot from the moulds to a perfected state, over bringing them to the same state by those other processes, and thus rendering them equally fit for the same service? That advantage is the measure of profits. It is quite unimportant what name was given to the products of the processes, whether one could be called annealed wheels and the other could not, except so far as affected their marketability.

"The record shows that the court overruled the alternative finding of the master, that if there is no infringement of the complainant's patent unless the wheels are subjected to the process of reheating, — that is to say, if the process of slow cooling used in connection with reheating is old, and not a part of the complainant's invention, no part of the profit derived by the defendant from the manufacture and sale of the wheels was due to the use by him of that invention. One exception taken to this finding was that not only the entire process described in the patent, but each part of such entire process, was the invention of the complainant; and the use of any material, substantial, and essential part of such entire process, the slow cooling being a substantial and material part, whereby only an improved chilled cast-iron railroad wheel could be made, and beneficial effects the same in kind if not in degree attained, that were attained by the complainant's entire process, is an infringement of complainant's patent, and the profits derived from the use of such material, substantial, and essential part should be accounted for in this case. This exception the court sustained, and thereby held that the defendant is chargeable with the profits he derived from slow cooling alone. We cannot assent to this. The patent is for an entire process, made up of several constituents. The patentee does not claim to have been the inventor of the constituents. The exclusive use of them singly is not secured to him. What is secured is their use when arranged in the process. Unless one of them is employed in making up the process, and as an element of it, the patentee cannot prevent others from using it. As well might the patentee of a machine, every part of which is an old and known device, appropriate the exclusive use of each device, though employed singly, and not combined with the others as a machine. The defendant was not, therefore, responsible for slow cooling alone, or from the profits derived from it. He was liable to account for such profits only when he used slow cooling in connection with reheating in the manner described in Whitney's claim substantially, or when extraneous heat was employed to retard the progress of cooling. We have said that slow cooling is not claimed in the specification as the invention of the patentee. And it is found by the master that there are other modes of slow cooling, and even other modes of relieving against the inherent strain caused by unretarded cooling, than that practised by the complainant and claimed by him. Though, therefore, slow cooling is an essential part of the complainant's process, it is an equally essential part of other processes which the defendant was at liberty to use in preparing his car-wheels for market.

"We add only that in our opinion the defendant should not have been charged with interest before the final decree. The profits which are recoverable against an infringer of a patent are in fact a compensation for the injury the patentee has sustained from the invasion of his right. They are the measure of his damages. Though called profits, they are really damages, and unliquidated until the decree is made. Interest is not generally allowable upon unliquidated damages. We will not say that in no possible case can interest be allowed. It is enough that the case in hand does not justify such an allowance. The defendant manufactured the wheels of which the complaint is made under a patent granted to him in 1861. His infringement of the complainant's patent was not wanton. He had before him the judgment of the Patent Office that his process was not an invasion of the patent granted to the complainant, and though this does not protect him against responsibility for damages, it ought to relieve him from liability to interest on profits."

§ 342. As to the time of the acts complained of as amounting to an infringement, it is obvious that the patent cannot be infringed by any thing done when the patent did not exist; and therefore it is no infringement to make or use a machine subsequently patented, or otherwise to practise the invention which is afterwards made the subject of a patent, before the patent is obtained. But when a patent is granted, the right in the subject-matter relates back to the time of the invention, so that the party who has practised the invention between the time of the discovery and the issuing of the patent must cease to do so. Any acts of infringement done after the issuing of the patent will be ground for the recovery of damages, although the previous acts were done at a time when it was uncertain whether there would be any patent issued.[1] The same is true of acts done in violation of a patent which is surrendered and renewed on account of defects in the specification. If a party erect and put in use a patented machine, during the existence of a defective patent which is afterwards surrendered, it will be an infringement of the new and reissued patent, if he continues the use of such machine after the renewal; and it seems that no notice of the renewal is necessary; and if it is, that knowledge of the original patent will be notice of the renewed patent granted in continuation of it, according to the provisions and principles of law.[2]

In conformity with this doctrine it has been recently held, that suits for infringement pending at the time of the surrender and reissue of letters-patent fall with such surrender, because the foundation on which they rested no longer exists.[3]

[1] Evans *v.* Weiss, 2 Wash. 342; Dixon *v.* Moyer, 4 Wash. 68.

[2] Ames *v.* Howard, 1 Sumner, 482, 488. In this case Mr. Justice Story said: "The next objection is, that in point of law the plaintiff is not entitled, without some previous notice or claim, to maintain this action under his patent against the defendants, for continuing the use of the machines erected and put in use by them before the patent issued. This objection cannot prevail. I am by no means prepared to say, that any notice is, in cases of this sort, ever necessary to any party who is actually using a machine in violation of the patent right. But it is very clear, that in this case enough was established in evidence to show that the defendants had the most ample knowledge of the original patent taken out by the plaintiff in 1822, and of which the present is only a continuation, being grounded upon a surrender of the first for mere defects in the original specification. Whoever erects or uses a patented machine does it at his peril. He takes upon himself all the chances of its being originally valid; or of its being afterwards made so by a surrender of it, and the grant of a new patent, which may cure any defects, and is grantable according to the principles of law. That this new patent was so grantable is clear, as well from the decision of the Supreme Court in Grant *v.* Raymond (6 Peters's R. 218), as from the act of Congress of the 3d of July, 1833, c. 162. There is no pretence to say that the defendants were *bonâ fide* purchasers without any knowledge or notice of any adverse claim of the plaintiff under this original patent; and the damages were by the court expressly limited to damages which accrued to the plaintiff by the use of the machine after the new patent was granted to the plaintiff."

[3] Moffitt *v.* Garr, 1 Black. 273. See, further, same case, sub-chapter on Action at Law.

§ 343. A patentee may recover damages for an infringement during the time which intervened between the destruction of the Patent Office by fire, in 1836, and the restoration of the records under the act of March 3, 1837.[1]

[1] Hogg *v.* Emerson, 6 How. 437.

CHAPTER IX.

OF THE REMEDY FOR AN INFRINGEMENT BY ACTION AT LAW.

§ 344. THE act of Congress of July 4, 1836, c. 357, § 14, provides that damages may be recovered for an infringement by "an action on the case," — a remedy which exists equally at common law, for the violation of the right secured by letters-patent.[1]

§ 345. I. *Parties.* — The statute also provides "that the action shall be brought in the name or names of the person or persons interested, whether as patentee, assignees, or as grantees of the exclusive right within and throughout a specified part of the United States."[2]

§ 345 *a.* The language of the latest patent law, that of 1870, is "that damages for the infringement of any patent may be recovered by action on the case in any circuit court of the United States, or district court exercising the jurisdiction of a circuit court, or in the Supreme Court of the District of Columbia, or of any Territory, in the name of the party interested, either as patentee, assignee, or grantee."

§ 346. Formerly, the grantee for a particular district could not bring an action on the patent in his own name.[3] But the statute has made him a party interested in the patent, and consequently, in his own district, he may sue in his own name.[4]

But in order that the assignee of a sectional interest may sue in his own name, the assignment must clearly convey to him the

[1] Bull. N. P. 76.

[2] Act of July 4, 1836, c. 357, § 14. It seems that no previous notice or claim of a right to the exclusive use of an invention is necessary to enable a patentee to maintain an action for an alleged violation of his patent right. Ames *v.* Howard, 1 Sumner, 482.

[3] Tyler *v.* Tuel, 6 Cranch, 324.

[4] Such a suit may be maintained although the plaintiff is the grantee of a right to use only a limited number of the patented machines in the particular district, provided it is an exclusive right, and it may be maintained against the patentee himself. Wilson *v.* Rousseau, 4 How. 646.

entire and unqualified monopoly which the patentee held in the specified territory, excluding the patentee himself as well as others; for any assignment short of this is a mere license.[1]

It has been recently held that the grant of a right to construct and use fifty machines within certain localities, reserving to the grantor the right to construct and to license others to construct, but not to use them therein, was the grant of an exclusive right under the patent of 1836, and that consequently the suit was rightly brought in the name of the assignees, although agreed to be at the expense of the grantor.[2]

An action may properly be brought by the patentee in behalf of one to whom he has granted an exclusive license and who has been damaged by the infringement.[3]

It has also been held that one joint owner of a patent can bring an action of infringement against his co-owner for making and selling machines in a manner which does not respect his rights.[4]

§ 347. Where the patentee has assigned his whole interest, either before or after the patent was taken out, the action can only be brought in the name of the assignee;[5] but where the assign-

[1] Gaylor *v.* Wilder, 10 How. 477, per Taney, C. J.

[2] Washburn *v.* Gould, 3 Story, 122.

[3] Goodyear *v.* McBurney, 3 Blatchf. 32.

[4] Pitts *v.* Hall, 3 Blatchf. 201.

[5] Herbert *v.* Adams, 4 Mass. 15. Affirmed by ruling in Gaylor *v.* Wilder, 10 How. 477. "The inventor of a new and useful improvement certainly has no exclusive right to it until he obtains a patent. This right is created by the patent, and no suit can be maintained by the inventor against any one for using it before the patent is issued. But the discoverer of a new and useful improvement is vested by law with an inchoate right to its exclusive use, which he may perfect and make absolute by proceeding in the manner in which the law requires. Fitzgerald possessed the inchoate right at the time of the assignment. The discovery had been made, and the specification prepared to obtain a patent. And it appears by the language of the assignment that it was intended to operate upon the perfect legal title which Fitzgerald then had a lawful right to obtain, as well as upon the imperfect and inchoate interest which he actually possessed. The assignment requests that the patent may issue to the assignee, and there would seem to be no sound reason for defeating the intention of the parties by restraining the assignment to the latter interest, and compelling them to execute another transfer, unless the act of Congress makes it necessary. The court thinks it does not. The act of 1836 declares that every patent shall be assignable in law, and that the assignment must be in writing, and recorded within the time specified. But the thing to be assigned is not the mere parchment on which the grant is written. It is the monopoly

ment is of an undivided part of the interest, the action should be brought in the joint names of the patentee and the assignee, as representing the whole interest.[1]

In a recent English case,[2] it was held that the assignee of a separate and distinct portion of a patent may sue for an infringement of that patent, without joining one who has an interest in another part, the damages to be recovered accruing to the former alone. The patentee, having obtained a patent for "improvements in lace *and other weavings*," assigned to the plaintiffs "all share and interest in it so far as it related to or concerned the making, using, exercising, and vending of the said invention of improvements in the manufacture of *close* weavings in lace, and of *twisted purle edges* of lace and other weavings in *twist lace machines*, as described in the *sixth* part of the specification," &c. The plaintiffs brought an action in their own name for alleged infringement of this part of the patent, to which the defendants pleaded want of right to sue. This was demurred to by plaintiffs, and the demurrer sustained by the court. Erle, C. J., said (Crowder and Byles, JJ.,

which the grant confers; the right of property which it creates. And when the party has acquired an inchoate right to it, and the power to make that right perfect and absolute at his pleasure, the assignment of his whole interest, whether executed before or after the patent issued, is equally within the province of the act of Congress.

"And we are the less disposed to give it a different construction, because no purpose of justice would be answered by it; and the one we now give was the received construction of the act of 1793, in several of the circuits. As long ago as 1825, it was held by Mr. Justice Story that, in a case of this kind, an action could not be maintained in the name of the patentee, but must be brought by the assignee. 4 Mason, 15 (Herbert *v.* Adams). We understand the same rule has prevailed in other circuits, and if it were now changed, it might produce much injustice to assignees who have relied on such assignments, and defeat pending suits brought upon the faith of long-established judicial practice and judicial decision. Fitzgerald sets up no claim against the assignment, and to require another to complete the transfer would be mere form. We do not think the act of Congress requires it; but that when the patent issued to him, the legal right to the monopoly and property it created was, by operation of the assignment then on record, vested in Enos Wilder." Per Taney, C. J.

[1] Whittemore *v.* Cutter, 1 Gallis. 429, 430. An assignee of the exclusive right to use a certain number of machines in a certain district, may join his assignor with him in a bill for an injunction. Woodworth *v.* Wilson, 4 How. 712.

[2] Dunnicliff *v.* Mallett, 7 C. B. N. S. 209.

concurring): "I am of opinion that the plaintiffs are entitled to judgment on these demurrers. The main question which has been argued before us arises apparently for the first time; therefore we must decide it according to general principles of law, no authority having been cited which bears any very close analogy. That question is, whether an assignment of part of a patent is valid. I incline to think that it is. It is every day's practice, for the sake of economy, to include in one patent several things which are in their nature perfectly distinct and severable. It is also every day's practice to get rid by disclaimer of part of a patent which turns out to be old. Being therefore inclined to think that a patent, severable in its nature, may be severed by the assignment of a part, I see no reason for holding that the assignee of a separate part, which is the subject of infringement, may not bring an action. Then, are the assignees, bringing an action for an injury done solely to them by an infringement of that part of the patent which is thus vested in them alone, liable to be defeated because they have not joined the assignees of other parts of the patent, who have no manner of interest in the damages sought to be recovered in such action? I see no reason why the action should be defeated on such ground. I see no reason why the plaintiffs should be put to the trouble and expense of applying for leave to use the names of the other parties, or of compelling them by means of a judge's order to permit their names to be used upon an indemnity, where no practical advantage whatever is to be gained by it, — the injury being to the assignees of part only, and the damages to be recovered being theirs only. It is said that the defendants may possibly be prejudiced by the non-joinder of the other parties, inasmuch as they might thereby be deprived of the advantage of any admissions which might have been made by them. I cannot think that it is a tenable ground of objection, because, if those parties were joined, any admissions by them would not be binding on the now plaintiffs, unless made in and for the purpose of the suit. Then, as to the alleged inconvenience of the matter being brought in question several times, I must confess I do not feel the force of the argument. In the ordinary case of a patentee trying the validity of the patent against several infringers, the power given to the judge to certify under 5 and 6 W. 4, c. 83, § 3, is only a provision in favor of the patentee, to entitle him to treble costs where the validity of the patent has already been established. I am not aware of any authority or of any principle which precludes the assignee of part of a patent from suing for an infringement of that part; nor do I think it would lead to any multiplying of actions to permit it. I am therefore of opinion that our judgment should be for the plaintiff on both these demurrers."

This opinion is not to be reconciled with that of Taney, C. J., in the case of Gaylor *v.* Wilder, *supra;* still less with that of Grier, J., in Blanchard *v.* Eldridge.[1] Here the plaintiff, having obtained a patent for turning every kind of irregular forms, assigned to one Carter "the full and exclusive license, right, and permission to have, hold, use, and enjoy Blanchard's patent for turning irregular forms, &c., *so far as said improvement* is or may be used for turning *shoe lasts, boot and shoe trees, and hat blocks, and also for turning spokes for wheels of all kinds of carriage-wheels,* and all *articles that form any part in the construction of carriages,* &c. He (the patentee, Blanchard) then brought the present suit for an alleged infringement of these rights, granted exclusively to Carter. The defendant moved for a new trial on the ground that the plaintiff was not entitled to sue, but the motion was refused. Grier, J.: "The point here raised by the defendant's counsel is not without its difficulty, and the force of his argument cannot be evaded, if his assumption be true, that this deed transfers to Carter the legal title of that portion of the patent which it purports to vest in him. But if it does not so operate, it cannot be noticed in a court of law, and cannot affect the case. As the grants of the crown were at common law construed with the greatest strictness, the privileges granted by a patent for a monopoly would probably not have been treated as capable of assignment unless made so by the letter of the grant. Since the statute 21 James I., patents for useful inventions (notwithstanding the statute itself mentions the 'inventor' only) have always granted the privilege or monopoly to the inventor, his executor, administrator, and assigns. These monopolies, therefore, are assignable as other personal chattels, by force of the grant which creates them. As a chattel, also, it might be held by two or more joint owners; hence any undivided portion or interest in the whole as a unity might be assigned, and if the original grantee

[1] 1 Wall. C. C. 337.

died, such assignees might join in action for infringement of their right.[1] But the patent right itself was insusceptible of local subdivision.[2] As a privilege or monopoly it was an entire thing, indivisible and incapable of apportionment.[3]

"But the act of Congress of 1836 has regulated the assignment of patents. Sec. 11 provides that a patent shall be assignable, — (1) As to the whole interest; (2) As to any undivided part thereof; (3) An exclusive right may be granted throughout any specified part or portion of the United States. Sec. 14 requires the action for infringement to be brought 'in the name or names of the person or persons interested, whether as patentee, assignees, or as grantees of the exclusive right within and throughout a specified part of the United States.' The word 'assignees' in this section must be construed by reference to the eleventh section, already referred to, which defines in what way a patent may be assigned, to wit, either the whole or any undivided portion of the whole. The statute also renders the monopoly capable of subdivision in the category of its locality, but in no other way. The patentee is not allowed to carve out his monopoly, which is a unity, into a hundred or more, all acting in the same place and liable to come into conflict. The grant to Carter, by the deed under consideration, is not of the whole monopoly, nor of any undivided portion of the whole, and though for an "exclusive right," it is not exclusive of all others within a certain district or *specified part* of the United States; on the contrary, it is an exclusive right to use the machine for a *specified purpose*. A machine for turning irregular figures may be used for numberless purposes. If the patentee or his assignee can assign to A. an exclusive right to use the machine for making shoe-lasts, to B. for turning spokes, to C. for axe-handles, and so on to the end of the alphabet, then may he, out of his one monopoly, carve out a thousand others, each subdivision, like a polypus, being itself a several monopoly, and having a separate existence in the same place. What endless perplexity and confusion must necessarily arise from the establishment of such a doctrine! Suppose the monopoly granted by this patent parcelled out to some twenty submonopolies, with an exclusive right to each to use his machine

[1] Boulton *v.* Bull, 2 H. Blackst. 463.
[2] Whittemore *v.* Cutter, 1 Gall. 429.
[3] Brooks *v.* Byam, 2 Story, 525.

for certain purposes in any given place; what remedy could A. have against B. for an infringement of his special privilege. The patentee or grantor might restrain his grantee of a machine for a special use, by a covenant; but, as between the several grantees, no action could lie, although they alone might suffer from a breach of the covenant.

"But it is sufficient for purposes of the present inquiry, that the act of Congress has not given a legal sanction to such transfers or assignments, nor subjected even a pirate of the machine to fifty different suits by fifty several assignees, whose several interests might be affected if a patent could be thus split up into numerous exclusive rights or sub-monopolies. Whether the deed confers on Carter and his assigns more than a special license, or what remedy a court of equity might be disposed to extend to him where his rights are infringed, it is not necessary now to inquire. As it does not confer a legal title to the whole or an undivided portion of the patent, nor grant 'an exclusive right within a specified part of the United States,' it cannot be received to affect this case. It was wholly irrelevant and ought not to be received in evidence. It adds to my confidence in the correctness of this view, that, as I have been informed, my brother Nelson has ruled the question in the same way in the second circuit."

In a subsequent English case,[1] it was held that the plaintiff, who had acquired, first, an undivided moiety from the patentees directly, and afterwards the remaining share indirectly, through a mesne assignment, was thereby vested with the entire right of the patentees, and could even bring an action against them for infringement. If the assignment has not been made, but has been merely agreed to be made, the action should be in the name of the patentee, the assignee not having the interest until the assignment has been made and recorded.[2] But it may be recorded at any time after the suit is brought and before trial.[3] An action for an infringement may be maintained against a corporation.[4]

§ 347 *a*. In the recent case of Moore *v*. Marsh,[5] in the Supreme

[1] Walton *v*. Lavater, 8 C. B. N. S. 162.
[2] Park *v*. Little, 3 Wash. 196.
[3] Pitts *v*. Whitman, 2 Story's R. 609, 614.
[4] Kneass *v*. The Schuylkill Bank, 4 Wash. 9.
[5] 7 Wall. 515.

Court of the United States, the issue was raised as to the true meaning of the words "name of the person interested" in the fourteenth section of the act of 1836, whether they meant persons interested in the patent at the time when the suit was brought, or when the cause of action accrued.

The facts in this case showed that Moore had brought suit against Marsh for infringement, the defence to which was that *after* the date of the alleged infringement, Moore had sold and assigned an undivided half of the patent for the district where the infringement was alleged to have been committed. The Court held that the right of action was given to the person or persons owning the exclusive right to the patent at the time of infringement. Otherwise there would be no redress, as a subsequent assignee or grantee can neither maintain an action in his own name, nor be joined with the patentee in maintaining it for any infringement of the exclusive right committed before he became interested in the patent. "The true meaning of the word 'interested,'" said Mr. Justice Clifford in pronouncing the judgment of the court, "as employed in the last clause of the fourteenth section of the Patent Act, when properly understood and applied, is that the right of action is given to the person or persons owning the exclusive right at the time the infringement is committed. Subsequent sale and transfer of the exclusive right are no bar to an action to recover damages for an infringement committed before such sale and transfer.

"The reason for the rule is, that the assignee or grantee is not interested in the damages for any infringement committed before the sale and transfer of the patent. Correct interpretation of the words, 'person or persons interested,' is that the words mean the person or persons interested in the patent at the time when the infringement was committed, which is the cause of action for which the damages may be recovered."[1]

§ 347 *b*. Where several persons are appointed as executors of the will of a deceased patentee, but provision is made for one to act independent of the others, and but one proves the will and receives the letters of administration, such executor can maintain an action for infringement of the letters-patent at common law without joining his co-executors. And where the patent

[1] Dean *v*. Mason, 20 How. 198.

was surrendered by such person as executor, and a reissue was made to him in the same character, it was held that this was a specific grant, and vested in him exclusively the legal title, and that the grantee could sustain a suit on the patent in all respects, as if he had been designated in it as *trustee* instead of executor.[1]

§ 348. The Supreme Court of the United States have held that a covenant by a patentee, made prior to the law authorizing extensions, that the covenantee should have the benefit of any improvement in the machinery, or alteration or renewal of the patent, did not include the extension by an administrator under the act of 1836; that it must be construed to include only renewals obtained upon the surrender of a patent on account of a defective specification, and, therefore, that a plaintiff who claimed under an assignment from the administrator could maintain a suit against a person who claimed under the covenant.[2]

§ 349. II. *The Declaration.* — The declaration, in an action for the infringement of a patent, should show a title in the plaintiff, with convenient certainty; and should set forth all the matters which are of the essence. Without these allegations, the plaintiff fails to show a right in point of law to ask the court for judgment in his favor. The several parts of the declaration may here be considered in the order in which they occur in pleading.

§ 350. The declaration should commence with a recital that the plaintiff was "the original and first inventor" of the subject-matter, the making, using, or vending of which is complained of. This averment is necessary, notwithstanding the letters-patent, afterwards referred to, recite that the plaintiff has alleged that he was the original and first inventor; because it must appear affirmatively, in point of fact, at the trial, that he was so, and the letters-patent can only be resorted to as *primâ facie* evidence of the fact. There must, therefore, be a distinct allegation of the fact, as one of the things essential to the plaintiff's title.[3] For the same reason, the declaration goes on to aver that the subject-matter was "new and useful," "not known or used before the plaintiff's invention or discovery," and "not at the time of his

[1] Rubber Co. *v.* Goodyear, 9 Wall. 788.

[2] Wilson *v.* Rousseau, 4 How. 646.

[3] The plaintiff must affirm the performance of all acts on which his title depends. Gray *v.* James, Peters, C. C. R. 476.

application for a patent in public use or on sale with his consent or allowance."

But while a declaration on letters-patent must tender issue on the novelty and utility of the invention patented, it need not aver at what specific time such invention was made, but only that it was before the application for the patent.[1]

§ 351. Whether it is necessary to aver the citizenship of the patentee has never been determined. In practice it is generally done, and it is safer to do so than to omit an averment which might on demurrer be held to be essential.[2] But it is absolutely necessary to aver that the plaintiff, being the original and first inventor, obtained letters-patent for his invention, in due form of law, under the seal of the Patent Office, signed by the Secretary of the Interior, and countersigned by the commissioner of patents.[3]

The declaration need not, however, show the regularity of the proceedings in the Patent Office preliminary to the grant, but may simply aver that the grant was duly obtained.[4]

[1] Wilder *v.* McCormick, 2 Blatchf. 31.

[2] Mr. Phillips suggests that the necessity for this averment will depend on the construction to be given to the fifteenth section of the act of 1836, by which, if the patentee be an alien, the defendant is permitted to show that the patentee has "failed and neglected for the space of eighteen months from the date of the patent to put and continue on sale to the public, on reasonable terms, the invention or discovery." Phillips on Patents, p. 520, *note*. This clause in the statute can scarcely be considered as imposing a burden of proof of citizenship on the plaintiff. It authorizes the defendant to avail himself of the fact that the plaintiff is an alien, by showing that the plaintiff has omitted to do certain acts; but is any thing more to be inferred from the clause than this, that if the defendant means to show the omission, he must first show that the plaintiff is an alien? I agree, however, with the learned author, that to aver the citizenship is the safest course.

[3] Formerly, patents bore the attestation of the President of the United States; and it was held to be necessary to aver that the letters had been so tested, and that the patent had actually issued, or been delivered; otherwise, the declaration would be bad on demurrer. Cutting and others, Executors *v.* Myers, 4 Wash. 220. For the same reason, the averment is now necessary that the letters were duly tested by the public officers whose duty it is to sign and countersign them; and the mode of averring the delivery, now usually practised, is to declare that the plaintiff, on such a day, "did obtain" them. But it is not necessary to aver that the preliminary steps to obtain a patent were taken, because if the declaration aver that the patent was granted in the form prescribed by law, the court, upon demurrer, will presume that every thing was rightly done to obtain it. Fulton's Executors *v.* Myers. *Vide* act of 1849, c. 108, § 2; modifying act of 1836, c. 357, § 5.

[4] Wilder *v.* McCormick, 2 Blatchf. 31. "The third and fourth causes of de-

§ 352. The substance of the grant should then be set forth, that is to say, that the letters-patent secured to the plaintiff, his

murrer cannot be sustained. The third is, that it does not appear that the application for the patent was in writing, nor to whom it was made. The fourth is that it does not appear that the commissioner of patents had any rightful authority to grant the patent. These causes are founded upon supposed requisites of the statute, not averred in the declaration to have been complied with, and are also supposed to be supported by general principles governing proceedings in tribunals of inferior jurisdiction. If the matters which it is alleged should be set forth in the declaration would call for the application of those principles in case they were pleaded by way of justification and in defence of acts done, or as a protection to the party pleading them, which would at least be a doubtful proposition (Martin *v.* Mott, 12 Wheat. 19), it would not necessarily follow that the same method of pleading must be pursued in declaring upon a private title or a grant emanating from functionaries acting under statutory authority. (Day *v.* Chism, 10 Wheat. 449; Bank of the United States *v.* Smith, 11 Wheat. 171; Carroll *v.* Peake, 1 Peters, 18, 23.) The third cause of demurrer rests upon the assumption that the plaintiff must, in his pleading, specify all the acts done by him to obtain a patent, in order that it may appear upon the face of the declaration that the mode of proceeding pointed out by the statute has been pursued. But the case of the Philadelphia & Trenton R.R. *v.* Stimpson, 14 Peters, 448, disposes of this and all the other objections that fall within the same class. The grant of the patent is itself sufficient evidence that all the preliminary steps required by law were properly taken. And, as the plaintiff may make his patent the direct and efficient proof, in the first instance, of his right to the grant, so *à fortiori* it would seem unnecessary for him to plead any of the particulars which conduced to the grant. It is sufficient to set forth the grant in substance (Tryon *v.* White, Peters, C. C. 96). The fourth cause of demurrer is founded upon a misapplication of a doctrine appertaining to the acts of legal tribunals, where a court of inferior jurisdiction takes cognizance of a case and renders judgment, and he who sets up such judgment in support of his own interests must aver and prove that the tribunal had jurisdiction in the matter. The authority of the commissioner of patents, or of the commissioner of the land office, or of the President to issue grants, is not of the nature of *jurisdiction* in its common-law and technical acceptation. As in regard to patents for land, so in regard to patents for inventions, the proper officer issues the grant when he has evidence satisfactory to his own mind that the claimant is entitled to receive it. But that adjudges nothing as to the real right. That question is unaffected, and remains to be examined and decided between parties contesting it, without prejudice or advantage from the letters-patent. We are not aware of any mode of pleading by which the courts can be called upon to settle the regularity of the preliminary proceedings in the patent office. Nor does there seem to be any utility in putting in issue the authority of the commissioner, upon the facts before him, to grant a patent, because, if the decision should negative his authority, it could not revoke or supersede the patent. The declaration must tender an issue upon the novelty and utility of the discovery patented, these being essential to the enforcement of any exclusive

heirs, administrators, &c., for the term of fourteen years, the full and exclusive right of practising the invention; which should be described briefly, as it is set forth in the letters-patent, of which profert should be made.[1] Where the declaration describes the plaintiff's invention in the words of the patent, it is not necessary that the description, as stated in the specification, should be set forth. If the defendant require the specification in his defence, he may have it placed in the record by praying oyer of it.[2]

§ 353. The declaration is concluded by an averment of the value of the patent right and of the breach by the defendant, and the damages sustained by the plaintiff.[3]

In this action for a breach of the patent, it is indispensable to establish a breach before suit brought. But in equity the doctrine is otherwise, as a bill for an injunction will lie upon sufficient proof of an intent to violate.[4] The declaration need not set forth the act complained of as contrary to the statute,[5] but may simply allege that the defendant "made, constructed, used, and vended to sundry persons," &c., the said invention.[6] Repeated infringements may be sued for in one action.[7] A declaration

privilege under the patent. But the question of the regularity of the proceedings in petitioning for and obtaining the patent, and that of the correctness of the judgment of the officer in awarding it, are not material, and cannot be inquired into."

[1] Chit. Pl. vol. 2. Profert of the letters-patent, in the declaration, makes them and the specification, when produced, a part of the declaration, and so gives all the certainty, as to the invention and improvement patented, required by law. Pitts *v.* Whitman, 2 Story's R. 609, 614.

[2] Gray *v.* James, Peters, C. C. R. 476.

[3] See the Precedents in the Appendix.

[4] Woodworth *v.* Stone, 3 Story, 749.

[5] Parker *v.* Haworth, 4 McLean, 370. "A motion was made in arrest of judgment, on the ground that the declaration does not set forth the act complained of as contrary to the statute. This is necessary when an action is brought on a penal statute, but not in the case like the present, where damages are sought for an injury done. Where the plaintiff sues for a penalty, as the statute is the only foundation for the action, the declaration must aver that the act is *contra formam statuti*. In Tyron *v.* White (Peters, C. C. R. 96), it is said, 'if the declaration in an action for the invasion of a patent right fails to lay the act complained *contra formam statuti*, the defect will be purged after the verdict.'"

[6] Case *v.* Redfield, 4 McLean, 526.

[7] Wilder *v.* McCormick, 2 Blatchf. 31. "A reiteration of infringements of a patent, like a repetition of torts of any other kind which are of the same

commencing in the form of action of trespass on the case, and concluding in the form of action of debt, is not demurrable.[1]

§ 354. If the plaintiff sues in the character of assignee of the patent, he must set forth both the patentee's title and his own, and should aver that the assignments were duly recorded in the Patent Office. If the declaration omit to state that the assignments were recorded, the omission will be cured by verdict, if the general terms of the declaration are otherwise sufficient to have authorized the admission of proof of the recording at the trial; upon the general principle, that, after verdict, all the facts necessary to have been proved to enable the jury to find a verdict for the plaintiff, will be presumed to have been proved, if the general terms of the declaration would have let them in.[2]

nature, may be sued for and recompensed in one action. There is no known doctrine of the law that requires a plaintiff to split up into separate actions grievances of that character."

[1] Ibid. "We do not perceive that there is any material incongruity between the commencement and the close of the declaration. The gravamen of the suit is the tortious infringement of the plaintiff's patent, and the conclusion of the declaration is a demand of damages in gross. They are averred to be 'actual damages,' but that allegation does not change the nature of the averment. It is still merely a demand of damages in compensation of the wrong."

[2] Dobson *v.* Campbell, 1 Sumner, 319, 326, Story, J. "We are of opinion that the motion in arrest of judgment ought to be overruled. We accede to the doctrine stated at the bar, that a defective title cannot, after verdict, support a judgment; and therefore it constitutes a good ground for arresting the judgment. But the present is not such a case; but is merely the case of a good title defectively set forth. The defect complained of is the omission to state that the assignments, on which the plaintiff's title is founded, were duly recorded in the office of the department of state, which is made essential to pass the title of the original patentee, by the fourth section of the Patent Act of the 21st of February, 1793, c. 55. The general principle of law is, that, where a matter is so essentially necessary to be proved, to establish the plaintiff's right to recovery, that the jury could not be presumed to have found a verdict for him, unless it had been proved at the trial, there the omission to state that matter in express terms, in the declaration, is cured by the verdict, if the general terms of the declaration are otherwise sufficient to comprehend it. This was the doctrine of Lord Ellenborough, in Jackson *v.* Pesked (1 M. & Selw. R. 234); and it is very elaborately expounded by Mr. Sergeant Williams, in his learned note to 1 Saunders' R. 228 *a*. The other authorities, cited on behalf of the plaintiff, are to the same effect. Now, it seems to us, that taking the whole declaration together (however inartificially drawn), the plaintiff sets up a title to the patent right by assignment, and an

§ 355. At the trial, proof may be given of the recording of an assignment, either before or after the action was brought.[1]

§ 356. III. *Pleadings and Defences.* — The fifteenth section of the act of 1836 provides that the defendant, in any action for the infringement of a patent, shall be permitted to plead the general issue, and to give the statute and any special matter in evidence, of which notice in writing may have been given to the plaintiff or his attorney, thirty days before trial, tending to prove that the description and specification of the patent does not contain the whole truth relative to the invention or discovery, or that it contains more than is necessary to produce the described effect; which concealment or addition shall fully appear to have been made for the purpose of deceiving the public; or that the patentee was not the original and first inventor or discoverer of the thing patented, or of a substantial and material part thereof claimed as new, or that it has been described in some public work anterior to the supposed discovery by the patentee, or had been in public use, or on sale, with his consent or allowance, before his application for a patent, or that he had surreptitiously or unjustly obtained a patent for that which was in fact invented or discovered by another, who was using reasonable diligence in adapting and perfecting the same; or that the patentee, if an alien at the time the patent was granted, had failed and neglected, for the space of eighteen months from the date of the patent, to put and continue on sale to the public, on reasonable terms, the invention or discovery for which the patent issued; in either of which cases, judgment is to be rendered for the defendant, with costs.

§ 357. The object of this provision was to enable the defendant to give certain special matters in evidence under the plea of the general issue. It seems to have been generally supposed, at a very early period in the history of our legislation, that under a plea of the general issue, the defendant could not be allowed to

enjoyment and use of the right under that title, and that he has been injured in that right, under that title, by the piracy of the defendant. This cannot be true, nor could a verdict for the plaintiff have been found by the jury, if the deeds of assignment had not been duly recorded; for, unless that was done, nothing could pass by the deeds. The cases of Hitchins *v.* Stevens (2 Shower R. 233), and McMurdo *v.* Smith (7 T. R. 518), cited at the bar, seem to us very strongly in point. So is France *v.* Fringer, Cro. Jac. 44."

[1] Pitts *v.* Whitman, 2 Story, 609. Of course, therefore, it is not necessary to aver that the assignment was recorded within three months. Ibid.

attack the validity of the patent, and that that plea only put in issue the question of infringement.[1] Accordingly, the act of 1793, § 6, enumerated certain special defences, which it declared the defendant "shall be permitted" to give in evidence under the general issue, by first giving notice thereof to the plaintiff. The Supreme Court of the United States construed the provision as intended to relieve the defendant from what were supposed to be the difficulties of pleading, by allowing him to give in evidence, under the plea of not guilty, certain matters affecting the patent, providing, at the same time, for the security of the plaintiff against surprise, by requiring notice to be given of the special matter to be relied on. This notice was substituted for a special plea.[2] The court also declared that the defendant was not obliged to pursue this course. He might plead specially, in which case the plea would be the only notice the plaintiff could claim; or he might plead the general issue, in which case he must give notice of the special matter on which he relied.[3] However,

[1] But it was not so in England. Until the act 5 and 6 Wm. IV., c. 83, § 5, the usual plea was *not guilty*, which, putting in issue the whole of the declaration, forced the plaintiff to support the grant in all its parts, and gave to the defendant the greatest latitude for evidence; but now the defendant must plead all the defences, and must also deliver in a list of the objections on which he intends to rely at the trial. Godson on Patents, 238, 2d ed.

[2] Evans *v.* Eaton, 3 Wheat. 454; Evans *v.* Kremer, Peters, C. C. R. 215. See, also, the elaborate note on the patent law in the Appendix to 3 Wheat., Note II. (written by Mr. Justice Story).

[3] Evans *v.* Eaton, 3 Wheat. 454, 503. In this case Mr. Chief Justice Marshall said: "The sixth section of the act appears to be drawn on the idea that the defendant would not be at liberty to contest the validity of the patent on the general issue. It therefore intends to relieve the defendant from the difficulties of pleading, when it allows him to give in evidence matter which does affect the patent. But the notice is directed for the security of the plaintiff, and to protect him against that surprise to which he might be exposed from an unfair use of this privilege. Reasoning merely on the words directing this notice, it might be difficult to define, with absolute precision, what it ought to include, and what it might omit. There are, however, circumstances in the act, which may have some influence on this point. It has been already observed, that the notice is substituted for a special plea; it is further to be observed, that it is a substitute to which the defendant is not obliged to resort. The notice is to be given only when it is intended to offer the special matter in evidence on the general issue. The defendant is not obliged to pursue this course. He may still plead specially, and then the plea is the only notice which the plaintiff can claim. If, then, the defendant may give in evidence, on a special plea, the prior use of the machine, at places not specified in his

where the defendant pleads specially and not under the general issue, the plea must still be filed thirty days before the term, or the plaintiff will be entitled to a continuance. The plaintiff has a right to the thirty days, whether the matter be set up by plea or by notice.[1]

§ 358. The fifteenth section of the act of 1836 is taken, with some additional defences, from the sixth section of the act of 1793, and has the same object in view. It differs from the former act, by omitting the provision that the patent "shall be declared void," if judgment is rendered for the defendant, and by providing that "when the defendant relies in his defence on the fact of a previous invention, knowledge, or use of the thing patented, he shall state in his notice of special matter the names and places of residence of those whom he intends to prove to have possessed a prior knowledge of the thing, and where the same thing had been used." This provision was added in consequence of the construction given to the former act, to the effect that notice of the places was not necessary to be given.[2] In other respects, the construction given to the act of 1793, section six, is applicable to the present law. The defendant is at liberty to plead specially, in which form of pleading he need give no other notice of his defence than the plea itself gives, or he may plead the general issue, and give notice of the special matter on which he relies. The statute does not undertake to enumerate all the defences which may be made to an action on a patent. It provides that when certain facts, which it enumerates, are to be relied on, and

plea, it would seem to follow that he may give in evidence its use at places not specified in his notice. It is not believed that a plea would be defective, which did not state the mills in which the machinery alleged to be previously used was placed.

"But there is still another view of the subject which deserves to be considered. The section which directs this notice also directs that if the special matter stated in the section be proved, 'judgment shall be rendered for the defendant, with costs, and the patent shall be declared void.' The notice might be intended not only for the information of the plaintiff, but for the purpose of spreading on the record the cause for which the patent was avoided. This object is accomplished by a notice which specifies the particular matter to be proved. The ordinary powers of the court are sufficient to prevent, and will undoubtedly be so exercised, as to prevent the patentee from being injured by the surprise."

[1] Phillips *v.* Comstock, 4 McLean, 525.

[2] Evans *v.* Eaton, ante, note ; Evans *v.* Kremer, Peters, C. C. R. 215.

the general issue is pleaded, the defendant shall give notice of the facts which he means to put in evidence.[1] The notice must be strictly construed; if the defendant gives notice that he will prove the prior use of the invention in the United States, he cannot be allowed to offer evidence of its prior use in England.[2]

§ 359. But it will be useful to make a particular enumeration of the defences that may be made under the general issue, without notice, before we turn our attention to those mentioned in the statute, of which notice must be given, when the general issue is pleaded.

§ 360. The defendant may show, under the general issue, without notice, that he never did the act complained of, that is, that he has not infringed the patent, or that he was acting under a license or purchase from the plaintiff.[3] He may show that the plaintiff is an alien, not entitled to a patent; or that the plaintiff has not a good title as assignee; or that his patent was not duly issued according to law, in respect of the signatures of the public officers, or of the public seal, &c.[4]

§ 361. He may also show that the invention is not a patentable subject; that is to say, admitting its novelty, he may show that it is not an "art, machine, manufacture, or composition of matter," in the sense of the statute.[5] But the defence that the subject is not patentable on the ground of want of novelty falls under the statute, and must be specified.

§ 362. In like manner, the defendant may show, under the general issue, without notice, that the invention, though new, fails in point of utility, and is worthless and frivolous.[6]

1 Whittemore *v.* Cutter, 1 Gallis. 429, 435; Grant *v.* Raymond, 6 Peters, 218.

2 Dixon *v.* Moyer, 4 Wash. 68.

3 Whittemore *v.* Cutter, 1 Gallis. 429, 435; 3 Wheaton's R. Appendix, Note II. p. 27.

4 Ibid.; Kneass *v.* The Schuylkill Bank, 4 Wash. 9, 11.

5 That the invention is not a patentable subject, admitting its novelty, is a different issue from any that is named in the fifteenth section of the statute, and it is one that is necessarily raised by the plea of "*not guilty*," since the declaration necessarily imports that the patentee had invented a patentable subject.

6 Want of novelty is one of the defences enumerated in the fifteenth section, but want of utility is not; but it is a clear bar to the action, upon the terms of the act, as well as upon the general principles of law.

§ 363. So, too, he may show that there is no specification, or that the specification is so ambiguous and unintelligible that the court cannot determine from it what the invention is that is intended to be patented. This is a different issue from that pointed out in the statute. If the specification do not describe the invention in clear and exact terms, so as to distinguish it from other inventions, but be so ambiguous and obscure that it cannot be ascertained with reasonable certainty for what the patent is taken, or what it includes, the patent is void for ambiguity; and this is put in issue by the plea of not guilty, because a clear and distinct specification of the invention is essential to the validity of the patent.[1] But if the invention is definitely described in the patent and specification so as to distinguish it from other inventions before known, there may still exist the defect described in the fifteenth section of the statute, of some concealment or addition made for the purpose of deceiving the public; and when it is intended to show this, under the general issue, notice must be given.

§ 364. We now come to the special defences enumerated in the fifteenth section of the statute. The statute provides that the defendant may, under the general issue, give the statute itself in evidence,[2] and certain special matters, of which he shall have given notice in writing to the plaintiff or his attorney thirty days before trial.[3]

§ 365. The first of these special defences is, "that the descrip-

[1] 3 Wheat. R. Appendix, Note II. p. 27; Phillips on Patents, p. 308; Kneass *v.* The Schuylkill Bank, 4 Wash. 9, 13. In this last case, Mr. Justice Washington intimates that the defendant may show under the general issue, and without notice, that the patent is broader than the discovery. But this must now be otherwise; since the fifteenth section of the act of 1836 describes one of the issues which require notice to be, that the patentee was not the original and first inventor of the thing patented, *or of a substantial and material part thereof.* This is the issue, that the patent is broader than the invention.

[2] The meaning of the permission to give the statute in evidence is, that the defendants shall be allowed to rely on any matter of law enacted in the statute, without pleading it specially, which must be done when the statute is a private one. The Patent Act is undoubtedly a public act; but from abundant caution, to prevent the question of the nature of the act from being raised, this provision was inserted. Kneass *v.* The Schuylkill Bank, 4 Wash. 9, 11.

[3] No witness can be examined, to prove a prior use of the invention, unless notice of his name and residence has been given. The Philadelphia and Trenton Railroad Co. *v.* Stimpson, 14 Peters, 448, 459.

tion and specification filed by the plaintiff does not contain the whole truth relative to his invention or discovery, or that it contains more than is necessary to produce the described effect; which concealment or addition shall fully appear to have been made for the purpose of deceiving the public." We have already seen what was the general purpose of Congress in providing that notice should be given, when certain facts were to be offered in evidence; but it is not very easy to define the scope of the issue intended by the above provision, or to distinguish the exact meaning of the statute in this particular. It is clear, however, that this issue, as we have already suggested, is distinguishable from the issue, which presents the naked question whether there is an intelligible description of the invention, which will enable the public to know what it is. It may help us to understand the present provision, if we review the corresponding provision in the former act, and the decisions made upon it.

§ 366. The corresponding provision in the act of 1793, § 6, was in the same terms, but that act also provided that, when judgment on this issue had been rendered for the defendant, "the patent shall be declared void"; which is omitted in the act of 1836, § 15. In one of the earliest reported cases in which this clause of the statute of 1793 came under consideration, Mr. Justice Story held that if the invention is definitely described in the patent and specification, so as to distinguish it from other inventions before known, the patent is good, although it does not describe the invention in such full, clear, and exact terms, that a person skilled in the art or science, of which it is a branch, would construct or make the thing, *unless such defective description or concealment was with intent to deceive the public.* The reasoning of the learned judge in this case tends to show that he considered the defect or concealment, with intent to deceive the public, to refer to the practicability of practising the invention from the specification; and in a subsequent case he seems to consider that the statute intended to alter the common law, and to declare the patent void, only when the concealment or defect was with such an intent. But it is not quite clear, whether he considered that the issue raised by an allegation that the specification would not enable a workman to make the thing described, is, as a defence to the action, not one of the special defences of the statute, and consequently that it is raised by the plea of not guilty, without notice.[1]

[1] Whittemore *v.* Cutter, 1 Gallis. 429, 433; Lowell *v.* Lewis, 1 Mas. 182, 187. The reasoning of the learned judge in both these cases was as follows: "Another objection is to the direction, that the oath taken by the inventor, not being conformable to the statute, formed no objection to the recovery in this action. The statute requires that the patentee should swear 'that he is the true inventor or discoverer of the art, machine, or improvement. The oath taken by Whittemore was, that he was the true *inventor* or *improver* of the machine." The taking of the oath was but a prerequisite to the granting of the patent, and in no degree essential to its validity. It might as well have been contended, that the patent was void, unless the thirty dollars, required by the eleventh section of the act, had been previously paid. We approve of the direction of the court on this point, and overrule this objection.

"Another objection is to the direction respecting the specification. It was as follows: "That if the jury should be satisfied that the specification and drawings, filed by the patentee in the office of the Secretary of State, were not made in such full, clear, and exact terms and manner as to distinguish the same from all other things before known, and to enable any person skilled in the art or science, of which it is a branch, or with which it is most nearly connected, to make and use the same, this would not be sufficient to defeat the rights of the plaintiffs to recover in this action, unless the jury were also satisfied that the specification and drawings were thus materially defective and obscure *by design*, and the concealment made for the purpose of deceiving the public. In this respect our law differed from the law of England, that, if the specification and drawings were thus materially defective, it afforded a presumption of a designed concealment, which the jury were to judge of. That in deciding as to the materiality of the deficiencies in the specification and drawings, it was not sufficient evidence to disprove the materiality, that, by studiously examining such specification and drawings, a man of extraordinary genius might be able to construct the machine, by inventing parts, and by trying experiments. The object of the law was to prevent the expenditure of time and money in trying experiments, and to obtain such exact directions, that, if properly followed, a man of reasonable skill in the particular branch of the art or science might construct the machine, and if, from the deficiencies, it was impracticable for such a man to construct it, the deficiencies were material.' In order fully to understand the objection to this direction, it is necessary to advert to the third section of the act of 1793, which specifies the requisites to be complied with in procuring a patent, and the sixth section of the same act, which states certain defences, of which the defendant may avail himself to defeat the action, and to avoid the patent. The third section, among other things, requires the party, applying for a patent, to deliver a written description of his invention, and of the manner of using, or process of compounding the same, in such full, clear, and exact terms, as to distinguish the same from all other things before known, and to enable any person skilled in the art or science of which it is a branch, or with

§ 367. In a subsequent case, the Supreme Court of the United States decided that, in order to justify a judgment declaring a

which it is most intimately connected, to make, compound, and use the same; and in the case of any machine, he shall fully explain the principle, and the several modes in which he has contemplated the application of that principle, or character, by which it may be distinguished from other inventions. The sixth section provides, among other things, that the defendant may give in his defence, that the specification filed by the plaintiff does not contain the whole truth relative to his discovery, or that it contains more than is necessary to produce the described effect, *which concealment or addition shall fully appear to have been made for the purpose of deceiving the public.*

"It is very clear that the sixth section does not enumerate all the defences of which the defendant may legally avail himself: for he may clearly give in evidence, that he never did the act attributed to him, that the patentee is an alien not entitled under the act, or that he has a license or authority from the patentee. It is, therefore, argued, that if the specification be materially defective, or obscurely or so loosely worded, that a skilful workman in that particular art could not construct the machine, it is a good defence against the action, although no intentional deception has been practised. And this is beyond all question the doctrine of the common law; and it is founded in good reason; for the monopoly is granted upon the express condition, that the party shall make a full and explicit disclosure, so as to enable the public, at the expiration of his patent, to make and use the invention or improvement in as ample and beneficial a manner as the patentee himself. If, therefore, it be so obscure, loose, and imperfect, that this cannot be done, it is defrauding the public of all the consideration upon which the monopoly is granted. (Buller, N. P. 77; Turner *v.* Winter, 1 T. R. 602.) And the motion of the party, whether innocent or otherwise, becomes immaterial, because the public mischief remains the same.

"It is said, that the law is the same in the United States, notwithstanding the wording of the sixth section, for there is a great distinction between a concealment of material parts, and a defective and ambiguous description of all the parts; and that, in the latter case, although there may be no intentional concealment, yet the patent may be avoided for uncertainty as to the subject-matter of it. There is considerable force in the distinction at first view; and yet, upon more close examination, it will be difficult to support it. What is a defective description but a concealment of some parts, necessary to be known in order to present a complete view of the mechanism? In the present case the material defects were stated, among other things, to consist in a want of a specific description of the dimensions of the component parts, and of the shapes and position of the various knobs. Were these a concealment of material parts, or a defective and ambiguous disclosure of them? Could the legislature have intended to pronounce that the concealment of a material spring should not, unless made with design to deceive the public, avoid the patent, and yet that an obscure description of the same spring should at all events avoid it? It would be somewhat hazardous to attempt to sustain such a proposition.

patent void, the defect or concealment must appear to have been made for the purpose of deceiving the public; but if the defendant

"It was probably with a view to guard the public against the injury arising from defective specifications, that the statute requires the letters-patent to be examined by the attorney-general, and certified to be in conformity to the law, before the great seal is affixed to them. In point of practice this must unavoidably be a very insufficient security, and the policy of the provision, that has changed the common law, may be very doubtful. This, however, is a consideration proper before another tribunal. We must administer the law as we find it. And, without going at large into this point, we think that the manifest intention of the legislature was not to allow any defect or concealment in a specification to avoid the patent, unless it arose from an intention to deceive the public. There is no ground, therefore, on which we can support this objection." 1 Gallis. 433.

"An objection of a more general cast (and which might more properly have been considered at the outset of the cause, as it is levelled at the sufficiency of the patent itself), is that the specification is expressed in such obscure and inaccurate terms, that it does not either definitely state in what the invention consists, or describe the mode of constructing the machine so as to enable skilful persons to make one. I accede at once to the doctrine of the authority, which has been cited (McFarlane *v.* Price, 1 Starkie's R. 192), that the patentee is bound to describe, in full and exact terms, in what his invention consists; and, if it be an improvement only upon an existing machine, he should distinguish what is new and what is old in his specification, so that it may clearly appear for what the patent is granted. The reason of this principle of law will be manifest on the slightest examination A patent is grantable only for a new and useful invention; and unless it be distinctly stated in what that invention specifically consists, it is impossible to say whether it ought to be patented or not; and it is equally difficult to know whether the public infringe upon or violate the exclusive right secured by the patent. The patentee is clearly not entitled to include in his patent the exclusive use of any machinery already known; and if he does, his patent will be broader than his invention, and consequently void. If, therefore, the description in the patent mixes up the old and the new, and does not distinctly ascertain for which, in particular, the patent is claimed, it must be void; since, if it covers the whole, it covers too much, and if not intended to cover the whole, it is impossible for the court to say what, in particular, is covered as the new invention. The language of the Patent Act itself is decisive on this point. It requires (§ 3) that the inventor shall deliver a written description of his invention, 'in such full, clear, and exact terms, as to distinguish the same from all other things before known; and in the case of any machine, he shall fully explain the principle, and the several modes, in which he has contemplated the application of that principle or character, by which it may be distinguished from other inventions.'

"It is, however, sufficient, if what is claimed as new appear with reasonable certainty on the face of the patent, either expressly or by necessary implication. But it ought to appear with reasonable certainty, for it is not to be left

merely seeks to defend himself, he may do so by showing that the patentee has failed in any of the prerequisites on which the authority to issue a patent depends. This decision made the evidence of fraudulent intent requisite only in the particular case

to minute references and conjectures from what was previously known or unknown; since the question is not, what was before known, but what the patentee claims *as new;* and he may, in fact, claim as new and patentable what has been long used by the public. Whether the invention itself be thus specifically described with reasonable certainty, is a question of law upon the construction of the terms of the patent, of which the specification is a part; and on examining this patent I at present incline to the opinion that it is sufficiently described in what the patented invention consists.

"A question nearly allied to the foregoing is, whether (supposing the invention itself be truly and definitely described in the patent) the specification is in such full, clear, and exact terms, as not only to distinguish the same from all things before known, but 'to enable any person skilled in the art or science, of which it is a branch, or with which it is most nearly connected, to make, compound, and use the same.' This is another requisite of the statute (§ 3), and it is founded upon the best reasons. The law confers an exclusive patent right on the inventor of any thing new and useful, as an encouragement and reward for his ingenuity, and for the expense and labor attending the invention. But this monopoly is granted for a limited term only, at the expiration of which the invention becomes the property of the public. Unless, therefore, such a specification was made as would, at all events, enable other persons of competent skill to construct similar machines, the advantage to the public, which the act contemplates, would be entirely lost, and its principal object would be defeated. It is not necessary, however, that the specification should contain an explanation level with the capacities of every person (which would, perhaps, be impossible); but, in the language of the act, it should be expressed in such full, clear, and exact terms, that a person skilled in the art or science of which it is a branch would be enabled to construct the patented invention. By the common law, if any thing material to the construction of the thing invented be omitted or concealed in the specification, or more be inserted or added than is necessary to produce the required effect, the patent is void. This doctrine of the common law our Patent Act has (whether wisely, admits of very serious doubts) materially altered; for it does not avoid the patent in such case, unless the 'concealment or addition shall fully appear to have been made for the purpose of deceiving the public.' (§ 6.) Yet, certainly, the public may be as seriously injured by a materially defective specification resulting from mere accident, as if it resulted from a fraudulent design. Our law, however, is as I have stated; and the question here is, and it is a question of fact, whether the specification be so clear and full that a pump-maker of ordinary skill could, from the terms of the specification, be able to construct one upon the plan of Mr. Perkins." 1 Mass. 187.

and for the particular purpose of having the patent declared void.[1]

[1] Grant *v.* Raymond, 6 Peters, 218, 246. Mr. C. J. Marshall, delivering the judgment of the court in this case, said: "Courts did not, at first, perhaps, distinguish clearly between a defence which would authorize a verdict and judgment in favor of the defendant in the particular action, leaving the plaintiff free to use his patent, and to bring other suits for its infringement; and one which, if successful, would require the court to enter a judgment not only for the defendant in the particular case, but one which declares the patent to be void. This distinction is now well settled.

"If the party is content with defending himself, he may either plead specially, or plead the general issue, and give the notice required by the sixth section of any special matter he means to use at the trial. If he shows that the patentee has failed in any of those prerequisites on which the authority to use the patent is made to depend, his defence is complete. He is entitled to the verdict of the jury and the judgment of the court. But if, not content with defending himself, he seeks to annul the patent, he must proceed in precise conformity to the sixth section. If he depends on evidence 'tending to prove that the specification filed by the plaintiff does not contain the whole truth relative to his discovery, or that it contains more than is necessary to produce the described effect,' it may avail him so far as respects himself, but will not justify a judgment declaring the patent void, unless such 'concealment or addition shall fully appear to have been made for the purpose of deceiving the public'; which purpose must be found by the jury to justify a judgment of *vacatur* by the court. The defendant is permitted to proceed according to the sixth section, but is not prohibited from proceeding in the usual manner, so far as respects his defence; except that special matter may not be given in evidence on the general issue unaccompanied by the notice which the sixth section requires. The sixth section is not understood to control the third. The evidence of fraudulent intent is required only in the particular case, and for the particular purpose stated in the sixth section.

"This instruction was material if the verdict ought to have been for the defendants, provided the allegations of the plea were sustained, and if such verdict would have supported a judgment in their favor, although the defect in the specification might not have arisen from design, and for the purpose of deceiving the public. That such is the law we are entirely satisfied. The third section requires, as preliminary to a patent, a correct specification and description of the thing discovered. This is necessary in order to give the public, after the privilege shall expire, the advantage for which the privilege is allowed, and is the foundation of the power to issue the patent. The necessary consequence of the ministerial character in which the secretary acts is that the performance of the prerequisites to a patent must be examinable in any suit brought upon it. If the case was of the first impression, we should come to this conclusion; but it is understood to be settled.

"The act of Parliament concerning monopolies contains an exception on which the grants of patents for inventions have issued in that country. The construction of so much of that exception as connects the specification with

§ 368. Now the statute of 1836 omits the provision that the patent shall be declared void, when judgment is rendered for the defendant, and it leaves the ground of a concealment or addition in the specification, with intent to deceive the public, simply a defence to the action, of a special nature. There can be no doubt, therefore, that when the defendant proposes to show that the specification contains more or less than a true description of the invention, and that the concealment or addition was made for the purpose of deceiving the public, his plea must either be special, setting forth the defects and charging the intent, or it must be

the patent, and makes the validity of the latter dependent on the correctness of the former, is applicable, we think, to proceedings under the third section of the American act. The English books are full of cases in which it has been held that a defective specification is a good bar when pleaded to, or a sufficient defence when given in evidence on the general issue, on an action brought for the infringement of a patent right. They are very well summed up in Godson's Law of Patents, title Specification ; and also in the chapter respecting the infringement of patents, also in Holroyd on Patents, where he treats of the specification, its form and requisites. It is deemed unnecessary to go through the cases, because there is no contrariety in them, and because the question is supposed to be substantially settled in this country. Pennock & Sellers *v.* Dialogue, 1 Peters, 1, was not, it is true, a case of defect in the specification or description required by the third section, but one in which the applicant did not bring himself within the provision of the first section, which requires that before a patent shall issue, the petitioner shall allege that he has invented a new and useful art, machine, &c., '*not known or used before the application.*' This prerequisite of the first section, so far as a failure in it may affect the validity of the patent, is not distinguishable from a failure of the prerequisites of the third section.

"On the trial, evidence was given to show that the patentee had permitted his invention to be used before he took out his patent. The court declared its opinion to the jury, that, if an inventor makes his discovery public, he abandons the inchoate right to the exclusive use of the invention. 'It is possible,' added the court, 'that the inventor may not have intended to give the benefit of his discovery to the public.' But it is not a question of intention, but of legal inference, resulting from the conduct of the inventor, and affecting the interests of the public. It is for the jury to say whether the evidence brings this case within the principle which has been stated. If it does, the court is of opinion that the plaintiff is not entitled to a verdict.'

"The jury found a verdict for the defendants, an exception was taken to the opinion, and the judgment was affirmed by this court. This case affirms the principle that a failure on the part of the patentee, in those prerequisites of the act which authorize a patent, is a bar to a recovery in an action for its infringement ; and that the validity of this defence does not depend on the intention of the inventor, but is a legal inference upon his conduct."

the general issue, accompanied by notice of the defects in the specification intended to be relied on. But I do not conceive that the statute means to say that no concealment or defect in a specification shall be available as a defence to the action, under the general issue, unless it was made with intent to deceive the public. The statute may be construed as if it read thus: "Whenever the defendant seeks to show that the specification does not contain the whole truth relative to the invention or discovery, or that it contains more than is necessary to produce the described effect, and that such concealment or addition was made for the purpose of deceiving the public, he may plead the general issue, and give such special matter in evidence, provided he shall have given notice," &c. On the other hand, if the defendant relies on a failure in the specification in respect of any of the prerequisites for issuing a patent, he may show such failure under a plea of the general issue, without any notice.

§ 369. The next special defence mentioned in the statute is, in substance, that the subject-matter is not new; that is, "that the patentee was not the original and first inventor or discoverer of the thing patented, or of a substantial and material part thereof, claimed as new; or that it had been described in some public work, anterior to the supposed discovery thereof by the patentee."[1]

§ 370. We have seen, in a former chapter of this work, when a party is or is not the original and first inventor of a patented sub-

[1] When this defence is relied upon, it will be incumbent on the defendant to show that the invention had been known, used, or described in a public work, *anterior to the supposed discovery of the patentee.* The plaintiff's right in his invention, therefore, relates back to the original discovery, which may be proved by parol, and is not necessarily presumed to have been made on the day when the patent issued; although the infringement must have taken place after the date of the patent. Dixon *v.* Moyer, 4 Wash. 68, 72. The conversations and declarations of a patentee, merely affirming that at some former period he had invented a machine, may well be objected to. But his conversations and declarations, stating that he had made an invention, and describing its details, and explaining its operations, are properly deemed an assertion of his right, at that time, as an inventor, to the extent of the facts and details which he then makes known, although not of their existence at an anterior time. Such declarations, coupled with a description of the nature and objects of the invention, are to be deemed part of the *res gestæ*, and they are legitimate evidence that the invention was then known and claimed by him; and thus its origin may be fixed, at least, as early as that period. The Philadelphia and Trenton Railroad Co. *v.* Stimpson, 14 Peters, 448.

ject; and also that a failure, in point of novelty, of any substantial and material part of the alleged invention, renders the patent *pro tanto*. In order to insure the plaintiff against surprise, whenever this defence is to be resorted to, the same section of the statute requires that the defendant "shall state in his notice of special matter the names and places of residence of those whom he intends to prove to have possessed a prior knowledge of the thing, and where the same had been used." This provision must be strictly complied with.[1] The statute does not, however, require notice of the *time* when such persons possessed the alleged knowledge and use of the invention.[2]

§ 371. It is also fairly to be inferred, from the requisition, that notice shall be given of "any special matter" intended to be offered in evidence "tending to prove" the particular defence relied upon, that the notice must describe whether the whole, or a part, and what part of the invention is to be charged with want of novelty, and in what public work or works the whole, or a part, or what part had been described before the supposed discovery by the patentee. There is no limitation of time within which this defence must be set up.[3]

§ 372. The stringent effect of this defence has been materially modified, however, by two other provisions. The first is contained in the two provisions which are found at the end of the same fifteenth section of the act of 1836: "provided that, whenever it shall satisfactorily appear that the patentee, at the time of making his application for the patent, believed himself to be the first inventor or discoverer of the thing patented, the same shall not be held to be void, on account of the invention or discovery, or any part thereof having been before known or used in any foreign country, it not appea ing that the same or any substantial part thereof had before been patented or described in any printed publication; *and, provided also*, that whenever the plaintiff shall fail to sustain his action, on the ground that in his specification of claim is embraced more than that of which he was the first inventor, if it shall appear that the defendant had used or violated any part of the invention justly and truly specified, and claimed as new, it shall be in the power of the court to

[1] Ibid.

[2] Phillips *v.* Page, 24 How. 164.

[3] Evans *v.* Eaton, Peters, C. C. R. 322, 348.

adjudge and award, as to costs, as may appear to be just and equitable."

In a recent case, Forbush *v.* Cook,[1] the defendants were allowed to introduce evidence tending to show that the plaintiff had had direct knowledge of two foreign machines, one of which had been patented and described in a printed publication, but the other not, previous to his obtaining his own patent. *Per contra*, in Beard *v.* Egerton,[2] a plea that the invention was communicated to the patentee by a foreigner was held bad on demurrer, inasmuch as such an allegation was no denial of the plaintiff's right as true and first inventor *within the realm*, under the statute 21 Jac. 1, c. 3. Also the plea that the real inventor had assigned his whole interest to the king of France, who had dedicated the same to the French public. The English patentee in this case was really nothing more than the agent and trustee of the inventor.[3]

§ 373. The other provision is contained in the act of March 3, 1837, § 7, 9, in relation to a disclaimer. The seventh section enacts as follows: "That, whenever any patentee shall have, through inadvertence, accident, or mistake, made his specification of claim too broad, claiming more than that of which he was the original or first inventor, some material and substantial part of the thing patented being truly and justly his own, any such patentee, his administrators, executors, and assigns, whether of the whole or of a sectional interest therein, may make disclaimer of such parts of the thing patented as the disclaimer shall not claim to hold by virtue of the patent or assignment, stating therein the extent of his interest in such patent; which disclaimer shall be in writing, attested by one or more witnesses, and recorded in the Patent Office, on payment, by the person disclaiming in manner as other patent duties are required by law to be paid, of the sum of ten dollars. And such disclaimer shall thereafter be taken and considered as part of the original specification, to the extent of the interest which shall be possessed in the patent or right secured thereby, by the disclaimant, and by those claiming by or under him subsequent to the record thereof. But no such disclaimer

1 20 Mon. Law Rep. 664.

2 3 Mann., Gr. & Scott, 97.

3 For a discussion of the specification itself, see s. c., 8 Mann., Gr. & Scott, 165; and 2 Carr. & Kirwan, 667.

shall affect any action pending at the time of its being filed, except so far as may relate to the question of unreasonable neglect or delay in filing the same."

§ 374. The ninth section is as follows: "Be it further enacted, any thing in the fifteenth section of the act to which this is additional to the contrary, notwithstanding, that, whenever by mistake, accident, or inadvertence, and without any wilful default, or intent to defraud or mislead the public, any patentee shall have in his specification claimed to be the original and first inventor or discoverer of any material or substantial part of the thing patented, of which he was not the first and original inventor, and shall have no legal or just right to claim the same, in every such case the patent shall be deemed good and valid for so much of the invention and discovery as shall be truly and *bonâ fide* his own: *Provided*, it shall be a material and substantial part of the thing patented, and be definitely distinguishable from the other parts so claimed without right as aforesaid. And every such patentee, his executors, administrators, and assigns, whether of the whole or a sectional interest therein, shall be entitled to maintain a suit at law or in equity on such patent for any infringement of such part of the invention or discovery as shall be *bonâ fide* his own, as aforesaid, notwithstanding the specification may embrace more than he shall have any legal right to claim. But, in every such case in which a judgment or verdict shall be rendered for the plaintiff, he shall not be entitled to recover costs against the defendant, unless he shall have entered at the Patent Office, prior to the commencement of the suit, a disclaimer of all that part of the thing patented which was so claimed without right: *Provided, however*, that no person bringing any such suit shall be entitled to the benefit of the provisions contained in this section, who shall have unreasonably neglected or delayed to enter at the Patent Office a disclaimer as aforesaid."[1]

[1] In Reed *v.* Cutter, 1 Story, 590, 600, Mr. Justice Story said: "In respect to another point, stated at the argument, I am of opinion that a disclaimer, to be effectual for all intents and purposes, under the act of 1837, c. 45 (§ 7 and 9), must be filed in the Patent Office before the suit is brought. If filed during the pendency of the suit, the plaintiff will not be entitled to the benefit thereof in that suit. But if filed before the suit is brought, the plaintiff will be entitled to recover costs in such suit, if he should establish at the trial that a part of the invention, not disclaimed, has been infringed by the defendant. Where a disclaimer has been filed, either before or after the suit is brought, the plain-

§ 375. The result of these various enactments is, that for so much of the invention as has been described in some public work anterior to the supposed discovery by the patentee, whether the description was known to him in point of fact or not, — if it be a substantial and material part of the thing invented, and be claimed as new, — and for so much as had been previously patented, the patent is inoperative. But the mere previous knowledge or use of the thing in a foreign country will not defeat a patent here, issued to an original inventor, provided it had not been previously patented or described in a printed publication.

§ 375 *a.* The law on this subject is now regulated by the statute of 1870. Section sixty-one of that act provides: "That in any action for infringement the defendant may plead the general issue, and having given notice in writing to the plaintiff or his attorney, thirty days before, may prove on trial any one or more of the following special matters: —

"First. That for the purpose of deceiving the public the description and specification filed by the patentee in the Patent Office was made to contain less than the whole truth relative to his invention or discovery, or more than is necessary to produce the desired effect; or,

"Second. That he had surreptitiously or unjustly obtained the patent for that which was in fact invented by another, who was using reasonable diligence in adapting and perfecting the same; or,

"Third. That it had been patented or described in some printed publication prior to his supposed invention or discovery thereof; or,

"Fourth. That he was not the original and first inventor or discoverer of any material and substantial part of the thing patented; or,

"Fifth. That it had been in public use or on sale in this country for more than two years before his application for a patent, or had been abandoned to the public.

"And in notices as to proof of previous invention, knowledge, or use of the thing patented, the defendant shall state the names of patentees and the dates of their patents, and when granted, and

tiff will not be entitled to the benefit thereof if he has unreasonably neglected or delayed to enter the same at the Patent Office. But such an unreasonable neglect or delay will constitute a good defence and objection to the suit.

the names and residences of the persons alleged to have invented or to have had the prior knowledge of the thing patented, and where and by whom it had been used; and if any one or more of the special matters alleged shall be found for the defendant, judgment shall be rendered for him with costs. And the like defences may be pleaded in any suit in equity for relief against an alleged infringement; and proofs of the same may be given upon like notice in the answer of the defendant, and with the like effect.

"SEC. 62. *And be it further enacted*, That whenever it shall appear that the patentee, at the time of making his application for the patent, believed himself to be the original and first inventor or discoverer of the thing patented, the same shall not be held to be void on account of the invention or discovery, or any part thereof, having been known or used in a foreign country, before his invention or discovery thereof, if it had not been patented, or described in a printed publication."

§ 376. It will be observed that the statute uses different phraseology in describing the kind of publication which is to have this effect. In the body of the fifteenth section of the act of 1836, it is declared to be a description in "some public work"; and in the proviso of the same section it is declared to be "any printed publication." This renders it somewhat doubtful as to what kind of publication is intended. The phrase "some public work" would seem to point to a class of regular, established publications, or to some book, publicly printed and circulated, so as to be open to the public; while the phrase "any printed publication" is broad enough to include any description printed in any form and published or circulated to any extent and in any manner. Taking the whole section together, however, and looking to the apparent policy of the statute, it is probable that the intention of Congress was to make it a conclusive presumption that the patentee had seen any printed description of the thing, which had been so printed and published as to be accessible to the public; but not to adopt that presumption in cases of printed descriptions published and circulated in such a manner as not to be accessible either to the public or to him. If the presumption were adopted in cases of the latter class of publications, an original and meritorious inventor might be defeated of his patent, by showing that the thing had, in a foreign country, been privately described in a printed paper published to a single individual; which certainly would not be a description in a "public work," although it would be a description in a "printed publication." When it is considered that the statute excepts cases even where the thing had been known or used abroad, provided it had not been patented or described in any printed publication, it seems reasonable to suppose that the publication intended is one to which the public could have access; and this construction is fortified by the consideration that the defence enacted in this section, to which the proviso establishes the exception, is that the thing had been described in "some public work." [1]

If this be so, it would seem to be a question for the jury, under all the circumstances under which the publication has taken place, to determine whether the description was so printed and published as to be accessible to the public, where the publication took place. If it was so accessible, the presumption is against the patentee, and his patent will be defeated, notwithstanding he may not have seen it; because the description was already in the possession of the public.

Upon this question of description by publication, the recent case of Lang *v.* Gisborne [2] has elicited an elaborate ruling of the Master of the Rolls. It appeared from the evidence that, in a book published at Paris in 1857, a plan for an electric target was described as having been then invented by a M. De Brettes, which plan was identical with that of the plaintiff's in the suit. It also appeared that a M. Ballière, bookseller in London, had sold one copy of the book to Dr. Wheatstone, another to the Cambridge University Library, a third to Dr. Richardson, and a fourth to some unknown party. The ruling, though made in an injunction

[1] The statute of 1799, § 6, used only the phrase "described in some public work," and did not contain the proviso introduced into the act of 1836. Marshall, C. J., in Evans *v.* Eaton, 3 Wheat. 454, 514, commenting on the former statute, said: "It may be that the patentee had no knowledge of this previous use or previous description; still his patent is void; *the law supposes he may have known it.*" It is, therefore, by adopting a presumption of knowledge, that the law declares the patent void. But there could be no reason or justice in adopting such a presumption, in cases where the printed description had not come into the possession of the public; and it is manifest that the former statute did not mean to adopt it in such cases, since it uses only the phrase "public work."

[2] 6 Law Times, N. S. 771.

suit, seems equally applicable to an action at law. The M. R. said: "Before I finally dispose of this case, I propose to read through the affidavits; but I will now state my view of the law, and also the general view which I take of the evidence. In the first place, I will state the law of the case as I take it to be, and as I should have instructed a jury, had I the jury before me. I will assume, for the present, that De Brettes's plan, described by the Vicomte du Moncel, is, in fact, identical with that of the plaintiff's. That plan appears to have been published in a book in Paris towards the end of December, 1857. That book was sent over to this country, and four copies of it were sold here: one on 31st December, 1857, to Professor Wheatstone; one on 6th May following to the library of the University of Cambridge; one on 21st August, 1858, to Dr. Richardson at Newcastle; and a fourth on 30th March, 1859, to some one whose name is not known. All these sales were made previous to the provisional and complete specification of the plaintiff's patent. Now, in my opinion, there are two modes by which an invention can be made public: the one is by a publication in fact or by user, such as that by the user alone the invention becomes a part of the general stock of public information; the other is by what is termed a publication in law. Upon these two modes of publication the authorities seem to establish this, that the requisition that an invention shall be made a part of the general stock of public information applies to cases where some one has used the invention either for the purpose of experiments or as a complete and perfect invention. In such cases it is no doubt very difficult to draw the line between the user of the invention as a mere experiment, and user of the invention in a complete state; that is, in such a state as that the inventor thinks he can then make no further addition to it. It is, however, to that class of cases that, in my opinion, the authorities refer. Now I think that there is a publication in law of an invention in this country, when the inventor of it makes, either by himself or his agent, a written description of it, puts that into a book, and sends that to a bookseller here, to be published by him. It is not necessary to prove, further, that any one volume of the book has been sold; for, according to the view which I have stated, the moment that the book is exposed in the publisher's shop for the purpose of sale, then there is in law a complete publication of the invention. I wish to state this view as broadly as I can, because, if this case should go further, it is very desirable that there should be no mistake as to my opinion of what the law is. Well, then, that is how the matter would stand, assuming the inventor to be an Englishman. But, assuming him to be a Frenchman, or any other foreigner, would the case be different? I think not. I think that if a foreigner writes a book in his own language, describing an invention of his, and hands it over to an English bookseller for the purpose of its being sold here, so soon as the book arrives here and is offered for sale in the public shop of the bookseller, then (assuming, of course, that the description of the invention is accurate) there is in law a publication of the invention. To come to any other conclusion would, in my opinion, lead to the most inextricable confusion. For instance, it would obviously be most difficult, if not impossible, to explain who or how many persons had actually bought the book; and then again the buying might be nothing if they had not read it. Who could say to how many persons the purchaser might have lent it, and of those persons who could say how many had read it? In the present case it is proved by the evidence that one of our large public libraries (that of the University of Cambridge) actually bought a copy of the Vicomte de Moncel's work. It may, therefore, well be that a thousand persons may have read it and considered De Brettes's invention before that of the plaintiff's was made; but how can that be proved? The courts would be involved in the most inextricable difficulties, if the onus of proof in such cases was thrown on the person who had made public an invention so far as he could do so, to show that the public had appreciated it by purchasing the book or making it common to others who had not actually purchased it. I am of opinion, therefore, that there was, in this case, a complete publication in law in this country of De Brettes's plan, as contained in the Vicomte de Moncel's book, in December, 1857, when it was offered for sale here."

A similar doctrine has been put forth by the Common Pleas, in the case of Stead *v.* Williams.[1] At the jury trial, Creswell, J., had given the following instructions: "But then the defendants do not bring home to the plaintiff the fact of his having seen any of these publications, and it is for you to judge, upon the whole of the matter, whether you think that he had seen those publica-

[1] 2 Webs. Pat. Cas. 137, 142.

tions and had derived his information from the stock of knowledge previously given to the public of this country, or whether he derived it from some person residing abroad, and therefore having a source of information which is considered as equivalent to his own invention." The defendants then moved for a new trial on the ground of improper instruction. Tindal, C. J., in granting the motion, said: "We think, if the invention has already been made public in England, by a description contained in a work, whether written or printed, which has been publicly circulated, in such case the patentee is not the first and true inventor, within the meaning of the statute, whether he has himself borrowed his invention from such publication or not; because we think the public cannot be precluded from the right of using such information as they were already possessed of at the time the patent was granted. It is obvious that the application of this principle must depend upon the particular circumstances which are brought to bear on each particular case. The existence of a single copy of a work, though printed, brought from a depository where it has long been kept in a state of obscurity, would afford a very different inference from the production of an Encyclopædia or other work in general circulation. Tbe question will be, whether, upon the whole evidence, there has been such a publication as to make the description a part of the public stock of information."

§ 377. The book must not only be specified, but the place in the book in which the alleged description is to be found. Thus, where the defendant specified in his notice that the invention claimed by the plaintiff was described in Ure's Dictionary of Arts, &c., and had been used by Andrew Ure of London, it was held not to be competent to the defendant to give the dictionary in evidence, no specification having been given of the place in the book where the description might be found; and also, that as the notice did not state the place where Andrew Ure had used the invention, the book was not competent evidence that Andrew Ure of London had a prior knowledge of the thing patented.[1]

[1] Silsby *v.* Foote, 14 How. 218. "The notice given in the case was as follows: 'The patentee was not the original and first inventor or discoverer of a substantial and material part thereof, claimed as new. That it had been described in a public work called "Ure's Dictionary of Arts, Manufactures, and Mines," anterior to the supposed invention thereof by the patentee; and also had been in public use and known before that time and used by Andrew

§ 378. What, then, constitutes a "description"? No judicial construction has yet been given to this term. It can scarcely be

Ure of London, the late M. Bonnemair of Paris, and George H. McCleary of Seneca Falls, New York.'

"Ure's Dictionary contains upwards of thirteen hundred pages, and the articles which the defendants offered to read were entitled Thermostad and Heat Regulator. The first question is, whether this was a sufficient notice of the special matter, tending to prove that the thing patented or some substantial part thereof, claimed as new, had been described in a patented publication. We are of opinion it was not. The act does not attempt to prescribe the particulars which such a notice shall contain. It simply requires notice. But the least effect which can be allowed to this requirement is, that the notice should be so full and particular as reasonably to answer the end in view. This end was, not merely to put the patentee on inquiry, but to relieve him from the necessity of making useless inquiries and researches, and enable him to fix with precision upon what is relied on by the defendants and to prepare himself to meet it at the trial. This highly salutary object should be kept in view, and a corresponding disclosure enacted from the defendant of all those particulars which he must be presumed to know, and which he may be safely required to state, without exposing him to any risk of losing his rights. Less than this would not be reasonable notice, and therefore would not be such a notice as the act must be presumed to have intended.

"Now, we do not perceive that the defendants would be exposed to the risk of losing any right, by requiring them to indicate in their notice what particular things, described in the printed publication, they intended to aver were substantially the same as the thing patented. This they might have done either by reference to pages or titles, and perhaps in other ways, for the particular manner in which the things referred to are to be identified must depend much upon the contents of the volume and their arrangement. It has been urged that a defendant may not have access to the book in season for the notice. But it must be remembered that, some considerable time before it is necessary to give such notice, the defendant has begun to use the thing patented, which *primâ facie* he has no right to use, and it would seem to be no injustice or hardship to expect him, before he begins to infringe, to ascertain that the patentee's title is not valid, and, if its invalidity depends upon what is in a public work, that he should inform himself what that work contains, and, consequently, how to refer to it. We do not think it necessary so to construe this act, designed for the benefit of patentees, as to enable the defendant to do, — what we fear is too often done, — infringe first, and look for defence afterwards.

"Nor does a notice that, somewhere in a volume of thirteen hundred pages, there is something which tends to prove that the thing patented, or some substantial and material part thereof, claimed as new, had been described therein, relieve the patentee from the necessity of making fruitless researches, to enable him to fix with reasonable certainty on what he must encounter at the trial. Upon this ground, therefore, the exception cannot be supported.

supposed, however, that a mere suggestion of the possibility of constructing the machine, or other thing, which may have been subsequently patented, is what the statute intends. The reason why the statute adopts the presumption of knowledge, on the part of the subsequent patentee, is that a knowledge of the thing was already in the possession of the public. It makes knowledge and the means of knowledge on the part of the public the same thing; and, acting upon this principle, it holds that the public have acquired nothing from the specification of the patentee which they did not possess before, and that the patentee has invented nothing which he, as one of the public, could not have derived from the means of knowledge which the public before possessed.[1] Hence it is, that the production of a prior description, which was in the possession of the public, negatives the title of the patentee as the first inventor. But it follows necessarily, from this view of the principle on which the law proceeds, that the description must be such as to give the public the means of knowledge, or, in other words, must of itself enable the public to practise the invention. It is not necessary that the invention should have been reduced to practice; but unless the description would enable the public, without further invention, to put the thing in practice, it cannot be said that a knowledge of that thing is in the possession of the public. Accordingly, it has been laid down by two eminent writers on the patent law, that the description which is to have the effect of defeating a subsequent patent

"But it is further urged, that the book ought to have been admitted as evidence that Andrew Ure of London had prior knowledge of the thing patented. This view cannot be sustained. For, although the name of Andrew Ure of London is contained in the notice of persons who are alleged to have had this prior knowledge, yet the defendants have not brought themselves within the act of Congress, because the notice did not state 'where the same was used' by Andrew Ure. Besides, inasmuch as the same section of the statute provides that a prior invention in a foreign country shall not avoid a patent, otherwise valid, unless the foreign invention had been described in a printed publication, the defendants are thrown back upon that clause of the act which provides for that defence arising from a printed publication which has already been considered." Per Curtis, J.

Compare Jones *v.* Berger, 5 Mann. & Grang. 208, for a construction of the somewhat similar statutory rule contained in 5 & 6 Wm. IV. c. 83, § 5.

[1] A man cannot be said to be the inventor of that which has been exposed to public view, and which he might have had access to if he had thought fit. Lord Abinger, C. B., in Carpenter *v.* Smith, Webs. Pat. Cas. 535.

ought to approach the character, and in some degree to answer the purposes, of a specification, by serving as a direction for making, doing, or practising the thing which is the subject of the patent.[1] But mere speculations or suggestions of an experimental kind, not stated in such a way as to serve for a practical direction, are entirely analogous in their character to abortive and unsuccessful experiments in practice. The Marquis of Worcester's Century of Inventions contained many hints and speculations, on which subsequent inventors have acted; but, as they were the mere speculations of an ingenious man, not reduced by him to practice, and not so stated that the statement would answer for a rule of working, without the exercise of invention on the part of the public, they have not been held to have defeated the patents to which they gave rise.[2]

§ 378 *a*. The following rule as to what a foreign publication should contain, in order to defeat a patented invention, was laid down by the Supreme Court of the United States in the recent case of Seymour *v*. Osborne:[3]—

"Patented inventions cannot be superseded by the mere introduction of a foreign publication of the kind, though of prior date, unless the description and drawings contain and exhibit a substantial representation of the patented improvement, in such full, clear, and exact terms as to enable any person, skilled in the art or science to which it appertains, to make, construct, and

[1] Phillips on Patents, p. 175. Mr. Webster (Pat. Cas. 719, note) says: "But whatever may be the peculiar circumstances under which the publication takes place, the account so published, to be of any effect in law as a publication, must, on the authority of the principal case, be an account of a complete and perfect invention, and published as such. If the invention be not described and published as a complete, perfected, and successful invention, but be published as account of some experiment, or by way of suggestion and speculation, as something which, peradventure, might succeed, it is not such an account as will vitiate subsequent letters-patent. It would appear to be a test not wholly inapplicable to cases of this nature, to inquire whether what is so published would be the subject of letters-patent, because, inasmuch as that which rests only in experiment, suggestion, and speculation, cannot be the subject of letters-patent, it would be unreasonable that what could not be the subject of letters-patent, supposing letters-patent granted in respect thereof, should vitiate letters-patent properly granted."

[2] See the observations of Lord Abinger, C. B., in Carpenter *v*. Smith, Webs. Pat. Cas. 534.

[3] 11 Wall. 516.

practise the invention to the same practical extent as they would be enabled to do if the information was derived from a prior patent. Mere vague and general representations will not support such a defence, as the knowledge supposed to be derived from the publication must be sufficient to enable those skilled in the art or science to understand the nature and operation of the invention, and to carry it into practical use. Whatever may be the particular circumstances under which the publication takes place, the account published, to be of any effect to support such a defence, must be an account of a complete and operative invention capable of being put into practical operation."

§ 378 *b*. Where the defence relied upon to defeat the novelty of the plaintiff's invention is the specification of a patent granted to some third party prior to the plaintiff's obtaining his own patent, the question arises, whether such specification must be so full and clear as to sustain the patent granted therefor, or whether, although incomplete itself, it will still be sufficient to show a want of novelty in any subsequent patent, if it contain a mere hint of the invention for which that subsequent patent was granted. This question has been ably and exhaustively treated in several leading English cases, and the House of Lords has decided that it is *not* sufficient that such prior specification contain a mere hint of the process contained in the subsequent one.[1]

Lord Chancellor Westbury, in moving the vote of the House, said: "My lords, I pass on to the next conclusion which is involved in the answer of the learned judges to your lordships' question, and that conclusion is, I think, also of great importance to the law of patents, because it results from an opinion that an antecedent specification ought not to be held to be an anticipation of a subsequent discovery, unless you have ascertained that the antecedent specification discloses a practicable mode of producing the result which is the effect of the subsequent discovery. My lords, here we attain at length to a certain, undoubted, and useful rule; for the law laid down with regard to the interpretation of an antecedent specification is equally applicable to the construction to be put upon publications or treatises previously given to the world, and which are frequently brought forward for the purpose of showing that the invention has been anti-

[1] Betts *v*. Menzies, 7 Law Times, N. S. 110; 4 Best & Smith, Q. B. 996.

cipated. The effect of this opinion I take to be this, — if your lordships shall affirm it, — that a barren, general description, probably containing some suggestive information, or involving some speculative theory, cannot be considered as anticipating, and therefore avoiding for want of novelty, a subsequent specification or invention, which involves a practical truth productive of beneficial effects, unless you ascertain that the antecedent publication involves the same amount of practical and useful information. Now, my lords, it will be evident, upon a comparison of the two specifications, that the one was a mere general suggestion, while the other is a specific, definite, practical invention. It is possible that a suggestion, such as that contained in the one, may lead to the discovery contained in the other. But it is the latter alone which does really add to the amount of useful knowledge; it is the latter alone which, by its practical operation, confers a benefit upon mankind, within the meaning of the patent law. In the present case, there was not only no evidence that what was contained in Dobb's specification was capable of practical operation, but in reality that conclusion was negatived by the verdict of the jury. Therefore, my lords, concurring, as I entirely do, in the conclusions which have been arrived at by the judges in answer to the second question, it results, as a necessary consequence, that the decision of the Court of Queen's Bench and of the Court of Exchequer Chamber ought to be reversed, and that the rule nisi, made absolute by the Court of Queen's Bench, ought to be discharged." The House of Lords voted, as here moved, reversing thereby the judgment appealed from,[1] and modifying the decision rendered in Bush *v.* Fox,[2] and sustaining Hill *v.* Evans,[3] where the Lord Chancellor had ruled as follows: "If appeal be made to an antecedently published book or specification, the question is, what is the nature and extent of the information thus acquired which is necessary to disprove the novelty of the subsequent patent? There is not, I think, any other general answer that can be given to the question than this, that the information as to the alleged invention, given by the prior publication, must, for the purpose of practical utility, be equal to that given by the subsequent patent. The invention must be shown to have been before made known.

[1] 8 Ell. & Blackb. 923.

[2] 38 E. L. & Eq. 1.

[3] 6 Law Times, N. S. 90.

Whatever, therefore, is essential to the invention must be read out of the prior publication. If specific details are necessary for the practical working and real utility of the alleged invention, they must be found substantially in the prior publication. Apparent generality, or a proposition not true to its full extent, will not prejudice a subsequent statement which is limited, accurate, and a specific rule of practical application. The reason is manifest, because much further invention, and therefore much further discovery, are required before the real truth can be extricated and embodied in a form to serve the uses of mankind. It is the difference between the ore, and the refined and pure metal which is extracted from it. Again, it is not in my opinion true in these cases to say that knowledge and the means of obtaining knowledge are the same. There is a great difference between them. To carry me to the place at which I wish to arrive is very different from merely putting me on the road that leads to it. There may be a latent truth in the words of a former writer not known even to the writer himself, and it would be unreasonable to say that there is no merit in discovering and unfolding it to the world. Upon principle, therefore, I conclude that the prior knowledge of an invention, to avoid a patent, must be knowledge equal to that required to be given by a patent, namely, such knowledge as will enable the public to perceive the very discovery and to carry the invention into practical use."

The result of these recent cases would accordingly seem to be that prior specifications are, in this respect, to be construed by the same principles as other publications.

§ 379. The defendant, therefore, — to return to the consideration of this defence, — who gives notice of the statute defence of want of novelty, will not be defeated in it, if he proves a material part of the invention to have been known or used before the discovery by the patentee, provided he shows that the specification was made broader than the real discovery of the plaintiff, with "wilful default or intent to defraud or mislead the public." But if it was made broader than the real discovery, through accident or inadvertence, the patent will still be good, and an action may be maintained for so much of the invention or discovery as is *bonâ fide* the invention or discovery of the patentee, provided it is a material and substantial part of the thing patented, and is definitely distinguishable from the other part which the patentee had no right to claim; unless there has been an unreasonable neglect or delay to file the disclaimer.[1] The question whether there has been unreasonable negligence or delay in entering a disclaimer is one which goes to the right of action, so that the *jury* may, on finding great negligence, say that the patent is void. This applies, however, only to the case where the part wrongly claimed by the patentee is a material and substantial part of the thing patented.[2] No costs, however, can be recovered in such an action, unless the plaintiff, before bringing his action, has filed in the Patent Office a disclaimer of all that part of the thing patented which his original specification should not have claimed. If the disclaimer is filed before the action is brought, but the entry of it at the Patent Office has been unreasonably neglected or delayed, the defence of a want of novelty in any material respect, from whatever cause the defect in the original specification arose, will be admitted as a bar to the action; and the question of unreasonable neglect or delay will be a question of law for the court.[3]

[1] It seems that the ninth section was intended to cover inadvertences and mistakes of law, as well as of fact; and, therefore, a claim of an abstract principle would be within its provisions. Wyeth *v.* Stone, 1 Story's R. 273, 295. See further as to Disclaimer, *ante.*

[2] Hall *v.* Wiles, 2 Blatchf. 194, per Nelson, J. Yet in another case, Seymour *v.* McCormick, 19 How. 96, the same judge, in giving the judgment of the Supreme Court, says: "In regard to the question of unreasonable delay in making the disclaimer, as going to the whole cause of action, the court are of opinion that the granting of the patent for this improvement, together with the opinion of the court below, maintaining its validity, repel any inference of unreasonable delay in correcting the claim; and that, *under the circumstances, the question is one of law.* This was decided in the case of O'Reilly *v.* Morse, 15 How. 121. The Chief Justice, in delivering the opinion of the court, observed that 'the delay in entering it (the disclaimer) is not unreasonable, for the objectionable claim was sanctioned by the head of the office; it has been held valid by a circuit court, and differences of opinion in relation to it are found to exist among the justices of this court. Under such circumstances the patentee had a right to insist upon it and not disclaim it until the highest court to which it could be carried had pronounced its judgment.'" But in the trial in the circuit court (3 Blatchf. 209), from which the above-cited appeal was taken, Judge Nelson used the following language: "If the *jury* are satisfied that there has been unreasonable negligence and delay on the part of the patentee in making a disclaimer as respects the invalid part of his patent, then the whole patent is inoperative, and the verdict must be for the defendant."

[3] McCormick *v.* Seymour, 3 Blatchf. 209; Seymour *v.* McCormick, 19 How. 96; Silsby *v.* Foote, 20 How. 378.

§ 380. Care is to be taken, therefore, in framing this defence, to ascertain, in the first place, whether the whole or only a part of the substance of the thing patented is open to the objection of prior use or knowledge; and, in the second place, whether a disclaimer has been filed. If a disclaimer has been filed in reasonable time, the defence of a want of novelty, that goes only to a part of the thing patented, and still leaves a material and substantial part unaffected by the objection, will not be an answer to the action, but will simply prevent the recovery of costs. But a defence which goes to the originality of the whole patent, and leaves nothing new that is material and substantial, and capable of distinction as the subject-matter of the plaintiff's invention, will be an answer to the action, notwithstanding any disclaimer. It is obviously necessary, therefore, to specify in the notice of defence the particular parts of the thing patented which it is intended to attack.[1]

§ 380 *a*. It may be well to add, by way of concluding the discussion of this statutory defence, that, although the statute requires notice to be given of any matter relied upon to defeat the patentee's claim on the ground of want of novelty, it does not prescribe any notice, previous to the admission of evidence, merely going to show the general state of the art at the time when the plaintiff made his invention. The distinction is, accordingly, to be drawn between evidence introduced for the purpose of defeating the patentee's claim and such as is offered by way of explanation. Thus in the case of Vance *v.* Campbell,[2] which turned chiefly upon the question of infringement, Nelson, J., rendering the opinion of the Supreme Court, says: "Several exceptions were taken to the admissibility of evidence offered by the defendants; but, without referring to them specially, it will be a sufficient answer to say, that it was competent and relative, as showing the state of the art in respect to improvements in the manufacture of cooking-stoves at the date of plaintiff's invention. No notice was necessary in order to justify the admission of evidence for this purpose."

§ 381. Another of the statute defences is, that the patentee

[1] See, further, an elaborate construction of the seventh and ninth sections, as to a disclaimer, in the opinion of Mr. Justice Story, in the case of Wyeth *v.* Stone, 1 Story's R. 273.

[2] 1 Black, 427.

had allowed his invention to become public, before his application for a patent, or, as it is expressed in the statute, that it "had been in public use, or on sale, with the consent or allowance of the patentee, before his application for a patent." This provision is intended to embody the defence of an abandonment or dedication to the public of his invention by the patentee, prior to his application for a patent. The question whether a patentee, by any and what degree of use of his invention before his application for a patent, could use his inchoate right in the thing invented, and not be able afterwards to resume it at his pleasure, arose before the statute of 1836 was passed, and the Supreme Court of the United States declared that an inventor might undoubtedly abandon his invention, and surrender or dedicate it to the public; and that the question which generally arises is, whether the acts or acquiescence of the party furnish, in the given case, satisfactory proof of such an abandonment or dedication to the public. The court held that the true construction of the then existing law was, that the first inventor cannot acquire a good title to a patent, if he suffers the thing invented to go into public use, or to be publicly sold for use, before he makes application for a patent; that such a voluntary act, or acquiescence in the public sale or use, is an abandonment of his right; or rather creates a disability to comply with the terms and conditions of the law, on which alone the public officer is authorized to grant a patent.[1] In a more recent case, the same court reaffirmed this construction of the patent laws, and held that the right of an alien patentee was vacated in the same manner by a foreign use or knowledge of his invention, under the then existing statutes.[2]

§ 382. It was the object of the clause now under consideration to make this defence of a prior abandonment or dedication to the public available under the general issue, upon notice of the facts intended to be proved. By "public use" is meant use in public; that is to say, if the inventor himself makes and sells the thing to be used by others, or it is made by one other person only, with his knowledge and without objection, before his application for a patent, *à fortiori*, if he suffers it to get into general use, it will

[1] Pennock *v.* Dialogue, 2 Peters, 1.

[2] Shaw *v.* Cooper, 7 Peters, 292.

have been in "public use."[1] But where the patentee alone makes the thing for the purposes of experiment and completion, without selling it to be used by others, the term "public use" is not applicable.[2]

§ 383. An important question next arises, as to what will constitute proof of the "consent and allowance" of the patentee to the "public use or sale" of his invention before his application. In the first place, a knowledge of such public use or sale by others, without objection on his part, will go far towards raising the presumption of an acquiescence, and in some cases will be a sufficient proof of it. The question in such cases is as to his consent; and if knowledge of the use of his invention by others is brought home to him, and no exclusive right has been asserted by him against that use, his silence will furnish very strong evidence that he has waived his right.[3] If the evidence shows a long acquiescence, or a very general use, it will be conclusive.[4]

§ 384. In the second place, although acquiescence cannot be presumed without knowledge, such knowledge may be presumed from the circumstances, and is not always required to be proved by direct evidence.[5]

§ 385. In the third place, no particular lapse of time is necessary to be shown, after knowledge and acquiescence are established, in order to prove an abandonment or dedication to the public. In one of the cases the invention was made in the year 1804, and suffered to go into general use without any claim of an exclusive right, or any objection, and without receiving any compensation, until the year 1822.[6] In another case, the invention was completed in 1811, and the letters-patent were obtained in 1818; in the interval, a single individual had made and publicly sold large quantities of the thing patented, under an agreement with the inventor as to price.[7] In a third case, the inventor, who was a foreigner, came to this country in 1817, and might lawfully have applied for a patent in 1819, but did not do so until three years afterwards. It appeared that he invented the

1 Pennock *v.* Dialogue; Shaw *v.* Cooper; Mellus *v.* Silsbee, 4 Mas. 108.

2 Shaw *v.* Cooper.

3 Mellus *v.* Silsbee.

4 Ibid.; Shaw *v.* Cooper.

5 Shaw *v.* Cooper, 7 Peters, 292, 321.

6 Mellus *v.* Silsbee, 4 Mas. 108.

7 Pennock *v.* Dialogue, 2 Peters, 1.

instrument in 1813 or 1814, and made it known to certain persons in England, by or through whom, contrary to his intention, it was publicly used and sold there.[1] In a fourth case, in England, the patentee had sold the article in the public market four months before the date of the patent.[2] In all these cases the patentee was held to have abandoned or dedicated to the public his right in the invention.

§ 386. But, on the other hand, it is a still further question, what constitutes a public use, with the consent or allowance of the patentee. What acts, in other terms, within a longer or shorter period of time, or what permission to use, granted or allowed to several persons, or restricted to a single instance, or what use by the patentee himself, will amount to an abandonment or dedication to the public? Is the intention with which the acts are done, or the use permitted, an element in the question, or is the intention wholly immaterial, provided certain acts are done, or a certain use is permitted? In determining these questions, it is necessary to discriminate between the cases of a use permitted to others, or of a knowledge imparted to others, and the exercise or practice of the invention by the patentee himself.

§ 387. In the case of Shaw *v.* Cooper, already referred to, the Supreme Court of the United States said that the intention of the inventor is not the true ground in these cases; that "whatever may be his intention, if he suffers the invention to get into public use, through any means whatsoever, without an immediate assertion of his right, he is not entitled to a patent; nor will a patent obtained under such circumstances protect his right."[3] The meaning of this obviously is, that no matter what the intention of the patentee was, in imparting to another a knowledge of his invention, if the person or persons, to whom he had so imparted it, afterwards, though fraudulently, use the invention in public, and the patentee looks on without objection, or assertion of his right, the public will have become possessed of the invention, and the patentee cannot resume his right in it by obtaining a patent. This meaning is apparent from other parts of the opinion in the same case; for the court say, that if the invention

[1] Shaw *v.* Cooper.

[2] Wood *v.* Zimmer, 1 Holt, N. P. C. 60.

[3] 7 Peters, 292, 323.

has become known to the public through fraudulent means, the patentee should assert his right immediately, and take the necessary steps to legalize it.[1] So, too, it is apparent from the opinion

[1] "Vigilance is necessary to entitle an individual to the privileges secured under the patent law. It is not enough that he should show his right by invention, but he must secure it in the mode required by law. And if the invention, through fraudulent means, shall be made known to the public, he should assert his right immediately, and take the necessary steps to legalize it.

"The patent law was designed for the public benefit, as well as for the benefit of inventors. For a valuable invention the public, on the inventor's complying with certain conditions, give him, for a limited time, the profits arising from the sale of the thing invented. This holds out an inducement for the exercise of genius and skill in making discoveries which may be useful to society and profitable to the discoverer. But it was not the intention of this law to take from the public that of which they were fairly in possession.

"In the progress of society the range of discoveries in the mechanic arts, in science, and in all things which promote the public convenience, as a matter of course, will be enlarged. This results from the aggregation of mind, and the diversities of talents and pursuits, which exist in every intelligent community. And it would be extremely impolitic to retard or embarrass this advance by withdrawing from the public any useful invention or art, and making it a subject of private monopoly. Against this consequence the legislature have carefully guarded, in the laws they have passed on the subject. It is undoubtedly just that every discoverer should realize the benefits resulting from his discovery, for the period contemplated by law. But these can only be secured by a substantial compliance with every legal requisite. His exclusive right does not rest alone upon his discovery, but also upon the legal sanctions which have been given to it, and the forms of law with which it has been clothed.

"No matter by what means an invention may be communicated to the public before the patent is obtained; any acquiescence in the public use, by the inventor, will be an abandonment of his right. If the right were asserted by him who fraudulently obtained it, perhaps no lapse of time could give it validity. But the public stand in an entirely different relation to the inventor. The invention passes into the possession of innocent persons, who have no knowledge of the fraud, and, at a considerable expense, perhaps, they appropriate it to their own use. The inventor or his agent has full knowledge of these facts, but fails to assert his right; shall he afterwards be permitted to assert it with effect? Is not this such evidence of acquiescence in the public use, on his part, as justly forfeits his right?

"If an individual witness a sale and transfer of real estate, under certain circumstances, in which he has an equitable lien or interest, and does not make known this interest, he shall not afterwards be permitted to assert it. On this principle it is, that a discoverer abandons his right, if, before the obtainment of his patent, his discovery goes into public use. His right would be secured by giving public notice that he was the inventor of the thing used, and that he should apply for a patent. Does this impose any thing more than reasonable

of the same court, in Pennock *v.* Dialogue, that it is the voluntary acquiescence of the inventor in the *public use*, and not his voluntarily imparting the knowledge to the person who fraudulently or otherwise uses it in public, that fastens upon him the presumption of a dedication.[1] It is also clear, that when the act or acts of user were by way of experiment, in order to perfect the invention, the inventor does not lose his right.

§ 388. Hence it appears, that the intention with which the inventor did the acts which are relied on as proof of "public use" is material, unless the evidence goes to the extent of showing that the invention had got beyond the control of the inventor, and he had not taken any steps to prevent its being thus situated.

diligence on the inventor? And would any thing short of this be just to the public? The acquiescence of an inventor in the public use of an invention can in no case be presumed, when he has no knowledge of such use. But this knowledge may be presumed from the circumstances of the case. This will, in general, be a fact for the jury. And if the inventor do not, immediately after this notice, assert his right, it is such evidence of acquiescence in the public use, as forever afterwards to prevent him from asserting it. After his right shall be perfected by a patent, no presumption arises against it from a subsequent use by the public.

"When an inventor applies to the department of state for a patent, he should state the facts truly; and indeed he is required to do so, under the solemn obligations of an oath. If his invention has been carried into public use by fraud, but for a series of months or years he has taken no steps to assert his right, would not this afford such evidence of acquiescence as to defeat his application, as effectually as if he failed to state that he was the original inventor. And the same evidence which should defeat his application for a patent would, at any subsequent period, be fatal to his right. The evidence he exhibits to the department of state is not only *ex parte*, but interested; and the questions of fact are left open, to be controverted by any one who shall think proper to contest the right under the patent.

"A strict construction of the act, as it regards the public use of an invention before it is patented, is not only required by its letter and spirit, but also by sound policy. A term of fourteen years was deemed sufficient for the enjoyment of an exclusive right of an invention by the inventor. But if he may delay an application for his patent, at pleasure, although his invention be carried into public use, he may extend the period beyond what the law intended to give him. A pretence of fraud would afford no adequate security to the public in this respect, as artifice might be used to cover the transaction. The doctrine of presumed acquiescence, where the public use is known, or might be known to the inventor, is the only safe rule which can be adopted on this subject." 7 Peters, 319, 320, 321, 322.

[1] 2 Peters, 1, 23.

In other words, it may be a material element, in determining whether the presumption of acquiescence in public use arises, to ascertain whether the inventor used the invention himself, or imparted a knowledge of it to others, with or without an intention to limit such use or knowledge, in respect to time, extent, or object.

§ 389. Where a party practises his invention himself, for the purposes of experiment or completion, before he takes out a patent, the inference that he intends to surrender his invention to the public does not arise; and, consequently, a dedication cannot be proved by evidence that shows only experimental practice by the inventor, whether in public or in private.[1] Indeed, it may

[1] Wyeth *v.* Stone, 1 Story's R. 273. In this case, Mr. Justice Story said: "In the next place, as to the supposed public use of Wyeth's machine before his application for a patent. To defeat his right to a patent, under such circumstances, it is essential that there should have been a public use of his machine, substantially as it was patented, with his consent. If it was merely used occasionally by himself in trying experiments, or if he allowed only a temporary use thereof by a few persons, as an act of personal accommodation or neighborly kindness, for a short and limited period, that would not take away his right to a patent. To produce such an effect, the public use must be either generally allowed or acquiesced in, or at least be unlimited in time, or extent, or object. On the other hand, if the user were without Wyeth's consent, and adverse to his patent, it was a clear violation of his rights, and could not deprive him of his patent."

See also Ryan *v.* Goodwin, 3 Sumner, 518; Bentley *v.* Fleming, 1 Car. & Kirw. 587. This last case shows a strong tendency to limit the effect of use in public, by the intention of the patentee. The patent in question had been obtained for making a card-machine; and there was evidence that, about five or six weeks before the letters-patent were obtained, the inventor, one Thornton, had lent the machine to one N., in order that he might try whether it would set the teeth of the cards. There was also evidence that N.'s room was in a mill, and that men were constantly going backwards and forwards to and from the said room. It appeared, moreover, that for some weeks before the time at which the machine was lent to N., it had been in complete working condition. On this evidence it was submitted, on the part of the defendant, that the plaintiff was out of court, — first, on the ground that the machine had been publicly used in N.'s room, which was a public room, before the granting of the letters-patent; and on this point the case of Wood *v.* Zimmer was referred to. Cresswell, J., said: "Have you any case that goes that length? The case referred to was the case of an absolute sale; but here there is no evidence that the machine was given to N. *for the purpose of giving it publicity.* The evidence merely is, that Thornton lent the machine to N. in order that he might discover whether it really was worth while to take out a patent for it or not. I cannot stop the case on that point."

be stated, as a general test, in cases of a supposed dedication through the using, exercising, or practising the invention by the patentee himself, previous to his application for a patent, that whenever the evidence stops short of proving such a use, exercise, or practice for the purpose of gain, a "public use" will not be proved.

The Court of Common Pleas, in England, has, in a recent case, gone still further, and ruled that an experiment performed in the presence of others, which not only turns out to be successful, but actually beneficial in the particular instance, is not *necessarily* a publication, so as to constitute a gift of the invention to the world. The facts are briefly as follows. Newall, claiming to be the inventor of an improved apparatus for laying submarine telegraph wires, brought a bill for injunction against Elliot and Glass, for alleged infringement of his patent. The defendants set up the plea of public use for gain, prior to obtaining letters-patent. This chancery suit was abandoned, in consequence of an agreement entered into by all parties, to have the case decided by an arbitrator, who should, if required, state a special case, to enable the parties to take the opinion of one of the superior courts of law on any point of law. The arbitrator found for the claimant, and the Common Pleas sustained his findings of law.[1] Byles, J., in giving the judgment of the court, said: "It must be, and is, conceded, on the part of the plaintiff, that an inventor's public use, for profit, of an invention already ascertained, by previous experiment, to be useful, is a gift of the invention to the public, and avoids a subsequent patent. And it is conceded by the defendant, that a use before the patent, merely experimental and tentative, does not avoid it. Now, the use here made of the invention, in actually laying down the cable, was a use which partook of both characters. On the one hand, it was experimental and tentative; but on the other, the experiment turned out not only successful, but beneficial to the inventor at the moment. The true question, therefore, looking at the decision of the arbitrator, seems to be this: is an experiment performed in the presence of others, which not only turns out to be successful, but actually beneficial in the present instance, necessarily a gift of the invention to the world? We think it is not. In the case under consideration, experiments on dry land are found to

[1] *In re* Newall and Elliot, 4 C. B. . s. 269.

be indecisive. The decisive experiment still remains to be made on a large scale and in deep water. An opportunity presents itself, in the course of a government contract, not a contract for the use of this particular apparatus, but a contract for laying down the cable by any means the contractor may select. The experimentor is obliged either to experiment in a way that may turn out to be useful in the particular instance, or else not to make any efficient and decisive experiment at all. The coincidence of an experiment with actual immediate profit or advantage from it, if successful, is unavoidable. Suppose, even, that this coincidence had been accidental; suppose that in the course of the voyage the inventor had tried some further and new experiment, with an alteration of the apparatus, which alteration had at once answered some useful purpose. Surely that further invention would have been his property. Otherwise a man cannot have the property in an invention, which starts from his brain so fully matured and armed that it not only succeeds at the first trial, but accomplishes on that very trial some profitable or useful purpose. If, indeed, the plaintiff in the present case had on other and subsequent voyages used his apparatus, and unnecessarily delayed his application for a patent, he would have given his invention to the public. But here the arbitrator must be taken to have found — as he well might on the evidence before him — that the inventor lost no time, but applied for his patent with reasonable expedition."

In this country, under the provisions of the act of 1839, this doctrine, if applicable at all, could or need only be applied to such profitable experiments as take place more than two years before the application for letters-patent.[1]

§ 389 *a*. Mere forbearance on the part of an inventor to apply for a patent during the progress of experiments, and until he has perfected his invention and tested its value by actual practice, affords no just grounds for presumption that the inventor intends to abandon his invention, or surrender and dedicate it to the public.

[1] Compare also *In re* Adamson's Patent, 35 E. L. & Eq. Rep. 327, where the Lord Chancellor refused to seal letters-patent for certain machinery, which has been used and open to public inspection several months before any application for a patent.

[2] Agawam Co. *v.* Jordan, 7 Wall. 583; Sisson *v.* Gilbert, 9 Blatchf. 185.

The fact that a patentee, before making his application to the Patent Office, had explained his invention orally to several persons, without making a drawing, model, or written specification thereof, and that subsequently, though prior to his application for a patent, the defendant had devised and perfected the same thing, and described it in the presence of the patentee, who made no claim to it, does not constitute a bar to an action for an infringement. Silence of a party works no estoppel unless it has misled another to his injury.[1]

§ 390. It has been held in England, where the "public use" must be a public use in England, that the making in England of a single pair of wheels, the subject of the patent, under the direction of the patentee, but under an injunction of secrecy, to be sent abroad for a person who intended to take a share in the patent, was not a public use within the realm.[2] But as our law

[1] Railroad Co. *v.* Dubois, 12 Wall. 47.

[2] Morgan *v.* Seaward, Webs. Pat. Cas. 189, 193. In this case Parke, B., said: "The evidence was, that before the date of the patent (which was the 22d of July, 1829), Curtis, an engineer, made for Morgan two pairs of wheels upon the principle mentioned in the patent, at his own factory. Galloway, the patentee, gave the instructions to Curtis, under an injunction of secrecy, because he was about to take out a patent. The wheels were completed and put together at Curtis's factory, but not shown or exposed to the view of those who might happen to come there. After remaining a short time, the wheels were taken to pieces, packed up in cases, and shipped in the month of April on board a vessel in the Thames, and sent for the use of the Venice and Trieste Company, of which Morgan was managing director, and which carried on its transactions abroad, but had shareholders in England. Curtis deposed, that 'they were sold to the company,' without saying by whom, which may mean that they were sold by Curtis to Morgan for the company; and Morgan paid Curtis for them. Morgan and Galloway employed an attorney, who entered a caveat against any patent on the 2d of March, and afterwards solicited the patent in question, which was granted to Galloway and assigned to Morgan. Upon these facts, the question for us to decide is, whether the jury must have necessarily found for the defendants, or whether they might have found that this invention, at the date of the letters-patent, was new in the legal sense of that word. The words of the statute are, that grants are to be good 'of the sole working or making of any manner of new manufactures within this realm, to the first and true inventor or inventors of such manufactures, which others at the time of the making of such letters-patent and grants did not use'; and the proviso in the patent in question, founded on the statute, is, that if the invention be not a new invention as to the public use and exercise thereof in England, the patent should be void. The word 'manufacture' in the statute must be construed in one of two ways; it

stood before the year 1839, if the inventor sold to any one who might choose to buy, although it was only a single specimen of

may mean the machine when completed, or the mode of constructing the machine. If it mean the former, undoubtedly there has been no use of the machine, as a machine, in England, either by the patentee himself or any other person ; nor indeed any use of the machine in a foreign country before the date of the patent. If the term 'manufacture' be construed to be 'the mode of constructing the machine,' there has been no use or exercise of it in England, in any sense which can be called 'public.' The wheels were constructed under the direction of the inventor, by an engineer and his servants, with an injunction of secrecy, on the express ground that the inventor was about to take out a patent, and that injunction was observed ; and this makes the case, so far, the same as if they had been constructed by the inventor's own hands, in his own private workshop, and no third person had seen them whilst in progress. The operation was disclosed, indeed, to the plaintiff, Morgan, but there is sufficient evidence that Morgan, at that time, was connected with the inventor, and designing to take a share of the patent. A disclosure of the nature of the invention to such a person, under such circumstances, must surely be deemed private and confidential. The only remaining circumstance is, that Morgan paid for the machines, with the privity of Galloway, on behalf of the Venice and Trieste Steam Company, of which he was the managing director ; but there was no proof that he had paid more than the price of the machines, as for ordinary work of that description ; and the jury would also be well warranted in finding that he did so with the intention that the machine should be used abroad only, by this company, which, as it carried on its transactions in a foreign country, may be considered as a foreign company ; and the question is, whether this solitary transaction, without any gain being proved to be derived thereby to the patentee or to the plaintiff, be a use or exercise in England, of the mode of construction, in any sense which can be deemed a use by others, or a public use, within the meaning of the statute and the patent. We think not. It must be admitted, that if the patentee himself had before his patent constructed machines for sale as an article of commerce, for gain to himself, and been in the practice of selling them publicly, that is, to any one of the public who would buy, the invention would not be new at the date of the patent. This was laid down in the case of Wood *v.* Zimmer (Holt, N. P. C. 58, and Webs. Pat. Cas. 44, n.), and appears to be founded on reason ; for if the inventor could sell his invention, keeping the secret to himself, and when it was likely to be discovered by another take out a patent, he might have, practically, a monopoly for a much longer period than fourteen years. Nor are we prepared to say, that if such a sale was of articles that were only fit for a foreign market, or to be used abroad, it would make any difference ; nor that a single instance of such a sale as an article of commerce, to any one who chose to buy, might not be deemed the commencement of such a practice, and the public use of the invention, so as to defeat the patent. But we do not think that the patent is vacated on the ground of the want of novelty, and

his invention, and sold for profit on it as an invention, such a sale would be a "public use," and the unlimited nature of the object with which a knowledge of the invention was imparted would prevent him from resuming his exclusive right by a subsequent patent.[1] It will presently be stated how far the law has been modified in this respect.

§ 391. Another limitation to the doctrine of presumptive dedication, or public use, with the consent, &c., is found in the case of a piratical user of the invention, by a party to whom the inventor has imparted a knowledge of it in confidence, before he has applied for a patent. Many inventions can be perfected and carried into practice only through the aid of workmen, servants, and other *employés*. We have seen that an inventor may intrust another person, confidentially, with a knowledge of his invention, for certain limited purposes; and if such a person afterwards fraudulently makes public the knowledge so acquired, the authorities seem to be agreed that the inventor may, if he takes immediate steps to give notice of his exclusive right, obtain a valid patent.[2] The words of the statute, describing the defence now under consideration, make it clear, that, if the invention has come into public use through a breach of confidence, it cannot be said to be in public use "with the consent or allowance" of the patentee; it is only when he has been silent after it has so become public, that the presumption of consent and allowance

the previous public use or exercise of it, by a single instance of a transaction such as this between the parties, connected as Galloway and the plaintiff are, which is not like the case of a sale to any individual of the public who might wish to buy; in which it does not appear that the patentee has sold the article, or is to derive any profit from the construction of his machine, nor that Morgan himself is; and in which the pecuniary payment may be referred merely to an ordinary compensation for the labor and skill of the engineer actually employed in constructing the machine; and the transaction might, upon the evidence, be no more in effect, than that Galloway's own servants had made the wheels; that Morgan had paid them for the labor, and afterwards sent the wheels to be used by his own copartners abroad. To hold this to be what is usually called a publication of the invention in England, would be to defeat a patent by much slighter circumstances than have yet been permitted to have that effect."

[1] Ibid.; Wood *v.* Zimmer, 1 Holt, N. P. C. 60.

[2] Pennock *v.* Dialogue, 2 Peters, 1; Shaw *v.* Cooper, 7 Peters, 292; Mellus *v.* Silsbee, 4 Mas. 108; Grant *v.* Raymond, 6 Peters, 248, 249; McClurg *v.* Kingsland, 1 How. 202, 207.

arises.[1] The act of 1839, as will appear hereafter, has made this point still more clear. Another instance of a use, which will not expose the patentee to the consequences of this defence, is that suggested on more than one occasion by Mr. Justice Story, where the use has been permitted to others, for other limited purposes than those of experiment or completion, as from motives of neighborly kindness and the like.[2] The test that is afforded by the case of Morgan *v.* Seaward, above cited, is applicable here also; namely, that the evidence excludes the supposition that the patentee had put the thing into public use, for the purpose of profit on it, as an invention.[3] If a patentee could show clearly that he had allowed to others a limited use of his invention, not for his own profit, but for their accommodation, in a manner consistent with a clear intention to hold the exclusive privilege, and the invention had not got beyond his control, with his apparent acquiescence, he would not be within the mischief of this part of the statute. Of course, mere delay to take out a patent, unaccompanied by public use or sale of the thing, with the consent or allowance of the patentee, before his application, however long may be the interval between the completion of the thing and the application, will have no effect upon the patent.[4] Mere delay has no other importance, than as it tends to show acquiescence in such public use as may have occurred, in the mean time; or to show that the acts of the inventor went beyond a use or permission to use, for the purpose of experiment, or other limited object.

§ 391 *a.* The recent case of Kendall *v.* Winsor [5] is instructive, as affording a complete *résumé* of the rulings upon the various

[1] Ryan *v.* Goodwin, 3 Sumner, 518; Pierson *v.* The Eagle Screw Company, 3 Story's R. 406, 407, 408.

[2] Mellus *v.* Silsbee, 4 Mas. 111; Wyeth *v.* Stone, 1 Story's R. 280, 281; Ryan *v.* Goodwin, 3 Sumner, 518.

[3] Webs. Pat. Cas. 189, 193.

[4] Ryan *v.* Goodwin, 3 Sumner, 519. In the case of Bentley *v.* Fleming, 1 Car. & Kirw. 587, 588, it was contended that, inasmuch as the machine in question was a complete workable machine for a long period before the letters-patent were taken out, it did not form the subject of a patent at all. Cresswell, J.: "A man cannot enjoy his monopoly by procuring a patent, after having had the benefit of the sale of his invention. But you cannot contend, that if a man were to keep his invention shut up in his room for twenty years, that circumstance merely would deprive him of his right to obtain a patent for it."

[5] 21 How. 322.

questions of abandonment, neglect to apply for letters-patent, piratical user, &c. The facts of the case are given in the opinion of Judge Daniel: —

"Upon the trial in the Circuit Court, in support of the defence, evidence was introduced tending to show that the plaintiff constructed a machine in substantial conformity with his specification as early as 1846, and that in 1849 he had several such machines in operation, on which he made harness to supply all such orders as he could obtain; that he continued to run these machines until he obtained these letters-patent; that he repeatedly declared to different persons that the machine was so complicated that he preferred not to take a patent, but to rely on the difficulty of imitating the machine and the secrecy in which he kept it. And the defendants also gave evidence tending to prove that the first of their machines was completed in the autumn of 1853, and the residue in the autumn of 1854, and that in the course of that fall the plaintiff had knowledge that the defendants had built or were building one or more machines like his invention, and did not interpose to prevent them. The plaintiff gave evidence tending to prove that the first machine built by him was never completed so as to operate; that his second machine was only partially successful, and improvements were made on it; that in 1849 he began four others, and completed them in that year, and made harness on them, which he sold when he could get orders; that they were subject to some practical difficulties, particularly as it respected the method of marking the harness and the liability of the bobbin to get out of the clutch; that he was employed in devising means to remedy these defects and did remedy them; that he also endeavored to simplify the machine by using only one ram-shaft; that he constantly intended to take letters-patent when he should have perfected the machine; that he applied to Mr. Keller for this purpose in February, 1853, but the model and specifications were not sent to Washington till November, 1854; that he kept the machines from the view of the public, allowed none of the hands employed in the mill to introduce persons to view them, and that the hands pledged themselves not to divulge the invention; that among the hands employed by the plaintiff was one Kendall Aldridge, who left plaintiff's employment in the autumn of 1852, and entered into an arrangement with the defendants to copy plaintiff's machine for them; and that it was by Aldridge, and under his superintendence, and by means of the knowledge which he had gained while in the plaintiff's employment, under a pledge of secrecy, that the defendants' machines were built and put in operation; and that one of the defendants had procured drawings of the plaintiff's machine, and has taken out letters-patent for it in England. Each party controverted the facts thus sought to be proved by the other. . . . The court set aside all those (defendants') prayers for instruction, and did instruct the jury as follows: —

"'1. That if Aldridge, under a pledge of secrecy, obtained knowledge of the plaintiff's machine, — and he had not abandoned it to the public, — and thereupon, at the instigation of the defendants, and with the knowledge, on their part, of the surreptitiousness of his acts, constructed machines for the defendants, they would not have the right to continue to use the same after the date of the plaintiff's letters-patent. *But if the defendants had these machines constructed before the plaintiff's application for his letters-patent, under the belief authorized by him that he consented and allowed them so to do*, then they might lawfully continue to use the same after the date of the plaintiff's letters-patent, and the plaintiff could not recover in this action. And that if the jury should find that the plaintiff's declaration and conduct were such as to justify the defendants in believing that he did not intend to take out letters-patent, but to rely on the difficulty of imitating his machine and the means he took to keep it secret, this would be a defence to the action. And they were further instructed, that to constitute such an abandonment to the public as would destroy the plaintiff's right to take a patent, in a case where it did not appear that any sale of the thing patented had been made, and there was no open public exhibition of the machine, the jury must find that he intended to give up and relinquish his right to take letters-patent. But if the plaintiff did intend not to take a patent, and manifested that intent by his declarations or conduct, and thereupon it was copied by the defendant, and so went into use, the plaintiff could not afterwards take a valid patent.' . . .

". . . Recurring now to the instruction from the judge at circuit in this case, we consider that instruction to be in strict conformity with the principles hereinbefore propounded, and with the doctrines of this court, as declared in the case of Pennock *v.* Dialogue and Shaw *v.* Cooper. That instruction diminishes or excludes no proper ground upon which the conduct and intent of the plaintiff below, as evinced ei her by declarations or acts, or by omissions to speak or act, and on which also the justice and integrity of the conduct of the defendants were to be examined and determined. It submitted the conduct and intentions of both plaintiff and defendants to the jury, as questions of fact to be decided by them, guided simply by such rules of law as had been settled with reference to issues like the one before them; and upon those questions of fact the jury have responded in favor of the plaintiff below, the defendant in error. . . . The decision of the Circuit Court is therefore affirmed, with costs."

§ 392. It now remains to be stated, how far this defence of a "prior public use or sale with the consent or allowance" of the patentee has been restricted or modified by subsequent legislation. Under this clause of the act of 1836, a use of the invention by a single person, or a sale of the thing invented to a single person, might, as we have seen, amount to a public use or sale, with the consent or allowance of the patentee. To remedy the inconvenience arising from this operation of the law, the act of 1839, § 7, provided "that every person or corporation, who has or shall have purchased or constructed any newly invented machine, manufacture, or composition of matter, prior to the application, by the inventor or discoverer, for a patent, shall be held to possess the right to use, and vend to others to be used, the specific machine, manufacture, or composition of matter, so made or purchased, without liability therefor to the inventor, or any other person interested in such invention; and no patent shall be held to be invalid, by reason of such purchase, sale, or use, prior to the application for a patent as aforesaid, except on proof of abandonment of such invention to the public; or that such purchase, sale, or prior use has been for more than two years prior to such application for a patent."

§ 393. This enactment enables a patentee to permit the use of his invention, by individuals, before his application, with more safety than he formerly could. Such use is not to invalidate the patent, except on proof of abandonment of the invention to the public, or that it had been continued for more than two years prior to the application for a patent. The question arises upon this provision, then, whether the particular purchase, sale, or prior use may of itself, under some circumstances, furnish proof of abandonment to the public, or whether such an abandonment must be proved by other cases, and by other evidence *dehors* the particular purchase, sale, or prior use, that happens to be in question. The obvious construction of the act is, that a purchase, sale, or prior use, before the application for a patent, shall not invalidate it, *unless* it amounts to an abandonment to the public; a purchase, sale, or prior use shall not have this effect, *per se*, but, if connected with facts which show an abandonment to the public, or if it has been for more than two years prior to the application, it will have this effect.[1] Thus, in the case of McClurg *v.* Kingsland, where the defendants used the invention for four months before the application of the inventor for a patent, such use being in public, with the consent and allowance of the patentee, he being in their employ, and making a part of the apparatus by which the invention was to be applied, but receiving no compensation for the use of his invention, and not giving any notice to the defendants not to use his invention, until, on a misunderstanding upon another subject, he left their employment; the Supreme Court of the United States said that it would be no strained construction, under such circumstances, to hold that the patent, subsequently obtained, was void; although the decision merely went to the point that the acts of the patentee justified the presumption of a license to the defendants.[2]

§ 394. The words of the statute which thus authorizes a public use or sale by or to individuals, prior to the application for a patent, make the subject of such use or sale "any newly invented machine, manufacture, or composition of matter"; and the purchaser is authorized to use, and vend to others to be used, "the specific machine, manufacture, or composition of matter," without liability to the inventor, &c.; and then the statute declares that the patent shall still be valid, notwithstanding such prior use or sale, except on proof of the abandonment of "such invention" to the public, &c. It might admit of some doubt, upon this language, whether the invention of a method of manufacture, a process, or an art, or any thing but a machine, a manufacture, or a

[1] See the comment of Mr. Justice Story on this statute, in Pierson *v.* The Eagle Screw Company, 3 Story's R. 402, 405, 407, cited *ante*.

[2] 1 How. 202, 208.

composition of matter, is within the scope of the provision, and whether the purchaser could do any thing more than use, or vend to others to be used, the specific thing which he had purchased. But the Supreme Court of the United States have construed the terms "newly invented machine, manufacture, or composition of matter" to mean "the invention patented," whatever it may be; and the words "the specific machine," to refer to the thing as originally invented, of which the right is afterwards secured by a patent; so that, according to the precedent afforded by the case in which this construction was adopted, this statute embraces whatever may be the subject-matter of a valid patent, although it may be a process, or method of manufacture, and not a machine, &c.[1]

[1] McClurg *v.* Kingsland, 1 How. 202, 209. The court said: "At the trial below and here, the plaintiff's counsel have contended, that this act cannot apply to the present case, inasmuch as the protection it affords to the person who had the prior use is confined to the specific machine, &c., and does not extend to such use of the invention, or thing patented, if it does not consist of a machine, &c., as contradistinguished from the new mode or manner in which an old machine or its parts operates, so as to produce the desired effect; but we think that the law does not admit of such construction, whether we look at its words or its manifest objects, when taken in connection with former laws, and the decisions of this court in analogous cases.

"The words 'such invention' must be referred back to the preceding part of the sentence, in order to ascertain the subject-matter to which it relates, which is none other than the newly invented machine, manufacture, or composition of matter constituting the thing patented, otherwise these words become senseless when the invention is not strictly of a machine, &c. Now, in the present case, we find the invention consists solely in the angular direction given to the tube through which the metal is conducted into the cylinder in which the roller is cast. Every part of the machinery is old, the roller itself is no part of the invention, and cannot be the machine, manufacture, or composition of matter contemplated by Congress, nor can the word 'specific' have any practical effect, unless it is applied to the thing patented, whatever it may be, without making a distinction between a machine, &c., and the mode of producing a useful result, by the mere direction given to one of the parts of an old machine. Such a construction is not justified by the language of the law, and would defeat both of its objects. If it does not embrace the case before us, the consequence would be that the use of the invention, under the circumstances in evidence, would, according to the decision in 2 Peters, 14, 15, invalidate the patent; for if the act operates to save the avoidance of the patent, it must, of consequence, protect the person who uses the invention before the application for a patent. Both objects must be affected, or both must fail, as both parts of the act refer to the same thing, and the same state of things, as affecting the person using the newly invented machine, or

§ 395. The result, therefore, of the different statute provisions and the authorities, is that this defence of a prior public use or sale, with the consent or allowance of the patentee, can now be made good so as to invalidate a patent, only by showing an abandonment to the public, or that the use or sale dates from a period more than two years before the application for a patent; that such an abandonment will not be proved by the particular act of use or sale alone, but that the act of use or sale may be attended with such circumstances as to amount to an abandonment; and that the abandonment may also be proved by other acts or omissions disconnected with the particular use or sale, which the patentee may have allowed to individuals, and which he can show did not alone amount to an abandonment.[1]

As the statute has been expounded in a recent case, "*it virtually extends the patentee's privilege to sixteen years instead of fourteen;*

the thing patented, as well as the inventor. Had the words 'invention,' or 'thing patented,' been used instead of machine, &c., there could have been no room for doubt of the application of the act to the present case; and, by referring to the phraseology of the different acts of Congress, denoting the invention, it is apparent that, though there is a difference in the words used, there is none as to their meaning or reference to the same thing. Thus, we find in the fourteenth section of the act of 1836, relating to suits for using the thing whereof the exclusive right is secured by any patent'; in the fifteenth, 'his invention, his discovery, the thing patented,' 'that which was in fact invented or discovered,' 'the invention or discovery for which the patent issued,' 'that of which he was the first inventor.' In the first section of the act of 1839, 'any patent for any invention, discovery, or improvement,' 'inventions and discoveries'; in the second section, 'the invention'; in the third, 'invention or discovery'; in the fourth, 'patented inventions and improvements'; in the fifth, 'the thing as originally invented.' 2 Story, 2510, 2511, 2546.

"We therefore feel bound to take the words 'newly invented machine, manufacture, or composition of matter,' and 'such invention,' in the act of 1839, to mean 'the invention patented,' and the words 'specific machine' to refer to 'the thing as originally invented,' whereof the right is secured by patent; but not to any newly invented improvement on a thing once patented. The use of the invention before an application for a patent must be the specific improvement then invented and used by the person who had purchased, constructed, or used the machine to which the invention is applied; so construed, the objects of the act of 1839 are accomplished; a different construction would make it necessary to carry into all former laws the same literal exposition of the various terms used to express the same thing, and thereby changing the law according to every change of mere phraseology, make it a labyrinth of inextricable confusion."

[1] See Railroad Co. *v.* Dubois, 12 Wall. 47.

that is, he may use his improvement by making and using his machines, and by vending and taking pay for them, for two years previous to his application, without forfeiting the benefits conferred upon him by his patent. But if he either sells a machine, or uses one, or puts one into public use, at any time more than two years before his application, it works a forfeiture of his right."[1]

The language of the act of 1870 in relation to the right of purchasers before patent is, "That every person who may have purchased of the inventor, or with his knowledge and consent may have constructed, any newly invented or discovered machine, or other patentable article, prior to the application by the inventor or discoverer for a patent, or sold or used one so constructed, shall have the right to use, and vend to others to be used, the specific thing so made or purchased, without liability therefor."[2]

§ 395 *a.* With regard to the question of abandonment or dedication *after* letters-patent have been obtained, it has been held, in the case of Wyeth *v.* Stone, that, at least in equity, the defence that the patentee had for some time acquiesced in open infringements of his right would be a sufficient ground for refusing an application for injunction, whatever the action of a court of law might be.[3]

Another question has arisen and received final adjudication in the Supreme Court, to wit, whether an inventor may, under certain circumstances, be presumed to make a formal dedication to the public *at the time* of filing his specification. The case arose under Battin's patent for a coal-breaking apparatus. The patentee, in his first specification, filed 1843, claimed as his invention merely the arrangement and combination of parts therein described, although he was, in fact, also the inventor of one or more of the parts themselves. In 1849 he surrendered his patent and took out a new one, in which he specified and claimed as new one of these parts. The Circuit Court, per Kane, J., held the prior specification had the effect of dedicating such parts to the public, who, being thus put in the enjoyment of the invention by the inventor himself, could not be dispossessed by any subsequent

[1] McCormick *v.* Seymour, 2 Blatchf. 240; affirmed in Seymour *v.* McCormick, 16 How. 480. Compare also Pitts *v.* Hall, 2 Blatchf. 229.

[2] Section 37.

[3] 1 Story's R. 273. *Vide* chapter on Remedy in Equity.

measures on his part, such as surrender or disclaimer.[1] On appeal to the Supreme Court[2] this opinion was reversed. McLean, J., in delivering the opinion of the Supreme Court, says: "The above instructions were, we think, erroneous. (They were these: 1. That a description by the applicant for a patent of a machine or a part of a machine, in his specification, unaccompanied by notice that he has rights in it or that he desires to secure title to it as a patent, is a dedication of it to the public; 2. That such a dedication cannot be revoked after the machine has passed into public use, either by surrender and reissue, or otherwise.) Whether the defect be in the specification or in the claim, under the thirteenth section, above cited, the patentee may surrender his patent, and by an amended specification or claim cure the defect. The reissued patent must be for the same invention substantially, though it be described in terms more accurate and precise than in the first patent. Under such circumstances, a new and different invention cannot be claimed. But where the specification or claim is made so vaguely as to be inoperative or invalid, yet an amendment may give to it validity, and protect the rights of the patentee against all subsequent infringements. So strongly was this remedy of the patentee recommended by a sense of justice and policy, that this court, in the case of Grant *v.* Raymond,[3] sustained a reissued and corrected patent, before any legislative provision was made on the subject. . . . How much stronger is a case under the statute which secures the rights of the patentee by surrender, and declares the effect of the reissued and corrected patent! By the defects provided for in the statute nothing passes to the public from the specification or claims, within the scope of the patentee's invention. And this may be ascertained by the language he uses. In the case of Stimpson *v.* West Chester R.R.,[4] it was held, that "where a defective patent had been surrendered and a new one taken out, and a patentee brought an action for a violation of his patent right, laying the infringement at a date subsequent to that of the reissued patent, proof of the use of the thing patented during the interval between the original and renewed patents will not defeat the same. In the same case it was also held, that the proceeding before the commis-

[1] Battin *v.* Taggert, 2 Wall. C. C. 101.

[2] Battin *v.* Taggert, 17 How. 74.

[3] 6 Pet. 218.

[4] 4 How. 380.

sioner, in the surrender and reissue of a patent, is not open for investigation except on the ground of fraud. The patent of 1843 was not surrendered on the obtainment of the patent of 1844. That was intended to be a new invention of arranging and combining the toothed rollers, which, the patentee says, was not made the subject of a claim in the patent of 1843. The patent of 1844 was cancelled but not reissued, when the patent of 1849 was issued. At that time the patent of 1843 and the improvement thereon, dated January 20, 1844, were surrendered and cancelled, and new letters-patent were issued on an amended specification. The cause of the surrender of the patent of 1843, as stated in the charge to the jury, was the ruling of the court in the case of Battin *v.* Clayton, and that the patent was consequently obtained. (That ruling was that the patent, being merely for the combination of machinery, could neither be supported by proof of the novelty, nor assailed by proof of the want of novelty, of the parts.) That ruling is not now before us, nor is it necessary to inquire whether the patent of 1843, on the specifications and claim, was sustainable. The plaintiff, by a surrender of that patent and the procurement of the patent of 1849 with amended specifications, abandoned his first patent and relied wholly on the one reissued. The claim and specifications in this patent, as amendatory of the first, were within § 13 of the act of 1836. It is said, with entire accuracy, in the charge, in regard to the amended specification of 1849, that it "described essentially the same machine as the former one did, but claimed as the thing invented the breaking apparatus only! And this the patentee had a right to do. He had a right to restrict or enlarge his claim, so as to give it validity and to effectuate his invention."

A somewhat similar point was involved in the very recent case of The Suffolk Co. *v.* Hayden.[1] We give the facts as they are presented by the reporter: "In December, 1854, Hayden, being the inventor of improvements in cotton-cleaners, made application for a patent therefor. The improvements consisted in certain described changes made by Hayden in the interior arrangements of an elongated trunk previously used. While this application was still pending, Hayden made another distinct improvement in the form of the trunk. . . . He desired, apparently, to claim this

[1] 3 Wall. 315.

new improvement in the form of the trunk, both separately and in combination with his other improvements in the interior arrangements. Accordingly, in November, 1855, he filed his application for a patent, and on March 17, 1857, letters were issued to him, in the specification whereof he claims the improvement in the form of the trunk, both separately and in combination with his improvements in the interior arrangements of the trunk; but he made no claim in this specification to his improvements in the interior arrangements of the trunk. It did not appear that Hayden was guilty of any laches in reference to the delay of the commissioner to act on his first application for a patent for the improvements in the interior arrangement, made in December, 1854. For some cause, however, the Patent Office did not act on that application till June, 1857. . . . Hayden having sued the Suffolk Manufacturing Company for breach of this last-mentioned patent, the defendant's counsel at the trial requested the judge to rule, that the patent was void (June, 1857), because the improvements in the interior arrangement, which were described and claimed in it, being also described but not claimed in the patent of March 17, 1857, were by the legal operation of that patent surrendered to the public use. The judge refused so to rule, and on error this refusal raised the first question." The refusal was sustained by the Supreme Court.

§ 396. The next special defence stated in the act of 1836 is "that the patentee had surreptitiously or unjustly obtained the patent for that which was in fact invented or discovered by another, who was using reasonable diligence in adapting and perfecting the same." This provision was intended to embrace the case of a patent being obtained fraudulently, when the party obtaining it was not the inventor, and also the case of two independent inventors, where the one makes his application before the other, who was the first inventor, and so obtains a patent for that which was previously invented by another.

§ 397. With regard to the first case, of a patent obtained by a person not the inventor, by a fraud on the rights of the real inventor, it is sufficient to observe that such a defence, if made out, would be a complete bar to the action, upon general principles, as well as upon other provisions of the statute. One of the modes in which a patent may be thus surreptitiously obtained is by obtaining a knowledge of the invention from the public records where the inventor has deposited a description of it. When the real inventor has filed such a description at the Patent Office, or has obtained a patent, he has given notice to every subsequent applicant for a patent for the same thing, of the fact that he invented it; and although others may not afterwards be able to offer direct evidence that a subsequent patentee had seen and pirated the machine or other thing invented by the former applicant or patentee, yet the jury may infer a piracy from the existence of the former record, of which every subsequent patentee is presumed to have knowledge.[1] As to the case of two independent inventors, one of whom makes an earlier application than another for a patent and succeeds in obtaining it, it will be a good defence to an action upon such a patent, if it can be shown that the same thing was first invented by another, although not actually perfected, provided the first inventor was at the time using reasonable diligence in adapting and perfecting the thing invented.[2]

[1] Odiorne *v.* Winkley, 2 Gallis. 51, 55. In this case, Mr. Justice Story said: "As to the question, whether the patent was surreptitiously obtained, there is no direct or positive proof that Reed had ever seen Perkins's machine before he obtained a patent, but there is evidence, from which the jury may legally infer the fact, if they believe that evidence. It is a presumption of law, that, when a patent has been obtained, and the specifications and drawings recorded in the Patent Office, every man who subsequently takes out a patent for a similar machine has a knowledge of the preceding patent. As in chancery it is a maxim, that every man is presumed to have notice of any fact, upon which he is put upon inquiry by documents within his possession, if such fact could, by ordinary diligence, be discovered upon such inquiry. It is also a presumption of fact, that every man, having within his power the exact means of information, and desirous of securing to himself the benefit of a patent, will ascertain for his own interest whether any one on the public records has acquired a prior right."

[2] Reed *v.* Cutter, 1 Story's R. 590, 599. In this case, Mr. Justice Story said: "The passage cited from Mr. Phillips's work on Patents (p. 395), in the sense in which I understand it, is perfectly accurate. He there expressly states, that the party claiming a patent must be the original and first inventor; and that his right to a patent will not be defeated by proof that another person had anticipated him in making the invention, unless such person 'was using reasonable diligence in adapting and perfecting the same.' These latter words are copied from the fifteenth section of the act of 1836, c. 357, and constitute a qualification of the preceding language of that section; so that an inventor, who has first actually perfected his invention, will not be deemed to have surreptitiously or unjustly obtained a patent for that, which was in fact first invented by another, unless the latter was at the time using reasonable dili-

§ 398. The last defence mentioned in the statute of 1836 is that the patentee, being an alien at the time the patent was granted, "had failed and neglected, for the space of eighteen months from the date of the patent, to put and continue on sale to the public, on reasonable terms, the invention or discovery for which the patent was issued." The object of this provision was to prevent foreigners from obtaining patents in this country, and afterwards withholding the use of their inventions from the public for an unreasonable length of time.[1]

§ 399. Apart, however, from the *general issue*, whether pleaded with or without statutory notice of the evidence to be offered, the defendant may plead *specially* in bar, that since the action was instituted the plaintiff has surrendered his letters-patent and

gence in adapting and perfecting the same. And this I take to be clearly law; for he is the first inventor, in the sense of the act, and entitled to a patent for his invention, who has first perfected and adapted the same to use; and until the invention is so perfected and adapted to use, it is not patentable. An imperfect and incomplete invention, resting in mere theory, or in intellectual notion, or in uncertain experiments, and not actually reduced to practice, and embodied in some distinct machinery, apparatus, manufacture, or composition of matter, is not, and indeed cannot be, patentable under our patent acts; since it is utterly impossible, under such circumstances, to comply with the fundamental requisites of those acts. In a race of diligence between two independent inventors, he who first reduces his invention to a fixed, positive, and practical form, would seem to be entitled to a priority of right to a patent therefor. Woodcock *v.* Parker, 1 Gallis. R. 438. The clause of the fifteenth section, now under consideration, seems to qualify that right, by providing that, in such cases, he who invents first shall have the prior right, if he is using reasonable diligence in adapting and perfecting the same, although the second inventor has, in fact, first perfected the same, and reduced the same to practice in a positive form. It thus gives full effect to the well-known maxim, that he has the better right who is prior in point of time, namely, in making the discovery or invention. But if, as the argument of the learned counsel insists, the text of Mr. Phillips means to affirm (what, I think, it does not) that he, who is the original and first inventor of an invention, so perfected and reduced to practice, will be deprived of his right to a patent, in favor of a second and subsequent inventor, simply because the first invention was not then known or used by other persons than the inventor, or not known or used to such an extent as to give the public full knowledge of its existence, I cannot agree to the doctrine; for, in my judgment, our patent acts justify no such construction."

[1] It has been held that this clause does not apply to American patentees; who became such as assignees of alien inventors, under § 6 of act of March, 1837. Tatham *v.* Lowber, 2 Blatchf. 49.

obtained a reissue. Thus in the case of Moffitt *v.* Garr,[1] the court said: "A surrender of the patent to the commissioner, within the sense of the provision, means an act which, in judgment of law, extinguishes the patent. It is a legal cancellation of it, and hence can no more be the foundation for the assertion of a right after the surrender, than could an act of Congress which has been repealed. It has frequently been determined that suits pending, which rest upon an act of Congress, fall with the repeal of it. The reissue of the patent has no connection with, or bearing upon, antecedent suits; it has as to subsequent ones. The antecedent suits depend upon the patent existing at the time they were commenced; and unless it exists and is in force at the time of trial and judgment, the suits fail. It is a mistake to suppose that, upon this construction, moneys recovered on judgment in suits, or voluntary payment under the first patent upon the surrender, might be recovered back. The title to these moneys does not depend upon the patent, but upon the voluntary payment or judgment of the court."

[1] 1 Black. 273.

CHAPTER X.

OF THE REMEDY IN EQUITY TO RESTRAIN INFRINGEMENTS.

§ 400. WE have seen that the common law and the statute both afford a remedy, by an action for damages, for the infringement of patent rights. But this remedy would be wholly inadequate to the protection of such rights, if it were not accompanied and fortified by another remedy, which flows from that great principle of equity jurisprudence, that where there is a legal right, and the nature of the injury to which it is exposed is such that a preventive remedy is indispensable, equity will afford that remedy by an injunction. The grounds of the equity jurisdiction in cases of patents are the prevention of irreparable mischiefs, the suppression of a multiplicity of suits and vexatious litigation, and the more complete discovery, from the party guilty of infringement, of the extent of the injury done to the patentee, than can be obtained in an action at law.[1] It does not belong to the purposes of this work to trace the origin of this branch of equity jurisdiction, nor is it necessary to do so, since the patent laws have expressly adopted in the broadest terms the remedy which it affords for the protection of patent rights, and have directed the proper courts "to grant injunctions according to the course and principles of courts of equity, to prevent the violation of the rights of any inventor, as secured to him by any law of the United States, on such terms and conditions as the said courts may deem reasonable."[2] All that is requisite, therefore, in the present work, is to develop the application of the doctrines and practice of courts of equity to the rights of inventors, in the remedy by injunction.

§ 401. As a preliminary remark, however, we may notice that the discretion vested in the court by the terms of the statute

[1] 2 Story's Eq. Jurisp. § 930, 931, 932, 933.

[2] Act of July 4, 1836, c. 357, § 17. Enlarged, as to powers of appeal, by act of February 18, 1861, c. 37.

above cited, to grant injunctions on such terms and conditions as the court may deem reasonable, is in perfect accordance with the principles of equity.[1] This discretion is not a wholly unregulated discretion, but the clause in which it is expressed is to be considered as affected by the previous direction that the injunction is to be granted according to the course and principles of courts of equity, which are guided by certain well-settled rules; so that the terms and conditions to be imposed in each case will be ascertained, by applying to the circumstances of the case those principles and that course of practice which have been usually followed, and which will admit of a "reasonable" application to the particular facts of the case.

[1] In Bacon *v.* Jones, 4 Mylne & Cr. 433, 436, Lord Cottenham made the following remarks on the granting of injunctions in cases of patents: "When a party applies for the aid of the court, the application for an injunction is made either during the progress of the suit or at the hearing; and in both cases, I apprehend, great latitude and discretion are allowed to the court in dealing with the application. When the application is for an interlocutory injunction, several courses are open: the court may at once grant the injunction, simpliciter, without more, — a course which, though perfectly competent to the court, is not very likely to be taken where the defendant raises a question as to the validity of the plaintiff's title; or it may follow the more usual, and, as I apprehend, more wholesome practice in such a case, of either granting an injunction, and at the same time directing the plaintiff to proceed to establish his title at law, and suspending the grant of the injunction until the result of the legal investigation has been ascertained, the defendant in the mean time keeping an account. Which of these several courses ought to be taken must depend entirely upon the discretion of the court, according to the case made.

"When the cause comes to a hearing, the court has also a large latitude left to it; and I am far from saying that a case may not arise in which, even at that stage, the court will be of opinion that the injunction may properly be granted without having recourse to a trial at law. The conduct and dealings of the parties, the frame of the pleadings, the nature of the patent right, and of the evidence by which it is established, — these and other circumstances may combine to produce such a result; although this is certainly not very likely to happen, and I am not aware of any case in which it has happened. Nevertheless, it is a course unquestionably competent to the court, provided a case be presented which satisfies the mind of the judge that such a course, if adopted, will do justice between the parties.

"Again, the court may, at the hearing, do that which is the more ordinary course; it may retain the bill, giving the plaintiff the opportunity of first establishing his right at law. There still remains a third course, the propriety of which must also depend upon the circumstances of the case, that of at once dismissing the bill."

§ 402. I. *The Parties.* — The parties entitled to relief in equity against the infringement of a patent are, first, the party or parties interested in the patent. As the remedy in equity is given in order to protect a legal right, and as the statute gives a right of action to the person or persons interested, whether as patentee, assignees, or grantees of the exclusive right for a particular district, it follows that any person holding the legal title, or the right to bring an action, may bring a bill for an injunction.

§ 403. We have seen when the assignee of a patent may sue at law in his own name, and when he should join his assignor. The same rules will govern in equity, in determining who are necessary parties to the bill. If the assignee has the whole interest, he may sue alone; but if he has less than the whole interest, he must join the patentee. If the assignment has not been recorded, the assignee is not substituted to the right and responsibility of the patentee, so as to maintain any suit at law or in equity, founded upon the patent;[1] and where there is a joint suit by the patentee and the assignee, and a disclaimer has been filed by the patentee, in which the assignee did not join, the disclaimer cannot operate in favor of the complainants in such a bill, or in an action at law.[2]

[1] Wyeth *v.* Stone, 1 Story's R. 273, 295. Story, J.: "The objection which I deem fatal is that the bill states and admits that the assignment to the plaintiff, Tudor (made in February, 1832), has never yet been recorded in the State department, according to the provisions of the Patent Act of 1793, c. 55, § 4. That act provides, 'that it shall be lawful for any inventor, his executor or administrator, to assign the title and interest in the said invention at any time; and the assignee, having recorded the said assignment in the office of the Secretary of State, shall thereafter stand in the place of the original inventor, both as to right and responsibility.' It seems a necessary, or, at least, a just inference, from this language, that until the assignee has so recorded the assignment, he is not substituted to the right and responsibility of the patentee, so as to maintain any suit at law or in equity, founded thereon. It is true, that no objection is taken in the pleadings on account of this defect; but it is spread on the face of the bill, and therefore the court is bound to take notice of it. It is not the case of a title defectively set forth, but of a title defective in itself, and brought before the court with a fatal infirmity, acknowledged to be attached to it. As between the plaintiffs and the defendants, standing upon adverse titles and rights (whatever might be the case between privies in title and right), Tudor has shown no joint interest sufficient to maintain the present bill; and therefore it must be dismissed with costs."

[2] Ibid. 294.

§ 404. There is, however, one distinction between an action at law and a suit in equity, in respect to the parties, and that is the case of an assignment of the exclusive right for a particular district. The grantee of such a right may bring an action at law, within his own district, for an infringement, even against the patentee himself, and, consequently, he may bring such an action always in his own name.[1]

§ 405. But in equity the patentee may be joined with the assignee of such an exclusive right, if it be a right to use a limited number of the patented machines in a particular district, because the interest of the patentee is not all vested in the grantee, who, although he may prevent the patentee from licensing other persons within the district, cannot obtain for himself the right to use more machines than the original grant authorized, without paying the patentee for such further license. This interest renders the patentee a proper party in such a bill.[2] Different persons, who have infringed a patent independently of each other, cannot be made defendants in the same bill.[3]

§ 405 *a*. It becomes at times important to know against whom a bill for injunction may be brought. Thus in the English case of Caldwell *v*. Van Vliessingen,[4] it was held that the Court of

[1] "The sixth question certified is as follows: whether the plaintiff, if he be an assignee of an exclusive right to use two of the patented machines within the town of Watervliet, has such an exclusive right as will enable him to maintain an action for an infringement of the patent within the said town; or whether, to maintain such action, the plaintiff must be possessed, as to that territory, of all the rights of the original patentee. The plaintiff is the grantee of the exclusive right to construct and use, and to vend to others to be used, two of the patented machines within the town of Watervliet, in the county of Albany. The fourteenth section of the patent law authorizes any person, who is a grantee of the exclusive right in a patent within and throughout a specified portion of the United States, to maintain an action in his own name for an infringement of the right. The plaintiff comes within the very terms of the section. Although limited to the use of two machines within the town, the right to use them is exclusive. No other party, not even the patentee, can use a right under the patent within the territory without infringing the grant." Wilson *v*. Rousseau, 4 How. 646, 686.

[2] Woodworth *v*. Wilson, 4 How. 712. It had been previously held that the grantee for a particular district can maintain a bill for an injunction and account. Ogle *v*. Edge, 4 Wash. 584.

[3] Dilly *v*. Doig, 2 Ves. Jr. 487.

[4] 9 E. L. & Eq. 51.

Chancery could enjoin the use in England of an English patented invention which had been made abroad, and attached to a foreign vessel as part of her equipment. But the Supreme Court of the United States, in the similar case of Brown *v.* Duchesne,[1] held directly the opposite opinion.

In Munz *v.* Grenfell,[2] an injunction was granted against one who had entered into partnership with the patentee for the joint prosecution of business connected with the invention, and then broken off, to patentee's detriment. The plaintiff was, however, ordered to bring an action at law.

Bewley *v.* Hancock [3] presents us with the case of four persons who, having taken out patents relative to the manufacture of goods from gutta-percha, entered into an agreement "that all patents taken out or in the course of being taken out by any or either of them, or on account of and for the benefit of any or either of them, in relation to the preparation or application of gutta-percha, or the manufacture of any articles therefrom, should be assigned to trustees and held for their joint account." Subsequently, one of the parties took out a patent for an apparatus and machinery for giving shape and configuration to elastic substances, and applied it to coating telegraph wires with gutta-percha, but refused to make any assignment. It was held that he could be restrained, as well as compelled to make specific performance.

On the other hand, in the very recent case of Mathers *v.* Green,[4] the Lord Chancellor decided, on appeal from the Master of the Rolls, that, in the absence of clear and unmistakable evidence of an agreement or contract between joint grantees or patentees, one of such patentees was not entitled to a share in the profits made by another in granting licenses. "The letters-patent grant to the three, their executors, administrators, and assigns, that they and every one of them, by themselves, their servants and agents, or such others as they may agree with, and no others, shall, for the term of fourteen years, use, exercise, and vend the same invention. The right conferred is a right to exclude all the world, other than the grantees, from using the

1 19 How. 183 (affirming 2 Curtis, C. C. 371).

2 2 Webs. Pat. Cas. 88.

3 35 E. L. & Eq. 545.

4 1 Law Rep. Eq. Ser. 29 (1865).

invention. But there is no exclusion in the letters-patent of any one of the patentees. The inability of any one of the patentees to use the invention, if any such inability exists, must be sought elsewhere than in the letters-patent. But there is no principle, in the absence of contract, which can prevent any persons not prohibited by statute from using any invention whatever. Is there, then, any implied contract, where two or more persons jointly obtain letters-patent, that no one of them shall use the invention without the consent of the others, or that if he does, he shall use it for their joint benefit. I can discover no principle for such a doctrine. It would enable one of two patentees either to prevent the use of the invention altogether, or else to compel the other patentee to risk his skill and capital in the use of the invention on the terms of being accountable for half the profit, if profit should be made, without being able to call on his co-patentee for contribution, if there should be loss. This would be placing the parties in a relation to each other which I think no court can assume to have been intended in the absence of express contract to that effect."

Similar language is used by Curtis, J., in Clum *v.* Brewer.[1] "One tenant in common has as good a right to use and to license third persons to use the thing patented as the other tenant has. Neither can come into a court of equity and assert a superior equity, unless it has been created by some contract modifying the rights which belong to them as tenants in common."

§ 406. II. *The Bill.* — A bill for an injunction to restrain the infringement of a patent, after the address to the court and the statement of the parties, should recite the application for the letters-patent, by the inventor, and the compliance by him with all the prerequisites for obtaining them, and the issue of the letters, giving the title as it is contained in them, *verbatim*, their attestation by the proper officers, and their delivery to the patentee. Profert of the letters should be made, but it is not necessary to set forth the description of the invention given in the specification.[2] It is necessary, however, to state that the plaintiff, after the issuing of the patent, put his invention into use, and is, at the time of filing the bill, in the exclusive possession of it.[3] If the

[1] 2 Curtis, C. C. 506.

[2] Kay *v.* Marshall, 1 Mylne & Cr. 373; Westhead *v.* Keene, 1 Beav. 287.

[3] Isaacs *v.* Cooper, 4 Wash. 259.

bill is brought upon the title of an assignee, either of the whole or a part of the interest, or of an administrator, or if the patent has been renewed, or extended, or amended by a disclaimer, the facts should be properly set forth, to show the present state of the title and the right for which protection is asked. The bill should further state the infringement complained of, whether it has been actually committed or is threatened; and if the right has been previously established by an action at law, against the same or any other party, or an injunction has been previously obtained against the same or any other party, the fact should be set forth.[1] These averments are usually followed by a statement that the defendant has been requested to desist from the use of the invention, and to account for the damages which the plaintiff has sustained. Then follows the charge of actual combination by the defendant with others, if the facts require it, and of a conspiracy, if one is intended to be proved, to destroy the plaintiff's exclusive privilege. The prayer of the bill is for a discovery upon oath and particular answers to the interrogatories, which should be pointed at all the previous material averments in the bill, for a general answer to the bill, for decree that the defendant account for and pay over the gains and profits which have accrued to him from using the invention for an injunction to restrain the defendant from the further use of the invention, and to compel the delivery or destruction of the machines or other things which he has made, and for further relief. The prayer should close with asking for a writ of injunction, and a subpœna. The bill should be sworn to by the usual affidavit.

The omission of the oath is not, however, a ground for demurrer after a hearing and order to file evidence. The objection should be made by motion, on the appearance of the respondents, when the oath will be directed, unless good cause to the contrary be shown.[2]

§ 407. It may often be a serious question, whether an original bill filed for an injunction and other relief is affected by a subsequent surrender and renewal of the patent, pending the proceedings. In a case where this had happened, and a temporary

[1] See the observations of Mr. Justice Story, cited from Woodworth *v.* Stone, *post.* See also Orr *v.* Littlefield, 1 Woodb. & M. 13.

[2] Woodworth *v.* Edwards, 3 Woodb. & M. 120.

injunction had been granted on the original bill, in which the patentee and certain assignees were plaintiffs, and upon the new patent a supplemental bill was filed against the defendant for the continuance of the injunction and other relief, the injunction was ordered to stand continued, as to the new patent, stated in the supplemental bill, until the hearing or further order. Hence it appears that, when a patent is surrendered and renewed, pending a temporary injunction, a supplemental bill is necessary, in order to continue the injunction as to the new patent.[1]

[1] Woodworth *v.* Stone, 3 Story's R. 749, 750. Story, J.: "If the present case had stood merely upon the original bill, it appears to me clear, that the motion to dissolve the injunction granted upon that bill ought to prevail, because, by the surrender of the patent, upon which that bill is founded, the right to maintain the same would be entirely gone. I agree that it is not in the power of the patentee, by a surrender of his patent, to affect the rights of third persons, to whom he has previously, by assignment, passed his interest in the whole or a part of the patent, without the consent of such assignees. But, here, the supplemental bill admits that the assignees, who are parties to the original and supplemental bill, have consented to such surrender. They have, therefore, adopted it, and it became theirs in the same manner as if it had been their personal act and done by their authority.

"The question, then, is precisely the same as if the suit were now solely in behalf of the patentee. In order to understand with clearness and accuracy some of the objections to the continuance of the injunction, it may be necessary to state that the original patent to William Woodworth (the inventor), who is since deceased, was granted on the 27th of December, 1828. Subsequently, under the eighteenth section of the act of 1836, c. 357, the commissioner of patents, on the 16th of November, 1842, recorded the patent in favor of William W. Woodworth, the administrator of William Woodworth (the inventor), for seven years from the 27th of December, 1849 (to which time the renewed patent extended); and the commissioner of patents was directed to make a certificate of such extension in the name of the administrator of William Woodworth (the inventor), and to append an authenticated copy thereof to the original letters-patent, whenever the same shall be requested by the said administrator or his assigns. The commissioner of patents, accordingly, on the 3d of March, 1845, at the request of the administrator, made such certificate on the original patent. On the 8th of July, 1845, the administrator surrendered the renewed patent granted to him 'on account of a defect in the specification.' The surrender was accepted, and a new patent was granted on the same day to the administrator, reciting the preceding facts, and that the surrender was 'on account of a defective specification,' and declaring that the new patent was extended for fourteen years from the 27th of December, 1828, 'in trust for the heirs at law of the said William Woodworth (the inventor), their heirs, administrators, or assigns.'

"Now, one of the objections taken to the patent is that it is for the term

By supplemental bill the plaintiff may also bring in new parties and enlarge the charges contained in the original bill.[1]

of fourteen years, and not for the term of seven years, or for two successive terms of seven years. But it appears to me that this objection is not well founded, and stands *inter Apices juris;* for the new patent should be granted for the whole term of fourteen years from the 27th of December, and the legal effect is the same as it would be if the patent was specifically renewed for two successive terms of seven years. The new patent is granted for the unexpired term only, from the date of the grant, viz., for the unexpired period existing on the 8th of July, 1845, by reference to the original grant in December, 1828. It is also suggested that the patent ought not to have been in trust for the heirs at law of the said William Woodworth, their heirs, administrators, or assigns. But this is, at most, a mere verbal error, if indeed it has any validity whatsoever ; for the new patent will, by operation of law, enure to the sole benefit of the parties, in whose favor the law designed it should operate, and not otherwise. It seems to me that the case is directly within the purview of the tenth and thirteenth sections of the act of 1836, c. 357, taking into consideration their true intent and objects.

"Another objection urged against the continuation of the injunction is, that the breach of the patent assigned in the original bill can have no application to the new patent, and there is no ground to suggest that, since the injunction was granted, there has been any new breach of the old patent, or any breach of the new patent. But it is by no means necessary that any such new breach should exist. The case is not like that of an action at law for the breach of a patent, to support which it is indispensable to establish a breach before the suit was brought. But in a suit in equity, the doctrine is far otherwise. A bill will lie for an injunction, if the patent right is admitted or has been established upon well-grounded proof of an apprehended intention of the defendant to violate the patent right. A bill, *quia timet*, is an ordinary remedial process in equity. Now, the injunction already granted (supposing both patents to be for the same invention) is *primâ facie* evidence of an intended violation, if not of an actual violation. And the affidavit of James N. Buffum is very strong and direct evidence to this same effect.

"But the most material objection taken is, that the new patent is not for the same invention as that which has been surrendered. And, certainly, if this be correct, there is a fatal objection to the prolongation of the injunction. But is the objection well founded in point of fact? It is said that the present

---

[1] Parkhurst *v.* Kinsman, 2 Blatchf. 78. Here the supplementary defendant claimed to be *bonâ fide* purchaser from the original defendant, and as such entitled to defend himself, without regard to the condition of such original defendant, who was precluded by his own agreement from denying the validity of the patent. But the court held, that the supplementary defendant had acquired his interest not merely *pendente lite*, but also with a full knowledge of the nature and state of the litigation, and therefore could take no higher rights than the original defendant possessed. The court added, that the plaintiff might even have enforced his decree without any supplementary bill.

§ 408. 3. *The Injunction.* — We have now to state, in the first place, the general principles on which courts of equity proceed in

patent is for a combination only, and that the old patent was for a combination and something more, or different. But I apprehend that, upon the face of the present patent, the question is scarcely open for the consideration of the court; and, at all events, certainly not open in this stage of the cause. I have already, in another cause, had occasion to decide, that where the commissioner of patents accepts a surrender of an old patent and grants a new one, under the act of 1836, c. 357, his decision, being an act expressly confided to him by law, and dependent upon his judgment, is not re-examinable elsewhere; and that the court must take it to be a lawful exercise of his authority, unless it is apparent upon the very face of the patent that he has exceeded his authority, and there is a clear repugnancy between the old and the new patent, or the new one has been obtained by collusion between the commissioner and the patentee. Now, upon the face of it, the new patent, in the present case, purports to be for the same invention, and none other, that is contained in the old patent. The avowed difference between the new and the old is, that the specification in the old is defective, and that the defect is intended to be remedied in the new patent. It is upon this very ground that the old patent was surrendered and the new patent was granted. The claim in the new patent is not of any new invention, but of the old invention more perfectly described and ascertained. It is manifest that, in the first instance, the commissioner was the proper judge whether the invention was the same or not, and whether there was any deficit in the specification or not, by inadvertence, accident, or mistake; and consequently he must have decided that the combination of machinery claimed in the old patent was, in substance, the same combination and invention claimed and described in the new. My impression is, that at the former trial of the old patent before me, I held the claim substantially (although obscurely worded) to be a claim for the invention of a particular combination of machinery for planing, tonguing, and grooving, and dressing boards, &c.; or, in other words, that it was the claim of an invention of a planing machine or planing apparatus such as he had described in his specification.

"It appears to me, therefore, that *primâ facie*, and, at all events, in this stage of the cause, it must be taken to be true, that the new patent is for the same invention as the old patent; and that the only difference is, not in the invention itself, but in the specification of it. In the old, it was defectively described and claimed. In the new, the defects are intended to be remedied. Whether they are effectually remedied is a point not now properly before the court. But as the commissioner of patents has granted the new patent as for the same invention as the old, it does not appear to me that this court is now at liberty to revise his judgment, or to say that he has been guilty of an excess of authority, at least (as has been already suggested), not in this stage of the cause; for that would be for the court of itself to assume to decide many matters of fact as to the specification and the combination of machinery in both patents, without any adequate means of knowledge or of guarding itself from gross error. For the purpose of the injunction, if for nothing

granting, continuing, or dissolving injunctions. To obtain an injunction, the plaintiff must accompany his application with an affidavit that he then believes himself to be the original and first inventor of the thing patented; for, it is said, although when he obtained his patent he might have very honestly sworn as to his belief of such being the fact, yet circumstances may have subsequently intervened, or information may have been communicated, sufficient to convince him that it was not his own original invention, and that he was under a mistake when he applied for his patent.[1] Such a special affidavit was required by Mr. Justice Washington to be subjoined to a bill.[2] And it is the usual practice, on moving for an injunction before the answer has been filed, to read such an affidavit, as well as others to the same purport.[3]

§ 409. In the courts of the United States, notice that an injunction is to be applied for must be served on the defendant, as no injunction, whether temporary or final, can be granted without reasonable previous notice to the adverse party or his attorneys, of the time and place of moving for the same.[4] Injunctions, therefore, are not granted in our courts on *ex parte* applications, in cases of patents, although they may be granted on filing the bill and before answer, on notice to the party to be affected, as well as after answer and upon the hearing.

In Bickford *v.* Skewes,[5] the vice-chancellor said that it was unusual to make an order for the indemnity of the defendant by the plaintiff in case the patent should not be sustained, adding that in one instance, Kay *v.* Marshall, where he had gone out of the way of the court to make such order, his order had been over-

else, I must take the invention to be the same in both patents, after the commissioner of patents has so decided, by granting the new patent.

"Upon the whole, therefore, I do order and direct, that the injunction do stand continued as to the new patent stated in the supplemental bill, until the hearing or further order of the court."

[1] Hill *v.* Thompson, 3 Meriv. 622, 624; Sturz *v.* De La Rue, 5 Russ. Ch. R. 322. The same reason exists at the time of the application, although the bill itself was sworn to when filed.

[2] Rogers *v.* Abbot, 4 Wash. 514; Ogle *v.* Edge, ibid. 584. See also Sullivan *v.* Redfield, 1 Paine, 441.

[3] See, further, as to affidavits, *post*, at the end of this chapter.

[4] Act 2d March, 1793, c. 22, § 5; Perry *v.* Parker, 1 Woodbury & M. 280, 281.

[5] 1 Webs. Pat. Cas. 214.

ruled on appeal. It results from this that courts of equity are loath to grant an injunction unless the plaintiff's right is very clear, especially in cases where an account will answer all reasonable purposes.

§ 410. The bill and the application being, then, in proper form, the first thing to be considered is, whether the court will require the patentee to establish his legal right by an action at law, before it grants the injunction, or whether it will grant the injunction, in the first instance, upon the proof of a legal right, furnished by the bill itself, and the accompanying affidavits. Upon this point, the rule, as it was laid down by Lord Eldon, is, that where a patent has been granted, and there has been an exclusive possession of some duration under it, the court will interpose its injunction, without putting the party previously to establish the validity of his patent by an action. Where the patentee has surrendered his original patent and taken out another one with an amended specification, the action of the commissioner in granting the subsequent patent is *primâ facie* evidence that the two patents are for the same invention, and can only be invalidated by clear proof of fraud, excess of authority, or manifest discrepancy.[1] But where the patent is but of yesterday, and, upon an application being made for an injunction, it is endeavored to be shown, in opposition to it, that there is no good specification, or otherwise, that the patent ought not to have been granted, the court will not, from its own notions upon the matter in dispute, act upon the presumed validity or invalidity of the patent, without the right having been ascertained by a previous trial, but will send the patentee to law to establish the validity of his patent in a court of law, before it will grant him the benefit of an injunction.[2]

§ 411. The rule thus stated has been followed by our own courts, with further explanations, which extend its application to the particular facts of the cases that have arisen. Thus, Mr. Justice Washington laid down the rule, as follows, that the practice is to grant an injunction upon the filing of the bill, and before a trial at law, if the bill state a clear right, and verify the same by affidavit. If the bill state an exclusive possession of the invention or discovery, an injunction is granted, although the court may feel

[1] Potter *v.* Holland, MS., per Ingersoll, J.

[2] Hill *v.* Thompson, 3 Meriv. 622, 624.

doubts as to the validity of the patent. But if the defects in the patent or specification are so glaring that the court can entertain no doubt as to that point, it would be most unjust to restrain the defendant from using a machine, or other thing, which he may have constructed, probably at great expense, until a decision at law can be had.[1] Upon another occasion, the same learned judge laid down the general rule in these terms, that, where the bill states a clear right to the thing patented, which, together with the alleged infringement, is verified by affidavit, if he has been in possession of it, by having used or sold it in part, or in the whole, the court will grant an injunction, and continue it till the hearing or further order, without sending the plaintiff to law to try the right. But, if there appeared to be a reasonable doubt as to the plaintiff's right, or as to the validity of the patent, the court will require the plaintiff to try his title at law, sometimes accompanied with an order to expedite the trial, and will permit him to return for an account, in case the trial at law should be in his favor. Mr. Justice Story, in Washburn *v.* Gould, referred to and adopted the general rule laid down by Lord Eldon, in Hill *v.* Thompson. In this case there had been a trial at law, which resulted in favor of the patentee.[2] Mr. Justice Woodbury has, in several cases, also acted upon it, with modifications, which will presently be stated.[3]

Where the defendant, in his answer, does not impeach the validity of the complainant's patent, but merely sets up a subsequent patent granted to himself, and denies that it is an infringement of the former one, the court is not precluded by the act of the commissioner in granting the subsequent patent without notice of interference to the prior patentee. According to the act of 1836, § 7, the commissioner of patents, when he thinks that there is a possibility of a patent interfering with one previously granted, must give notice to such prior patentee. But his action is not conclusive. For, says Kane, J., in giving the opinion of the court in Wilson *v.* Barnum:[4] "It cannot be asked that a third person shall have his legal rights impaired or his legal remedies impeded by any proceeding to which he was not made

[1] Isaacs *v.* Cooper, 4 Wash. 259, 260.

[2] 3 Story's R. 156, 169.

[3] Orr *v.* Littlefield, 1 Woodb. & M. 13; Woodworth *v.* Hall, ibid. 248; Hovey *v.* Stevens, ibid. 290. See also Sullivan *v.* Redfield, 1 Paine, 441.

[4] 1 Wallace, C. C. 347.

and could not have made himself a party. To hold ourselves concluded by the action of the Patent Office, where that action has been without notice, would be as perilous to the interest of inventors as to that of the public." The conclusion drawn by the learned judge was, that the grant of the subsequent patent, under such circumstances, served merely to indicate the opinion which highly respectable officers had formed on an *ex parte* examination of the subject, but was not a case where the action of the Patent Office was conclusive or even *primâ facie* evidence. In this case it was decided that the district judge, sitting for the circuit court and being well satisfied of the fact of infringement, may grant an interlocutory injunction, although a majority of the experts examined thought that there was no infringement.

§ 412. It appears, therefore, that, upon the question of first sending the plaintiff to law to try the validity of his patent, the general rule must be subdivided according to the aspect and position of the case before the court. The cases may be ranged under three different classes: *first*, where there is nothing before the court, as evidence, but the bill and the affidavits in support of it; *second*, where the injunction is asked before the final hearing, and the respondent offers evidence, either in the answer or by affidavits, affecting the validity of the patent; *third*, where the question comes on upon the hearing, and the full proofs taken in the cause.

§ 413. These different aspects of the cause may now be considered separately, with reference to this question. *First*, where the plaintiff asks for an injunction upon the bill and affidavits, and no opposing evidence is adduced, but the respondent appears and objects. In such cases, the bill and the affidavits must show the issuing of the patent, and an exclusive possession of the right of some duration; and, when these are shown, although the court may feel some doubts as to the validity of the patent, the injunction will be granted without a previous trial at law; but if the patent contains glaring defects, so that no doubt can be entertained, or the bill is defective in material allegations, the injunction will not be granted, but the plaintiff will be required to try his title at law.[1] Some additional evidence, besides the mere issue

[1] Hill *v.* Thompson, 3 Meriv. 622; Harmer *v.* Plane, 14 Ves. 130, 133; Isaacs *v.* Cooper, 4 Wash. 259; Ogle *v.* Edge, ibid. 584; Woodworth *v.* Hall, 1 Woodb. & M. 248. Length of enjoyment is to be looked to in answer to a

of the patent, must be offered; and this evidence will be the fact that, after he had procured his patent, the plaintiff proceeded to put that right into exercise or use for some time without being disturbed; a circumstance that strengthens the probability that the patent is good, and renders it so likely as alone often to justify the issue of an injunction in aid of it.[1] It will also be further additional evidence, in support of the *primâ facie* right to an injunction, that the patentee has successfully prosecuted other persons for violating it.[2]

If a patentee has established his title under original letters-patent, he is entitled to a temporary injunction under an extension of those letters-patent, without a trial at law or evidence of long possession.[3] Furthermore, where the right to a temporary injunction does not depend upon any controverted and doubtful facts, but upon the interpretation to be put upon a written instrument, it is the duty of the court to interpret it and to grant or refuse the injunction accordingly.[4]

With regard to the question of infringement, it may be added, that it is not sufficient to produce the machine of the plaintiff and that of the defendant and submit them to an examination and

theoretical objection to the specification. Bickford *v.* Skewes, Webs. Pat. Cas. 211, 213.

[1] Orr *v.* Littlefield, 1 Woodb. & M. 13, 16. As to length of possession, see the observations of Mr. Justice Woodbury, cited from this case, *post.*

[2] Ibid.

[3] Clum *v.* Brewer, 2 Curtis, C. C. 506.

[4] Ibid. "There may be cases in which there is so much doubt what the parties to an instrument intended to effect by it, that the court may think it proper to suspend its judgment until the surrounding circumstances can be more fully and safely examined on a final hearing. It is possible, also, that where there are grave doubts concerning the legal effect of an instrument, the court might decline to interfere by special injunction, even though, if compelled to decide, their decision must be in favor of the complainant. Probably the circumstances of the case, and the degree of mischief which would be suffered by refusing the injunction, compared with the inconvenience and loss occasioned by granting it, would control the action of the court in the case supposed. But, in general, I apprehend, if the title to a temporary injunction depends on the construction of a deed, the court will construe it, and act accordingly, whatever view of that question the answer may have presented." Per Curtis, J. It may be well to add, by way of explanation, that the instrument in discussion was a deed of articles of agreement under the patent, and that the defendants claimed under a license from one of the grantees.

comparison by the court; at least where such a comparison would involve more than the usual amount of mechanical knowledge.[1]

§ 414. *Secondly*, where the injunction is asked for before the hearing, but opposing evidence is adduced by the respondent against the validity of the patent. In these cases, several elements enter into the rule that is to guide the discretion of the court. How far, and for what length of time, there has been an exclusive possession or assertion of the right; how far the respondent has succeeded in raising doubts as to the novelty of the invention, or as to its being a patentable subject, or as to the infringement; and how far a long possession will go to counteract evidence impeaching the validity of the patent, — are some of the circumstances to be weighed in determining whether the plaintiff's *primâ facie* right to an injunction has been answered by the respondent, to that extent that the court will suspend the injunction until the plaintiff has established his right by an action. It seems to be the result of all the authorities that there is a *primâ facie* right to an injunction, without a trial at law, upon certain things being shown, namely, a patent, long possession, and infringement.[2] The question will therefore be, in cases of opposing evidence, where that right has been shown, whether it has been displaced by the respondent.

Where the patentee has made a partial assignment and entered into an agreement with the assignee in the nature of a copartnership, the assignee cannot, in a bill for an injunction, deny the validity of the patent, or set up in defence an outstanding patent which he has bought up from some third party, by way of impeaching the originality.[3]

[1] Per Sprague, J., Howe *v.* Morton *et al.*, MS.

[2] In Neilson *v.* Thompson, Webs. Pat. Cas. 277, Sir L. Shadwell, V. C., said: "It seems to me, on these affidavits, that it is sufficiently made out that there has been a use of the patent in this sense, that the right of the patentee to the benefit of the patent has been submitted to where there has been a contest, and it does not at all appear to me that the general way in which the defendants, on their affidavit, state the mode by means of which the plaintiffs succeeded in establishing the patent, is at all an answer to the two cases which are stated in Mr. Blunt's affidavit. Then I have the case of a patent having been obtained in the year 1828, and actually enjoyed by the patentee for upwards of twelve years. *Primâ facie*, I apprehend, that gives a right to the patentee to come into court in a case in which he can show an infringement; and the question is, has there been an infringement?"

[3] Kinsman *v.* Parkhurst, 18 How. 289.

§ 415. When the presumption in favor of the validity of the patent has been strengthened by evidence of enjoyment and possession undisturbed for several years, and recoveries against other persons for violating it, it will not be sufficient to deprive the plaintiff of the injunction before a trial at law, for the defendant to read affidavits tending to cast doubts on the originality of the invention, especially if that evidence is answered by what is stronger on the part of the patentee.[1]

[1] Orr *v.* Littlefield, 1 Woodb. & M. 13. In this case, Mr. Justice Woodbury said: "It is not enough that a party has taken out a patent, and thus obtained a public grant, and the sanction or opinion of the Patent Office, in favor of his right, though that opinion, since the laws were passed, requiring some examination into the originality and utility of inventions, possesses more weight. But the complainant must furnish some further evidence of a probable right; and though it need not be conclusive evidence, else additional hearing on the bill would thus be anticipated and superseded, yet it must be something stronger than the mere issue, however careful and public, of the patent, conferring an exclusive right; as, in doing that, there is no opposing party, no notice, no long public use, no trial with any one of his rights. The kind of additional evidence is this: if the patentee, after the procurement of his patent, conferring an exclusive right, proceeds to put that right into exercise or use for some years, without its being disturbed, that circumstance strengthens much the probability that the patent is good, and renders it so likely, as alone often to justify the issue of an injunction in aid of it. Ogle *v.* Edge, 4 Wash. C. C. 584; 2 Story's Eq. Jur. 210; Drew on Injunc. 222; Phil. on Pat. 462. After that, it becomes a question of public policy, no less than private justice, whether such a grant of a right exercised and in possession so long, ought not to be protected until avoided by a full hearing and trial. Harmer *v.* Plane, 14 Ves. 130.

"In this case, the evidence is plenary and uncontradicted, as to the use and sale of this patent, by the inventor and his representative, for several years, publicly and without dispute. Computing from the original grant, the time is over nine years, and since the reisssue of the letters-patent it is nearly three. I concur in the opinion delivered by Judge Sprague, in Orr *v.* Badger, that the time to be regarded under this view is what has elapsed since the original issue or grant. Law Reporter for February, 1845. In Thompson *v.* Hill, 3 Meriv. 622, the time was only three years from the first grant. In Ogle *v.* Edge, 4 Wash. C. C. 584, it was but six years. And though, in some cases reported, it had been thirteen, and in others twenty years (14 Ves. 120), yet it is believed that seldom has a court refused an injunction in applications like this, on account of the shortness of time after the grant, however brief, if long enough to permit articles or machines to be constructed by the patentee in conformity to his claim, and to be sold publicly, and repeatedly, and they have been so used and sold, under the patent, without dispute. Here the sales were extensive and profitable, from 1836, downwards, and the right as

§ 416. But when an injunction is asked before the trial and resisted, and doubts are cast on the originality and validity of

well as the possession does not appear to have been contested till 1842. In Hill *v.* Thompson, 3 Meriv. 622, 624, it is true that the court dissolved an injunction when only about one year had elapsed since any work had been completed under the patent, and only two years since the specification was filed, the chancellor calling it a patent 'but of yesterday,' but he added that he would not dissolve it if 'an exclusive possession of some duration' had followed; though an answer had been put in denying all equity, and doubts existed as to the validity of the patent, and no sales under it were proved in that case. So, though the patent had been issued thirteen years, and the evidence is doubtful, as to *acquiescence* in the possession or use, an injunction may be refused. Collard *v.* Allison, 4 Mylne & Craig, 487. But in the present case, the acquiescence appears to have been for several years universal.

"Another species of evidence, beside the issue of the patent itself, and long use and possession under it, so as to render it probable the patent is good, and to justify an injunction, is the fact that if the patent becomes disputed, the patentee prosecutes for a violation of his rights, and recovers. Same authorities; Kay *v.* Marshall, 1 Mylne & Craig, 373. This goes upon the ground that he does not sleep over his claims or interests, so as to mislead others, and that, whenever the validity of his claim has been tried, he has sustained it as if good. But such a recovery is not regarded as binding the final rights of the parties in the bill, because the action was not between them; though, when the judgment is rendered without collusion or fraud, it furnishes to the world some strong as well as public assurance that the patent is a good one. In this view of the evidence of this character in the present action, it is not contradicted nor impaired at all by the judgments having been given on verdicts and defaults, under agreements. Such judgments, when, as is admitted here, not collusive, are as strong, if not stronger evidence of the patentee's rights, than they would have been if the claim was so doubtful as to be sent to a jury for decision, rather than to be so little doubtful as to be admitted or agreed to after being legally examined. Both of these circumstances, therefore, possession and judgments, unite in support of an injunction in the present case.

"The only answer to the motion, as made out on these grounds, is the evidence offered, by affidavits, on the part of the respondents, tending to cast doubt on the originality of the invention of the patentee. I say, tending to this, because some of the affidavits, at least, do not distinctly show that the persons making them intended to assert that the whole of any one of the combination of particulars contained in Dr. Orr's claim, in his specification, had been used before his patent issued; because they are counteracted by other testimony from the witnesses of the complainants, more explicit and in larger numbers; and because, in this preliminary inquiry, where the evidence is taken without the presence or cross-examination of the opposite party, it would be unsafe to settle and decide against the validity of the patent, when a full and formal trial of it is not contemplated till further progress is made

the patent, if the counterbalancing and fortifying circumstances of long possession, use, or sale to a considerable extent, and

in the case. All that is required in this stage is the presumption before named that the title is good. This presumption is stronger here than usual, as it arises from the issue of the patent, and an enjoyment and possession of it undisturbed for several years, beside the two recoveries against those charged with violating it.

"After these, other persons can, to be sure, contest the validity of the patent, when prosecuted either in equity or at law; but it is hardly competent for them to deprive the complainant of her right, thus acquired, to an injunction, or, in other words, to be protected in so long a use and possession, till her rights are disproved, after a full hearing; surely it is not reasonable to permit it when the affidavits of the respondents to invalidate or cast a shade over her right are met by that which is stronger, independent of the long possession, judgments, and presumptions before mentioned. But another objection has been urged in argument. When an answer to the bill denies all equity in it, the respondents contend that an injunction would be dissolved, and hence it ought not to be imposed, if the respondent denies equity by affidavit. This may be correct, in respect to injunctions termed *common*, as these affidavits and counter-affidavits are inadmissible. Eden, 117, 326. Yet, in these, the denial must be very positive and clear. Ward *v.* Van Bokkelen, 1 Paige, 100; Noble *v.* Wilson, ibid. 164. But the position cannot be correct in the case of injunctions called *special*, like the present one, and where facts and counter-evidence show the case to be different from what is disclosed in the affidavits, or an answer of the respondents alone. No usage or cases are found where the injunctions are dissolved, as a matter of course, on such answers, if the complainant has adduced auxiliary presumptions in favor of his right, like those in the present instance. On the contrary, the cases are numerous where the whole is regarded as still within the sound discretion of the court, whether to issue the injunction or refuse it; or, if issued, to dissolve or retain it. 3 Meriv. 622, 624; 2 Johns. Ch. R. 202; 3 Sumn. 74; Livingston *v.* Van Ingen, 9 Johns. R. 507, 570; Rodgers *v.* Rodgers, 1 Paige, 426. And where the complainant has made out not merely a grant of the patent, but possession and use, and sale under it, for some time, undisturbed, and beside this, a recovery against other persons using it, the courts have invariably held that such a strong color of title shall not be deprived of the benefit of an injunction till a full trial on the merits counteracts or annuls it. In several cases, where the equities of the bill were even denied, and in others, where strong doubts were raised, whether the patent could, in the end, be sustained as valid, the courts decided, that injunctions should issue under such circumstances, as have before been stated in favor of the plaintiff, till an answer or final hearing; or, if before issued, should not be dissolved till the final trial, and then cease, or be made perpetual, as the result might render just. The Chancellor, in Roberts *v.* Anderson, 2 Johns. Ch. R. 202, cites 2 Vesey, 19, and Wyatt's P. R. 236; Boulton *v.* Bull, 3 Ves. 140; Universities of Oxford and Cambridge *v.* Richardson, 6 Ves. 689, 705; Harmer *v.* Plane,

former recoveries under it, do not exist, the injunction will not be allowed before trial.[1]

§ 417. Where the patentee has been guilty of laches in not bringing his injunction bill, the court will not entertain a motion for an interlocutory injunction. Thus, where the bill was filed in July, and it appeared that the plaintiff wrote to the defendant in November of the year preceding, complaining of the infringement, and knew of the same even as far back as August of that year, a motion for an interlocutory injunction was dismissed.[2]

§ 418. If the respondent succeeds in raising doubts both as to the exclusive possession and as to the novelty of what is claimed, and the evidence on these points is conflicting, the injunction will be refused until a trial.[3]

§ 418 *a*. The issue of novelty may, in an injunction bill, be raised in a manner such as to warrant a peremptory refusal of the patentee's application, name'y, by the defendants alleging a so-called publication in law. This topic has already been fully discussed in the chapter on Action at Law, and the ruling of the Master of the Rolls quoted at length. Here we only purpose giving the words of the refusal: "I have now examined the affidavits in this case, and I find in them nothing to alter the opinion I have already expressed. I think it is clearly proved that the principle of these targets (plaintiffs') was first discovered by De

14 Ves. 130; and Hill *v*. Thompson, 3 Meriv. 622, 624." See also Sargent *v*. Seagrave, 2 Curtis, C. C. 553; Sargent *v*. Carter, 21 Mon. Law Rep. 651; Newall *v*. Wilson, 19 E. L. & Eq. 156, where it was held to be no acquiescence in an infringement, that the patentee had not caused a subsequent patent to be repealed by *scire facias*, such patent not having been put in use. Potter *v*. Holland, MS. per Ingersoll, J.

There was a case before Sir L. Shadwell, V. C., where a good deal of doubt, as to the originality of the invention, was raised, by the introduction of a former patent and specification, but the plaintiff had enjoyed uninterrupted possession for seven years; and the infringement being clearly shown, the injunction was granted before trial, and a trial ordered. Losh *v*. Hague, Webs. Pat. Cas. 200. In like manner, Mr. Justice Story held that the affidavit of a single witness, after long possession, and other recoveries on the patent, would not outweigh the oath of the patentee, and the general presumption arising from the grant of the patent. Woodworth *v*. Sherman, 3 Story's R. 171, 172. See also Orr *v*. Badger, 10 Law Reporter, 465.

[1] Hovey *v*. Stevens, 1 Woodb. & M. 290. The patent in this case had been issued less than a month before the infringement complained of.

[2] Bovill *v*. Crate, 1 Law Rep. Eq. 387.

[3] Collard *v*. Allison, 4 Mylne & Cr. 487, 488.

Brettes, was published in a foreign country by the Vicomte du Moncel, in his book, and that that book was afterwards sold and made common here in 1857. (The plaintiffs' specification was filed in 1860.) As *a question of law*, therefore, there was an actual publication of the plans claimed by the plaintiffs as theirs; and that question cannot obviously be affected by any consideration of the number of persons among the public who may have thought proper to avail themselves of the publication. It may be very hard on the plaintiffs, especially when they have taken every possible pains to ascertain whether their invention has been previously made public, to find that it has been anticipated; but still that will not alter the case. There will yet be the question — and, as in this case, the only one — whether the Vicomte du Moncel's book, having been sent, as it was, to this country for the purpose of sale, there was *in law a publication* of the plan claimed by the plaintiffs prior to their specification. As I have said, I think there was such a publication, and the decree must be in accordance with that view."[1]

On the other hand, in a case which at first would appear similar, but in which the questions of identity and sufficiency were as matters of fact involved, the Lord Chancellor said: —

"But it is contended that the invention is not new, and that the patent is therefore invalid, and reference is made, for the purpose of establishing this case, to a patent obtained by one Collins, as far back as 1800, the object of which was, among other things, to manufacture sheathing of a mixture of copper and zinc; but although this patent was obtained upwards of forty years ago, it does not appear that the article was ever introduced into use, or a single sheet of sheathing ever manufactured under it. If it ever attracted public notice, it appears to have been long since forgotten. I am satisfied, on the evidence, that it was unknown to Mr. Muntz at the time when he obtained his patent, and I am further satisfied the object would not have been accomplished by ordinary copper and zinc united according to Collins's process; that any attempt made to effect this would have failed, which may well account for no public use having been made during so long a period of this patent. It was said, indeed, by the defendants, that the sheathing manufactured by them was made

[1] Lang *v.* Gisborne, 6 Law Times, N. S. 771.

according to Collins's specification, but this sheathing appears to have been subjected to a third analysis, and it turns out to be composed of the purest copper and the purest zinc, in the same proportions as are recommended by Mr. Muntz in his specification. It follows, therefore, that the two component articles must either have originally been not of the ordinary, but of the purest quality, or, which appears from the evidence to have been the most probable case, that they must have been purified in the course of the process, by some mode which is not described or suggested in Collins's specification. As the evidence, therefore, does not satisfy me that sheathing could be manufactured according to the former patent, I do not consider the novelty of Mr. Muntz's specification successfully impeached by reference to that patent." [1]

§ 419. If the question of infringement is doubtful, it must be tried by a jury; and in a case of this kind, Sir L. Shadwell, V. C., dissolved an injunction, and ordered an action to be brought to try the infringement, the respondents being ordered to keep an account, and to admit the plaintiff's title to the patent.[2] The same rule would be applicable to the granting an injunction in the first instance.

Thus, in an injunction bill arising under Muntz's patent, Vice-Chancellor Shadwell said, that, although he would not then put any construction on the patent, it was impossible not to see that the rolling hot was a material feature in the invention; and as the defendants did not roll hot, he would not grant the injunction, but would leave the plaintiff to his action.[3]

It is, however, for the court alone to decide whether there is any doubt as to the matter of infringement, and the granting of a feigned issue is not a matter of right. Thus, in the case of Van Hook *v.* Pendleton,[4] a motion for a feigned issue was denied. Nelson, J., said: "If we do not entertain doubts on that question (of infringement), it will be our duty to decide it; for we are not aware of any principle that will justify us in sending the case to a jury, unless we shall be brought to doubt on the question of identity." Similarly, Betts, J.: "It is not a matter of

[1] Muntz *v.* Foster, 2 Webs. Pat. Cas. 95.
[2] Morgan *v.* Seaward, 1 Webs. Pat. Cas. 167.
[3] Muntz *v.* Vivian, 2 Webs. Pat. Cas. 87.
[4] 2 Blatchf. 87.

course to order a feigned issue; but the party applying must lay a foundation for it. . . . A feigned issue is not to be granted unless the opinion of a jury on the question is found to be needed. And after a jury shall have passed upon the matter, it will be for the court to say, whether the verdict is right, and the court may set it aside."[1]

§ 420. It seems, also, that another element to be considered is the effect of the injunction on the defendant's business. As the granting of an injunction rests in the discretion of the court exercised upon all the circumstances of the case; and as the object of the injunction is to prevent mischief, it is said that where irreparable mischief would ensue from it to the defendant, it ought not to be granted.[2] But this must be understood as applying to a case where the plaintiff would not be injured by the delay, but would be left in *statu quo* after a trial establishing the validity of his patent; or at least, where the rights of the plaintiff are capable of being fully protected by an account to be kept in the interim; because the object of the court is to preserve to each party the benefit to which he is entitled.

The ruling of Judge Curtis, in the case of Forbush *v.* Bradford,[4] contains a full and clear enunciation of the doctrines of equity applicable to such cases: "In acting on applications for temporary injunctions to restrain the infringement of letters-patent, there is much latitude for discretion. The application may be granted or refused unconditionally, or terms may be imposed on either party as conditions for making or refusing the order. And the state of the litigation, where the plaintiff's title is denied, the nature of the improvement, the character and extent of the infringement complained of, and the comparative inconvenience which will be occasioned to the respective parties, by allowing or denying the motion, must all be considered in determining whether it shall be allowed or refused, and if at all, whether absolutely or upon some and what conditions. In this case the thing patented is an improvement on a loom. The loom itself is not claimed; but only a particular modification of a loom already in use.

[1] Compare, *infra*, Goodyear *v.* Day, 2 Wall. C. C. 283.

[2] Neilson *v.* Thompson, Webs. Pat. Cas. 278, 286.

[3] Ibid.

[4] 21 Mon. Law Rep. 471.

"The defendants in these cases do not make and sell looms having the patented improvement; they only use in their mills a certain number of such looms. The complainants are makers of looms, but do not use them. So that this particular mode of infringement, by the use of the thing patented, though it is a violation of the exclusive right claimed by the complainants, does not deprive them of a monopoly which they desire to retain in their own hands, because, practically, it deprives them only of what they would be entitled to receive for a license to use the thing patented, nor does it, like the manufacture and sale of the thing patented, constantly widen the field of litigation, and render it more and more difficult for the complainants to vindicate their rights.

"On the other hand, the defendants cannot be prohibited from using the thing patented without, at the same time, being deprived of the use of the entire loom. For though it is possible to alter the looms and work them without the patented improvement, it is shown that, in the present state of the business, and while this litigation is pending, no prudent man would do this. The practical effect of an injunction would, therefore, be to stop all these looms, and thus deprive the defendants of the use of a large amount of capital lawfully invested, and which they have the right to the benefit of; and it would also throw out of employment a large number of operatives who are now engaged in running the looms, and in the processes of manufacture which depend upon their use. All this would not prevent the court from granting an injunction, if the right had been finally established at law. But a bill of exceptions has been taken, upon points which involve the validity of the patent. This again does not present an insuperable objection to a temporary injunction. The court is bound to exercise its own judgment upon the questions involved in the bill of exceptions, with a view to see whether the litigation that remains presents such serious doubts concerning the title as ought to influence its judgment in granting or withholding the injunction. I can conceive of many cases in which a temporary injunction ought to issue, where there has been a trial at law and a bill of exceptions taken, even though serious questions are raised, upon which the court of errors may reverse the judgment.[1] And *à fortiori*, when the

[1] Budson *v.* Benecke, 12 Beavan, 1. See further on the subject of prelim-

court that tried the cause, and is applied to for an injunction, is fully satisfied of the correctness of its judgment. But even in such a case, when the bill of exceptions is not merely frivolous, as the litigation is not in fact terminated, and its result may be adverse to the complainant's title, it is necessary for the court to contemplate that as a possible result, and look at the consequences in that event of allowing or refusing the injunction.

"Upon the particular facts of these cases, I am of opinion that an injunction should issue, unless, within ten days after notice of the order, the defendants shall give a bond with sufficient surety, to be judged of by the clerk of this court, conditioned to keep an account of the quantity of cloth made on each of the looms in question, and to file such account under oath, once in three months in the clerk's office of this court, and to pay the amount of any final decree in the cause."

§ 421. Nor will an injunction be granted, where the plaintiff has permitted the defendant to go on and incur expense under the expectation of receiving a certain sum, if the relations between them are such as to allow of the defendant's disputing the plaintiff's right as patentee.[1] But it seems that where the defendant is estopped at law from denying the validity of the patent, an injunction will be granted; but if there is a real question to be tried, and a year's rent for the use of the invention is due, the court will order the money to be paid into court, to wait the event of the trial.[2]

Where it appeared that the defendant was engaged in fulfilling a contract which was confessedly in violation of the patentee's right, but into which he (defendant) entered with the implied understanding that the question between him and the patentee was to be merely one of damages, it was held that no injunction ought to issue restraining him from completing the contract.[3]

§ 422. If the plaintiff shows the necessary possession, and an infringement has actually been committed by the defendant, the

inary injunctions after a trial and questions arising thereon, Morris *v.* Lowell Manuf. Co., 3 Fisher's Pat. Cas. 67.

[1] Neilson *v.* Thompson, Webs. Pat. Cas. 278, 286.

[2] Neilson *v.* Fothergill, Webs. Pat. Cas. 287, 289, 290. See further as to injunctions against licensees, *post.* As to effect of previous compromise between patentee and alleged defendant, see Sargent *v.* Larned, 2 Curtis, C. C. 340.

[3] Smith *v.* Sharp Manuf. Co., 3 Blatchf. 545.

injunction will be granted, notwithstanding the defendant admits the infringement and promises not to repeat it.[1]

Furthermore, in an application for an injunction, it is not a sufficient answer to allege that the infringement has been discontinued, without offering compensation for such unlawful use.[2]

§ 423. *Third.* — The third class of cases is where the question of granting the injunction comes on upon the final hearing; and here the situation of the parties is entirely different from the state of things on an interlocutory motion. The object of a bill in equity to protect a patent is a perpetual injunction; and this in general can only be granted at the hearing; and if granted at the hearing, it will necessarily be perpetual. Objections raised by the defendant, therefore, to the validity of the patent, at the hearing, require a very different consideration from the court; because the question is, whether the court will give any assistance to a party, who might have applied for an interlocutory hearing, and so have given the defendant an opportunity to have the legal title investigated, but has not done so. In such cases, where there are no circumstances shown which would have prevented the plaintiff from asking for an injunction in the progress of the cause, it will not only not be granted at the hearing, but the bill will be dismissed with costs, if it has been pending for a long time, and the answer had denied the validity of the patent and the fact of infringement.[3]

[1] Losh *v.* Hague, 1 Webs. Pat. Cas. 200. Sir L. Shadwell, V. C.: "It really seems to me that this is a case in which I must grant the injunction, because, as I understand it, the wheels that the defendant has made are certainly wheels made according to that thing for which, as I understand it, the plaintiff has taken out his patent, — the substance of part of the patent being for making wheels that shall have the spoke and the felloe in parts of the same piece, that is, in other words, the spoke is to be made with an elbow bend, which elbow bend will constitute a part of the felloes. Now it seems to me that there can be no question, but that the wheels complained of as having been made by the defendant do answer the description of the plaintiff's wheels, and I do not think it enough, on a question of injunction, for the defendant to say why he has done the thing complained of, but will not do it again. That is not the point, because, if a threat had been used, and the defendant revokes the threat, that I can understand as making the plaintiff satisfied; but if once the thing complained of has been done, I apprehend this court interferes, notwithstanding any promise the defendant may make not to do the same thing again."

[2] Sickels *v.* Mitchell, 3 Blatchf. 548.

[3] Bacon *v.* Jones, 4 Mylne & Cr. 433. In this case Lord Cottenham said:

§ 424. The next question is, supposing that an injunction is not to be granted *simpliciter*, what course is to be taken. This part

"Generally speaking, a plaintiff who brings his cause to a hearing is expected to bring it on in such a state as will enable the court to adjudicate upon it, and not in a state in which the only course open is to suspend any adjudication until the party has had an opportunity of establishing his title by proceedings before another tribunal. And I think the court would take a very improper course, if it were to listen to a plaintiff who comes forward at the hearing, and asks to have his title put in a train for investigation, without stating any satisfactory reason why he did not make the application at an earlier stage. When he comes forward upon an interlocutory motion, the court puts the parties in the way of having their legal title investigated and ascertained; but when a plaintiff has neglected to avail himself of the opportunity thus afforded, it becomes a mere question of discretion, how far the court will assist him at the hearing, or whether it will then assist him at all.

"If, indeed, any circumstances had occurred to deprive him of that opportunity in the progress of the cause, the question might have been different. But in this case I have not heard any reason suggested why the plain and ordinary course was not taken by the plaintiffs of previously establishing their right at law. They might have brought their action before filing the bill, or they might, after the bill was on the file, have had their right put in a train for trial. Instead of that, they have allowed the suit to remain perfectly useless to them for the last four years. They knew of the alleged infringement in the month of August, 1835; and from that time till the hearing there was no moment at which they might not, by applying to the court, have had liberty to bring an action to establish their title at law. It is obvious that such a line of proceeding exposes a defendant to inconveniences which are by no means necessary for the protection of the plaintiff. It is no trifling grievance to have a chancery suit hanging over him for four years, in which, if the court shall so determine at the hearing, he will have to account for all the profits he has been making during the intermediate period. Is a defendant to be subject to this annoyance without any absolute necessity, or even any proportionate advantage to his adversary, and without that adversary being able to show any reason why he did not apply at an earlier time. It appears to me that it would be very injurious to sanction such a practice, more especially when I can find no case in which the court has thought it right to retain a bill, simply for the purpose of enabling a plaintiff to do that which these plaintiffs might have done at any time within the last four years. It was much more regular and proper that the plaintiffs should have taken steps for putting the legal right in a course of trial. Those steps they have not chosen to take, and it is now impossible to put the defendants in the same position in which they would have stood if such a course had been originally adopted.

"For these reasons, I am of opinion that the Master of the Rolls, finding that the evidence in the cause was not such as he could act upon with safety, came, in the exercise of his discretion, to a sound conclusion, when he refused to grant the injunction or retain this bill. I have purposely abstained from

of the subject embraces the cases where the plaintiff will be sent to try his title at law, without an injunction; and the cases where an injunction will be granted, but the plaintiff will be required to establish his patent at law. The plaintiff will be sent to a court of law to establish the validity of his patent without a previous injunction, if he does not show long possession and exercise of his exclusive right, where the injunction is resisted by evidence which casts doubt on the originality of his invention, or on the question of infringement, or where the patent contains gross and obvious defects.[1]

In a motion for an interlocutory injunction, the defendant, claiming under a patent subsequent to that of the plaintiff, cannot set up the action of the commissioner in granting his own patent as a bar upon the issue of infringement, where the commissioner had given no notice of interference to the prior patentee. In some respects, it is true, the action of the commissioner has a quasi-judicial character; but where he perceives no interference and issues no notice to the prior patentee, such patentee is not bound by his subsequent action. His grant of letters-patent to the subsequent patentee is nothing more than an *ex parte* opinion formed by a highly respectable and intelligent officer.[2]

In Sickels *v.* Young,[3] the court ruled that a motion for a preliminary injunction was not to be granted unless the right was clear in favor of the complainants, and that it, the court, was not even bound by the verdict of a jury appointed to try the special issue of infringement, where the evidence was very conflicting.

§ 425. With regard to the length of time during which possession and exercise of the exclusive right must be shown, it does not appear that any specific lapse of time has been adopted as a

saying any thing as to the legal rights of the parties, because I do not think the case in such a state as to enable me to adjudicate upon it. The appeal must be dismissed with costs."

[1] Hovey *v.* Stevens, 1 Woodb. & M. 290; Ogle *v.* Edge, 4 Wash. 584; Collard *v.* Allison, 4 Mylne & Cr. 488; Morgan *v.* Seaward, Webs. Pat. Cas. 167. By defects is to be understood such as raise doubts as to the merits, — that is, the originality or usefulness of the patent, or the patentee's own error in the specification. Woodworth *v.* Hall, 1 Woodb. & M. 400. As to defects arising from the acts of public officers, see *post*.

[2] Wilson *v.* Barnum, 1 Wall. C. C. 347.

[3] Sickels *v.* Young, 3 Blatchf. 293.

standard; and, indeed, it is manifest that no positive rule can be assumed, applicable to all cases. The general principle is, as we have seen, that the time elapsed between the granting of the patent and the application for an injunction must have been sufficient to have permitted articles or machines to be constructed by the patentee in conformity with his claim, and to be sold publicly and repeatedly.[1] It must also appear, that the thing has in fact been sold publicly, if that is the kind of possession relied on;[2] and where the proof of possession consists of former recoveries, or licenses granted to parties who have been sued and have submitted, if it appears doubtful whether such recoveries and submissions were not collusively obtained, the necessary kind of possession will not be made out, and the right will first have to be tried at law.[3] But it does not impair the effect of such recoveries or submissions, that they were obtained by agreement and without trial, if there was at first a real contest.[4]

§ 426. Where, however, former use or former recoveries are relied upon, as proof of the possession of the exclusive right, they must have been under the same patent, or under a patent connected in law with that under which the application is made; otherwise it will not appear that they related to the same right.[5] But under our system of amending specifications, or of surrender-

[1] See the observations of the court, cited *ante*, from Orr *v.* Littlefield, 1 Woodb. & M. 13, 17.

[2] Ibid.; Hovey *v.* Stevens, 1 Woodb. & M. 290, 303.

[3] Collard *v.* Allison, 4 Mylne & Cr. 487, 488; Kay *v.* Marshall, 1 Mylne & Cr. 373; Orr *v.* Badger, 10 Law Reporter, 465; Orr *v.* Littlefield, 1 Woodb. & M. 13, 17, 18.

[4] Orr *v.* Littlefield, 1 Woodb. & M. 13, 17, 18; Orr *v.* Badger, 10 Law Rep. 465. In Neilson *v.* Thompson, Webs. Pat. Cas. 275, 276, the plaintiff's solicitor proved the preparation and granting of fifty or sixty licenses, and also various infringements by parties who submitted and took a license on proceedings being commenced against them. Sir L. Shadwell, V. C., said: "It seems to me, on these affidavits, that it is sufficiently made out that there has been a use of the patent in this sense, that the right of the patentee to the benefit of the patent has been submitted to where there has been a contest, and it does not at all appear to me that the general way in which the defendants on their affidavit state the mode by means of which the plaintiffs succeeded in establishing the patent is at all an answer to the two cases which are stated in Mr. Blunt's affidavit. Then I have the case of a patent having been obtained in the year 1828, and actually enjoyed by the patentee for upwards of twelve years."

[5] Hovey *v.* Stevens, 1 Woodb. & M. 290.

ing an old patent and taking out a new one on account of informalities, the right in contemplation of law remains the same, after the issue of the new patent, if it is in fact for the same invention; and, consequently, a former possession under the old patent will be ground for granting an injunction, without a previous trial, under the amended patent.[1] Usually, where an injunction is not granted, but the plaintiff is required to establish his title at law, the defendant will be ordered to keep an account until the question is determined.[2]

§ 427. The cases where an injunction will be granted, but the plaintiff will be required to establish his patent at law, do not admit of any very precise classification under a distinct rule. The court must exercise its discretion upon the circumstances.[3]

1 Orr *v.* Badger, 10 Law R. 465.

2 See *post*, as to the account.

3 In Harmer *v.* Plane, 14 Ves. 130, 131, Lord Eldon thus explained the grounds on which an injunction should be granted in cases where there is so much doubt as to require further investigation. "The ground upon which, where doubt is excited in the mind of the court, an injunction is granted until the legal question can be tried, a ground that was acted upon in the case of Boulton *v.* Watt (Boulton *v.* Bull, 2 Hen. Black. 453; 3 Ves. 140; Hornblower *v.* Boulton, 8 Term Rep. 95; Hill *v.* Thompson, 3 Mer. 622), in some cases preceding that, and some that have occurred since, is this: Where the crown on behalf of the public grants letters-patent, the grantee, entering into a contract with the crown, the benefit of which contract the public are to have, and the public have permitted a reasonably long and undisputed possession under color of the patent, the court has thought, upon the fact of that possession proved against the public, that there is less inconvenience in granting the injunction until the legal question can be tried, than in dissolving it at the hazard, that the grant of the crown may in the result prove to have been valid. The question is not really between the parties on the record; for, unless the injunction is granted, any person might violate the patent, and the consequence would be that the patentee must be ruined by litigation. In the case of Boulton and Watt, therefore, though a case of great doubt, upon which some of the ablest judges in Westminster Hall disagreed, yet upon the ground of the possession by the patentees against all mankind, the injunction was granted until the question could be tried; and the result of the trial, being in favor of the patent, proved that the conduct of the court, in that instance, was at least fortunate.

"The first of these patents, granted in the 27th year of his present majesty, is expired, and the patent for the improvements was granted in the 34th Geo. III. The agreement entered into by this defendant for a license to work under the patentee, would not bind the defendant. If the plaintiff could not legally grant that license, there was no consideration; and the question between them,

If the plaintiff has, by proof of possession and enjoyment, made out a *primâ facie* case for an injunction, it will then be for the court to consider whether the nature of the case entitles the defendant to a farther investigation into the validity of the patent or into the fact of infringement. The defendant will have a right to farther investigation, if he shows that there are any questions of fact or of law which a court of equity does not ordinarily undertake to settle; and this investigation will generally be ordered to take place in an action at law, although it is competent for the court to direct an issue out of chancery.[1]

therefore, is entirely open. Still, however, the patentee has had possession against all the world; and if he can maintain its validity by a due performance of the condition as to enrolment of the specification, by dissolving the injunction in the mean time, I should act both against principle and practice; not only enabling this defendant against law to exercise a right in opposition to the patent, but also encouraging all mankind to take the same liberty."

[1] Harmer *v.* Plane, 14 Ves. 130, 131; Hill *v.* Thompson, 3 Meriv. 622, 630; Wilson *v.* Tindal, Webs. Pat. Cas. 730, note. In this case, Lord Langdale, M. R., said: "Having regard to the arguments on the validity of the patent, to the enjoyment of it by the plaintiffs, and to the evidence which appears upon the affidavits which have been made in this case, I am of opinion that the injunction which is applied for ought to be granted.

"The question for consideration is, whether any terms ought to be imposed upon the plaintiffs, or whether any other mode of investigating the facts than that which is adopted in the usual course of proceeding in this court, ought to be adopted. It is to be observed, that all orders made on applications of this kind are merely interlocutory orders; they do not bind the right between the parties. The injunction which I have stated it to be my intention to grant will be an injunction only until further order. It will not be a perpetual injunction; not an injunction to continue during the continuance of the patent. Notwithstanding this order, the defendant may put in his answer, he may displace all the affidavits which have been filed on both sides. The plaintiff and the defendant may respectively proceed to evidence, they may bring their cause on for a hearing, and upon the hearing of the cause, the whole case, the law regarding the patent, and the facts which will appear upon the depositions, will have to be reconsidered; and that reconsideration may, for any thing that can be known to the contrary, justly end in a result different from that which I have come to upon the present occasion.

"The defendant, having his option to adopt this course of proceeding, has at the bar expressed his desire to have this matter tried at law. If he was left merely to prosecute a *scire facias* for the repeal of the patent, that would be one part of the question which he might in that way try. But there are other questions subsisting between the parties regarding matters of fact, which could not be tried in that way.

"Now it has been stated by Lord Cottenham, that he recollected no in-

§ 428. Under our system it has been held, that, if the defendant wishes to have the question of originality tried by an issue out of chancery, he must set out in his answer the names of places and persons where and by whom the invention had previously been used, because the act of Congress peremptorily requires notice of these facts in a trial of this question at law.[1]

§ 429. In the previous editions of this work it was intimated that an injunction would not be granted without a trial at law, in cases where both parties claimed under patents, or where generally the question of novelty was directly at issue. The subsequent case of Goodyear *v.* Day[2] has, however, elicited from Judge Grier a ruling in direct opposition to such opinion. We state the case as it is given by the reporter, and quote also *in extenso* from the decision of the court: —

"The bill prayed a perpetual injunction. The answer denied the allegations, and concluded by praying 'a trial by jury of the various issues of fact formed by it.' The argument involved

stance in which the court has not adopted the course of directing the trial of an action; he has stated that to be the result of his experience. I certainly am very reluctant to try my own memory against that, but I should have supposed that there were instances in which that had been done. It is not the right of parties in every case to have an action tried in a court of law: it is a question of convenience, and the court is to exercise a fair discretion. I have no doubt, whatever, of the competency of this court to grant an injunction *simpliciter*. Neither had Lord Cottenham any doubt of it. But the question is, whether, when there is an opportunity for carrying the matter further, it is not, on the whole, a convenient course of proceeding to have it tried before the tribunal which is most proper for the consideration of the legal question, and by which the facts can be better investigated than they can here. It is not, therefore, upon the ground of any doubt as to the validity of the patent that I make the order which I am about to make, but it is because the nature of the case entitles the defendant to a further investigation in one form or other, and the most convenient and most effective mode appears to me to be that which has been mentioned, namely, by bringing an action in a court of law. Notwithstanding, therefore, the very forcible arguments I have heard upon this subject, I think I must, in this case, as has been done in so many other cases, direct the plaintiff to bring an action to try this right, the injunction being granted in the terms of the notice of motion." See also Stevens *v.* Keating, 2 Webs. Pat. Cas. 175.

In Russell *v.* Barnsley, Webs. Pat. Cas. 472, Sir L. Shadwell, V. C., said that he did not recollect a case where a defendant had stated his wish to try the question at law, that the court had refused to give him the opportunity.

[1] Orr *v.* Merrill, 1 Woodb. & M. 376.

[2] 2 Wall. C. C. Rep. 283.

many interesting inquiries; but facts were so interfused throughout the whole case, in the questions of law, that these last have not been found very capable of being reported. The pleadings were long; the proof and exhibits very full, amounting to about four thousand printed pages; and they had been taken under an order that they should be read either at law or in equity. The witnesses were numerous and the questions were of a kind requiring much attention and intelligence. Both parties assumed to act under patents. The case having been set down for final hearing on the proofs and exhibits, and having been fully, ably, and learnedly argued by counsel on both sides for several days, the main question of law was, whether, in the face of the answer, denying positively the complainant's merits and all infringement of his patent, and praying for a trial by jury, of the issues involved, the court would, under any circumstances, grant a perpetual injunction without a previous verdict. Another question, partially mingled with a question of fact, was what amount of prior discovery is necessary to deprive a subsequent discoverer of the merit of such originality as the law requires for the protection of a patent."

The court said: "It is true that in England the chancellor will generally not grant a final and perpetual injunction in patent cases, when the answer denies the validity of the patent, without sending the parties to law to have that question decided. But even there the rule is not absolute or universal; it is a practice founded more on convenience than on necessity. It always rests in the sound discretion of the court. A trial at law is ordered by the chancellor, to inform his conscience; not because either party may demand it as a right, or that a court of equity is incompetent to judge of questions of facts or of legal titles. In the courts of the United States the practice is by no means so general as in England, or as it would be here, if the trouble of trying issues at law devolved upon a different court. Cases involving inquiries into the most complex and difficult questions of mechanics and philosophy are becoming numerous in the courts. Often questions of originality and infringement of patents do not depend so much on the credibility of witnesses or the weight of oral testimony, as on the application of principles of science and law to admitted facts. It is true that, in matters of opinion, both mechanics and learned professors will differ widely.

But still the question is not to be decided by the number, credibility, or respectability of such witnesses, but by the force and weight of the reasons given for their respective opinions. It is no reflection on trial by jury to say that cases frequently occur, in which ten out of twelve jurors do not understand the principles of science, mathematics, or philosophy, necessary to a correct judgment of the case. Besides, much of the time of the courts is lost, where twelve men will not agree upon any verdict; or where they have agreed, the conscience of the chancellor, instead of feeling enlightened, rejects it altogether. A select or special jury of philosophers, if they could be got, would perhaps not prove more satisfactory, or obviate the difficulty. In a late case, involving the validity of Morse's telegraph patents, which was heard in Philadelphia, a final injunction was decreed without a verdict to establish the patents; and many other cases might be cited from other circuits, if necessary, in support of this practice, showing that the courts of the United States do not always consider it a proper exercise of their discretion to order such issues to be tried at law, before granting a final injunction. In the present case there are many reasons why the court will not thus exercise their discretion: —

"1. Because this case has been set down for final hearing on the exhibits and proofs, without any motion or order of the court for such an issue.

"2. After a patient hearing of very able counsel, and a careful consideration of the testimony, the court feel no doubt or difficulty on these questions, which would be removed or confirmed by a verdict.

"3. It would require three or four weeks at least to try this case before a jury, if this library of testimony were read to them; and at least as many months if the witnesses were examined *viva voce*, as they probably would be; and, after all this expenditure of time and labor, it is even more than probable, that, from the confusion created by the great length of the testimony and argument in court, or the force and effect of those urged from without, no verdict would be obtained, and most certainly none that would alter the present conviction of the court. Without requiring the aid of a jury, we shall, therefore, proceed to examine the questions, both of fact and law, which affect the validity of complainant's patent."

The court then concluded with the following remarks: —

"But notwithstanding the indomitable energy and perseverance with which this attempt to invalidate the patent has been pursued, the volumes of testimony with which it has been oppressed, and the great ability with which it has been canvassed in the argument, we are of opinion that the defendant has signally failed in the attempt to show that himself or any other person discovered and perfected the process of manufacturing vulcanized india-rubber before Goodyear. We shall, therefore, give our decree of perpetual injunction."

§ 430. The practice of the court in dissolving, reviving, continuing, or making final injunctions, previously granted, is regulated in general by the same rules as the practice of granting them in the first instance. On a motion on affidavits to dissolve an injunction, the defendant's proofs must overcome the equity of the bill and the evidence in its support.[1] A motion to dissolve an injunction may be made at any time. If made after a trial has been ordered at law, or while an action at law is pending, or while the plaintiff is preparing to bring an action, the decision of the court will be made upon the same principles which governed the granting of the injunction in the first instance; that is to say, the defendant will not succeed in displacing the plaintiff's *primâ facie* right to an injunction, merely by filing an answer, or reading affidavits casting doubts on the validity of the patent, provided the plaintiff is guilty of no unreasonable delay in bringing on the trial; especially, if the plaintiff adduces auxiliary evidence in favor of his right.[2]

§ 431. Where the motion to dissolve is made after a trial at law has been had, the court will have to look at the result of that trial, and will be governed by the position in which the plaintiff's right has been left. If the proceedings at law are not in a state to be regarded as final, the court will choose to be informed as to the further questions which remain to be investigated. If a verdict has been rendered for the plaintiff, but a new trial has been,

[1] Sparkman *v.* Higgins, 1 Blatchf. 205.

[2] Orr *v.* Merrill, 1 Woodb. & M. 376; Orr *v.* Littlefield, Ib. 13; Orr *v.* Badger, 10 Law Rep. 465. In such cases the injunction should be continued to the next term after that at which the suit at law might be tried to test the title. Orr *v.* Merrill. See also Woodworth *v.* Rogers, 3 Woodb. & M. 135, where the question of dissolving an injunction is amply discussed.

or is to be moved for, and if the court can see that there is a question on which an argument might be addressed to the court of law, which might induce it to grant a new trial, the injunction will not be continued, as a matter of course, but the court will endeavor to leave the parties in a situation that will produce, on the whole, the least inconvenience, having regard to all the circumstances of their respective situations.[1]

[1] Hill *v.* Thompson, 3 Meriv. 622, 628. In this case, the injunction had been dissolved, a trial at law had resulted in a verdict for the plaintiff, who came before the court with a motion to *revive* the injunction. On the part of the defendants, it was stated to be their intention to move for a new trial at law, at the next term, which was as soon as the motion could be made. Lord Eldon said: "In this case, the injunction was first granted upon the strength of the affidavits, which were contradicted, as to their general effect, in the most material points, when it afterwards came before the court upon a motion to dissolve the injunction so obtained. Many topics were then urged on both sides, and fully discussed in argument. It was insisted, on the part of the plaintiff, and the court agreed to that position, that where a person has obtained a patent, and had an exclusive enjoyment under it, the court will give so much credit to his apparent right, as to interpose immediately, by injunction, to restrain the invasion of it, and continue that interposition until the apparent right has been displaced. On the other hand, it was with equal truth stated, that, if a person takes out a patent, as for an invention, and is unable to support it, except upon the ground of some alleged improvement in the mode of applying that which was previously in use, and it so becomes a serious question, both in point of law and of fact, whether the patent is not altogether invalid, then, upon an application to this court for what may be called the extra relief which it affords on a clear *primâ facie* case, the court will use its discretion; and, if it sees sufficient ground of doubt, will either dissolve the injunction absolutely, or direct an issue, or direct the party applying to bring his action, after the trial of which, either he may apply to revive, if successful, or else the other party may come before the court, and say, I have displaced all his pretensions, and am entitled to have my costs and the expenses I have sustained, by being brought here upon an allegation of right which cannot be supported. And as, in this instance, the court will sometimes add to its more general directions, that the party against whom the application is made shall keep an account pending the discontinuance of the injunction, in order that, if it shall finally turn out that the plaintiff has a right to the protection he seeks, amends may be made for the injury occasioned by the resistance to his just demands. In his directions to the jury, the judge has stated it as the law on the subject of patents, — first, that the invention must be novel; secondly, that it must be useful; and thirdly, that the specification must be intelligible. I will go further, and say, that not only must the invention be novel and useful, and the specification intelligible, but also that the specification must not attempt to cover more than that which,

§ 432. Sometimes the court will direct a motion for an injunction to stand over, when none has been granted, until it can be

being both matter of actual discovery and of useful discovery, is the only proper subject for the protection of a patent. And I am compelled to add, that, if a patentee seeks, by specification, any more than he is strictly entitled to, his patent is thereby rendered ineffectual, even to the extent to which he would be otherwise fairly entitled. On the other hand, there may be a valid patent for a new combination of materials, previously in use, for the same purpose, or for a new method of applying such materials. But, in order to its being effectual, the specification must clearly express that it is in respect of such new combination or application, and of that only, and not lay claim to the merit of original invention in the use of materials. If there be a patent both for a machine and for an improvement in the use of it, and it cannot be supported for the machine, although it might for the improvement merely, it is good for nothing altogether, on account of its attempting to cover too much. Now, it is contended, that what is claimed by the present patent is not a novel invention; that the extraction of iron from slags or cinders was previously known and practised; that the use of lime in obstructing 'cold short' was likewise known. But to all this it is answered, that the patent is not for the invention of these things, but for such an application of them as is described in the specification. Now, the utility of the discovery, the intelligibility of the description, &c., are all of them matters of fact proper for a jury. But whether or not the patent is defective, in attempting to cover too much, is a question of law, and as such, to be considered in all ways that it is convenient for the purposes of justice that it should be considered. This specification generally describes the patent to be 'for improvements in the smelting and working of iron'; and it then goes on to describe the particulars in which the alleged improvements consist, describing various proportions in the combination of materials, and various processes in the adhibition of them. The question of law, upon the whole matter, is, whether this is a specification by which the patentee claims the benefit of the actual discovery of lime as a preventive of 'cold short,' or whether he claims no more than the invention of that precise combination and those peculiar processes which are described in the specification. And, when I see that this question clearly arises, the only other question which remains is, whether I can be so well satisfied with respect to it as to take it for granted that no argument can prevail upon a court of law to let that first question be reconsidered by granting the motion for a new trial. If this be a question of law, I can have no right whatever to take its decision out of the jurisdiction of a court of law, unless I am convinced that a court of law must and will consider the verdict of the jury as final and conclusive. But this only brings it back to the original question; and I see enough of difficulty and uncertainty in the specification, and enough of apparent repugnance between the specification and the patent itself, to say that it is impossible I can arrive at such a conclusion respecting it, as to be satisfied that there is no ground for granting a new trial. In the order I formerly pronounced was contained a direction, that the defendant should keep

ascertained what the result of an application for a new trial is to be; and where a rule, to show cause why a new trial should not be had, had been granted, an injunction was refused, it not having been allowed before.[1]

§ 433. This course of proceeding shows that when a new trial has been or is intended to be applied for, a court of equity will generally leave the parties in the situation in which they stood before the trial. If no injunction had been previously granted, the court will not increase the defendant's burdens by imposing one, as long as the plaintiff's right remains doubtful at law. But if an injunction has been granted and the plaintiff has succeeded at law, it would seem that the injunction ought not to be dissolved, on the mere suggestion that there is ground for a new trial, unless the court sees what Lord Eldon called "sufficient ground of doubt" of the plaintiff's right; but that the court will exercise its discretion, and if it sees reason for dissolving the injunction, it will direct the defendant to keep an account pending the discontinuance of the injunction, in order that, if it finally turns out that the plaintiff has a valid patent, he may receive amends for the injury occa-

an account of iron produced by their working in the manner described in the injunction. If the injunction is to be now revived, the whole of their establishment must be discharged between this and the fourth day of next term, when it is intended to move for a new trial, the result of which may be, that the defendants have a right to continue the works; to do which, they will then be under the necessity of recommencing all their operations, and making all their preparations and arrangements *de novo*. It appears to me that this would be a much greater inconvenience than any that can result from my refusal, in the present instance, to revive the injunction. My opinion, therefore, is, that this matter must stand over till the fifth day of next term, when I may be informed of the result of the intended application for a new trial; the account to be taken in the mean time as before."

[1] There is a recent case where an injunction was applied for and refused, and the plaintiff was directed to bring an action, which was tried and a verdict found for the plaintiff. The motion for the injunction was then renewed; but it appeared, on affidavit, that a bill of exceptions had been tendered, and that the defendants also intended to move for a new trial. The Lord Chancellor directed the application to stand over until the result of these proceedings should be known. Shortly afterwards a rule *nisi*, for a new trial, was obtained, and then the motion for the injunction was brought on again. The Lord Chancellor said, that under the circumstances in which the case stood at law, a rule to show cause why a new trial should not be had, having been granted, he must consider the legal title of the parties as still undecided; and he therefore refused the application. Collard *v.* Allison, 4 Myl. & Cr. 487, 490.

sioned by the resistance to his just demands.[1] After a trial and judgment at law, in favor of the plaintiff, the injunction will be revived or granted as matter of course.[2] How far the court will undertake to look into the regularity of such a judgment, and to determine, on the suggestion of the defendant, whether there is probable ground for a writ of error, and therefore to suspend the injunction, is a question which has not arisen in this country; but it seems that in England, the Lord Chancellor has so far entertained an application of this kind, as to look into the proceedings at law and the grounds of the judgment, and to satisfy himself that no good reason existed for departing from the usual course of reviving the injunction after a judgment in favor of the plaintiff.[3]

§ 434. An important part of the remedial process in equity is the account of profits made by the defendant. Sometimes an account is ordered to be kept, in lieu of granting or continuing an injunction; and it is always ordered when the injunction is made perpetual, unless the amount would be very small. The cases in which an account is ordered to be kept, either with or without an injunction, during the pendency of an action in which the right is to be tried, proceeded upon the principle that the plaintiff may turn out to be entitled to the right, and he is more secure of ample justice if the account of the defendant's profits is kept while he is using the invention, than if it were deferred to be taken at a future time, especially if the defendant is left at liberty to make new contracts.[4] Such an account will be ordered, if the injunction is dissolved, by reason of the irreparable injury it would do to the defendant's business.[5]

[1] See the observations cited, *ante*, from Hill *v.* Thompson. See further, as to ordering an account, *post.*

[2] Neilson *v.* Harford (Cor. Lord Lyndhurst in 1841), Webs. Pat. Cas. 373.

[3] Ibid.

[4] Hill *v.* Thompson, 3 Meriv. 626, 631; Crossley *v.* Derby Gas Light Company, Webs. Pat. Cas. 119; Neilson *v.* Fothergill, ibid. 290; Morgan *v.* Seaward, ibid. 168; Bacon *v.* Jones, 4 Myl. & Cr. 436; Foster *v.* Moore, 1 Curtis, C. C. 279.

[5] Neilson *v.* Thompson, Webs. Pat. Cas. 278, 285. In this case, Lord Cottenham said: "Nothing that took place could preclude the defendants from the right of disputing the plaintiff's right as a patentee, but they have, at very considerable expense, erected this machinery, and from that time to the present have been using it, the plaintiff being aware of it, at least from

§ 435. Sometimes, as a further means of doing justice between the parties, upon the question of infringement, when an action at law is to be tried, the court will order a mutual inspection of the plaintiff's and defendant's works. The object in so doing is to enable the parties, on the trial, to give such evidence as will tend

some time in 1839 (the precise day is not stated), and having stood by and permitted them to do this. If he is entitled as patentee, it would be extremely hard for the court to do any thing to prevent his receiving that which he is entitled to receive, and in expectation of which he permitted the defendants to go on with their works. But, on the other hand, it would be extremely hard indeed to tell the defendants that they shall not use the works which, with the plaintiff's knowledge, they have prepared at a very considerable expense ; and as to telling them they may go on with the cold blast instead of the hot blast, I am told that the difference between the use of the one and the other is an expense of nearly double, even if it were possible ; at all events they may sustain that loss in the interval until the right is tried. It seems to me that stopping the works by injunction, under these circumstances, is just inverting the purpose for which an injunction is used. An injunction is used for the purpose of preventing mischief; this would be using the injunction for the purpose of creating mischief, because the plaintiff cannot possibly be injured. All that he asks, all that he demands, all that he ever expects from these defendants, is one shilling per ton. He has not a right to say to them, you shall not use this apparatus ; he cannot do so after the course of conduct he has adopted ; he may, no doubt, say with success, if he is right, you shall pay me that rent which the others pay, and in the expectation of which I permitted you to erect this machinery. Therefore, in no possible way can the plaintiff be prejudiced ; but the prejudice to the defendants must be very great indeed, if they are for a short period prevented from using at their furnaces that apparatus which, with the consent of the plaintiff, they have erected. The object, therefore, is, pending the question, which I do not mean to prejudice one way or the other by any thing I now say, to preserve to the parties the opportunity of trying the question, with the least possible injury to the one party or the other ; and I think the injunction would be extremely prejudicial to the defendants, and do no possible good to the plaintiff for the purpose for which it may be used. It may, by operating as a pressure upon the defendants, produce a benefit, but that is not the object of the court : the object of the court is to preserve to each party the benefit he is entitled to, until the question of right is tried, and that may be entirely secured by the defendants undertaking to keep an account, not only for the time to come, but from the time when the connection first commenced, and undertaking to deal with that account in such a way as the court may direct ; and if the plaintiff is entitled, the court will have an opportunity of putting the plaintiff precisely in the situation in which he would have stood if the question had not arisen. If it shall turn out that the patent is not valid, the court will deal with it accordingly, and that will, I think, most effectually prevent all prejudice."

to prove or disprove the fact of infringement. For this purpose inspectors or viewers are appointed, under the direction of the court, who are to be admitted as witnesses on the trial at law. If the parties do not agree on the persons to be appointed, the court will appoint them.[1]

§ 436. When the validity of the patent is fully established, an account will be ordered of all the profits made by the defendant, to be taken by a master; and if the patent has expired, the account and the injunction will extend to all the articles piratically made during the existence of the patent, though some of them may remain unsold.[2] The master is not limited to the date of the decree, but may take the account down to the time of the hearing before him.[3] The proper form of the decree for profits is to direct the taking of an account of all the profits made by the defendant in violation of the plaintiff's patent, by making, using, or vending the articles named in the bill.[4]

It has been decided, in the case of Livingston *v.* Woodworth,[5] that the account of profits granted by a court of equity comprises only such profits as have been actually made by the defendant, and not such as he might have made with reasonable diligence, nor interest from the date of filing the bill. The original bill filed in the Circuit Court by the appellees concluded with a prayer that the defendants (here the appellants) may be decreed to account for and pay over to the complainants (appellees) "all *gains*

[1] Morgan *v.* Seaward, Webs. Pat. Cas. 168; Russell *v.* Cowley, ibid. 457. See these cases for the decrees appointing such inspectors. Also Jones *v.* Lee, 36 E. L. & Eq. 558.

[2] Crossley *v.* Beverley, Webs. Pat. Cas. 119; Crossley *v.* Derby Gas Light Company, ibid. 119, 120. In this case a very curious difficulty occurred in estimating the "profits." The plaintiff was the owner of a patent for making gas meters, which the defendants had made and sold and employed in their works. The profits to be ascertained were the benefits derived from the use of the meters, in enabling the defendants to furnish gas to their customers at a lower rate than they could have done without them, and so to obtain additional profits from an increased consumption. It was a case, therefore, presenting the uncertain elements of profits made by the application of particular means, and a just distribution of those profits to a particular agent employed. The case, as it is reported, does not furnish any principles. See s. c. 3 Mylne & Cr. 428, 430.

[3] Rubber Company *v.* Goodyear, 9 Wallace, 788.

[4] Ibid.

[5] Livingston *v.* Woodworth, 15 How. 546.

and profits which have accrued from using their said machines since the expiration of the said original patent." Under this bill the master to whom the account was referred made a report which was not confirmed; the court made a further decretal order, with instructions to ascertain the amount of profits which may have been, *or with due diligence might have been, realized by the defendants.* The report made in pursuance of this order was confirmed, and interest from the time of filing the bill added by the court. On appeal to the Supreme Court the rulings of the Circuit Court were reversed, and an entirely different measure of damages and profits established. The Supreme Court ruled as follows: "On the part of the appellees (the complainants in the Circuit Court), it has been insisted that the decretal order, made in this cause by consent, covered and ratified in advance all the subsequent proceedings on the part of the court, rendering those proceedings, inclusive of the final decree, a matter of consent, which the appellants could have no right to retract, and from which, therefore, they could not legally appeal. In order to try the accuracy of this argument and of the conclusions sought to be deduced therefrom, it is proper to examine the order which is alleged in support of them. The words of that order are as follows: 'This cause came on, &c., and by consent of parties it declared by the court,'—what? 'That the complainants are entitled to the perpetual injunction and the *account prayed for by the bill.*' It seems to us incomprehensible, that, by this consent of the defendant below, he had consented to any thing precise and unchangeable beyond the perpetual injunction, much more so that he had thereby bound himself to acquiesce in any shape or to any extent of demand which might be made against him, under the guise of an account. Indeed, the complainants below, and the circuit court itself, have shown by their own interpretation of this decretal order, that they did not understand it to mean, as in truth by no just acceptation it could mean, any thing fixed, definite, or immutable; for the complainants below excepted to the report of the master; and the court recommitted that report with a view to its alteration. Nor can we regard the reference to the master as in the nature of an arbitration; for, if so deemed, the award of that officer must have been binding, unless it could be assailed for fraud, misbehavior, or gross mistake of fact. In truth, the account consented to was the account prayed for by the bill, namely: 'That the defendants may be decreed to account for and pay over all such gains and profits as have accrued to them from using the said machines since the expiration of said original letters-patent.' This language is particularly clear and significant, — such gain and profits, and such only as have actually accrued to the defendants; and we are unable to perceive how, by such an assent, the defendants below could have been concluded against exceptions to any thing and every thing which might have been involved by that report, however illegal or oppressive.

"Considering next the decretal order for the recommitment of the first report, the second report made in obedience to that order, and the final decree made upon that second report, we are constrained to regard them all as alike irreconcilable with the prayer of the bill, with the just import of the consent decree, and with those principles which control courts of equity. In the instructions to the master, it will be seen that he is ordered 'to ascertain and report the amount of profits which may have been, or which with due diligence and prudence might have been, realized by the defendants for the work done by them or by their servants, computing the same upon the principles set forth in the opinion of the court, and that the account of such profits commence from the date of the letters-patent issued with the amended specification. The master, in his report made in pursuance of the instructions just adverted to, admits that the account is not constructed upon the basis of actual gains and profits acquired by the defendants by the use of the inhibited machine, but upon the theory of awarding damages to the complainants for an infringement of their monopoly. He admits, too, that the rate of profits assumed by him was conjectural, and not governed by the evidence; but he attempts to vindicate the rule he had acted upon by the declaration, that he was not aware that he had 'infused into the case any element too unfavorable to the defendants. That by the decision of the court they were trespassers and wrong-doers, in the legal sense of these words, and consequently in a position to be mulcted in damages greater than the profits they have actually received, the rule being, not what benefit they have received, but what injury the plaintiffs have sustained.' To what rule the master has reference in thus stating the grounds on which his calculations have been based, we do not know. We are aware of no rule which converts a court of equity into an instrument for the punishment of simple torts; but upon this principle of chastisement the master admits that he has been led, in contravention of his original view of the testimony and upon conjecture as to reality of the facts, and not upon facts themselves, to double the amount which he had stated to be a compensation to the plaintiffs below, and the compensation prayed for by them; and the circuit court has, by its decree, pushed this principle to its extreme, by adding to this amount the penalty of interest thereon, from the time of filing the bill to the date of the final decree.

"We think that the second report of the master, and the final decree of the circuit court, are warranted neither by the prayer of the bill, by the justice of this case, nor by the well-established rules of equity jurisprudence. If the appellees, the plaintiffs below, had sustained an injury to their legal rights, the courts of law were open to them for redress, and in those courts they might, according to a practice which, however doubtful in point of essential right, is now too inveterate to be called in question, have claimed not merely compensation, but vengeance for such injury as they could show that they had sustained. But before a tribunal which refuses to listen even to any save those acts and motives which are perfectly fair and liberal, they cannot be permitted to contravene the highest and most benignant principle of the being and constitution of that principle."[1]

§ 436 *a*. Profits are rightly estimated by finding the difference between cost and sales. In estimating cost, the elements of cost of materials, interest, expense of manufacture and sale, and bad debts, considered by a manufacturer in estimating his profits, are to be taken into account, and no others. Interest on capital stock and "manufacturers' profits" are not to be allowed. Profits due to elements not patented, which entered into the composition of the patented article, may sometimes be allowed, but not always. Extraordinary salaries, being in fact dividends of profits allowed under that name, should not be allowed.[2]

§ 437. An injunction should not be dissolved merely on account of doubts as to the validity of the patent, which arises from objections to the technical form or signature of the letters, or other

[1] These principles have been applied in the subsequent case of Dean *v.* Mason, 20 How. 198. See also Silsby *v.* Foote, 20 How. 378; and Elwood *v.* Christy, 18 C. B. N. S. 494. Rubber Company *v.* Goodyear, 9 Wallace, 788.

[2] Rubber Company *v.* Goodyear, 9 Wallace, 788.

acts or omissions of the public officers, and not from any neglect or wrong of the patentee.[1]

Nor is it sufficient ground for dissolving an injunction, that there has been delay in the several steps necessary to the acquisition of the patent, provided that such delay was not usual, and that the application was followed up with reasonable diligence. Or that the patentee has in the mean while sold the manufactured article. And if third parties, inquiring at the Patent Office, are informed that no patent has been obtained for such articles, and act upon the information, the patentee is not bound by such action of the Patent Office officials, and a temporary injunction granted him cannot be dissolved on that ground.[2]

§ 438. Upon the question of granting an injunction against a party who has had the use of the invention by permission or grant of the patentee, the doctrine seems to be this. A licensee who derives his license from one tenant in common of a patent cannot

[1] Woodworth *v.* Hall, 1 Woodb. & M. 389, 400. In this case, Mr. Justice Woodbury said: "Finally, it is contended that if any doubt exists as to the validity of a patent, as some assuredly does here, as before stated, the injunction should be dissolved. This may, with some qualification as to the matters connected with the subject, be true in granting an injunction, as laid down in 4 Wash. C. C. 584, if the doubt relate to the merits, that is, the originality or usefulness of a patent, or a patentee's own error in his specification. But when the objection relates to the technical form or signature of papers connected with the letters, and the doubts arise from acts of public officers, and not any neglect or wrong of the patentee, the position seems to me not sound. More especially should an injunction, once granted, not be disturbed for such doubts, when, as in this case, the term for trial of the merits is near; and the allowing such doubts to prevail, even to the extent of dissolving an injunction, might not merely affect the present patent and present parties, but operate injuriously on all other patents and parties where, for the last ten years, by a contemporaneous and continued construction of the patent law, chief clerks have, under its authority, signed patents or other important papers as acting commissioner, in the necessary absence of the commissioner, or made mistakes of a clerical character in the form of the letters. In my opinion, so far from its being proper, under such circumstances, to dissolve an injunction for doubts on such technical objections, it is rather the duty of the court, if, as here, mischievous consequences are likely to ensue to others from interfering, and if, as here, legislative measures have been recommended by the public officers, which are pending, to remedy or obviate the possible evil from any public mistakes, not to dissolve an injunction already granted, unless required to do it by imperative principles of law, showing the letters-patent to be clearly void."

[2] Sparkman *v.* Higgins, 1 Blatchf. 205.

be enjoined by another cotenant.[1] A party who has had the use of an invention, under a contract for an annual rent, or other estimated rate of payment, may discontinue the payment, and, if he still use the invention, the patentee may sue him for the rent due, or for an infringement. If an action is brought for the rent, and the defendant is not estopped by the terms of his contract from denying the validity of his patent, the plaintiff cannot recover without giving him an opportunity to do so.[2] The same is true under an action for the infringement, if the defendant is not estopped.[3] Where, therefore, a court of equity does not see that the defendant is estopped from denying the validity of the patent, but that he has a right to resist the patent, it will deal with a defendant who has used under a license or other contract, or under permission, upon the question of injunction, as it deals with other defendants; and, as we have seen, if the bill which prays for an injunction also shows that rent is due by contract, the court will order the money to be paid into court, to await the result of an action at law.[4]

[1] Clum *v.* Brewer, 2 Curtis, C. C. 506.

[2] Hayne *v.* Maltby, 3 T. R. 438.

[3] As to estoppel and failure of consideration, see Bowman *v.* Taylor, 2 Ad. & Ell. 278, and other cases collected in Webs. Pat. Cas. 290, note.

[4] Neilson *v.* Fothergill, Webs. Pat. Cas. 287, 288. The bill showed that the plaintiffs had called on the defendants for an account of the iron smelted by the use of the invention, in order to ascertain the sum due, and that the defendants had rendered an account in writing of all the iron smelted by them up to the 2d of August, 1839, and duly paid one shilling per ton on the same; that the plaintiff had applied to the defendants for an account of the iron smelted since the 2d day of August, 1839, and for like payments, but the defendants had refused. It appeared that the draft of a license was sent to the defendants, containing amongst others a clause for revoking the license upon the nonpayment of the rent, *and that this license was kept;* that the payments were made in conformity to it, and that the plaintiffs, after August, 1839, *revoked the license.* An injunction had been granted, which the defendants now moved to discharge. Lord Cottenham, L. C.: "This case is deprived of those circumstances upon which I acted in the other, namely, the party who claims to be patentee permitting them to incur expense, in the expectation of being permitted to use the furnaces upon the payment of the rent, which is all the plaintiff requires. But here, all that is accounted for, because that was done under a contract, and for two years at least the party has had the benefit of the works which he has so erected, and the patentee has kept his contracts with the defendants; he has not interposed and endeavored to deprive them of the benefit of their expenditure. It is the act of the manufacturer which has put an end to this connection; he has,

§ 438 *a*. A licensee, who has obtained a license upon certain terms, will be held by a court of equity to a compliance with those

therefore, exposed himself to any degree of injury that may arise from the expenditure upon these works, and it appears that there is no answer to the claim to this rent from August, 1839, to August, 1840. I shall have to consider, if your client declines to escape from the injunction upon the terms I propose to him, whether the injunction should not go in a case which is deprived of those equitable circumstances which induced me to dissolve it in the others. (Wigram: Your lordship will give me the benefit of the supposition, that, at law, I have a defence if the patent is good for nothing.) If you can show me that there is a real question to try, the money must be paid into court instead of being paid to the parties; but at all events, I do not see how far that year, from August, 1839, to August, 1840, when you went on under the contract without giving notice to determine, you can escape paying it, either into court to abide the event of the trial of the question at law, or paying it to the party, if there is no question to try.

Wigram, in reply. "Your lordship said you should consider, whether, since August, 1840, we were to be considered as holding adversely, and, therefore, whether liable or not to pay for what was gone by, we were at all events wrong-doers. And then you put me to show, whether I could not in law defend myself for what was said to be due in August, 1840. The principle which I have always understood to govern cases of this sort is this, that, excluding the law of estoppel, if you go into a court of law, and can show a total failure of consideration for the contract, there you may always defend yourself; if, on the other hand, you cannot make out a case of total failure of consideration, you are liable upon your contract, and you may or may not have your cross action. This is the general principle in these cases, subject to the question, whether that which has been done may or may not amount to an estoppel. The whole question in the case of Bowman *v.* Taylor, relied upon for the plaintiff, was, whether or not there could be an estoppel by recital, and it was held that there could. In Hayne *v.* Maltby, the question was, whether there was any estoppel, there being no recital of the plaintiff's title, but only an agreement and a covenant to pay, and the court held that there was not. In that case, Mr. Justice Ashurst said, the plantiffs use this patent as a fraud on all mankind, and they state it to be an invention of the patentee, when in truth it was no invention of his. The only right conferred on the defendant by the agreement was that of using this machine, which was no more than which he in common with every other subject has, without any grant from the plaintiff. That is exactly our case. We say that all mankind have a right to use it, but that some people have taken licenses, supposing it to be the plaintiff's invention. On the money then being paid into court, the injunction should be dissolved."

Lord Cottenham, L. C.: "The case of Hayne *v.* Maltby appears to me to come to this, — that although a party has dealt with the patentee and has carried on business, yet that he may stop, and then the party who claims to be patentee cannot recover without giving the other party the opportunity of

terms. In such cases, however, the court will act with due regard to the substantial rights of both parties, neither permitting on the one hand the licensee to continue his use in disregard of the agreement, nor on the other hand working an unreasonable forfeiture of the license. Thus, in Brooks *v.* Stolley,[1] the defendant in an injunction bill had been allowed to use the plaintiff's machine on certain conditions, viz.: "that the said John Stolley should pay the said Brooks and Morris one dollar and twenty-five cents for each and every thousand feet of boards he may plane, payable on Monday of every week," &c. The defendant admitted failure of payment. The court ruled that the terms of the agreement made the performance of its stipulations by the defendant a condition to his continued use of the machine, and that the case was one in which equitable relief was in place, but that, unlike an ordinary case of infringement, an unconditional injunction which would virtually annul the agreement would be excessive. Said the court: "The complainants invoke the aid of equity, not to decree a specific performance of the contract, but to protect their rights as assignees of the patent. This right, they allege, has been infringed. The defendant relies on the license contained in the contract; but having failed to make the weekly payments, he has no pretence of right to run the machine. To entitle himself to the benefit of the license, it is incumbent on the defendant to do all that he is bound to do. . . . A question is made whether the failure of the defendant to make the weekly payments operates as

disputing his right, and that if the defendant successfully dispute his right, that notwithstanding he has been dealing under a contract, it is competent to the defendant so to do. That is exactly coming to the point which I put, whether at law the party was estopped from disputing the patentee's right, after having once dealt with him as the proprietor of that right; and it appears from the authority of that case, and from the other cases, that from the time of the last payment, if the manufacturer can successfully resist the patent right of the party claiming the rent, that he may do so in answer to an action for the rent for the use of the patent during that year. That being so, I think that, upon the money being paid into court, that is to say, upon the amount of the rent for that year being paid into court (if required), and the same undertaking being given to account for the subsequent period, the same order ought to be made in this case as in the others. There must be an undertaking to deal with the amount of that in the same way as before. The great difficulty in this case, which, however, is surmounted in the undertaking, is that the said suit does not go to that year's rent."

[1] 3 McLean, 523.

a forfeiture of the contract. There is no condition of forfeiture in the contract. Whether it has been abandoned by the defendant must depend upon the circumstances of the case. A court of chancery will not decree the cancelment of a contract, except for fraud or mistake. . . . An injunction is prayed which, in effect, will annul the patent. Now, although it may be admitted that the defendant, as the facts in the case stand, could not successfully invoke in his behalf the action of a court of equity or law, yet, under the relief asked by the complainants, a somewhat different view may be taken. Are the complainants entitled to an absolute injunction, which shall annihilate the contract? It appears to me that short of this adequate relief may be given." It will be observed that the breach in question consisted in a mere non-payment of money.

In the similar case of Wilson *v.* Sherman (under the same, Woodworth's, patent),[1] the court decided that one ground for granting an injunction failed, inasmuch as the contract constituting the alleged violation of the agreement had been fully completed before the bringing of the bill; also that the grant of an injunction, on the ground of forfeiture of the license, would, under the circumstances of the case, be too rigorous an exercise of the power of the court. The violation was, in this case, selling outside of the county agreed upon in the license the materials manufactured by the patented machine.

But perhaps the fullest exposition of the equitable rights existing mutually between patentee and licensee is contained in the decision of the Lord Chancellor in Warwick *v.* Hooper:[2] "From what I have stated, it appears that the equity relied on, on the part of the plaintiffs, results from the following facts: that the plaintiff are assignees of a certain patent; that the defendant accepted a license to use the patent invention upon certain terms, one of which was to pay a royalty or rent to the amount of at least £2,000 a year, to be made up at the end of each year, in manner stated in the license, and that in default of such payment being made, the license might be determined; that the defendant has made default in such payment in every year except the first, since the license was granted; and that the plaintiffs have in consequence determined the license according to the proviso in that behalf enabling them to do so. On the

[1] 1 Blatchf. 536.

[2] 3 E. L. & Eq. 233.

defendant's behalf . . . it is insisted, first, that the condition as to the payment of the £2,000 yearly was dispensed with by the agreement embodied in the letter of the 4th of November, 1845; and, secondly, that if the condition as to the payment of the £2,000 yearly was not dispensed with, and the covenant to pay such sum had been broken by non-payment of such sum, yet that the plaintiffs had elected not to treat such breach as a forfeiture of the license, but to continue the license by the acceptance of payment of the royalties under the license, accruing due for a period subsequent to the last breach of covenant.

"I shall first consider the point whether the license granted to the defendant by those under whom the plaintiffs claim, has been legally determined, so as to make the defendant a wrong-doer, as against the plaintiffs, by continuing to use the patented invention; because, if the license has not determined, there is an entire failure of the equity set forth in the plaintiff's bill; and I think this point may be determined upon principles and authorities which can be open to very little doubt or dispute. The proviso contained in the license for determining the same, upon default being made in the payment of the £2,000 a year, was inserted exclusively for the benefit of the grantors, and the defendant, the grantee, could in no manner, by any option or act of his, determine the license; nor were the grantors bound, in the event of default being made in the stipulated payments, to avoid the license or to treat it as determined; and until they, the grantors, should in the prescribed manner declare the option and exercise the right to treat the default as a ground of forfeiture, the license would continue in full force notwithstanding any breaches of covenants and conditions on the part of the defendant which might have occurred. It is not necessary to cite authority for this well-established proposition. The question to be determined is, whether the plaintiffs, by receiving royalties which accrued for two quarters after the expiration of the year ending July 27, 1849, did not treat and act upon the license as an existing and continuing license, and thereby elect conclusively not to treat the previous breaches of covenant as grounds of forfeiture, and thereby preclude themselves from afterwards determining the license upon the ground of any previous breach of covenant." The Chancellor then discusses the principles recognized and adopted in similar cases arising between landlord and tenant, and concludes: "I cannot perceive any distinction between the present case and the case of landlord and tenant under a lease; and it seems to me to be clear that the receipt of the royalty under the license for the two quarters commencing after the alleged ground of forfeiture had occurred, was a conclusive election by the plaintiffs not to act upon the previous breaches of the covenants as a ground of forfeiture."

For a full discussion of the question, whether the Federal courts had or had not jurisdiction in the two American cases above cited, see *infra*, chapter on Jurisdiction. It may suffice here to observe that the question was decided affirmatively, on the ground that a non-compliance with the terms of the license, coupled with a continued use of the patented invention, constituted an infringement of the patent, and on that ground alone was a proper subject of adjudication in the Federal courts. The case of Goodyear *v.* The Congress Rubber Co.[1] may be regarded as modifying, or, to speak perhaps more accurately, limiting the doctrines already stated. The patentee, Charles Goodyear, had given to Horace Day an exclusive license for a specified purpose, Day covenanting to use it for no other purpose. Day subsequently using it for other purposes, Goodyear brought a bill in New Jersey to restrain the violation, and obtain a decree of account. The decree was granted, but after its rendition, and pending the accounting under it, Day assigned his license to the Congress Rubber Co., who took with full knowledge of the facts. Day also disposed of his property with intent to defeat the decree of account. The Congress Rubber Co. proceeded to manufacture articles under the license assigned to them. The bill in question was thereupon brought to restrain them from so doing, on two grounds, first, that the assignor, the original licensee, had violated his covenant, and that any one holding under him was bound by equities against him; secondly, that the Company had not themselves fulfilled the terms of the license, by paying the fees agreed upon. This last ground was sustained, but the first was overruled on demurrer. The Court ruled: 1. That the patentee had no lien on the license to secure the tariffs. 2. That the unpaid tariffs due by the assignor afforded no ground for enjoining the assignees under the license, and that the question whether the assignment was fraudulent or

[1] 3 Blatchf. 449.

not, did not respect the patentee. 3. That the question respecting any attempt to evade the New Jersey decree could not arise until that decree became final. 4. That the bill could not be sustained against the assignees, to aid either in enforcing that decree or in collecting the tariffs due from the licensee to the patentee at the time of the assignment.

It may be well to observe that this case differs from Brooks *v.* Stolley and Wilson *v.* Sherman, in that the license here in question was an exclusive one, and from Warwick *v.* Hooper, in that it contained no provision for determining the license in default of non-payment. The question of jurisdiction moreover was not raised, inasmuch as the court had jurisdiction for another reason, the plaintiff being a citizen of Connecticut and the defendants citizens of New York.

In conclusion, where the patentee assigns his whole interest in the patent, reserving merely an annual income to be paid by the grantee, he can have no action either at law or in equity under the patent, but his only remedy in case the income is not paid is an action upon the covenant. Thus, in Hartshorn *v.* Day,[1] the recital mentioned that the grantee had stipulated to pay $1,200 and the expenses, and the body of the instrument declared: "Now I, Chaffee, do hereby in consideration of the premises, &c., &c., nominate, constitute, and appoint said William Judson my trustee and attorney irrevocable, to hold said patent and have the control thereof, &c." This was held to pass the entire equitable and legal title in the letters-patent to said Judson, for the benefit of Goodyear, so that if the annuity was not paid, the patentee had no right to revoke the power of attorney and assign the patent to another party. Nelson, J., in giving the opinion of the Supreme Court, expressly declares the doctrine of Brooks *v.* Stolley inapplicable to this case.

§ 439. It has been held that in a bill in equity for a perpetual injunction, it is a good defence, that, prior to the granting of the patent, the inventor had allowed the invention to go into public use, without objection; but that it should be clearly established by proof, that such public use was with the knowledge and consent of the inventor.[2] This is the same as one of the statute defences against an action at law, which may all be made, pursuant to the statute, in equity, if the defendant chooses, although

[1] 19 How. 211.

[2] Wyeth *v.* Stone, 1 Story's R. 273.

the statute has expressly made them defences only in an action at law.

§ 440. The general principle of equity jurisprudence, that the court will not lend its extraordinary aid to any claimant who has encouraged or acquiesced in an infringement of his right, or who has unreasonably delayed prosecuting for such violation, is fully recognized in the case of patentees applying for an injunction. Where a patentee seeks an injunction against an alleged infringer, and the evidence shows that this infringer or others have been in the habit of disregarding the exclusive right conferred upon the patentee, and this with knowledge either actual or implied, on the part of the patentee, the court will dismiss the bill on the ground that the plaintiff has been guilty of laches, or that there is a want of that exclusive possession which lies at the foundation of every claim to an injunction.

This principle has been acknowledged and applied in several copyright and patent cases. Thus, in Lewis *v.* Chapman,[1] the Master of the Rolls said: "The two works were preparing for publication at the same time. The publication of the defendants began first, and the attention of the plaintiffs was drawn to it at the commencement and afterwards during the process of the defendants' publication, which was completed six years and a half before the bill was filed; and for more than one year before the bill was filed, a complete copy of the defendants' work was in possession of the plaintiffs, and had been obtained by them for the express and avowed purpose of investigating the contents and comparing them with the contents of the plaintiffs' work and the contents of Fullarton's book, which at that time was under consideration here. The delay of the plaintiffs is accounted for by reasons which affect them and relate to their own convenience only; . . . and although the small extent to which the plaintiffs from time to time made themselves acquainted with the contents of the defendants' work may in point of fact be entirely true; yet it appears to me that the plaintiffs, having so strong an interest in the subject, having such powerful motives for vigilant attention, and having such means of information, cannot be allowed in a court of justice to state that they remained ignorant of that which they had the perfect means of knowing, and which it was their avowed purpose as well as their strong interest to

[1] 3 Beav. 133.

learn; and under these circumstances I think it my duty to impute to them such a knowledge of the contents of defendants' work as made it their duty to apply for an injunction, if at all, at a much earlier period. And *on the ground of delay and not for any other reason*, I think that the injunction moved for must be refused."

So, also, in Saunders *v.* Smith,[1] we find the Lord Chancellor ruling as follows: "When I look at this book (the defendants', viz., Smith's Leading Cases), I see that it is a work of very great labor, and I find the principle is to take, first, the marginal note, sometimes with some alteration, and then to take the leading case as a principle, and then, by very voluminous and obviously very laborious notes, to work out the principle. It is clear, therefore, that the work is one of great labor, and that this was evident from the first volume; and I find that the plaintiffs were informed, in March, 1837, of an intention (on the part of the defendant) to deal with the existing reports (the copyright in which had vested, by assignment, in the plaintiffs) in the manner now complained of. I find the first volume published, announcing the intention of going on with the same plan, which necessarily would run over the period to which the copyrights of the plaintiffs relate, and that no remonstrance is made to Mr. Smith upon the nature of his work, but he is permitted to go on with this laborious undertaking until the period at which the first part of the second volume is published. In the mean time there was a communication between the plaintiffs and Mr. Maxwell, who was interested in the publication of the work, and who has as much right to the protection of the court as Mr. Smith; and in the proposal which he makes to the plaintiffs, he deals with the work as property he is entitled to deal with, wishing to make it the subject of arrangements between himself and the plaintiffs; and I do not find that this leads to any caution or interference on the part of the plaintiffs as to that course which Mr. Smith had pursued in part, and which the plaintiffs must have been aware that he intended to pursue further. I do not give any opinion upon the legal question. I am only to decide whether the plaintiffs are entitled, under the circumstances, to the interposition of the court to protect their legal right, when that legal right has not yet been established. But I assume the existence

[1] 3 Mylne & Cr. 711.

of the legal right, and I say that whatever legal rights the plaintiffs may have, the circumstances are such as to make it the duty of a court of equity to withhold its hand and to abstain from exercising its equitable jurisdiction, at all events until the plaintiffs shall come here with the legal title established."[1]

In Collard *v.* Allison,[2] the Chancellor ruled thus: "But then it is said there is possession of the patent, and that possession of a patent for a certain length of time gives such a title as the court will protect until a trial at law can be had. And certainly, if I found that manufacturers of piano-fortes had acquiesced, and that there was no doubt upon that point, to which I have before referred, I should have adopted the course which Lord Eldon adopted and which I have followed, of protecting the right until the trial should have been had. For that purpose, however, I ought to have very satisfactory evidence of exclusive possession. Now, I find here, that certain manufacturers state that they abstained from making piano-fortes in this manner, out of respect for the plaintiffs as having a patent; while other manufacturers, again, say that they have always made them in this way. Which of these statements is true I am not called upon to decide; but the discrepancy does throw sufficient doubt on the case to prevent my interfering by injunction. The result is, that this case, in my opinion, wants that evidence of exclusive possession upon which Lord Eldon acted in the case that has been referred to, and that there is so much doubt as to the novelty of what is claimed, and as to the validity of a patent for such a manufacture, that I do not feel that I ought to interfere."

But the case bearing most strongly on this question, and containing the development and further application of the principles already embodied in those just cited, is that of Wyeth *v.* Stone.[3] Here Mr. Justice Story said: "In the next place, as to Wyeth's supposed abandonment of his invention to the public since he obtained his patent, I agree that it is quite competent for a patentee at any time, by overt acts or by express dedication, to abandon or surrender to the public, for their use, all the rights

[1] See also Rundell *v.* Murray, 1 Jac. 311; Baily *v.* Taylor, 1 Russ. & Myl. 73; Platt *v.* Button, 19 Vesey (Sumn. ed.), 447; Southey *v.* Sherwood, 2 Meriv. 435.

[2] 4 Mylne & Cr. 487.

[3] 1 Story's Rep. 273.

secured by his patent, if such is his pleasure, clearly and deliberately expressed. So if, for a series of years, the patentee acquiesces, without objection, in the known public use by others of his invention, or stands by and encourages such use, such conduct will afford a very strong presumption of such an actual abandonment or surrender. *A fortiori*, the doctrine will apply to a case, where the patentee has openly encouraged or silently acquiesced in such use by the very defendants, whom he afterwards seeks to prohibit by injunction from any further use; for in this way, he may not only mislead them into expenses, or acts, or contracts, against which they might otherwise have guarded themselves; but his conduct operates as a surprise, if not as a fraud upon them. At all events, if such a defence were not a complete defence at law, in a suit for any infringement of the patent, it would certainly furnish a clear and satisfactory ground why a court of equity should not interfere either to grant an injunction, or to protect the patentee, or to give any other relief. This doctrine is fully recognized in Rundell *v.* Murray,[1] and Saunders *v.* Smith.[2] But if there were no authority on the point, I should not have the slightest difficulty in asserting the doctrine, as founded in the very nature and character of the jurisdiction exercised by courts of equity on this and other analogous subjects.

"There is certainly very strong evidence in the present case, affirmative of such an abandonment or surrender, or at least of a deliberate acquiescence by the patentee in the public use of his invention by some or all of the defendants, without objection, for several years. The patent was obtained in 1829; and no objection was made, and no suit was brought against the defendants for any infringement until 1839, although their use of the invention was, during a very considerable portion of the intermediate period, notorious and constant, and brought home directly to the knowledge of the patentee. Upon this point I need hardly do more than refer to the testimony of Stedman and Barker, who assert such knowledge and acquiescence for a long period, on the part of the patentee, in the use of these ice-cutters by different persons (and among others by the defendants), on Fresh Pond, where the patentee himself cut his own ice. It is no

[1] 1 Jacobs, 311.

[2] 3 Mylne & Cr. 711, 728, 730, 735.

just answer to the facts so stated, that until 1839 the business of Wyeth, or rather of his assignee, the plaintiff, Tudor, was altogether limited to shipments in the foreign ice-trade, and that the defendant's business, being confined to the domestic ice-trade, did not interfere practically with his interest under the patent. The violation of the patent was the same, and the acquiescence the same, when the ice was cut by Wyeth's invention, whether the ice was afterwards sold abroad or sold at home. Nor does it appear that the defendants have as yet engaged at all in the foreign ice-trade. It is the acquiescence in the known user by the public without objection or qualification, and not the extent of the actual user, which constitutes the ground upon which courts of equity refuse an injunction in cases of this sort. The acquiescence in the public use, for the domestic trade, of the plaintiff's invention for cutting ice, admits that the plaintiff no longer claims or insists upon an exclusive right in the domestic trade under the patent; and then he has no right to ask a court of equity to restrain the public from extending the use to foreign trade or for foreign purposes. If he means to surrender his exclusive right in a qualified manner, or for a qualified trade, he should at the very time give public notice of the nature and extent of his allowance of the public use, so that all persons may be put upon their guard, and not expose themselves to losses or perils, which they have no means of knowing or averting, during his general silence and acquiescence.

"The cases which have been already cited fully establish the doctrine, that courts of equity constantly refuse injunctions, even where the legal right and title of the party are acknowledged, when his own conduct has led to the very act or application of the defendants, of which he complains, and for which he seeks redress. And this doctrine is applied, not only to the case of the particular conduct of the party towards the persons, with whom the controversy now exists, but also to cases where his conduct with others may influence the court in the exercise of its equitable jurisdiction. Under such circumstances, the court will leave the party to assert his rights, and to get what redress he may at law, without giving him any extraordinary aid or assistance of its own."

§ 441. But although it is a principle of equity, that a patentee must not lie by, and by his silence or acquiscence induce another to go on expending his money and incurring risk, and afterwards, if profit is made, come and claim a share in the profit, without having been exposed to share in the losses; yet delay to institute his proceedings may be explained by the difficulty of getting evidence of the infringement.[1]

§ 442. It has already been stated that in all cases of proceedings in equity to restrain the infringement of patents, in the courts of the United States, the injunction can, at no time, be applied for without notice to the adverse party, giving him an opportunity to oppose it; and, therefore, the injunction is always *special*.[2] Where the injunction is applied for before an answer has been filed, the plaintiff, in addition to the allegations in his bill, must read affidavits to show his title, and the fact of infringement, especially if the defendant appears and offers evidence against the one or the other; and these affidavits should, in strictness, cover the issue of the patent, the novelty of the invention, and all other facts necessary to the title.[3] It is believed, however, that in our practice, where the whole title is set out in the bill, which is sworn to, if the defendant does not read affidavits denying the title, it is not usual to read them in support of the title, which is considered as verified by the bill itself. But, if the defendant attacks the title by affidavit, it must be supported by auxiliary proof in addition to the bill, in order to make out the *primâ facie* right to an injunction.

§ 443. In one of the circuit courts of the United States some doubt has been thrown over the question, whether the plaintiff is at liberty to read affidavits in support of his title, after an answer denying it. Mr. Justice McLean has held, that on an application for an injunction, after an answer, the plaintiff is not entitled to read affidavits to contradict the answer upon the point of title.[4] Mr. Justice Woodbury, on the contrary, has held, that the plaintiff may show from counter-evidence that the case is different from that disclosed in the affidavits, or answer of the defendant,

[1] Crossley *v.* Derby Gas Light Company, Webs. Pat. Cas. 119, 120. As to what would be reasonable time, in certain circumstances, see Losh *v.* Hague, Webs. Pat. Cas. 200, 201.

[2] For the distinction between *common* and *special* injunctions, see 2 Story's Eq. Jurisp. § 892.

[3] 3 Daniels Ch. Pr. 1890, 1891, Amer. edit. 1846; Hindmarch on Patents, 332, and cases cited.

[4] Brooks *v.* Bicknell, 3 McLean, 250, 255.

and thus proceed to fortify his right to an injunction.[1] I am inclined, after some examination of the point, to think that the latter is the more correct opinion.[2] It is settled, in the first cir-

[1] Orr *v.* Littlefield, 1 Woodb. & Min. 13, 19. See the observations cited from this case, *ante.*

[2] If Mr. Justice McLean is to be understood to mean that the plaintiff is not at liberty to read affidavits in support of the novelty of his invention, after an answer denying it, it would seem that the practice and other authorities are opposed to his position. In the case above cited (Brooks *v.* Bicknell), the principal ground of objection to the plaintiff's title was, that the patent had been illegally extended; and the opinion does not expressly affirm that the plaintiff may not adduce evidence against the answer, to support the novelty of his invention, although this is implied in the observations of the court. It is, however, clear that there is a distinction between common and special injunctions on this point. In Hill *v.* Thompson, 3 Meriv. 622, 624, the leading case on the subject of injunctions in patent causes, where Lord Eldon laid down the rules that have since been followed by all judges, an injunction had been obtained until answer, or further order; on the coming in of the answer, the defendants moved to dissolve. The report does not expressly state that the answer denied the validity of the patent, but as this was the only question discussed, it is obvious that the answer must have contained such a denial; and it appears that a variety of affidavits were produced on both sides, tending respectively to impeach, and to assert the validity of the patent, and of the injunction to restrain the breach of it; and amongst them, was an affidavit by the plaintiff on the point of novelty. The same reasons for allowing affidavits of title to be read on a motion for dissolving an injunction apply to motions for granting it, in the first instance, where the answer has been filed. Now, upon the practice of reading such affidavits on a motion to dissolve, there has been a considerable conflict of decisions. But a distinction was adopted, at a very early period, with regard to injunctions for restraining certain wrongful acts of a special nature, as distinguished from the common injunction for staying proceedings at law. It is the settled practice of the court, in England, to allow affidavits to be read, at certain stages, against the answer, in cases of waste, and of injuries in the nature of waste; but, in cases of waste, they must be confined to the acts of waste, and the title, it is said, must be taken from the answer. Drewry on Injunc. 429; Gibbs *v.* Cole, 3 P. Will. 255; Norway *v.* Rowe, 19 Ves. 146, 153; Smythe *v.* Smythe, 1 Swanst. 254, and cases collected in the note. The question is, whether the same rule applies to cases of patents, or, whether they do not stand, in respect to the admission of affidavits on the point of title, upon the reason of the rule which permits affidavits in cases of waste upon the facts of waste. The ground of permitting affidavits to be read on the part of the plaintiff, in cases of waste, is that the mischief is irreparable; the timber, if cut, cannot be set up again, so that the mischief, if permitted, cannot be retrieved. The same reason exists in cases of partnership, by analogy to waste. Peacock *v.* Peacock, 19 Ves. 49. Does not this reason apply to a denial of the novelty of the plaintiff's invention?

cuit, by a decision referred to in the note below, by Mr. Justice Story, that the whole question of granting or dissolving injunctions, in cases of irreparable mischief, rests in the sound discretion of the court, after answer, as well as before.

It is also decided, in the second circuit, that where in an application for a provisional injunction the plaintiffs read affidavits in support of the bill, which are met by affidavits from the defendant setting up a license in defence, there the court may, under rule 107, and the emendation of May, 1846, permit the plaintiff to put in proofs of rebuttal of the defence, but that the defendant cannot reply to such rebutting proofs by further evidence on his part. Also, that the order admitting such proofs is regular, although not made until such rebutting proofs are received.[1]

Such a denial in the answer the defendant has a right to make, and to have it tried at law; but if the denial is to be taken as true, on a motion to grant or to dissolve an injunction, it may work an irreparable mischief before the plaintiff can establish his right at law; and yet this is the consequence of adopting the rule, that, in cases of patents, the title is to be taken from the answer, on motions for an injunction. The court must either assume that the denial in the answer, upon the point of novelty, is true; and, therefore, the plaintiff cannot have an injunction in any case, of however long possession, where the defendant chooses to make this denial; or it must say, that, however strong the denial in the answer, the plaintiff shall always have his injunction; or it must look into the evidence on both sides sufficiently to determine whether it is probable that the plaintiff will be able to establish his patent, and grant or withhold the injunction accordingly. The latter was the course taken by Mr. Justice Woodbury, in Orr *v.* Littlefield, where, however, an answer had not been filed, the defendant relying on affidavits; but the reasoning of the learned judge makes the same course applicable to cases where the equity of the bill is denied by the answer. See the observations of the court, cited *ante*. There is a dictum of Lord Langdale, M. R., in Wilson *v.* Tindal, Webs. Pat. Cas. 730, note (cited *ante*), that "notwithstanding this order (the injunction) the defendant may put in his answer, he may displace all the affidavits which have been filed on both sides." This I conceive to mean merely, that the defendant may show such a case in his answer, as to control the *primâ facie* case made by the plaintiff; and not that the answer necessarily displaces the affidavits before filed. In Poor *v.* Carleton, 3 Sumner, 70, 83, Mr. Justice Story reviewed this whole subject, and laid down the broad doctrine that the granting and dissolving injunctions, in cases of irreparable mischief, rests in the sound discretion of the court, whether applied for before or after answer; and that affidavits may, after answer, be read by the plaintiff to support the injunction, as well as by the defendant to repel it, although the answer contradicts the substantial facts of the bill, and the affidavits of the plaintiff are in contradiction of the answer.

[1] Day *v.* New England Car Spring Co., 3 Blatchf. 154. "The rule of pro-

ceeding applicable to injunctions must govern this case. The plaintiff has set out his rights and his injuries by his bill; and the defendants must be prepared to make their entire defence thereto, by showing in the first instance, by their answer or by affidavits, a want of right in the plaintiffs or a superior right in themselves. The law allows the plaintiff to obviate such defence by suppletory or rebutting evidence, and precludes the defendants from replying to such rebutting evidence by further proofs on their part. This is alike the rule at law and in equity. No court permits a defendant to make a new defence to proofs or arguments made in reply to his own. He has one hearing or chance alone, and must abide the advantage placed in the hands of the plaintiff. But this disadvantage to a defendant is not perpetual. The defendants can file their answer to the bill and move to dissolve the injunction; or they can appeal to the discretion of the court to award only a qualified one, &c.

"As this case stands, the defendants can meet it upon this motion, only by showing, from the depositions and documents before the court, that the plaintiff has no title, or that a paramount legal or equitable right is vested in them. This I understand to be, in a proceeding by injunction bill to stay waste or prevent the infringement of patent rights, the established practice of this court and of the English Court of Chancery." Rule 107 of this court, in Eq.; Rule, May, 1846; 1 Blatchf. 656; 3 Daniels, Ch. Pract. 1885, 1886, notes; 2 Waterman's Eden on Injunct. 384, 385, notes.

CHAPTER XI.

QUESTIONS OF LAW AND QUESTIONS OF FACT.

§ 444. THE several provinces of the court and the jury in the trial of patent causes have already been incidentally alluded to, but it may be proper to give here a summary of the principal questions which constitute matters of fact and matters of law.

§ 445. As to *novelty*. Under this general head there are several distinctions to be carefully observed. Novelty, as the term is generally employed, embraces only the topics of invention and identity. But it is evident that, where there is no dispute either as to identity or invention, the question may arise: granting the patent to be what the patentee claims it to be, can the *court*, without aid of the jury, say that the invention as it stands has been made known to the public? This issue arose in the case of Lang *v.* Gisborne [1] (already discussed in the chapter on Action at Law). The plan of the target invented and patented by the plaintiff was admitted to be identical with that made by the defendant, and also with one described in a work which was published in Paris before the patentee's application, and of which several copies had been sold in England. The only question, therefore, before the court, was whether the sale of a few copies, unaccompanied by evidence of subsequent public user, did amount to a publication in law such as would entitle the court to reject the plaintiff's application. The Master of the Rolls held that such a sale was a publication in law, and that the question could not be affected by any consideration of the number of the persons who might or might not be proved to have thought it proper to avail themselves of the publication.

This opinion is, we think, substantially embodied in the ruling of the Court of Common Pleas, in the case of Stead *v.* Williams.[2] It must, however, be observed, that this latter case differs from

[1] 6 Law Times, N. S. 771.

[2] 2 Webs. Pat. Cas. 126.

that of Lang *v.* Gisborne, inasmuch as the question of identity was also raised, and that therefore it was not only proper, but necessary, for the court to submit the question of prior publication to the jury, upon the whole of the evidence. In Lang *v.* Gisborne, on the contrary, no such point was at issue, but the whole resolved itself into a question of pure law. Making, then, this qualification, we think that the Common Pleas and the Master of the Rolls are of accord on the question what effect is to be given to publications. At the jury trial, Creswell, J., had instructed the jury thus: "But then the defendants do not bring home to the plaintiff the fact of his having seen any of those publications; and it is for you to judge, upon the whole of the matter, whether you think that he had seen those publications, and had derived his information from the stock of knowledge previously given to the public of this country," &c. This ruling was appealed from, and a new trial was granted on the ground of misdirection. Tindal, C. J., observes: "On a full consideration of the subject, we have come to the conclusion that the view taken by the defendants' counsel is substantially correct: for we think, if the invention has already been made public in England, by a description contained in a work whether written or printed, which has been publicly circulated, in such case the patentee is not the first and true inventor within the meaning of the statute, whether he has himself borrowed his invention from such publication or not; because we think the public cannot be precluded from the right of using such information as they were already possessed of at the time the patent was granted. It is obvious that the application of this principle must depend upon the particular circumstances which are brought to bear on each particular case. The existence of a single copy of a work, though printed, brought from a depository where it has long been kept in a state of obscurity, would afford a very different inference from the publication of an encyclopædia or other work in general circulation."

§ 446. Passing then to the question whether the patentee was the inventor of the thing patented, and whether the thing patented is substantially different from any thing before known, — an issue which, in distinction from the one treated of in the preceding paragraph, might be called the *material* one, — we find it broadly stated in a number of cases, that it is a question for the decision of the jury, and that the sole province of the court consists in giving the proper instructions as to what constitutes novelty and sufficiency of invention to sustain a patent.[1]

Here, again, there is a distinction, which was formerly much dwelt upon, and which gave rise to much discussion. The defendant, who is charged with infringement of a patent and raises the issue of novelty, may do so in two ways. He may simply allege that the plaintiff's invention is really no invention at all, but that it was in public use at the time the letters-patent were obtained. The evidence to support such an allegation would consist, then, of what is called evidence *in pais*, and, as such, could be weighed and decided upon only by the jury. All that the court can do in such cases is to instruct the jury that if they are satisfied that the plaintiff's invention is borrowed from some third party, or *substantially* contained in some printed publication (i. e. where there is a dispute as to identity), or substantially in public use at the time of the alleged invention, they must find for the defendant.[2] On this point all the decisions agree that in such cases the issue of novelty and identity is, under proper instructions, to be left to the jury.

It was, however, supposed — and the supposition lies at the foundation of a number of important English cases — that where the defendant, in a patent suit, claims himself to be acting under a patent, or asserts that the plaintiff's invention is contained in a patent granted to some third party, in such a case the court alone, by virtue of its acknowledged authority to be the sole interpreter of written instruments, could pronounce upon the question of identity. In other words, the court could say that the process or the machine claimed in A.'s patent is identical with that of B.

[1] Whittemore *v.* Cutter, 1 Gall. 478; Lowell *v.* Lewis, 1 Mas. 182; Carver *v.* Braintree Manuf. Co., 2 Story's R. 432; Washburn *v.* Gould, 3 Story's R. 122; Steiner *v.* Heald, 6 E. L. & Eq. 536, reversing s. c. 2 Carr. & Kirw. N. P. 1022. The patentee here had taken out letters-patent for the manufacture of garancine from spent madder. For a long while this spent madder had been worthless, although still containing a percentage of coloring matter. It was then discovered that by treating *fresh* madder with acid and hot water, *all* the coloring matter could be extracted. The plaintiff's invention consisted in treating the previous spent madder in the same way. Held by the Exchequer Chamber that it was a question for the jury, whether this was a new manufacture of garancine.

[2] Stead *v.* Williams, 2 Webs. Pat. Cas. 126; Stead *v.* Anderson, ibid. 147.

Thus, in Bovill *v.* Pimm,[1] the Court of Exchequer say, "We think this is a question of law, where the facts are not disputed." Also, in the recent case (1860) of Betts *v.* Menzies,[2] it was held by the Exchequer Chamber, on appeal from the Queen's Bench, that the comparison of two specifications was exclusively within the province of the court. The decision assumed that this point had been decided in Bush *v.* Fox,[1] a case which had been before the House of Lords in 1856.

In March, 1862, the case of Hills *v.* Evans[4] came up before the Lord Chancellor Westbury, and received from him a ruling in direct opposition to that of the Exchequer Chamber, in Betts *v.* Menzies. In rendering his decision his lordship entered into an elaborate discussion of the case of Bush *v.* Fox, and showed that the House of Lords, in that case, had not, as was commonly supposed, pronounced directly upon the question, but that the Exchequer, in giving their decision in Betts *v.* Menzies, had been misled by *obiter dicta* of Lord Cranworth in moving the vote of the house. In June, 1862, Betts *v.* Menzies came up to the House of Lords, on appeal from the Court of Exchequer Chamber. The decision of the Exchequer Chamber was thereupon reversed, and the ruling of Lord Westbury sustained.

In Hills *v.* Evans the Lord Chancellor said: "Now the argument has been, that it is the duty of the court and the right of the court to construe these earlier specifications, and that if I found, from the specifications so construed, when collated and compared with the specification of the plaintiff's patent, that the invention described in the one was identical with the invention described in the other, the court might at once arrive at the conclusion that there was no novelty in the invention, and deal with the whole matter as matter of law, and not as matter to be submitted to the jury, and that undoubtedly is a question deserving of very serious consideration. It is undoubtedly true as a proposition of law, that the construction of a specification, as the construction of all other written instruments, belongs to the court; but a specification of an invention contains, most generally, if not always, some technical terms, some phrases of art, and requires generally the aid of the light derived from what are called surrounding circumstances. It is therefore an admitted rule of law,

[1] 36 E. L. & Eq. 441.
[2] 1 Ell. & Ell. Q. B. 990.
[3] 38 E. L. & Eq. 1.
[4] 6 Law Times, N. S. 90.

that the explanation of the words or technical terms of art, the phrases used in commerce, and the proof and results of the processes which are described (and in a chemical patent, the ascertainment of chemical equivalents), that all these are matters of fact, upon which evidence may be given, and upon which undoubtedly it is the province and right of a jury to decide. But when those portions of a specification are abstracted and made the subject of evidence, and therefore brought within the province of the jury, the direction to be given to the jury must be a direction given only conditionally; that is to say, a direction as to the meaning of the patent, upon the hypothesis or basis of the jury arriving at a certain conclusion with regard to the meaning of those terms, the signification of those phrases, the truth of those processes, and the result of the technical procedure described in the specification. . . . [Citing from the opinion of Baron Parke, in Neilson *v.* Harford.] Now, adopting that as the rule in the comparison of two specifications, each of which is filled with terms of art and with the description of technical processes, the duty of the court would be confined to this, to give the legal construction of such document taken independently. But after that duty is discharged, there would remain a most important function to be still performed, which is the comparison of the two instruments, when they have received their legal exposition and interpretation; and, as it is always a matter of evidence what external thing is indicated and denoted by any description, when the jury have been informed of the meaning of the description contained in each specification, the work of comparing the two and ascertaining whether the words (as interpreted by the court) contained in specification *A* do or do not denote the same external matter as the words (interpreted and explained by the court) contained in specification *B*, is a matter of fact, and is, I conceive, a matter within the province of the jury, and not within the function of the court. Granting, therefore, to the full extent the propriety of the expression of the rule which is here contained, and taking either specification as so interpreted, whether the two specifications that are brought into comparison do or do not indicate the same external matter must be determined by the jury, and not as matter of law by the court. And I find that this has been the case and the course adopted by learned judges in a great variety of reported cases at Nisi Prius." The Chancellor then cites Muntz *v.* Foster, and Walton *v.* Potter, and proceeds to show that a seemingly contrary opinion, expressed by a former Lord Chancellor in Bush *v.* Fox, in moving the judgment of the House of Lords, was a mere *obiter dictum*, and not embraced in that judgment.

Similar language is employed by Lord Chancellor Westbury, in Betts *v.* Menzies,[1] before the House of Lords: "My Lords, the second question was this, 'can the court pronounce Betts's patent to be void, simply on the comparison of the two specifications, without evidence to prove identity of invention; and also without evidence that Dobb's specification disclosed a practicable mode of producing the result or some part of the result described in Betts's patent.[1] The answer of the learned judges involves, therefore, two conclusions which are extremely material to the patent law. One is this, — that even if there be identity of language in two specifications, remembering that those specifications describe external objects, even if the language be verbatim the same, yet if there be terms of art found in the other specification, it is impossible to predicate of the two with certainty that they describe the same identical external object, unless you ascertain that the terms of art used in the one have precisely the same signification and denote the same external objects at the date of the one specification as they do at the date of the other. And, my Lords, this is obvious; for if we take two specifications dated as the present are, one in 1804 and the other in 1849, even if the terms employed in the one were identical with the terms employed in the other, — supposing that each of them contained a term of art, e. g. a denomination of some engine, some instrument, some drug, some chemical compound, — it might well be that the thing denoted by that name in 1804 is altogether different from the thing denoted by the same name in 1849. If it were necessary to enter into such a subject, I could give numerous examples — say in chemistry — of things that were denoted by one name in 1804 and which have retained the denomination, but which, by improved processes of chemical manufacture, are at present perfectly different in their results, their qualities, and their effects, from the things denoted by the same name some forty or fifty years ago. It is perfectly clear, therefore, that if you compare two specifications, even if the language be the same, you cannot arrive at a certainty that they denote the same external object and the same

[1] 4 Best & Smith, 9 B. 996; 7 Law Times, N. S. 110.

external process, unless you enter into an inquiry, and ascertain as a fact, that the thing signified by the nouns substantive contained in the one specification are precisely the same as the things signified by the same nouns substantive contained in the other. In all cases, therefore, where the two documents profess to describe an external thing, the identity of signification between the two documents containing the same description, must belong to the province of evidence, and not to that of construction."[1]

In England, therefore, it must be regarded as settled by the court of ultimate appeal, that wherever there are terms of art employed, the court cannot compare two specifications and pronounce the inventions contained therein to be identical; and that the former cases holding a different doctrine are overruled. Thus, Booth *v.* Kennard,[2] as supporting the statement that the court may, on the issue of novelty, compare two specifications, is no longer law. The right of the court, however, to pronounce upon the patentability of an invention as there stated remains unaffected.

§ 446 *a.* It has recently been held by the Supreme Court of the United States, that where a prior patent is offered to invalidate the patent in suit, it is not for the court to instruct the jury, as matter of law, that the two specifications cover inventions which are or are not identical. It is a question for the jury, on the evidence, under general instructions as to the rules by which they are to consider the evidence.[3]

[1] Compare Hills *v.* London Gas Co., 3 Hurls. & Nor. 920; 5 ibid. 311.

[2] 2 Hurls. & Nor. 84; 1 ibid. 527.

[3] Bischoff *v.* Wethered, 9 Wall. 812. In this case Mr. Justice Bradley, delivering the opinion of the court, said: "The precise question has recently undergone considerable discussion in England, and has finally resulted in the same conclusion to which we have arrived. The cases will be found collected in the last edition of Curtis on Patents (§ 446). It was at first decided in the cases of Bovill *v.* Pimm, Betts *v.* Menzies, and Bush *v.* Fox, that it was the province and duty of the court to compare and decide on the identity or diversity of the two inventions. But in 1862 Lord Westbury, in two very elaborate judgments, one of which was delivered in the House of Lords, on occasion of overruling the decision in Betts *v.* Menzies, held that it belonged to the province of evidence, and not that of construction, to determine this question. 'In all cases, therefore,' he concludes, 'where the two documents profess to describe an external thing, the identity of signification between the two documents containing the same description must belong to the province of evidence, and not that of construction.' Lord Westbury very justly re-

§ 447. It is, however, to be kept in mind that the patentee, who is the real inventor of some useful machinery or process, may, nevertheless, by an improper wording of his claim, avoid the whole patent. The jury may find, as a matter of fact, that he is the inventor of the various steps in the process or the various items in the machinery; and yet, if the claim is so clumsily drawn up as to comprise other matters of which the patentee is not the inventor, the court must pronounce the patent invalid, either in whole or in part. This principle lies at the foundation of the decisions in Kay's ill-fated patent for flax-spinning.[1] Here the real invention consisted in macerating flax, and spinning it at a short ratch (two and a half inches) by machinery already known. The jury found for the patentee, Kay, that he was the inventor, and that his invention had been of great public utility. But, unfortunately, he claimed in his specification to be the inventor of the machinery, and the court (the House of Lords) held that such a claim was invalid.[2]

§ 448. The question whether a renewed patent is for the same invention as the original patent is also a question of fact for the jury;[3] as is likewise the question whether the invention has been abandoned to the public.[4]

§ 449. The question of *utility* is a question of fact, under some circumstances, and under other circumstances it may be for the court, without referring it to the jury, to pronounce the patent void. We have seen that a "useful invention," in the sense of

marks, that two documents using the same words, if of different dates, may intend diverse things, as indeed was actually decided by this court in the case of The Bridge Proprietors *v.* The Hoboken Company. . . . This view of the case is not intended to, and does not trench upon the doctrine that the *construction* of written instruments is the province of the court alone. It is not the *construction of the instrument*, but the *character of the thing invented*, which is sought in questions of identity or diversity of inventions."

[1] 2 Webs. Pat. Cas. 34–84.

[2] See chapter of Specifications, where this patent is discussed at length.

[3] Carver *v.* Braintree Manuf. Co., 2 Story's R. 432.

[4] Pennock *v.* Dialogue, 2 Pet. 16; Grant *v.* Raymond, 6 Pet. 248; Shaw *v.* Cooper, 7 Pet. 313; McClurg *v.* Kingsland, 1 How. 202; Kendall *v.* Winsor, 21 How. 322. Yet in Pennock *v.* Dialogue, 2 Pet. 1, Story, J., rules: "The question which generally arises at trials is a question of fact rather than of law; whether the acts or acquiescence of the party furnish, in the given case, satisfactory proof of an abandonment or dedication to the public. But when all the facts are given, there does not seem any reason why the court may not

our law, is one not injurious or mischievous to society, and not frivolous or insignificant, but capable of use for a purpose from which some advantage can be derived; and that when an invention is useful in this sense, the degree or extent of its usefulness is wholly unimportant. There are, therefore, two modes in which the utility of an invention may be impeached: first, when it appears, on the face of the letters-patent and specification, that the invention is injurious to the morals or health of society; secondly, when it appears, on evidence, that the thing invented, although its object may be innocent or useful, is not capable of being used to effect the object proposed.

§ 450. The question whether the invention is useful, in the first sense, is a question whether the patent is void, on the face of it, as being against public policy; or, in other words, because the subject-matter disclosed by the patent is not a patentable subject. This is a question of law for the court.[1] But when it does not appear that the invention has any noxious or mischievous tendency, but on the contrary that its object is innocent or salutary, there may be a further question, whether the means by which the inventor professes to accomplish that object will in practice succeed or fail. It is not essential to the validity of a patent that the success of the means made use of should be complete, or that the thing invented should supersede any thing else used for the same purpose; because the law looks only to the fact that the invention is capable of some use. Thus, if a machine is useful for some of the cases for which it is intended, although cases may occur in which it does not answer, it is still useful, in this sense of the patent law;[2] but if any thing claimed as an essential part of the invention is useless altogether, the patent is invalid, because there is a total failure in point of usefulness.[3] These questions, whether the invention is capable of use for the purpose for which it is claimed, and whether any thing claimed as essential is entirely useless, depend upon evidence, and are questions of fact for the jury.[4]

state the legal conclusions deducible from them. In this view of the matter, the only question would be, whether, upon general principles, the facts stated by the court would justify the conclusion."

[1] Langdon *v.* De Groot, 1 Paine's C. C. R. 203; Lowell *v.* Lewis, 1 Mason, 182; Phillips on Patents, 432.

[2] Haworth *v.* Hardcastle, Webs. Pat. Cas. 480.

[3] Lewis *v.* Marling, Webs. Pat. Cas. 490, 495.

[4] Haworth *v.* Hardcastle, *ut sup.*; Lewis *v.* Marling, *ut sup.*; Hill *v.*

§ 451. In like manner, the question whether an invention is frivolous or insignificant is a question of law. If the object proposed to be accomplished is a frivolous or insignificant object, from which no advantage can be derived to the public, it is for the court to pronounce the patent void, as not being for a patentable subject. But if the object proposed is not clearly frivolous and unimportant, but the means by which it is proposed to be accomplished do not succeed in producing the result, the question returns to the usefulness of the means, and this again becomes a question of fact for the jury.

§ 452. The construction of the specification, as to the extent of the claim, belongs to the province of the court. The court must determine, upon the whole instrument, what the claim actually covers, and whether the patent is valid in point of law. The jury are, therefore, to take the construction of the patent, as to the extent of the claim, from the court, and to determine whether any thing that is included in the claim is not new. But if the specification contains terms of art, which require explanation, by means of evidence, it is for the jury to find the meaning of those terms.

Nevertheless, even in such cases, the construction of the claim itself as such, that is, as a statement in a written instrument, belongs to the court, and cannot be left by them to the jury. On this point, the ruling in Emerson *v.* Hogg[1] is very precise and lucid: "We think the exception well taken to the fourth instruction given by the court to the jury, which is as follows: 'Whether the specification be ambiguous is generally a question of law to be decided by the court. In this case it is compounded of law and fact, and if the jury find the fact to be that a *spiral wheel* and a *spiral propeller* are the same thing in ordinary acceptation, then the specification is sufficiently definite and certain in this respect.' The part of the specification to which this instruction is applicable is this: 'I employ an improved *spiral paddle-wheel*, differing essentially from those which have heretofore been essayed. This *spiral* I make by taking a piece of metal of such length as I intend the *spiral propeller* to be, and of a suitable width, say, for example, eighteen inches; this I bend along the centre, so as to form two sides, say of nine inches in width, standing at right angles, or

Thompson, 3 Meriv. 630, 632; Lowell *v.* Lewis, 1 Mason, 182; Bedford *v.* Hunt, ibid. 302.

[1] 2 Blatchf. 1.

nearly so, to each other, and give to it, longitudinally, the spiral curvatures which I wish. Of these pieces I prepare two, three, or more, and fix them on the outer end of the paddle-shaft, by means of arms of a suitable length, say of two feet, more or less, in such a position that the trough form given to them longitudinally shall be effective in acting upon the water. It must be entirely under water, and operate in the direction of the boat's way. Instead of metal, the *spiral propeller* may be formed of wood and worked into the proper form, — the shape, and not the material thereof, being the only point of importance.'

"The specification was objected to, on the trial, as ambiguous, and one of the particulars urged in support of the objection was, that it was uncertain, upon the face of the specification, whether the patentee claimed a *wheel* constructed *spirally*, or only *spiral paddles* attached to a wheel. The court did not dispose of the point as a question of construction merely, but left a fact to be found by the jury, and indicated the rule of law that would govern when that fact should be ascertained. This was undoubtedly error. It is the province and the duty of the court to settle the meaning of the patent; and if that cannot be ascertained satisfactorily, upon the face of the specification, the law declares it insufficient for ambiguity and uncertainty. The meaning of the terms employed, in view of the object the inventor had in contemplation, and to ascertain the extent of his claim, must be determined and declared by the court. The specification is laid before the jury as defined and settled by the exposition of the court, and the matters of fact presented by the respective parties to support or defeat the patent are then to be examined and applied as if the construction fixed by the court had been incorporated in the specification. It accordingly devolved upon the court to dispose of the question as a point of law, and either to decide in this respect that the patent was ambiguous, and therefore void, and direct the jury to find a verdict for the defendants, or to rule against the objection and decide that the patent conveyed, in this particular, a meaning sufficiently certain, and point out what its claim was."

§ 453. And here it is very important to ascertain whether there are any principles, which are to guide the court in construing patents, peculiar to these instruments, or whether they are to be construed in all respects like other written instruments, and without the aid of extrinsic evidence. In one sense, a patent is a deed, being a grant of the government under seal; the letters-patent, the specification, and the drawings annexed being taken together as one instrument. But it often happens that the extent of the claim is not manifest on the face of the specification itself. The question arises, therefore, how is the court to ascertain the precise extent of the claim, as matter of law? The specification is a written instrument, in which the patentee has undertaken to state the invention which he professes to have made, and for which he has obtained letters-patent. In determining the real extent of the claim thus made, it is obvious that the actual invention of the party is a necessary auxiliary to the construction of the language which he has employed in describing it. The thing of which the patentee was the real inventor is what he was entitled to claim, and the question, in all cases requiring construction, will be, whether he has claimed more or less than that thing, or exactly what that thing is. If he has claimed more than his actual invention, that is, more than that of which he was an original and the first inventor, his claim is inoperative, under our law, *pro tanto*. If he has claimed less, his exclusive right is restricted to what he has claimed. If he has claimed the just extent of his actual invention, he is entitled to hold it in all its length and breadth.

§ 454. There are two sources to which the court is entitled to resort in construing a claim. In the first place, resort may be had to the descriptive parts of the specification, where the patentee has undertaken to state what his invention is; in other words, the court is to inquire what the patentee has said that he has invented. If his statement or description of the invention is clear and explicit, then the language in which he has made his claim, which is generally to be found in a summary statement of the subject-matter for which he asks a patent, may and should be construed so as to include the actual invention previously set forth, if it can be so construed without violation of principle;[1]

[1] See Russell *v.* Cowley, Webs. Pat. Cas. 469, 470; Davoll *v.* Brown, 1 Woodbury & M. 53, 59. Where the construction depends, as it generally does, in the first instance, on the terms of the specification, the preamble may sometimes be resorted to. Winans *v.* Boston & Providence Railroad, 2 Story's R. 412; sometimes the body of the specification, Russell *v.* Cowley, *ut sup.*, sometimes the summing up, Moody *v.* Fiske, 2 Mason, 112, 118. Generally, the whole is examined together, unless the summary seems explicitly to exclude

for the general maxim, under which the construction is to be pursued, is, according to the spirit of the modern authorities, *ut res magis valeat quam pereat.*

§ 455. But it may be uncertain, upon the terms of the descriptive parts of the specification, if unaided by evidence, what the precise extent of the invention was; and this may happen, without that degree and kind of ambiguity which renders a patent void for uncertainty, or because the directions could not be carried out by a competent workman. For instance, the patentee may state that he employs something which turns out not to be new; and the question will then be, whether he has so described that thing as to claim it as part of his invention; or his invention may be so stated as to render it doubtful whether he has invented or discovered the general application of a principle to produce a particular effect, and is therefore entitled to claim all the forms in which the same principle can be applied to produce the same effect, or whether he has only invented or discovered a from of giving effect to a principle the application of which was known before. So, too, on the general description of a machine, or a manufacture, which, as a whole, may be new, it may be uncertain whether the party invented the various parts of which that whole is composed, or only invented the combined whole, as he has produced it; and, if the latter, whether he invented the whole, as it may embrace all the forms and dimensions in which that whole can be produced, or whether his claim is to be confined to certain forms and dimensions, there being other wholes, of the same general character, of other forms and dimensions, which it does not include.

§ 456. In such cases, the character and scope of the invention can only be ascertained by attending to what the evidence shows is new or old; to the state of the art; to the fact of whether the principle, which the patentee has employed, had been discovered and applied before, and therefore that he could have invented only a new form of the application, or whether he has invented the application of the principle itself, and consequently is entitled, if he has not restricted himself, to claim the same applica-

the rest of the specification and to require a construction by itself alone. MacFarlane *v.* Price, Webs. Pat. Cas. 74; 1 Starkie, 199; The King *v.* Cutler, Webs. 76, note; 1 Starkie, 354; Ames *v.* Howard, 1 Sumner, 482, 485. See Davoll *v.* Brown, *ut sup.*

tion of the same principle, under other forms or dimensions, or by other means, than those which he has specifically described. The question, whether he has limited himself to particular forms, dimensions, or methods, necessarily involves an inquiry into the substance and essence of his invention. In other words, before it can be ascertained, in doubtful cases, what he has claimed, some attention must be paid to his actual invention, as ascertained on the evidence.

§ 457. To what extent, then, is the court entitled to receive evidence of the actual invention, and how is that evidence to be applied to the construction of the claim? In the progress of a *nisi prius* trial, the state of the art, the surrounding circumstances in which the inventor was placed, the previous existence of some things mentioned or referred to in the patent, will all be likely to be developed on the evidence; and these facts may materially affect the construction to be given to the claim. It has been said, and with great propriety, that in the exercise of the duty of determining what the claim is, in point of law, the judge must gather as he goes along; informing himself upon the evidence, and observing what facts are controverted, and what facts are not controverted, which bear upon the meaning of the claim, in reference to its extent.[1] If the facts material to the construction are not left in doubt on the evidence, the construction will be given to the jury, absolutely; but, if the evidence requires a finding of facts by the jury, the construction will be given to them conditionally.[2]

§ 458. Among the facts which will thus exercise an important influence on the extent of the claim, is the previous existence of something mentioned in the specification. If it is manifest, on the face of the terms in which the patentee has described his invention, that he has included something of which he was not the inventor, his patent cannot be allowed to cover it. But it may be doubtful whether he has so included the thing which the evidence shows to be old; and then the degree or extent to which that thing was known before, its great familiarity and constant use for analogous purposes, will be important elements in the question, whether the patentee has claimed it as of his own

[1] Per Lord Abinger, C. B., in Neilson *v.* Harford, Webs. Pat. Cas. 350, 351.

[2] Ibid., p. 370.

invention. This consideration has given rise to the rule, that the patentee is to be presumed not to intend to claim things which he must know to be in use; which is only another application of the broader rule, that a specification should be so read as, consistently with the fair import of language, will make the claim coextensive with the actual discovery or invention.[1]

§ 459. Another important consideration will be the state of the art. If, for instance, a patent contemplates the use of certain substances, although it may make use of terms extensive enough to embrace other substances, which, in the progress of the art, have been ascertained to be capable of the same use, but at the time of the patent were not known to be so, or, being known at the time to be capable of the same use, were yet so expensive as not to be expected to be in use for the same purpose, the general terms of the specification will be so interpreted as to include only those substances *ejusdem generis* with the particular substances mentioned, which may reasonably be supposed, on the state of the art, to have been contemplated at the time. This is to be ascertained by evidence.

§ 460. Thus, on a specification describing "An improved gas apparatus, for the purpose of extracting inflammable gas by heat from pit coal, or tar, *or any other substance* from which gas, or gases capable of being employed for illumination, can be extracted by heat," it appeared that it was known, at the date of the patent, as a philosophical fact, that oil would yield inflammable gas, but that the apparatus described in the specification could not be used advantageously, if at all, for the making of gas from oil; it was answered, that it was a general opinion at the time that nothing but coal would be cheap enough for purposes of illumination; and the court held that the patentee must be understood to mean things that were in use, and not every thing which would produce gas, but, from being so expensive, was never expected to be in use.[2]

§ 461. Sometimes the construction may rest on facts which are so referred to as to make a part of the description and to govern it. If these facts are controverted they are to be left to the jury. But if they are proved or admitted, the court will take notice of

[1] Haworth *v.* Hardcastle, Webs. Pat. Cas. 484, 485.
[2] Crossley *v.* Beverley, Webs. Pat. Cas. 106.

them in giving a legal construction to the instrument. Thus, where the question was, whether, in the specification of an improvement in a machine known by the name of speeder, double-speeder, or fly-frame used for roving cotton preparatory to spinning, the patentee had confined himself to the use of the bow-flier, that is, a flier in "one continuous piece," as part of his new combination; it appeared that the specification thus described the invention: "It will be seen that the fliers, as used by me, and shown at, &c., *are made in one continuous piece, instead of being open at the bottom, as is the case with those generally used in the English fly-frame*, and this, among other reasons, enables me to give the increased velocity above referred to." The patentee then summed up his claim as follows: "What I claim as new, &c., is the arrangement of the spindles and fliers, in two rows, *in combination with the described arrangement of gearing*," which he had previously pointed out. Although the language here did not admit of much doubt as to the kind of flier intended to be claimed, the court took notice of the admitted or apparent facts, which tended to show that the bow-flier alone was intended; one of which was, that the bow-flier alone could be geared as the patentee had described his flier to be, in two places, through its bottom; the other form of the open-flier having no bottom susceptible of being used or geared in that manner.[1]

[1] Davoll *v.* Brown, 1 Wood. & M. 53. In this case, Mr. Justice Woodbury said: "The construction seldom rests on facts to be proved by parol, unless they are so referred to as to make a part of the description and to govern it; and when it does at all depend on them, and they are proved or admitted, and are without dispute, as here, it is the duty of the court, on these facts, to give the legal construction to the instrument. But whether the court gave the right construction to the patent in dispute, so far as regards the kind of flier to be used in it, is a proper question for consideration now; and, if any mistake has occurred in relation to it, in the hurry and suddenness of a trial, it ought to be corrected, and will be most cheerfully. There is no doubt, as to the general principle contended for by the defendant in this case, that a patentee should describe, with reasonable certainty, his invention. Several reasons exist for this. One is, the act of Congress itself requires that he 'shall particularly specify and point out the part, improvement, or combination which he claims as his own invention.' And another is, that unless this is done, the public are unable to know whether they violate the patent or not, and are also unable, when the term expires, to make machines correctly, and derive the proper advantages from the patent. These principles, how-

§ 462. The sufficiency of the description to enable competent persons to apply the invention is a question of fact for the jury,

ever, are not inconsistent with another one, equally well settled, which is, that a liberal construction is to be given to a patent, and inventors sustained, if practicable, without a departure from sound principles. Only thus can ingenuity and perseverance be encouraged to exert themselves in this way usefully to the community; and only in this way can we protect intellectual property, the labors of the mind, productions and interests, as much a man's own, and as much the fruit of his honest industry as the wheat he cultivates or the flocks he rears. Grant *v.* Raymond, 6 Peters, 218. See also Ames *v.* Howard, 1 Sumner, 482, 485; Wyeth *v.* Stone, 1 Story, 273, 287; Blanchard *v.* Sprague, 2 Story, 164. The patent laws are not now made to encourage monopolies of what before belonged to others or to the public, which is the true idea of a monopoly, but the design is to encourage genius in advancing the arts, through science and ingenuity, by protecting its productions of what did not before exist, and of what never belonged to another person or the public. In this case, therefore, the jury were instructed to consider the case under these liberal views, unless the invention, such as the court construed it to be, in point of law, was described with so much clearness and certainty that other machines could readily be made from it by mechanics acquainted with the subject.

"Looking to the whole specification and drawing, both the figure and language, could any one doubt that bow-fliers were intended to be used in the new combination which was patented? The figure is only that of a bow-flier; so is the language. First, the spindles are described as working up and down 'through the bottom of the fliers, as seen at *a*,' which is not possible in the case of the open-flier, as that has no bottom for the spindle to work in.

"Again, the specification says, 'to the bottom of each flier a tube is attached, as seen at *b*, figures 1 and 2,' which is impracticable with an open-flier. Again, it says, 'motion is communicated to the flier independently,' but that is not feasible with the open-flier. And finally, towards the close, in order to remove all possible doubt, the specification adds, 'it will be seen that the fliers, as used by me, and shown at *ii* and *kk*, are made in *one continuous piece*, instead of being open at the bottom, as is the case with those generally used in the English fly-frames.' All know that the flier in one continuous piece is the bow-flier. Besides this, other admitted or apparent facts tended to show that the bow-flier alone was intended. One great advantage claimed from the new combination in the patent was an increased velocity of the spindle. Thus, in the early part of the specification, it is stated, among the advantages of his improvement, that 'the machine will bear running at a much higher velocity than the English fly-frame.' And towards the close he says, that it is the use of the flier in 'one continuous piece,' that is, the bow-flier, instead of the open one, as in the English fly-frame, which, 'among other reasons, enables me to give the increased velocity above referred to.' How could there, then, be any reasonable doubt, that in his patent it was this bow-flier he intended to use in his new combination?

"In truth, he not only says so, and could not otherwise obtain one of his

on the testimony of experts and the language itself.[1] But it does not follow from this that the construction of the specification is to be drawn into the province of the jury. Their province is, after having been informed what the specification has said, to determine whether the directions are sufficiently clear and explicit to enable a competent workman to practise the invention. Still, where it is evident on the face of the specification that no one could use the invention without first ascertaining by experiment the exact proportion of the different ingredients, the court must pronounce the patent invalid.[2] The information of what the specification has said is to come from the court; although it may happen, that in determining the meaning of the specification, the aid of the jury will be required to ascertain the meaning of words of art, or the surrounding circumstances, which govern that meaning. When such words of art or such surrounding circumstances do affect the meaning, the court will instruct the jury that the specification has said so and so, according as they find the meaning of the scien-

principal objects and advantages, but it is manifest from the form of the flier itself, and was not doubted at the trial, that only the bow-flier could be geared, as he described his flier to be, in two places, through its bottom ; the other form of the open flier confessedly having no bottom susceptible of being used, or geared in this manner. . . . There was no fact in doubt about this, to be left to the jury; and there was but one construction as to the kind of flier intended to be used, that was consistent either with the drawings, or the express language employed, or the chief object of the machine in its increased velocity, or in the practicability of gearing it in the manner before described by him in two important particulars, or of giving motion to it 'independently.' It is as clear and decisive on this point as if he had said *the before-described* spindles and fliers, because he says the spindles and fliers 'with the described arrangement of the gearing,' and no other spindles or fliers, but the short spindles and bow-fliers could be geared in the manner before described, through the bottoms of the latter. Matters like these must be received in a practical manner, and not decided on mere metaphysical distinctions. (Crossley *v.* Beverley, 3 Carr. & Payne, 513, 514.) Taking with us, also, the settled rules, that specifications must be sustained if they can be fairly (Russell *v.* Cowley, 1 Cromp., Mees. & Rosc. 864, 866; Wyeth *v.* Stone, 1 Story, 273, 287), that we should not be astute to avoid inventions, and that it is a question for the court, and not the jury, whether the specification can be read and construed intelligibly in a particular way (Whitney *v.* Emmett, 1 Baldw. 303, 315; Blanchard *v.* Sprague, 2 Story, 164, 169), we think the instructions given at the trial in this case were correct, and that no sufficient ground has been shown for a new trial."

[1] Lowell *v.* Lewis, 1 Mason, 190, 191.

[2] Wood *v.* Underhill, 5 How. 1.

tific terms, or the existence of the surrounding circumstances. If there are no words of art and no surrounding circumstances to be ascertained, the court, as we have seen, will instruct the jury what the specification has said; and then the jury will determine, the specification having said so and so, whether the description is sufficient to enable a competent workman to put the invention in practice.[1]

§ 463. There is no positive rule by which it can be determined, in a given case, *à priori*, whether the meaning of words of art, or the bearing of surrounding circumstances, affects the sense of the specification; or which limits the right of the plaintiff to offer evidence to show that its meaning is so affected. The plaintiff is always entitled to say that his specification requires the explanation of facts, to determine the extent of his claim and the character of his invention; and the only course that can be taken is for the court to receive and watch the evidence, and to apply it to the construction, taking care that it be not allowed to go so far as to supply positive omissions, which would render the specification defective. Within this limit, the construction, which is nothing more than the ascertaining of the meaning of what is written, may always be affected by evidence; which is to be taken into view, although no conflict arises requiring a finding of the jury, because the court can have no judicial knowledge either of the terms of art, or of the surrounding circumstances, and cannot say, until it has heard the evidence, that the meaning is not to be affected by them.

§ 464. The provinces of the court and the jury, then, are distinct, and upon this particular question of the practicability of the specification, it is of consequence that they should not be confounded. When it is put to a jury to determine whether a specification has so fully and accurately described the invention that others can practise it from the description, the danger sometimes arises of their undertaking to determine what the claim is; because the extent and character of the claim itself may depend on the same words on which they are to decide the intelligibility

[1] It follows, from the proposition that the court are to declare what the specification has said, that it is also a question of law upon the construction of the specification, whether the invention has been specifically described with reasonable certainty. This is a distinct question from the intelligibility of the practical directions, although both may arise upon the same passages.

of the directions, and may thus seem to be inseparably blended with the question of that intelligibility. But in truth these questions are always separable, and care should be taken to separate them. In one aspect, every thing is for the jury which bears on the question whether the specification sufficiently describes the mode of carrying the invention into effect; but on the other hand the meaning of the very passages on which this question arises, in relation to the prior question of what the specification has said, is for the court, after the facts which bear upon that meaning have been ascertained.

Thus, in Davis *v.* Palmer,[1] Marshall, C. J., says: "It may not, perhaps, be easy to draw a precise line of distinction between a specification so uncertain as to claim no particular improvement, and a specification so uncertain as not to enable a skilful workman to understand the improvement and construct it. Yet we think the distinction exists. If it does, it is within the province of the jury to decide whether a skilful workman can carry into execution the plan of the inventor."

§ 465. The case of Neilson *v.* Harford presents an apt illustration of the nicety and importance of these distinctions. Mr. Neilson invented the application of the hot blast to smelting furnaces, by introducing between the blowing apparatus and the furnace a chamber or receptacle, in which the air was to be heated on its passage, before it entered the furnace. After describing the mode in which this was to be accomplished, his specification said: "The form or shape of the vessel or receptacle [the vessel in which the air was to be heated] is immaterial to the *effect*, and may be adapted to the local circumstances or situation." This direction, it was contended, was calculated to mislead a workman, because it was not true; it was said, in point of fact, that the size or shape of the heating vessel was immaterial to the "effect" on the air in that vessel; and this, it was argued, was the "effect" concerning which this delusive statement was made in the specification. On the other hand, the plaintiff contended that the meaning of this passage was, that the size and shape of the heating vessel were immaterial to the effect *on the furnace*, and that it was true, in point of fact, that some beneficial effect might be produced on the furnace, whatever the size or

[1] 2 Brock. 298.

shape of the heating vessel might be, provided the temperature of the air be sufficiently raised.

§ 466. The principal question raised upon the pleadings was, whether the directions were calculated to mislead a workman who might be employed to construct such an apparatus, by stating that which was not true. This, it was allowed, was a question for the jury, but before it could be determined, it was necessary to ascertain what the specification had said; since the fact of its having or not having stated what was not true, would depend altogether upon the sense in which the words were to be received. At the trial, the presiding judge construed the word "effect" to mean the effect on the air in the heating vessel; and the jury having found that the size and shape of the heating vessel were material to the extent of beneficial effect produced, a verdict was entered for the defendants.

§ 467. Upon a motion to enter the verdict for the plaintiff, on this issue, founded on the special verdict, which also ascertained that some beneficial result would be produced from any shape of the heating vessel, it was argued with great force and ingenuity, that the question being whether the specification could or could not be carried into effect, which is confessedly a question for the jury, the whole question of the meaning of the passages on which they were to decide the sufficiency of the specification, was also for the jury, who were to say whether the words were or were not sufficient for carrying into practical effect the invention or discovery which the patentee supposed he had made. It was further argued, that the meaning of the words depended upon evidence; whereas, if the court were to pass upon the meaning of the paper, they must act upon the written paper alone, without evidence. But the court laid down the doctrine that in all cases the meaning of the specification is for the court; and, although the question which goes to the jury is whether the directions in the specification are sufficient or not, it is necessary for the court to declare what the specification has said. This must be done, either by taking into view at the time the evidence which bears upon the meaning, where it is not controverted, or by leaving to the jury, as matters of fact, to pass upon that evidence, in order to ascertain the meaning of scientific words, or the surrounding circumstances on which the construction depends. In the one case, the construction is given absolutely; in the other, it is given conditionally, because dependent upon facts to be found by the jury.[1]

[1] Neilson *v.* Harford, Webs. Pat. Cas. 295, 349. Sir W. Follett argued as follows: "I submit to your lordships that the whole question upon the validity of the specification, that is, on the meaning of the specification, and whether it can or cannot be carried into effect, is a question for the jury and not for the court, and that the jury are to put their construction upon the meaning of the words, and that the jury are to say whether the words are or not sufficient, and that it is for them to say whether the specification does sufficiently show the mode of carrying the invention and discovery which the patentee supposed he had made into practical effect. [Lord Abinger, C. B.: Why is the specification, which is a written instrument, more particularly to be considered by a jury, than any other instrument? The meaning of scientific words must be matter of evidence.] [Alderson, B.: The construction of it is surely for the court.] I do not know quite the extent to which it is supposed the authorities have gone in stating that certain papers are for the court. In many cases, undoubtedly, written papers are for the court, but I apprehend that is by no means a general doctrine of law; but that written papers, which involve a question of fact like this, whether or not the party has sufficiently described the invention, that that written paper is for the jury and not for the court, because it is for the jury to say, as a matter of fact, whether there be or not a sufficient description in that instrument to enable parties to carry it into effect. That I apprehend to be a question entirely for the jury. Certainly, the whole of this is a question of evidence, and a question of fact. It is a question of fact as relates to the paper; it is a question of fact as regards the evidence at the trial; it is not a question of law at all; and I do not know any rule which is to say that the court is to construe that specification, and to take it from the jury, because, supposing the fact to be that evidence was given at the trial on scientific matters, which evidence would aid the meaning or the construing of the instrument, your lordships can have no judicial notice of that at all. If it be a written paper for your lordships to decide upon, it must be without evidence. It is not that your lordships can come to a conclusion upon the meaning of the paper by looking at the evidence at the trial, but if it comes within the rule, that it is a written paper which the court is to act upon, then it must act upon the written alone. I think I can show your lordships that in every single case in which any question has arisen, it has been submitted to the jury, not decided by the court. [Lord Abinger, C. B.: Not consistently with my recollections; I have always thought that the meaning of the specification was to be determined by the court. That meaning may be varied by the evidence of particular words. A man must gather as he goes along in order to construe the written instrument. It is quite new to me that it is not to be considered by the court.] [Alderson, B.: Surely the court is to tell the jury what the specification has said. If the specification contains words of art, the court is to say, — If you believe these words of art to mean so and so, the specification has said so and so; leaving the question of words of art to the jury. But if

§ 468. The question whether the invention disclosed by the specification is a proper subject for a patent, is a question of law, on which the court will instruct the jury. It may involve the finding of a variety of facts; but when the facts are all ascertained, it is purely a question of law, whether the invention or discovery is a patentable subject. This is a distinct and very different question from that of the novelty of the invention. The thing claimed as the subject of a patent may be entirely new, and yet it may not fall wi hin that class of discoveries or inventions recognized by the patent law as the subjects of patents, and as such comprehended within the description of the statute. Thus, the subject-matter may turn out to be the application of an old or well-known thing, to a new purpose, constituting a new use only so far as the occasion is concerned; which the law decides is not the subject of a patent.[1] Or, on the other hand, the claim may be for the use of a known thing in a known manner, to produce effects already known, but producing those effects so as to be more economically or beneficially enjoyed by the public; which the law decides is a patentable subject.[2] In these and other

there are no words of art, what the specification has said is to be construed by the court. Then it is to be left to the jury, whether the specification having so said, it is or not a sufficient description of the invention according to their judgment.] I do not mean the validity of the specification as to questions in which you may direct nonsuits in point of law arising out of objections of a different kind, but that this question, whether or not the specification sufficiently describes the mode of carrying the invention into effect, that every thing relating to that is for the jury, and not for the court, — the meaning of the passages in the specification, and every thing. I should submit to your lordships that the whole of it was for the jury, and not for the court. [Alderson, B.: That there are some things in the specification which are questions of fact is true, and there are some things in the specification which are questions of law; the construction is to be given by the court, but the intelligibility of it is for the jury.] That is all I am contending. [Lord Abinger, C. B.: The intelligibility means with reference to words of science, or matters in it which persons may explain so as to satisfy the jury. You are discussing an abstract principle where it is not necessary: if you take an abstract principle, I must say the meaning of the specification is a matter of law, and that the judge must be informed, by evidence, of the facts, and then he must leave those facts to the jury, for them to find whether they be true or not.] See also *ante*, note.

[1] Losh *v.* Hague, Webs. Pat. Cas. 202, 207; Howe *v.* Abbott, 2 Story's R. 190.

[2] Crane *v.* Price, Webs. Pat. Cas. 408, 409.

cases where the question arises, upon all the facts attending and surrounding the alleged invention, whether it is a patentable subject, it is for the court to settle that question. Of course the novelty of the invention is a prerequisite to the validity of the patent, and this is a question of fact; but the alleged invention being ascertained to be new, it is still to be determined whether it is that species of invention to which the law gives the protection of a patent.

§ 469. The question of infringement is, as has already been stated, a question whether the invention of the defendant is substantially the same thing as that of the plaintiff. The identity of two things is a matter of fact, depending upon evidence; and although it is to be determined under the guidance of those principles which determine what constitutes identity and diversity in the sense of the patent law, yet it is for the jury to determine, as matter of fact, under proper instructions, whether the two things are the same or different.[1]

This is true even where there is no dispute as to the particular process or machine employed by the defendant, but only whether that process or machine is an infringement. The court cannot compare the plaintiff 's invention with that which is used by the defendant and say that the two are identical.[2]

For a full discussion of the question, what is proper evidence of the infringement, by means of chemical equivalents, of a chemical process, see Heath's patent and the numerous decisions elicited by it,[3] *supra*, chapter on Infringement.

§ 469 *a*. On the question of infringement, the issue is between the plaintiff's machine, as described in his patent, and the machine made, used, or sold by the defendant; and it is no answer for the defendant to show that he is a licensee under another patent, and that his machine is made in accordance with that patent.[4]

[1] Boulton *v*. Bull, 2 H. Bl. 463; Whittemore *v*. Cutter, 1 Gallis. 478; Pennock *v*. Dialogue, 4 Wash. 538; Lowell *v*. Lewis, 1 Mason, 191; Phillips on Patents, 431.

[2] Delarue *v*. Dickenson, 7 Ell. & Blackb. 738. Compare a similar question as to the provinces of court and jury on the issue of novelty, at the commencement of the present chapter.

[3] 2 Webs. Pat. Cas. 213; 32 E. L. & Eq. 45.

[4] Blanchard *v*. Putnam, 8 Wallace, 420.

CHAPTER XII.

EVIDENCE.

§ 470. The evidence appropriate to the different stages of a patent cause may be divided into (1) the evidence of title, and (2) the evidence upon the point of infringement. Evidence of title relates to the letters-patent and the plaintiff's interest therein, the novelty and utility of the invention, and the sufficiency of the specification. Evidence of the infringement relates to the identity of the thing made, used, or practised by the defendant, with the invention of the patentee.

§ 471. I. *As to the plaintiff's title.* With regard to the letters-patent, the statute of 1836, §§ 4, 5, makes a copy under the seal of the Patent Office and the signature of the commissioner competent evidence that a patent has been granted by the government for the invention described in the specification annexed. If the patent produced in evidence refers to the description in a former patent, it is necessary to produce and read that former patent, in order to show what the invention is, if it is not made entirely clear and intelligible by the patent on which the action is brought.[1]

§ 471 *a*. Where the patentee has surrendered his original patent and taken out a reissue with an amended specification, the action of the commissioner of patents in granting the reissue is conclusive evidence upon the question of "inadvertence, accident, or mistake." The decision of the commissioner is not re-examinable elsewhere, except upon the ground of fraud or evident want of jurisdiction. Such is the ruling of the Supreme Court in the case of Stimpson *v.* Westchester Railroad,[2] confirm-

[1] Lewis *v.* Davis, 3 Carr. & Payne, 502. A drawing filed subsequent to the destruction by fire of the original patent is admissible in evidence. Emerson *v.* Hogg, 2 Blatchf. 1.

[2] 4 How. 380.

ing the decision in Woodworth *v.* Stone,[1] under the provisions of the act of 1836, c. 357, § 13, although the same court had previously decided, in the case of Philadelphia and Trenton Railroad *v.* Stimpson,[2] that the action of the commissioner was only *primâ facie* evidence. The opinion of Judge Story in the case of the Philadelphia and Trenton Railroad, as cited in the note to the following paragraph, must accordingly be understood with this modification. So also, in the case of an extension of the term of letters-patent, the action of the commissioner is conclusive evidence of all the facts that he is required to find, and is impeachable only for fraud.[3] The signature of one styling himself "acting commissioner," attached to letters-patent, is sufficient in controversies between the patentee and third parties.[4]

§ 472. The letters-patent being thus proved to have issued, they are *primâ facie* evidence that the patentee was the first inventor of the thing patented.[5] The reason upon which this is held is that our statute requires the patentee to make oath that he is the first and true inventor of the thing; and when the patent has issued, supported by this oath, the burden of proofs is cast upon the party who would object, to show that the grant has been improperly obtained by the patentee; because the law presumes, in the first instance, that the patent has been granted upon the proofs which the statute requires to be laid before the officers of the government, and that those proofs were satisfactory.[6]

[1] 3 Story's R. 749.

[2] 14 Pet. 448. See *ante*, § 279 *et seq.*

[3] Clum *v.* Brewer, 2 Curt. C. C. 506; Colt *v.* Young, 2 Blatchf. 471.

[4] Woodworth *v.* Hall, 1 Woodb. & Min. 248, 389.

[5] Alden *v.* Dewey, 1 Story's R. 336; Woodworth *v.* Sherman, 3 Story's R. 172; Stearns *v.* Barrett, 1 Mason, 153. It is also held in England that the patent is *primâ facie* evidence, on the part of the person claiming the right, that he is so entitled. Minter *v.* Wells, Webs. Pat. Cas. 129.

[6] In the Philadelphia and Trenton Railroad Company *v.* Stimpson, 14 Peters, 458, Mr. Justice Story, delivering the opinion of the Supreme Court of the United States, said: "Now the objection is, that the present patent does not contain any recitals that the prerequisites thus stated in the act have been complied with, viz., that the error in the former patent has arisen by inadvertency, accident, or mistake, and without any fraudulent or deceptive intention; and that without such recitals, as it is the case of a special authority, the patent is a mere nullity and inoperative. We are of opinion that the objection cannot, in point of law, be maintained. The patent was issued under the great sale of the United States, and is signed by the President, and countersigned by the Secretary of State. It is a presumption of law, that all

Where the defendant wishes to set up a merely equitable title against one who possesses the full legal title, he must distinctly allege such defence in his answer, and establish it on the title. The burden of proof is against him.[1]

§ 473. When the patentee wishes to strengthen this evidence, either in the opening of his case or to rebut any evidence offered by the defendant which may have tended to show that he was not the first inventor, he can only call persons who were in the way of hearing of the invention if it had existed before, to testify that they have not heard of it. The proposition which the plaintiff has to establish is, strictly, a negative; he is to prove that the invention did not exist before; and therefore, as has been said, he must proceed by exhausting the affirmative instances of it, by calling those persons who might have known of it, if it had existed before, but who never have heard of it; and the more those persons, from their acquaintance with the particular trade or manufacture, were in the way of hearing of or meeting with it, the stronger the evidence will be.[2]

public officers, and especially such high functionaries, perform their proper official duties until the contrary is proved. And where, as in the present case, an act is to be done, a patent granted upon evidence, and proofs to be laid before a public officer, upon which he is to decide, the fact that he has done the act or granted the patent is *primâ facie* evidence that the proofs have been regularly made, and were satisfactory. No other tribunal is at liberty to re-examine or controvert the sufficiency of such proofs, if laid before him, when the law has made such officer the proper judge of their sufficiency and competency. It is not, then, necessary for the patent to contain any recitals that the prerequisites to the grant of it have been duly complied with, for the law makes the presumption; and if, indeed, it were otherwise, the recitals would not help the case without the auxiliary proof that these prerequisites had been, *de facto*, complied with. This has been the uniform construction, as far as we know, in all our courts of justice, upon matters of this sort. Patents for lands, equally with patents for inventions, have been deemed *primâ facie* evidence that they were regularly granted whenever they have been produced under the great seal of the government, without any recitals or proofs that the prerequisites under which they have been issued have been duly observed. In cases of patents, the courts of the United States have gone one step further, and as the patentee is required to make oath that he is the true inventor, before he can obtain a patent, the patent has been deemed *primâ facie* evidence that he has made the invention." See Pitts *v.* Hall, 2 Blatchf. 229.

[1] Gibson *v.* Cook, 2 Blatchf. 144.

[2] Cornish *v.* Keene, Webs. Pat. Cas. 503; Galloway *v.* Bleaden, ibid. 526; Pennock *v.* Dialogue, 4 Wash. 538. "The fact of making or exhibiting an

§ 474. Although this evidence is only general and negative, it is not, on that account, without weight. To illustrate its force as well as its proper office, we may suppose a case where the defendant had succeeded in showing that some prior inventor had made experiments in the same line as the patentee, and that this evidence goes so far as to show that that person had probably accomplished the same result as the patentee; but the point is still left in doubt, whether he had actually reached and perfected the invention for which the plaintiff has obtained a patent.[1] The rule of law in such cases is that if the prior efforts of some preceding inventor rested in experiment alone, his experiments, however near they may have been carried to the complete production of the thing, will not prevent a subsequent, more successful inventor, who has produced the perfect result at which both may have aimed, from obtaining a valid patent. The question for the jury will therefore be, in such cases, whether the efforts of the prior inventor rested in experiment alone, without coming to the point of completion, both in the theory and the actual application of the invention. Upon this question, the fact that the invention was never heard of until it was known to have proceeded from the present patentee, is of great weight. If it had been heard of among those persons who make it the business

article never before seen or heard of by the witnesses who prove the fact, is at least *primâ facie* evidence of invention, until other evidence is given to prove that the same article was invented, known, or in use, at an antecedent period of time, and that the patentee had only embodied the conceptions and the discovery of some other person."

[1] The remarks of Nelson, J., in Many *v.* Jagger, 1 Blatchf. 372, seem to be here in point: "But there is one fact to which we will call your attention, that is entitled to some consideration, although it is not decisive. The James wheel was in general use on the Harlem R.R. in 1834, and to some extent on the New Jersey R.R. Baldwin in Philadelphia in 1835, and Tiers in the same city in 1836, one of them a year, the other a year and a half after the James wheel was in common use on these two roads, made trial to cast the double-plate wheel; and we think, on the evidence in the case, it is fair to infer that they made their experiments with full knowledge of the James wheel. . . . If this inference be a fair one, and it is for the jury to say whether it is or not, then, with the James wheel before them, Baldwin and Tiers both failed to make a double-plate wheel. They had the idea of such a wheel in their minds, but were unable to perfect it. The conclusion would seem to follow, that the James wheel and the double-plate wheel were not necessarily identical, or that the former would necessarily lead to the latter without any ingenuity other than ordinary mechanical skill."

of their lives to know what is going on in the particular trade or art which it concerns, or to know what inventions in all arts or trades are from time to time produced, prior to the time when it was made by the patentee, the presumption would be very strong, that the person who is proved to have made near experiments towards it had actually accomplished the perfect result.[1] Still the evidence would not be conclusive, because the report that such an invention had been made might have arisen from what had been done in the way of experiment alone. But it would be very strong presumptive evidence that the experiments had terminated successfully, if persons who were in the way of hearing of such inventions should testify that they had heard of such an invention having been announced, although they had not seen it. On the other hand, if such persons had not heard of such an invention, the evidence would not show conclusively that the prior experiments rested in experiment alone, but it would have a very strong tendency to establish this conclusion, because there is an irresistible tendency in inventions to become known, as to their results, if not as to their processes, whenever the results are accomplished.[2]

§ 475. There is one other species of evidence, applicable to the issue of novelty, when the question is as to the time when the patentee had completed his invention. It may be necessary for the plaintiff to rebut evidence offered by the defendant as to the invention and use of the same thing by other persons before the date of his patent, and hence it may be important to show

[1] If such persons had *seen* the thing, no further inquiry would be necessary, for the proof would be positive that the thing existed before. But the evidence we are here considering relates merely to the fact of such persons having or not *heard of* the invention, which fact, if shown in the affirmative, of course must be aided by proof of its having been made by somebody, and would not alone be conclusive proof of its actual previous existence.

[2] The case of Galloway *v.* Bleaden, Webs. Pat. Cas. 521, 525, presents a state of facts similar to that which we have supposed in the text. Two witnesses conversant with subjects of the description of the patented invention, and who devoted themselves to the knowledge of the inventions made from week to week, testified that they had not before heard of such a discovery previous to the issuing of the plaintiff's patent. The court said this was enough to call on the other side to show affirmatively that the invention was not new, and that it was for the jury to say whether the evidence as to what had been done by the antecedent experiments or efforts of others, in the way in which it ought to be understood, had brought their minds to that conclusion.

the precise time when the invention was completed by the patentee. For this purpose the patentee may give in evidence his own declarations, as part of the *res gestæ*, describing the nature and object of the invention, to an extent which has been defined by the Supreme Court of the United States.[1]

But where the inventor has parted with his interest in the letters-patent, e. g. by assignment, any subsequent declarations made by him are wholly inadmissible, either to show a want of title in him, or to affect the quality of the article, or to impair in any way the rights of the assignee.[2]

§ 476. Sometimes the issue of novelty involves the identity or diversity of the thing patented, compared with something before known or used, on which the defendant relies to defeat the

[1] "In many cases of inventions, it is hardly possible in any other manner to ascertain the precise time and exact origin of the particular invention. The invention itself is an intellectual process or operation; and, like all other expressions of thought, can in many cases scarcely be made known, except by speech. The invention may be consummated and perfect, and may be susceptible of complete description in words, a month, or even a year before it can be embodied in any visible form, machine, or composition of matter. It might take a year to construct a steamboat, after the inventor had completely mastered all the details of his invention, and had fully explained them to all the various artisans whom he might employ to construct the different parts of the machinery. And yet, from those very details and explanations, another ingenious mechanic might be able to construct the whole apparatus, and assume to himself the priority of the invention. The conversations and declarations of a patentee, merely affirming that at some former period he invented that particular machine, might well be objected to. But his conversations and declarations, stating that he had made an invention, and describing its details and explaining its operations, are properly to be deemed an assertion of his right, at that time, as an inventor, to the extent of the facts and details which he then makes known, although not of their existence at an antecedent time. In short, such conversations and declarations, coupled with a description of the nature and objects of the invention, are to be deemed a part of the *res gestæ*, and legitimate evidence that the invention was then known to and claimed by him; and thus its origin may be fixed at least as early as that period." The Philadelphia and Trenton Railroad Company *v.* Stimpson, 14 Peters, 462. In Pettibone *v.* Derringer, 4 Wash. 215, the patentee was allowed to give in evidence his letters to the Secretary of State, containing applications and specifications, and certified under the department seal as papers remaining in that office. See Allen *v.* Blunt, 2 Woodb. & Min. 121, where a motion for a new trial, on the ground that such letters had been admitted in evidence, was refused.

[2] Many *v.* Jagger, 1 Blatchf. 376.

patent. The nature of the evidence, and the sources from which it is to be drawn, are the same upon this issue as when the question of identity or diversity arises under the issue respecting an infringement; and the consideration of the principles of evidence on both of these issues may here be postponed until we come to the general discussion of the question of identity.

§ 476 *a*. Where the patent is for a combination, the patentee is not permitted, on the trial, to abandon a part of the combination as useless, still less can he be suffered to prove it useless.[1]

With regard to the evidence of damages in an action for infringement, see *ante*, chapter on Infringement, where this topic is discussed at length. Here it may suffice to state that, in the absence of a license fee, actual damages must be proved by evidence bearing directly on the point, so that the jury may be furnished with sufficient data, and not left to the exercise of their ingenuity in guessing probable damages.[2]

§ 477. The plaintiff must also offer some evidence of the utility of his invention. The degree of utility, as we have seen, is not material; but the invention must be capable of some use, beneficial to society. This is ordinarily proved by the evidence of persons conversant with the subject, who may be called upon to say whether the thing invented is or is not capable of the use for which it is designed, or whether it is an improvement upon what had been in use before. But it may also be proved by other testimony, which will show that large orders have been given for the article by the public, or that licenses have been taken for the exercise of the right.

§ 478. The plaintiff, in addition to the *primâ facie* evidence of the novelty of his subject-matter, must also offer some proof of the sufficiency of his specification. In other words, he must show, to use the language of the statute, that his specification is "in such full, clear, and exact terms, as to enable any person, skilled in the art or science to which it appertains, to make, construct, compound, or use" the thing patented. This may be

[1] Vance *v.* Campbell, 1 Black. 427.

[2] Seymour *v.* McCormick, 16 How. 480; City of New York *v.* Ransom, 23 How. 487; Suffolk Co. *v.* Hayden, 3 Wall. 315. In view of these subsequent cases, it may be questioned whether the rule on the evidence and measure of damages, as laid down by Judge Nelson, in Stevens *v.* Felt, 2 Blatchf. 37, is still to be considered as law.

apparent to the jury on the face of the specification itself, from its simplicity and the absence of technical terms and descriptions; but where the invention is at all complicated, or terms of art or science are made use of, requiring the exercise of technical knowledge to determine whether the specification is sufficient, it is at least advisable, if not necessary, for the plaintiff, in opening his case, to give some evidence that his specification can be applied by those to whom the law supposes it to be addressed. If the sufficiency of the specification is disputed, the plaintiff must go into evidence to sustain it. How much of this evidence may properly be reserved for answer to the defendant's case, and how much should be introduced in the plaintiff's opening, must depend on the circumstances of the trial, although it may be stated, as a general rule, that slight evidence of sufficiency is all that is necessary to be offered at first, in order to make it incumbent on the defendant to falsify the specification.[1]

§ 479. The nature and source of the evidence, to show the sufficiency of a specification, present a topic of much interest, under that somewhat difficult branch of the law of evidence which relates to experts. What is the meaning of the statute, when it refers to the ability of persons "skilled in the art or science" to which the invention appertains, "or with which it is most nearly connected," to make, construct, compound, and use the same? Does it mean to adopt as witnesses those only who have the practical skill of artisans in the art or science, and to make their ability to understand and apply the specification the test of its sufficiency, or does it include that higher class of persons, who, from general scientific knowledge, or from a theoretical acquaintance with the principles of the art or science involved, might be able to teach an artisan or practical workman how to practise the invention? It is apparent that both of these classes of persons may be within the

[1] It seems to be the rule in England that the plaintiff must open with some evidence of the sufficiency of his specification, unless the defendant admits that it was tried and succeeded. Turner *v.* Winter, Webs. Pat. Cas. 81; 1 T. R. 602; Cornish *v.* Keene, Webs. Pat. Cas. 503. And if a whole class of substances be stated as suitable, the plaintiff must show that each of them will succeed. Bickford *v.* Hewes, ibid. 218. Under our system of pleading, the same rule should be followed. Although the defendant is obliged to give notice if he intends to rely on the insufficiency of the specification, the plea of not guilty puts the sufficiency of the specification in issue, and the plaintiff must therefore prove it as one of the things necessary to found his action.

literal meaning of the phrase "skilled in the art or science"; but the question is, whether the law contemplates one only, or both of them, as the proper witnesses to determine the sufficiency of a specification. It seems to me very clear that the law means to adopt, as a general standard of the sufficiency of a specification, the ability of skilful practical workmen to practise the invention from the directions given in the specifications. The standard of acquirement and knowledge may vary with the nature of the subject-matter; but where the invention falls within the province of an art or science, which is practised by a particular class of mechanics, operators, manufacturers, or other workmen, who possess and whose vocation it is to apply technical knowledge in that particular branch of industry, the patent law refers to their capacity to take the specification and carry out in practice the direction which it contains, without invention or addition of their own.

§ 480. Thus, if the invention be of a pump, or of some improvement in pumps, the question will be whether a pump-maker of ordinary skill could construct one upon the plan given in the specification, from the directions given.[1] If it be a composition of matter falling within the art of practical chemistry, the question on the specification will be whether its directions are so clear and intelligible that a practical chemist of ordinary skill could make the compound by following out the directions.[2] If it be a process involving the application of a principle in physics to a particular branch of manufacture, to be carried into effect in a particular manner, the question will be whether the directions, if fairly followed out by a competent workman, of the class ordinarily employed to construct an apparatus of that kind, would produce the effect intended.[3] This seems to be the general rule, applicable to a very large proportion of the inventions which become the subjects of patents; and accordingly it may be stated as a general rule that the proper witnesses to determine on the sufficiency of a specification are practical workmen of ordinary skill in the particular branch of industry to which the patent relates, because it is to them that the specification is supposed to be addressed.[4]

1 Lowell *v.* Lewis, 1 Mason, 182.
2 Ryan *v.* Goodwin, 3 Sumner, 514.
3 Neilson *v.* Harford, Webs. Pat. Cas. 371.
4 Gibson *v.* Brand, Webs. Pat. Cas. 629; Bickford *v.* Skewes, ibid. 219;

§ 481. At the same time, there may be another class of witnesses, of much higher character, competent to be examined on

Arkwright *v.* Nightingale, ibid. 61; Elliott *v.* Aston, ibid. 224; Huddart *v.* Grimshaw, ibid. 87; Morgan *v.* Seaward, ibid. 174; Neilson *v.* Harford, ibid. 371. The following instructive charge, given by Alderson, B., to the jury in Morgan *v.* Seaward, contains an elaborate illustration of the law on this point of intelligibility. "I will now begin with the specification. It is the duty of a party who takes out a patent to specify what his invention really is, and although it is the bounden duty of a jury to protect him in the fair exercise of his patent right, it is of great importance to the public, and by law it is absolutely necessary, that the patentee should state in his specification, not only the nature of his invention, but how that invention may be carried into effect. Unless he be required to do that, monopolies would be given for fourteen years to persons who would not, on their part, do what in justice and in law they ought to do, state fairly to the public what their invention is, in order that other persons may know what is the prohibited ground, and in order that the public may be made acquainted with the means by which the invention is to be carried into effect. That is the fair premium which the patentee pays for the monopoly he receives. The question is, whether Mr. Galloway has in the specification, and which is accompanied by a drawing which you ought to take as part of the specification, described with sufficient clearness and distinctness the nature of his invention, and the mode by which it is to be carried into effect. He has described two inventions, and if either of those inventions is not sufficiently specified, the patent fails; for if a person runs the hazard of putting two inventions into one patent, he cannot hold his patent, unless each can be supported as a separate patent. In order to support each, the invention must be useful, and must be described in the specification in such a manner as to lead people clearly to know what the invention is, and how it is to be carried into effect. That doctrine must be applied to each of the two inventions contained in this patent, that is, to the invention of the steam-engine, and the invention of the machinery for propelling vessels.

"To begin, therefore, with the steam-engine. Has Mr. Galloway sufficiently described it so as to enable any one to know what he has invented, and so as to enable a workman of competent skill to carry the invention into effect? Mr. Justice Buller, in the case of the King *v.* Arkwright, lays down as the criterion that a man, to entitle himself to the benefit of a patent of monopoly, must disclose his secret and specify his invention in such a way that others of the same trade, who are artists, may be taught to do the thing for which the patent is granted, by following the directions of the specification, without any new invention or addition of their own. That is reasonable and proper; for people in trade ought to be told the manner in which the thing may be done in respect of which the patent is granted. How? Not by themselves becoming inventors of a method of carrying it into effect, but by following the specification, without making a new invention, or making any addition to the specification. If the invention can only be carried into effect by persons setting themselves a problem to solve, then they who solve the

this point. These are persons who possess a thorough scientific knowledge, of a theoretical nature, of the principles of the art or

problem become the inventors of the method of solving it, and he who leaves persons to carry out his invention by means of that application of their understanding, does not teach them in his specification that which, in order to entitle him to maintain his patent, he should teach them, the way of doing the thing, but sets them a problem, which, being suggested to persons of skill, they may be able to solve. That is not the way in which a specification ought to be framed. It ought to be framed so as not to call on a person to have recourse to more than those ordinary means of knowledge (not invention) which a workman of competent skill in his art and trade may be presumed to have. You may call upon him to exercise all the actual existing knowledge common to the trade, but you cannot call upon him to exercise any thing more. You have no right to call upon him to tax his ingenuity or invention. Those are the criteria by which you ought to be governed, and you ought to decide this question according to those criteria. You are to apply those criteria to the case now under consideration, and you should apply them without prejudice, either one way or the other, for it is a fair observation to make, that both parties here stand, so far as this objection is concerned, on a footing of perfect equality. The public, on the one hand, have a right to expect and require that the specification shall be fair, honest, open, and sufficient; and, on the other hand, the patentee should not be tripped up by captious objections which do not go to the merits of the specification. Now, applying those criteria to the evidence in the cause, if you shall think that this invention has been so specified that any competent engineer, having the ordinary knowledge which competent engineers possess, could carry it into effect by the application of his skill, and the use of his previous knowledge, without any inventions on his part, and that he could do it in the manner described by the specification, and from the information disclosed in the specification, then the specification would be sufficient. If, on the other hand, you think that engineers of ordinary and competent skill would have to set themselves a problem to solve, and would have to solve that problem before they could do it, then the specification would be bad.

"Further, if a patentee is acquainted with any particular mode by which his invention may be most conveniently carried into effect, he ought to state it in his specification. That was laid down in a case before Lord Mansfield. There the question arose on a patent for steel trusses. It appeared that the patentee, in some parts of his process, used tallow to facilitate the invention for which he had obtained a patent, and in his specification he made no mention of the use of the tallow. The court held the specification to be bad, because, they said, you ought not to put people to find out that tallow is useful in carrying into effeot the invention of steel trusses. You ought to tell the public so, if that is the best mode of doing it, for you are bound to make a *bonâ fide* full and candid disclosure. So again in the case of the malt. That was a patent for drying malt, and one of the objections taken was that the patentee did not state in his specification the degree of heat to which the

science to which the patent relates, but who do not, as an habitual occupation, devote themselves to the application of those princi-

malt should be exposed. The argument there was this. They said, it appeared that the specification was not sufficient, inasmuch as it did not describe the extent of heat to which the malt should be exposed, for it only said, 'the proper degree of heat and time of exposure will be easily learned by experience, the color of the internal part of the prepared grain affording the best criterion.' Surely, there it would have been competent to the patentee to say, any person of ordinary skill, in such a business, would be able to judge what color the malt ought to be, and that, by experiment, he would learn what degree of temperature was exhibited at the time when that proper degree of color was obtained; therefore the plaintiff contended that there was enough stated in the specification to enable the public to carry the invention into effect, and that the patent ought to be supported, because skilful malsters and skilful driers of malt would easily know where to stop, and what degree of heat was requisite for the purpose. There is no doubt that when a man was told that a certain effect might be produced upon the malt by shaking it and subjecting it to a certain degree of heat, his mind would be set on float; he would be at work upon it to ascertain what that degree of heat should be, and he would probably find it out. But that is not enough. The specification of a patent must not merely suggest something that will set the mind of an ingenious man at work, but it must actually and plainly set forth what the invention is, and how it is to be carried into effect, so as to save a party the trouble of making experiments and trials. The court in that case said, that a specification that casts upon the public the expense and labor of experiments and trials, is undoubtedly bad. Here, in this case, the defendants take that line of argument; they say that experiments and trials are necessary. If it be said that all these matters will be well or easily known to a person of competent skill (and to such only the patentee may be allowed to address himself), then the invention will not in reality have given any useful or valuable information to the public.

"Now, let us apply the principle of this case to the present, and see whether or not the patentee here has given that full information by the specification and drawing, which, being addressed to persons of competent skill and knowledge, would enable them, from that specification and drawing, to carry the invention into effect. On that subject there is, undoubtedly, contradictory evidence, but you see a specification is addressed to all the world, and therefore all the world, at least those possessed of a competent skill, ought to be able to construct the machine by following that specification. It is not fair to you or to me, if we happen to be less inventive than our neighbors, that we should be prevented from constructing these machines by reason of the specification not giving a clear exposition of the way in which it is to be done. In the case of the steam-engine, there was put in on the part of the defendants a model made, as it was said, according to the specification, which model would not work. The model was a copy of the drawing, and would not work, because one part happened to be a little too small, whereas, if it had been a little

ples in the practical exercise of that art, science, or manufacture. Such persons may, without doubt, be examined as to the suffi-

larger, it would have worked. Now a workman of ordinary skill, when told to put two things together so that they should move, would of course, by the ordinary knowledge and skill he possesses, make them of sufficient size to move. There he would have to bring to his assistance his knowledge that the size of the parts is material to the working of the machine. That is within the ordinary knowledge of every workman. He says, 'I see this will not work because it is too small,' and then he makes it a little larger, and finds it will work. What is required is, that the specification should be such as to enable a workman of ordinary skill to make the machine; with respect to that, therefore, I do not apprehend you will feel much difficulty, but with respect to the other there is a good deal more difficulty. I will not sum up the evidence upon the subject of the steam-engine, but I will confine myself to the second invention, and see whether that can be carried into effect by means of the specification and the drawings, for it is to that question that the whole is directed. That invention is in two parts: first, he says, it is an improvement on paddle-wheels for propelling vessels, whereby the float-boards or paddles are made to enter and come out of the water at positions the best adapted, as far as experiments have determined the angle, for giving full effect to the power applied. He says, as far as experiments have determined the angle. That clearly speaks of an invention for enabling a party to use paddle-wheels for propelling vessels, which may be adjusted in such a way as that they may enter and come out of the water in angles the best adapted to give effect to the power of the engine, that is to say, at the angle *a*, if that shall be the best position for giving full effect to the power of the engine, or at the angle *b*, if that shall, hereafter, by experiment, be determined to be the proper angle. It appears from his statement here, that the proper angle was a matter of considerable doubt at that time; and, therefore, he does not profess to set down an individual angle as the best, which appears to have been one of the ideas of the defendant, as to the effect of the plaintiff's specification. But he says, I will give you a method of enabling the paddle-wheels to enter and come out of the water, with the position the best adapted for giving full effect to the power of the engine. Then, at the end of the specification, after having described the manner in which it is to be done, he says, that his claim is 'for the mode hereinbefore described of giving the required angle to the paddles (that is, any angle which may be required by the person ordering the machinery) by means of the rods *g*, *h*, *i*, *j*, and *k*, the bent stems marked *f*, the disk *a*, and the crank *b*.' Now, I do not think that means he is to give you a machine, the angle of which may now be *a*, and now *b*, but that if you wish to have a machine, the paddles of which shall enter at angle *a*, which you tell him, and go out at angle *b*, which you tell him, he ought to be able to construct a machine which shall answer to your order. That I take to be what the inventor says he has enabled the public to do by means of his specification and plan. He then describes the invention. In Fig. 4, you have the shape of the stem, and a particular angle is mentioned, but it is obvious that that is

ciency of a specification; but the question which should be propounded to them, in cases where there is a recognized class of

not an angle to which the parties are necessarily to be confined. Then he says, '*g*, *h*, *i*, *j*, and *k* are connecting rods attached at one of their ends by pins or bolts, *r*, to the bent stems, *f*, of the float-boards, and the other ends of all these rods, excepting *g*, are attached to the disk, *a*, by pins or bolts, *s*, as shown in Fig. 5.' The only observation is, that he gives no dimensions; he fixes no points either for the centre or the eccentric, or for the crank to which the eccentric centre is attached; therefore, if those can only be ascertained by experiments subsequently to be made, then the specification is bad. The whole, in some degree, turns upon the length of the rods and the position of the centre of the eccentric. The principle upon which these parties proceed, and upon which all the inventions in that respect proceed, is that the wheel, with its spokes, to which the floats are attached, turns round on an axis, and the floats are made to turn by means of an eccentric, and therefore the floats bend as the wheel revolves, and they bend in a particular manner, according as the floats are disposed and according to the position of the centre of the eccentric, by which they are regulated. They are regulated by means of a fixed bar, which is attached to the centre of the eccentric disk. The others are movable boards, which are attached apparently to the circumference of that same disk, and the whole is made to revolve by the fixed bar being attached to a fixed point of the wheel itself, and therefore the revolution of the wheel forcing that fixed point round, turns round the eccentric disk, and with it changes continually the position of all those rods which are affixed to the circumference of that disk, and, according to their being on one or the other side of that disk, they operate on the respective float-boards to which they are attached. All that turns upon the position of the eccentric axis and the length of the respective rods operating through the medium of this centre upon the respective float-boards. Now the question is, whether, in the absence of any statement as to the dimensions of these different parts, and of any directions for finding the centre of the eccentric, you think the specification is sufficient or not, and that must be determined by the evidence which has been given by the witnesses on the one side and on the other.

"Now, gentlemen, you cannot treat the actual picture which is given in the drawing as any guide to the particular angle or to the particular position of the eccentric; and for this simple reason. If that were the criterion, then the substance of the invention would be the particular angle contained in the particular drawing, and, in order to show an infringement, they ought to have shown that Mr. Seaward's wheel entered the water at the same angle as the angle described by the drawing, and therefore, in that case, you would be bound to find the first issue for the defendant, namely, that there was no infringement. If, however, you treat the picture or the drawing as only an illustration of the invention, and not as confining the invention to the particular angle there described, then you ought to find in the specification some directions which should enable you to construct the machine in a new form, or you ought to be satisfied that, without any instructions, a workman of ordinary and

practical workmen, who would be called upon to apply the directions of the specification, is whether a person of that class, of

competent skill and knowledge would be able to do it. Now, I do not think that Mr. Carpmael gives any evidence to that point; but Mr. Brunel says, 'I have read the specification, and I think I could construct by it a machine at any required angle without difficulty.' You see he says, 'I think I could construct by it a machine at any required angle without difficulty'; but whether Mr. Brunel could do it or not, is not the point. I dare say Mr. Brunel, the inventor of the block machinery, could invent any thing of this sort, the moment it was suggested to him, but that is not the criterion. The question is, whether a man of ordinary knowledge and skill, bringing that ordinary knowledge and skill to bear upon the subject, would be able to do it.

"Then the evidence of Mr. Park is much more material. He says, 'I could, without any difficulty, make the machine so that the paddles could enter the water at any angle.' He prepared the models which have been used. Now, the criterion is, whether, at the time when the specification was introduced to the world, Mr. Park would have been able to construct the machine with his ordinary knowledge and skill, without the peculiar knowledge he has since obtained upon the subject, from being employed to make the models for Mr. Morgan, because it would not be at all fair to allow your verdict to be influenced by knowledge so acquired; but he says, with his ordinary knowledge and skill he could, without difficulty, construct a wheel, so that the paddles should enter the water at any angle. He says, if the diameter of the wheel is given, which it is fair should be given, and the immersion of the float, and that is also fair to be given, he could do it. Those are reasonable data for him to require, and if, with his ordinary skill and knowledge, and without that peculiar knowledge which he has obtained, in consequence of his connection with the plaintiffs, and with this cause, he could do it, that would be evidence on which you would be entitled to place reliance. Then he tells you how he could do it: now, I do think it would have been a vast deal better if the specification had given us the same information, for that is what a specification ought to do.

"The specification ought to contain a full description of the way in which it is to be done. The question really is, whether, upon the whole evidence, you are of opinion that the specification does fairly and fully and properly give to the public that information which the public are entitled to receive, that is to say, whether it tells them, without having recourse to experiments, how to do it, or whether it even tells them what is the course their experiments ought to take, — to what point their examinations and experiments should be directed. He says, he could do it with the skill he possesses; and he has described the manner in which he proposes to do it. He says, 'I have seen this drawing'; then he produces a drawing, and he says, 'This represents my plan of drawing it. An engineer of competent skill would have no difficulty in doing it.' His doing it himself I do not consider so material, but he says an engineer of competent skill would have no difficulty in doing it. That is material.

ordinary skill, could practise the invention from these directions. There does not seem to be any authority, which goes the length

"Then, when that drawing was shown, some of the gentlemen appearing on behalf of the defendants drew an angle upon it as the angle of entering, and asked him how that could be done. No doubt his principle would enable him to work out any angle, but there are a set of angles which would cause the centre of the eccentric to go beyond the wheel itself, which, therefore, it is impossible to carry into effect, but those angles are such as would not be required in ordinary practice by any persons. You should discard, on both sides, all exaggerated cases, and look to the substance of the thing. If you think, in substance, that the information really communicated would be enough in all ordinary cases, or in such cases as are likely to occur, then that would do; but if it is not a clear statement, and if it does not give such information as will render it unnecessary for parties to make experiments, then the specification would, in that respect, be insufficient. It is most important that patentees should be taught that they are bound to set out fully and fairly what their invention is; for, suppose a person were to make an invention, and get a right of making it for fourteen years, to the exclusion of all other persons, it would be a very great hardship upon the public, if he were to be allowed to state his specification in such a way, that, at the expiration of the term of his patent, he might laugh at the public, and say, I have had the benefit of my patent for fourteen years, but you, the public, shall not now carry my invention into effect, for I have not shown you how it is to be done. I have got my secret, and I will keep it.

"Mr. George Cottam says, 'It is a common problem to find a centre from three given points, and a person of ordinary engineering skill ought to be able to do that.' The question is, whether it ought not to be suggested to him by the specification, that that is the problem to be solved. Then Mr. Curtis says, 'I have made wheels on this plan.' You see he made the two wheels which were sent to the Venice and Trieste Company, but those were made under the direction of Mr. Galloway, the inventor. Now, it somewhat detracts from the weight due to his testimony, not as to his respectability, but as to the value of his evidence to you, that he had received the verbal instructions of Mr. Galloway. It may be, that he could do it, because of his practice under Mr. Galloway; and it must be recollected that people in other places would not have that advantage. He says, he would not have any difficulty in doing it; and he says, 'I should not consider my foreman a competent workman unless he were able to make the wheel from the specification and drawings.' He says, 'I could alter the angle by altering the cranks.' The question is not, whether he could do that, but whether he could alter the angle to a particular angle by altering the cranks in a particular way, that is, whether, having the angle given to him, he could make the alteration that was desired. Then Mr. Joseph Clement says, he is a mechanic, and did the work of Mr. Babbage's calculating-machine; that he has seen the model of the steam-engine and paddle-wheels. He speaks of the similarity of the plaintiffs' and defendants' wheels, and says, 'I could make the machine from the specification and drawing. The float

of saying that a specification, in cases of this kind, would be good, if every competent artisan who might be called were to testify

ought to enter the water at a tangent to the epicycloid.' That is only his opinion as to the most convenient angle. The real motion of the boat is this: The wheel keeps turning round and round on its own axis; during that time the boat has a progressive motion. The wheel, therefore, has a double motion; therefore every point of the wheel does not move in a circle, but in a cycloid, that being the curve described by the rolling of a circle on a flat surface. He says, it should enter at a tangent, that is, that the angle should be such that it will enter the water perpendicularly, in consequence of the motion of the boat, and of the point of the wheel. He says, in like manner, it ought to go up. That is, probably, a very correct view of the case. He says, 'I should have no difficulty in constructing a float to enter at any angle ordinarily required. A man, properly instructed in mechanics, would have no difficulty in doing it.' That is his evidence, which it is material for you to consider; and he is a mechanic himself.

"Then, Henry Mornay, a young gentleman in Mr. Morgan's employment, where he has been apparently studying the construction of engines, speaks of a circumstance which does appear to me to be material. He says, Mr. Morgan, in practice, makes his rods of different lengths. He must necessarily do so, in order that the floats may follow at the same angle as that at which the driving float enters the water. The problem which Mr. Park solved is a problem applying to three floats only; but it appears that the other floats will not follow in the same order, unless some adjustment of the rods is made. Now, suppose it was to be desired that the floats should all enter the water at the given or required angle, if one should go in at one angle, and one at another, the operation of the machine would not be uniform; and the specification means that the party constructing a wheel should be able to make a wheel, the floats of which shall all enter at the same angle, and all go out at the same angle. Now, in order in practice to carry that into effect, if there are more than three floats, something more than Mr. Park's problem would be required; and Mr. Mornay says, actually, that Mr. Morgan, in practice, makes his rods of different lengths, and he must necessarily do that, in order that the floats may follow at the same angle as the driving float enters the water. If so, he should have said in his specification, 'I make my rods of different lengths, in order that the rest of my floats may enter at the same angle; and the way to do that is so and so.' Or, he might have said, 'It may be determined so and so.' But the specification is totally silent on the subject; therefore, a person reading the specification would never dream that the other floats must be governed by rods of unequal length; and least of all could he ascertain what their lengths should be, until he had made experiments. Therefore, it is contended that the specification does not state, as it should have stated, the proper manner of doing it. He says, if they are made of equal lengths, though the governing rod would be vertical at the time of entering, and three would be so when they arrived at the same spot, by reason of the operation Mr. Park suggests, yet the fourth would not come vertical

that he could not apply the directions successfully, provided a scientific witness of the other class were to testify that he could

at the proper point, nor would the fifth, sixth, or seventh. Then they would not accomplish that advantage which professes to be acquired. The patentee ought to state in his specification the precise way of doing it. If it cannot completely be done by following the specification, then a person will not infringe the patent by doing it. If this were an infringement, it would be an infringement to do that perfectly, which, according to the specification, requires something else to be done to make it perfect. If that be correct, you would prevent a man from having a perfect engine. He says, practically speaking, the difference in the length of the rods would not be very material, the difference being small. But the whole question is small, therefore it ought to have been specified; and if it could not be ascertained fully, it should have been so stated. Now, this is the part to which I was referring, when, in the preliminary observations I addressed to you, I cited the case before Lord Mansfield, on the subject of the introduction of tallow, to enable the machine to work more smoothly. There, it was held, that the use of the tallow ought to have been stated in the specification. This small adjustment of these different lengths may have been made for the purpose of making the machine work more smoothly; if so, it is just as much necessary that it should be so stated in the specification, as it was that the tallow should be mentioned. The true criterion is this, — has the specification substantially complied with that which the public has a right to require? Has the patentee communicated to the public the manner of carrying his invention into effect? If he has, and if he has given to the public all the knowledge he had himself, he has done that which he ought to have done, and which the public has a right to require from him.

"I will now read the defendant's evidence, and you will see whether, upon the whole, there is evidence before you, on which you think you can come to any reasonable conclusion.

"Now, first of all, Mr. Donkin, a man of considerable experience, is called; but before I go to his evidence, I will remark, that I have always found that there is a great deal of contradiction in questions of this description; but that is not to be attributed, in the least degree, to corruption, or to any intention to misrepresent or mislead, — people's opinions vary. They come to state to you not matters of fact, but matters of opinion, and they tell you, conscientiously, what their opinion really is. You may have a great difference of opinion among scientific men on a question relating to science; but though, by their evidence, they contradict one another, they are not influenced by a corrupt desire to misrepresent.

"Now, Mr. Donkin says, 'On first reading the specification, I thought there was a defect in its not explaining the mode of obtaining the required angle. In my judgment, a workman of ordinary skill would not be able to find out any mode of obtaining the required angle.' He says, a geometrician might discover the mode of adjusting the three angles, the angle of immersion, the vertical angle, and the angle of emersion; but, in order to discover

teach or demonstrate to an artisan how to apply them;[1] although

the mode by which all the paddles may enter at the same angle, another discovery must be made. He says, it requires to be ascertained, by experiment or diagram, whether the adjustment is to be made by altering the bent stem, or by varying the length of the rods, and you have nothing but the drawing to guide you in that respect. He says, he must first ascertain whether he is to produce the effect by altering the centre, or by altering the bent stem, or varying the lengths of the movable rods. What are those but experiments to ascertain how the thing should be done, all of which he ought to have been saved, by its being stated in the specification how to do it. However, that is his evidence; he says, the angle must depend on the dimensions of the several parts of the wheel. Then he goes on to the other parts of the case, and, on his cross-examination, he says, 'I think a competent workman would be able to do it if he made the previous discovery; but he would not do it unless a careful investigation was gone into.' He says, 'Few ordinary workmen would be able to get the desired angle; I think my foreman would. I think a person moderately acquainted with geometry might do it, but he must find it out; he could sit down and determine it. If he possessed proper information, he ought to be able to do it. An engineer properly skilled in geometry ought to be able to find out how the angle was to be determined. If he sat down and referred to his general knowledge, he would find it out.' Now, the criterion is not, whether he could find it out or not, but whether he could do it by means of the information contained in this specification and drawing, calling in aid his general knowledge, and those mechanical means with which he may reasonably be expected to be familiar; but if he is to sit down and consider how it is to be done, that is not sufficient. You will judge, whether or not the evidence of this witness satisfies you on these points, and whether it makes out the proposition for which the defendants contend.

"Then, Mr. Brunton says, 'I think a workman of competent skill could not construct a machine so as to have the floats enter at any particular

---

[1] In Allen *v.* Blunt, 3 Story's R. 747, 748, Mr. Justice Story made use of the following language: "As to the relative weight of the evidence of persons practically engaged in the trade, employment, or business of the particular branch of mechanics to which the patent right applies, and the evidence of persons who, although not practical artisans, are thoroughly conversant with the subject of mechanics as a science. It appears to me that the Patent Acts look to both classes of persons, not only as competent, but as peculiarly appropriate witnesses, but for different purposes. Two important points are necessary to support the claim to an invention: First, that it should be substantially new, as, for example, if it be a piece of mechanism, that it should be substantially new in its structure or mode of operation. Secondly, that the specification should express the mode of constructing, compounding, and using the same in such full, clear, and exact terms, 'as to enable any person skilled in the art or science to which it appertains, or with which it is most nearly connected, to make, construct, compound, and use the same.'

proof may be offered of the opinions of scientific witnesses, that

angle and leave at a particular angle.' He says, if the required angle was different from the drawing, it would be an exceedingly difficult thing, and he is not prepared to say how he could do it. Then, Mr. Hawkins says, 'I do not think a workman of ordinary skill could, from the plan and specification, make a wheel that should enter and quit the water at a different angle from that given in the drawing, unless he possessed considerable ingenuity for inventing the method of doing it.'

"Then, Mr. Peter Barlow says, 'There are not, I think, sufficient data to adjust the angle.' He says, if the length of the stems was given, the difficulty would be very great, but it would have been a guide, and it ought to have been explained. That appears to me to be a very good common-sense observation. Then, Mr. John Donkin says, 'I think an ordinary workman would find considerable difficulty in altering a paddle-wheel to suit a particular angle, and I doubt whether he could do it.' On his cross-examination, he says, 'It requires more than a common knowledge of geometry; I think a man moderately acquainted with geometry might do it, but he would have to make experiments, and his first experiments would fail. A skilful engineer would have less difficulty in it, but he ought to be able to find it out.' Then, Mr. Bramah says, 'I think I could discover how to do it.' He has been an engineer many years, and he says, 'I think I could discover it, but I do not know at present how to do it. Yesterday I attended to the evidence, and this morning I tried to find out how it was to be done, but I could not.' Supposing Mr. Bramah had to make a machine of this kind, is he to sit down

---

Now, for the latter purpose, a mere artisan skilled in the art with which it is connected, may in many cases be an important and satisfactory witness. If, as a mere artisan, he can, from the description in the specification, so make, construct, compound, and use the same, it would be very cogent evidence of the sufficiency of the specification. Still, it is obvious, that, although a mere artisan, who had no scientific knowledge on the subject, and who was unacquainted with the various mechanical or chemical equivalents employed in such cases, might not be able to make and compound the thing patented, from the specification; yet a person who was skilled in the very science on which it depended, and with the mechanical and chemical powers and equivalents, might be able to teach and demonstrate to an artisan, how it was to be made or constructed, or compounded or used. *A fortiori*, he would be enabled so to do, if he combined practical skill with a thorough knowledge of the scientific principles on which it depended." It is not quite clear, upon this passage, whether the learned judge did or did not mean to intimate, that a specification would be good, if a scientific witness could teach an artisan how to make, compound, or use the thing patented, although the artisan could not practise the invention without such aid. The sense in which he seems to oppose the word "artisan" to that class of persons who are not practical artisans, but who are "thoroughly conversant with the subject of mechanics as a science," or are "skilled in the very science on which the

a particular means which might be used to carry out the general

and invent a mode of doing it, or ought he not to have such information afforded as would enable him to do it at once by means of the specification? Then, Mr. Francis Bramah says, 'I have examined the specification: I could not make a machine from the specification, the floats of which should enter and leave the water at any required angle. Till I came into court yesterday, I presumed that the angle given in the drawing was the best angle, that is, that the specification had not only stated how to do it, but had described the best angle.' If so, it would be a specification only for that particular angle. He says, 'I can go as far as I was told yesterday, but no farther.'

"Now, gentlemen, I have gone through the evidence on both sides on this point, and the question, upon this part of the case, revolves itself into this : Do the witnesses on the plaintiff's side satisfy you that the patentee has, in his specification, given to the public the means of making a machine which shall enter and leave the water at any angle that may be ordered : that is, if a man ordered a machine at an angle likely to be required for entering and going out, and to be vertical at the bottom, could an ordinary workman, with competent skill, execute that order by following the directions given in this specification? If you think he could, then the specification would be sufficient. If, on the other hand, you think he would not be able to execute the order, unless he sat down and taxed his invention to find out a method of doing that which has not been sufficiently described in the specification, then the specification would be bad. If you think the specification good, then you ought to find for the plaintiffs upon that issue; if you think the specification bad, then you ought to find for the defendants."

---

invention depends," would seem to imply that an obscurity or other defect in a specification, which would embarrass an artisan, may be cured by a scientific person, whose superior knowledge of the principles of the science might be used to teach the workman from the specification; if so, this is not the standard which the same learned judge adopted on other occasions. In Lowell *v.* Lewis, 1 Mas. 190, he instructed the jury, that the question was, whether the specification was so clear and full, that *a pump-maker of ordinary skill* could, from the terms of the specification, construct a pump on the plan described. Perhaps, however, in the more recent case, he intended only to draw a distinction between mere mechanics or laborers in a particular art, manufacture, or trade, and persons conversant with the science on which it depends; and to say that the latter are competent, and often the most satisfactory witnesses, which is certainly obvious. It is scarcely to be presumed that he meant to say, that where the description in a patent is of a thing which a particular class of mechanics would be employed to make, the specification would be sufficient, although it could not be carried out by a workman of that class having ordinary skill, provided it could be understood by a "person thoroughly conversant with the subject of mechanics as a science." This, as a general proposition, would confine the practice of many inventions, after the patent had expired, to the latter class of persons, which the patent law does not intend.

directions of a specification, would succeed, without showing that that means had actually been tried and had succeeded.[1]

§ 482. Whether there is a class of inventions addressed so entirely to scientific witnesses, as to render their knowledge and skill requisite, in the practical application of the directions, so that there cannot be said to be any recognized class of artisans, to whose capacity the directions can be referred, is another question. This must depend on the nature of the invention.

§ 483. Before it can be determined, in any case, what class of persons are to be taken as those, whose ability to apply the directions furnishes the standard of the sufficiency of the specification, it must first be ascertained to what class of persons the specification is presumed to be addressed, as being those who are to carry out the directions. If the inquiry arose after the patent had expired, this class of persons would, in most cases, be readily ascertained by observing what persons applied themselves to the practice of the invention. But it actually arises before the patent has expired, and before its dedication to the public enables us to see what persons will undertake to practise the invention. That state of things must, therefore, be anticipated, so far as to ascertain what persons will undertake practically to carry out the directions of the patent, for the purpose for which the invention is designed. The standard, therefore, will vary greatly, according to the nature of the invention. In some cases the persons who will undertake to practise it will be very numerous, in others very limited, in point of numbers. In some cases the qualifications will be very moderate, in others, a very high state of accomplishment, skill, and knowledge will be requisite. The nature and objects of the invention must be resorted to, to see to what persons the specification is to be presumed to be addressed. If it be a machine destined to a particular use, the workmen whose vocation it is to make similar machines for similar purposes, will be the persons who would be called upon to make the machine after the patent has expired. If it be a composition of matter, involving the knowledge of practical chemists, such persons will attempt to practise the invention, when they are at liberty to do so. If it be a manufacture of an improved character, the persons whose business it has been to make the

[1] Neilson *v.* Harford, Webs. Pat. Cas. 295, 315, 316.

old article, will be the persons who will make the new one. In all these and similar cases, where there is a class of workmen who are habituated to the practical exercise of the art or science under which the patented invention falls, the specification is to be presumed to be addressed to them; and, although scientific witnesses may be examined as to the clearness and fulness of the specification, its sufficiency must be referred to the ability of competent practical workmen, of ordinary skill, to understand and apply it. This limitation of the evidence follows, necessarily, from the principle that the specification cannot be supported by the fresh invention and correction of a scientific person. The ordinary knowledge and skill of practical workmen being the standard, where the specification is for the benefit of a particular trade, the evidence cannot be carried so far as to include the degree of skill and knowledge possessed by a scientific person, who could, on a mere hint, invent the thing proposed to be accomplished; although such a witness may be asked whether a competent workman could attain the object of the patent by following out the directions.[1]

§ 484. But if the invention be of a character entirely novel, embodying an effect never before produced, and which it is not within the province of any particular class of workmen to produce, but which it belongs rather to the province of men possessed of some science to apply, by directing the labors of common artisans, upon principles which such artisans do not commonly understand or undertake to use, then the specification may be presumed to be addressed to men capable of applying those principles, and not to mere artisans, who have previously been employed in the construction of things of the same class which it is the object of the invention to supersede. Thus, in the case of an invention, which consisted in an improvement on paddle-wheels for propelling vessels, by a mode of constructing them, so that the floats might enter and quit the water at any required angle, the specification would be addressed to engineers capable of determining what angle was required, and it ought to furnish the rules by which such persons could ascertain the angle, and the mechanical means by which it could be applied in practice.[2]

[1] Morgan *v.* Seaward, Webs. Pat. Cas. 174; Neilson *v.* Harford, ibid. 371; The Househill Co. *v.* Neilson, ibid. 692.

[2] Morgan *v.* Seaward, Webs. Pat. Cas. 170.

The understanding of such a specification would be somewhat above the range of acquirements belonging to mechanics employed in the manual labor of constructing the machinery, that is to say, the specification would be addressed to competent engineers, of ordinary skill in that profession.[1]

§ 485. But it should be remembered that whenever, in a case of this kind, as in all other cases, the persons to whom the specification is to be presumed to be addressed have been ascertained, a rule becomes applicable, which defines the nature and scope of the evidence that may be offered, to explain the specification. This rule is, that the patentee must not, in framing his specification, call upon the persons to whom it is addressed to exercise more than the actual existing knowledge common to their trade or profession. He has a right to exhaust this knowledge; but if, in order to apply his directions, the members of the trade or profession are required to tax their ingenuity or invention, so that, beyond the exercise of ordinary and competent skill, they would have to solve a problem or supply something in the process, by the exercise of the inventive faculty, the specification would be bad.[2]

§ 486. II. *As to the Infringement.*—Upon the question of infringement, the point to be determined is, whether the thing made or used by the defendant is, in the sense of the patent law, identical with the invention of the patentee.[3] This is the same question as that which arises on the issues of novelty, when it is necessary to determine whether the invention of the patentee is the same as some former thing, or different, and therefore entitled to be regarded as a novelty. We may, therefore, here consider the principles of evidence applicable to the inquiry, whether two things are identical in the sense of the patent law.

§ 487. It is obvious that there may be two kinds of evidence applicable to this issue, both of which may be drawn from experts. Whether one thing is like another, is a matter of judg-

[1] Morgan *v.* Seaward, Webs. Pat. Cas. 170.

[2] Ibid. It should also be remembered that the court, in construing the *claim*, is not bound to receive the testimony of experts. Winans *v.* N. Y. & Erie R.R., 21 How. 88.

[3] In equity suits, if the defendant means to contest the alleged infringement at the hearing, he should take proofs of non-infringement. Bennet *v.* Fowler, 8 Wallace, 445.

ment, to be determined on the evidence of our own senses, or the senses of others. If we rely on the senses of others, the sole testimony which they can bear is, either as to the matters of fact which constitute the precise differences or resemblances between the two things, or as to matter of opinion, by which they infer that these differences or resemblances do or do not affect the question of the substantial identity of the two things. Both of these kinds of evidence, however, run so nearly into each other, and the boundaries between them are often so shadowy, that it is sometimes difficult to draw the line between fact and opinion. The actual differences or resemblances between two things are *primâ facie* matters of fact, to be observed by the senses; but, with the act of observing these differences or resemblances, we blend the process of reasoning, by which we determine, for our own satisfaction, what is a real, and what only an apparent difference or resemblance; what constitutes a difference or resemblance, in point of principle; and the result of this process, expressed in the conclusion, that the two things are, or are not identical, is matter of opinion. Between these two branches of evidence it is exceedingly difficult to draw the line so as to define the true office of an expert, and to admit all proper evidence of facts and opinions, without leaving to the witness the whole determination of the issue.[1]

§ 488. At the same time it is certain that a boundary exists somewhere. The question whether two things are identical, in the sense of the patent law, is a mixed question of law and fact; and when it is submitted to a jury, it is for the court to instruct them, after the actual differences or resemblances are ascertained, what constitutes, in point of law, a difference or identity.[2] There is, therefore, a most important function to be discharged, if one

[1] In Dixon *v.* Moyer, 4 Wash. 68, 71, Mr. Justice Washington said: "In actions of this kind, persons acquainted with the particular art to which the controversy relates are usually examined for the purpose of pointing out and explaining to the jury the points of resemblance, or of difference, between the thing patented and that which is the alleged cause of the controversy; and the opinions of such witnesses, in relation to the materiality of apparent differences, are always entitled to great respect. But, after all, the jury must judge for themselves, as well upon the information so given to them, as upon their own view, where the articles, or models of them, are brought into court."

[2] Barrett *v.* Hall, 1 Mas. 447, 470.

may so say, by the law itself; for it has to determine, upon all the facts open to the observation of the senses, whether guided by the superior facility for observation enjoyed by experts, or not so assisted, whether, in the sense of the law, there is an identity or a difference. This function is always in danger of being encroached upon by a loose mode of receiving the testimony of experts, by whom the whole question is often in reality left to be decided.[1]

§ 489. The testimony of persons skilled in the particular subject is undoubtedly admissible for two purposes: *first*, to point out and explain the points of actual resemblance or difference; *secondly*, to state, as matter of opinion, whether these resemblances or differences are material; whether they are important or unimportant; whether the changes introduced are merely the substitution of one mechanical or chemical equivalent for another, or whether they constitute a real change of structure or composition, affecting the substance of the invention. But when these facts and opinions have been ascertained, the judgment of the jury is to be exercised upon the whole of the evidence, under the instructions of the court as to what constitutes such a change as will in point of law amount to a fresh invention and therefore will not be an infringement.[2]

§ 490. The duty of giving this instruction should not be surrendered by the court. A scientific witness may be asked, for instance, whether in his opinion a particular machine is substantially new in its structure or mode of operation, or whether it is substantially the same thing as another, with only apparent differences of form and structure. But when the differences or

[1] Thus in U. S. Annunciator Co. *v.* Sanderson, 3 Blatchf. 184, it was held that where two machines were to all appearance the same, the positive testimony of an expert that they were in principle different, was not to be followed, unless such expert should show satisfactorily wherein the difference consisted.

[2] In Allen *v.* Blunt, 3 Story's R. 742, 748, 749, Mr. Justice Story, discussing the relative value of scientific witnesses and mere artisans, said: "The very highest witnesses to ascertain and verify the novelty of an invention, and the novelty or diversity of mechanical apparatus and contrivances and equivalents, are beyond all question, all other circumstances being equal, scientific mechanics; they are far the most important and useful to guide the judgment and *to enable the jury to draw a safe conclusion whether the modes of operation are new or old, identical or diverse.*"

resemblances have been pointed out, and when the view that science takes of their relative importance has been ascertained; when the fact appears of whether a particular change is or is not regarded by mechanicians as the substitution of one mechanical equivalent for another, the court must instruct the jury whether the particular change amounts, in point of law, to a change of what is commonly called the principle of the machine. This is a question wholly aside from the function of a witness. The most skilful and scientific mechanician in the world can only say what, in his opinion, are the differences or resemblances between one machine and another, and how far they are regarded by mechanicians as material or substantial. But the question of what constitutes a fresh invention, or what, upon a given state of facts, amounts to a change so great as to support an independent patent for a new thing, is a question of law; and this question is involved in every issue as to the identity of two things, whether it relates to the question of infringement or of prior invention.[1]

§ 491. The evidence for the defendant, upon the question of novelty, will of course consist of proof, positive in its nature, that the thing patented existed before; and if any credible evidence of this is adduced, it will outweigh all the negative evidence that can be offered by the plaintiff.[2] Thus, in Parker *v.* Ferguson,[3] where a witness testified to his having assisted in the construction of a single water-wheel exactly similar to that of the plaintiff, for a person who removed it to a place some twelve miles off, so that witness never again saw it, the court instructed the jury, that, if they were satisfied of the credibility of the witness, they must consider the proof of want of novelty as established. But testimony by a witness that he had seen an article which might have been made by a machine similar to that of the plaintiff, is not sufficient to defeat the latter's title.[4] But whenever the defendant relies on the fact of a previous invention, knowledge, or use of the thing patented, he must give notice of the names and

[1] See the instructions of the court in Walton *v.* Potter, Webs. Pat. Cas. 585, 586, 587, 589, 591; Huddart *v.* Grimshaw, ibid. 85, 86, 91, 92, 95. See also the examination of certain experts in Russell *v.* Cowley, ibid. 462, before Lord Lyndhurst, in the exchequer, cited *ante.*

[2] Manton *v.* Manton, Dav. Pat. Cas. 250.

[3] 1 Blatchf. 407.

[4] Treadwell *v.* Bladen, 4 Wash. 703.

places of residence of the persons whom he intends to prove as having possessed a prior knowledge or had a prior use of it.[1]

§ 491 *a*. In an action for infringement, evidence going to show the superiority of defendant's machine to that of the patentee is improper, except to prove a substantial difference between the two.[2] In one case where the defendant and the plaintiff had executed a bond, in which the former acknowledged the validity of the latter's patent and recited a previous infringement, it was held that this, together with other evidence, might be received as tending to show a subsequent breach, but did not of itself raise any implication.[3]

In a recent English case, where the patentee had a patent for a process of treating chemically sewage matter with the view of thereby obtaining a valuable manure, a similar process used by the Board of Health simply for the purpose of disinfection, so that this product was rejected as a by-product, was to be regarded as no evidence of infringement.[4]

§ 492. Persons who have used the machine patented are not thereby rendered incompetent as witnesses, on account of interest.[5] It has been held that a witness who was patentee in another patent, and had sold to the defendant the right to use the machine, the use of which was complained of as an infringement, was a competent witness, since any verdict that the plaintiff might recover could not be given in evidence by the plaintiff in an action against the witness.[6] A patentee who has assigned the whole of his interest in the patent is a competent witness for the assignee in support of it.[7] It is not, however, admissible to

[1] See *ante*, chapter on Action at Law. The notice need not, however, specify the places in which such user was made. Where the defence is prior publication in some printed work, the notice must specify the particular part of the work referred to, if the same be one of a general character, e. g. a scientific dictionary. Foote *v*. Silsby, 1 Blatchf. 445. Compare Vance *v*. Campbell, 1 Black. 427.

[2] Alden *v*. Dewey, 1 Story, 336.

[3] Byam *v*. Eddy, 2 Blatchf. 521.

[4] Higgs *v*. Goodwin, 1 Ell. Bl. & Ell. 529. See also chapter on Infringement.

[5] Evans *v*. Eaton, 7 Wheat. 356; Evans *v*. Hettich, ibid. 453; 2 Greenl. on Evid. § 508. It is no objection to the competency of a witness, that he is sued in another action for infringement of the same patent. Ibid.

[6] Treadwell *v*. Bladen, 4 Wash. 704.

[7] Bloxam *v*. Elsee, 1 Carr. & Payne, 563.

offer evidence going to show that the patentee, after assigning his entire interest, had declared the patent abandoned and worthless.[1] The assignee of the exclusive right for a certain county or district is to be received as witness in an action for infringement in another district in which he has no direct interest.[2] Where evidence of prior user by some third party is attempted to be shown, the declaration of such party as to his motives for such user are inadmissible as mere hearsay.[3] A licensee is a competent witness for the patent, in an action for an infringement, for he has no direct pecuniary interest in supporting the patent, but it may be for his advantage that it should not be supported.[4] Evidence, on the part of the plaintiff, that the persons, of whose prior use of a patented machine the defendant had given evidence, had paid the plaintiff for licenses, ought not to be absolutely rejected, though entitled to very little weight.[5]

§ 492 *a*. In several recent cases, the Supreme Court, in construing the Judiciary Act of 1789, § 34, has decided that where, under the laws of any State, parties may be examined in their own behalf, the plaintiff, in an action for infringement brought in a district embracing such a State, is a competent witness.[6]

§ 493. Where the defence is set up that the patentee being an alien has not complied with § 13 of the act of 1836, which requires that such patentee must put and continue on sale to the public, on reasonable terms, the invention for which the patent was granted, the burden of proof rests on the defendant.[7]

§ 493 *a*. Fraud in obtaining an extension of a patent can only be tried in a direct proceeding to impeach the patent, and not in a collateral proceeding, as in a suit in equity to recover for infringements.[8]

[1] Wilson *v*. Simpson, 9 How. 109; Many *v*. Jagger, 1 Blatchf. 372.

[2] Buck *v*. Hermance, 1 Blatchf. 322.

[3] Hyde *v*. Palmer, 7 Law Times, N. S. 823.

[4] Derosne *v*. Fairie, Webs. Pat. Cas. 154.

[5] Evans *v*. Eaton, 3 Wheat. 454.

[6] Vance *v*. Campbell, 1 Black. 427; Haussknecht *v*. Claypool, ibid. 431.

[7] Tatham *v*. Lowber, 2 Blatchf. 49.

[8] Rubber Company *v*. Goodyear, 9 Wallace, 788.

CHAPTER XIII.

JURISDICTION.

§ 494. The Constitution of the United States confers upon Congress power "to promote the progress of science and useful arts, by securing for limited times, to authors and inventors, the exclusive right to their respective writings and discoveries." This power is general; there is no distinction which limits it to cases where the invention has not been known or used by the public. Accordingly it is well settled that Congress may pass general or special laws in favor of inventors; and they may leave a particular inventor to the protection afforded by a general law, or they may pass a special law in his behalf, or they may exempt his case from the operation of a general law by extending his exclusive right beyond the term fixed by such general law.[1] They may even grant to an inventor the exclusive right to his invention after the same has gone into public use. The grant does not imply an irrevocable contract with the public that, at the expiration of the period, the invention shall become public property. Where, however, Congress does, by special law, grant to an inventor the monopoly of his invention after the same has gone into public use, such enactment will not, without unmistakable language to that effect, be construed to work retrospectively, by rendering the use of a machine embraced under the patent unlawful for the time previous to the enactment.[2]

[1] Evans *v.* Eaton, 3 Wheat. 454; s. c. Pet. C. C. 332; Evans *v.* Hettich, 7 Wheat. 453; Blanchard *v.* Sprague, 2 Story's Rep. 164; s. c. 3 Sumn. 535; Woodworth *v.* Hall, 1 Woodb. & Min. 248.

[2] Blanchard *v.* Sprague, *supra*. Letters-patent were granted to the plaintiff, Thomas Blanchard, on the 6th of September, 1819; and being deemed inoperative, by reason of defects in the specification, new letters-patent were granted on the 20th of January, 1820, for the space of fourteen years. Afterward, by act of Congress, passed the 30th of June, 1834, the sole right was granted to the plaintiff to make, use, and vend his invention for the term of fourteen years, from the 12th of January, 1834. This act not being thought

§ 495. In accordance with the general powers thus constitutionally conferred, Congress has regulated the matter of the

to describe with sufficient accuracy the letters-patent, to which it was intended to refer, an additional act was passed on the 6th of February, 1839, renewing the act of the 30th of June, 1834, and correcting the date of the 12th of January, 1834, to the 20th of January, 1834. This last act was as follows: "*An act to amend and carry into effect the intention of an act entitled An Act to renew the patent of Thomas Blanchard, approved June 30th*, 1834. Sec. 1. Be it enacted, &c., That the rights secured to Thomas Blanchard, a citizen of the United States, by letters-patent granted on the sixth of September, eighteen hundred and nineteen, and afterwards on a corrected specification on the 20th day of January, Anno Domini eighteen hundred and twenty, be granted to the said Blanchard, his heirs and assigns, for the further term of fourteen years from the 20th of January, eighteen hundred and thirty-four, said invention so secured being described in said last-mentioned letters as an engine for turning or cutting irregular forms out of wood, iron, brass, or other material which can be cut by ordinary tools. Provided, that all rights and privileges heretofore sold or granted by said patentee to make, construct, use, or vend the said invention, and not forfeited by the purchasers or grantees, shall enure to and be enjoyed by such purchasers or grantees respectively, as fully and upon the same conditions during the period hereby granted as for the term that did exist when such sale or grant was made. Sec. 2. And be it further enacted, that any person who had *bonâ fide* erected or constructed any manufacture or machine for the purpose of putting said invention into use, in any of its modifications, or was so erecting or constructing any manufacture or machine for the purpose aforesaid, between the period of the expiration of the patent heretofore granted on the thirtieth day of June, one thousand eight hundred and thirty-four, shall have and enjoy the right of using said invention in any such manufacture or machine erected or erecting as aforesaid, in all respects as though this act had not passed. Provided, that no person shall be entitled to the right and privilege by this section granted, who has infringed the patent right and privilege heretofore granted, by actually using or vending said machine before the expiration of said patent, without grant or license from said patentee or his assignees, to use or vend the same."

Upon this act, Mr. Justice Story said: "Then it is suggested, that the grant of the patent by the act of Congress of 1839, c. 14, is not constitutional; for it operates retrospectively to give a patent for an invention, which, though made by the patentee, was in public use and enjoyed by the community at the time of the passage of the act. But this objection is fairly put at rest by the decision of the Supreme Court in the case of the patent of Oliver Evans. Evans *v.* Eaton, 3 Wheat. 454. For myself I never have entertained any doubt of the constitutional authority of Congress to make such a grant. The power is general to grant to inventors; and it rests in the sound discretion of Congress to say, when and for what length of time and under what circumstances the patent for an invention shall be granted. There is no restriction which limits the power of Congress to cases where the invention has not been known or used by the public. All that is required is, that the patentee should be the

jurisdiction in patent cases by two enactments. The act of July 4, 1836, c. 357, § 17, declares: —

"That all actions, suits, controversies, and cases arising under any law of the United States, granting or confirming to inventors the exclusive right to their inventions or discoveries, shall be originally cognizable, as well in equity as in law, by the circuit courts of the United States, or any district court having the powers and jurisdiction of a circuit court, which courts shall have power, upon bill in equity filed by any party aggrieved, in any such case, to grant injunctions, according to the course and principles of courts of equity, to prevent the violation of the rights of any inventor, as secured to him by any law of the United States, on such terms and conditions as said courts may deem reasonable. *Provided*, however, that from all judgments and decrees from any such court, rendered in the premises, a writ of error or appeal, as the case may be, shall lie to the Supreme Court of the United States, in the same manner and under the same circumstances as is now provided by law in other judgments and decrees of circuit courts, and in all other cases in which the court shall deem it reasonable to allow the same." [1]

inventor. The only remaining objection is, that the act is unconstitutional, because it makes the use of a machine constructed and used before the time of the passage of the act of 1834, c. 213, and the grant of the patent under the act of 1839, c. 14, unlawful, although it has been formerly decided that, under the act of 1834, the plaintiff had no valid patent; and so the defendant, if he constructed and used the machine during that period, did lawful acts, and cannot now be retrospectively made a wrong-doer. If this were the true result of the language of the act, it might require a good deal of consideration. But I do not understand that the act gives the patentee any damages for the construction or use of the machine, except after the grant of patent under the act of 1839, c. 14. If the language of the act were ambiguous, the court would give it this construction, so that it might not be deemed to create rights retrospectively, or to make men liable for damages for acts lawful at the time when they were done. The act of Congress passed in general terms ought to be so construed, if it may, as to be deemed a just exercise of constitutional authority; and not only so, but it ought to be construed, not to operate retrospectively or *ex post facto*, unless that construction is unavoidable; for even, if a retrospective act is or may be constitutional, I think I may say that, according to the theory of our jurisprudence, such an interpretation is never adopted without absolute necessity; and courts of justice always lean to a more benign construction. But in the present case there is no claim for any damages but such as have accrued to the patentee from a use of his machine since the grant of the patent under the act of 1839, c. 14."

[1] See also act of February 15, 1819, c. 19.

The right of appeal, as thus conferred, has been recently modified by the act of 1861, c. 37, § 1, which provides: —

"That from all judgments and decrees of any circuit court rendered in any action, suit, controversy, or case at law or in equity, arising under any law of the United States, granting or confirming to authors the exclusive right to their inventions or discoveries, a writ of error or appeal, as the case may be, shall lie at the instance of either party, to the Supreme Court of the United States, in the same manner and under the same circumstances as is now provided by law in other judgments and decrees of such circuit courts, without regard to the sum or value in controversy in the action."

§ 496. The judicial interpretation of these enactments has been to the effect, that the jurisdiction thereby conferred upon the circuit and district courts in the first instance, and to the Supreme Court on appeal, is not merely an original one, but also an exclusive one, so that the State courts have no cognizance whatever of actions in which the validity or force of letters-patent is involved.[1]

But where the controversy at issue does not turn upon the letters-patent themselves, but rather upon the force of some contract under them, e. g. an assignment or license, which acknowledges their validity, in such cases the jurisdiction appertains, as in other contracts, to the State courts, and can only be brought into the United States courts on some other ground, e. g. that of citizenship or residence, which would justify the application. Thus, in a recent case,[2] a bill for injunction was brought upon a special agreement entered into between the plaintiff and the defendant, adjusting several suits pending between them concerning patent rights claimed by the plaintiff. It charged a breach of the agreement and prayed for an account. Nelson, J., in dismissing the bill, said: "It was attempted to sustain the jurisdiction on the ground that the suit is brought under the Patent Act, where jurisdiction depends on the subject-matter, and that the *gravamen* laid was the infringement of patent rights. But there is no foundation for this position. The bill is not constructed for the purpose of presenting a question of the

[1] Dudley *v.* Mayhew, 3 Comst. 14; Elmer *v.* Pennel, 40 Maine, 434; Parsons *v.* Barnard, 7 Johns. 144.

[2] Goodyear *v.* Day, 1 Blatchf. 565.

infringement of a patent, but is brought for the violation of a contract."

Hence a bill brought to enforce the specific performance of a contract to convey a patent is not cognizable in the United States courts; but, *semble*, that an objection, on that account, should be taken before the pleadings are closed and the evidence published.[1] Nor a suit brought to enforce the covenants of a licensee.[2]

While, however, it is true that a contract under a patent, e. g. a license, is not *per se* cognizable in the United States courts, so as to permit a suit to be brought there for the recovery of the sums agreed upon, still a licensee, whose right is conditioned upon the weekly payment of a certain sum, and who neglects to pay the same, but continues to use the invention, is virtually guilty of an infringement of the patent, and may, like any other infringer, be enjoined by a United States court. This point was decided in the case of Brooks *v.* Stolley,[3] where the Court said: —

"It is suggested, that, as the whole controversy in the case arises under the contract of license, the parties to which being citizens of this State, the Federal court cannot take jurisdiction. This objection would be unanswerable if no right were involved in the controversy except what arises out of the contract; as, for instance, the Circuit Court could take no jurisdiction, under the contract, of an action merely to recover the sums agreed to be paid by the defendant; but, in the present aspect of the case, it is not limited to the contract. The complainants set up their right under the patent, and allege that the defendant is infringing that patent; that the license affords no justification to the defendant. The right then of the complainants to an injunction is not founded by them on the contract, but on the assignment of the patent.

"Now the terms of the contract make the performance of its stipulations by the defendant a condition to his continued use of the machine; and if the words of the contract did not import and indeed clearly sustain this view, equitable considerations, arising from the nature of the contract, would require such a

[1] Nesmith *v.* Calvert, 1 Woodb. & Min. 34.

[2] Goodyear *v.* Union Rubber Co., MS., Ingersoll, J.

[3] 3 McLean, 523.

construction of it. The payment is to be made weekly. Could any reasonable construction of the contract give the right to run the machine by the defendant, in default of such payment? The frequent settlement and payment show that longer indulgence was not intended by the parties, and that a remedy at law would be no adequate relief to the complainants. To enforce the payment by legal means would require a weekly suit; and this would subject the complainants to inconvenience, delay, and expense, which would be nearly, if not quite, equal to the amount recovered. Such a construction of the contract would be as inequitable as the remedy proposed would be inadequate. The complainants invoke the aid of equity, not to decree a specific execution of the contract, but to protect their rights as assignees of the patent. This right they allege has been infringed. The defendant relies on the license contained in the contract; but having failed to make the weekly payment, he has no pretence of right to run the machine."

§ 497. With regard to the question, in what district an action for the infringement of patent rights may or must be brought, it has been held in the case of Chaffee *v.* Hayward,[1] that such action can only be brought in the district in which the defendant resides or in which he is personally served with the summons, and that the commencement of an action by attaching the property of a non-resident defendant was not sufficient to confer jurisdiction. It was urged *arguendo* that the Circuit Court, having jurisdiction of the *subject-matter*, was by the Process Act of 1792, § 2, at liberty to issue its process in the same form as a process from the Supreme Court of any State comprised in that district, and that if the service by attachment was good by the laws of that State, as they stood at the time of the passage of the Process Act, then it was good under the laws of the United States. But the Supreme Court did not accept these conclusions. Catron, J., in rendering the opinion of the court, said: "By § 11 of the Judiciary Act of 1789, it is provided, 'That no civil suit in a circuit or district court shall be brought against an inhabitant of the United States by any original process in any other district than that whereof he is an inhabitant or in which he shall be found at the time of serving the writ.' It has been several times

[1] 20 How. 208.

held by this court as the true construction of the foregoing section, that jurisdiction of the person of a defendant (who is an inhabitant of another State) can only be obtained in a civil action, by service of process on his person within the district where the suit is instituted; and that no jurisdiction can be acquired by attaching property of a non-resident defendant, pursuant to a State attachment law.[1] It is insisted, however, that these rulings were had in cases arising where the jurisdiction depended on citizenship; whereas here the suit is founded on an act of Congress conferring jurisdiction on the Circuit Courts of the United States in suits by inventors against those who infringe their patents, including all cases both at law and in equity, arising under the patent laws, without regard to the citizenship of the parties or the amount in controversy, and that therefore the eleventh section of the Judiciary Act does not apply, but the process acts of the State where the suit is brought must govern, and that the act of Congress, May 8, 1792, so declares. . . . That act (§ 2) declares that until further provision shall be made, and except where by this act 'or *other statutes of the United States is otherwise* provided,' the forms of writs and executions and modes of processes in suits at common law shall be the same in each State respectively as are now used or allowed in the Supreme Court of the same. This was to be the mode of process, unless provision had been made by Congress; and to the extent that Congress had provided, the State laws should not operate. Now the only statute of the United States then existing regulating practice was the Judiciary Act of 1789, which is above recited. The eleventh section is excepted out of and stands unaffected by the subsequent process acts, and is as applicable in this case as it was to those where jurisdiction depended on citizenship. It applies in its terms to *all* civil suits; it makes no exceptions, nor can the courts of justice make any. The judicial power extends to all cases in law and equity arising under the Constitution and laws of the United States; and it is pursuant to this clause of the Constitution that the United States courts are vested with power to execute the laws respecting inventors and patented inventions; but where the suits are to be brought is left to the general law, to wit, to the eleventh section of the Judiciary Act, which requires personal

[1] Toland *v.* Sprague, 12 Pet. 327; also 15 Pet. 171; 17 How. 424.

service of process within the district where the suit is brought, if the defendant be an inhabitant of another State."

This decision affirms the rulings in Saddler *v.* Hudson,[1] and Allen *v.* Blunt;[2] and is followed in Goodyear *v.* Chaffee.[3]

The case of Day *v.* Newark Rubber Co.[4] goes still further. Here the defendant was a corporation chartered under the laws of New Jersey, but having an agency and store in New York. The suit was commenced by attaching the goods in the store, and also by serving a summons on its president in New York. The motion to quash the writ of foreign attachment and summons was allowed, on the ground that the corporation was not an inhabitant of the New York district, nor found within it at the time of serving the process, — a corporation having no corporate existence out of the State under whose laws it is created. The court said: "Without pursuing the examination of the case further, we are satisfied, for the reasons stated, that neither the levying of the writ of attachment upon the goods of the defendants in this district, nor the service of the summons upon their president within it, nor both together, have the effect to give jurisdiction to the court in this case against the defendants; and further, that, according to the true construction of the eleventh section of the Judiciary Act of 1789, the court would have no jurisdiction in suits instituted against foreign corporations, even in cases where the State practice, if adopted by it, would authorize the institution of such suits by the attachment of their goods found within their jurisdiction."

§ 498. Where, however, the court has jurisdiction of the person of the defendant, it may restrain him from violating the patent in a district other than the one in which the suit is brought. Still, where it may be necessary to proceed directly against the machine itself, as in cases of extreme contumacy or of fraudulent contrivance to evade an injunction, *semble*, proceedings must be instituted in the district in which the machine is located.[5]

The equity jurisdiction conferred upon the circuit courts by the

[1] Saddler *v.* Hudson, 2 Curtis, C. C. 6.

[2] Allen *v.* Blunt, 1 Blatchf. 480.

[3] Goodyear *v.* Chaffee, 3 Blatchf. 268.

[4] 1 Blatchf. 628.

[5] Boyd *v.* McAlpin, 3 McLean, 427; Wilson *v.* Sherman, 1 Blatchf. 536, citing Simpson *v.* Wilson, 4 How. 709, and Wilson *v.* Simpson, 9 How. 109.

act of 1836, § 17, is irrespective of the right of the plaintiff to an injunction or his demand for one. Consequently the patentee is entitled to a discovery and account after the expiration of the term for which the patent is granted.[1]

§ 499. With regard to the appellate jurisdiction of the Supreme Court, it may be stated that it does not extend by virtue of the act of 1836, § 17, to cases where the matter in controversy is, not the settlement of the claims and rights of a patentee, but the mere amount of costs. Such a question is left for decision under the provisions of the Judiciary Act of 1789, and consequently the amount in issue must exceed $2,000.[2] This limitation would still seem applicable under the provisions of the act of 1861, c. 37, whereby an appeal lies to the Supreme Court irrespective of the value or amount in controversy.

In Hogg *v.* Emerson, 6 How. 439, it was held, that when a case is sent up to the Supreme Court, under the discretion conferred upon the court below, by the act of 1836, the whole case must go up; the word "reasonable," in the statute, applying rather to the cases themselves than to the points of the cases.

[1] Nevins *v.* Johnson, 3 Blatchf. 80. "The arrangement of the provisions of sec. 17 may be fairly referred to, as implying that the power to award injunctions was introduced by Congress, rather as ancillary to the general equity jurisdiction imparted, than as the substantive and primary purpose of the enactment. It bears more the aspect of an incident to the jurisdiction before conferred than a condition of the jurisdiction itself."

[2] Sizer *v.* Many, 16 How. 98.

CHAPTER XIV.

REPEAL OF PATENTS. INTERFERING PATENTS OR APPLICATIONS.

§ 500. THE sixteenth section of the act of 1836 made provision for suits by bill in equity to declare void either of two interfering patents, or an existing patent where a subsequent applicant claimed the invention on the ground of priority, and the application had been refused on the ground that to grant it would interfere with the existing patent. The court was empowered, in the case of two interfering patents, to declare either of them void, in the whole or in part, or invalid or inoperative in any part or portion of the United States, according to the interest which the parties to the suit might possess in the inventions patented; and in the case of an application for a patent rejected on account of interference with an existing patent, to adjudge the patent to the applicant, as the fact of priority of right or invention might appear; *provided*, that the adjudication should not affect the rights of any person except the parties to the action, and those claiming title from or under them subsequent to the rendition of the judgment. With regard to the effect of this *proviso*, it has been held that, in order to affect parties who were not parties to the suit for interference, the judgment must be direct and affirmative, declaring the interference and that one of the patents is void in the whole or in part, or inoperative, or invalid in some particular part of the United States.[1]

§ 501. The act of 1870 makes corresponding but separate provisions on this subject of interference. The case of an application for a patent finally refused, *for any reason whatever*, which, of course, includes a refusal on the ground of interference with an existing patent, is provided for under section fifty-two of the new act, by giving the applicant a remedy by bill in equity; which, in fact, operates as a review of the grounds on which the

[1] Tyler *et al.* *v.* Hyde *et al.*, 2 Blatchf. 308.

application was finally rejected, the adjudication under the bill being that the applicant is entitled to the patent, if it so appears. Such a decision operates, it would seem, as an annulment of the patent previously granted, so far as the interference extends.

§ 502. The 58th section of the act of 1870 provides, that when there are interfering patents, any person interested in any one of them, or in the working of the invention claimed under either of them, may have relief by bill in equity against the interfering patentee and all persons interested under him ; the judgment and its effect being the same as under section sixteen of the act of 1836.[1]

§ 503. But neither the act of 1836 nor the act of 1870 has made provision for vacating or declaring void any existing patent excepting upon the ground of interference, and that too at the suit of some rival patentee, or applicant, or of some person claiming under them. Parties who are sued, or are liable to be sued as infringers, — in other words, the general public, — are not embraced in these provisions. It has therefore been held by the Supreme Court of the United States, that when it is sought to vacate or annul a patent, on the ground that it was obtained by a fraud on the government, a private individual cannot maintain a bill in equity in his own name. But it has also been held that the general chancery jurisdiction of the courts of the United States affords a remedy in cases of this kind in the name of the attorney-general, on the relation of some one who is injured specially or as a part of the general public. What was formerly done in England by *scire facias* came afterwards to be done by a bill in chancery, as the more convenient remedy ; and this jurisdiction has been held to extend, in the courts of the United States, to patents granted by the government through mistake or inadvertence as well as fraud. This was so held in the case of a patent for lands,[2] and now patents for inventions have been placed upon the same footing, by a recent decision, which denies that an individual can maintain a suit in chancery for the repeal of a patent, in his own name, excepting in interference cases, but intimates that the proper remedy is in the name of the attorney-

[1] For the provisions respecting the court in which the suit may be brought, notice to adverse parties, and the method of proceeding generally, see §§ 52, 58, act of 1870.

[2] United States *v.* Stone, 2 Wall. 525.

general, or in the name of the United States.[1] Undoubtedly, the proper course is to institute the suit in the name of the attorney-general, or of the United States, *on the relation* of some one who is interested adversely to the patent.

§ 504. Whether this remedy can be resorted to in the case of a patent that has expired, is doubtful. In Bourne *v.* Goodyear, which appears to have been a proceeding in the name of the United States, on the relation of Bourne, to vacate an extended patent, it was held that the extended patent having expired before the bill was filed, there was no equity to support a suit to set it aside, because there was nothing for the bill to operate upon.[2] But this cannot be universally true. A patent may have expired, and yet the patentee may collect for past infringements; and it would seem that in a suit to declare the patent void *ab initio*, the court might entertain a prayer to restrain the patentee from making such collections. In the subsequent case of Maury *v.* Whitney, it was made one ground of demurrer to the bill that the extended patent had expired by its own limitation before the bill was filed. The court did not decide this question, because the suit to declare the patent void was brought in the name of an individual, and not in the name of the United States. But in delivering the opinion of the court, Mr. Justice Miller said that where a case arises in which the United States or the attorney-general shall institute a suit to have a patent declared null *ab initio*, which, though no longer in force as to present or future infringements, *is used* to sustain suits for infringements during its vitality, the question will be considered.[3] Bourne *v.* Goodyear, therefore, is not to be regarded as decisive on this question. It was apparently decided without considering that there may be such a case as Mr. Justice Miller described in the subsequent decision, and was therefore made more comprehensive than it should have been.

[1] Maury *v.* Whitney, 14 Wall. 434.
[2] Bourne *v.* Goodyear, 9 Wall. 811.
[3] Maury *v.* Whitney, 14 Wall. 434.

APPENDIX.

LAWS OF THE UNITED STATES

RELATING TO

PATENTS, &c.

PATENT LAWS.

ACT OF 1790, CHAPTER 7.

1 STATUTES AT LARGE, 109.

Repealed by Act of 1793, Chap. 11, § 12.

An Act to promote the progress of useful arts.

SECTION 1. *Be it enacted by the Senate and House of Representatives of the United States of America in Congress assembled,* That upon the petition of any person or persons to the Secretary of State, the Secretary for the Department of War, and the Attorney-General of the United States, setting forth that he, she, or they hath or have invented or discovered any useful art, manufacture, engine, machine, or device, or any improvement therein not before known or used, and praying that a patent may be granted therefor, it shall and may be lawful to and for the said Secretary of State, the Secretary for the Department of War, and the Attorney-General, or any two of them, if they shall deem the invention or discovery sufficiently useful and important, to cause letters-patent to be made out in the name of the United States, to bear teste by the President of the United States, reciting the allegations and suggestions of the said petition, and describing the said invention or discovery, clearly, truly, and fully, and thereupon granting to such petitioner or petitioners, his, her, or their heirs, administrators, or assigns for any term not exceeding fourteen years, the sole and exclusive right and liberty of making, constructing, using, and vending to others to be used, the said invention or discovery; which letters-patent shall be delivered to the Attorney-General of the United States to be examined, who shall, within fifteen days next after the delivery to him, if he shall find the same conformable to this act, certify it to be so at the foot thereof, and present the letters-patent so certified to the President, who shall cause the seal of the United States to be thereto affixed, and the same shall be good and available to the grantee or grantees by force of this act, to all and every intent and purpose herein contained, and shall be recorded in a book to be kept for that purpose in the office of the Secretary of State, and delivered to the patentee or his agent, and the delivery thereof shall be entered on the record and indorsed on the patent by the said Secretary at the time of granting the same.

SECTION 2. *And be it further enacted*, That the grantee or grantees of each patent shall, at the time of granting the same, deliver to the Secretary of State a specification in writing, containing a description, accompanied with drafts or models, and explanations and models (ir the nature of the invention or discovery will admit of a model), of the thing or things by him or them invented or discovered, and described as aforesaid, in the said patents; which specification shall be so particular, and said models so exact, as not only to distinguish the invention or discovery from other things before known and used, but also to enable a workman or other person skilled in the art of manufacture, whereof it is a branch, or wherewith it may be nearest connected, to make, construct, or use the same, to the end that the public may have the full benefit thereof, after the expiration of the patent term; which specification shall be filed in the office of the said Secretary, and certified copies thereof shall be competent evidence in all courts and before all jurisdictions, where any matter or thing, touching or concerning such patent, right, or privilege shall come in question.

SECTION 3. *And be it further enacted*, That upon the application of any person to the Secretary of State, for a copy of any such specification, and for permission to have similar model or models made, it shall be the duty of the Secretary to give such a copy, and to permit the person so applying for a similar model or models, to take, or make, or cause the same to be taken or made, at the expense of such applicant.

SECTION 4. *And be it further enacted*, That if any person or persons shall devise, make, construct, use, employ, or vend, within these United States, any art, manufacture, engine, machine, or device, or any invention or improvement upon, or in any art, manfuacture, engine, machine, or device, the sole and exclusive right of which shall be so as aforesaid granted by patent to any person or persons, by virtue and in pursuance of this act, without the consent of the patentee or patentees, their executors, administrators, or assigns, first had and obtained in writing, every person so offending shall forfeit and pay to the said patentee or patentees, his, her, or their executors, administrators, or assigns, such damages as shall be assessed by a jury, and moreover shall forfeit to the person aggrieved, the thing or things so devised, made, constructed, used, employed, or vended, contrary to the true intent of this act, which may be recovered in an action on the case founded on this act.

SECTION 5. *And be it further enacted*, That upon oath or affirmation made before the judge of the district court where the defendant resides, that any patent which shall be issued in pursuance of this act, was obtained surreptitiously by, or upon false suggestion, and motion made to the said court, within one year after issuing the said patent, but not afterwards, it shall and may be lawful to and for the judge of the said district court, if the matter alleged shall appear to him to be sufficient, to grant a rule that the patentee or patentees, his, her, or their executors, administrators, or assigns, show cause why process should not issue against him, her, or them, to repeal such patents; and if sufficient cause shall not be shown to the contrary, the rule shall be made absolute, and thereupon the said judge shall order process to be issued as aforesaid, against such patentee or patentees, his, her, or their executors, administrators, or assigns. And in case no sufficient cause shall be shown to the contrary, or if it shall appear that the patentee was not the first and true inventor or discoverer, judgment shall be rendered by such court for the repeal of such patent or patents; and if the party at whose complaint the process issued shall have judgment given against him, he shall pay all such costs as the defendant shall be put to in defending the suit, to be taxed by the court, and recovered in such manner as costs expended by defendants shall be recovered in due course of law.

SECTION 6. *And be it further enacted,* That in all actions to be brought by such patentee or patentees, his, her, or their executors, administrators, or assigns, for any penalty incurred by virtue of this act, the said patents or specifications shall be *primâ facie* evidence that the said patentee or patentees was or were the first and true inventor or inventors, discoverer or discoverers, of the thing so specified, and that the same is truly specified; but that nevertheless the defendant or defendants may plead the general issue, and give this act, and any special matter whereof notice in writing shall have been given to the plaintiff, or his attorney, thirty days before the trial, in evidence tending to prove that the specification filed by the plaintiff does not contain the whole of the truth concerning his invention or discovery; or that it contains more than is necessary to produce the effect described; and if the concealment of part, or the addition of more than is necessary, shall appear to have been intended to mislead, or shall actually mislead the public, so as the effect described cannot be produced by the means specified, then, and in such cases, the verdict and judgment shall be for the defendant.

SECTION 7. *And be it further enacted,* That such patentee as aforesaid shall, before he receives his patent, pay the following fees to the several officers employed in making out and perfecting the same, to wit: For receiving and filing the petition, fifty cents; for filing specifications, per copy-sheet containing one hundred words, ten cents; for making out patent, two dollars; for affixing great seal, one dollar; for indorsing the day of delivering the same to the patentee, including all intermediate services, twenty cents.

Approved April 10, 1790.

ACT OF 1793, CHAPTER 11.

1 STATUTES AT LARGE, 318.

Repealed by Act of 1836, Chap. 357, § 21.

An Act to promote the progress of useful arts, and to repeal the Act heretofore made for that purpose.

SECTION 1. *Be it enacted by the Senate and House of Representatives of the United States of America in Congress assembled,* That when any person or persons, being a citizen or citizens of the United States, shall allege that he or they have invented any new and useful art, machine, manufacture, or composition of matter, or any new and useful improvement on any art, machine, manufacture, or composition of matter, not known or used before the application, and shall present a petition to the Secretary of State, signifying a desire of obtaining an exclusive property in the same, and praying that a patent may be granted therefor, it shall and may be lawful for the said Secretary of State to cause letters-patent to be made out in the name of the United States, bearing teste by the President of the United States, reciting the allegations and suggestions of the said petition, and giving a short description of the said invention or discovery, and thereupon granting to such petitioner or petitioners, his, her, or their heirs, administrators, or assigns, for a term not exceeding fourteen years, the full and exclusive right and liberty of making, constructing, using, and vending to others to be used, the said invention or discovery, which letters-patent shall be delivered to the Attorney-General of the United States, to be examined; who, within fifteen days after such delivery, if he finds the same conformable to this act, shall certify accordingly, at the foot thereof, and return the same to the Secretary of State, who shall present the letters-patent, thus certified, to be signed, and shall cause the seal of the United States to be thereto affixed; and the same shall be good and available to the grantee or grantees, by force of this act, and shall be recorded in a book, to be kept for that purpose, in the office of the Secretary of State, and delivered to the patentee or his order.

SECTION 2. *Provided always, and be it further enacted,* That any person who shall have discovered an improvement in the principle of any machine, or in the process of any composition of matter, which shall have been patented, and shall have obtained a patent for such improvement, he shall not be at liberty to make, use, or vend the original discovery, nor shall the first inventor be at liberty to use the improvement: And it is hereby enacted and declared, that simply changing the form or the proportions of any machine, or composition of matter, in any degree, shall not be deemed a discovery.

SECTION 3. *And be it further enacted,* That every inventor, before he can receive a patent, shall swear or affirm, that he does verily believe that he is the true inventor or discoverer of the art, machine, or improvement for which he solicits a patent, which oath or affirmation may be made before any person authorized to administer oaths, and shall deliver a written description of his invention, and of the manner of using, or process of compounding the same, in such full, clear, and exact terms, as to distinguish the same from all other things before known, and to enable any person skilled in the art or science of which it is a branch, or with which it is most nearly connected, to make, compound, and use the same. And in the case of any machine, he shall fully explain the principle, and the several modes in which he has contemplated the application of that principle or character, by which it may be distinguished from other inventions; and he shall accompany the whole with drawings and written references, where the nature of the case admits of drawings, or with specimens of the ingredients, and of the composition of matter, sufficient in quantity for the purpose of experiment, where the invention is of a composition of matter; which description, signed by himself, and attested by two witnesses, shall be filed in the office of the Secretary of State, and certified copies thereof shall be competent evidence in all courts, where any matter or thing, touching such patent right shall come in question. And such inventor shall, moreover, deliver a model of his machine, provided the Secretary shall deem such model to be necessary.

SECTION 4. *And be it further enacted,* That it shall be lawful for any inventor, his executor or administrator, to assign the title and interest in the said invention, at any time, and the assignee, having recorded the said assignment in the office of the Secretary of State, shall thereafter stand in the place of the original inventor, both as to right and responsibility, and so the assignees of assigns, to any degree.

SECTION 5. *And be it further enacted,* That if any person shall make, devise, and use, or sell the thing so invented, the exclusive right of which shall, as aforesaid, have been secured to any person by patent, without the consent of the patentee, his executors, administrators, or assigns, first obtained in writing, every person so offending shall forfeit and pay to the patentee a sum that shall be at least equal to three times the price for which the patentee has usually sold or licensed, to other persons, the use of the said invention, which may be recovered in an action on the case founded on this act, in the circuit court of the United States, or any other court having competent jurisdiction.

SECTION 6. *Provided always, and be it further enacted,* That the defendant in such action shall be permitted to plead the general issue, and give this act, and any special matter, of which notice in writing may have been given to the plaintiff or his attorney, thirty days before trial, in evidence, tending to prove that the specification filed by the plaintiff does not contain the whole truth relative to his discovery, or that it contains more than is necessary to produce the described effect, which concealment or addition shall fully appear to have been made for the purpose of deceiving the public, or that the thing thus secured by patent was not originally discovered by the patentee, but had been in use, or had been described in some public work anterior to the supposed discovery of the patentee, or that he had surreptitiously obtained a patent for the discovery of another person; in either of which cases judgment shall be rendered for the defendant, with costs, and the patent shall be declared void.

SECTION 7. *And be it further enacted*, That where any State, before its adoption of the present form of government, shall have granted an exclusive right to any invention, the party claiming that right shall not be capable of obtaining an exclusive right under this act, but on relinquishing his right under such particular State, and of such relinquishment, his obtaining an exclusive right under this act shall be sufficient evidence.

SECTION 8. *And be it further enacted*, That the persons whose applications for patents were, at the time of passing this act, depending before the Secretary of State, Secretary at War, and Attorney-General, according to the act passed the second session of the first Congress, entituled "An Act to promote the progress of useful arts," on complying with the conditions of this act, and paying the fees herein required, may pursue their respective claims to a patent under the same.

SECTION 9. *And be it further enacted*, That in case of interfering applications, the same shall be submitted to the arbitration of three persons, one of whom shall be chosen by each of the applicants, and the third person shall be appointed by the Secretary of State; and the decision or award of such arbitrators, delivered to the Secretary of State in writing, and subscribed by them, or any two of them, shall be final, as far as respects the granting of the patent. And if either of the applicants shall refuse or fail to choose an arbitrator, the patent shall issue to the opposite party. And where there shall be more than two interfering applications, and the parties applying shall not all unite in appointing three arbitrators, it shall be in the power of the Secretary of State to appoint three arbitrators for the purpose.

SECTION 10. *And be it further enacted*, That upon oath or affirmation being made before the judge of the District Court where the patentee, his executors, administrators, or assigns reside, that any patent, which shall be issued in pursuance of this act, was obtained surreptitiously, or upon false suggestion, and motion made to the said court, within three years after issuing the said patent, but not afterwards, it shall and may be lawful for the judge of the said District Court, if the matter alleged shall appear to him to be sufficient, to grant a rule, that the patentee, or his executor, administrator, or assign show cause why process should not issue against him to repeal such patent. And if sufficient cause shall not be shown to the contrary, the rule shall be made absolute, and thereupon the said judge shall order process to be issued against such patentee, or his executors, administrators, or assigns, with costs of suit. And in case no sufficient cause shall be shown to the contrary, or if it shall appear that the patentee was not the true inventor or discoverer, judgment shall be rendered by such court for the repeal of such patent; and if the party, at whose complaint, the process issued, shall have judgment given against him, he shall pay all such costs as the defendant shall be put to in defending the suit, to be taxed by the court, and recovered in due course of law.

SECTION 11. *And be it further enacted*, That every inventor, before he presents his petition to the Secretary of State, signifying his desire of obtaining a patent, shall pay into the treasury thirty dollars, for which he shall take duplicate receipts; one of which receipts he shall deliver to the Secretary of State, when he presents his petition; and the money thus paid shall be in full for the sundry services to be performed in the office of the Secretary of State, consequent on such petition, and shall pass to the account of clerk-hire in that office: *Provided nevertheless*, That for every copy, which may be required at the said office, of any paper respecting any patent that has been granted, the person obtaining such copy shall pay, at the rate of twenty cents, for every copy-sheet of one hundred words, and for every copy of a drawing, the party obtaining the same, shall pay two dollars, of which payments an account shall be rendered, annually, to the treasury of the United States, and they shall also pass to the account of clerk-hire in the office of the Secretary of State.

SECTION 12. *And be it further enacted*, That the act, passed the tenth day of April, in the year one thousand seven hundred and ninety, intituled "An Act to promote the progress of useful arts," be, and the same is hereby, repealed: *Provided always*, That nothing contained in this act shall be construed to invalidate any patent that may have been granted under the authority of the said act; and all patentees under the said act, their executors, administrators, or assigns, shall be considered within the purview of this act, in respect to the violation of their rights; provided such violations shall be committed after the passing of this act.

Approved February 21, 1793.

ACT OF 1794, CHAPTER 58.

1 STATUTES AT LARGE, 393.

Repealed by Act of 1836, Chap. 357, § 21.

An Act supplementary to the Act intituled "An Act to promote the progress of useful arts."

Be it enacted by the Senate and House of Representatives of the United States of America in Congress assembled, That all suits, actions, process and proceedings, heretofore had in any District Court of the United States, under an act passed the tenth day of April, in the year one thousand seven hundred and ninety, intituled "An Act to promote the progress of useful arts," which may have been set aside, suspended, or abated, by reason of the repeal of the said act, may be restored, at the instance of the plaintiff or defendant, within one year from and after the passing of this act, in the said courts, to the same situation, in which they may have been when they were so set aside, suspended, or abated; and that the parties to the said suits, actions, process or proceedings be, and are hereby, entitled to proceed in such cases, as if no such repeal of the act aforesaid had taken place: *Provided always*, That before any order or proceeding, other than that for continuing the same suits, after the reinstating thereof, shall be entered or had, the defendant or plaintiff, as the case may be, against whom the same may have been reinstated, shall be brought into court by summons, attachment, or such other proceeding as is used in other cases for compelling the appearance of a party.

Approved June 7, 1794.

ACT OF 1800, CHAPTER 25.

2 STATUTES AT LARGE, 37.

Repealed by Act of 1836, Chap. 357, § 21.

An Act to extend the privilege of obtaining patents for useful discoveries and inventions, to certain persons therein mentioned, and to enlarge and define the penalties for violating the rights of patentees.

SECTION 1. *Be it enacted by the Senate and House of Representatives of the United States of America in Congress assembled*, That all and singular the rights and privileges given, intended or provided to citizens of the United States, respecting patents for new inventions, discoveries, and improvements, by the act intituled "An Act to promote the progress of useful arts, and to repeal the Act heretofore made for that purpose," shall be, and hereby are, extended and given to all aliens who at the time of petitioning in the manner prescribed by the said act, shall have resided for two years within the United States, which privileges shall be obtained, used, and enjoyed by such persons, in as full and ample manner, and under the same conditions, limitations, and restrictions, as by the said act is provided and directed in the case of citizens of the United States: *Provided always*, That every person petitioning for a patent for any invention, art, or discovery, pursuant to this act, shall make oath or affirmation before some person duly authorized to administer oaths before such patent shall be granted, that such invention, art, or discovery hath not, to the best of his or her knowledge or belief, been known or used either in this or any foreign country, and that every patent which shall be obtained pursuant to this act, for any invention, art, or discovery, which it shall afterward appear had been known or used previous to such application for a patent, shall be utterly void.

SECTION 2. *And be it further enacted*, That where any person hath made, or shall have made, any new invention, discovery, or improvement, on account of which a patent might, by virtue of this or the above-mentioned act, be granted to such person, and shall die before any patent shall be granted therefor, the right of applying for and obtaining such patent, shall devolve on the legal representatives of such person in trust for the heirs at law of the deceased, in case he shall have died intestate; but if otherwise, then in trust for his devisees, in as full and ample manner, and under the same conditions, limitations, and restrictions as the same was held, or might have been claimed or enjoyed by such person, in his or her lifetime; and when application for a patent shall be made by such legal representatives, the oath or affirmation, provided in the third section of the before-mentioned act, shall be so varied as to be applicable to them.

SECTION 3. *And be it further enacted*, That where any patent shall be or shall have been granted pursuant to this or the above-mentioned act, and any person without the consent of the patentee, his or her executors, administrators, or assigns, first obtained in writing, shall make, devise, use, or sell the thing whereof the exclusive right is secured to the said patentee by such patent, such person so offending shall forfeit and pay to the said patentee, his executors, administrators, or assigns, a sum equal to three times the actual damage sustained by such patentee, his executors, administrators, or assigns, from or by reason of such offence, which sum shall and may be recovered by action on the case founded on this and the above-mentioned act, in the Circuit Court of the United States, having jurisdiction thereon.

SECTION 4. *And be it further enacted*, That the fifth section of the above-mentioned act, intituled "An Act to promote the progress of useful arts, and to repeal the Act heretofore made for that purpose," shall be, and hereby is, repealed.

Approved April 17, 1800.

ACT OF 1819, CHAPTER 19.

3 Statutes at Large, 481.

Repealed by Act of 1836, Chap. 357, § 21.

An Act to extend the jurisdiction of the Circuit Courts of the United States to cases arising under the law relating to patents.

Be it enacted by the Senate and House of Representatives of the United States of America in Congress assembled, That the Circuit Courts of the United States shall have original cognizance, as well in equity as at law, of all actions, suits, controversies, and cases arising under any law of the United States, granting or confirming to authors or inventors the exclusive right to their respective writings, inventions, and discoveries; and upon any bill in equity, filed by any party aggrieved in any such cases, shall have authority to grant injunctions, according to the course and principles of courts of equity, to prevent the violation of the rights of any authors or inventors, secured to them by any laws of the United States, on such terms and conditions as the said courts may deem fit and reasonable: *Provided however,* That from all judgments and decree of any Circuit Courts rendered in the premises, a writ of error or appeal, as the case may require, shall lie to the Supreme Court of the United States, in the same manner, and under the same circumstances, as is now provided by law in other judgments and decrees of such circuit courts.

Approved February 15, 1819.

ACT OF 1832, CHAPTER 162.

4 Statutes at Large, 559.

Repealed by Act of 1836, Chap. 357, § 21.

An Act concerning patents for useful inventions.

Section 1. *Be it enacted by the Senate and House of Representatives of the United States of America in Congress assembled,* That it shall be the duty of the Secretary of State, annually, in the month of January, to report to Congress, and to publish in two of the newspapers printed in the city of Washington, a list of all the patents for discoveries, inventions, and improvements, which shall have expired within the year immediately preceding, with the names of the patentees, alphabetically arranged.

SECTION 2. *And be it further enacted*, That application to Congress to prolong or renew the term of a patent shall be made before its expiration, and shall be notified at least once a month, for three months before its presentation, in two newspapers printed in the city of Washington, and in one of the newspapers in which the laws of the United States shall be published in the State or Territory in which the patentee shall reside. The petition shall set forth particularly the grounds of the application. It shall be verified by oath; the evidence in its support may be taken before any judge or justice of the peace; it shall be accompanied by a statement of the ascertained value of the discovery, invention, or improvement, and of the receipts and expenditures of the patentee, so as to exhibit the profit or loss arising therefrom.

SECTION 3. *And be it further enacted*, That wherever any patent which has been heretofore, or shall be hereafter, granted to any inventor in pursuance of the act of Congress, entitled "An Act to promote the progress of useful arts, and to repeal the Act heretofore made for that purpose," passed on the twenty-first day of February, in the year of our Lord, one thousand seven hundred and ninety-three, or of any of the acts supplementary thereto, shall be invalid or inoperative, by reason that any of the terms or conditions prescribed in the third section of the said first-mentioned act, have not, by inadvertence, accident, or mistake, and without any fraudulent or deceptive intention, been complied with on the part of the said inventor, it shall be lawful for the Secretary of State, upon the surrender to him of such patent, to cause a new patent to be granted to the said inventor for the same invention for the residue of the period then unexpired, for which the original patent was granted, upon his compliance with the terms and conditions prescribed in the said third section of the said act. And, in case of his death, or any assignment by him made of the same patent, the like right shall vest in his executors and administrators, or assignee or assignees: *Provided however*, That such new patent so granted shall, in all respects, be liable to the same matters of objection and defence as any original patent granted under the said first-mentioned act. But no public use or privilege of the invention so patented, derived from or after the grant of the original patent, either under any special license of the inventor, or without the consent of the patentee that there shall be a free public use thereof, shall, in any manner, prejudice his right of recovery for any use or violation of his invention after the grant of such new patent as aforesaid.

Approved July 3, 1832.

ACT OF 1832, CHAPTER 203.

4 Statutes at Large, 577.

Repealed by Act of 1836, Chap. 357, § 21.

An Act concerning the issuing of patents to aliens, for useful discoveries and inventions.

Be it enacted by the Senate and House of Representatives of the United States of America in Congress assembled, That the privileges granted to the aliens described in the first section of the act, to extend the privilege of obtaining patents for useful discoveries and inventions to certain persons therein mentioned, and to enlarge and define the penalties for violating the rights of patentees, approved April seventeenth, eighteen hundred, be extended in like manner to every alien who, at the time of petitioning for a patent, shall be resident in the United States, and shall have declared his intention, according to law, to become a citizen thereof: *Provided,* That every patent granted by virtue of this act and the privileges thereto appertaining, shall cease and determine and become absolutely void without resort to any legal process to annul or cancel the same in case of a failure on the part of any patentee, for the space of one year from the issuing thereof, to introduce into public use in the United States the invention or improvement for which the patent shall be issued; or in case the same for any period of six months after such introduction shall not continue to be publicly used and applied in the United States, or in case of failure to become a citizen of the United States, agreeably to notice given at the earliest period within which he shall be entitled to become a citizen of the United States.

Approved July 13, 1832.

ACT OF 1836, CHAPTER 357.

5 Statutes at Large, 117.

An Act to promote the progress of the useful arts, and to repeal all Acts and parts of Acts heretofore made for that purpose.

Section 1. *Be it enacted by the Senate and House of Representatives of the United States of America in Congress assembled,* That there shall be established and attached to the Department of State an office to be denominated the Patent Office; the chief officer of which shall be called the Commissioner of Patents, to be appointed by the President, by and with the advice and consent of the Senate, whose duty it shall be, under the direction of the Secretary of State, to superintend, execute, and perform all such acts and things touching and respecting the granting and issuing of patents for new and useful discoveries, inventions, and improvements, as are herein provided for, or shall hereafter be, by law, directed to be done and performed, and shall have the charge and custody of all the books, records, papers, models, machines, and all other things belonging to said office. And said commissioner shall receive the same compensation as is allowed by law to the Commissioner of the Indian Department, and shall be entitled to send and receive letters and packages by mail, relating to the business of the office, free of postage.

SECTION 2. *And be it further enacted*, That there shall be in said office an inferior officer, to be appointed by the said principal officer, with the approval of the Secretary of State, to receive an annual salary of seventeen hundred dollars, and to be called the Chief Clerk of the Patent Office; who, in all cases during the necessary absence of the commissioner, or when the said principal office shall become vacant, shall have the charge and custody of the seal, and of the records, books, papers, machines, models, and all other things belonging to the said office, and shall perform the duties of commissioner during such vacancy. And the said commissioner may also, with like approval, appoint an examining clerk, at an annual salary of fifteen hundred dollars; two other clerks at twelve hundred dollars each, one of whom shall be a competent draughtsman; one other clerk at one thousand dollars; a machinist at twelve hundred and fifty dollars; and a messenger at seven hundred dollars. And said commissioner, clerks, and every other person appointed and employed in said office shall be disqualified and interdicted from acquiring or taking, except by inheritance, during the period for which they shall hold their appointments, respectively, any right or interest, directly or indirectly, in any patent for an invention or discovery which has been, or may hereafter be granted.

SECTION 3. *And be it further enacted*, That the said principal officer, and every other person to be appointed in the said office, shall, before he enters upon the duties of his office or appointment, make oath or affirmation truly and faithfully to execute the trust committed to him. And the said commissioner and the chief clerk shall also, before entering upon their duties, severally give bonds, with sureties, to the Treasurer of the United States, the former in the sum of ten thousand dollars, and the latter in the sum of five thousand dollars, with condition to render a true and faithful account to him or his successor in office, quarterly, of all moneys which shall be by them respectively received for duties on patents, and for copies of records and drawings, and all other moneys received by virtue of said office.

SECTION 4. *And be it further enacted*, That the said commissioner shall cause a seal to be made and provided for the said office, with such device as the President of the United States shall approve; and copies of any records, books, papers, or drawings belonging to the said office, under the signature of the said commissioner, or, when the office shall be vacant, under the signature of the chief clerk, with the said seal affixed, shall be competent evidence in all cases in which the original records, books, papers, or drawings could be evidence. And any person making application therefor may have certified copies of the records, drawings, and other papers deposited in said office, on paying for the written copies the sum of ten cents for every page of one hundred words; and for copies of drawings the reasonable expense of making the same.

SECTION 5. [See act of 1837, ch. 45, § 6.] *And be it further enacted*, That all patents issued from said office shall be issued in the name of the United States, and under the seal of said office, and be signed by the Secretary of State, and countersigned by the commissioner of the said office, and shall be recorded, together with the descriptions, specifications, and drawings, in the said office, in books to be kept for that purpose. Every such patent shall contain a short description or title of the invention or discovery, correctly indicating its nature and design, and in its terms grant to the applicant or applicants, his or their heirs, administrators, executors, or assigns, for a term not exceeding fourteen years, the full and exclusive right and liberty of making, using, and vending to others to be used, the said invention or discovery, referring to the specifications for the particulars thereof, a copy of which shall be annexed to the patent, specifying what the patentee claims as his invention or discovery.

SECTION 6. *And be it further enacted*, That any person or persons, having discovered or invented any new and useful art, machine, manufacture, or composition of matter, or any new and useful improvement on any art, machine, manufacture, or composition of matter, not known or used by others before his or their discovery or invention thereof, and not, at the time of his application for a patent, in public use or on sale, with his consent or allowance, as the inventor or discoverer; and shall desire to obtain an exclusive property therein, may make application, in writing, to the Commissioner of Patents, expressing such desire, and the commissioner, on due proceedings had, may grant a patent therefor. But before any inventor shall receive a patent for any such new invention or discovery, he shall deliver a written description of his invention or discovery, and of the manner and process of making, constructing, using, and compounding the same, in such full, clear, and exact terms, avoiding unnecessary prolixity, as to enable any person skilled in the art or science to which it appertains, or with which it is most nearly connected, to make, construct, compound, and use the same; and in case of any machine, he shall fully explain the principle, and the several modes in which he has contemplated the application of that principle or character by which it may be distinguished from other inventions; and shall particularly specify and point out the part, improvement, or combination, which he claims as his own invention or discovery. He shall, furthermore, accompany the whole with a drawing or drawings, and written references, where the nature of the case admits of drawings, or with specimens of ingredients, and of the composition of matter, sufficient in quantity for the purpose of experiment, where the invention or discovery is of a composition of matter; which descriptions and drawings, signed by the inventor and attested by two witnesses, shall be filed in the Patent Office; and he shall moreover furnish a model of his invention, in all cases which admit of a representation by model, of a convenient size to exhibit advantageously its several parts. The applicant shall also make oath or affirmation that he does verily believe that he is the original and first inventor or discoverer of the art, machine, composition, or improvement, for which he solicits a patent, and that he does not know or believe that the same was ever before known or used; and also of what country he is a citizen; which oath or affirmation may be made before any person authorized by law to administer oaths.

SECTION 7. [See act of 1839, ch. 88, §§ 7-12, and act of 1863, ch. 102, § 1.] *And be it further enacted*, That, on the filing of any such application, description, and specification, and the payment of the duty hereinafter provided, the commissioner shall make, or cause to be made, an examination of the alleged new invention or discovery; and if, on any such examination, it shall not appear to the commissioner that the same had been invented or discovered by any other person in this country prior to the alleged invention or discovery thereof by the applicant, or that it had been patented or described in any printed publication in this or any foreign country, or had been in public use or on sale with the applicant's consent or allowance prior to the application, if the commissioner shall deem it to be sufficiently useful and important, it shall be his duty to issue a patent therefor. But whenever, on such examination, it shall appear to the commissioner that the applicant was not the original and first inventor or discoverer thereof, or that any part of that which is claimed as new had before been invented or discovered, or patented, or described in any printed publication in this or any foreign country, as aforesaid, or that the description is defective and insufficient, he shall notify the applicant thereof, giving him, briefly, such information and references as may be useful in judging of the propriety of renewing his application, or of altering his specification to embrace only that part of the invention or discovery which is new. In every such case, if the applicant shall elect to withdraw his application, relinquishing his claim to the model, he shall be entitled to receive back twenty dollars, part of the duty required by this act, on filing a notice in writing of such election in the Patent Office, a copy of which, certified by the commissioner, shall be a sufficient warrant to the treasurer for paying back to the said applicant the said sum of twenty dollars. But if the applicant in such case shall persist in his claims for a patent, with or without any alteration in his specification, he shall be required to make oath or affirmation anew, in manner as aforesaid. And if the specification and claim shall not have been so modified as, in the opinion of the commissioner, shall entitle the applicant to a patent, he may, on appeal, and upon request in writing, have the decision of a board of examiners, to be composed of three disinterested persons, who shall be appointed for that purpose by the Secretary of State, one of whom at least, to be selected, if practicable and convenient, for his knowledge and skill in the particular art, manufacture, or branch of science to which the alleged invention appertains; who shall be under oath or affirmation for the faithful and impartial performance of the duty imposed upon them by said appointment. Said board shall be furnished with a certificate in writing, of the opinion and decision of the commissioner, stating the particular grounds of his objection, and the part or parts of the invention which he considers as not entitled to be patented. And the said board shall give reasonable notice to the applicant, as well as to the commissioner, of the time and place of their meeting, that they may have an opportunity of furnishing them with such facts and evidence as they may deem necessary to a just decision; and it shall be the duty of the commissioner to furnish to the board of examiners such information as he may possess relative to the matter under their consideration. And on an examination and consideration of the matter by such board, it shall be in their power, or of a majority of them, to reverse the decision of the commissioner, either in whole or in part, and their opinion being certified to the commissioner, he shall be governed thereby in the further proceedings to be had on such application: *Provided however*, That before a board shall be instituted in any such case, the applicant shall pay to the credit of the treasury, as provided in the ninth section of this act, the sum of twenty-five dollars, and each of said persons so appointed shall be entitled to receive for his services in each case a sum not exceeding ten dollars, to be determined and paid by the commissioner out of any moneys in his hands, which shall be in full compensation to the persons who may be so appointed, for their examination and certificate as aforesaid.

SECTION 8. [See act of 1839, ch. 88, § 6.] *And be it further enacted*, That whenever an application shall be made for a patent which, in the opinion of the commissioner, would interfere with any other patent for which an application may be pending, or with any unexpired patent which shall have been granted, it shall be the duty of the commissioner to give notice thereof to such applicants, or patentees, as the case may be; and if either shall be dissatisfied with the decision of the commissioner on the question of priority of right or invention, on a hearing thereof, he may appeal from such decision, on the like terms and conditions as are provided in the preceding section of this act; and the like proceedings shall be had, to determine which or whether either of the applicants is entitled to receive a patent as prayed for. But nothing in this act contained shall be construed to deprive an original and true inventor of the right to a patent for his invention, by reason of his having previously taken out letters-patent therefor in a foreign country, and the same having been published, at any time within six months next preceding the filing of his specification and drawings. And whenever the applicant shall request it, the patent shall take date from the time of the filing of the specification and drawings, not however exceeding six months prior to the actual issuing of the patent; and on like request, and the payment of the duty herein required, by any applicant, his specification and drawings shall be filed in the secret archives of the office until he shall furnish the model and the patent be issued, not exceeding the term of one year, the applicant being entitled to notice of interfering applications.

Section 9. [See act of 1861, ch. 88, § 10.] *And be it further enacted*, That before any application for a patent shall be considered by the commissioner as aforesaid, the applicant shall pay into the treasury of the United States, or into the Patent Office, or into any of the deposit banks, to the credit of the treasury, if he be a citizen of the United States, or an alien, and shall have been resident in the United States for one year next preceding, and shall have made oath of his intention to become a citizen thereof, the sum of thirty dollars; if a subject of the king of Great Britain, the sum of five hundred dollars; and all other persons the sum of three hundred dollars; for which payment duplicate receipts shall be taken, one of which to be filed in the office of the Treasurer. And the moneys received into the treasury under this act shall constitute a fund for the payment of the salaries of the officers and clerks herein provided for, and all other expenses of the Patent Office, and to be called the Patent Fund.

Section 10. *And be it further enacted*, That where any person hath made, or shall have made, any new invention, discovery, or improvement, on account of which a patent might by virtue of this act be granted, and such person shall die before any patent shall be granted therefor, the right of applying for and obtaining such patent shall devolve on the executor or administrator of such person, in trust for the heirs at law of the deceased, in case he shall have died intestate: but if otherwise, then in trust for his devisees, in as full and ample manner, and under the same conditions, limitations, and restrictions as the same was held, or might have been claimed or enjoyed by such person in his or her lifetime; and when application for a patent shall be made by such legal representatives, the oath or affirmation provided in the sixth section of this act shall be so varied as to be applicable to them.

SECTION 11. *And be it further enacted*, That every patent shall be assignable in law, either as to the whole interest, or any undivided part thereof, by any instrument in writing; which assignment, and also every grant and conveyance of the exclusive right, under any patent, to make and use, and to grant to others to make and use the thing patented within and throughout any specified part or portion of the United States, shall be recorded in the Patent Office within three months from the execution thereof, for which the assignee or grantee shall pay to the commissioner the sum of three dollars.

SECTION 12. [See act of 1861, ch. 88, §§ 9, 10.] *And be it further enacted*, That any citizen of the United States, or alien, who shall have been a resident of the United States one year next preceding, and shall have made oath of his intention to become a citizen thereof, who shall have invented any new art, machine, or improvement thereof, and shall desire further time to mature the same, may, on paying to the credit of the treasury, in manner as provided in the ninth section of this act, the sum of twenty dollars, file in the Patent Office a caveat, setting forth the design and purpose thereof, and its principal and distinguishing characteristics, and praying protection of his right till he shall have matured his invention; which sum of twenty dollars, in case the person filing such caveat shall afterwards take out a patent for the invention therein mentioned, shall be considered a part of the sum herein required for the same. And such caveat shall be filed in the confidential archives of the office, and preserved in secrecy. And if application shall be made by any other person within one year from the time of filing such caveat, for a patent of any invention with which it may in any respect interfere, it shall be the duty of the commissioner to deposit the description, specifications, drawings, and model, in the confidential archives of the office, and to give notice, by mail, to the person filing the caveat, of such application, who shall, within three months after receiving the notice, if he would avail himself of the benefit of his caveat, file his description, specifications, drawings, and model; and if, in the opinion of the commissioner, the specifications of claim interfere with each other, like proceedings may be had in all respects as are in this act provided in the case of interfering applications: *Provided however*, That no opinion or decision of any board of examiners, under the provisions of this act, shall preclude any person, interested in favor or against the validity of any patent which has been or may hereafter be granted, from the right to contest the same in any judicial court in any action in which its validity may come in question.

SECTION 13. [See act of 1837, ch. 45, §§ 5–8, and act of 1861, ch. 88, § 9.] *And be it further enacted*, That whenever any patent which has heretofore been granted, or which shall hereafter be granted, shall be inoperative, or invalid, by reason of a defective or insufficient description or specification, or by reason of the patentee claiming in his specification as his own invention more than he had or shall have a right to claim as new; if the error has or shall have arisen by inadvertency, accident, or mistake, and without any fraudulent or deceptive intention, it shall be lawful for the commissioner, upon the surrender to him of such patent, and the payment of the further duty of fifteen dollars, to cause a new patent to be issued to the said inventor, for the same invention, for the residue of the period then unexpired for which the original patent was granted, in accordance with the patentee's corrected description and specification. And in case of his death, or any assignment by him made of the original patent, a similar right shall vest in his executors, administrators, or assignees. And the patent, so reissued, together with the corrected description and specification, shall have the same effect and operation in law, on the trial of all actions hereafter commenced for causes subsequently accruing, as though the same had been originally filed in such corrected form, before the issuing out of the original patent. And whenever the original patentee shall be desirous of adding the description and specification of any new improvement of the original invention or discovery which shall have been invented or discovered by him subsequent to the date of his patent, he may, like proceedings being had in all respects as in the case of original applications, and on the payment of fifteen dollars, as hereinbefore provided, have the same annexed to the original description and specification; and the commissioner shall certify, on the margin of such annexed description and specification, the time of its being annexed and recorded; and the same shall hereafter have the same effect in law, to all intents and purposes, as though it had been embraced in the original description and specification.

Section 14. *And be it further enacted*, That whenever, in any action for damages for making, using, or selling the thing whereof the exclusive right is secured by any patent heretofore granted, or by any patent which may hereafter be granted, a verdict shall be rendered for the plaintiff in such action, it shall be in the power of the court to render judgment for any sum above the amount found by such verdict as the actual damages sustained by the plaintiff, not exceeding three times the amount thereof, according to the circumstances of the case, with costs; and such damages may be recovered by action on the case, in any court of competent jurisdiction, to be brought in the name or names of the person or persons interested, whether as patentees, assignees, or as grantees of the exclusive right within and throughout a specified part of the United States.

Section 15. [See act of 1837, ch. 45, § 9; and by act of 1839, ch. 88, § 7.] *And be it further enacted*, That the defendant in any such action shall be permitted to plead the general issue, and to give this act and any special matter in evidence, of which notice in writing may have been given to the plaintiff or his attorney, thirty days before trial, tending to prove that the description and specification filed by the plaintiff does not contain the whole truth relative to his invention or discovery, or that it contains more than is necessary to produce the described effect; which concealment or addition shall fully appear to have been made for the purpose of deceiving the public, or that the patentee was not the original and first inventor or discoverer of the thing patented, or of a substantial and material part thereof claimed as new, or that it had been described in some public work anterior to the supposed discovery thereof by the patentee, or had been in public use or on sale with the consent and allowance of the patentee before his application for a patent, or that he had surreptitiously or unjustly obtained the patent for that which was in fact invented or discovered by another, who was using reasonable diligence in adapting and perfecting the same; or that the patentee, if an alien at the time the patent was granted, had failed and neglected, for the space of eighteen months from the date of the patent, to put and continue on sale to the public, on reasonable terms, the invention or discovery for which the patent issued; in either of which cases judgment shall be rendered for the defendant with costs. And whenever the defendant relies in his defence on the fact of a previous invention, knowledge, or use of the thing patented, he shall state, in his notice of special matter, the names and places of residence of those whom he intends to prove to have possessed a prior knowledge of the thing, and where the same had been used: *Provided however*, That whenever it shall satisfactorily appear that the patentee, at the time of making his application for the patent, believed himself to be the first inventor or discoverer of the thing patented, the same shall not be held to be void on account of the invention or discovery or any part thereof having been before known or used in any foreign country, it not appearing that the same or any substantial part thereof had before been patented or described in any printed publication. *And provided also*, That whenever the plaintiff shall fail to sustain his action on the ground that in his specification of claim is embraced more than that of which he was the first inventor, if it shall appear that the defendant had used or violated any part of the invention justly and truly specified and claimed as new, it shall be in the power of the court to adjudge and award as to costs, as may appear to be just and equitable.

SECTION 16. [See act of 1839, ch. 88, § 10.] *And be it further enacted*, That whenever there shall be two interfering patents, or whenever a patent on application shall have been refused on an adverse decision of a board of examiners, on the ground that the patent applied for would interfere with an unexpired patent previously granted, any person interested in any such patent, either by assignment or otherwise, in the one case, and any such applicant in the other case, may have remedy by bill in equity; and the court having cognizance thereof, on notice to adverse parties, and other due proceedings had, may adjudge and declare either the patents void in the whole or in part, or inoperative or invalid in any particular part or portion of the United States, according to the interest which the parties to such suit may possess in the patent or the inventions patented, and may also adjudge that such applicant is entitled, according to the principles and provisions of this act, to have and receive a patent for his invention, as specified in his claim, or for any part thereof, as the fact of priority of right or invention shall in any such case be made to appear. And such adjudication, if it be in favor of the right of such applicant, shall authorize the commissioner to issue such patent, on his filing a copy of the adjudication, and otherwise complying with the requisitions of this act. *Provided however*, That no such judgment or adjudication shall affect the rights of any person except the parties to the action and those deriving title from or under them subsequent to the rendition of such judgment.

SECTION 17. [See act of 1861, ch. 37.] *And be it further enacted*, That all actions, suits, controversies, and cases arising under any law of the United States, granting or confirming to inventors the exclusive right to their inventions or discoveries, shall be originally cognizable, as well in equity as at law, by the Circuit Courts of the United States, or any District Court having the power and jurisdiction of a Circuit Court; which courts shall have power, upon a bill in equity filed by any party aggrieved, in any such case, to grant injunctions, according to the course and principles of Courts of Equity, to prevent the violation of the rights of any inventor as secured to him by any law of the United States, on such terms and conditions as said courts may deem reasonable: *Provided however*, That from all judgments and decrees from any such court rendered in the premises, a writ of error or appeal, as the case may require, shall lie to the Supreme Court of the United States, in the same manner and under the same circumstances as is now provided by law in other judgments and decrees of Circuit Courts, and in all other cases in which the court shall deem it reasonable to allow the same.

SECTION 18. [See act of 1848, ch. 47, § 1, and act of 1861, ch. 88, §§ 12, 16.] *And be it further enacted*, That whenever any patentee of an invention or discovery shall desire an extension of his patent beyond the term of its limitation, he may make application therefor, in writing, to the Commissioner of the Patent Office, setting forth the grounds thereof; and the commissioner shall, on the applicant's paying the sum of forty dollars to the credit of the treasury, as in the case of an original application for a patent, cause to be published in one or more of the principal newspapers in the city of Washington, and in such other paper or papers as he may deem proper, published in the section of country most interested adversely to the extension of the patent, a notice of such application and of the time and place when and where the same will be considered, that any person may appear and show cause why the extension should not be granted. And the Secretary of State, the Commissioner of the Patent Office, and the Solicitor of the Treasury shall constitute a board to hear and decide upon the evidence produced before them both for and against the extension, and shall sit for that purpose at the time and place designated in the published notice thereof. The patentee shall furnish to said board a statement, in writing, under oath, of the ascertained value of the invention, and of his receipts and expenditures, sufficiently in detail to exhibit a true and faithful account of loss and profit in any manner accruing to him from and by reason of said invention. And if, upon a hearing of the matter, it shall appear to the full and entire satisfaction of said board, having due regard to the public interest therein, that it is just and proper that the term of the patent should be extended, by reason of the patentee, without neglect or fault on his part, having failed to obtain, from the use and sale of his invention, a reasonable remuneration for the time, ingenuity, and expense bestowed upon the same, and the introduction thereof into use, it shall be the duty of the commissioner to renew and extend the patent, by making a certificate thereon of such extension, for the term of seven years from and after the expiration of the first term; which certificate, with a certificate of said board of their judgment and opinion as aforesaid, shall be entered on record in the Patent Office; and thereupon the said patent shall have the same effect in law as though it had been originally granted for the term of twenty-one years. And the benefit of such renewal shall extend to assignees and grantees of the right to use the thing patented, to the extent of their respective interests therein: *Provided however*, That no extension of a patent shall be granted after the expiration of the term for which it was originally issued.

SECTION 19. *And be it further enacted*, That there shall be provided for the use of said office, a library of scientific works and periodical publications, both foreign and American, calculated to facilitate the discharge of the duties hereby required of the chief officers therein, to be purchased under the direction of the Committee of the Library of Congress. And the sum of fifteen hundred dollars is hereby appropriated for that purpose, to be paid out of the patent fund.

SECTION 20. *And be it further enacted*, That it shall be the duty of the commissioner to cause to be classified and arranged, in such rooms or galleries as may be provided for that purpose, in suitable cases, when necessary for their preservation, and in such manner as shall be conducive to a beneficial and favorable display thereof, the models and specimens of compositions and of fabrics and other manufactures and works of art, patented or unpatented, which have been, or shall hereafter be, deposited in said office. And said rooms or galleries shall be kept open during suitable hours for public inspection.

SECTION 21. *And be it further enacted*, That all acts and parts of acts heretofore passed on this subject be, and the same are hereby repealed: *Provided however*, That all actions and processes in law or equity sued out prior to the passage of this act may be prosecuted to final judgment and execution, in the same manner as though this act had not been passed, excepting and saving the application to any such action of the provisions of the fourteenth and fifteenth sections of this act, so far as they may be applicable thereto; *And provided also*, That all applications or petitions for patents, pending at the time of the passage of this act, in cases where the duty has been paid, shall be proceeded with and acted on in the same manner as though filed after the passage hereof.

Approved July 4, 1836.

ACT OF 1837, CHAPTER 45.

5 STATUTES AT LARGE, 191.

An Act in addition to the act to promote the progress of science and useful arts.

SECTION 1. *Be it enacted by the Senate and House of Representatives of the United States of America in Congress assembled*, That any person who may be in possession of, or in any way interested in, any patent for an invention, discovery, or improvement, issued prior to the fifteenth day of December, in the year of our Lord one thousand eight hundred and thirty-six, or in an assignment of any patent, or interest therein, executed and recorded prior to the said fifteenth day of December, may, without charge, on presentation or transmission thereof to the Commissioner of Patents, have the same recorded anew in the Patent Office, together with the descriptions, specifications of claim and drawings annexed or belonging to the same; and it shall be the duty of the commissioner to cause the same, or any authenticated copy of the original record, specification, or drawing which he may obtain, to be transcribed and copied into books of record to be kept for that purpose; and wherever a drawing was not originally annexed to the patent and referred to in the specification, any drawing produced as a delineation of the invention, being verified by oath in such manner as the commissioner shall require, may be transmitted and placed on file, or copied as aforesaid, together with certificate of the oath; or such drawings may be made in the office, under the direction of the commissioner, in conformity with the specification. And it shall be the duty of the commissioner to take such measures as may be advised and determined by the Board of Commissioners provided for in the fourth section of this act, to obtain the patents, specifications, and copies aforesaid, for the purpose of being so transcribed and recorded. And it shall be the duty of each of the several clerks of the judicial courts of the United States, to transmit as soon as may be, to the Commissioner of the Patent Office, a statement of all the authenticated copies of patents, descriptions, specifications, and drawings of inventions and discoveries made and executed prior to the aforesaid fifteenth day of December, which may be found on the files of his office; and also to make out and transmit to said commissioner, for record as aforesaid, a certified copy of every such patent, description, specification, or drawing, which shall be specially required by said commissioner.

SECTION 2. *And be it further enacted*, That copies of such record and drawings, certified by the commissioner, or, in his absence, by the chief clerk, shall be *primâ facie* evidence of the particulars of the invention and of the patent granted therefor in any judicial court of the United States, in all cases where copies of the original record or specification and drawings would be evidence, without proof of the loss of such originals; and no patent issued prior to the aforesaid fifteenth day of December shall, after the first day of June next, be received in evidence in any of the said courts in behalf of the patentee or other person who shall be in possession of the same, unless it shall have been so recorded anew, and a drawing of the invention, if separate from the patent, verified as aforesaid, deposited in the Patent Office; nor shall any written assignment of any such patent, executed and recorded prior to the said fifteenth day of December, be received in evidence in any of the said courts in behalf of the assignee or other person in possession thereof, until it shall have been so recorded anew.

SECTION 3. [See act of 1842, ch. 263, § 2.] *And be it further enacted*, That whenever it shall appear to the commissioner that any patent was destroyed by the burning of the Patent Office building on the aforesaid fifteenth day of December, or was otherwise lost prior thereto, it shall be his duty, on application therefor by the patentee or other person interested therein, to issue a new patent for the same invention or discovery, bearing the date of the original patent, with his certificate thereon that it was made and issued pursuant to the provisions of the third section of this act, and shall enter the same of record: *Provided however*, That before such patent shall be issued the applicant therefor shall deposit in the Patent Office a duplicate, as near as may be, of the original model, drawings, and description, with specification of the invention or discovery, verified by oath, as shall be required by the commissioner; and such patent, and copies of such drawings and descriptions, duly certified, shall be admissible as evidence in any judicial court of the United States, and shall protect the rights of the patentee, his administrators, heirs, and assigns, to the extent only in which they would have been protected by the original patent and specification.

SECTION 4. *And be it further enacted*, That it shall be the duty of the commissioner to procure a duplicate of such of the models, destroyed by fire on the aforesaid fifteenth day of December, as were most valuable and interesting, and whose preservation would be important to the public; and such as would be necessary to facilitate the just discharge of the duties imposed by law on the commissioner in issuing patents, and to protect the rights of the public and of patentees in patented inventions and improvements: *Provided*, That a duplicate of such models may be obtained at a reasonable expense: *And provided also*, That the whole amount of expenditure for this purpose shall not exceed the sum of one hundred thousand dollars. And there shall be a temporary board of commissioners, to be composed of the Commissioner of the Patent Office and two other persons to be appointed by the President, whose duty it shall be to consider and determine upon the best and most judicious mode of obtaining models of suitable construction; and also to consider and determine what models may be procured in pursuance of, and in accordance with, the provisions and limitations in this section contained. And said commissioners may make and establish all such regulations, terms, and conditions, not inconsistent with law, as in their opinion may be proper and necessary to carry the provision of this section into effect, according to its true intent.

SECTION 5. [See act of 1836, ch. 357, § 13.] *And be it further enacted*, That, whenever a patent shall be returned for correction and reissue under the thirteenth section of the act to which this is additional, and the patentee shall desire several patents to be issued for distinct and separate parts of the thing patented, he shall first pay, in manner and in addition to the sum provided by that act, the sum of thirty dollars for each additional patent so to be issued: *Provided however*, That no patent made prior to the aforesaid fifteenth day of December shall be corrected and reissued until a duplicate of the model and drawing of the thing as originally invented, verified by oath as shall be required by the commissioner, shall be deposited in the Patent Office;

Nor shall any addition of an improvement be made to any patent heretofore granted, nor any new patent be issued for an improvement made in any machine, manufacture, or process, to the original inventor, assignee, or possessor of a patent therefor, nor any disclaimer be admitted to record, until a duplicate model and drawing of the thing originally invented, verified as aforesaid, shall have been deposited in the Patent Office, if the commissioner shall require the same; nor shall any patent be granted for an invention, improvement, or discovery, the model or drawing of which shall have been lost, until another model and drawing, if required by the commissioner, shall, in like manner, be deposited in the Patent Office;

And in all such cases, as well as in those which may arise under the third section of this act, the question of compensation for such models and drawings shall be subject to the judgment and decision of the commissioners, provided for in the fourth section, under the same limitations and restrictions as are therein prescribed.

SECTION 6. [See act of 1836, ch. 357, § 5.] *And be it further enacted*, That any patent hereafter to be issued may be made and issued to the assignee or assignees of the inventor or discoverer, the assignment thereof being first entered of record, and the application therefor being duly made, and the specification duly sworn to by the inventor. And in all cases hereafter, the applicant for a patent shall be held to furnish duplicate drawings, whenever the case admits of drawings, one of which to be deposited in the office, and the other to be annexed to the patent, and considered a part of the specification.

SECTION 7. *And be it further enacted*, That, whenever any patentee shall have, through inadvertence, accident, or mistake, made his specification of claim too broad, claiming more than that of which he was the original or first inventor, some material or substantial part of the thing patented being truly and justly his own, any such patentee, his administrators, executors, and assigns, whether of the whole or of a sectional interest therein, may make disclaimer of such parts of the thing patented as the disclaimant shall not claim to hold by virtue of the patent or assignment, stating therein the extent of his interest in such patent; which disclaimer shall be in writing, attested by one or more witnesses, and recorded in the Patent Office, on payment by the person disclaiming in manner as other patent duties are required by law to be paid, of the sum of ten dollars. And such disclaimer shall thereafter be taken and considered as part of the original specification, to the extent of the interest which shall be possessed in the patent or right secured thereby, by the disclaimant, and by those claiming by or under him subsequent to the record thereof. But no such disclaimer shall affect any action pending at the time of its being filed, except so far as may relate to the question of unreasonable neglect or delay in filing the same.

SECTION 8. [See act of 1861, ch. 88, § 9.] *And be it further enacted*, That, whenever application shall be made to the commissioner for any addition of a newly discovered improvement to be made to an existing patent, or whenever a patent shall be returned for correction and reissue, the specification of claim annexed to every such patent shall be subject to revision and restriction, in the same manner as are original applications for patents; the commissioner shall not add any such improvement to the patent in the one case, nor grant the reissue in the other case, until the applicant shall have entered a disclaimer, or altered his specification of claim in accordance with the decision of the commissioner; and in all such cases, the applicant, if dissatisfied with such decision, shall have the same remedy, and be entitled to the benefit of the same privileges and proceedings as are provided by law in the case of original applications for patents.

SECTION 9. [See act of 1836, ch. 357, § 15.] *And be it further enacted* (any thing in the fifteenth section of the act to which this is additional to the contrary notwithstanding), That, whenever by mistake, accident, or inadvertence, and without any wilful default or intent to defraud or mislead the public, any patentee shall have in his specification claimed to be the original and first inventor or discoverer of any material or substantial part of the thing patented, of which he was not the first and original inventor, and shall have no legal or just right to claim the same, in every such case the patent shall be deemed good and valid for so much of the invention or discovery as shall be truly and *bonâ fide* his own; *Provided*, It shall be a material and substantial part of the thing patented, and be definitely distinguishable from the other parts so claimed without right as aforesaid. And every such patentee, his executors, administrators, and assigns, whether of the whole, or of a sectional interest therein, shall be entitled to maintain a suit at law or in equity on such patent for any infringement of such part of the invention or discovery as shall be *bonâ fide* his own as aforesaid, notwithstanding the specification may embrace more than he shall have any legal right to claim. But, in every such case in which a judgment or verdict shall be rendered for the plaintiff, he shall not be entitled to recover costs against the defendant, unless he shall have entered at the Patent Office, prior to the commencement of the suit, a disclaimer of all that part of the thing patented which was so claimed without right. *Provided however*, That no person bringing any such suit shall be entitled to the benefits of the provisions contained in this section, who shall have unreasonably neglected or delayed to enter at the Patent Office a disclaimer as aforesaid.

SECTION 10. [See act of 1861, ch. 88, § 6.] *And be it further enacted*, That the commissioner is hereby authorized and empowered to appoint agents, in not exceeding twenty of the principal cities or towns in the United States as may best accommodate the different sections of the country, for the purpose of receiving and forwarding to the Patent Office all such models, specimens of ingredients and manufactures, as shall be intended to be patented or deposited therein, the transportation of the same to be chargeable to the patent fund.

SECTION 11. *And be it further enacted*, That, instead of one examining clerk, as provided by the second section of the act to which this is additional, there shall be appointed, in manner therein provided, two examining clerks, each to receive an annual salary of fifteen hundred dollars; and also, an additional copying clerk, at an annual salary of eight hundred dollars. And the commissioner is also authorized to employ, from time to time, as many temporary clerks as may be necessary to execute the copying and draughting required by the first section of this act, and to examine and compare the records with the originals, who shall receive not exceeding seven cents for every page of one hundred words, and for drawings and comparison of records with originals, such reasonable compensation as shall be agreed upon or prescribed by the commissioner.

SECTION 12. [See act of 1861, ch. 88, § 9.] *And be it further enacted*, That, wherever the application of any foreigner for a patent shall be rejected and withdrawn for want of novelty in the invention, pursuant to the seventh section of the act to which this is additional, the certificate thereof of the commissioner shall be a sufficient warrant to the treasurer to pay back to such applicant two thirds of the duty he shall have paid into the treasury on account of such application.

SECTION 13. *And be it further enacted*, That in all cases in which an oath is required by this act or by the act to which this is additional, if the person of whom it is required shall be conscientiously scrupulous of taking an oath, affirmation may be substituted therefor.

SECTION 14. *And be it further enacted*, That all moneys paid into the treasury of the United States for patents and for fees for copies furnished by the Superintendent of the Patent Office prior to the passage of the act to which this is additional, shall be carried to the credit of the patent fund created by said act; and the moneys constituting said fund shall be, and the same are hereby, appropriated for the payment of the salaries of the officers and clerks provided for by said act, and all other expenses of the Patent Office, including all the expenditures provided for by this act; and also for such other purposes as are or may be hereafter specially provided for by law. And the commissioner is hereby authorized to draw upon said fund, from time to time, for such sums as shall be necessary to carry into effect the provisions of this act, governed, however, by the several limitations herein contained. And it shall be his duty to lay before Congress, in the month of January, annually, a detailed statement of the expenditures and payments by him made from said fund; And it shall also be his duty to lay before Congress, in the month of January, annually, a list of all patents which shall have been granted during the preceding year, designating, under proper heads, the subjects of such patents, and furnishing an alphabetical list of the patentees, with their places of residence; and he shall also furnish a list of all patents which shall have become public property during the same period; together with such other information of the state and condition of the Patent Office as may be useful to Congress or the public.

Approved March 3, 1837.

ACT OF 1839, CHAPTER 88.

5 STATUTES AT LARGE, 353.

An Act in addition to "An Act to promote the progress of the useful arts."

SECTION 1. *Be it enacted by the Senate and House of Representatives of the United States of America in Congress assembled,* That there shall be appointed, in manner provided in the second section of the act to which this is additional, two assistant examiners, each to receive an annual salary of twelve hundred and fifty dollars.

SECTION 2. *And be it further enacted,* That the commissioner be authorized to employ temporary clerks to do any necessary transcribing, whenever the current business of the office requires it; *Provided, however,* That instead of salary, a compensation shall be allowed, at a rate not greater than is charged for copies now furnished by the office.

SECTION 3. *And be it further enacted,* That the commissioner is hereby authorized to publish a classified and alphabetical list of all patents granted by the Patent Office previous to said publication, and retain one hundred copies for the Patent Office and nine hundred copies to be deposited in the library of Congress, for such distribution as may be hereafter directed; and that one thousand dollars, if necessary, be appropriated, out of the patent fund, to defray the expense of the same.

SECTION 4. *And be it further enacted,* That the sum of three thousand six hundred and fifty-nine dollars and twenty-two cents be, and is hereby, appropriated from the patent fund, to pay for the use and occupation of rooms in the City Hall by the Patent Office.

SECTION 5. *And be it further enacted,* That the sum of one thousand dollars be appropriated from the patent fund, to be expended under the direction of the commissioner, for the purchase of necessary books for the library of the Patent Office.

SECTION 6. [See act of 1836, ch. 357, § 8.] *And be it further enacted,* That no person shall be debarred from receiving a patent for any invention or discovery, as provided in the act approved on the fourth day of July, one thousand eight hundred and thirty-six, to which this is additional, by reason of the same having been patented in a foreign country more than six months prior to his application: *Provided,* That the same shall not have been introduced into public and common use in the United States, prior to the application for such patent: *And provided also,* That in all cases every such patent shall be limited to the term of fourteen years from the date or publication of such foreign letters-patent.

SECTION 7. [See act of 1836, ch. 357, §§ 7, 15.] *And be it further en-*

acted, That every person or corporation who has, or shall have, purchased or constructed any newly invented machine, manufacture, or composition of matter, prior to the application by the inventor or discoverer for a patent, shall be held to possess the right to use, and vend to others to be used, the specific machine, manufacture, or composition of matter so made or purchased, without liability therefor to the inventor, or any other person interested in such invention; and no patent shall be held to be invalid by reason of such purchase, sale, or use prior to the application for a patent as aforesaid, except on proof of abandonment of such invention to the public; or that such purchase, sale, or prior use has been for more than two years prior to such application for a patent.

SECTION 8. *And be it further enacted*, That so much of the eleventh section of the above recited act as requires the payment of three dollars to the Commissioner of Patents for recording any assignment, grant, or conveyance of the whole or any part of the interest or right under any patent, be, and the same is hereby, repealed; and all such assignments, grants, and conveyances shall, in future, be recorded, without any charge whatever.

SECTION 10. [See act of 1836, ch. 357, § 16.] *And be it further enacted*, That the provisions of the sixteenth section of the before-recited act shall extend to all cases where patents are refused for any reason whatever, either by the Commissioner of Patents or by the Chief Justice of the District of Columbia, upon appeals from the decision of said commissioner, as well as where the same shall have been refused on account of, or by reason of, interference with a previously existing patent; and in all cases where there is no opposing party, a copy of the bill shall be served upon the Commissioner of Patents, when the whole of the expenses of the proceeding shall be paid by the applicant, whether the final decision shall be in his favor or otherwise

SECTION 11. [See act of 1836, ch. 357, § 7.] *And be it further enacted*, That in all cases where an appeal is now allowed by law from the decision of the Commissioner of Patents to a board of examiners, provided for in the seventh section of the act to which this is additional, the party, instead thereof, shall have a right to appeal to the Chief Justice of the District Court of the United States for the District of Columbia, by giving notice thereof to the commissioner, and filing in the Patent Office, within such time as the commissioner shall appoint, his reasons of appeal, specifically set forth in writing, and also paying into the Patent Office, to the credit of the patent fund, the sum of twenty-five dollars. And it shall be the duty of said Chief Justice, on petition, to hear and determine all such appeals, and to revise such decisions in a summary way, on the evidence produced before the commissioner, at such early and convenient time as he may appoint, first notifying the commissioner of the time and place of hearing, whose duty it shall be to give notice thereof to all parties who appear to be interested therein, in such manner as said judge shall prescribe. The commissioner shall also lay before the said judge all the original papers and evidence in the case, together with the grounds of his decision, fully set forth in writing, touching all the points involved by the reasons of appeal, to which the revision shall be confined. And at the request of any party interested, or at the desire of the judge, the commissioner and the examiners in the Patent Office may be examined under oath, in explanation of the principles of the machine or other thing for which a patent, in such case, is prayed for. And it shall be the duty of said judge, after a hearing of any such case, to return all the papers to the commissioner, with a certificate of his proceedings and decision, which shall be entered of record in the Patent Office; and such decision, so certified, shall govern the further proceedings of the commissioner in such case: *Provided however*, That no opinion or decision of the judge in any such case shall preclude any person interested in favor or against the validity of any patent which has been or may hereafter be granted from the right to contest the same in any judicial court, in any action in which its validity may come in question.

SECTION 12. [See act of 1836, ch. 357, § 7, and act of 1861, ch. 88, § 1.] *And be it further enacted*, That the Commissioner of Patents shall have power to make all such regulations, in respect to the taking of evidence to be used in contested cases before him, as may be just and reasonable. And so much of the act to which this is additional, as provides for a board of examiners, is hereby repealed.

SECTION 13. [See act of 1852, ch. 107, § 3.] *And be it further enacted*, That there be paid annually, out of the patent fund, to the said Chief Justice, in consideration of the duties herein imposed, the sum of one hundred dollars.

Approved March 3, 1839.

ACT OF 1842, CHAPTER 263.

5 STATUTES AT LARGE, 543.

An Act in addition to "An Act to promote the progress of the useful arts," and to repeal all acts and parts of acts heretofore made for that purpose.

SECTION 1. *Be it enacted by the Senate and House of Representatives of the United States of America in Congress assembled*, That the Treasurer of the United States be, and he hereby is, authorized to pay back, out of the patent fund, any sum or sums of money, to any person who shall have paid the same into the Treasury, or to any receiver or depositary to the credit of the Treasurer, as for fees accruing at the

Patent Office through mistake, and which are not provided to be paid by existing laws, certificate thereof being made to the said Treasurer by the Commissioner of Patents.

SECTION 2. [See act of 1837, ch. 45, § 3.] *And be it further enacted,* That the third section of the act of March, eighteen hundred and thirty-seven, which authorizes the renewing of patents lost prior to the fifteenth of December, eighteen hundred and thirty-six, is extended to patents granted prior to said fifteenth day of December, though they may have been lost subsequently: *Provided however,* The same shall not have been recorded anew under the provisions of said act.

SECTION 3. [See act of 1861, ch. 88, § 11.] *And be it further enacted,* That any citizen or citizens, or alien or aliens, having resided one year in the United States, and taken the oath of his or their intention to become a citizen or citizens, who by his, her, or their own industry, genius, efforts, and expense, may have invented or produced any new and original design for a manufacture, whether of metal or other material or materials, or any new and original design for the printing of woollen, silk, cotton, or other fabrics, or any new and original design for a bust, statue, or bas relief or composition in alto or basso relievo, or any new and original impression or ornament, or to be placed on any article of manufacture, the same being formed in marble or other material, or any new and useful pattern, or print, or picture, to be either worked into or worked on, or printed or painted or cast or otherwise fixed on, any article of manufacture, or any new and original shape or configuration of any article of manufacture not known or used by others before his, her, or their invention or production thereof, and prior to the time of his, her, or their application for a patent therefor, and who shall desire to obtain an exclusive property or right therein to make, use, and sell and vend the same, or copies of the same, to others, by them to be made, used, and sold, may make application in writing to the Commissioner of Patents expressing such desire, and the commissioner, on due proceedings had, may grant a patent therefor, as in the case now of application for a patent: *Provided,* That the fee in such cases, which by the now existing laws would be required of the particular applicant, shall be one half the sum, and that the duration of said patent shall be seven years, and that all the regulations and provisions which now apply to the obtaining or protection of patents not inconsistent with the provisions of this act shall apply to applications under this section.

SECTION 4. *And be it further enacted,* That the oath required for applicants for patents may be taken, when the applicant is not, for the time being, residing in the United States, before any minister, plenipotentiary, *chargé d'affaires,* consul, or commercial agent holding commission under the government of the United States, or before any notary public of the foreign country in which such applicant may be.

SECTION 5. *And be it further enacted*, That if any person or persons shall paint or print or mould, cast, carve, or engrave, or stamp, upon any thing made, used, or sold, by him, for the sole making or selling which he hath not or shall not have obtained letters-patent, the name or any imitation of the name of any other person who hath or shall have obtained letters-patent for the sole making and vending of such thing, without consent of such patentee, or his assigns or legal representatives; or if any person, upon any such thing not having been purchased from the patentee, or some person who purchased it from or under such patentee, or not having the license or consent of such patentee, or his assigns or legal representatives, shall write, paint, print, mould, cast, carve, engrave, stamp, or otherwise make or affix the word "patent," or the words "letters-patent," or the word "patentee," or any word or words of like kind, meaning, or import, with the view or intent of imitating or counterfeiting the stamp, mark, or other device of the patentee, or shall affix the same, or any word, stamp, or device, of like import, on any unpatented article, for the purpose of deceiving the public, he, she, or they, so offending, shall be liable for such offence to a penalty of not less than one hundred dollars, with costs, to be recovered by action in any of the Circuit Courts of the United States, or in any of the District Courts of the United States having the powers and jurisdiction of a Circuit Court; one half of which penalty, as recovered, shall be paid to the patent fund, and the other half to any person or persons who shall sue for the same.

SECTION 6. [See act of 1861, ch. 88, § 13.] *And be it further enacted*, That all patentees and assignees of patents hereafter granted are hereby required to stamp, engrave, or cause to be stamped or engraved, on each article vended, or offered for sale, the date of the patent; and if any person or persons, patentees, or assignees, shall neglect to do so, he, she, or they shall be liable to the same penalty, to be recovered and disposed of in the manner specified in the foregoing fifth section of this act.

Approved August 29, 1842.

ACT OF 1848, CHAPTER 47.

9 STATUTES AT LARGE, 231.

An Act to provide additional examiners in the Patent Office, and for other purposes.

SECTION 1. [See act of 1836, ch. 357, § 18.] *Be it enacted by the Senate and House of Representatives of the United States of America in Congress assembled*, That there shall be appointed, in the manner provided in the second section of the act entitled "An Act to promote the progress of useful arts, and to repeal all acts and parts of acts heretofore made for that purpose," approved July fourth, eighteen hundred and thirty-six, two principal examiners, and two assistant examiners, in addition to the number of examiners now employed in the Patent Office; and that hereafter each of the principal examiners employed in the Patent Office shall receive an annual salary of twenty-five hundred dollars, and each of the assistant examiners an annual salary of fifteen hundred dollars: *Provided*, That the power to extend patents, now vested in the board composed of the Secretary of State, Commissioner of Patents, and Solicitor of the Treasury, by the eighteenth section of the act approved July fourth, eighteen hundred and thirty-six, respecting the Patent Office, shall hereafter be vested solely in the Commissioner of Patents; and when an application is made to him for the extension of a patent according to said eighteenth section, and sixty days' notice given thereof, he shall refer the case to the principal examiner having charge of the class of inventions to which said case belongs, who shall make a full report to said commissioner of the said case, and particularly whether the invention or improvement secured in the patent was new and patentable when patented; and thereupon the said commissioner shall grant or refuse the extension of said patent, upon the same principles and rules that have governed said board; but no patent shall be extended for a longer term than seven years.

SECTION 2. [See act of 1861, ch. 88, § 10.] *And be it further enacted*, That hereafter the Commissioner of Patents shall require a fee of one dollar for recording any assignment, grant, or conveyance of the whole or any part of the interest in letters-patent, or power of attorney, or license to make or use the thing patented, when such instrument shall not exceed three hundred words; the sum of two dollars when it shall exceed three hundred and shall not exceed one thousand words; and the sum of three dollars when it shall exceed one thousand words; which fees shall in all cases be paid in advance.

SECTION 3. *And be it further enacted*, That there shall be appointed, in manner aforesaid, two clerks, to be employed in copying and recording, and in other services in the Patent Office, who shall each be paid a salary of one thousand two hundred dollars per annum.

SECTION 4. *And be it further enacted*, That the Commissioner of Patents is hereby authorized to send by mail, free of postage, the annual reports of the Patent Office, in the same manner in which he is empowered to send letters and packages relating to the business of the Patent Office.

Approved May 27, 1848.

ACT OF 1849, CHAPTER 108.

9 Statutes at Large, 395.

Extract from the Act entitled "An Act to establish the Home Department, and to provide for the Treasury Department an Assistant Secretary of the Treasury and a Commissioner of the Customs."

Section 2. *And be it further enacted,* That the Secretary of the Interior shall exercise and perform all the acts of supervision and appeal in regard to the office of Commissioner of Patents, now exercised by the Secretary of State; and the said Secretary of the Interior shall sign all requisitions for the advance or payment of money out of the Treasury on estimates or accounts, subject to the same adjustment or control now exercised on similar estimates or accounts by the First or Fifth Auditor and First Comptroller of the Treasury.

Approved March 3, 1849.

ACT OF 1852, CHAPTER 107.

10 Statutes at Large, 75.

An Act in addition to "An Act to promote the progress of the useful arts."

Section 1. [See act of 1839, ch. 88, § 11.] *Be it enacted by the Senate and House of Representatives of the United States of America in Congress assembled,* That appeals provided for in the eleventh section of the act entitled An act in addition to an act to promote the progress of the useful arts, approved March the third, eighteen hundred and thirty-nine, may also be made to either of the assistant judges of the Circuit Court of the District of Columbia, and all the powers, duties, and responsibilities imposed by the aforesaid act, and conferred upon the chief judge, are hereby imposed and conferred upon each of the said assistant judges.

Section 2. *And be it further enacted,* That in case appeal shall be made to the said chief judge, or to either of the said assistant judges, the Commissioner of Patents shall pay to such chief judge or assistant judge the sum of twenty-five dollars, required to be paid by the appellant into the Patent Office by the eleventh section of said act, on said appeal.

Section 3. *And be it further enacted,* That section thirteen of the aforesaid act, approved March the third, eighteen hundred and thirty-nine, is hereby repealed.

Approved August 30, 1852.

ACT OF 1859, CHAPTER 80.

11 STATUTES AT LARGE, 422.

Extract from "An Act making appropriations for the legislative, executive, and judicial expenses of the government," &c.

SECTION 4. *And be it further enacted*, That the Secretary of the Interior be, and he is hereby, directed to cause the annual report of the Commissioner of Patents on mechanics hereafter to be made to the Senate and House of Representatives to be prepared and submitted in such manner as that the plates and drawings necessary to illustrate each subject shall be inserted so as to comprise the entire report in one volume not to exceed eight hundred pages.

Approved March 3, 1859.

ACT OF 1861, CHAPTER 37.

12 STATUTES AT LARGE, 130.

An Act to extend the right of appeal from the decisions of Circuit Courts to the Supreme Court of the United States.

SECTION 1. [See act of 1836, ch. 357, § 17.] *Be it enacted by the Senate and House of Representatives of the United States of America in Congress assembled*, That from all judgments and decrees of any Circuit Court rendered in any action, suit, controversy, or case, at law or in equity, arising under any law of the United States granting or confirming to authors the exclusive right to their respective writings, or to inventors the exclusive right to their inventions or discoveries, a writ of error or appeal, as the case may require, shall lie, at the instance of either party, to the Supreme Court of the United States, in the same manner and under the same circumstances as is now provided by law in other judgments and decrees of such Circuit Courts, without regard to the sum or value in controversy in the action.

Approved February 18, 1861.

ACT OF 1861, CHAPTER 88.

12 STATUTES AT LARGE, 246.

An Act in addition to "An Act to promote the progress of the useful arts."

SECTION 1. [See act of 1839, ch. 88, § 12.] *Be it enacted by the Senate and House of Representatives of the United States of America in Congress assembled*, That the Commissioner of Patents may establish rules for taking affidavits and depositions required in cases pending in the Patent Office, and such affidavits and depositions may be taken before any justice of the peace, or other officer authorized by law to take depositions to be used in the courts of the United States, or in the State courts of any State where such officer shall reside; and in any contested case pending in the Patent Office it shall be lawful for the clerk of any court of the United States for any district or territory, and he is hereby required, upon the application of any party to such contested case, or the agent or attorney of such party, to issue subpœnas for any witnesses residing or being within the said district or territory, commanding such witnesses to appear and testify before any justice of the peace, or other officer as aforesaid, residing within the said district or territory, at any time and place in the subpœna to be stated; and if any witness, after being duly served with such subpœna, shall refuse or neglect to appear, or, after appearing, shall refuse to testify (not being privileged from giving testimony), such refusal or neglect being proved to the satisfaction of any judge of the court whose clerk shall have issued such subpœna, said judge may thereupon proceed to enforce obedience to the process, or to punish the disobedience in like manner as any court of the United States may do in case of disobedience to process of *subpœna ad testificandum* issued by such court; and witnesses in such cases shall be allowed the same compensation as is allowed to witnesses attending the courts of the United States: *Provided*, That no witness shall be required to attend at any place more than forty miles from the place where the subpœna shall be served upon him to give a deposition under this law: *Provided also*, That no witness shall be deemed guilty of contempt for refusing to disclose any secret invention made or owned by him: *And provided further*, That no witness shall be deemed guilty of contempt for disobeying any subpœna directed to him by virtue of this act, unless his fees for going to, returning from, and one day's attendance at the place of examination, shall be paid or tendered to him at the time of the service of the subpœna.

SECTION 2. *And be it further enacted*, That for the purposes of securing greater uniformity of action in the grant and refusal of letters-patent, there shall be appointed by the President, by and with the advice and consent of the Senate, three examiners in chief, at an annual salary of three thousand dollars each, to be composed of persons of competent legal knowledge and scientific ability, whose duty it shall be, on the written petition of the applicant for that purpose being filed, to revise and determine upon the validity of decisions made by examiners when adverse to the grant of letters-patent; and also to revise and determine in like manner upon the validity of the decisions of examiners in interference cases, and when required by the commissioner in applications for the extension of patents, and to perform such other duties as may be assigned to them by the commissioner; that from their decisions appeals may be taken to the Commissioner of Patents in person, upon payment of the fee hereinafter prescribed; that the said examiners in chief shall be governed in their action by the rules to be prescribed by the Commissioner of Patents.

SECTION 3. *And be it further enacted*, That no appeal shall be allowed to the examiners in chief from the decisions of the primary examiners, except in interference cases, until after the application shall have been twice rejected; and the second examination of the application by the primary examiner shall not be had until the applicant, in view of the references given on the first rejection, shall have renewed the oath of invention, as provided for in the seventh section of the act entitled "An Act to promote the progress of the useful arts, and to repeal all Acts and parts of Acts heretofore made for that purpose," approved July fourth, eighteen hundred and thirty-six.

SECTION 4. *And be it further enacted*, That the salary of the Commissioner of Patents, from and after the passage of this act, shall be four thousand five hundred dollars per annum, and the salary of the chief clerk of the Patent Office shall be two thousand five hundred dollars, and the salary of the librarian of the Patent Office shall be eighteen hundred dollars.

SECTION 5. *And be it further enacted*, That the Commissioner of Patents is authorized to restore to the respective applicants, or when not removed by them, to otherwise dispose of such of the models belonging to rejected applications as he shall not think necessary to be preserved. The same authority is also given in relation to all models accompanying applications for designs. He is further authorized to dispense in future with models of designs when the design can be sufficiently represented by a drawing.

SECTION 6. [Repealing act of 1837, § 10.] *And be it further enacted*, That the tenth section of the act approved the third of March, eighteen hundred and thirty-seven, authorizing the appointment of agents for the transportation of models and specimens to the Patent Office, is hereby repealed.

SECTION 7. *And be it further enacted*, That the commissioner is further authorized, from time to time, to appoint, in the manner already provided for by law, such an additional number of principal examiners, first assistant examiners, and second assistant examiners as may be required to transact the current business of the office with despatch, provided the whole number of additional examiners shall not exceed four of each class, and that the total annual expenses of the Patent Office shall not exceed the annual receipts.

SECTION 8. *And be it further enacted*, That the commissioner may require all papers filed in the Patent Office, if not correctly, legibly, and clearly written, to be printed at the cost of the parties filing such papers; and for gross misconduct he may refuse to recognize any person as a patent agent, either generally or in any particular case; but the reasons of the commissioner for such refusal shall be duly recorded, and be subject to the approval of the President of the United States.

SECTION 9. [See act of 1836, ch. 357, §§ 7, 12, 13.] *And be it further enacted*, That no money paid as a fee, on any application for a patent after the passage of this act, shall be withdrawn or refunded, nor shall the fee paid on filing a caveat be considered as part of the sum required to be paid on filing a subsequent application for a patent for the same invention. That the three months' notice given to any caveator, in pursuance of the requirements of the twelfth section of the act of July fourth, eighteen hundred and thirty-six, shall be computed from the day on which such notice is deposited in the post-office at Washington, with the regular time for the transmission of the same added thereto, which time shall be indorsed on the notice; and that so much of the thirteenth section of the act of Congress, approved July fourth, eighteen hundred and thirty-six, as authorizes the annexing to letters-patent of the description and specification of additional improvements is hereby repealed, and in all cases where additional improvements would now be admissible, independent patents must be applied for.

SECTION 10. *And be it further enacted*, That all laws now in force fixing the rates of the Patent Office fees to be paid, and discriminating between the inhabitants of the United States and those of other countries, which shall not discriminate against the inhabitants of the United States, are hereby repealed, and in their stead the following rates are established: —

On filing each caveat, ten dollars.

On filing each original application for a patent, except for a design, fifteen dollars.

On issuing each original patent, twenty dollars.

On every appeal from the examiner in chief to the commissioner, twenty dollars.

On every application for the reissue of a patent, thirty dollars.

On every application for the extension of a patent, fifty dollars; and fifty dollars in addition, on the granting of every extension.

On filing each disclaimer, ten dollars.

For certified copies of patents and other papers, ten cents per hundred words.

For recording every assignment, agreement, power of attorney, and other papers, of three hundred words or under, one dollar.

For recording every assignment, and other papers, over three hundred and under one thousand words, two dollars.

For recording every assignment or other writing, if over one thousand words, three dollars.

For copies of drawings, the reasonable cost of making the same.

SECTION 11. [See act of 1842, ch. 263, § 3.] *And be it further enacted*, That any citizen or citizens, or alien or aliens, having resided one year in the United States, and taken the oath of his or their intention to become a citizen or citizens, who, by his, her, or their own industry, genius, efforts, and expense may have invented or produced any new and original design, or a manufacture, whether of metal or other material or materials, and original design for a bust, statue, or bas-relief, or composition in alto or basso relievo, or any new and original impression or ornament, or to be placed on any article of manufacture, the same being formed in marble or other material, or any new and useful pattern, or print, or picture, to be either worked into or worked on, or printed, or painted, or cast, or otherwise fixed on any article of manufacture, or any new and original shape or configuration of any article of manufacture, not known or used by others before his, her, or their invention or production thereof, and prior to the time of his, her, or their application for a patent therefor, and who shall desire to obtain an exclusive property or right therein to make, use, and sell, and vend the same, or copies of the same, to others, by them to be made, used, and sold, may make application, in writing, to the Commissioner of Patents, expressing such desire; and the commissioner, on due proceedings had, may grant a patent therefor, as in the case now of application for a patent, for the term of three and one half years, or for the term of seven years, or for the term of fourteen years, as the said applicant may elect in his application: *Provided*, That the fee to be paid in such application shall be for the term of three years and six months, ten dollars, for seven years, fifteen dollars, and for fourteen years, thirty dollars: *And provided*, That the patentees of designs under this act shall be entitled to the extension of their respective patents for the term of seven years, from the day on which said patent shall expire, upon the same terms and restrictions as are now provided for the extension of letters-patent.

SECTION 12. [See act of 1836, ch. 357, § 18.] *And be it further enacted*, That all applications for patents shall be completed and prepared for examination within two years after the filing of the petition, and in default thereof they shall be regarded as abandoned by the parties thereto; unless it be shown to the satisfaction of the Commissioner of Patents that such delay was unavoidable; and all applications now pending shall be treated as if filed after the passage of this act, and all applications for the extension of patents shall be filed at least ninety days before the expiration thereof; and notice of the day set for the hearing of the case shall be published, as now required by law, for at least sixty days.

SECTION 13. [See act of 1842, ch. 263, § 6.] *And be it further enacted*, That in all cases where an article is made or vended by any person under the protection of letters-patent, it shall be the duty of such person to give sufficient notice to the public that said article is so patented, either by fixing thereon the word "patented," together with the day and year the patent was granted; or when, from the character of the article patented, that may be impracticable, by enveloping one or more of the said articles, and affixing a label to the package, or otherwise attaching thereto a label on which the notice, with the date, is printed; on failure of which, in any suit for the infringement of letters-patent by the party failing so to mark the article the right to which is infringed upon, no damage shall be recovered by the plaintiff, except on proof that the defendant was duly notified of the infringement, and continued after such notice to make or vend the article patented. And the sixth section of the act entitled "An Act in addition to an Act to promote the progress of the useful arts," and so forth, approved the twenty-ninth day of August, eighteen hundred and forty-two, be, and the same is hereby, repealed.

SECTION 14. [See act of 1862, ch. 182.] *And be it further enacted*, That the Commissioner of Patents be, and he is hereby, authorized to print, or in his discretion to cause to be printed, ten copies of the description and claims of all patents which may hereafter be granted, and ten copies of the drawings of the same, when drawings shall accompany the patents: *Provided*, The cost of printing the text of said descriptions and claims shall not exceed, exclusive of stationery, the sum of two cents per hundred words for each of said copies, and the cost of the drawing shall not exceed fifty cents per copy; one copy of the above number shall be printed on parchment to be affixed to the letters-patent; the work shall be under the direction, and subject to the approval, of the Commissioner of Patents, and the expense of the said copies shall be paid for out of the patent fund.

SECTION 15. *And be it further enacted*, That printed copies of the letters-patent of the United States, with the seal of the Patent Office affixed thereto and certified and signed by the Commissioner of Patents, shall be legal evidence of the contents of said letters-patent in all cases.

SECTION 16. [See act of 1836, ch. 357, §§ 5, 18.] *And be it further enacted*, That all patents hereafter granted shall remain in force for the term of seventeen years from the date of issue; and all extension of such patents is hereby prohibited.

SECTION 17. *And be it further enacted*, That all acts and parts of acts heretofore passed, which are inconsistent with the provisions of this act, be, and the same are hereby, repealed.

Approved March 2, 1861.

ACT OF 1862, CHAPTER 182.

12 Statutes at Large, 583.

An Act making supplemental appropriations for sundry civil expenses, &c.

Section 4. [See act of 1861, ch. 88, § 14.] For the fund of the Patent Office, fifty thousand eight hundred and fifty-five dollars and forty-nine cents, to supply a deficiency existing under the act of March second, eighteen hundred and sixty-one, entitled "An Act in addition to an Act to promote the progress of the useful arts": *Provided*, That the fourteenth section of said act be, and the same is hereby, repealed.

Approved July 16, 1862.

ACT OF 1863, CHAPTER 102.

12 Statutes at Large, 796.

An Act to amend an Act entitled "An Act to promote the progress of the useful arts."

Section 1. [See act of 1836, ch. 357, § 7.] *Be it enacted by the Senate and House of Representatives of the United States of America in Congress assembled*, That so much of section seven of the act entitled "An Act to promote the progress of the useful arts," approved July fourth, eighteen hundred and thirty-six, as requires a renewal of the oath, be, and the same is hereby, repealed.

Section 2. *And be it further enacted*, That, whereas the falling off of the revenue of the Patent Office required a reduction of the compensation of the examiners and clerks, or other employees in the office, after the thirty-first day of August, eighteen hundred and sixty-one, that the Commissioner of Patents be, and he is hereby, authorized, whenever the revenue of the office will justify him in so doing, to pay them such sums, in addition to what they shall already have received, as will make their compensation the same as it was at that time.

Section 3. [See act of 1864, ch. 159.] *And be it further enacted*, That every patent shall be dated as of a day not later than six months after the time at which it was passed and allowed, and notice thereof sent to the applicant or his agent. And if the final fee for such patent be not paid within the said six months, the patent shall be withheld, and the invention therein described shall become public property as against the applicant therefor: *Provided*, That in all cases where patents have been allowed previous to the passage of this act, the said six months shall be reckoned from the date of such passage.

Approved March 3, 1863.

ACT OF 1864, CHAPTER 159.

13 STATUTES AT LARGE, 194.

An Act amendatory of "An Act to amend an Act entitled an Act to promote the progress of the useful arts," approved March three, eighteen hundred and sixty-three.

[See act of 1863, ch. 102, § 3.] *Be it enacted by the Senate and House of Representatives of the United States of America in Congress assembled*, That any person having an interest in an invention, whether as the inventor or assignee, for which a patent was ordered to issue upon the payment of the final fee, as provided in section three of an act approved March three, eighteen hundred and sixty-three, but who has failed to make payment of the final fee, as provided by said act, shall have the right to make the payment of such fee, and receive the patent withheld on account of the non-payment of said fee, provided such payment be made within six months from the date of the passage of this act: *Provided*, That nothing herein shall be so construed as to hold responsible in damages any persons who have manufactured or used any article or thing for which a patent, as aforesaid, was ordered to be issued.

Approved June 25, 1864.

ACT OF 1865, CHAPTER 112.

13 STATUTES AT LARGE, 533.

An Act amendatory of "An Act to amend an Act entitled An Act to promote the progress of the useful arts," approved March three, eighteen hundred and sixty-three.

[See act of 1863, ch. 102, § 3.] *Be it enacted by the Senate and House of Representatives of the United States of America in Congress assembled*, That any person having an interest in an invention, whether as inventor or assignee, for which a patent was ordered to issue upon the payment of the final fee, as provided in section three of an act approved March three, eighteen hundred and sixty-three, but who has failed to make payment of the final fee, as provided in said act, shall have the right to make an application for a patent for his invention, the same as in the case of an original application, provided such application be made within two years after the date of the allowance of the original application: *Provided*, That nothing herein shall be so construed as to hold responsible in damages any persons who have manufactured or used any article or thing for which a patent aforesaid was ordered to issue. This act shall apply to all cases now in the Patent Office, and also to such as shall hereafter be filed. And all acts or parts of acts inconsistent with this act are hereby repealed.

Approved March 3, 1865.

ACT OF JULY 8, 1870, CHAPTER 230.

An Act to revise, consolidate, and amend the Statutes relating to Patents and Copyrights.

SECTION 1. *Be it enacted by the Senate and House of Representatives of the United States of America in Congress assembled*, That there shall be attached to the Department of the Interior the office, heretofore established, known as the Patent Office, wherein all records, books, models, drawings, specifications, and other papers and things pertaining to patents shall be safely kept and preserved.

SECTION 2. *And be it further enacted*, That the officers and employees of said office shall continue to be: one commissioner of patents, one assistant commissioner, and three examiners-in-chief, to be appointed by the President, by and with the advice and consent of the Senate; one chief clerk, one examiner in charge of interferences, twenty-two principal examiners, twenty-two first assistant examiners, twenty-two second assistant examiners, one librarian, one machinist, five clerks of class four, six clerks of class three, fifty clerks of class two, forty-five clerks of class one, and one messenger and purchasing clerk, all of whom shall be appointed by the Secretary of the Interior, upon nomination of the Commissioner of Patents.

SECTION 3. *And be it further enacted*, That the Secretary of the Interior may also appoint, upon like nomination, such additional clerks of classes two and one, and of lower grades, copyists of drawings, female copyists, skilled laborers, laborers and watchmen, as may be from time to time appropriated for by Congress.

SECTION 4. *And be it further enacted*, That the annual salaries of the officers and employees of the Patent Office shall be as follows: —

Of the commissioner of patents, four thousand five hundred dollars.

Of the assistant commissioner, three thousand dollars.

Of the examiners-in-chief, three thousand dollars each.

Of the chief clerk, two thousand five hundred dollars.

Of the examiner in charge of interferences, two thousand five hundred dollars.

Of the principal examiners, two thousand five hundred dollars each.

Of the first assistant examiners, one thousand eight hundred dollars each.

Of the second assistant examiners, one thousand six hundred dollars each.

Of the librarian, one thousand eight hundred dollars.

Of the machinist, one thousand six hundred dollars.

Of the clerks of class four, one thousand eight hundred dollars each.

Of the clerks of class three, one thousand six hundred dollars each.

Of the clerks of class two, one thousand four hundred dollars each.

Of the clerks of class one, one thousand two hundred dollars each.

Of the messenger and purchasing clerk, one thousand dollars.

Of laborers and watchmen, seven hundred and twenty dollars each.

Of the additional clerks, copyists of drawings, female copyists, and skilled laborers, such rates as may be fixed by the acts making appropriations for them.

SECTION 5. *And be it further enacted,* That all officers and employees of the Patent Office shall, before entering upon their duties, make oath or affirmation truly and faithfully to execute the trusts committed to them.

SECTION 6. *And be it further enacted,* That the commissioner and chief clerk, before entering upon their duties, shall severally give bond, with sureties, to the Treasurer of the United States, the former in the sum of ten thousand dollars, and the latter in the sum of five thousand dollars, conditioned for the faithful discharge of their duties, and that they will render to the proper officers of the treasury a true account of all money received by virtue of their office.

SECTION 7. *And be it further enacted,* That it shall be the duty of the commissioner, under the direction of the Secretary of the Interior, to superintend or perform all the duties respecting the granting and issuing of patents which herein are, or may hereafter be, by law directed to be done; and he shall have charge of all books, records, papers, models, machines, and other things belonging to said office.

SECTION 8. *And be it further enacted,* That the commissioner may send and receive by mail, free of postage, letters, printed matter, and packages relating to the business of his office, including Patent Office reports.

SECTION 9. *And be it further enacted,* That the commissioner shall lay before Congress, in the month of January, annually, a report, giving a detailed statement of all moneys received for patents, for copies of records or drawings, or from any other source whatever; a detailed statement of all expenditures for contingent and miscellaneous expenses; a list of all patents which were granted during the preceding year, designating under proper heads the subjects of such patents; an alphabetical list of the patentees, with their places of residence; a list of all patents which have been extended during the year; and such other information of the condition of the Patent Office as may be useful to Congress or the public.

SECTION 10. *And be it further enacted,* That the examiners-in-chief shall be persons of competent legal knowledge and scientific ability, whose duty it shall be, on the written petition of the appellant, to revise and determine upon the validity of the adverse decisions of examiners upon applications for patents, and for reissues of patents, and in interference cases; and when required by the commissioner, they shall hear and report upon claims for extensions, and perform such other like duties as he may assign them.

SECTION 11. *And be it further enacted*, That in case of the death, resignation, absence, or sickness of the commissioner, his duties shall devolve upon the assistant commissioner until a successor shal be appointed, or such absence or sickness shall cease.

SECTION 12. *And be it further enacted*, That the commissioner shall cause a seal to be provided for said office, with such device as the President may approve, with which all records or papers issued from said office, to be used in evidence, shall be authenticated.

SECTION 13. *And be it further enacted*, That the commissioner shall cause to be classified and arranged in suitable cases, in the rooms and galleries provided for that purpose, the models, specimens of composition, fabrics, manufactures, works of art, and designs, which have been or shall be deposited in said office; and said rooms and galleries shall be kept open during suitable hours for public inspection.

SECTION 14. *And be it further enacted*, That the commissioner may restore to the respective applicants such of the models belonging to rejected applications as he shall not think necessary to be preserved, or he may sell or otherwise dispose of them after the application has been finally rejected for one year, paying the proceeds into the treasury, as other patent moneys are directed to be paid.

SECTION 15. *And be it further enacted*, That there shall be purchased, for the use of said office, a library of such scientific works and periodicals, both foreign and American, as may aid the officers in the discharge of their duties, not exceeding the amount annually appropriated by Congress for that purpose.

SECTION 16. *And be it further enacted*, That all officers and employees of the Patent Office shall be incapable, during the period for which they shall hold their appointments, to acquire or take, directly or indirectly, except by inheritance or bequest, any right or interest in any patent issued by said office.

SECTION 17. *And be it further enacted*, That for gross misconduct the commissioner may refuse to recognize any person as a patent agent, either generally or in any particular case; but the reasons for such refusal shall be duly recorded, and be subject to the approval of the Secretary of the Interior.

SECTION 18. *And be it further enacted*, That the commissioner may require all papers filed in the Patent Office, if not correctly, legibly and clearly written, to be printed at the cost of the party filing them.

SECTION 19. *And be it further enacted*, That the commissioner, subject to the approval of the Secretary of the Interior, may from time to time establish rules and regulations, not inconsistent with law, for the conduct of proceedings in the Patent Office.

SECTION 20. *And be it further enacted*, That the commissioner may print or cause to be printed copies of the specifications of all letters-patent and of the drawings of the same, and copies of the claims of current issues, and copies of such laws, decisions, rules, regulations, and circulars as may be necessary for the information of the public.

SECTION 21. *And be it further enacted*, That all patents shall be issued in the name of the United States of America, under the seal of the Patent Office, and shall be signed by the Secretary of the Interior and countersigned by the commissioner, and they shall be recorded, together with the specification, in said office, in books to be kept for that purpose.

SECTION 22. *And be it further enacted*, That every patent shall contain a short title or description of the invention or discovery, correctly indicating its nature and design, and a grant to the patentee, his heirs or assigns, for the term of seventeen years, of the exclusive right to make, use, and vend the said invention or discovery throughout the United States and the Territories thereof, referring to the specification for the particulars thereof; and a copy of said specifications and of the drawings shall be annexed to the patent and be a part thereof.

SECTION 23. *And be it further enacted*, That every patent shall date as of a day not later than six months from the time at which it was passed and allowed, and notice thereof was sent to the applicant or his agent; and if the final fee shall not be paid within that period, the patent shall be withheld.

SECTION 24. *And be it further enacted*, That any person who has invented or discovered any new and useful art, machine, manufacture, or composition of matter, or any new and useful improvement thereof, not known or used by others in this country, and not patented, or described in any printed publication in this or any foreign country, before his invention or discovery thereof, and not in public use or on sale for more than two years prior to his application, unless the same is proved to have been abandoned, may, upon payment of the duty required by law, and other due proceedings had, obtain a patent therefor.

SECTION 25. *And be it further enacted*, That no person shall be debarred from receiving a patent for his invention or discovery, nor shall any patent be declared invalid, by reason of its having been first patented or caused to be patented in a foreign country: *Provided*, The same shall not have been introduced into public use in the United States for more than two years prior to the application, and that the patent shall expire at the same time with the foreign patent, or, if there be more than one, at the same time with the one having the shortest term; but in no case shall it be in force more than seventeen years.

SECTION 26. *And be it further enacted*, That before any inventor or discoverer shall receive a patent for his invention or discovery, he shall make application therefor, in writing, to the commissioner, and shall file in the Patent Office a written description of the same, and of the manner and process of making, constructing, compounding, and using it, in such full, clear, concise, and exact terms as to enable any person skilled in the art or science to which it appertains, or with which it is most nearly connected, to make, construct, compound, and use the same; and in case of a machine, he shall explain the principle thereof, and the best mode in which he has contemplated applying that principle so as to distinguish it from other inventions; and he shall particularly point out and distinctly claim the part, improvement, or combination which he claims as his invention or discovery; and said specification and claim shall be signed by the inventor and attested by two witnesses.

SECTION 27. *And be it further enacted*, That when the nature of the case admits of drawings, the applicant shall furnish one copy signed by the inventor or his attorney in fact, and attested by two witnesses, which shall be filed in the Patent Office; and a copy of said drawings, to be furnished by the Patent Office, shall be attached to the patent as part of the specification.

SECTION 28. *And be it further enacted*, That when the invention or discovery is of a composition of matter, the applicant, if required by the commissioner, shall furnish specimens of ingredients and of the composition, sufficient in quantity for the purpose of experiment.

SECTION 29. *And be it further enacted*, That in all cases which admit of representation by model, the applicant, if required by the commissioner, shall furnish one of convenient size to exhibit advantageously the several parts of his invention or discovery.

SECTION 30. *And be it further enacted*, That the applicant shall make oath or affirmation that he does verily believe himself to be the original and first inventor or discoverer of the art, machine, manufacture, composition, or improvement for which he solicits a patent; that he does not know and does not believe that the same was ever before known or used; and shall state of what country he is a citizen. And said oath or affirmation may be made before any person within the United States authorized by law to administer oaths, or, when the applicant resides in a foreign country, before any minister, *chargé d'affaires*, consul, or commercial agent, holding commission under the government of the United States, or before any notary public of the foreign country in which the applicant may be.

SECTION 31. *And be it further enacted*, That on the filing of any such application and the payment of the duty required by law, the commissioner shall cause an examination to be made of the alleged new invention or discovery; and if on such examination it shall appear that the claimant is justly entitled to a patent under the law, and that the same is sufficiently useful and important, the commissioner shall issue a patent therefor.

SECTION 32. *And be it further enacted*, That all applications for patents shall be completed and prepared for examination within two years after the filing of the petition, and in default thereof, or upon failure of the applicant to prosecute the same within two years after any action therein, of which notice shall have been given to the applicant, they shall be regarded as abandoned by the parties thereto, unless it be shown to the satisfaction of the commissioner that such delay was unavoidable.

SECTION 33. *And be it further enacted*, That patents may be granted and issued or reissued to the assignee of the inventor or discoverer, the assignment thereof being first entered of record in the Patent Office; but in such case the application for the patent shall be made and the specification sworn to by the inventor or discoverer; and also, if he be living, in case of an application for reissue.

SECTION 34. *And be it further enacted*, That when any person, having made any new invention or discovery for which a patent might have been granted, dies before a patent is granted, the right of applying for and obtaining the patent shall devolve on his executor or administrator, in trust for the heirs at law of the deceased, in case he shall have died intestate; or if he shall have left a will, disposing of the same, then in trust for his devisees, in as full manner and on the same terms and conditions as the same might have been claimed or enjoyed by him in his lifetime; and when the application shall be made by such legal representatives, the oath or affirmation required to be made shall be so varied in form that it can be made by them.

SECTION 35. *And be it further enacted*, That any person who has an interest in an invention or discovery, whether as inventor, discoverer, or assignee, for which a patent was ordered to issue upon the payment of the final fee, but who has failed to make payment thereof within six months from the time at which it was passed and allowed, and notice thereof was sent to the applicant or his agent, shall have a right to make an application for a patent for such invention or discovery the same as in the case of an original application: *Provided*, That the second application be made within two years after the allowance of the original application. But no person shall be held responsible in damages for the manufacture or use of any article or thing for which a patent, as aforesaid, was ordered to issue, prior to the issue thereof: *And provided further*, That when an application for a patent has been rejected or withdrawn, prior to the passage of this act, the applicant shall have six months from the date of such passage to renew his application, or to file a new one; and if he omit to do either, his application shall be held to have been abandoned. Upon the hearing of such renewed applications abandonment shall be considered as a question of fact.

SECTION 36. *And be it further enacted*, That every patent or any interest therein shall be assignable in law, by an instrument in writing; and the patentee or his assigns or legal representatives may, in like manner, grant and convey an exclusive right under his patent to the whole or any specified part of the United States; and said assignment, grant, or conveyance shall be void as against any subsequent purchaser or mortgagee for a valuable consideration, without notice, unless it is recorded in the Patent Office within three months from the date thereof.

SECTION 37. *And be it further enacted*, That every person who may have purchased of the inventor, or with his knowledge and consent may have constructed any newly invented or discovered machine, or other patentable article, prior to the application by the inventor or discoverer for a patent, or sold or used one so constructed, shall have the right to use, and vend to others to be used, the specific thing so made or purchased, without liability therefor.

SECTION 38. *And be it further enacted*, That it shall be the duty of all patentees, and their assigns and legal representatives, and of all persons making or vending any patented article for or under them, to give sufficient notice to the public that the same is patented, either by fixing thereon the word "patented," together with the day and year the patent was granted; or when, from the character of the article, this cannot be done, by fixing to it or to the package wherein one or more of them is enclosed, a label containing the like notice; and in any suit for infringement, by the party failing so to mark, no damages shall be recovered by the plaintiff, except on proof that the defendant was duly notified of the infringement, and continued, after such notice, to make, use, or vend the article so patented.

SECTION 39. *And be it further enacted*, That if any person shall, in any manner, mark upon any thing made, used, or sold by him for which he has not obtained a patent, the name or any imitation of the name of any person who has obtained a patent therefor, without the consent of such patentee, or his assigns or legal representatives; or shall in any manner mark upon or affix to any such patented article the word "patent" or "patentee," or the words "letters-patent," or any word of like import, with intent to imitate or counterfeit the mark or device of the patentee, without having the license or consent of such patentee or his assigns or legal representatives; or shall in any manner mark upon or affix to any unpatented article the word "patent," or any word importing that the same is patented, for the purpose of deceiving the public, he shall be liable for every such offence to a penalty of not less than one hundred dollars, with costs; one moiety of said penalty to the person who shall sue for the same, and the other to the use of the United States, to be recovered by suit in any district court of the United States within whose jurisdiction such offence may have been committed.

SECTION 40. *And be it further enacted*, That any citizen of the United States, who shall have made any new invention or discovery, and shall desire further time to mature the same, may, on payment of the duty required by law, file in the Patent Office a caveat setting forth the design thereof, and of its distinguishing characteristics, and praying protection of his right until he shall have matured his invention; and such caveat shall be filed in the confidential archives of the office and preserved in secrecy, and shall be operative for the term of one year from the filing thereof; and if application shall be made within the year by any other person for a patent with which such caveat would in any manner interfere, the commissioner shall deposit the description, specification, drawings, and model of such application in like manner in the confidential archives of the office, and give notice thereof, by mail, to the person filing the caveat, who, if he would avail himself of his caveat, shall file his description, specifications, drawings, and model within three months from the time of placing said notice in the post-office in Washington, with the usual time required for transmitting it to the caveator added thereto, which time shall be indorsed on the notice. And an alien shall have the privilege herein granted, if he shall have resided in the United States one year next preceding the filing of his caveat, and made oath of his intention to become a citizen.

SECTION 41. *And be it further enacted*, That whenever, on examination, any claim for a patent is rejected for any reason whatever, the commissioner shall notify the applicant thereof, giving him briefly the reasons for such rejection, together with such information and references as may be useful in judging of the propriety of renewing his application or of altering his specification; and if, after receiving such notice, the applicant shall persist in his claim for a patent, with or without altering his specifications, the commissioner shall order a re-examination of the case.

SECTION 42. *And be it further enacted*, That whenever an application is made for a patent which, in the opinion of the commissioner, would interfere with any pending application, or with any unexpired patent, he shall give notice thereof to the applicants, or applicant and patentee, as the case may be, and shall direct the primary examiner to proceed to determine the question of priority of invention. And the commissioner may issue a patent to the party who shall be adjudged the prior inventor, unless the adverse party shall appeal from the decision of the primary examiner, or of the board of examiners-in-chief, as the case may be, within such time, not less than twenty days, as the commissioner shall prescribe.

SECTION 43. *And be it further enacted*, That the commissioner may establish rules for taking affidavits and depositions required in cases pending in the Patent Office, and such affidavits and depositions may be taken before any officer authorized by law to take depositions to be used in the courts of the United States, or of the State where the officer resides.

SECTION 44. *And be it further enacted*, That the clerk of any court of the United States, for any district or territory wherein testimony is to be taken for use in any contested case pending in the Patent Office, shall, upon the application of any party thereto, or his agent or attorney, issue [a] subpœna for any witness residing or being within said district or territory, commanding him to appear and testify before any officer in said district or territory authorized to take depositions and affidavits, at any time and place in the subpœna stated; and if any witness, after being duly served with such subpœna, shall neglect or refuse to appear, or after appearing shall refuse to testify, the judge of the court whose clerk issued the subpœna, may, on proof of such neglect or refusal, enforce obedience to the process, or punish the disobedience as in other like cases.

SECTION 45. *And be it further enacted*, That every witness duly subpœnaed and in attendance shall be allowed the same fees as are allowed to witnesses attending the courts of the United States, but no witness shall be required to attend at any place more than forty miles from the place where the subpœna is served upon him, nor be deemed guilty of contempt for disobeying such subpœna, unless his fees and travelling expenses in going to, returning from, and one day's attendance at the place of examination, are paid or tendered him at the time of the service of the subpœna; nor for refusing to disclose any secret invention or discovery made or owned by himself.

SECTION 46. *And be it further enacted*, That every applicant for a patent or the reissue of a patent, any of the claims of which have been twice rejected, and every party to an interference, may appeal from the decision of the primary examiner, or of the examiner in charge of interference[s], in such case to the board of examiners-in-chief, having once paid the fee for such appeal provided by law.

SECTION 47. *And be it further enacted*, That if such party is dissatisfied with the decision of the examiners-in-chief, he may, on payment of the duty required by law, appeal to the commissioner in person.

SECTION 48. *And be it further enacted*, That if such party, except a party to an interference, is dissatisfied with the decision of the commissioner, he may appeal to the Supreme Court of the District of Columbia, sitting in banc.

SECTION 49. *And be it further enacted*, That when an appeal is taken to the Supreme Court of the District of Columbia, the appellant shall give notice thereof to the commissioner, and file in the Patent Office, within such time as the commissioner shall appoint, his reasons of appeal, specifically set forth in writing.

SECTION 50. *And be it further enacted*, That it shall be the duty of said court, on petition, to hear and determine such appeal, and to revise the decision appealed from in a summary way, on the evidence produced before the commissioner, at such early and convenient time as the court may appoint, notifying the commissioner of the time and place of hearing; and the revision shall be confined to the points set forth in the reasons of appeal. And after hearing the case, the court shall return to the commissioner a certificate of its proceedings and decision, which shall be entered of record in the Patent Office, and govern the further proceedings in the case. But no opinion or decision of the court in any such case shall preclude any person interested from the right to contest the validity of such patent in any court wherein the same may be called in question.

SECTION 51. *And be it further enacted*, That on receiving notice of the time and place of hearing such appeal, the commissioner shall notify all parties who appear to be interested therein in such manner as the court may prescribe. The party appealing shall lay before the court certified copies of all the original papers and evidence in the case, and the commissioner shall furnish it with the grounds of his decision, fully set forth in writing, touching all the points involved by the reasons of appeal. And at the request of any party interested, or of the court, the commissioner and the examiners may be examined under oath, in explanation of the principles of the machine or other thing for which a patent is demanded.

SECTION 52. *And be it further enacted*, That whenever a patent on application is refused, for any reason whatever, either by the commissioner or by the Supreme Court of the District of Columbia upon appeal from the commissioner, the applicant may have remedy by bill in equity; and the court having cognizance thereof, on notice to adverse parties and other due proceedings had, may adjudge that such applicant is entitled, according to law, to receive a patent for his invention, as specified in his claim, or for any part thereof, as the facts in the case may appear. And such adjudication, if it be in favor of the right of the applicant, shall authorize the commissioner to issue such patent, on the applicant filing in the Patent Office a copy of the adjudication, and otherwise complying with the requisitions of law. And in all cases where there is no opposing party a copy of the bill shall be served on the commissioner, and all the expenses of the proceeding shall be paid by the applicant, whether the final decision is in his favor or not.

SECTION 53. *And be it further enacted*, That whenever any patent is inoperative or invalid, by reason of a defective or insufficient specification, or by reason of the patentee claiming as his own invention or discovery more than he had a right to claim as new, if the error has arisen by inadvertence, accident, or mistake, and without any fraudulent or deceptive intention, the commissioner shall, on the surrender of such patent and the payment of the duty required by law, cause a new patent for the same invention, and in accordance with the corrected specification, to be issued to the patentee, or, in the case of his death or assignment of the whole or any undivided part of the original patent, to his executors, administrators, or assigns, for the unexpired part of the term of the original patent, the surrender of which shall take effect upon the issue of the amended patent; and the commissioner may, in his discretion, cause several patents to be issued for distinct and separate parts of the thing patented, upon demand of the applicant, and upon payment of the required fee for a reissue for each of such reissued letters-patent. And the specifications and claim in every such case shall be subject to revision and restriction in the same manner as original applications are. And the patent so reissued, together with the corrected specification, shall have the effect and operation in law, on the trial of all actions for causes thereafter arising, as though the same had been originally filed in such corrected form; but no new matter shall be introduced into the specification, nor in case of a machine patent shall the model or drawings be amended, except each by the other; but when there is neither model nor drawing, amendments may be made upon proof satisfactory to the commissioner that such new matter or amendment was a part of the original invention, and was omitted from the specification by inadvertence, accident, or mistake, as aforesaid.

SECTION 54. *And be it further enacted*, That whenever, through inadvertence, accident, or mistake, and without any fraudulent or deceptive intention, a patentee has claimed more than that of which he was the original or first inventor or discoverer, his patent shall be valid for all that part which is truly and justly his own, provided the same is a material or substantial part of the thing patented; and any such patentee, his heirs or assigns, whether of the whole or any sectional interest therein, may, on payment of the duty required by law, make disclaimer of such parts of the thing patented as he shall not choose to claim or to hold by virtue of the patent or assignment, stating therein the extent of his interest in such patent; said disclaimer shall be in writing, attested by one or more witnesses, and recorded in the Patent Office, and it shall thereafter be considered as part of the original specification to the extent of the interest possessed by the claimant and by those claiming under him after the record thereof. But no such disclaimer shall affect any action pending at the time of its being filed, except so far as may relate to the question of unreasonable neglect or delay in filing it.

SECTION 55. *And be it further enacted*, That all actions, suits, controversies, and cases arising under the patent laws of the United States shall be originally cognizable, as well in equity as at law, by the circuit courts of the United States, or any district court having the powers and jurisdiction of a circuit court, or by the Supreme Court of the District of Columbia, or of any territory; and the court shall have power, upon bill in equity filed by any party aggrieved, to grant injunctions according to the course and principles of courts of equity, to prevent the violation of any right secured by patent, on such terms as the court may deem reasonable; and upon a decree being rendered in any such case for an infringement, the *claimant* [complainant] shall be entitled to recover, in addition to the profits to be accounted for by the defendant, the damages the complainant has sustained thereby, and the court shall assess the same or cause the same to be assessed under its direction, and the court shall have the same powers to increase the same in its discretion that are given by this act to increase the damages found by verdicts in actions upon the case; but all actions shall be brought during the term for which the letters-patent shall be granted or extended, or within six years after the expiration thereof.

SECTION 56. *And be it further enacted*, That a writ of error or appeal to the Supreme Court of the United States shall lie from all judgments and decrees of any circuit court, or of any district court exercising the jurisdiction of a circuit court, or of the Supreme Court of the District of Columbia, or of any territory, in any action, suit, controversy, or case, at law or in equity, touching patent rights, in the same manner and under the same circumstances as in other judgments and decrees of such circuit courts, without regard to the sum or value in controversy.

SECTION 57. *And be it further enacted*, That written or printed copies of any records, books, papers, or drawings belonging to the Patent Office, and of letters-patent under the signature of the commissioner or acting commissioner, with the seal of office affixed, shall be competent evidence in all cases wherein the originals could be evidence, and any person making application therefor, and paying the fee required by law, shall have certified copies thereof. And copies of the specifications and drawings of foreign letters-patent, certified in like manner, shall be *primâ facie* evidence of the fact of the granting of such foreign letters-patent, and of the date and contents thereof.

SECTION 58. *And be it further enacted*, That whenever there shall be interfering patents, any person interested in any one of such interfering patents, or in the working of the invention claimed under either of such patents, may have relief against the interfering patentee, and all parties interested under him, by suit in equity against the owners of the interfering patent; and the court having cognizance thereof, as hereinbefore provided, on notice to adverse parties, and other due proceedings had according to the course of equity, may adjudge and declare either of the patents void in whole or in part, or inoperative, or invalid in any particular part of the United States, according to the interest of the parties in the patent or the invention patented. But no such judgment or adjudication shall affect the rights of any person except the parties to the suit and those deriving title under them subsequent to the rendition of such judgment.

SECTION 59. *And be it further enacted*, That damages for the infringement of any patent may be recovered by action on the case in any circuit court of the United States, or district court exercising the jurisdiction of a circuit court, or in the Supreme Court of the District of Columbia, or of any territory, in the name of the party interested, either as patentee, assignee, or grantee. And whenever in any such action a verdict shall be rendered for the plaintiff, the court may enter judgment thereon for any sum above the amount found by the verdict as the actual damages sustained, according to the circumstances of the case, not exceeding three times the amount of such verdict, together with the costs.

SECTION 60. *And be it further enacted*, That whenever, through inadvertence, accident, or mistake, and without any wil[l]ful default or intent to defraud or mislead the public, a patentee shall have (in his specification) claimed to be the original and first inventor or discoverer of any material or substantial part of the thing patented, of which he was not the original and first inventor or discoverer as aforesaid, every such patentee, his executors, administrators, and assigns, whether of the whole or any sectional interest in the patent, may maintain a suit at law or in equity, for the infringement of any part thereof, which was *bonâ fide* his own, provided it shall be a material and substantial part of the thing patented, and be definitely distinguishable from the parts so claimed, without right as aforesaid, notwithstanding the specifications may embrace more than that of which the patentee was the original or first inventor or discoverer. But in every such case in which a judgment or decree shall be rendered for the plaintiff, no costs shall be recovered unless the proper disclaimer has been entered at the Patent Office before the commencement of the suit; nor shall he be entitled to the benefits of this section if he shall have unreasonably neglected or delayed to enter said disclaimer.

SECTION 61. *And be it further enacted*, That in any action for infringement the defendant may plead the general issue, and having given notice in writing to the plaintiff or his attorney, thirty days before, may prove on trial any one or more of the following special matters: —

First. That for the purpose of deceiving the public the description and specification filed by the patentee in the Patent Office was made to contain less than the whole truth relative to his invention or discovery, or more than is necessary to produce the desired effect; or,

Second. That he had surreptitiously or unjustly obtained the patent for that which was in fact invented by another, who was using reasonable diligence in adapting and perfecting the same; or,

Third. That it had been patented or described in some printed publication prior to his supposed invention or discovery thereof; or,

Fourth. That he was not the original and first inventor or discoverer of any material and substantial part of the thing patented; or,

Fifth. That it had been in public use or on sale in this country, for more than two years before his application for a patent, or had been abandoned to the public.

And in notices as to proof of previous invention, knowledge, or use of the thing patented, the defendant shall state the names of patentees and the dates of their patents, and when granted, and the names and residences of the persons alleged to have invented, or to have had the prior knowledge of the thing patented, and where and by whom it had been used; and if any one or more of the special matters alleged shall be found for the defendant, judgment shall be rendered for him with costs. And the like defences may be pleaded in any suit in equity for relief against an alleged infringement; and proofs of the same may be given upon like notice in the answer of the defendant, and with the like effect.

SECTION 62. *And be it further enacted*, That whenever it shall appear that the patentee, at the time of making his application for the patent, believed himself to be the original and first inventor or discoverer of the thing patented, the same shall not be held to be void on account of the invention or discovery, or any part thereof, having been known or used in a foreign country, before his invention or discovery thereof, if it had not been patented or described in a printed publication.

SECTION 63. *And be it further enacted*, That where the patentee of any invention or discovery, the patent for which was granted prior to the second day of March, eighteen hundred and sixty-one, shall desire an extension of his patent beyond the original term of its limitation, he shall make application therefor, in writing, to the commissioner, setting forth the reasons why such extension should be granted; and he shall also furnish a written statement under oath of the ascertained value of the invention or discovery, and of his receipts and expenditures on account thereof, sufficiently in detail to exhibit a true and faithful account of the loss and profit in any manner accruing to him by reason of said invention or discovery. And said application shall be filed not more than six months nor less than ninety days before the expiration of the original term of the patent; and no extension shall be granted after the expiration of said original term.

SECTION 64. *And be it further enacted*, That upon the receipt of such application, and the payment of the duty required by law, the commiss'oner shall cause to be published in one newspaper in the city of Washington, and in such other papers published in .he section of the country most interested adversely to the extension of the patent as he may deem proper, for at least sixty days prior to the day set for hearing the case, a notice of such application, and of the time and place when and where the same will be considered, that any person may appear and show cause why the extension should not be granted.

SECTION 65. *And be it further enacted*, That on the publication of such notice, the commissioner shall refer the case to the principal examiner having charge of the class of inventions to which it belongs, who shall make to said commissioner a full report of the case, and particularly whether the invention or discovery was new and patentable when the original patent was granted.

SECTION 66. *And be it further enacted*, That the commissioner shall, at the time and place designated in the published notice, hear and decide upon the evidence produced, both for and against the extension; and if it shall appear to his satisfaction that the patentee, without neglect or fault on his part, has failed to obtain from the use and sale of his invention or discovery, a reasonable remuneration for the time, ingenuity, and expense bestowed upon it, and the introduction of it into use, and that it is just and proper, having due regard to the public interest, that the term of the patent should be extended, the said commissioner shall make a certificate thereon, renewing and extending the said patent for the term of seven years from the expiration of the first term, which certificate shall be recorded in the Patent Office, and thereupon the said patent shall have the same effect in law as though it had been originally granted for twenty-one years.

SECTION 67. *And be it further enacted*, That the benefit of the extension of a patent shall extend to the assignees and grantees of the right to use the thing patented to the extent of their interest therein.

SECTION 68. *And be it further enacted*, That the following shall be the rates for patent fees: —

On filing each original application for a patent, fifteen dollars.

On issuing each original patent, twenty dollars.

On filing each caveat, ten dollars.

On every application for the reissue of a patent, thirty dollars.

On filing each disclaimer, ten dollars.

On every application for the extension of a patent, fifty dollars.

On the granting of every extension of a patent, fifty dollars.

On an appeal for the first time from the primary examiners to the examiners-in-chief, ten dollars.

On every appeal from the examiners-in-chief to the commissioner, twenty dollars.

For certified copies of patents and other papers, ten cents per hundred words.

For recording every assignment, agreement, power of attorney, or other paper, of three hundred words or under, one dollar; of over three hundred and under one thousand words, two dollars; of over one thousand words, three dollars.

For copies of drawings, the reasonable cost of making them.

SECTION 69. *And be it further enacted,* That patent fees may be paid to the commissioner, or to the treasurer or any of the assistant treasurers of the United States, or to any of the designated depositaries, national banks, or receivers of public money, designated by the Secretary of the Treasury for that purpose, who shall give the depositor a receipt or certificate of deposit therefor. And all money received at the Patent Office, for any purpose, or from any source whatever, shall be paid into the treasury as received, without any deduction whatever; and all disbursements for said office shall be made by the disbursing clerk of the Interior Department.

SECTION 70. *And be it further enacted,* That the Treasurer of the United States is authorized to pay back any sum or sums of money to any person who shall have paid the same into the treasury, or to any receiver or depositary, to the credit of the treasurer, as for fees accruing at the Patent Office through mistake, certificate thereof being made to said treasurer by the Commissioner of Patents.

SECTION 71. *And be it further enacted,* That any person who, by his own industry, genius, efforts, and expense, has invented or produced any new and original design for a manufacture, bust, statue, alto-relievo, or bas-relief; any new and original design for the printing of wool[l]en, silk, cotton, or other fabrics; any new and original impression, ornament, pattern, print, or picture, to be printed, painted, cast, or otherwise placed on or worked into any article of manufacture; or any new, useful, and original shape or configuration of any article of manufacture, the same not having been known or used by others before his invention or production thereof, or patented or described in any printed publication, may, upon payment of the duty required by law, and other due proceedings had the same as in cases of inventions or discoveries, obtain a patent therefor.

SECTION 72. *And be it further enacted,* That the commissioner may dispense with models of designs when the design can be sufficiently represented by drawings or photographs.

SECTION 73. *And be it further enacted,* That patents for designs may be granted for the term of three years and six months, or for seven years, or for fourteen years, as the applicant may, in his application, elect.

SECTION 74. *And be it further enacted,* That patentees of designs issued prior to March two, eighteen hundred and sixty-one, shall be entitled to extension of their respective patents for the term of seven years, in the same manner and under the same restrictions as are provided for the extension of patents for inventions or discoveries issued prior to the second day of March, eighteen hundred and sixty-one.

SECTION 75. *And be it further enacted*, That the following shall be the rates of fees in design cases:—

For three years and six months, ten dollars.

For seven years, fifteen dollars.

For fourteen years, thirty dollars.

For all other cases in which fees are required, the same rates as in cases of inventions or discoveries.

SECTION 76. *And be it further enacted*, That all the regulations and provisions which apply to the obtaining or protection of patents for inventions or discoveries, not inconsistent with the provisions of this act, shall apply to patents for designs.

. . . .

GENERAL INDEX.

GENERAL INDEX.

N.B. — The references are to the Sections, unless indicated by the abbreviation p., which refers to the *page*.

A.

E.

F.

G.

I.

P.

R.

V.

W.

Cambridge: Press of John Wilson & Son.

www.ingramcontent.com/pod-product-compliance
Lightning Source LLC
LaVergne TN
LVHW081943200926
848484LV00009B/2503
* 9 7 8 1 5 8 4 7 7 5 8 0 5 *